THE PRESIDENT'S SCHEDULE

Friday - January 21, 1977

9:00
(15 min.)

Dr. Zbigniew Brzezinski - The Oval Office.

10:00
(90 min.)

Reception: Hosts and Hostesses During Campaign and Inaugural Host Committee. The State Floor.

12:00
(60 min.)

Reception Honoring Governors of the States and Members of the Cabinet. The State Floor.

1:30
(90 min.)

Reception: DNC, Democratic Finance Committee, State Campaign Managers, Labor/ Business and Entertainers - The State Floor.

3:05
(5 min.)

Mr. Robert Fulbright - The Map Room.

3:15
(15 Min.)

Mr. Enno (Hank) Knoche, Acting Director, Central Intelligence Agency, and Dr. Zbigniew Brzezinski - The Map Room.

4:00
(90 min.)

Reception: Georgians and Friends. The State Floor.

POWER

AND

PRINCIPLE

POWER
AND
PRINCIPLE

Memoirs of the

National Security Adviser

1977–1981

Zbigniew Brzezinski

Farrar · Straus · Giroux

NEW YORK

Library of Congress Cataloging in Publication Data

Brzezinski, Zbigniew K.
Power and principle.
Includes index.
1. Brzezinski, Zbigniew K.   2. Carter,
Jimmy.   3. United States—Foreign relations
—1977-1981.   4. United States—National security.
5. Statesmen—United States—Biography.   I. Title.
E840.8.B79A36 1983   327.73′092′2   83-1598

To my NSC colleagues

Contents

Illustrations

FOLLOWING PAGE 398

Preface

From January 20, 1977, to January 20, 1981, I served in the White House as the Assistant to the President for National Security Affairs. These memoirs are intended as my contribution to the historical record and need, I think, no other explanation. Nonetheless, one of my strongest motives for having written them is my belief that public service in our democracy carries with it the obligation to inform the citizens of the United States of how the major decisions—decisions which affected and in some cases continue to affect their well-being and their security—were debated and made by the President and his top advisers. In presenting these memoirs, I am discharging a fundamental democratic responsibility.

It would be absurd to pretend that mine is not a subjective account. All volumes of memoirs present a view of the events from the vantage point of the memorialist, and it is possible that I have not entirely avoided the common pitfall of enhancing my own role. The recognition of this danger has led me to restrict myself largely to describing those matters in which I was personally involved and to eschew the tempting but in the end unsound project of re-creating the totality of the Carter Administration's foreign policy. For example, I do not deal in detail with the various negotiations or foreign trips undertaken by my colleagues in the Cabinet unless I was also directly engaged in them. It is surely not subjectivity per se which distorts our view of history but rather the temptation to include everything, even to the point of relying on speculation and hearsay.

I feel it is important to convey to the reader a sense of how the great issues of those four years appeared to me *at the time,* as well as to provide a more systematic analysis of how policy was made and what roles key individuals played. Thus, my goal has been both to provide a narrative account of the issues as they arose and as we confronted them and, equally importantly, to explore in depth those central issues of American foreign policy which were my main concern during the Carter Administration. These were the U.S.–Soviet relationship, the Middle East, the evolving U.S.–Chinese relationship, and the Iranian tragedy. In briefer chapters, I have also summarized our overall goals, including that emphasis on human rights which so distinguished the Carter Administration, and some of our initiatives toward the Third World. I end the book with an attempt to draw some conclusions from the Carter experience for America's position in the world of the eighties. Throughout, the conceptual framework for the book remains the centrally important question of whether it is possible to blend a concern for moral principle with the imperatives of national power so as to create a meaningful policy that is understood and supported by a large democratic society.

If this book is about policies, it is also about processes. The general reader may occasionally feel that I devote too much attention to the mechanics of governance, but I would argue that the absence of this dimension from all too many volumes of memoirs seriously limits any understanding of the way the U.S. government actually functions. Policy is made within the framework of a complicated network of institutional arrangements, and if the personal in politics plays a surprisingly large role, so, too, does the more neglected realm of the organizational. In trying to give this element its due, I hope I have provided the reader with a more accurate insight into the workings of the U.S. government at its highest level and a feel for the concerns and preoccupations of its policy makers.

Given my purposes in writing this book, I faced a major organizational decision: whether to structure my account chronologically or to focus more systematically on some key topics. I have chosen the latter approach because I felt that it permitted a fuller, more nuanced treatment of events. The chronological approach, though at first sight appearing truer to the events as they occurred, is in fact as much of a distortion as an account that moves topic by topic. The general reader probably cannot imagine the extraordinary pressures of time under which those engaged in shaping America's global policy operate. The President's advisers are like jugglers: moving from meeting to meeting, from topic to topic, dealing with developments as they occurred in an increasingly disorganized world. There is probably no effective way of conveying this atmosphere, for which the overused simile of the pressure cooker is, if anything, an understatement.

The insufficiency of the chronological approach becomes apparent when one realizes that each problem, no matter how urgent, remained only one of a number of pressing concerns which had to be dealt with *simultaneously*. Thus, we were dealing at once with subjects which, in this memoir, I have treated separately—each in its own chapter. To get a sense of this, the reader has only to refer to the chronological tables at the beginning of each major section of the book; I have included them in order to show how the various issues under discussion overlapped in time. I do think, however, that the Carter Administration can be considered in some rough chronological order, and, accordingly, I have divided this book into three parts, corresponding to what I view as three major phases of the Administration: the first, in which we undertook broad foreign policy initiatives; the second, which focuses on several major turning points in which our foreign policy either scored major successes or suffered severe setbacks; and the third, which describes how the Carter policy was tempered by these conflicting experiences.

I have made every attempt, in writing this book, not to simply reconstruct the past from hindsight. To this end, I have carefully reviewed the record of my various memoranda to the President, the minutes of various meetings in which I participated or which I chaired, contemporary news clippings, as well as my own notes on the more important events, which I dictated fresh, usually late the same night. Thus, all quotations of verbatim remarks either by me or attributed to others that appear in this book are taken either from the actual minutes of meetings or from my notes dictated on the same day. In no case have I used reconstructions attempted months or years later. In some cases, I quote my journal notes directly. Longer passages are indented for easier recognition. These journal excerpts are reproduced verbatim, for which I beg the reader's indulgence; dictation at the end of a tiring day is not likely to be conducive to literary elegance.

In writing this book I benefited from the help of many friends and colleagues. President Carter generously—and without any restrictions—opened to me his Presidential archives and permitted quotations from his papers and instructions to me (including Annex I in full) and from my memoranda to him. His generosity is gratefully acknowledged—and I only hope that in the pages that follow I have done justice to his dedicated leadership and to his historic accomplishments in the area of foreign policy. I have tried to be honest in reviewing our occasional disagreements and even tensions, but I trust that I succeeded in conveying my genuine affection for this remarkable man and President.

My successor, Richard Allen, was most gracious in facilitating access to my official papers and in arranging some of the necessary clearances for my staff. His truly helpful attitude made my transition out of office —as well as the needed research for this book—so much easier. I am pleased to acknowledge this, as well as the equally cooperative attitude of Allen's successor, William Clark. Ms. Brenda Reger of the National Security Council coordinated the interagency clearance process of portions of the manuscript, and her efficient and timely actions (so in keeping with the NSC tradition) greatly expedited the routine. I thank her warmly. Finally, on the governmental side, at the U.S. Archives,

E. Alan Thompson, Director of the Records Declassification Division, and his staff were always eager to assist me and my research associates, and it pleases me to be able to register my debt to them.

Special acknowledgment is due to a number of my close associates. Trudy Werner, who worked for me first at the Trilateral Commission and then for many endless hours in that crowded, always busy annex to my office in the West Wing of the White House, provided vitally important continuity in my present office, tirelessly supervising the preparation of the manuscript as well as many other aspects of this project. She was an essential alternative to chaos! Three other former NSC colleagues were intimately associated with the research and development of this volume. Madeleine Albright participated in the early shaping of its structure and provided the much-needed intellectual as well as political critique of my recollections. Her good judgment and friendship were invaluable. Nicholas Spiliotes, with genuine devotion and high intelligence, was heavily engaged in archival research and in reviewing my initial drafts, and he himself integrated my diary entries with official memoranda in drafting the first versions of Chapters 4 and 8. He and his able successor, Carol Hansen, were relentlessly honest in criticizing my manuscript and in pointing out its deficiencies. Carol also devotedly edited my final draft. To these four go my very special gratitude, for without them I simply would have produced much later a product in which I would take much less pride.

Individual chapters were reviewed carefully by Michel Oksenberg, William Odom, William Quandt, and Gary Sick, all of whom were also direct actors in the story recounted therein. Their suggestions and accounts of what transpired greatly strengthened the accuracy and the analysis presented in this memoir. More specific segments of the book were also reviewed by Jody Powell and by my other former NSC associates, notably Guy Erb, Gerald Funk, Robert Kimmitt, Jessica Tuchman Mathews, Robert Pastor, James Thomson, and Victor Utgoff. To all of them go my friendship and appreciation.

A special debt is owed to Christine Dodson, the NSC Staff Secretary, who played a central role in organizing the NSC files and who, together with Carol Cleveland, George Van Eron and Madeleine Albright, made the necessary arrangements for their safeguarding. All those who have an appreciation for historical research owe them a special obligation.

The publisher of this book, Roger Straus, gave me both encouragement and much-needed advice. In working with him I came to appreciate more fully why he has been so often described as the dean of America's publishers. His associate, David Rieff, helped to smooth out the manuscript and to improve its organization, bringing to bear on this task his good judgment, felicity of style, and—very important—unperturbed patience.

It is not only a bow to convention to end this expression of gratitude by registering the unique editorial and intellectual role played by my wife, Muska. She has edited all my previous books and her standards remain painfully high. I have never met them, but even trying was critically helpful.

Zbigniew Brzezinski
October 1982

POWER
AND
PRINCIPLE

Prologue

At 3 p.m. on January 20, 1977, I left the rather cold Presidential box at the Inaugural Parade and went over to my office in the White House. My staff was already present, moving in papers and arranging the files. I knew that I was assuming a major responsibility and I had given a great deal of thought to what my priorities ought to be. I was determined to focus my energies while in the White House on the attainment of three broad objectives:

First, I felt it important to try to increase America's ideological impact on the world and to infuse greater historical optimism into our outlook on the world. In my view the preceding years had seen a striking decline in the relevance of the American message to the world, and I believed that by emphasizing human rights America could again make itself the carrier of human hope, the wave of the future. This would help to overcome the spreading pessimism, which in the realm of action is particularly dangerous because it can become a self-fulfilling prophecy.

The second was to improve America's strategic position, and that meant primarily in relationship to the Soviet Union. I had become increasingly concerned about the longer-term political implications of growing Soviet military power, and I feared that the Soviet Union would become increasingly tempted to use its power either to exploit Third World turbulence or to impose its will in some political contest with the United States. Accordingly, I also believed that an improvement in the U.S.–Chinese relationship was in the strategic interest of the United States.

The third was to restore America's political appeal to the Third World. Prior to the assumption of office I felt strongly that the policies of the preceding years had resulted in America's undue isolation in the world, and I feared the consequences for our own society of a lonely America in a hostile world.

For me, the period of waiting ended on December 15, 1976, when my wife and I were attending a large pre-Christmas party at Automation House in New York City given by our good friend Ted Kheel, the highly respected labor negotiator. All of a sudden, I was jabbed in the shoulder and informed by an obviously awed young lady that "Governor Carter is trying to reach you on the telephone." I had the premonition this might be "it." I asked my wife to accompany me, and we went to Kheel's secluded office on the third floor where I could receive the call in privacy. Carter's voice was cheerful, slightly teasing:

"Zbig, I want you to do me a favor. . . . I would like you to be my National Security Adviser."

"That's no favor—that is an honor. And I hope and feel confident that you won't regret your decision," I replied.

"Actually, I knew as of some months ago that you were my choice, but I had to go through these processes of selection. But I knew all along," added Carter.

Then we talked briefly about various staffing decisions, and I stressed that I wanted a lean and efficient staff, not a small State Department. Carter heartily agreed. Then Hamilton Jordan came on the phone, and after some jocular exchanges regarding his comments during the election campaign about Vance and me (to the effect that Jordan would view it as a defeat if Establishment figures like Vance or me came to hold high posts under Carter), we discussed the arrangements for my trip down to Plains the very next morning, so that I could be properly "anointed" in front of the press.

I must confess to a moment of discomfort when Carter opened the conversation. When he uttered his opening sentence, "I want you to do me a favor," the thought flashed through my mind: he is going to offer me one of the lower-level positions that we had earlier discussed. He had called me on November 29 to ask me for my suggestions and comments on people for the top foreign policy positions in his Administration. Toward the end of the conversation, he asked me, "And what about you?" I said that I could see myself working for him either as an Under Secretary of State, or a Deputy Secretary with a Secretary like Cyrus Vance (to whom I could perhaps be helpful in conceptual terms), or as his NSC man, the integrator and energizer of policy for the President. At the time Carter replied noncommittally, "This is very helpful to me"—and now in a flashback it occurred to me that perhaps he was calling to ask me as "a favor" to take the slot of Under Secretary of State. His next few words dispelled that concern.

It was no secret that I wanted to be the President's Assistant for National Security Affairs. I expected Carter to be an activist President, and I felt that being close to him was the best spot for an activist person like myself. The press occasionally speculated that I might be appointed Secretary of State. I felt that this would not be the case. I sensed that

Carter wanted to be his own Secretary of State and that he would therefore be in control over foreign policy in the White House. The press speculation, however, was helpful to me because it deflected public attention from what was my goal, namely the White House slot. Accordingly, I did not object to the public speculation about the Secretaryship of State, though I did reiterate publicly—and quite sincerely—that I did not desire the position.

I first met Jimmy Carter at one of the early meetings of the Trilateral Commission, which I directed in the early 1970s. I remember discussing his membership with my two principal Trilateral Commission colleagues, Gerard Smith and George Franklin. We wanted a forward-looking Democratic governor who would be congenial to the Trilateral perspective. Reubin Askew of Florida was mentioned as a logical candidate, but then one of them noted that Jimmy Carter, the newly elected governor of Georgia, courageous on civil rights and reportedly a bright and upcoming Democrat, was interested in developing trade relations between his state of Georgia and the Common Market and Japan. I then said, "Well, he's obviously our man," and George Franklin went down to Atlanta to explore his background further and came back enthusiastic. Jimmy Carter was invited to join and he accepted.

In the course of 1974 I was told that Jimmy Carter had declared his candidacy for the Presidency and that he needed advice. I decided, therefore, to approach him, largely because I felt that he would spread the Trilateral Commission's concept of closer and more cooperative relations between the United States on the one hand and Europe and Japan on the other. I did not then think of him as a candidate with whom I would become closely identified. I wrote him a note making an offer of help, and received in return a handwritten note, dated December 31, 1974: "To Zbigniew Brzezinski— Thank you for your offer to help me with analyses of foreign affairs issues. I look forward to meeting with you for a personal discussion, and hope that in the meantime you would let me have any memos or articles which would be instructive to me. The Trilateral Com experience has been a wonderful opportunity for me, and I have used it perhaps even more than you could know. Your friend, Jimmy."

Through the spring of 1975 I sent Jimmy Carter various materials, including some of my speeches. I would receive from time to time handwritten notes expressing appreciation, occasionally praising me for the ideas that I had expressed, and reserving "the right to plagiarize freely." I became increasingly impressed by him, but the turning point came in the summer of 1975 when Carter and I, as well as other Commission members, attended a Trilateral meeting in Kyoto, Japan. At the Commission meeting itself, Carter spoke forcefully and clearly on behalf of a fair Middle East settlement as very much in the U.S.

national interest. Accordingly, I complimented him publicly at one of the plenary sessions. Afterwards, and quite unexpectedly, he asked me if I would be willing to attend a press conference, dealing with his candidacy, that he was giving to a group of American newspapers. I was a little surprised at the time, but concluded that he probably wanted to show the newspapermen that his candidacy was being taken seriously and that he could count on expert advice in his campaign.

His press conference made a believer of me. The American newspapermen were skeptical, sardonic, and even patronizing. "Well, Governor, how's your candidacy going? Anybody take it seriously back home? Tell us, your hope is to get a shot at the Vice Presidency, isn't it?" Carter withstood the barrage with a patient smile and simply responded: "The first test will be in Iowa, and I have really campaigned hard. I have done more in that state than the other candidates, and I expect to win. You fellows will probably ignore the victory. But then will come the New Hampshire primary. I have campaigned all over the state and as hard as I have ever campaigned in Georgia. I will win, and then your headlines will say 'Southerner wins in the North,' and after that will come Florida. It is right next to my home state, and I think I can knock Wallace below the 40 percentage line, thus lifting the scourge of Wallace from the Democratic Party; or I might even beat him. And then your headlines will say 'Carter Front-runner.' "

After returning home from Kyoto, I told my wife about this exchange and how impressed I was by Carter generally. I mentioned his comments on the Middle East and his demeanor under antagonistic questioning, and said that he struck me as a new and fresh face. This was the time when putative Presidential candidates were beginning to sign up advisers as evidence of their seriousness. I had been invited to meetings by Senators Kennedy, Jackson, and Mondale, and also by Congressman Udall. Walter Mondale withdrew from the race; Edward Kennedy struck me as electorally very attractive but I had misgivings about the Camelot crowd returning to Washington; Morris Udall, I feared, might repeat in the foreign affairs area the disastrous McGovern phenomenon; while Henry Jackson, who appealed to me the most on substantive grounds, was vulnerable as a relatively colorless candidate. Jimmy Carter thus came along at the right moment. I saw in him decency and humaneness, and I also felt that there was a great deal of steel underneath. As a result, I hoped that in the area of foreign policy he would be able to combine principle with power, the only prescription in my judgment for a successful American foreign policy.

My wife, who believes in getting to the point, simply said, "Put your money where your mouth is. If you like him and believe in him, don't wait for developments, come out and support him." I sent Carter a small check, and started writing foreign policy papers for him on a more systematic basis. I may add that at the time his national recognition factor in public opinion polls was less than 2 percent! He was not considered to be a serious candidate, and I was often asked why I was backing such an obscure figure.

By the end of 1975 I had emerged as Carter's principal foreign policy adviser. In late December he asked me "to develop for me the outline of a basic speech/statement on foreign affairs. . . . I agree with your order of priorities. I would also like to talk to you re more definite analyses and your personal campaign help. Your friend, Jimmy." Shortly thereafter I wrote him a letter in which I said: "As a framework for your own foreign affairs approach let me suggest that your basic case ought to be that our national purpose must be (1) as the first priority to create a stable inner core for world affairs, based on closer collaboration among the advanced democracies (open-ended trilateralism); (2) secondly, to shape on the above basis more stable North–South relations, which means (i) more cooperation with the emerging Third World countries (the richer and more successful), through such devices as the tripartite Paris conferences, etc.; (ii) compassionate aid to the Fourth World, which the U.S. should grant as a matter of conscience as well as interest, but in which it ought to also engage other states on a multilateral basis; (3) thirdly, to promote detente with the Soviet Union and to court China. Detente, of course, is desirable but it ought to be more reciprocal. Moreover, since the element of rivalry remains a reality, it cannot be the basis for coping with global problems."

Carter agreed, and that skeleton was then given more substance in a memorandum to the candidate at the end of January 1976 which I submitted jointly with Richard Gardner, a respected professor at Columbia University's Law School and also a very early Carter supporter. We argued that American foreign policy should seek to promote more international cooperation and more self-reliance in development by the Third World; that it should strive to make detente both more comprehensive and more reciprocal (these words "comprehensive" and "reciprocal" later became code words in my debates with Cyrus Vance) and that there should be continued efforts to reach agreement with the Soviet Union on arms control, particularly an effort to lower the present SALT ceilings; that more attention should be paid to China, since the Chinese–American relationship bore directly on the American–Soviet relationship, and hence we should further upgrade our political relations with China; and that all of this ought to be derived from an effort to create a stable inner core for world cooperation through closer consultations with Western Europe and Japan. This outline was later developed into a speech Carter delivered on June 23 to the Foreign Policy Association in New York. The speech was Carter's major statement on foreign policy, and it foreshadowed many of his actions and concerns as President.

The development of the speech gave me the first opportunity to work more closely with the Presidential candidate. I noted in my journal: "Have a good working relationship—he is calm, pleasant, and to the point. Funny, he inserted a lot of anti-Kissinger stuff (which he got from Ball) and I had to argue for omitting it. He was quite dogged, and finally we compromised on one 'Lone Ranger' reference to H.K." in Carter's speech.

A week after the speech was delivered I sent him a little note saying, "I concede! Your instincts were absolutely right—see enclosed." And I attached various newspaper clippings, praising the speech and heavily focusing on the "Lone Ranger" remark. As I often experienced later, the American press is not likely to give a serious speech much coverage unless there is some newsworthy twist to it which satisfies its taste for personal color.

During the campaign I remained in close touch with Carter, developing various memos for him, dealing either with current affairs or with long-range plans. We would often talk on the phone. On one occasion he asked me for my characterizations of the various people he was considering for the Vice-Presidential nomination. After sharing my views, I noted in my journal that "my gut feeling is that it will be Muskie or Mondale." On July 17, he asked me for some suggestions for his acceptance speech, and I recorded that "to my amazement he did use most of the language I dictated to him by telephone. Actually, I don't think it really fitted the speech, but it was gratifying." Toward the end of July, I traveled with Carter's foreign policy panel to meet with the candidate at his home in Plains.

Shortly thereafter, Carter asked me to develop, together with Henry Owen, the extraordinarily industrious former head of the State Department Policy Planning Council, and Richard Gardner, a joint foreign policy paper for the transition period. He also quizzed me at some length regarding George Ball. Ball had sent Carter a copy of his new book on foreign policy, a move obviously designed to register his availability. Carter was concerned because some people in the campaign were very opposed to Ball, largely on account of his allegedly anti-Israel views on the Middle East. As a result, it was agreed that Ball would be asked to prepare a separate paper, one which would identify him less directly with the campaign. At the same time, I did tell Carter that whatever people might be saying about Ball because of his views on Israel, he did have strong views and was not afraid to express them.

The foreign policy debate between Carter and Ford in San Francisco was a major turning point in the campaign. It had been preceded by the first debate, which focused largely on domestic issues. Much to everyone's surprise, Carter did not do quite as well as had been expected. He was clearly defensive about his performance. I talked to him on the telephone a few days after, and "when I said that he must now feel good to be at home, after such a tough week, he immediately, almost defensively, said, 'It was a *good* week.' "

In fact, it had not been a good week. Carter's campaign was for the first time on the defensive, and we were all concerned that he do better in the foreign policy debate. I was asked by the campaign staff to meet with Jimmy Carter in San Francisco on the morning of that debate. I briefed him for about two and a half hours over breakfast on October 5. I still did not know him well, and I was struck by the fact that he was wearing blue jeans and was barefoot; I said on greeting him, "Ah, our barefoot candidate," and I had the impression that he was not amused. I was taken by the fact that he said grace in a totally private fashion, simply by closing his eyes and bowing his head for two or three seconds. Having been accustomed in New England to rather officious sayings of grace before meals, which always struck me as somewhat hypocritical, I sensed in Carter a deep religiosity which at the same time was quite private and personal. Until that moment, I had wondered whether his proclaimed religious convictions were real or simply politically expedient. The feeling that I was dealing with a man of genuine conviction was important in shaping my own personal commitment to Jimmy Carter.

In addition to the substantive briefing, I stressed to the candidate (and I gave him a memo to that effect) that he ought to make leadership, both Presidential and of America in the world, the major theme of the debate. In fact, the memo argued that "if you are asked to make the opening response, use the initial part of the first three minutes for stating . . . that the major issue confronting us is the absence of effective Presidential leadership. . . . If your opening comment involves a reaction to Ford's response, you can use that opportunity to raise the above theme very briefly, indicating to the public that this is the key question for Americans to ponder. . . . In general, I should think that a major purpose of the debate on foreign policy will be to leave the public with a clear impression that Ford has provided no leadership." I stressed this theme because I felt that Carter had missed the chance to assert himself in the first debate and only by putting Ford on the defensive could he shatter the advantage of Presidential incumbency.

Carter "won" the debate—at least in terms of its political effects. Not only did Ford make a major gaffe on Poland, but Carter succeeded in putting him on the defensive throughout the entire debate. His opening words defined the theme: "Well, I think this Republican Administration has been almost all style and spectacular and not substance. We've got a chance tonight to talk about, first of all, leadership, the current character of our country and a vision of the future." On matters of substance, the debate was probably a standoff, but the combined effects of Ford's misstep on Poland and his defensive demeanor served to project Carter as genuinely Presidential, the dynamic and fresh leader that the country so badly needed after the crises of Watergate and Vietnam.

The period after the elections was spent by the President-elect in the development of position papers and in the selection of his new Administration. Those of us who had supported Carter from quite early on, notably Richard Gardner and Henry Owen, as well as myself, now found ourselves engulfed by offers of "help" from various colleagues. It was both a surprise and a pleasure to discover how many of them had apparently always thought of Carter as the outstanding political figure on the American scene and the extent to which they were prepared to make a personal sacrifice by joining him in Washington! As in every post-electoral phase, this was also a time of quiet maneuvering and positioning. I was aware of the fact that the anti-Kissinger mood that had developed in the course of 1976 worked to my disadvantage. I decided, therefore, simply to wait, while helping as best I could in the development of a joint longer-range foreign policy paper, which Carter had asked Gardner, Owen, and me to prepare. I felt that by then Carter must have formed some view of me and, even if only subconsciously, must have some notion of how he would like to involve me in his Administration.

I bided my time, though admittedly with mounting impatience. Toward the end of November, Carter called me in a very cheerful mood, saying—perhaps somewhat teasingly—that he would like to talk to me about people and appointments. He was particularly interested in what I had to say regarding top-level appointments in the area of foreign policy, and he asked me to call him back in two hours. Needless to say, the thought did cross my mind whether I should say something about myself, but, on balance, I decided that the better part of wisdom would be not to refer to myself at all. Instead, I started off by saying that he ought to think of appointments within the context of three alternative types of foreign policy leadership: there was direct and dominant Presidential leadership, in which a strong President (like Nixon) is assisted by a dominant White House (Kissinger) overshadowing a weak Secretary of State; there was, secondly, the model of a predominant Secretary of State, as with Dulles under Eisenhower or Kissinger under Ford, with a relatively passive President and nonobtrusive White House; and, thirdly, there could be a more balanced "team" arrangement, combining a strong President (like Kennedy) with a relatively secure and strong Secretary of State (Rusk) and an equally confident and energetic White House (Bundy). I said that I assumed that Carter would strive for the third model. In the back of my mind I did have the feeling that although he might naturally gravitate toward the first model, in view of the Kissinger legacy he would find it awkward to admit it. Moreover, at this stage, I did genuinely believe that the team approach could work.

I then went on to assess for Carter some possible candidates. In each case I outlined the strengths and weaknesses of each as I saw them and the organizational and international implications of his selection. I described George Ball as a strong conceptualizer but probably a poor organizer, an assertive individual but probably somewhat handicapped by his controversial position on the Middle East, and finally perhaps somewhat too Atlanticist in his overall outlook. I foresaw that Ball's appointment would be received extremely well in Western Europe and Japan, probably somewhat less so in the developing countries, and negatively in Israel. He would be a dominant Secretary of State, and one implication of that ought to be that the National Security Adviser should be a weaker person, not likely to engage in a policy contest. I sensed that Carter was not enthusiastic, and I added that he ought to consider Ball for the post of Secretary of the Treasury as well.

The second obvious candidate was Cyrus Vance, whom I described as a skillful negotiator, probably a very good manager, with a broad range of experience. I added that he might be overly concerned with the UN and with a U.S.–Soviet accommodation, and that he probably was not enough of a conceptualizer—though the President could compensate for that. The international reception to the appointment would be uniformly good. I said that Vance was a team player who would fit well into my third model of a balanced leadership in the area of foreign affairs.

We went on to discuss Paul Warnke, whom I described as highly articulate, possessing a quick mind and a broad intelligence, a skilled debater, though perhaps identified in the public mind as overly "soft" in his views on East–West relations. Warnke's appointment would be a strong signal of Carter's commitment to detente, but he would probably have to be matched internally by a "hard line" appointment, and I mentioned Paul Nitze as an example. We also discussed James Schlesinger and Senator John Culver (both of them praised by Carter), but it seemed to me that the President-elect was not giving much consideration to any of them. For the NSC, I suggested that he consider Harold Brown, unless he had him in mind for the Defense slot, or Henry Owen, or Richard Gardner. I noted, not without some personal interest, that Carter was extremely noncommittal on this subject.

After putting down the telephone receiver it dawned on me that I had in effect recommended Cyrus Vance to him as Secretary of State. I have no illusion that my recommendation was the determining factor, but I suspect in retrospect that it had a great deal to do with his choice of me to be his Assistant for National Security Affairs. My unplanned endorsement of Vance gave Carter the feeling that Vance and I could collaborate, a view which Vance apparently expressed to Carter in their discussions, when Carter was selecting Vance as his Secretary of State.

I felt very good about Cy's selection. I was also extremely pleased with Harold Brown's appointment. I had worked with both of them on the Trilateral Commission, but did not know Harold as well as I had gotten to know Cy. I was most impressed with Brown's credentials as the president of the California Institute of Technology, the first scientist to fill the job of Secretary of Defense. He had a reputation as a brilliant physicist with proven managerial ability and previous experience at the Pentagon. He understood the technological complexities of modern warfare. I thought that he was an excellent choice for that key Cabinet post.

On the evening of December 5, Carter called to tell me that Vance, whose selection had already been announced, had been the unanimous choice of all of his advisers. I told him that in the early summer I had been leaning toward George Ball, but had subsequently concluded that he would not really work out well as part of the team, and that Vance had become my number-one choice by the fall. Carter then asked me to come down to Atlanta to discuss what role I might play in the new Administration. On the evening of December 7, I met with him in the Governor's Mansion, and the two positions we discussed were those of the Assistant for National Security Affairs and Deputy Secretary of State. I made it clear that I preferred the former, and most of the discussion was spent on how I might operate, what might be my relationship to Vance, what is the proper role for the NSC. Carter stressed that he hoped that the NSC would assert itself particularly in relation to the Department of Defense. He felt that in the past the Department had not been adequately integrated into the decision-making process and that greater control from the White House would be needed. However, he made me no offer. At the end he merely asked me to sign some FBI security forms, and when I asked him how long it would take for them to be screened by the FBI, he said, laughing teasingly, "Usually only two or three days, but in your case probably no less than five or six weeks."

The phone call to the party at Automation House followed a week later, and the formal announcement of my appointment was made on December 16. I immediately plunged into two all-absorbing activities: developing an appropriate organization for the NSC and formulating the basic foreign policy goals for the new President. In a brief statement in Plains, when introduced to the press by the President-elect as his designated Assistant for National Security Affairs, I said, "We as a nation confront two fundamental alternatives—either the imperative of increased international cooperation or the specter of increasing global turbulence. It will be a time which will demand the very best from us, not only intellectually but morally."

The beginning was hectic. I was struck right away by "the fantastic pace of work. . . . Today I worked part of it literally standing up because there was practically no time to sit down; constant phone calls; papers crossing my desk; people to see; issues to respond to. And you wonder if it can be like this for four years, although the excitement and the challenge is probably more than enough to keep one going." It did stay that way.

During this early phase, I tried to keep away from journalists, but I noted that "escaping from the press might be a problem." I was swamped by requests for interviews and was even interviewed by an enterprising Washington *Post* journalist while walking to lunch. After an off-the-record supper with a few reporters in early February, during which there was a general discussion of foreign policy, I wrote that "I do have the feeling that this Administration is not going to be given much credit by these fellows and that criticism will come much sooner. There were questions on our policy toward the Soviet Union, human rights, where is the architectural effort, and all that. Somehow, they seem to have expected that these things will have been done within the first ten days. Their attitude varied from reasonably friendly to skepticism and doubt."

I was uneasy even in these early days about the policy orientation of some of Carter's foreign policy appointments. I feared that he would not be obtaining, especially from the State Department, the kind of realistic and hard-nosed advice which should balance his more idealistic views. On January 11, I wrote that "I will try to sensitize [Carter] to the need to have somewhat more tough-minded a group in security and arms control-oriented areas. I have a slight sense that perhaps too homogeneous a group is emerging insofar as these areas are concerned." The next day I reported that "I discussed with him the need for greater diversity in the defense/arms control cluster and I have the feeling that he may look into this issue more fully. Otherwise, there is the real prospect that the advice that he will be getting from the different departments and sectors of the government will be of a very similar outlook and substance." This theme cropped up several more times in the early weeks, but actually Carter left second-level appointments entirely to the discretion of his principal Cabinet Secretaries, thereby depriving himself of more effective personal and political control over the upper echelons of the State Department.

After our first Cabinet meeting I scribbled down a few vignettes: "So far in the Cabinet meeting I have been struck by how much [HEW Secretary Joseph] Califano flatters Carter in a way calculated to please him. [Commerce Secretary] Juanita Kreps maintains a standoffish, rather disdainful attitude, but it obviously makes Carter want to be nice to her. Toward [Energy Secretary] Schlesinger, Carter obviously defers to a considerable and highly visible degree. It will be interesting to see how quickly and how soon Schlesinger begins to move into the strategic and international areas."

My initial impressions of Washington social life were less than ecstatic. After attending the Alfalfa Club dinner, where "the old elite of Washington were mingling with the new," I commented on the extraordinary hypocrisy that seemed to dominate the atmosphere of the evening: "Everybody is greeting me so warmly, so friendly, with such amity, as if one was a bosom pal of people one hardly knows. Hypocrisy seems to be the dominant style in personal relationships around here."

Throughout, I kept observing closely the new President, my new boss. At a meeting on St. Simon after Christmas with the newly selected Cabinet, "I followed closely Carter's performance to get a sense of the man. I was on the whole struck by his coolness, deliberateness, and his obvious sense of systematic planning priorities. I also spent a little bit of time with Mrs. Carter and was quite impressed by her clear involvement in everything that he does. For example, she even sat in on the Cabinet meeting, sitting part of the time on the arm of his chair and part of the time at his feet." A week after the inaugural, I wrote: "In general, I am quite struck by how systematic Carter is in his approach to decision making and by the degree to which he wishes to immerse himself in detail. For example, today after a half-hour overview of the budget issue he asked for a four-hour briefing next Monday to go into these issues in depth." That session, held on February 1, "began at 4:30 and lasted, believe it or not, until almost 11:30 p.m. Carter went into every item in enormous detail, with great attention to specific data, both weapons specifications and finances. I occasionally wondered if he was doing this deliberately in order to impress us with his stamina or whether he was really fascinated. This morning when I talked to him about it, I could tell that he was quite pleased that I noticed that he was so determined to get into detail, and he stressed to me that he never likes to make a decision without being fully familiar with all the details."

Prior to the inaugural, Carter met on several occasions with the Joint Chiefs, to learn from them about our strategic plans but also to obtain their views on arms control, to which he was clearly dedicated. It was my first exposure to Carter as a negotiator, and I emerged from the experience feeling that he was unusually skilled in giving his interlocutors "a sense of confidence and yet encouraging them to moderate and modify their positions."

Despite such auspicious beginnings, I should also record that my career as Assistant for National Security Affairs almost came to an end on the evening of January 28, 1977. Having earlier discussed with the President the various emergency procedures to be followed in the event of an imminent nuclear attack on the United States, "I called in the person responsible for evacuating the President in the event of a crisis. I obtained a detailed account on how long it actually would take to evacuate the President by helicopter. . . . I ordered him to run a simulated evacuation right now, turning on my stopwatch. The poor fellow's eyes . . . practically popped; he looked so surprised. He said, 'Right now?' and I said, 'Yes, right now.' He reached for the phone and could hardly speak coherently when he demanded that the helicopter immediately come for a drill. I took one of the secretaries . . . along to simulate Mrs. Carter, and we proceeded to the south lawn to wait for the helicopter to arrive. It took roughly two and a half times as long to arrive as it was supposed to. We then flew to a special site from where another evacuation procedure would be followed. To make a long story short, the whole thing took roughly twice as long as it should have. Moreover, on our return we found that the drill somehow did not take into account the protective service and we were almost shot down."

1

Relating to Key Players

It would be hard to equal what Fritz Mondale has meant to me, but I believe I will become equally close to the Cabinet members and other leaders that will be sworn in this afternoon.

Cy and I have spent a lot of time together in the last couple of years. I guess of all the Cabinet members who were recommended to me, he had the closest to unanimous recommendation, and I am very grateful that Cy has come.

The next man who has been strongly recommended, both for the position he will hold and also as a chief scientific adviser for the President—he is a man who has had exceptional leadership background as Secretary of the Air Force. . . . I would like Harold Brown to come forward.

He has been an incisive analyst of the international field. He will be my closest adviser in tying together our economics, foreign policy, and also defense matters. . . . He will put together the most intimate preparations for any kind of crisis that affects our nation. . . . I would like to introduce to you Dr. Zbigniew Brzezinski.

> —President Jimmy Carter,
> remarks at swearing-in ceremony
> for Cabinet members, January 23, 1977

To the President

My position in the Administration depended entirely on my relationship with Jimmy Carter. Although I was given Cabinet status, my situation was different from that of other Cabinet officers. We all served at the pleasure of the President, but the Assistant for National Security Affairs derives his ability to exercise authority exclusively from the President himself. The Assistant neither runs a large department nor has a precisely defined mandate. Carter's desire to be an active, dominant President thus automatically enhanced my role as his stand-in on national security matters. But so much depended on how enduring that relationship would be, on whether I could count on his support, on the extent to which our ideas meshed, and—terribly important in Washington—on the degree to which I was perceived as being close to him personally. How that relationship would evolve in the White House pressure cooker would determine both my effectiveness and my survival.

Like Truman, Johnson, and Ford—and unlike Eisenhower, Kennedy, and Nixon—Carter entered the White House knowing little about foreign affairs. He was neither self-conscious nor embarrassed about this, and gained expertise by assiduously reading books and discussing foreign policy as much as he could. During the early stages of his Presidency, we had many wide-ranging discussions. Later, there was less time and maybe less inclination on his part to engage in such broad debate, and I missed them particularly during those periods in 1978–79 when I thought our policy was not sufficiently assertive.

I realized very quickly that it would be unwise to try to cultivate anything but a rigorously formal relationship with the President, given both the sense of distance that the Presidency inevitably engenders and Carter's own somewhat reticent personality. I noted in my journal that "in personal relations he is . . . somewhat cold; but in front of groups he is warm and highly complimentary about me." Accordingly, I concluded that I had better lead from strength; not being myself a jolly backslapper, I had better concentrate on providing Carter with crisp briefings, frank even if irritating comments, clear memos, and effective support. Reliance and trust rather than warmth, I felt, would work best in consolidating the relationship that had developed during the campaign.

Accordingly, I did not use the morning briefings, or the many other occasions when we were either traveling together or in some other one-on-one situation, to try to cultivate a personal friendship. I made it a point to be concise, businesslike, and utterly forthright—so that he would know that when I agreed with what he was saying it was an honest agreement, and that if I disagreed there were solid reasons for my dissent. It was also a point of honor with me, and I felt that Carter appreciated it, that I never used the many opportunities I had in being alone with Carter to engage in any personal sniping at Vance, Brown, or my other colleagues.

Not that the relationship was devoid of any human warmth. Carter must have sensed that I genuinely liked him, respected him, and grieved at his (our) setbacks. I also felt that in his own way he was fond of me and took me seriously. The highest compliment he paid me was that during the entire four years, with only two very special exceptions (after the normalization of relations with China and when awarding me the Presidential Medal of Freedom), he never thanked me for anything, nor did he ever rebuke me sharply (which he did occasionally to every one of his other senior officials, including Vance and Brown). I considered that to be a token of a special closeness, in which certain things need not be said, whether positive or negative.

There were disagreements, to be sure, though I tried to confine them, if I could, to one-on-one situations. I felt that it would be awkward for the President to be debated by his subordinate, and therefore I challenged him only at the NSC meetings or at our breakfasts if I felt that a wrong decision was about to be made. Otherwise, I would wait until I could speak to him alone, and then—as he sometimes complained—I would make my case strongly and persistently. Occasionally, this prompted some heat, of a very human and even peevish type. Once, when Carter produced his own version of a letter to Brezhnev instead of my draft, I told him of four specific and substantive objections to his version, adding (doubtless gratuitously) that I felt that his draft did not say much and that Brezhnev would not be impressed by it. Carter responded by saying that in that case he wouldn't write Brezhnev at all. I said that perhaps I could leave him with both versions and that he might want to think about it. "No," he snapped. "What should I do with the two drafts, then?" I inquired. "Throw them away" was his hurt conclusion.

There were also times when Carter tried to reach out in a personal way. There is no doubt in my mind that a barrier did arise between us as the years went on. I gradually came to think of him more and more as an institution—"the President"—and less and less as a human being —"Jimmy Carter" or even just "Carter." It had to be that way, and yet we were still human beings with our own personal ambitions and hopes intertwined by fate. There were times when I felt that he was trying to puncture that barrier, to reestablish some measure of warmth and communion. Sometimes it was through a personal phone call, just to say something pleasant or funny; more often it was through an abrupt, unexpected turn in a conversation, with him mentioning—in a totally unrelated fashion—something highly personal. One day, after we finished playing tennis, he suddenly started telling me about his difficulties with one of his sons; on another occasion, when we were discussing world affairs, he shared with me the details of an awkward ailment from which he was temporarily suffering. At other times, such diverse subjects as jogging (including what kind of shoes I ought to buy), tennis, family affairs, religion, Georgia, and Carter's family history served to convey a measure of personal warmth.

The best time to talk to the President was on Saturday mornings. After the formal national security briefing, he would often lean back in his chair and engage me in a conversation, on any subject. We might talk about history, or religion, or speculate about politics. It was on a Saturday morning quite early in the term that I suggested to him that he ought to record his recollections of the day in a systematic fashion, for otherwise he would have no record of what he actually thought and felt as President. Documents could never re-create that, I said.

Occasionally there would also be little gestures of personal friendship. It might come through an invitation to join him and Rosalynn in the Family Theater for movies. He told me once that he and Rosalynn were particularly fond of the movies of the thirties and forties, and I recall his enthusiasm in re-creating for me Gene Kelly's masterful dancing. Personal warmth could also surface, as it did one Saturday, in the form of a semi-shy request: "Would you have just Roz and me to supper tonight?"—with the disarming afterthought that hamburgers would do, that my wife need not prepare anything special (we had venison!). More often, though I suspect it was part a friendly challenge, it came in the form of an invitation to jog with him—something that I initially did until he simply left me behind both in distance and in speed.

I particularly recall our trip to Korea. As we were approaching Camp Casey in our helicopter, just south of the DMZ, where we were supposed to spend the night, Carter suggested that I join him and some troops in a morning jog. I asked at what time this invigorating event was to take place, and on learning that "it will be at 5:15 a.m., I politely declined on the grounds that I did not have any [running] shoes. Carter smilingly offered me his own. After a moment's reflection, I pointed out that I did not have any shorts. He said he would share an extra pair with me. Shortly after retiring, his valet showed up bringing me shorts and shoes. Thus early the next morning I proceeded to jog. He set off at the head of a platoon or two, approximately sixty men and a few uniformed women. We jogged for three miles, with him setting a really frenetic pace. About 20 percent of the troops fell out and all of the women. We were photographed by the press on the way out and on the way back. Unfortunately, [Jerrold] Schecter [the NSC press spokesman] and I couldn't quite keep up and there was a large gap between the President, the company, and the two of us coming in last. The press cheered wildly as we approached, and I raised my hands in a victory gesture and shouted to them that we did an extra lap and therefore we were coming in first."

I often wondered what it was that made for a bond between us—a bond that withstood four tough years, during which there were some occasions when each felt distressed by the other and yet mutual commitment and loyalty survived. In part, it was doubtless that mysterious interpersonal quality called "chemistry"; in part, it might also have been a curious cultural affinity. We were both outsiders, not just to Washington but in a larger sense to contemporary America. I was a naturalized American, even though politically probably more intensely American than most; Carter was very conscious and proud of his Southern background, but sensitive to any slight or cultural condescension from Northerners, and especially from established Washingtonians. I once came across a passage in William Styron's *Sophie's Choice* in which the author describes a surprising affinity between Poland and the South, two peoples bred on a history that overcame defeat, on a code of chivalry and honor that proudly compensated for backwardness:

"Poland is a beautiful, heart-wrenching, soul-split country which in many ways . . . resembles or conjures up images of the American South—or at least the South of other, not-so-distant times. . . .

"Despoiled and exploited like the South, and like it, a poverty-ridden, agrarian, feudal society, Poland has shared with the Old South one bulwark against its immemorial humiliation, and that is pride. Pride and the recollection of vanished glories. Pride in ancestry and family name, and also, one must remember, in a largely factitious aristocracy, or nobility. . . . In defeat both Poland and the American South bred a frenzied nationalism. Yet, indeed, even leaving aside these most powerful resemblances, which are very real and which find their origin in similar historical fountains (there should be added: an entrenched religious hegemony, authoritarian and puritanical in spirit), one discovers more superficial yet sparkling cultural correspondences: the passion for horseflesh and military titles, domination over women (along with a sulky-sly lechery), a tradition of storytelling, addiction to the blessings of firewater. And being the butt of mean jokes." I read that passage to Carter, for I thought that in a strange way it conveyed something about the relationship between the two of us.

But beyond that cultural affinity, there was perhaps another reason for the compatibility between us. For most of the four years no one in the White House close to the President except me was Carter's own age. All of his senior staff were much younger. The two closest to the President, Jody Powell and Hamilton Jordan, could have been his sons and had that kind of relationship with him. They could speak up to him in ways that I could not, but at the same time they could be chastised in a manner that would have been inappropriate in Carter's relationship with me. I think Carter took my criticisms more seriously, for, in effect, I was his only peer. There was, of course, Carter's very close personal friend Bert Lance. I believe that the Carter Presidency, and especially economic policy, might have taken a different turn if Lance had not been forced out. His departure was a searing experience for Carter; I remember entering Carter's small private office on the morning of Lance's resignation to find the two of them sitting there in obvious distress. Without having to be told, I knew what was about to happen. With the departure of Lance, Carter lost the one person in the White House who was genuinely his peer, and I certainly was only a partial substitute.

As time went on, I got to know the man better, to sense what he was about, and to interpret his moods and signals. Carter was famous for his smile. I soon learned that he in fact had several smiles. There was first of all the genial smile for public consumption. I was initially deceived by it because it seemed so warm and so forthcoming, and yet once you got to know him you knew that this was an outward smile, one with little individual affection in it, a "political" smile, as it were. Then there was the smile which he used to mask anger. More often than not, when angry, he would smile even while expressing displeasure, but only if one knew him well did one sense that behind the mask was unadulterated fury. Then there was a shy, relaxed smile, the expression of the individual at ease, which Carter revealed only occasionally to his intimates. This was the Carter who would exchange a private joke about some very pompous official, the Carter who would kid you about your personal habits. This Carter revealed himself rarely, but when he did you knew his friendship was without affectation.

Carter had a few pet sayings which I also came to interpret more accurately once I got to know him better. When he said, "I understand," he was saying, "I don't want to argue the subject with you anymore, and I don't want you to go away feeling that I have disagreed with you, but I am not going to say anything which you can later use to the effect that I had agreed with you." In effect, "I understand" was a pacifier— and it often produced misunderstandings with those who concluded that "I understand" meant "I agree." He would often say, "I will stand firm," or "I have no political interest in this." These were signals to me that he was weighing the possibility of a change of position or that he was concerned about political costs of a particular stand. Similarly, he would sometimes say, "This doesn't bother me at all," and I knew that he was reassuring himself precisely because he was deeply troubled. The key to working with him effectively was to recognize these signals for what they were.

I soon learned how, when necessary, to distract him from affairs of state and how to engage him intellectually. It goes without saying that I did this rarely, most often on Saturday mornings, and only when I knew the President had time for the luxury of a personal conversation. I would appeal to his strong and instinctive desire to be both a teacher and a student. For example, I would ask if he knew the background to, say, the Soviet nationalities problem, and the chances were that we would then become engaged in a prolonged discussion of the subject, with Carter literally lapping up facts and concepts. Alternatively, he would be the teacher, explaining with relish to his ignorant student some of the mysteries of nuclear fusion or the origins of Southern Baptist fundamentalism. All I had to do was ask for an explanation, and off he would go. His memory was phenomenal, his reading voracious, and his thirst for more knowledge unquenchable.

At times, Carter could also be extremely pedantic. Memos addressed to him would come back with penciled corrections of spelling mistakes or grammatical improvements. He also delighted in giving me lists of security violations committed by my staff (such as leaving a safe unlocked) that had been brought to his attention by the security office. I would make copies of such lists, with the President's initials on them, and give them to the perpetrators; the unintended result was that these came to be much appreciated as valued souvenirs of Presidential attention. Secretaries would frame and hang them. I found the whole thing amusing, for it showed the extent to which he was still a Navy lieutenant who very much enjoyed keeping the ship in trim and proper shape.

He was also very interested in the arts, and I suspect that to some extent his eagerness to immerse himself in culture reflected his small-town origins. Culture was something to absorb and to enjoy because early in life it was primarily derivative and secondhand, despite the fact that Carter's family was unusually well read and that as a child he was made conscious of the better things in life. Classical music would be played quietly as he worked in his small White House study, and more than once I was engaged (with a sense of some discomfort, because my expertise is more than limited) in a discussion of the relative merits of Rubinstein vs. Horowitz, of Nureyev vs. Baryshnikov. Once I was summoned by the special phone linking his office and mine to come over (it was 1:45 p.m. and I was just finishing lunch at my desk) to listen to a recording of a violin concerto. On another occasion, after Horowitz's concert in the White House, Carter told me that "during the entire concert Horowitz missed only one note and that this was something that he himself observed. A couple of times he urged me to have the concert replayed by [White House closed-circuit] TV so that I could listen to it. . . . What I didn't say was that a piano concert on television isn't exactly the same thing as a piano concert listened to directly."

I never doubted that I was dealing with a shrewd, rather deliberate, yet fundamentally very decent and engaging person who combined high intelligence with occasionally surprising naïveté, genuine dedication to principle with sometimes excessive tactical flexibility. Carter had real feeling for the nuances of language and was a master at leaving himself room for maneuver; yet on occasion, as after the Soviet invasion of Afghanistan, he would overstate what he wanted to say quite grossly and pay a high political price for it. He was generally very serene, and this helped to maintain a stable relationship—but one could also sense within that relationship major shifts from genuine warmth to sudden distance. The latter was especially the case when events, and perhaps my persuasion, made him do things that instinctively he would have preferred not to do.

Of course, it helped that over the years he and I developed somewhat the same dislikes (especially Schmidt and López Portillo) and similar favorites (Sadat, Giscard, and Deng Xiaoping—though for me the Pope came first). At the same time, domestically we did not concur to nearly the same extent. For example, I thought highly of Howard

Baker and tried hard to get Carter to engage him in what I hoped would become a bipartisan foreign policy. Carter simply did not get along well with him; the chemistry just was not there. And chemistry plays a far more crucial role in politics than is usually imagined.

On some Saturday mornings in his office or when traveling, Carter and I would gossip a bit, comparing notes on people. His clear favorite was Sadat. It was love at first sight and quite genuine, I think, on both sides. There is not the slightest doubt that Carter deeply cared for that expansive, impetuous, bold Egyptian, who embodied qualities so different from those of the highly controlled, precise Georgian with the computerlike mind. We would laugh together at Sadat's inaccuracies and sweeping assertions, and yet at the same time we marveled at his courage and the grandiose scope of his historical vision. I told Carter about one of my meetings, in which Sadat clapped his hands and had a huge globe brought into his living room, on which with a pointer he gave me a lecture on what U.S. global policy ought to be. His prescriptions would have made Theodore Roosevelt sound like a pacifist!

Carter spoke of Sadat as his dearest friend, a person who would do anything for Carter and to whom Carter was utterly committed. For Carter, Sadat was quite literally family, in the Southern sense. Carter identified with Sadat in an extraordinary way. There was also a bit of hero worship. I almost felt a degree of deference in Carter's feeling, a touch of loving envy for Sadat's boldness and a great deal of protective concern.

In the case of Valéry Giscard d'Estaing, there was no question of feeling. Rather, Carter's relationship with the President of France was that of one well-functioning mind admiring another. Both Carter and I were struck by the detached, aloof, cold quality of Giscard's reasoning. His mind seemed almost disembodied. It functioned by itself, lodged in an elongated and elegant casing, which was immobile, passive, and projected coldness. It was the mind that worked, spoke, queried, and dissected. Of all the foreign statesmen we met, Giscard had by far the best mind and yet he was almost impossible to reach personally.

Giscard was invariably haughtily polite. Whenever I went to Paris, he would invite me to his ornate office for a talk, treating me in these sessions as a fellow intellectual with whom it was worthwhile to analyze and reflect on problems. Sitting in his study, often dimly lit by a desk lamp, with logs burning in the fireplace, one was first queried systematically, asked for one's analysis of current issues, and then treated to a subtle, sometimes slightly ironic commentary. From some of his asides about American attitudes, I had the feeling that my Polish patrimony and my Ivy League professorship were more important reasons for being taken seriously than my formal position.

I could never figure out what Giscard thought of Carter. But Carter valued his relationship with Giscard, especially as his disenchantment with German Chancellor Helmut Schmidt mounted. He would interrogate me on my talks with the French President and would recount, I thought with a touch of pride, his own exchanges with "Valéry." I felt that Carter was gratified that Giscard treated him as an intellectual peer, and I detected a touch of the country boy's awe for the elegance of the Parisian's intellect. However, affection never intruded into that relationship.

I had the feeling that Carter saw in Sadat, in Giscard, and in the Chinese leader Deng Xiaoping traits he hoped others would see also in him. When Deng Xiaoping, the diminutive but dangerous leader of China, whose capacity for political survival others had painfully underestimated, came to Washington, he impressed Carter, as he had earlier impressed me in Beijing, with his quickness of mind, his acerbic tongue, and—above all—his cold and even ruthless appreciation of the uses of power. His discussion with us of the Chinese plans for a military operation against Vietnam (see Chapter 11), and of possible Soviet moves against China and of China's reactions, was the single most impressive demonstration of raw power politics that I encountered in my four years in the White House. As I listened to Deng's calm, determined dissection of a possible Sino-Soviet power confrontation, I could not help but think that this discussion was taking place in the midst of a most acute debate in Washington on how we ought to respond to the disintegration of the pro-American regime in Iran, and I secretly wished that Deng's appreciation of the uses of power would also rub off on some of the key U.S. decision makers.

Deng was tough, even brutal, but his most important asset was his straightforward and lucid sense of strategic direction. He understood that a new global balance of power was in the making, that China and the United States shared common geopolitical interests, and that concrete political conclusions needed to be drawn from that reality. Deng wasted no time on irrelevancies, concentrating rather on the key objective, and that quality both awed and attracted Carter and me.

If the President and I admired the same people, we also shared similar dislikes. Among them the Chancellor of Germany, Helmut Schmidt, took the undisputed first place. This need not have been the case, for Carter's initial attitude toward Schmidt was one of respect and even deference. He knew that Schmidt had a better grasp of world economics, not to speak of the advantage of having inherited from his predecessors a healthy domestic economy. I had known Schmidt for at least a decade and a half prior to my going to the White House, and I had briefed Carter on Schmidt, presenting a most attractive and favorable picture. Prior to their first meeting Carter was eager to learn from, and to work closely with, the German Chancellor. That attitude was unfortunately not reciprocated. Schmidt, almost from the very first encounter, adopted a patronizing attitude, mixed with less than persuasive protestations of friendship. Invariably there followed nasty behind-the-scenes gossip to sundry American and German journalists.

I often suspected that Schmidt's attitude became hostile after Carter's success at the London Economic Summit of 1977. Schmidt had dominated the earlier summits and had come to this one expecting to continue in his starring role. Yet the summit was unquestionably Carter's triumph, and the Western press hailed him as the new leader. I sensed that Schmidt resented this bitterly. Matters were not made better by an incident in which Carter embarrassed Schmidt into retracing his steps when the two of them were leaving 10 Downing Street. After saying goodbye to the Prime Minister, Carter followed his usual routine of shaking hands with the lowly staff; Schmidt, obviously flustered, then detoured himself in his elevator shoes in order to repeat Carter's act.

Invidious gossip and derogatory asides followed almost immediately and became the standard follow-up to any personal meeting between the two men. At such meetings Schmidt volubly professed his personal friendship. Then within a day or two would come reports on Schmidt's expressed contempt for the American President. There is no doubt in my mind that Schmidt's conduct contributed greatly to the deterioration in American–German relations in that it made it both fashionable and legitimate in Germany to derogate the U.S. President in a manner unthinkable in earlier times.

Understandably, Carter developed a strong dislike for Schmidt, considering him to be a bully and a hypocrite. I tried to get leading Germans to help muzzle the Chancellor, but to no avail. I brought the matter up with Foreign Minister Hans-Dietrich Genscher, a thoughtful and most responsible German statesman, and with Berndt von Staden, the diligent and discreet German Ambassador in Washington. At first, Genscher laughed and said, "Well, he's known in Germany as 'the Lip.' He speaks the same way about other Cabinet members." I told Genscher that this might be so, but that he was talking about the American President and it was having a terrible effect on American–German relations. On more than one occasion Genscher assured me that he would do what he could. So did von Staden. But in fact there was nothing to be done since the difficulty was rooted in Schmidt's character. A revealing insight into the nature of that personality came to me when, on one occasion, I was talking with him privately about sensitive NATO affairs. We were having a perfectly good and normal discussion until two of Schmidt's aides entered the room. In an instant, he changed the tone of his voice and began to shout at me and did not desist until I started replying in kind.

Carter's dislike for the other statesman was less specific, more instinctive, and certainly had less impact on our relations. Neither he nor I had any particular grievances against the President of Mexico, José

López Portillo. It was more a matter of his attitude and manner, which combined pomposity with vanity. For example, when the Carters arrived in Mexico City on a state visit, they were made to walk a couple of hundred feet on a red carpet toward a platform with an immobile statue on it, which on closer examination turned out to be the Mexican President. Perhaps this act of imposed homage had some special meaning to the Mexican leader and his associates, but it struck both of us as silly and vainglorious.

I never discussed the Pope in any detail with Carter, but in the course of several exchanges with Pope John Paul II (see also p. 461), whom I came to admire enormously both for his conviction and for his extraordinary political grasp, His Holiness did make one very perceptive comment about my President. Recounting his Washington conversations, the Pope smiled and said, "You know, after a couple of hours with President Carter I had the feeling that two religious leaders were conversing." I told this to Carter, who was immensely pleased by that comment, and I thought that this, too, was in itself quite revealing.

Personal likes and dislikes were not the only bond between us. Humor was also a catalyst and a safety valve in maintaining the relationship. From time to time, I would send in a memo designed to amuse or to tease. When the press reported (erroneously) that Amy Carter had been in touch with a Soviet dissident, I sent him a memorandum, on which he responded with humorous references to Amy's cats. On the occasion of his birthday, I sent to Camp David a message, allegedly from Brezhnev, contrived to precipitate predictable marginal comments. First of all, I deliberately overstated his age by three years, prompting him to write on the margin (before he realized it was a fake): "Zbig— tell Brezhnev: 53"; then indicated in stilted Soviet language that in honor of the President's birthday the Soviets were now prepared to accept U.S. SALT proposals but only if the limits on the Soviet aggregates were *more restrictive* than those on the American, thereby alerting him to the spoof; and, finally, requested "as a step towards greater trade between us . . . that you let me have here your assistant, Mr. Brzezinski, for a few weeks. I would personally take care of his human rights and return him to you in a deserving condition." Carter wrote on the margin: "OK, but will not take him back—entire package stacked against US because of Brzezinski item."

On another occasion, the President's secretary, Susan Clough, showed him a picture of me having lunch with Soviet Ambassador Anatoly Dobrynin, with a vodka bottle on the table, and another of the two of us reclining on lounge chairs in the Rose Garden. The second picture came back to me with a unique dedication: "Zbig—this is a predictable aftermath of the vodka luncheon. At least the bird looks sober and alert. Jimmy" (referring to a little bird that seemed to be planted near our feet). On another occasion, I read to the President an account of a

MEMORANDUM

THE WHITE HOUSE
WASHINGTON

June 17, 1977

MEMORANDUM FOR THE PRESIDENT

TOP SECRET

FROM: ZBIGNIEW BRZEZINSKI ᏃᏅ .

SUBJECT: White House Contacts with Soviet Dissidents

I have seen press reports that a member of the White House community, a Miss Amy Carter, has been in direct touch with Soviet dissidents. A check of our files reveals that such correspondence was undertaken outside of the NSC process and was not subject to normal staffing procedures.

In view of the foregoing, you may wish to consider the following options:

1. A call to the President's Office for a personal report (on the model of General Singlaub);

2. A personal reprimand;

3. Request for a clarification;

4. Reassignment;

5. Commendation for personal initiative;

6. None of the above.

Your instruction regarding the above is hereby requested for appropriate action.

This is very serious. Because of the sensitivity of the subject & the difficulty, have of my dealing with a superior, CIA check with her associates clandestinely before I see her. Begin with the Grits and Misty Malarkey Ying Yang.

J.C.

profile of leading Washington figures submitted by an ambassador. One person was described as very calculating, cold, and determined. Carter smiled and said, "Aah, they're describing you," and with some relish I responded, "No, Mr. President, they're describing you."

I liked Carter's sense of humor. It was quick and dry and quite spontaneous. I remember, for example, a day in the summer of 1979, shortly after the massive purge of the Cabinet, walking "into the President's Oval Office this morning to give him the briefing before our early foreign affairs breakfast; he was sitting near the fireplace reading the newspapers. The front page of the newspaper was covered with pictures of people he had fired. He looked at me, smiled, and said, 'I am looking in the newspaper to see whether you are still in the Cabinet.' "

Another shared form of cultural appreciation was an eye for attractive women. During the first Economic Summit in London in May 1977, while riding in a car, Carter and I shared a good laugh when we caught each other craning our necks for a better look at an extremely attractive woman walking along the sidewalk. On another trip, while in Belgrade in 1980, the Yugoslav President's translator was an unusually striking and very well-endowed Serbian lady. At one point the President passed me a note asking if I knew the Serbo-Croat translation for an appropriate and concise description. In my response I complimented the President on his strategic vision.

Little instances like that, in themselves not significant or even (I realize) amusing to others, helped to reduce the inevitable tensions in the relationship, especially during the various policy disputes that took place.

I have no doubt that Carter both respected and resented the fact that I pushed hard on some key issues (as the chapters that follow show), that I became a protagonist as well as a coordinator of policy. Yet I think he knew my role changed in part because events bore out my grimmer assessments of the Soviet role and because increasingly the Administration needed an articulate voice to explain what it was trying to do. Initially, I was very conscious that "people are laying for Brzezinski all over town, ready to pounce on any sign of assertiveness" (as the Washington *Post* put it on March 28, 1977—my birthday), and therefore I really wanted to lie low. I also believed, probably naïvely, that our collegial system would work well, with the public case for our foreign policy being made primarily by the President and the Secretary of State.

In practice, it turned out that Vance, for all of his many gifts and personal qualities, was not an effective communicator, and the President started encouraging me to speak up more. Indeed, after my appearances on the Sunday talk shows he would phone me, as sometimes did Rosalynn, to tell me how well I had done. On other occasions, he sent back to me press dispatches on my comments with marginal notes, such as "Zbig—perfect" (referring to a speech I made at the National Press Club urging our allies to stand more steadfastly with us against the Soviet Union on the Afghanistan issue). Unfortunately, and with adverse consequences not only for me personally but more significantly for the President himself, these public appearances did fuel the image of an Administration in which the National Security Adviser overshadowed the Secretary of State, and in retrospect it probably would have been wiser for me to have been the invisible man.

Yet none of that affected my relationship with Carter. If anything, press attacks on me strengthened his support. When the New York *Times* published in early 1979 an account of our Iranian policy, apparently based on deliberate State Department leaks designed to embarrass me, Carter really lit into Vance (at the January 12 breakfast), saying that "if this goes on I will make my decisions only with Fritz and Zbig and simply not tell anybody else." On more than one occasion, he asked me how I was bearing up under the press attacks that became especially frequent after Vance's resignation in the late spring of 1980, and then again during the highly inflated "Billy Carter affair," reassuring me that as far as he was concerned the attacks were having an opposite effect.

It would be wrong to conclude, however, that my relationship with the President was without its ups and downs. The White House, after all, is a beehive of activity which includes also a large dose of backstabbing and intense personal rivalries. I was the object of envy and resentment, and also of much criticism (some of it, doubtless, more than merited). I never knew how much of it was filtered directly to Carter, but I cannot think of any instance in which adverse gossip visibly affected my standing. The only known case, that of Chancellor Schmidt's attempt to undermine me (see p. 463), clearly backfired; in the very last phases of the Presidential campaign Carter was probably concerned that the extreme left of the Democratic Party was hostile to me, but he personally never made me feel it.

In reviewing my journal, I am struck that at different times I noted periods of special closeness and chumminess in my relation with Carter; at other times, I felt some distance, even coldness. Paradoxically, but also perhaps revealingly, the periods of relaxed warmth coincided more with times when U.S. policy was less concerned with the problems of power, when (putting it very simply) it more reflected Vance's concerns. When my stock on the outside was highest, especially after the Soviet invasion of Afghanistan, on the inside I felt sometimes that it was sinking. Perhaps it was my imagination, but in early 1980 I noted on several occasions that Carter seemed to resent my efforts to make him into a successful Truman rather than a Wilson. Of course, events, their educational impact, and Carter's own underlying toughness had more to do with his increasing acceptance of the hard line from 1979 on than any persuasiveness on my part. But in those difficult days I was especially sensitive to any change in Carter's attitude toward me.

Most important to me—and something which I will always cherish—was the underlying feeling that I had throughout the entire four years that my loyalty to Carter as a person and as the President was reciprocated by his loyalty to me. This was a priceless asset in those very difficult days of continuous political conflict in which one was inevitably and endlessly engaged. He gave moving testimony to this on the day when, shortly before leaving office, he awarded me the Presidential Medal of Freedom. Speaking quite spontaneously and with evident emotion to the assembled audience, he stated, "I doubt that anyone in my own Administration has been more controversial than Dr. Brzezinski and the reason for it is manifold, but I would like to say two reasons: One is that he is evocative. He is a person who explores constantly better ways to do things. . . . I don't know of a single time in the last four years when he has ever made a public statement of any kind, privately or publicly, which was not compatible with my own policies. The other reason that he has been somewhat controversial is that he has never tried to take credit for a success, nor has he ever tried to blame me as President or anyone else for a failure. To me this is a wonderful evidence of courage because it's so easy for someone who works within the inner circles of the White House in particular and other places of leadership when something goes wrong very quietly, very subtly to say I recommended one thing, the President or the Secretary of State or the Secretary of Defense did something else. Zbigniew Brzezinski has never done that. I am deeply indebted to him and I think the nation shares that debt with me. . . ."

To Rosalynn Carter

Throughout the four years a special reinforcement to this relationship was Rosalynn's attitude toward me. Carter once said something quite revealing: that while he would reassess over time his view of a person, and often revise it quite drastically, for Rosalynn her first impression was decisive; it never altered. I had the feeling that her view of me was good, though she never said anything explicitly to indicate that, and I sensed that I had in her an important ally.

Her influence on her husband was considerable and was exercised almost openly. Carter—at least to me—was not embarrassed to admit it. The two of them were extremely close. Once, late in the evening, I had to give Carter a memorandum personally, and I went over to the Family Theater, since my electronic guide indicated that the President was there. I found the theater empty, except for Carter and Rosalynn, sitting together on a sofa, holding hands while watching a movie. Carter also told me that every evening the two of them would read jointly a chapter from the Bible and (typical of his unending quest for self-improvement) that during the first year of the Presidency they did so in Spanish so that they could also enhance their mastery of that language.

He was even a bit of a protective husband. I recall one moonlit night in the bay of Rio de Janeiro, on a yacht, when Carter—while talking to me in the bow—all of a sudden asked Rosalynn to dance. As just the two of them were gracefully gliding, with the rest of us, including the Brazilian Foreign Minister, standing and watching, I decided that I did not wish to be a courtier and I simply cut in on them. During the dance, I suggested to Rosalynn that after docking we should all go to a nightclub. As soon as we stopped, she purred to the President, "Jimmy, Zbig suggests we go to a nightclub. Let's . . ." Carter looked at her coldly, gave me a passing glance, and in very slow and deliberate tones muttered, "Rosalynn, if you want to go to a nightclub with Zbig, it's all right with me." (We did go . . . the *three* of us.)

Rosalynn could be as tough as she was charming and gracious. I felt strongly that one of the unkindest, and totally undeserved, cuts inflicted on the Carters was Hugh Sidey's column in *Time* magazine celebrating the alleged return with the Reagans of culture to the White House. Rosalynn gave the White House both grace and warmth and did so without flaunting either status or power or, as lately has been the case, wealth. For Carter, she was a tower of strength, a source of serene affection and of good judgment. Whenever an important issue arose, she would quietly sit and listen—and later share with him her views. She had a knack for getting to the guts of a problem. When I briefed her on the crisis that had developed over the Soviet brigade in Cuba and commented that the President had ordered us to protest to Brezhnev, she cuttingly observed, "But Brezhnev already has a cabinet-ful of our protests."

On another occasion I noted (August 29, 1979) after giving Rosa-lynn an extensive briefing: "She is really quite a charmer. She sat there like a demure schoolgirl, taking notes, asking questions, but beneath that innocent air there is a very purposeful and politically shrewd individual. It is good to have her on one's side." That she was sympathetic to me and to my approach greatly fortified my standing with Carter, and it would have been a major source of strength for me in the event of a major showdown over my role, which might have taken place if Carter had been reelected.

To Walter Mondale

The challenge would have come probably from Mondale as well as from Vance's successor, Muskie—if late-1980 White House whispers were to be believed. Initially my relations with the Vice President could not have been better or warmer. Our offices in the West Wing of the White House were adjoining, and that made for easy and informal contact. When there was something to talk about, Fritz (as the Vice President was called by his friends) would simply pop into my office, or I would stick my head into his. Carter was determined to make Fritz a genuinely active Vice President, and it was my task to make certain that Fritz knew what was going on in the national security area.

Fritz and I hit it off well. Ten or so days after assuming office, I jotted in my journal: "One of the more pleasant relationships I am developing is with Mondale. He really is a delightful and amiable guy, extremely easygoing, very direct and to the point. Very bright and cooperative. I think it is a relationship which I will very much enjoy. Moreover, I hope he will get more actively engaged in foreign affairs." Ten days later in a similar entry: "It is quite striking how often Mondale now drops by to chat. . . . For example, today he came in to talk about our relations with Europe. . . . He has a knack of looking at problems with a sense of detachment and this prevents him from becoming absorbed in too much detail."

These initial impressions, by and large, stood the test of time. Mondale throughout impressed me as quick, alert, possessing a quiet wit and—if necessary—a sharp tongue. "It's always amusing to talk to him, and a great deal of our time is spent simply joking around," I observed on another occasion, and this shared element of humor was of some importance, given the inevitable tensions enveloping the Oval Office. Fritz also had much more relaxed working habits than Carter; he would arrive in his office at a civilized hour, was not embarrassed to take an occasional nap during the day, and would smilingly depart in the later afternoon, bidding us toilers a cheerful goodbye.

But Mondale managed to be on top of issues, not by doing as much reading as Carter, but by relying more on timely briefings. This made for a more superficial grasp of affairs, but Fritz compensated for that with his innate ability to focus on the truly significant or central, without getting bogged down in minutiae. When he discovered that CIA Director Admiral Stansfield Turner's weekly, and later biweekly, briefings of the President were somewhat less than useful, he simply stopped coming. His reliance on oral presentations did increase the importance of those who had access to him, and in some instances of the last person to talk to him before he made his final recommendations to Carter.

As I got to know him better, I discovered that underneath the genial demeanor there was also some inner tension and insecurity. Though he did not mind lighthearted sparring, he tended to become irritated when challenged more seriously. He hated to be interrupted, even though he would do so often himself to others; on one occasion, he even complained to David Aaron, my deputy, that I had dared to interrupt him at a session of the Special Coordination Committee (SCC) which I was chairing. On another occasion, he got exceedingly exercised, and even called me from Mexico, because an obscure State Department official had said to a newspaperman that Fritz's visit to Mexico was a trip in search of a mission. On several occasions when we discussed articles about him, I was struck how put off he was by a few passing critical comments in otherwise remarkably laudatory treatments. I was also amused by the loving way he would comb his hair in front of the mirror in his office before proceeding to any meeting.

Mondale's most important substantive contribution was his political judgment. He was a vital political barometer for the President, and Carter respected his opinion on the domestic implications of foreign policy decisions. I also felt that Mondale had a good sense of political timing. For example, in the early months he was quite keen on pushing hard with our Middle East peace initiatives, even if it meant some transitory conflicts with the Israelis. He became particularly tough-minded after Begin's accession to power and following Sadat's Jerusalem initiative. "He feels that we are coming to a crunch and in that crunch we ought to be prepared to take a firm stand even on the fundamental issues of arms transfers and aid policy," I noted on January 23, 1978. A few days later (February 10) I returned to the theme again, observing that Mondale "has become remarkably hard on the Middle Eastern issue and is really in a fighting mood insofar as the Israelis are concerned."

As discussed more fully later, Fritz was also helpful in the effort to move forward the normalization process with China, and strongly backed my desire to go on a special mission to Beijing. I later reciprocated in facilitating the President's approval of a similar visit to China by Mondale, something that he very much wanted for political reasons. In the early months we also worked closely in an attempt to infuse some order into the President's agenda, restricting the number of issues that we were tackling, lest our congressional calendar become overloaded. Here, too, Mondale showed good judgment and his experience was of immeasurable help.

In time, disagreements between us gradually surfaced. For one thing, I could sense that Fritz was uneasy about my inclination to make an issue early on of the Soviet aggressiveness in the Third World. I argued that otherwise detente would be jeopardized, while Fritz felt that my reactions were endangering SALT. In that sense, he was closer to

Vance's view. I also did not share his strong inclination to impose very strict restrictions on CIA activities; I was concerned about revitalizing the Agency's capacity for activity abroad, while Fritz approached the issue from the standpoint of domestic civil liberties.

We also had some disagreements on how to respond to the crisis in Iran, but the most significant difference involved our Middle East efforts. By late 1978, with the congressional elections near and with the Presidential season gradually beginning, Fritz became an advocate of a rather passive U.S. posture, tilted in favor of the Israelis. References to this started cropping up in my journal: "During the day I had a sharp disagreement with the Vice President. He was beating up on [NSC Middle East specialist] Bill Quandt over some relatively tough language that we are proposing to put before the Israelis and Egyptians. The thrust of the tough language will be critical of the Israelis. The Vice President was insisting that this be softened, and as a result he and I had a rather sharp exchange. I told him flatly that if he wants to change the Presidential strategy he ought to discuss it with the President. . . . Policy should not be changed by surreptitious changing of wording which then has the effect of changing policy," I wrote on July 11, 1978. Such disagreements, not just with me but also with Vance, became more frequent in 1979 and 1980, with Fritz feeling very strongly that our Middle East policy, particularly the public clashes with Begin, was damaging our domestic political prospects.

In general, Carter rarely, if ever, thought of foreign policy in terms of domestic politics, while Mondale rarely, if ever, thought of it otherwise. With national security my preeminent concern, I inevitably shared some of Carter's predilection, though my experience in the White House gradually educated me to a much higher awareness of the importance of domestic politics to our effectiveness. Fritz, in effect, provided a needed corrective, though I did feel at times that he was too much inclined to defer to special domestic interests in fashioning his priorities. He probably felt that I was excessively insensitive to such matters. By late 1980, with the left-liberal segments of the Democratic Party gunning for me, I felt that Fritz concluded that I was a liability, and this is why I gave some credence to the whispers that he would join Muskie in a post-election showdown over my role.

But with the basic directions of Carter's foreign policy set quite firmly after the Soviet invasion of Afghanistan, I was not too worried. Moreover, despite the disagreements we had in the latter phases of the Carter Administration, the working relationship between us was both harmonious and quite genial, and I particularly respected the manner in which Fritz complemented Carter both as a person and as a politician. Together, they made a team that was much more effective than either of them would have been by himself.

To Cyrus Vance

On a day-to-day basis, the key working relationship, second in importance only to that with the President, was with Cyrus Vance, the Secretary of State. We had known each other in New York City, where we
had both been active in various internationally oriented organizations,
most notably the Council on Foreign Relations and the Trilateral Commission. We were not especially close, but we had collaborated on a
number of projects and thus knew each other's mind. As Carter's campaign developed steam, Vance, who had earlier backed Sargent Shriver
for the Presidency, became a valued member of our advisory group,
and we grew closer. In the early-morning hours of election night we
toasted Carter's victory together.

After Carter had selected Vance to be Secretary of State (some two
weeks or so before my own appointment), Cy and I discussed by telephone the prospect of working together, and Cy said that he had told
Carter that he had no apprehension about my becoming Assistant for
National Security Affairs. On my part, I had earlier made it plain to
the President-elect that Vance would be my choice for the post of
Secretary of State. Carter must have found all of that quite reassuring.

This is not to say that I had no apprehensions. I have already noted
my misgivings over what seemed to me to be ideologically a one-sided
slate of appointments made by Cy to fill the second-level echelons at
State. (There were exceptions, to be sure. For example, Matt Nimetz,
who handled some critical European issues, proved to be tough-minded
and a loyal colleague.) For his part, Cy, a touch anxiously, mentioned
to me at the late December 1976 meeting at St. Simon his desire that I
see no foreign ambassadors. I explained that as a matter of practicality
his request was impossible to satisfy: occasionally, ambassadors would
be delivering special messages from heads of state for the President, and
other White House staff would doubtless see ambassadors socially or
even in their offices. Moreover, I would also be on the lunch or dinner
circuit, and hence it would be deceptive to pretend that there were no
conversations or exchanges of views. What I could assure him was that
I would not meet with foreign ambassadors secretly; that I would inform
him of what was said at any meetings with me; and that I would not
engage in back-channel negotiations without the President's and his
dispensation. And that was what I did.

The beginnings were generally encouraging. As with Mondale, I was
extremely happy that we were able to work as a team. Vance, as I saw
it, was going to be the principal negotiator and spokesman; thanks to
my closer relationship with Carter, I would work on the inside; with
Brown completing the triumvirate in the area of national security. My
first impressions of Cy as a colleague and as Secretary of State were

most positive. After roughly three months of working together, I summed him up in my journal as "very well informed, very much to the point, well briefed on most issues, shows a much more factual grasp of international affairs than I ever expected, in many cases better informed than I, quick in responding, quite decisive in tone and in speech, very much interested in negotiating and in procedure. I think he is weaker on the longer-range perspective, overoptimistic on our relations with the Soviets, and does not stand up strongly enough to the President on really important issues." But I really admired his dedication, the long hours he was putting in, and his readiness to fulfill any Presidential requirement.

In this early period, Cy did not seem to be worried about my closeness to Carter or about my role generally. If he was, he certainly managed not to convey it. He made no secret to me, however, over his growing irritation about the various public pronouncements emanating from our irrepressibly outspoken and charmingly disarming UN Ambassador, Andrew Young. "I have not seen him so put off for quite a long time, and I think it's obvious that Andy is beginning to get under his skin," I observed on April 15.

That some differences between us would eventually emerge was inevitable. For one thing, our vantage points prompted different emphases: his was on diplomacy, mine on national security. That meant that our priorities were likely to diverge, not to speak of more personal concerns or jealousies. His reluctance to speak up publicly, to provide a broad conceptual explanation for what our Administration was trying to do, and Carter's lack of preparation for doing it himself, pushed me to the forefront. (I will not claim I resisted strongly.) That in turn fueled resentments, if not initially on Cy's part, then clearly so on the part of his subordinates. I remember one July evening in 1978 when the President, Vance, Brown, and I were briefing the congressional leaders on our overall foreign policy. I was originally supposed to speak on my just-completed China trip, but, after the other presentations, the President announced that I would provide a general overview of our foreign policy. I did so, evoking a private comment to me from Senator Adlai Stevenson that he was much impressed by what I had to say but that my talk should have been given by the Secretary of State (who himself concentrated his remarks on the Middle East).

I was struck, even in the very early months (in fact, my first notation on this subject was dated January 21, 1977), by how much pressure there is from one's own subordinates to engage in conflict with one's principal peers. More than once, David Aaron would alert me to an encroachment on NSC turf by State, urging me to assert myself strongly. One could resist such pressures up to a point, but one was also conscious that the loyalty and morale of one's own staff were at stake; and I suspect that Cy was subjected to far greater pressures from the much larger, extraordinarily turf-conscious, and more insecure State Department bureaucracy.

More importantly, by the spring and summer of 1978, some substantive differences on policy had arisen. Though Cy and I both tried to confine them to our in-house discussions, the varying viewpoints filtered down to the bureaucracy, became increasingly the object of interagency conflicts and of gossip, and then started to leak out. This was the case, first, over the issue of the Soviet–Cuban role in the African Horn and the likely impact of that on SALT; then came the China question; and in the final year and a half we differed on how to respond to the Iranian crisis.

The press seized on these disagreements with a passion and a vengeance. Since the prevailing Washington expectation had been all along that Vance and I would fight, the first year must have been frustrating for the columnists and social gossips who thrive on registering every blow and on assessing in the greatest detail one's rise or decline on the barometer of power. But by 1978 almost weekly communiqués, in the form of highly exaggerated accounts of the "Vance–Brzezinski struggle," started appearing prominently in the press, particularly in the Washington *Post*. "Vance Wins" would be the headline one day, to be followed by "Brzezinski Dominates Foreign Policy" on another—each enraging our associates, each further straining the direct relationship between us. It got to a point that I was not sure whether I was more outraged by pieces portraying Vance as the winner or mortified by ones that celebrated my alleged predominance. Painfully I noted down after a piece particularly critical of Vance, "I don't need articles like that. They simply contribute to ill feeling and they cause reactions against me" (February 15, 1980).

But the press kept it up, thereby harming everyone concerned, while in fact considerably exaggerating the split between us. On most issues, at most times we were in basic agreement. Cy took the lead on the Middle East, and I backed him strongly. I did not inject myself much into the African issues and generally supported his and Andy Young's efforts. We were in agreement regarding the importance of improving U.S. relations with the Third World, and we both felt that we had to bite the bullet on the politically sensitive Panama Canal Treaties. We were united in a commitment to our human-rights policy.

Yet the press insisted on inventing disagreement even when there was none. On Tuesday, January 16, 1979, I noted in my journal: "I was infuriated this morning to read in the New York *Times* a front-page headline to the effect and I quote: 'Vance and Brzezinski Differ Again on Peking Tie and Effect on Soviet.' This was in reference to the speeches that Cy and I gave yesterday at the State Department to 600 people, with Cy speaking on U.S.–Chinese relations and my speaking on the global context of this new relationship. We had closely coordinated those speeches, we had exchanged drafts, the President had reviewed both drafts, and I even phoned up [*Times* journalist Bernard] Gwertzman to tell him in advance that we were making these speeches and that they were closely coordinated. Nonetheless, the whole thrust of the story was that we were again in disagreement."

Moreover, despite our three major disagreements—and I do not wish to minimize their importance—we managed, or so I felt at my end, to disagree in a civil and honorable fashion. Never once did I feel that we were somehow enemies. Never did I feel that Vance did anything dishonorable toward me. And my sincere conviction is that neither did I toward him. On the contrary, when the press was attacking Vance's effectiveness, I urged Carter on two specific occasions to go to the airport to greet him on his return from foreign missions as a gesture of Presidential support. At this stage, Cy seemed to think of me as an ally, as the following account (dated September 13, 1977) reveals:

". . . Cy came to see me in the early evening. He had heard rumors that people are talking that he may wish to resign and that [an NSC staffer] has been saying that he has a bad back and he was very concerned about this; but in effect primarily wanted to know whether that reflects in any way the President's thinking. . . . In fact he asked me for my assessment of the President's attitude, saying that if 'the President and you here were not satisfied' he would only be too happy to step aside. Considering the pressures under which he has been working and some of the unfair criticism to which he has been subjected, I am not surprised that he might feel this way, and I can only hope that I reassured him enough. I was quite sincere in saying to him that I feel confident that the President feels that he couldn't get a better man to work for him in this spot, and I also added that as far as I am concerned I certainly would not wish to exchange jobs and feel that we each complement the other extremely well."

More than a year later, when the prevailing wisdom in Washington was that Vance and I were bitter enemies, and in fact after some genuine policy differences between Vance and me had surfaced, I wrote in my journal (on November 8, 1978): "I must say [Vance] is really a very pleasant person to deal with. It would be difficult to imagine someone better as Secretary of State in terms of the personal relationship, even though I am often frustrated by what the Department of State stands for. There is no doubt he is a very good person—extremely loyal, highly dedicated, and willing to do what the President wishes without too much questioning. Moreover, he is really a very decent person. Finally, what is quite impressive is how well briefed he is on most of the issues he has to deal with. He obviously has a lot of energy and a very good memory."

For my part, while I continued to feel to the very end of Cy's tenure that our disagreements were handled in a civil fashion, there was one particular matter on which I harbored some resentment. Though there were no personal attacks on Vance attributed by the press to the NSC, some of Vance's immediate subordinates deliberately fed the press stories designed to present me in a very unfavorable light. They caricatured me personally as well as my views, while more generally contributing to the impression of an Administration that continually zigzagged. After leaving office, both Hodding Carter, Vance's press secretary, and Leslie Gelb, a journalist whom Vance hired to handle political-military affairs, attacked me publicly and on the record in terms very similar to those that originated from the State Department under the protective shield of nonattribution. I often wondered why Cy could not put a stop to that sniping.

I was also a little hurt that Cy never showed me any sympathy when I was the object of occasionally very vicious ad hominem attacks, especially in late 1979 by the Washington *Post*. Yet when he became the object of particularly nasty treatment, notably by syndicated columnist Joseph Kraft, he did expect sympathy. For example, in March 1980, Kraft, who had previously attacked me for attempting to oppose the Soviets in Ethiopia, wrote a column describing Vance as a beaten man who could not reason clearly, who was discredited by the events in Afghanistan, and a Secretary of State whom the President should replace. Vance was understandably hurt and in the course of the day mentioned this column to me at least twice. Since he was already under enormous pressure, some of it unfair, from the White House on the Middle East question (see Chapter 12), I did feel for him.

But the only really head-on confrontation with Cy, forcing the President to make something close to a choice, occurred immediately after the normalization of relations with China in December 1978. Cy was away in the Middle East until the day of the announcement, and much of the final process of normalization was handled, with the President's express approval, by me. Not unexpectedly, this produced bitter resentment in State. Moreover, the issue of the Shah was at a critical point, and former Under Secretary of State George Ball had been brought in as a consultant; apparently he falsely told Vance that I had been sending instructions behind Cy's back to the U.S. Embassy in Tehran. Vance's resentment over the general thrust of events (for the normalization of relations with China coincided with the stalemate in both the Middle East and SALT negotiations which he was handling) boiled over.

On December 19, four days after the startling Washington–Beijing announcement, after my early-morning briefing, the President told me that Cy had phoned him earlier in the morning, very upset, complaining that the NSC–State relationship had greatly deteriorated and saying that he wanted to discuss it with the President. Carter told me that he would like to meet with us over lunch, and asked me whether any of Cy's immediate associates ought to be included. I suggested that he limit it to Warren Christopher, Cy's deputy, and David Aaron, so that we could have an open discussion. Later, the Vice President and Ham Jordan were added to the group. We met for lunch in the Roosevelt Room, and Carter opened by saying that he thought he had a united team but he understood that some differences had surfaced and he wanted to know why. He asked Cy to comment, and Cy startled me with the sharpness of his attack. He asserted that cables had been sent by me to his ambassadors without his knowledge, that on the China issue Warren Christopher was not brought into the decision-making process until the last moment and Dick Holbrooke, Assistant Secretary for the Far East, was brought in even later, that I negotiated with the Chinese on normalization without informing the State Department, that NSC committee procedures should be changed, and that I should not see foreign ambassadors.

The President, reserving comment, asked me for my reaction. I pointed out that I had thought until now that the system was working well, that it was simply untrue that I was sending messages to ambassadors behind Cy's back, that Christopher was brought into the China decision-making process actually on my recommendation, for until then the President wanted no one else involved, that handling the China relationship was assigned by the President to me (though much of the negotiations were conducted in tandem with U.S. Ambassador Leonard Woodcock in Beijing), and that as far as NSC procedures were concerned the President should also check with Harold Brown to see whether State's complaints were shared by other participants. I also added that for the last twenty months there had been a fairly sustained press campaign directed at me, with much of it openly derived from State Department officials, and that I would like to be shown a single personal attack on Vance which clearly emanated from the NSC.

When I finished, the President stated that in his view State was much more responsible for the personal leaks, mentioning both Gelb and Holbrooke in this connection. He added that I had been attacked more than any member of his Administration, in part as a surrogate for attacks on himself. As far as the NSC system was concerned, the President said that he was satisfied with it and did not wish any changes. With regard to China, the President simply confirmed that while Cy was taking the lead on SALT and the Middle East he had wanted me to take the lead on China, especially since the Chinese trusted me. He endorsed my earlier observation that the circle of participants in the normalization was limited by him personally and was not part of some intrigue by me designed to undermine State.

It would be wrong to conclude from this account that Carter was always on my side. He was very sensitive to Cy's occasional sense of isolation, and from time to time he went out of his way to reassure him on a personal basis. He invited Vance to Camp David more frequently than he did me, and there is no doubt that he worked hard at making their relationship more cordial. For his part, Cy was extraordinarily deferential to the President; he had a way of very pleasantly blinking his eyelashes to indicate agreement and deference, and I was struck by how often that habit manifested itself in Cy's dealings with the President. Yet I could not help but notice also some tension in the relationship, springing probably from different backgrounds and ages. While leaning over backwards to be nice to Vance, Carter would occasionally also be extremely sharp. When Vance once sent over to Carter's office a comment on the President's personal correspondence with Brezhnev, using in it the word "we," Carter immediately circled the "we," adding a marginal note: "This correspondence is personal between me and Brezhnev. It is not to the State Department!" As I noted in my journal, "The President is rightly touchy on this subject but I felt a little sorry that Cy would be receiving such a sharp reminder."

In a revealing comment, Carter once told me in the fall of 1979 that he was frustrated by the inability of the State Department to come up with any innovative ideas. He also seemed a little hurt in noting that he had volunteered more than once to speak personally to Cy's subordinates by paying a visit to the State Department, and Cy never picked him up on this offer. At the same time, he added that he found Cy's restraining influence useful, since, as he said, both he and I were activists and needed someone like Cy to rein us in.

I was struck by that observation, and it made me reflect on why Cy and also his deputy, Warren Christopher, were so much better when playing supporting roles than when given predominant responsibility for coping with the ugly realities of the contemporary world. Vance, in my judgment, was at his very best when working closely with Carter in dealing with such matters as the Middle East, and he deserves more credit for the accomplishments at Camp David than he was given. Similarly, Christopher was at his best when supporting Vance, or when negotiating on the President's behalf on the hostage issue. But when diplomacy yielded to power politics, Vance—and later Christopher when he became in effect Muskie's alter ego, given Muskie's relative unfamiliarity with key problems—preferred to litigate issues endlessly, to shy away from the unavoidable ingredient of force in dealing with contemporary international realities, and to have an excessive faith that all issues can be resolved by compromise. Unfortunately, in a revolutionary age, such an approach more often than not tends to be exploited by the Qaddafis, Khomeinis, or even the Brezhnevs or Begins of our age.

Vance was a gentleman lawyer, patient, cooperative, and clearly a good sport. Typical of Vance's gentlemanly approach to the world was his reluctance to approve intelligence activities directed at some foreign embassies. Like Secretary Henry Stimson earlier, he seemed to feel that one should not read other people's mail. He was successful on Wall Street because he was methodical and congenial. But the contractual-litigational approach which works so successfully in a large law firm was less than suited for shaping a foreign policy in an age that has become both ideological and revolutionary.

I felt that the litigational approach suffered from the handicap of not bringing issues to a head. I noted on June 29, 1978: "The basic problem remains that our foreign policy is being conducted essentially on a contractual-legal basis, as if we were negotiating some legal contract. Unless we bring some situations to a head, be it in southern Africa or in the Middle East, or even occasionally through a confrontation with the Soviets, we will not resolve the outstanding issues." After all, at least to some, Gordian knots exist to be cut.

Vance was also not predisposed to engage in wide-ranging doctrinal and strategic dialogues about historical trends or in the kind of sharp debates which are needed to rebut the arguments of our adversaries. And yet, in my judgment, even to reach an accommodation with the Soviets required us to engage them in a historical-philosophical dialogue about the current state of the world. Specific negotiations needed to be reinforced by broader discussions, especially with Communist leaders who tend to think in strategic categories. Only out of such a dialogue could we eventually fashion some shared understandings and some principles of reciprocity.

Ultimately, the deepest differences between Vance and me were philosophical. Our differing backgrounds had produced substantially different conceptions of how the world works and consequently a different estimate of the proper balance between power and principle in our age. That balance cannot be easily struck, and the boundary between equilibrium and excess in either direction is truly an elusive one. I could not help reflecting on the extent to which Vance seemed to be the quintessential product of his own background: as a member of both the legal profession and the once-dominant Wasp elite, he operated according to their values and rules, but those values and rules were of declining relevance not only in terms of domestic American politics but particularly in terms of global conditions.

In a striking historical coincidence, the decline of the Anglo-American hegemony in the world coincided with the decline of Wasp predominance in America. Yet Vance, and also Christopher, epitomized that which is best in both the Anglo-American tradition and Wasp values. All in all, in temperament and in training, Vance was representative of an elite that was no longer dominant either in the world or in America. Carter certainly never was part of that America, and it certainly was not easy for me to relate to it either.

In my judgment, Cy would have made an extraordinarily successful Secretary of State in a more tranquil age. There his strongest qualities would have stood out, reinforcing this country's basic decency and commitment to fundamental principle. He was at his best when negotiating with decent parties in the world: the British over Zimbabwe or the Israelis and Egyptians regarding Middle East peace; he was at his worst in dealing with the thugs of this world. His deep aversion to the use of force was a most significant limitation on his stewardship in an age in which American power was being threatened on a very broad front. This was put most trenchantly by Harold Brown when he said to the New York *Times* on December 7, 1980, that "Secretary Vance was persuaded that anything that involved the risk of force was a mistake."

To Harold Brown

Brown's comment was revealing not only about Vance but about Brown himself. I doubt that he would have characterized Vance in that manner in 1977 or even in 1978, for initially his views were closer to Vance's than to mine. But from mid-1978 on, and certainly during the second half of the Carter Administration, Harold Brown became an articulate exponent of the need to build up American power and to project it assertively. He and I were on the same side in our internal debates over China, increasingly so on the broad question of U.S.–Soviet relations, on the need to revive the CIA, and especially on the defense budget. On some issues regarding the U.S. position in the SALT II negotiations with the Soviets, he took a tougher line than I, in part because he had to be careful not to lose the confidence of the military chiefs. Possessing a technical expertise considerably superior to mine, he was especially effective in rebutting the arguments of Vance and Paul Warnke, the Director of the Arms Control and Disarmament Agency, in favor of greater U.S. concessions.

Brown, Vance, and I worked very much together as a team, and in that triangular relationship Brown's gradual shift to a harder line made for a subtle but important change of balance. Initially, I had expected—knowing of earlier contests between strong-willed Secretaries of State and of Defense—to be the man in the middle. Indeed, for tactical reasons I hoped that this would be the case. I would then have been the mediator. To some extent, I played that role in our SCC debates on SALT. But on larger strategic geopolitical issues Harold during the initial two years or so was the man in the middle, siding first with me, then with Vance, and sometimes (and he could do so quite effectively with his agile mind) with both of us at the same time. This was exasperating, and privately I would egg him on, reminding Harold that Secretaries of Defense should be more forceful in promoting our defense interests.

As time went on, and particularly as Soviet strategic and geopolitical assertiveness coincided with a tightening budget squeeze, Harold became more of a protagonist, clashing head on with Vance and even more so with Vance's more outspoken successor, Edmund Muskie. I noted on January 1, 1979: "In general, I must say I find Brown good to work with and on the larger issues now increasingly tough-minded. Perhaps the remark that I made to him some months ago, namely that he is running the risk of going down in history as a very brillant Louis Johnson [Secretary of Defense in the Truman Administration], has had some effect. He has certainly become my staunchest ally in the Administration—intelligent, tough-nosed, very supportive. Given the situation in the State Department, I would have much tougher sledding, and it's tough enough, if I didn't have Brown to work with." He and I pushed the President hard on the need to increase defense spending, gradually overcoming the resolute efforts of Mondale, Stuart Eizenstat of the Domestic Policy Staff, and others to protect our domestic programs from the inevitable cuts. In doing so, Harold had the great advantage of possessing a virtuoso mastery of technical detail, of weapons characteristics, and of the budgetary process itself. These were matters on which I was much weaker, and I had less interest in them; I could back him but certainly not take the lead. There was thus a marked difference in this respect between the budget process of 1977 and that of 1978. Harold was relatively passive during the first year and I was simply unwilling to use up my capital, and not sufficiently versed to debate the Office of Management and Budget on my own, in order to fight on Harold's behalf for larger defense funds; in 1978, Harold pushed hard and I simply supported him.

This even led to some tension between Carter and Brown, which was unusual. Brown was generally very deferential to Carter, while the President respected Brown's intellect and appreciated the subtle but effective way in which Brown subordinated the Joint Chiefs of Staff to Presidential wishes. (This was especially the case with the decision to abandon the expensive development of a new manned bomber, the B-1, which had threatened to explode into a political embarrassment.) At first, Carter had been a little uneasy that Brown would interpose himself excessively between the President and the JCS. Indeed, just a few days after the inaugural Carter asked me what I thought of Brown's request that the President deal with the JCS only through his office. I backed Harold strongly, telling the President that it was in his interest that his civilian defense chief be firmly in charge. However, I found that Harold was equally resistant to any close relationship with the NSC and it took me quite a bit of effort to break through. "I have finally worked out an arrangement with Harold Brown for earlier intrusion of NSC personnel into the work of DOD. It was like negotiating with a foreign state," I noted on November 5, 1977. But in time, particularly over the B-1 issue and then in overcoming military resistance to SALT, I felt the President came to appreciate Harold's protective attitude regarding his position in DOD.

In late 1978 Carter became increasingly unhappy over Harold's pressure to increase defense spending and on several occasions complained to me that Brown did not make his own position clear and instead propounded uncritically the Defense Department perspective. Carter asked me to assess both Brown's requests and the OMB (Office of Management and Budget) rebuttals, making no secret of his aggravation. The President openly stated that he was irritated both by Brown's pressure for larger expenditures and by his inclination to make his own position somewhat ambiguous. Carter was also clearly egging me on to assert myself more effectively in the budget process, which I never quite succeeded in doing.

The President's frustration with Harold's ambiguity was in part justified. Occasionally, I also felt that out of both personal caution and intellectual agility Harold tended to see every side of an issue, edge up to a firm view, and then quickly again hedge it. He was tougher in the SCC discussions, where his support vis-à-vis Vance was invaluable, but in the NSC, with the President in the chair, I occasionally found myself left out on a limb by upholding a tough position. In that regard, I found his two immediate deputies, Charles Duncan and Graham Claytor, to be extraordinarily helpful, strong-willed, and hardnosed. They would stiffen the DOD position when necessary, as for instance on the East–West technology transfer question. And it was to Harold's credit that he selected them to work with him and took their advice seriously. Brown also occasionally annoyed me by very pleasantly agreeing to a point of view in a personal conversation and then attempting to score points in front of the President by suddenly debating the matter. His mind and mine must have worked along a similar track, because I was particularly put off by his tendency to interrupt me in mid-sentence and to complete for me the argument that I was making before then plunging into his own rebuttal of it.

My most serious complaint over our relations was that on two critical issues—the Soviet proxy expansion into Ethiopia, next to the vital Arabian peninsula, and then the fall of the Shah—I was unable to obtain Harold's clear-cut support. Without it, I could not generate the kind of response I felt was needed. Harold was generally inclined to agree with my concerns, but at the critical juncture he was not quite prepared to cross the t's and dot the i's. When we discussed foreign affairs, we found ourselves much in agreement, sharing some of the same anxieties. For example, I noted in December 1978: "We are both worried that SALT will be used to generate such euphoria about American–Soviet relations that it will be difficult to face realistically either the Soviet military or the Soviet regional challenge. Harold appears to be increasingly worried about longer-range trends." On another occasion, approximately a year later, I told Brown that "I certainly don't look forward to leaving office with a general public perception of us having been weak and indecisive and I wonder how he feels. He was rather shaken up by my comments and very much in agreement. I think he and I are going to be pushing harder and harder. He is particularly irritated because he is concerned that his trip to China, which Mondale has previewed with the Chinese, will now be canceled at Vance's insistence because the Soviets might not like it."

But when it came to action, there was in him an ambivalence and a lack of interest in broader strategy which reduced the impact of what we had to say to the President. I wondered sometimes why this was so, and I suspect that the reason was rooted partly in intellectual brilliance, which often is an enemy of clear-cut action, and partly in the fact that broader strategy was not his central concern. This occasionally created a Hamlet-like impression. My own inclination was to make judgments about geopolitical and strategic stakes involved and then to derive from such conclusions the needed action. Harold, a superb analyst, tended, on the other hand, to dissect the problem and then to examine alternative responses to its more immediate manifestations. That did not always result in the effective meshing of our policy prescriptions.

Nonetheless, he was my closest partner and I greatly admired him. As his concern over America's deteriorating power grew, he became more outspoken and assertive. Indeed, during the last months my position in the debates between Brown and Muskie was what I hoped it would have been between Vance and Brown. Without Brown, I would have been much more isolated on the critical issues during the more difficult phases of the Carter Presidency; with his growing help and forceful propounding of the need for a greater defense effort, I felt that President Carter was fashioning a policy truly responsive to our geopolitical and strategic dilemmas.

2

Power and Policy

I believe that we can have a foreign policy that is democratic, that is based on fundamental values, and that uses power and influence, which we have, for humane purposes. We can also have a foreign policy that the American people both support and, for a change, know about and understand.

—President Jimmy Carter, speech at
the University of Notre Dame, May 22, 1977

With the elections over, and the key appointments made, our immediate priorities in the area of foreign affairs were to organize the decision-making process at home and to define our goals abroad. At stake was both the organizational and the conceptual framework of the new Administration's foreign policy. The decisions that the new President would make would greatly influence the distribution of power within his team and shape at least the initial character of his policies.

As early as January 11, I wrote in my journal: "It is . . . increasingly evident that the coordination of foreign policy and the infusion of it with strategic content will have to come from this office. The way the Executive Branch has been set up, and particularly the staffing of the State Department, seems to indicate that operational decisions, negotiating, and so forth may well be handled from the State Department, Defense Department, and other agencies, but that there is no single source of larger strategic thinking and innovation in the government."

Defining Our Goals

Carter's personal philosophy was the point of departure for the foreign policy priorities of the new Administration. He came to the Presidency with a determination to make U.S. foreign policy more humane and moral. In part because of his religious feelings, in part because it was useful in the campaign, he went on record not only in rejecting the "Lone Ranger" style of the preceding Administration but in criticizing it for an excessive preoccupation with practicing balance-of-power politics. I know he genuinely believed that as President he could shape a more decent world.

I shared in that belief, up to a point. For me, the highest form of attainment is to combine thought with action, and I believed that power should be a means for attaining morally desirable ends. Accordingly, I felt that the United States should use its power to improve the human condition, but I put stronger emphasis perhaps than Carter on the notion that strengthening American power was the necessary point of departure. Indeed, later on, when a choice between the two had to be made, between projecting U.S. power or enhancing human rights (as, for example, in Iran), I felt that power had to come first. Without credible American power, we would simply not be able either to protect our interests or to advance more humane goals.

The new President's specific views on foreign affairs—going beyond his desire for a foreign policy governed by humane and moral concerns —had been formed during his time with the Trilateral Commission. Contrary to the current myth, the Trilateral Commission is not a conspiracy designed to dominate the world but genuinely strives to engage Americans, Western Europeans, and Japanese in a common endeavor to shape a more cooperative world. Many of its sessions and papers are dedicated to such themes as aid for the developing countries, arrangements for the fairer exploitation of the oceans, or programs to delay or halt the proliferation of nuclear weapons. Carter absorbed many of these themes and he actively participated in some of the discussions.

The electoral campaign, quite naturally, focused on the real or alleged inadequacies of the incumbent Administration. Thus it was inevitable that both the style and the substance of President Ford's policies were attacked in the various policy papers that were developed for Carter. That being said, these attacks did reflect the sincerely held view that America had come to be seen as Machiavellian, preoccupied with the status quo, out-traded by the Soviets on detente, agreeing to a SALT I arrangement with excessively high and unequal numbers, unable to move forward on the Middle East problem, and too passive in regard to the justified aspirations of the Africans or Latin Americans.

The commitment to human rights reflected Carter's own religious beliefs, as well as his political acumen. He deeply believed in human rights and that commitment remained constant during his Administration. At the same time, he sensed, I think, that the issue was an appealing one, for it drew a sharp contrast between himself and the policies of Nixon and Kissinger. Both during the campaign and afterwards Vance and I supported this policy, while Andy Young gave it a special Third World orientation, with emphasis on Africa, and that, too, had some domestic appeal in the black community.

Another important and distinctive theme of Carter's early foreign policy views was his preoccupation with nuclear nonproliferation. During the campaign, he gave a major speech on this subject before a UN group which was extremely well received. Prepared largely by Richard Gardner, it reflected Carter's own very solid background in nuclear affairs, and thus he spoke with a sense of moral conviction and technical expertise. The subject was very much his own, and there is no doubt that among political leaders he stood out as the one who had a genuine and highly personal familiarity with the scientific intricacies of the nuclear problem.

A related concern was SALT, which Carter saw as a means for stabilizing the U.S.–Soviet relationship and also for reducing the nuclear threat to human survival. Vance backed him strongly on the subject and encouraged him to assign the highest priority to SALT, largely because he saw in SALT the opportunity for establishing a more cordial relationship with the Soviet Union on a wider front. I also supported SALT because I regarded it as a useful means for publicly testing Soviet intentions and, if the Soviets responded favorably, for halting the momentum of the Soviet military buildup.

In my own contributions to Carter's early thinking, I stressed the need for an affirmative and morally appealing American leadership worldwide. I repeatedly emphasized that detente with the Soviet Union was bound to be competitive and that we must strive to inject into it some genuine reciprocity. American foreign policy, I argued, ought to be based on trilateral cooperation with Western Europe and Japan as its point of departure. I related all of that to the proposition that the President must project a certain aura of historical optimism in order to galvanize our friends and to infuse greater confidence in America itself.

In many of his campaign speeches Carter was critical of the way the previous Administration had developed policy—out of sight of the American public and without the participation of Congress. Accordingly, on the eve of the third and final debate with Ford, I proposed to Carter that he let it be known that after the elections he would hold a comprehensive day-long meeting between the Executive Branch and legislative leaders on the subject of foreign policy goals. My intent in part was tactical: to show that the new President would narrow the existing gap between the two branches of government insofar as foreign policy was concerned and that he would hold genuine consultations. I also saw in such a meeting an opportunity to have Carter speak out more broadly on his foreign policy strategy, thereby making certain that the new Administration would be committed to commonly shared goals as defined by him. He accepted that proposal, referred to it briefly in the course of the campaign, and after the elections asked me to organize such a meeting.

In the meantime, Henry Owen, Richard Gardner, and I developed for him a memorandum outlining the goals that his new Administration should pursue in foreign affairs. It was written immediately after the election and delivered to Carter shortly thereafter. After Vance's selection as Secretary of State-designate, I sent him a copy of the memo and the document was used in our first internal discussions regarding the aims of the new Administration. On January 5, 1977, we held our first informal NSC meeting, at which Vice President-elect Mondale presided. In attendance were Vance and Warren Christopher, Vance's designated deputy; Harold Brown and Charles Duncan, his designated deputy; Andrew Young, the Ambassador to the UN-designate; as well as Charles Schultze of the Council of Economic Advisers and Ted Sorensen, then still the designee as CIA Director. In addition, David Aaron, Rick Inderfurth, and I represented the NSC. The meeting produced two decisions which subsequently proved to be important: the first was to move rapidly with the conclusion of the Panama Canal Treaties, and the second was for Vance to go to the Middle East as early as February. Thus both Panama and the Middle East emerged as our immediate tangible priorities.

Later on, it was sometimes said that the Panama ratification effort proved excessively debilitating and politically costly for the President. This may be the case, but it has to be remembered that at the time the negotiations were in a critical stage and we were faced with the possibility of the talks breaking down. It was generally felt that violence would then ensue, and every intelligence assessment pointed to the likelihood that it would spread to other parts of Central America. Moreover, there would be a strong wave of anti-Yankee sentiment throughout Latin America. Accordingly, the rapid conclusion of the negotiations, which still seemed on track, was thought by all concerned to be justified. In regard to the Middle East, Vance believed that it was important for him to meet with the principals in the region and to move forward on the negotiations sometime in the spring. The substantive character of the U.S. strategy for the Middle East was to be defined later.

The broad scope of the new President's policies was reflected by the studies that were commissioned by this first informal session of the NSC: (1) a Presidential Review Memorandum (PRM) was to be rapidly developed on Panama, so that we could meet in order to make more substantive decisions during the week of January 24; (2) a PRM on SALT was to be submitted for NSC consideration by January 31; (3) a PRM on the Middle East was to be completed by January 31; (4) a PRM on South Africa and the Rhodesia negotiations was to be completed by January 31; (5) a PRM on Cyprus and the Aegean was to be completed by January 31, and Vance proposed that a special envoy be sent to the region during the first week of February; (6) a PRM on the mutual and balanced force reduction negotiations (MBFR) in Vienna was to be completed by January 31; (7) a PRM on the economic summit and trilateral policies was to be completed by the end of March; (8) a PRM on North–South strategy was to be prepared by mid-March; (9) a PRM on our European policy was to be completed by mid-April; (10) a PRM on our comprehensive military force posture was to be ready by midsummer; (11) a PRM on our intelligence structure and mission was to be completed by February 15; (12) a PRM on our arms sales policy was to be finished by April 1; (13) a PRM on our policy toward Korea was to be undertaken and a date was to be set; (14) a PRM on our Philippine base negotiations was to be undertaken and a date was to be set later; (15) a PRM on nuclear proliferation was to be undertaken, with a date also to be set later. The bureaucracy was stunned by the scope and the urgency of such immediate assignments.

Thus, two weeks before the inaugural, the Carter Administration had in place its foreign policy team, the NSC machinery was yet to be approved officially by the President, but at least he and I knew how it would operate, policy papers had been assigned, and the initial policy commitments were set in motion. Moreover, these decisions were to serve as the basis for the meeting with congressional leaders which I had earlier proposed.

It was held on January 12 at the Smithsonian Institution. It was agreed that Carter would introduce the initial discussion and that then it would be led by Vance. My intention was to remain silent and to let the President-elect and the Secretary of State-designate do all of the talking. However, during the meeting Carter called upon me to speak more than once, and thus I took an active part, stressing that we had inherited a stalemated situation in some parts of the world and that the agenda that Vance had outlined was required, lest America be seen worldwide as still paralyzed by the Vietnam and Watergate experiences. Prior to the congressional meeting, I mentioned to Carter that it would be useful for me to develop for him, on a more systematic basis, a briefing book containing the four-year goals of his Administration in the area of foreign policy; the idea appealed immensely to him and he announced it at this meeting, saying that such an undertaking would be conducted by me and the NSC.

Shortly thereafter I reviewed the original memo that Owen, Gardner, and I had prepared during the transition phase, updated it in the light of the subsequent discussions with Carter and Vance (including the informal NSC meeting of January 5), and invited Professor Samuel Huntington of Harvard to work on this with me. I was pleased by the President's interest, and I hoped that the document, as I wrote in my journal on January 13, "will enable us to integrate on an interagency basis the various objectives that different departments have and to shape them into one comprehensive plan. It could become a vehicle for influencing the general strategic thrust of the foreign policy of the Carter Administration."

The completed paper, containing forty-three pages, was submitted to the President on April 30. It was designed to give him a sense of our strategic priorities, to indicate more specifically what our goals would be in different regional and functional areas, and then to outline what might be the steps to accomplish these goals, quite literally on a year-by-year basis. Some of these objectives were necessarily vague, but others were quite tangible. For example, we set for ourselves the end of 1978 as the goal for normalization of relations with China. In my cover memo to this book of goals, I tried to summarize the principal priorities and the "general philosophical presentation." I suggested that the Carter policy ought to be defined as one of *constructive global engagement.*

As I wrote, I saw the need not for a new anti-Communist coalition, nor for an updated Atlanticism, nor for a policy focused only on the new nations, and certainly not for protectionism and isolationism. Rather, as I wrote at the time, ". . . it requires a *broad architectural process* for an unstable world organized almost entirely on the principle of national sovereignty and yet increasingly interdependent socially and economically. In that process of widening cooperation, our relationships will have to involve varying degrees of intimacy: (1) with our closest friends in the industrial world; (2) with the emerging states; (3) with states with which we compete militarily and ideologically, with whom we will seek through appropriate arrangements to reduce the chances of war and to codify more precise rules of reciprocal restraint."

As they appeared in the book, the original ten goals were fairly detailed and turned out to be the working blueprints for the next four years. We looked at the book frequently, assessed how successful we were in meeting the targets, refined and in some cases reordered them; but generally we stuck to them. As written in 1977, we set out:

1. To engage Western Europe, Japan, and the other advanced democracies in a closer political cooperation through the increasing institutionalization of consultative relationships, and thereby to promote wider macroeconomic coordination pointing toward a stable and open monetary and trade system.

Among the targets we set for ourselves were: to reintegrate Greece into the NATO command structure in 1978, achieve a peaceful resolution of outstanding issues on Cyprus and in the Aegean during 1977–78, and complete and ratify the Multilateral Trade Negotiations in the course of 1978–79. Throughout our four years we wanted to improve coordination of Western economic policies toward the Soviet Union and Eastern Europe.

2. To weave a worldwide web of bilateral, political, and, where appropriate, economic relations with the new emerging regional "influentials," thereby widening, in keeping with historical circumstances, our earlier reliance on the Atlantic community.

We set for ourselves the goal of consulting on critical issues with such countries as Venezuela, Brazil, Nigeria, Saudi Arabia, Iran, India, and Indonesia. Specifically we developed a list, appropriate to each country, of positive acts which would symbolize our new relationship. At the same time we prepared a list of actions we could avoid taking, without jeopardizing U.S. interest, which would be particularly troublesome to these countries.

3. To develop more accommodating North–South relations, political as well as economic, so as to develop greater economic stability and growth in the Third World, diminish hostility toward the U.S., lessen Soviet influence, and increase the stake those nations would have in good relations with the North and the West.

We set out to support the Global Development Budget, institutionalize the North–South dialogue in the Conference on International Economic Cooperation (CIEC), and shape links between the OECD and OPEC. Our most specific target was to have a ratified Panama Canal Treaty by the end of 1978, as a symbol of our understanding of the change in the Third World and of our willingness to cooperate with the newly emerging nations.

4. To push U.S.–Soviet strategic arms *limitation* talks into strategic arms *reduction* talks, using the foregoing as an entering wedge for a more stable U.S.–Soviet relationship. At the same time, we wanted to rebuff Soviet incursions both by supporting our friends and by ameliorating the sources of conflict which the Soviets exploit. We wanted to match Soviet ideological expansion by a more affirmative American posture on global human rights, while seeking consistently to make detente both more comprehensive and more reciprocal.

We wanted to have a completed and ratified SALT Treaty by early 1978, and thus be ready to seek a SART (Strategic Arms Reduction Treaty) by 1980. We wanted to achieve a phased mutual and balanced force reduction by 1980 and to initiate discussions on military restraints in the Indian Ocean.

5. To normalize U.S.–Chinese relations because we saw that relationship as a central stabilizing element of our global policy and a keystone for peace.

We wanted to initiate talks with the P.R.C. and complete the claims negotiations during 1977 and to establish full diplomatic relations by 1979. We wanted, in 1978, to facilitate Chinese acquisition of nondefense and possibly even defense-oriented Western technology and by 1979 to host a visit by a leading P.R.C. political figure, sign trade and cultural agreements, and lay the basis for a long-term cooperative relationship. At the same time we were determined to maintain adequate security, economic, and cultural relations with Taiwan.

6. To obtain a comprehensive Middle East settlement, without which the further radicalization of the Arab world and the reentry of the Soviet Union into the Middle East could not be avoided. Failure to

do so would pose serious consequences for Western Europe, Japan, and the United States.

During 1977 we would work to establish a framework for Israeli–Arab negotiations and secure an agreement on the part of all parties to a set of basic principles. In the following year we would help with negotiating agreements on specific trade-offs.

7. To set in motion a progressive and peaceful transformation of South Africa toward a biracial democracy while in the meantime forging elsewhere a coalition of moderate black African leaders in order to stem continental radicalization and eliminate the Soviet–Cuban presence from the continent.

We wanted to help achieve majority rule in Zimbabwe by helping to convene a constitutional conference by mid-1977, participating in the mechanics of transfer in 1977–78, and seeing a new government installed by 1978. We wanted to keep up pressure so that by 1980 there would be marked progress in dismantling apartheid in South Africa itself. If possible, we wanted to withdraw completely in parallel with the Soviets from the arms-sales business in Africa by 1979.

8. To restrict the level of global armaments, unilaterally and through international agreements. We were determined to reduce by 15 percent, with the exclusion of transfers to NATO, Australia, New Zealand, and Japan, the dollar value of transfers from the 1976 totals. We wanted to cooperate in the international restraints on nuclear proliferation and sign a Comprehensive Test Ban Treaty (CTB) and ratify it in 1977–78, as well as ratify the Threshold Test Ban Treaty (TTB) and its companion treaty, the Peaceful Nuclear Explosion Treaty (PNE), in 1977.

9. To enhance global sensitivity to human rights through actions designed to highlight U.S. observance of such rights and through multilateral and bilateral initiatives meant to influence other governments to give a higher priority to such human rights.

We wanted, in 1977, to complete U.S. adherence to five major international human-rights treaties. We wanted to have a full review of international human-rights issues (the so-called Basket III issues) at the Belgrade Helsinki review conference. We wanted, in 1978, to propose acceptable and appropriate human-rights criteria to be considered in the International Financial Institution (IFI) loan program. We also wanted to expand our refugee programs to accept those seeking refuge from repressive regimes of the left and the right.

10. To maintain a defense posture capable of deterring the Soviet Union, both on the strategic and the conventional level, from hostile acts and from political pressure.

We realized that this would require the United States to modernize and reconceptualize its defense posture in keeping with the broad changes in the world, to improve NATO military strength and readiness, and to develop capabilities to deter or to counter Soviet military intervention in the Third World. We began to examine U.S. commitments and bases abroad, to seek greater budgetary efficiency, and to look at ways to standardize NATO equipment.

The President was quite taken with the book and the goals project, and referred to it on several occasions, praising it as an unusually useful document. In our daily operations we were guided by its general outline, and thoughts from it would appear in briefings with members of Congress, press backgrounders, and in Presidential responses during press conferences.

Four months after the inauguration, the President delivered a major foreign policy speech at the Notre Dame commencement ceremonies. On a scorching May 22 in South Bend, Indiana, a heavily perspiring President explained the premises on which his foreign policy would be founded and presented the goals we had developed with him. The speech was well received. *The Times* of London described it as providing a "stirring vision," while *The Financial Times* declared: "The world not only calls for a new American foreign policy, it is actually getting it."

I thought it was a landmark speech because while it recommitted the United States to our allies, it dedicated this country to a policy of global involvement. It proclaimed human rights as a basic tenet of U.S. foreign policy and identified this country with the aspirations of the politically awakened world. The President gave the Soviets a choice. He stressed the need for SALT and at the same time made clear that while we believed in detente as a step toward peace, we hoped to persuade the Soviet Union not to impose its system on others, either through direct military intervention or through the use of proxy military forces, as had been the case with the Cuban intervention in Angola.

The President concluded by summarizing all that we had talked about during the campaign and in the first exhilarating months of the Administration: "Our policy is based on an historical vision of America's role. Our policy is derived from a larger view of global change. Our policy is rooted in our moral values, which never change. Our policy is reinforced by our material wealth and by our military power. Our policy is designed to serve mankind. And it is a policy that I hope will make you proud to be Americans."

It has often been said that the Carter Administration had no central strategy. I believe this to be incorrect. A review of the ten goals in the light of the four-year experience of the Carter Administration suggests that by and large it did have a defined philosophical perspective and certain basic priorities. However, events later on, notably growing Soviet self-assertiveness, did deflect the Administration from some of its original goals. Moreover, policy disagreements both vis-à-vis Soviet actions and over Iran created the impression of an Administration whose objectives were not coherent.

In my opinion, a more accurate indictment of the Carter Administration foreign policy performance is that we were overly ambitious and that we failed in our efforts to project effectively to the public the degree to which we were motivated by a coherent and well-thought-out viewpoint. Although the President had made a point of stressing the need to keep the U.S. public involved in foreign policy making, we failed in our duty to educate the people about what we were doing and where we were heading. Although we knew that we were conducting policy in an unprecedentedly complex world which did not lend itself to demagogy and easy solutions, we failed to point out the difficulties of achieving some of the tasks we had set for ourselves.

As early as February 8, 1977, feeling some uneasiness with the scope of our publicly proclaimed foreign policy goals, I urged the President "to emphasize more the things that we can accomplish, as for example the trilateral summit and closer cooperation with Japan and Europe, and less the things in which we are likely to have fewer successes—as for example Africa, the Middle East, and for that matter SALT. He agreed with the advice, though I am not sure he was delighted by it." To a degree, I believe we all also failed to follow it.

Organizing Power

The effective implementation of Presidential policy requires a system which can initiate, coordinate, and supervise the execution of policy. Carter wanted a system that would be simple and responsive to his personal control. I did, too, for I felt that this would permit the NSC to play the central role.

Shortly after Christmas 1976, Carter summoned the members of his new Cabinet and his principal staff assistants to a meeting on St. Simon, an island off the Georgia coast. The purpose was to review our longer-term policy and to discuss our operating procedures. As it turned out, there was no significant discussion of policy issues at the meeting, but it did provide me with the opportunity to raise with Carter directly the question of how the NSC process should be organized.

Few people outside the upper levels of government realize the extent to which there is institutional flexibility and inherent ambiguity in the way foreign policy is made. The Cabinet as such is not designed to make it. The National Security Council in the statutory sense merely means a meeting, involving the President, the Vice President, the Secretary of State, the Secretary of Defense, and—when the President so decides—also the Director of Central Intelligence and the Chairman of the Joint Chiefs, as well as the President's Assistant for National Security Affairs. But who decides that it should be held? How is that meeting prepared? Who develops for the President the basic policy options? Who integrates the dozens of policy issues and the several agencies that have some responsibility for coping with these issues? On all of these matters in recent years each President has developed his own style and his own procedures.

In his memoirs, Henry Kissinger describes at some length the protracted negotiations that took place between him and his principal colleagues, notably Secretary of Defense Melvin Laird and Secretary of State William Rogers, regarding the proposed reorganization of the NSC machinery. President Nixon had decided that the "influence of the State Department establishment must be reduced," but how that was to be done and what role Kissinger, as the President's Assistant for National Security Affairs, should play took some two and a half weeks to resolve. In the end, Kissinger came to exercise control by chairing a series of sub-Cabinet committees, attended by sub-Cabinet-level senior officials. After the election of President Reagan, the new Secretary of State, Alexander Haig, attempted a strategy of preemption by submitting to the new President, immediately after the inauguration, a document giving him central direction over the process, including crisis machinery. This generated a strong reaction from the other key officials, and in a highly publicized compromise announced two full months after the inaugural, the crisis machinery was assigned to the Vice President. The Secretary of State did, however, retain control over most of the other NSC committees. The Reagan Administration took far longer than its predecessors in organizing its foreign policy decision-making process.

In our case, the situation unfolded somewhat differently. President Carter had assumed office proclaiming that there would be no "Lone Ranger" in his Administration. Accordingly, in preparing the new decision-making format for his approval, I drew a table of organization in which a majority of the NSC committees would be chaired by the Secretary of State, the Secretary of Defense, the Secretary of the Treasury, or even occasionally the Director of the CIA (DCI). After consulting with my newly chosen deputy, David Aaron, Senator Mondale's foreign affairs adviser and a person whom I remembered favorably from an earlier stint in Washington, I proposed to the President that only three of the seven NSC committees be chaired by me, namely those dealing with arms control matters, sensitive intelligence activity, and crisis management. In each case, my chairmanship was justified on the grounds that these matters potentially involved jurisdictional conflicts between interested agencies and that the President's Assistant was the only one who could provide the needed coordination. Aaron, an energetic and competitive official, was especially persuasive in arguing that I insist on controlling crisis management.

I presented the revised table of organization to Carter at a private meeting with him in the course of the St. Simon sessions. He rejected it out of hand. "Too many committees," he said. "I want a simple, cleaner structure." (At the time, one of his pet goals was to reduce the number of governmental agencies, and that apparently included NSC committees as well.) I went back to the drawing board, but this time I made certain that Carter himself was involved in the new design. We sat down together in his cottage at St. Simon, and I outlined to him the types of issues that were likely to come up for Presidential consideration through the NSC machinery. I pointed out that they fall essentially into the following categories:

Foreign policy issues—both regional (e.g., Europe) and topical
   (e.g., human rights)
Defense policy issues—budgetary, strategic, and doctrinal
International economic issues—especially those that impinge on
   U.S. national security (e.g., oil prices)
Intelligence policy issues—approval of sensitive operations or of
   covert activity, as well as budgetary matters
Arms control—notably SALT, MBFR, a comprehensive test ban
   (CTB), nonproliferation, etc.
Crisis management

I suggested that the work of the NSC, in deference to the President's desire for simplicity, be organized into only two committees. One was to be the Policy Review Committee, to deal with the first three of the above categories and to be chaired by the appropriate Secretary. (In practice, the PRC subsequently met most often under the chairmanship of the Secretary of State, occasionally under the Secretary of Defense, and only two or three times under the Secretary of the Treasury.) I also proposed that the PRC be chaired by the DCI on the two occasions per year when the intelligence budget and annual intelligence priorities were reviewed. The second NSC committee was to be called the Special Coordination Committee, and I recommended to the President that its very title required a chairman who was not a departmental head. It was to be charged with decisions regarding sensitive intelligence and covert activity, with the development of U.S. policy on arms control (and especially SALT), as well as with crisis management. I stated that all of these matters not only posed potential jurisdictional conflicts but in one way or another touched upon the President's own political interests. It followed that the Assistant for National Security Affairs should chair the Special Coordination Committee and that this committee ought to be the decision-making framework for the three types of issues mentioned above.

Though I had a fairly clear notion in advance of the meeting with the

President-elect of what ought to be the functional distribution of responsibility, the actual proposal for the two committees, including their names, emerged in the discussion with Carter. Especially important was the assignment to the SCC of responsibility for SALT and for crisis management. It was also agreed that, whenever possible, appropriate Cabinet members themselves would attend the SCC or the PRC meetings. (Carter, incidentally, at the very first Cabinet meeting gave me Cabinet status—unlike my predecessors and my successor.) The idea was to engage the Cabinet more fully in the national security decision-making process and to accustom Cabinet members to working as a team under each other's chairmanship and that of the President's Assistant for National Security Affairs.

On the last day of the St. Simon deliberations, Carter surprised me, and doubtless Vance and Brown even more, by announcing to the assembled group that he and I (and he mentioned no one else) had worked out a new NSC system. He then outlined its basic principles, roughly along the aforementioned lines. Since the President-elect stated that this was the system which he himself had helped to design, everyone at the meeting nodded his head and indicated his approval. As I wrote in my journal: "This will enable me on my return to Washington to draft or actually to redraft my proposals on the NSC, to send them down for his approval, and thereby establish the basis for a system that I can use effectively."

One issue that was not resolved was how to achieve effective international economic coordination. Here again the St. Simon "public" announcement by Carter was useful. I subsequently noted in my journal that "it appears that Blumenthal and Schultze would like to move all international economics to the new Economic Policy Group. In the wake of my discussion with Carter, I met with them, had a prolonged argument, but succeeded, by invoking his name and the documents he approved, in preserving the notion that the NSC would be involved in those international economic matters which have a large political-strategic dimension." I was, however, a little premature in my judgment. A few days later I noted that "Mike Blumenthal is quite anxious about controlling the whole process," and in registering another encounter on the subject with Blumenthal, I concluded that "I anticipate that there will be some clashes."

In fact, the issue was never fully resolved. I did succeed later in persuading the President to appoint Henry Owen as Ambassador-at-Large, associated with the NSC and reporting to the President through me, to coordinate the preparation for the annual Economic Summit meetings (involving our principal Western European allies as well as Japan and Canada). In that capacity, Henry Owen became gradually the de facto coordinator for international economic policy. His role expanded particularly after Blumenthal left, and the coordinating function was then exercised relatively smoothly from the White House.

As a result of the organization scheme designed with Carter, the paperwork for Presidential decisions came to be structured in terms of three successive stages:

1. Prior to a PRC or SCC meeting on a given subject either a formal PRM (Presidential Review Memorandum) would be commissioned or more simple option papers would be requested. In the case of the PRC, the department whose Secretary would chair the meeting would take the lead for the preparation of the papers; in the case of an SCC, the lead would be taken by the NSC staff. (On issues which did not demand immediate Cabinet-level attention, a "mini-SCC" or "mini-PRC" met under the chairmanship of David Aaron or the relevant department under secretary.)

2. The PRC or the SCC session would generate either a unanimous recommendation for a Presidential decision or a report to the President on alternative policy recommendations. In either case, this would take the form of a very brief summary of the meeting, including sometimes the actual minutes of the discussion, as well as the recommendation for approval or a request for a decision. Alternatively, a PRC or an SCC could result in option papers for a more formal and full NSC meeting. In either case, the report to the President, including the minutes of the meeting, or the option papers for the full NSC meeting would be prepared by the NSC staff and submitted by me to the President directly. In other words, though the PRC would be chaired by a Secretary, the report on the meeting would go from me to the President.

3. The Presidential decision would be transmitted to the pertinent departments either through a formal Presidential Directive, in the case of particularly important decisions, or by a decision memo, reflecting the President's reaction to the report received from me. The decision memo, which would be sent to the pertinent Secretaries, would be signed by me; some of the Presidential Directives were also signed by me, once the President had approved their text. The more important ones, notably the ones dealing with strategic decisions, were always signed by the President himself.

The very first Presidential Directives codified this arrangement. After my return to Washington, David Aaron, Rick Inderfurth (my very able special assistant and a member of the transition team), and I developed the two formal Presidential Directives, which were submitted to the President-elect for his approval on January 15. The first, Presidential Directive/NSC-1, established the system of Presidential Review Memoranda (PRM)/NSC and of Presidential Directives (PD)/NSC, replacing the National Security Study Memoranda (NSSM) and National Security Decision Memoranda (NSDM) which existed under the previous Administration. The second, Presidential Directive/NSC-2, dealt with the National Security Council system. It opened with the statement: "To assist me in carrying out my responsibilities for the conduct of national security affairs, I hereby direct the reorganization of the National Security Council system. The reorganization is intended to place more responsibility in the Departments and Agencies while insuring that the NSC, with my Assistant for National Security Affairs, continues to integrate and facilitate foreign and defense policy decisions." It then specified: "The Assistant to the President for National Security Affairs, at my direction and in consultation with the Secretaries of State and Defense and, when appropriate, the Secretary of the Treasury and the Chairman, Council of Economic Advisers, shall be responsible for determining the agenda and insuring that the necessary papers are prepared. Other members of the NSC may propose items for inclusion on the agenda. The Assistant to the President shall be assisted by National Security Council staff, as provided by law." The Directive went on to delineate the respective responsibilities of the SCC and the PRC. I worried somewhat whether Carter would approve the assignment of SALT and crisis management to the SCC, and in my journal I noted that day: "The next two hurdles are whether Carter will approve it so that it can be promulgated and whether there will be a counterattack after the promulgation. That will probably take place in the week after the inaugural."

My premonition was justified. Carter signed the Presidential Directives on the eve of his inaugural. He was attending the Presidential Gala at the Kennedy Center when Harold Brown and I went to obtain his approval for some sensitive national security arrangements, which he endorsed, and at the same time he signed the proposed Presidential Directives. The next day, minutes after the inaugural, the directives were hand-delivered by messenger to the Secretary of State and to the Secretary of Defense. Shortly thereafter, I received a call from Cy Vance, who protested that he had not been consulted. I reminded him of what the President had said at St. Simon, and assured him that there was no desire to circumvent his authority but that the directives reflected the President's own decisions. Though mollified somewhat, Vance did indicate that he wished to discuss the matter with me further.

When we met two days later, Vance first registered his unhappiness with the assignment of SALT to the SCC, but desisted when I asked him whether in that case he felt that meetings on SALT, if conducted within the PRC, should be chaired by the Secretary of Defense. He then focused on crisis management, saying that this was properly the responsibility of the Secretary of State. I countered that if a crisis was genuinely serious it most certainly would command Presidential attention. Thus the President himself would be the crisis manager. Given the fact that the essential communications were located in the Situation Room and given the high probability of the President's own personal involvement, it followed that until the very moment when he assumed command it ought to be his Assistant who coordinated the crisis management. Though obviously not pleased, Vance did concede that these arguments had some merit and, in any case, he acceded to the new system. I noted down in my journal shortly after this meeting: "I must say that in general my relationship with Vance so far is excellent. He is a gentleman, and both of us have been leaning over backwards to be accommodating, and we have avoided too many difficulties. In fact, our difficulties so far have been minor and each of us has gone out of his way to reassure the other."

Though I was gratified with the outcome, I did not feel that I had usurped excessive authority. Under the new system, the PRC was to be responsible for setting broad and longer-term policy lines; at the same time, I did preserve NSC control over especially sensitive or potentially important matters. Through coordination of the SALT decision process, I would have a major input on our policy toward the Soviet Union, while retention of crisis control meant that in the event of major difficulties I would be in a position to shape the agenda and thus to influence the outcome of our deliberations. The role of the Secretaries was formally enhanced, but certain key levers were reserved for the President's Assistant.

That seemed compatible with the kind of personal leadership which I felt Carter wished to project and the kind of team spirit he wanted to achieve. I knew full well that Carter would not wish me to be another Kissinger. At the same time, I also felt confident that he would not let Vance become another Dulles. He wanted to be the decision maker and, even more important, to be perceived as one. What I sought, therefore, was to have an institutional arrangement whereby I could help to shape those decisions. The new system made that eminently feasible.

Making Policy

Coordination is predominance. I learned that lesson quickly. And the key to asserting effective coordination was the right of direct access to the President, in writing, by telephone, or simply by walking into his office. I was one of three Assistants who had such direct access at any time, not subject to anyone's control. I tried not to abuse it, mindful of Henry Kissinger's frustrations over Haldeman's control of his access to President Nixon and aware that excess would easily prompt the erection of barriers by Carter's solicitous personal aides. At the same time, I was determined to maintain an active and personal dialogue with the President on foreign policy issues because only then could I assert my own authority in a manner consistent with his views.

From the very first day of the Presidency, I insisted that the morning intelligence briefing be given to the President by me and by no one else. The CIA tried to have me take a briefing officer with me, but I felt that this would inhibit candid talk. Shortly after becoming Director of Central Intelligence, Admiral Stansfield Turner showed up in my Situation Room, quizzed my staff on how the intelligence briefing for the President was prepared, and then appeared in my office "to discuss" the President's morning briefing. In doing so, he not too subtly reminded me that he was the principal intelligence officer of the U.S. government and that it was therefore odd that I should be giving the President an intelligence briefing every morning. Just to drive the point home, he also noted that Allen Dulles used to brief President Kennedy. I merely nodded my head and told Stan that he obviously had a point. As soon as he left, I went over to Carter's Appointments Secretary, Tim Kraft, and told him that as of the next morning the President's schedule (which was always published in the Washington morning paper), instead of listing me as giving the President the "intelligence briefing," should say that I was giving the "national security briefing." The next day I phoned Stan and drew his attention to the President's schedule as published in the morning paper, adding that I felt the problem was now resolved. The matter was never again raised, and I continued to brief the President alone during the entire four years.

Every morning I would arrive in my office at least half an hour before my scheduled appointment with the President. I would obtain from the CIA briefing officer a copy of the President's Daily Brief, prepared overnight in Turner's office, which I would then review and supplement with additional intelligence items assembled for me by my staff in the Situation Room. I would select some pages from the State Department intelligence reports, perhaps some extracts from key cables, as well as an occasional clip from a more important newspaper or magazine article, especially from abroad. Such a package might contain up to twenty or so pages, which I knew the President would read in full, being a quick reader. In addition, on a sheet of White House stationery I would write out for myself five to eight points which I wished to raise with the President in the course of my oral presentation. I was deliberately quite brief, so that the President would have time to react to me and then to read the materials. I would typically highlight some of the key information and brief him on the SCC or PRC meetings scheduled for the day, telling him what position on his behalf I intended to take. From time to time I would summarize for him any ongoing policy discussions involving me or Vance or Brown and obtain his guidance as to the positions that I should take; I might explain to him why I disagreed with some recommendations submitted to him by his other advisers; and I might also then touch upon appointments, the political impact of foreign policy decisions, or any other matter that seemed particularly timely. Carter would always listen very attentively, reserving comment until I was finished.

In effect, the morning briefing involved a touching of bases, some prodding of the President to think about problems that in my judgment needed attention, the planting of basic ideas, and—especially in the first months of his Presidency—some wider discussions of conceptual or strategic issues. This was particularly important in the initial stages, when we were defining our broad goals and setting our priorities. I also used the sessions occasionally to make suggestions to Carter as to what he ought to stress in his public statements, including possible formulations or wordings. He was extremely good at picking up phrases, and I was often amazed how after such a morning briefing he would use in a later press conference or public appearance words almost identical to those we had discussed.

In the course of a typical day, the President would phone me several times, asking me to drop by, or to make a factual inquiry, or to convey a message to Brown or to Vance. He would from time to time also send me handwritten notes, including even comments on the latest press dispatches. For example, when the President read a dispatch on October 12, 1978, to the effect that the Israelis were completing plans for the construction of new settlements on the West Bank, he sent the dispatch over to me with a marginal note: "Prepare for another serious confrontation." On another occasion, when the Soviet Tass service reporter filed a particularly uncomplimentary account of Carter's press conference, the President sent the news clip to me with a marginal note: "This reporter would fit in well at the Washington *Post*." The material that I had given to him in the morning would also come back annotated, and I would use his annotations as the basis for written or oral instructions to the Secretaries of State or Defense, or to the Director of Central Intelligence.

To maintain the dialogue with the President, particularly on larger issues, I also initiated, approximately a month after his inaugural, the practice of sending him a weekly NSC report. It was meant to be a highly personal and private document, for the President alone. It contained usually some additional intelligence information or reports on policy implementation, as well as an occasional summary of more incisive papers written by NSC staffers, and frequently the report was opened by a brief one-page-long editorial piece by me, entitled "Opinion." In it I commented in a freewheeling fashion on the Administration's performance, alerted him to possible problems, conveyed occasionally some criticism, and attempted to impart a global perspective (see Annex II).

The reports also provided useful clues to the President's thinking. If his interest was engaged, even if he did not entirely agree, he would make copious marginal comments. On the other hand, if he was simply irritated by my report, as he sometimes was, it would come back with just the initial "C" on the upper right-hand margin. What with holidays, trips abroad, and other bureaucratic disruptions, reports were not submitted every single week, but the four-year total amounted to 159 reports. All of that made for a continuing dialogue, which kept me informed of the President's thinking and also perhaps influenced it.

Our policy decisions were formally developed in the various sessions of the PRC and SCC held in the Situation Room of the White House. In the four years to follow, I spent hundreds of hours in that room, either chairing SCC meetings or attending PRC meetings chaired by my Cabinet colleagues. A windowless, elm-paneled, softly lit room, with a table that can seat only about ten people, the Situation Room had a certain mystique, dating back to the days of the Cuban missile crisis. Moreover, under Carter, precisely because the SCC and the PRC met most often at the senior Cabinet level, the Situation Room did become the locale where most of the coordination and joint decision making in the area of national security policy took place.

The PRC/SCC system had the effect of engaging Carter's principal associates, on the Cabinet level, in an ongoing process of discussion and debate. It was, to be sure, time-consuming, but it also meant that any decision that went up to the President had been fully vetted. During the early phases of the Carter Administration, the PRC met more frequently, usually under Vance's chairmanship. In time, however, the SCC became more active. I used the SCC to try to shape our policy toward the Persian Gulf, on European security issues, on strategic matters, as well as in determining our response to Soviet aggression. Moreover, right from the very start of the Carter Administration, the SCC was the central organ for shaping our SALT policy.

Whenever there was disagreement either in the PRC or in the SCC, the President would resolve it, either by responding in writing to my report on the meeting (usually submitted on the same day) or by convening a smaller meeting, usually with Vance, Brown, Mondale, occasionally Turner, as well as myself. In the latter phases of the Administration, as the President became increasingly absorbed in domestic matters, I tried to relieve him of the time-consuming task of having to resolve issues of secondary importance. Thus at SCC sessions I would announce my interpretation of our consensus, leaving it up to any individual to appeal to the President if he so wished. This put the burden of bothering the President on the dissenter. At one point, this prompted a slightly exasperated Harold Brown to complain: "Well, I hope this isn't like Lincoln's Cabinet, with you feeling that you have all of the votes even if you are in the minority." I assured him that I was simply acting as the catalyst for needed decisions.

Formal but relatively infrequent NSC meetings were reserved for larger decisions. For example, the definition of our basic position on SALT, some crucial decisions pertaining to the Middle East, our reaction to the Soviet invasion of Afghanistan, and the rescue mission in Iran were discussed at formal NSC sessions. I also exploited the scheduling of such sessions to try to inject a more coherent and disciplined approach to our foreign policy by giving the President broader strategic memos on the eve of such meetings.

The NSC meetings typically included the Vice President, the Secretary of State, the Secretary of Defense, the Director of Central Intelligence, the Chairman of the Joint Chiefs, and sometimes Hamilton Jordan, Jody Powell, or Lloyd Cutler. Domestic advisers were included more frequently from approximately 1979 on, and the President's Counsel, Lloyd Cutler, an established and very astute Washington lawyer, was especially insistent on attending. On truly sensitive matters, however, all but the statutory members were excluded. The meeting would usually open by my summarizing the agenda. I would then pose the key questions to which attention ought to be given and on which policy decisions were needed. The President would chair the meeting, commenting quite often and quizzing the participants. There was no doubt that he was in charge, and he would make his decisions in a very clear-cut fashion. He would listen very attentively to debates among us, and on one occasion he told me that he particularly enjoyed disagreements between Harold Brown and me, since the debates between us involved such quick and sharp sparring.

I should add that the Cabinet meetings never dealt with foreign policy issues. Moreover, they were almost useless. The discussions were desultory, there was no coherent theme to them, and after a while they were held less and less frequently. (Not wanting to waste time, I used the Cabinet sessions to dispose surreptitiously of my light reading; since they took place on Monday mornings, I would use them to go through the latest editions of the weekly magazines, carefully hidden on my knees below the edge of the Cabinet table.)

The output from the NSC sessions was usually summarized either in formal Presidential Directives, and during Carter's Administration sixty-three of these were issued on matters of genuine importance, or in directives signed by me on behalf of the President, summarizing the decisions that the President had reached. We deliberately limited Presidential Directives to a smaller number than was the case with our predecessors, feeling that it would enhance their impact to confine them to matters of great significance.

The basic system endured the entire four years. However, not long after the President's inaugural it was reinforced by two informal procedures which filled an obvious gap. Since Carter preferred to confine formal NSC meetings to issues of major importance, there was the need for a supplementary mechanism which involved the President in the decision-making process. The Friday Presidential breakfast filled that need. Its origin, however, was more personal. In late June 1977, Carter told me that he had decided to hold a breakfast once a week, involving Vance, Fritz Mondale, and me. He explained that Vance lacked personal contact with him, in contrast to my daily morning session, and this would permit us all to have a freewheeling discussion. I noted in my journal after the first session, which was held on June 25: "I am delighted because I have been sensing the need for more effective integration of our foreign policy efforts, and it is difficult to do that through quick personal meetings with the President but without substantive discussion involving others as well. This will enable us now to review foreign policy more coherently. I hope we will stick to these meetings and that we will not have to abandon them."

These weekly Presidential breakfasts quickly became important executive sessions. The President wanted to keep them informal and resisted my suggestion that I develop an agenda for each of them, but after a while I started doing so indirectly, simply by suggesting to the President at the Friday-morning briefing (held before the breakfast) what topics he might wish to bring up. He would add these to the list he would normally draw up himself. Sometimes as many as ten topics would be covered, and the format permitted closer discussion, more intimacy and confidentiality than the formal NSC meetings. On the other hand, there was some disadvantage in the casual way some decisions were made and interpreted. For example, each participant would write down for himself the President's decisions as guidance for implementation. It was only after the flap over the UN vote on Jerusalem in the spring of 1980 (see Chapter 12) that Carter authorized me to provide an authoritative summary of his decisions as guidance for the participants.

Participation in the Friday breakfast increased as the session grew in importance. In early 1978, Ham Jordan was added by the President, on the grounds that he could help us by injecting political judgments into our discussions, and later in the year Brown prevailed on the President to admit him. In the latter phases of the Administration, the President added Hedley Donovan (Carter's Senior Adviser) and Lloyd Cutler to the group, and occasionally Jody Powell would come. Moreover, when Vance was replaced by Muskie, Warren Christopher (the Deputy Secretary) attended regularly to provide the expertise and continuity on issues that Muskie lacked. In spite of my repeated efforts, and for reasons which I could never understand, I was unable to prevail on the President to include Turner in the breakfast. I succeeded in having him invited to one breakfast in mid-September 1980, but no more than that. I felt that this was regrettable, for it made Turner's job more difficult, but the President was adamant in his insistence that the breakfast was already too large.

The breakfast itself was held in the Cabinet Room. Normally all of the participants would assemble a minute or so before 7:30, at which point the President would enter. He would sit at the end of the table, with his back to the door leading to the Oval Office. Vance usually sat on the President's right, with Brown next to him, and I would sit at the President's left, with Mondale to the left of me. After sitting down, the President would bow his head and ask one of the participants to say grace. For some reason he asked me to do so only once in the course of the four years. I could never figure out why, because he and I often had private discussions on religion and this was, in fact, an important bond between us. Perhaps he felt that the influence of the National Security Adviser in divine counsels was somewhat suspect. (A minor footnote: each breakfast participant was charged $1.75 for the occasion.)

A typical day did not leave much time for reflection.

Zbigniew Brzezinski: Record of Schedule

Tuesday, September 19, 1978

6:45	Arrived at office.
7:15	The President (7:25): morning briefing.
7:40	Took call from Secretary of State Vance.
7:45	Mike Oksenberg, NSC Staff member for China.
7:55	Took call from Secretary Vance.
7:57	Congressional Breakfast (9:03).
9:24	The President called; to President's office (9:27).
9:28	Stu Eizenstat of the White House (9:34).
9:34	Took call from Secretary Vance.
10:06	Roosevelt Room, Briefing for Jewish Leaders (10:37).
10:44	Madeleine Albright (NSC Staff member, Congressional relations) called.
10:52	Took call from the President.
11:11	Took call from Secretary Vance.
11:12	Jody Powell, White House press secretary, and Jerry Schecter, associate White House press secretary.
11:26	Took call from Secretary Vance.
11:30	The President—meeting with Chinese; and Israeli Prime Minister Begin's farewell call (12:50).
12:50	Col. Wm. Odom, military assistant.
12:55	Called Sen. Robert Byrd, Senate majority leader.
12:59	Called Ambassador Roy Atherton.
1:00	Lunch with Gen. Bernard Rogers at Pentagon (2:27).

2:28   To Oval Office for Sadat's farewell call (3:02).
3:02   David Aaron, my deputy; and Bill Quandt, NSC Staff
       member for Middle East.
3:10   Called Sec. Vance.
3:28   Madeleine Albright (3:29).
3:56   Chaired SCC (SALT) meeting—Sec. Vance, Sec. Brown,
       Adm. Turner, Paul Warnke, David Aaron.
4:30   Energy Secretary James Schlesinger (4:58).
5:40   Called Mike Oksenberg.
5:42   Called Soviet Ambassador Anatoly Dobrynin.
5:47   Called Iranian Ambassador Ardeshir Zahedi.
5:54   Called Edgar Bronfman, Jewish leader.
5:58   Seweryn Bialer of Columbia University (6:09).
6:24   Jerry Schecter.
6:52   Deputy Secretary of State Warren Christopher (6:54).
9:50   Departed for the day.

The other informal mechanism of considerable importance was the so-called V–B–B luncheon, later renamed the M–B–B luncheon. This weekly event would bring Vance (later Muskie), Brown, and me together for a session designed to resolve issues for which we felt there was no need to convene a formal SCC or PRC. I initiated this practice in early March 1977, and we quickly established the tradition of each of us acting sequentially as the host. Our respective staffs would prepare the agenda, each of us would have a briefing book containing the necessary background, and we would then expeditiously resolve, usually in very good spirit, a dozen or even more issues. As the months went on, more often than not Brown and I were on the same side, and the absence of staff made it easier for Vance to accommodate without loss of face. Our sessions became somewhat more lengthy after Muskie became Secretary in the spring of 1980, for he had a tendency to roam all over the field, discussing things leisurely and philosophizing at length. On the other hand, he tended to be less contentious than Vance, and as a result the sessions continued to produce quick and clear-cut decisions. After each lunch I would prepare a memorandum listing the decisions on which we had agreed, sending a copy to each of the other two participants, as well as a report to the President.

The President insisted on such immediate reporting, for he wanted to keep decisions in the area of foreign policy firmly under his control. On numerous occasions he urged me to be more assertive, particularly in controlling the Defense Department and its budgetary process. In late October 1977, I used the weekly report to give him a questionnaire on the performance of the NSC, focusing particularly on the NSC paper flow, policy innovation, and the President's involvement. His responses indicated that he felt he was kept adequately informed of the PRC and

SCC activities, that the paper flow was generally satisfactory, but he explicitly stated that I should make certain that DOD was subjected to more scrutiny and that the NSC develop more policy initiatives for him.

Carter made no secret of the fact that he thought that State was sluggish in developing policy initiatives, and he was particularly impatient with State Department double-talk. When in early April 1979 I forwarded to him some language proposed by State for a message to Brezhnev regarding a possible summit meeting, the President sent it back to me with an ironic handwritten note which said: "Zbig—I think, in the future, if you agree, perhaps it might be possible, if no unforeseen obstacles arise, under some circumstances, for you to permit me to express my opinion that I might know if it is your reading on the subject that both of us might benefit if in texts of letters, including those to heads of state, some circumlocutions could be avoided—unless Cy and you think otherwise. JC."

At times, Carter's impatience produced circumstances in which he would make decisions ahead of the NSC coordinating process, prompting me to complain to him. Moreover, whenever I tried to relieve him of excessive detail, Carter would show real uneasiness, and I even felt some suspicion, that I was usurping authority. For example, my journal for February 12, 1980, contains the following: "I told Carter at the morning briefing that coordination isn't working well. The message to Gromyko was brought to him before Brown and I could comment on it to Vance. The plans for dealing with the Iranians were discussed with the President before they could be clearly discussed among ourselves. The President is being entangled in a discussion of the Palestinian issue before we refine the options. He himself talked with Giscard and changed the seven-power conference into a five-power conference, omitting the Canadians and the Japanese. Etc., etc. He really got rather furious. He told me in an icy fashion that I just want to be involved in everything. I told him that that was not the point. That if he wants to do all the work himself he can, but if he wants issues coordinated for him, he shouldn't encourage this kind of thing. He gave me a rather silent and icy stare." Nonetheless, coordination was usually effectively maintained, in large measure because Carter's own involvement in foreign affairs made it possible for the NSC to exercise strict control on his behalf.

While this made delegation of authority more difficult—and to relieve the President's burden sometimes I had to act on his behalf without his direct knowledge—it did have the effect of reinforcing central control. Indeed, whenever the State Department or Defense tried to evade NSC coordination, all I had to do was mention it to the President. He would either phone or fire off a note to Vance or Brown, reiterating his interest in being kept promptly informed. For example, in the spring of 1980 I had the feeling that the conversations with Soviet Ambassador

Dobrynin on Afghanistan were going beyond the limits set by our NSC deliberations, and I showed the President a cable which the State Department was sending out to our embassies concerning the April 19, 1980, meeting between Secretary Vance and Ambassador Dobrynin. The President immediately dashed off a note to Cy and to Warren Christopher, insisting that "meetings and assessments like this should be reported to the White House immediately."

Such direct Presidential involvement generated the impetus for close NSC coordination of the policy-making output of both State and the Defense Department. All major cables with policy implications had to be cleared with relevant NSC staff before they could be sent out. Since much of policy is made by cables, control in this area gave the NSC staff considerable leverage over both the making and the implementation of policy. In addition, before any major foreign discussions, talking points used by the Secretaries of State and Defense were sent over to the NSC for Presidential clearance. This meant, in practice, that I would review them, recommend changes, and, if necessary, carry the argument to the President. Usually, when Vance or Brown traveled abroad, I would prepare prior to their departure Presidential instructions for them. I would usually review with Vance or with Brown such drafts or talking points before submitting them to the President, and I want to emphasize that here because I do not wish to imply that such procedural control meant simply dictation from me.

Major Presidential speeches on foreign policy were also prepared under NSC supervision. Typically, I would develop the initial outline, submit it for Presidential approval, and then the speech writers would flesh it out. I would rewrite the draft and submit it for comments to Vance, Brown, and Mondale. I would then incorporate their comments into the finished draft or, in the case of truly serious disagreements, give the President a draft with occasionally some alternative wordings in key places (indicating who stood behind which language and why). When Ham Jordan officially became Chief of Staff, his deputy, Alonzo McDonald, tried to gain control over the speech-writing process, but I made it very clear that as far as foreign policy was concerned the NSC remained in charge.

The NSC was also made responsible for clearing foreign travel by the Cabinet, and this involved me on several occasions in some unpleasantness with Cabinet members. Travel abroad was a popular activity, and China became a particularly desirable watering spot. As a result, I got into some acrimonious hassles when I had to tell Cabinet members that their planned trips, usually with large staffs, had to be canceled or postponed.

It is generally not well known that during the Carter years the CIA was also held under very strict control by the NSC. The Director of the CIA had relatively limited access to the President, briefing him only once a week and then, later, only twice a month, and always with me in attendance. He had throughout the four years practically no one-on-one meetings with the President, and all CIA reporting was funneled to the President through me. Moreover, all major decisions regarding the CIA had to be vetted by the SCC or in private one-on-one meetings between Turner and me. These weekly meetings between the two of us dealt with the most sensitive internal CIA matters, and I would report on them to the President when appropriate. In brief, the CIA was effectively supervised by the NSC, in keeping with the National Security Act of 1947. Turner and I, after some initial frictions, developed a good working relationship, and I was certainly supportive of his efforts to revitalize the Agency.

Finally, policy was controlled through supervision of implementation. David Aaron chaired the mini-SCCs and participated in similar sub-Cabinet-level PRC activity designed to make certain that Presidential instructions were implemented faithfully. Much of policy is made by the bureaucracy through implementation of policy, often deliberately skewing such implementation in directions that the bureaucracy would prefer to go. Aaron, with his aggressive personality and keen intellect, was a particularly effective manager of this process, though I was often amazed at how skillful the State Department was in delaying the execution of decisions which it had not in the first place favored.

Maintaining tight control was more difficult with the domestic political advisers of the President, whose participation I tried to limit since so much of the discussion was based on extraordinarily sensitive information and the domestic people often had no basis for judging what was sensitive or not. This made for damaging leaks as well as occasionally for less than useful discussions. At the same time, we clearly needed the input of the President's domestic advisers, because the foreign policy of a democracy is effective only as long as it is sustained by strong popular support. Insensitivity to domestic concerns could produce calamities, as was shown early in the Administration by the joint U.S.–Soviet statement on the Middle East which so outraged American friends of Israel.

To strike some sort of balance between these conflicting concerns, the President would often consult Mondale on the domestic implications of foreign policy decisions, and approximately a year or so after the Administration took office Ham Jordan became more actively engaged in our discussions. Moreover, as I got to know him and Jody Powell better, I found them to be useful allies, who often shared my feeling that the Carter Administration needed to project a tougher profile on the central issue of the American–Soviet relationship. As a result, I became more sympathetic to drawing them into foreign policy deliberations, knowing that their voices carried weight with the President and needing their reinforcement in my occasional disagreements with Vance. In doing so I learned why Carter valued them so: they were both very decent, extremely bright, and extraordinarily dedicated individuals.

In the latter phase of the Administration, Ham Jordan was designated as Chief of Staff, but this in no way affected either my relationship with the President or my dealings with Jordan. Carter made it very clear, and I heartily agreed, that his appointment did not alter either my status or my relationship with the President, or my control over the NSC machinery. (In a bizarre move, when Jordan's appointment was announced, the senior staff received questionnaires from Ham's office on their respective staffs with instructions that these evaluations were to be completed and submitted for Jordan's approval within forty-eight hours. I simply ignored them.)

Ultimately every decision-making system is a creature of the President, and each President has his own distinctive style. Carter's was perhaps formally the most centralized of all in the postwar era, even though that did not prevent some internal and even public disputes. Nonetheless, it was a system and a process that actively involved the President and his Cabinet-level advisers in day-to-day deliberations and intensive participation in foreign policy decision making.

Further, it enabled President Carter toward the end of his term (October 9, 1980) to state quite accurately and with obvious pride: "There have been Presidents in the past, maybe not too distant past, that let their Secretaries of State make foreign policy. I don't."

Staffing

The new NSC system was in place on Inauguration Day. So was the NSC staff. I was especially proud of that because actually I had very little time for recruiting. I moved to Washington right after Christmas, staying in a small bachelor apartment graciously provided me by Averell and Pamela Harriman. This was to be my home away from home until my family moved to Washington in the early summer of 1977. Until then, I was under Pamela's protective wing, and that made survival somewhat easier.

Knowing of Carter's reputation as an efficient manager, I was determined to have my staff ready to serve him the moment he moved into the Oval Office. At his insistence, but with my concurrence, the policy-oriented NSC staff was to be cut from approximately fifty under Kissinger to no more than thirty. This made recruitment somewhat easier, and I was further aided by a widespread sense of enthusiasm which Carter's election had generated. As a result, I had no refusals.

In selecting my staff, I very deliberately sought to balance three different groups: professionals from within the bureaucracy; forward-looking and more liberal foreign affairs experts from the non-Executive part of the Washington political community; and some strategic thinkers from academia whose views closely corresponded to my own. I felt that the professionals would provide bureaucratic expertise and continuity. I knew from my own service in the State Department in the mid-sixties that especially State and the CIA were full of underutilized talent. The very size of these departments and their multilayered systems of clearances work against the assertion of individuality, and service on the NSC staff could thus give promising officials a unique opportunity to spread their wings. I was not disappointed, and some of my very best staff members came from this category. In addition, two outstanding examples of collective institutional memory, especially valuable in the months ahead, were Roger Molander, the in-house expert on SALT, and Robert Hormats, international economist, both possessing lengthy experience of NSC service.

Secondly, I intentionally recruited several individuals whose views were more "liberal" than mine, but whose expertise on foreign affairs I very much respected. I knew that at some point I would be attacked from the left, both on the Hill and by the press, and that the attack would focus on my alleged reputation as a "hawk." I felt, therefore, that a liberal presence on the staff would give me a more diversified perspective and would also be politically helpful. I thus recruited Jessica Tuchman from Congressman Morris Udall's staff, to be responsible for global issues, including human rights; I also succeeded in recruiting Robert Hunter from Senator Kennedy's staff, placing him in charge of Western Europe. I asked Robert Pastor, staff director of the Linowitz Commission on U.S.–Latin American relations, to handle Latin American and Caribbean affairs. All three proved to be exemplary colleagues in areas of genuine sensitivity.

Finally, I wanted on the NSC staff some individuals who shared my broad strategic perspectives, and who could undertake the needed review of our military doctrine, of our basic assumptions about global power, and thus help to define new longer-range goals for the United States. Given the centrality of this undertaking, it was important that the staffers involved share some of my basic assumptions and be close to me personally. With this thought in mind, I recruited Colonel William Odom, who later became a general while on the NSC staff, from the U.S. Military Academy at West Point. I knew him from an earlier association with me at the Research Institute on International Change at Columbia, I respected his views on Soviet military affairs and strategy, and I considered him to be an innovative strategic thinker. Then I was extremely fortunate in drawing to the NSC Professor Samuel Huntington of Harvard, the director of its Center for International Affairs. A creative and broadly gauged thinker, he undertook immediately the very difficult assignment of assessing the overall global balance between the United States and the Soviet Union, relating the more conventional military comparisons to the intellectually more difficult endeavor of making some overall political judgments regarding the rivalry between the two superpowers.

As my deputy, I selected David Aaron. I met him first in 1967, when I was developing in the State Department a more forward-looking approach toward Eastern Europe. He was at that time involved in Western European affairs, and I was very impressed by him. In the early seventies, Senator Mondale asked me for some recommendations for a foreign affairs expert who would work with him during his drive for the Presidency. I recommended to him David Aaron, who at the time was working on Kissinger's NSC staff.

I mention this because it was later often alleged in Washington that Mondale imposed Aaron on me. This was far from the case. When I came to Washington after my designation by Carter, Aaron was already in the Executive Office Building, ensconced as the transition chief for the NSC. He and Rick Inderfurth, a young but politically very sensitive staffer from the Senate Intelligence Committee, had assembled various briefing books dealing with the likely policy and staffing issues that I would have to face as the new NSC chief. After working with them for approximately two weeks, I concluded that I wanted each of them to continue on. I asked Rick to be my immediate assistant, and on my own initiative, and without either consulting Mondale or being pressed by him, I invited Aaron to be my deputy.

Aaron and Inderfurth worked in small offices adjoining mine in the West Wing of the White House and were my closest collaborators. During the four years, I "burned out" three special assistants, with first Robert Gates of the CIA and then Les Denend of the Air Force serving as Rick's successors. Rick was politically savvy, Bob Gates the epitome of discretion and good judgment, and Les Denend exemplary in his penetrating insight, personal dedication, and efficiency. They and the several secretaries in the office leading to mine (notably Trudy Werner, my personal assistant, Lora Simkus, Florence Gantt, Pat Battenfield, Wilma Hall, and Kathy McGraw) formed a family which made the system tick.

In a special category was my choice in 1978 for congressional liaison, Madeleine Albright. A close associate of Senator Muskie and an extremely able supporter of Democratic causes, Albright not only became a key NSC staffer but greatly reinforced the occasionally sputtering overall White House coordination with Congress. To fill the critical position of Staff Secretary—the person who really makes the NSC staff run—I called upon Christine Dodson, my former associate from Columbia. Christine had served as Administrative Director of the institute I directed at Columbia before moving on to work in systems analysis and computers. She brought a personal commitment to the job in addition to her administrative ability, and not only ruled the NSC with an "iron hand" but succeeded in modernizing the NSC data system and significantly innovated internal NSC procedures.

The new staff was generally well received. The Washington *Post* in its account of the new NSC stressed (on January 24) that "the new NSC staff accents youth, imaginativeness, doctoral degrees and a more liberal political orientation than the staffs that more recently worked for Kissinger or his successor, Brent Scowcroft. . . ." The article went on to add that "the declared purpose of the NSC staff is to coordinate policy and to serve as a 'think tank' rather than to make policy. That distinction disappeared in the Kissinger years—and may again." It noted with approval the fact that I had created a special office for "global issues" designed to cover a range of subjects from UN affairs to arms sales, nuclear weapons proliferation, and human rights—all matters dear to the new President's heart.

Two of my appointments quickly became controversial. The first involved William Quandt, my selection for the Middle East slot. As early as a week before the inaugural I noted in my journal that there were rumblings against this selection. Morris Amitay, the head of the American–Israeli Political Action Committee, phoned me to register his concern on the grounds that Quandt was pro-Palestinian. Shortly thereafter I was visited by Senator Richard Stone of Florida, who voiced the same concern. I assured both of them that I had checked Quandt's credentials carefully, that in my view he was an objective and serious student of Middle East affairs, and that such objections were therefore groundless. Nonetheless, for many months to come, objections to Quandt kept percolating and they probably contributed to some later tensions between a portion of the Jewish community and myself.

The second controversial appointment involved not the individual but the slot which he filled. I asked Jerrold Schecter, a respected veteran correspondent from *Time* magazine, to serve as the NSC press spokesman, with the title of Associate Press Secretary. This was subsequently often portrayed as an attempt by me to build up my personal image. In fact, though perhaps mistakenly, my intention was the very opposite. I had at the time felt that it would be wiser for me to maintain a low profile with the press. This meant that I would not engage in frequent formal or informal briefings but would leave the task to the White House Press Office. However, there existed a problem: the new Press Secretary, Jody Powell, for all of his extraordinary talents, did not know much about foreign affairs, and I felt that his office needed reinforcement. The solution, in my mind, was to appoint someone as the NSC press spokesman who would serve at the same time as Jody's "associate press secretary." This would give his office the needed expertise and enable me, working through Schecter, to make certain that the President's line on foreign affairs was properly articulated. It worked out that way, but—alas—it was not perceived that way.

Schecter skillfully and with humor worked in that thankless capacity for three years, bearing up cheerfully under attack and instructing me in the art of cultivating the Washington press corps. I am afraid that I was a poor student. In the last year, Jerry was seduced by private business and replaced by Alfred Friendly, Jr., a highly sophisticated journalist and Soviet expert. His style was less combative than Schecter's and his attitude more detached. He guided me with subtle skill through some difficult controversies, but by then I also had developed a greater immunity to that widespread Washington disease known as "mass media neurosis."

On Monday, January 24, I held my first NSC staff meeting. I established in it the practice, which I followed for the subsequent four years, of first briefing the staff on my encounters with the President during the preceding week. I told them of my conversations with him and what his major concerns were. My purpose in this was to give the staff a sense of direct engagement with the President. I knew that they would have to work extraordinarily hard, and I felt that I could sustain that commitment only if they felt personally engaged with the President. Since they could not meet with him directly as often as I would, I believed that by sharing with them my conversations and by giving them a feel of his thinking, I would vicariously establish the same personal link. I have to say that in the course of the four years I was never disappointed by any violation of confidentiality in this regard.

I was also able to prevail on Carter to come to the first NSC staff meeting. This was an important gesture by him, demonstrating to the staff that they would be working for a President who would be himself deeply involved in foreign affairs.

Part I
COMPREHENSIVE INITIATIVES

Every new Administration feels it has a mandate for new foreign policy. This is especially the case when the new President comes from a different party than his predecessor. To be sure, the new men soon discover that the problems they face are more intractable and lasting than they had expected—and the virtues of continuity come to be appreciated more than the merits of innovation. Proud claims of originality quietly give way to statesmanlike appeals for bipartisanship on behalf of the enduring national interest.

But, typically, each new President tries to imprint a distinctively new stamp on foreign policy. For Eisenhower, it was to replace containment with proclamations of liberation; for Kennedy, it was "to move America forward again" and in the process to make it more appealing to the developing world; for Nixon, it was to free America from the paralysis induced by the Vietnam War.

When Jimmy Carter assumed office, U.S. foreign policy appeared to him and to his team to be stalemated on the level of power and excessively cynical on the level of principle. The new Administration therefore decided to move on a broad front and to tackle several key issues at once while the President's prestige was at its highest. We were determined to demonstrate also the primacy of the moral dimension in foreign policy.

Translated into policy decisions, this involved an effort to infuse new life into the paralyzed Middle East peace process, to conclude a SALT II agreement better than SALT I, to improve relations with Latin America through the ratification of the Panama Canal Treaties, to reactivate NATO, while also advancing such causes as human rights, nuclear nonproliferation, and majority rule in southern Africa. Inevitably, such widely gauged activism came close to overloading the decision-making process itself and put enormous pressure on the Presidential schedule. The competing goals came into conflict and, indeed, one additional major objective—normalizing relations with China—was put temporarily on hold.

In brief, the first phase of Carter's foreign policy, which lasted till early 1978, was thus dominated by high expectations and ambitious goals.

Part I: Comprehensive Initiatives

Middle East

1977

February	NSC outlines policy seeking comprehensive settlement
March–May	Carter meets key Middle East leaders
May 18	Menachem Begin elected Prime Minister of Israel
July 19–20	Carter meets Begin in Washington
October 1	U.S.–Soviet joint statement on Middle East
November 19–21	Sadat in Jerusalem
December 17	Begin briefs Carter on Sinai–West Bank autonomy proposals

1978

January	U.S. assumes initiative in trilateral talks among U.S., Egypt, and Israel

Other Issues

1977

January–April	Policy development on broad range of global issues
April	President approves U.S. support for Common Fund for Commodities
April 14	President Carter's Pan-American Day speech outlines Latin American policy
September 7	Panama Canal Treaties signed
October 5	Carter signs International Covenants on Human Rights
October 25	Brzezinski speech in Bonn on "regional influentials"
November	International Nuclear Fuel Cycle Evaluation (INFCE) 2-year program inaugurated

1978

January 1–2	Carter visits New Delhi: discussion of Indian delay on full-scope nuclear safeguards
March 10	Nuclear Nonproliferation Act signed into law: establishes criteria for export of nuclear material
March 22	First, formal steps to majority rule in Rhodesia
April 25	South Africa accepts UN plan for Namibia
April 28	Shipment of enriched uranium to India
March–April	Panama Canal Treaties ratified
December 6	30th anniversary of UN Declaration of Human Rights commemorated at White House

U.S.–Soviet Relations

1977

January–March	Two U.S. SALT II proposals formulated
February	Carter letter to Andrei Sakharov
March 30	Soviets reject both proposals
May 18–19	Vance–Gromyko talks resume SALT negotiations
May 22	Carter speech at Notre Dame outlines U.S. foreign policy: sends signal to China
June 30	Carter announces B-1 bomber production will be halted
July	Cuban deployments to Horn of Africa
August 24	PD-18 issued on "essential equivalence"
September 23	Carter–Gromyko meeting in Washington revives SALT progress
September 27	Carter reaches agreement with Gromyko on framework for SALT II

1978

March 17	Carter Wake Forest speech stresses U.S. defense efforts
Spring	Disagreement among top U.S. officials on "linkage" between SALT and Soviet adventurism

3

Not Geneva, but Jerusalem

I don't think that there can be any reasonable hope for a settlement of the Middle Eastern question, which has been extant now on a continuing basis now for more than twenty-nine years, without a homeland for the Palestinians.

—President Jimmy Carter, press conference,
May 12, 1977

Peace in the Middle East was an urgent priority of the new Administration. The new team believed that the stalemate that existed in 1977 would gradually fragment, with disastrous consequences for world peace as well as for the United States itself. A new war would likely generate a major U.S.–Soviet confrontation, more intense and direct than the one that almost came to a head in 1973. Apart from all other considerations, I was convinced that only through progress toward peace could the United States achieve both greater security for Israel and a more solid position for itself among the more moderate Arab states. In the process the Soviet Union would be frozen out of much of the Middle East.

To be sure, the policy of "small steps" had already resulted in a limited, but historically significant, accommodation between Israel and Egypt. The Egyptians had regained control over the Suez Canal, and the United States had become engaged in monitoring the armistice in the Sinai. But what next? By the end of 1976 there was widespread agreement among experts that whoever won the U.S. Presidential elections would have to make a major effort to infuse new life into the peace process. There were simply no more "small steps" to be taken; one now had to deal somehow with the complicated issues of the Sinai, the West Bank, the Golan Heights, Jerusalem, and more generally of peace and security for Israel.

Prior to the 1976 elections, I undertook to familiarize myself more deeply with the Middle East problem. In the summer of 1976, I visited Israel. In the course of the trip I met with the various top Israeli leaders, received extensive briefings, and was taken by the military to the Golan Heights. Particularly valuable were my discussions with

Yigal Allon and Abba Eban. Both men had been blessed with subtle and incisive minds, and both had the facility to look at the problem of Israel in a wider regional perspective. Finally, both impressed me as flexible, and encouraged me to think that Israeli political leadership could generate the needed imagination and historical vision for overcoming the Middle East logjam.

Two occasions on that trip were also especially memorable. I met for dinner with the Defense Minister, Shimon Peres. Dinner was a private, hospitable affair at his house, despite the enormous tension that was in the air: as we dined the lives of some 100 Israeli hostages were being threatened by reckless kidnappers at an airport in distant Uganda. The terrorists were making demands on the Israeli government which it was apparently getting ready to accept. I will never forget the stunned and suspicious look on Peres's face when I said to him, "Why don't you send some commandos down to Uganda and storm the damn airport terminal?" The very next morning I heard on the air the triumphant announcement of the successful Entebbe raid!

The other was my visit with the leader of the opposition, Menachem Begin, and his wife. As a young man, I had greatly admired the heroism of the Jewish underground fighters and was familiar with some of their epic. It was thus a specially meaningful moment for me to meet the Irgun's fabled leader—and in the very apartment in which he used to hide from the British authorities. I suspected that Begin was surprised by my interest and familiarity with Irgun exploits.

In any case, the trip to Israel helped me to reach an important conclusion. Probably contrary to the expectations of my Israeli hosts, my trip to the Golan and my travels within the country convinced me of the futility of seeking security through the acquisition of territory. It became clear to me that Israel could never acquire enough territory to compensate for Arab hostility—and that therefore Israeli security would have to be decoupled from the question of territorial sovereignty. The extension of Israeli sovereignty would not in and of itself create security, especially if that extension generated greater Arab hostility, but security could be created by arrangements that extended Israel's security lines beyond formal and sovereign borders. In other words, a formula combining mutually acceptable borders (and hence only limited changes in the 1967 lines) with security outposts *beyond such borders* had to be contrived.

My second "learning" process involved participation in an extensive project on peace in the Middle East, sponsored by the Brookings Institution. A distinguished group of American experts on the Middle East, including also some leaders of the American Jewish community (such as Rita Hauser and Phil Klutznick), met during much of 1975 and hammered out a series of policy recommendations which struck me as both timely and realistic.* Some of the more ticklish issues were not resolved, but the group believed that a process pointing toward a settlement should be launched on a broad front, at least on the basis of an Arab–Israeli consensus on some broad principles. I agreed with the report, for I felt the recommendations protected Israeli security while enhancing the prospects for a constructive U.S. relationship with the Arab world, something clearly in the U.S. interest. I shared these findings with Jimmy Carter during the campaign, and I knew from his earlier remarks in Kyoto that he would be sympathetic. I also discussed them with Vance, who generally agreed and who also believed that an active U.S. policy in the region was needed.

The Long March to Geneva

The basic approach of the new Administration was formulated in the course of three sessions: an informal meeting on January 30 involving just the President, Cyrus Vance, Andrew Young, and me; a formal

---

* The study reached five main conclusions:

"1. *U.S. interests.* The United States has a strong moral, political, and economic interest in a stable peace in the Middle East. It is concerned for the security, independence, and well-being of Israel and the Arab states of the area and for the friendship of both. Renewed hostilities would have far-reaching and perilous consequences which would threaten those interests.

"2. *Urgency.* Whatever the merits of the interim agreement on Sinai, it still leaves the basic elements of the Arab–Israeli dispute substantially untouched. Unless these elements are soon addressed, rising tensions in the area will generate increased risk of violence. We believe that the best way to address these issues is by the pursuit of a comprehensive settlement.

"3. *Process.* We believe that the time has come to begin the process of negotiating such a settlement among the parties, either at a general conference or at more informal multilateral meetings. While no useful interim step toward settlement should be overlooked or ignored, none seems promising at the present time and most have inherent disadvantages.

"4. *Settlement.* A fair and enduring settlement should contain at least these elements as an integrated package:

"(a) *Security.* All parties to the settlement commit themselves to respect the sovereignty and territorial integrity of the others and to refrain from the threat or use of force against them.

"(b) *Stages.* Withdrawal to agreed boundaries and the establishment of peaceful relations carried out in stages over a period of years, each stage being undertaken only when the agreed provisions of the previous stage have been faithfully implemented.

"(c) *Peaceful relations.* The Arab parties undertake not only to end such hostile actions against Israel as armed incursions, blockades, boycotts, and propaganda attacks, but also to give evidence of progress toward the development of normal international and regional political and economic relations.

"(d) *Boundaries.* Israel undertakes to withdraw by agreed stages to the

PRC meeting on February 4, chaired by Cyrus Vance; and a formal NSC meeting on February 23, chaired by the President, held immediately upon Vance's return from his week-long trip to the Middle East. Both at the private meeting with the President and in the more formal meeting in the Situation Room, chaired by Vance, it was agreed the peace initiative in the Middle East was of the highest importance.

The PRC of February 4 also recommended to the President that in our substantive approach we should seek to obtain a clear definition of the Arab commitment to peace, that we should get the parties to recognize the distinction between secure defense lines and final borders, and that our objective would be to obtain an agreed set of principles before actually convening the Geneva Conference. It was also decided that Vance should go to the area to discuss both substance and procedure.

I made a very strong case for concentrating on substance rather than on the process. My argument was essentially as follows: the time was

---

June 5, 1967, lines with only such modifications as are mutually accepted. Boundaries will probably need to be safeguarded by demilitarized zones supervised by UN forces.

"(e) *Palestine.* There should be provision for Palestinian self-determination, subject to Palestinian acceptance of the sovereignty and integrity of Israel within agreed boundaries. This might take the form either of an independent Palestine state accepting the obligations and commitments of the peace agreements or of a Palestine entity voluntarily federated with Jordan but exercising extensive political autonomy.

"(f) *Jerusalem.* The report suggests no specific solution for the particularly difficult problem of Jerusalem but recommends that, whatever the solution may be, it meet as a minimum the following criteria:

—there should be unimpeded access to all of the holy places and each should be under the custodianship of its own faith;

—there should be no barriers dividing the city which would prevent free circulation throughout it; and

—each national group within the city should, if it so desires, have substantial political autonomy within the area where it predominates.

"(g) *Guarantees.* It would be desirable that the UN Security Council endorse the peace agreements and take whatever other actions to support them the agreements provide. In addition, there may well be need for unilateral or multilateral guarantees to some or all of the parties, substantial economic aid, and military assistance pending the adoption of agreed arms control measures.

"5. *U.S. role.* The governments directly concerned bear the responsibility of negotiation and agreement, but they are unlikely to be able to reach agreement alone. Initiative, impetus, and inducement may well have to come from outside. The United States, because it enjoys a measure of confidence of parties on both sides and has the means to assist them economically and militarily, remains the great power best fitted to work actively with them in bringing about a settlement. Over and above helping to provide a framework for negotiation and submitting concrete proposals from time to time, the United States must be prepared to take other constructive steps, such as offering aid and providing guarantees where desired and needed. In all of this, the United States should work with the U.S.S.R. to the degree that Soviet willingness to play a constructive role will permit."

ripe for a new U.S. initiative and we should seek to develop a comprehensive framework of principles that would serve to guide the ensuing negotiations; vital U.S. national interests were at stake and that justified an active U.S. role; the Soviets should not be involved substantively in the negotiations, but the prospect of a Geneva Conference—which the Soviets would co-chair—should be used as a form of pressure on the Israelis and inducement for the Arabs, though not as an end in itself; moreover, Geneva should not be used for negotiations as such but should be held to legitimize any agreement previously reached by the parties through U.S. efforts.

I felt particularly strongly that we should strive to make the parties to the conflict recognize the basic incompatibility between acceptable and secure frontiers for Israel. In my view, the two were in fact a contradiction in terms: genuinely defensible frontiers could not be acceptable to the Arabs because they would have to involve major acquisition of territory by Israel, while what would be acceptable to the Arabs would definitely leave Israel vulnerable. As I wrote to the President before the NSC meeting of February 23: "We should be prepared to go very far with the Israelis in talking about how their security can be assured in a peace settlement, while stating our view that the Arabs will not accept substantial changes in sovereignty beyond the 1967 lines." I believed that mutually acceptable frontiers would have to be reinforced by some special security lines or zones, designed to enhance Israeli security. I further argued that we needed to press the Arabs to be more forthcoming in their concept of peace and emphasize to them that we expected them to produce an acceptable formula on the Palestinian question. Growing U.S. influence in the region, I felt, would also help Assad and Sadat to make efforts to get the PLO under control, and we should continue to play a discreet role in encouraging this.

Specifically as far as convening the Geneva Conference was concerned, I felt very strongly in those first months of our Administration that we should obtain as much substantive agreement as possible before actually going to Geneva, since progress at a large multilateral conference was unlikely. I advocated that we keep the Soviets informed of our efforts—since they would serve as co-chairmen of any Geneva Conference—but that we not involve them prematurely. At the NSC meeting of February 23, I said, "If we only resolve procedural questions before going to Geneva, Geneva will break down and the Soviets will try to exploit the situation." In a memorandum to the President following up on the NSC meeting, I elaborated on the point by arguing that going to Geneva should be seen as a concession to the U.S.S.R. for which the Soviets should make some concession to us. As I pointed out, the Soviets had always adopted the position of the most radical Arabs. It was now time for them to use their influence for peace. I wrote to the President: "Until we have an understanding with the

Soviets that they will, in fact, play a constructive role, we should avoid getting publicly committed to holding a Geneva Conference. In other words, we should hold out the promise of a Geneva Conference this fall and work toward it but stop short of being committed to holding it."

In making my case I relied on the advice of my NSC staffer for the Middle East, Bill Quandt, from the University of Pennsylvania and one of the contributors to the earlier Brookings study on Peace in the Middle East. He developed a close working relationship with his State Department counterparts, notably Roy Atherton and Hal Saunders, and this helped to generate effective teamwork. Subsequently, his replacement, Robert Hunter, continued working in the same spirit, and as a result there was never any of the institutional backbiting between NSC and State that occasionally characterized our work in other areas.

I favored as rapid movement as possible. I felt the President enjoyed maximum leverage during the first year, and that his ability to deal with the problem would decline as he approached the congressional elections of late 1978, not to speak of the later 1980 Presidential elections. With public opinion behind him, and with Congress not willing to undermine the President in a crucial area of national security, I believed that Carter stood a good chance of achieving a breakthrough —provided he moved firmly and rapidly.

I also told the President on more than one occasion that there would be no breakthrough to peace without U.S. persuasion of Israel. Israeli internal politics were so stalemated that no Israeli politician could take the responsibility for advocating a genuine compromise unless he could make also the added argument that otherwise U.S.–Israeli relations would suffer. Given the centrality of the U.S. pipeline to Israel's survival, most Israelis instinctively would shrink back from overt defiance of the United States, *provided* they were convinced the United States meant business.

But that in turn raised the question of timing. The nature of American domestic politics was such that the President had the greatest leverage in his first year of office, less so in the second, and so forth. The more time he had for persuasion and for the subsequent progress toward peace to be manifest, the more opportunity he had to act. Friction with Israel made little sense in the third or fourth Presidential years, for such conflict would be adversely reflected in the mass media and in financial support for the Democratic Party. This case was supported, sometimes tacitly, sometimes explicitly, by Mondale, Jordan, and Powell, though in the later phases of the Presidency both Jordan and Mondale swung around and urged Carter to avoid any actions which might irritate the American Jewish community.

Vance also favored rapid movement. Though at first he felt that we should engage in some preparatory fact-finding (viewing his mission to the Middle East primarily in those terms), his sense of urgency increased after his trip, and on his recommendation it was agreed at the February 23 NSC meeting that our target for the convening of the Geneva Conference should be September of the same year. Accordingly, we would have to reach agreement on the procedures for such a conference. In addition we would also seek some agreement on principles dealing with the nature of peace, withdrawal and security, and the Palestinian question. After the NSC meeting, I noted that Cy, the President, and I "are very much on the same wavelength insofar as the Middle East is concerned . . . all of that makes me feel that we can perhaps work together now in pushing the Middle East issue toward some reasonable solution."

In the months that followed, Carter plunged heavily into the negotiating process himself. An intense schedule of meetings with Middle Eastern heads of state was prepared for him, and he was visited on March 7–8 by Prime Minister Yitzhak Rabin of Israel, on April 4–5 by President Anwar Sadat of Egypt, on April 25–26 by King Hussein of Jordan, on May 24 by Crown Prince Fahd of Saudi Arabia, and Carter traveled to Geneva on May 9 to meet with President Assad of Syria.

Prior to the President's meeting with Rabin, I had one of the best conversations yet with him. It dealt not only with the Middle East but also with the President's religious beliefs, and revealed a lot to me about the man with whom I would work so closely for the next four years. Our talk took place on a Saturday morning (March 5), and it was very relaxed because Carter was quite free and had no other appointments except my morning briefing.

> . . . We talked about the forthcoming Rabin visit. I went over his briefing materials, and we spent quite a bit of time talking about the frontiers of Israel. I brought in a number of maps, and we looked over the Sinai, the West Bank, and Golan, and compared the various approaches of the Israelis and the Arabs and even of the various Israelis, some of whom have rather different ideas one from the other. Our discussion of Jerusalem led us to a discussion of religion. We first compared impressions of Jerusalem, including even such matters as to where Christ was buried, and then we got into a discussion of what religion means to us respectively. I pointed out to him that to me religion is a search, whereas he and his sister seem to have found in religion the answer and a much more direct relationship to God. He partially disagreed, pointing out that even though that is true, it still entails a search for the real meaning in life, and that to him the real message from Christ is that of humility. He spoke quite a bit and

rather warmly about that. This led us into a discussion of children and religion. I told him how difficult it is for my children to become really religiously involved. And he talked about his, telling me that his older children are much more skeptical but that Amy, for example, is remarkably well informed about religion, that she reads every evening something like two hours on religious matters, and that she listens to religious tapes, which gives her much more of a feeling for the reality of religion. He himself reads the Bible every evening. He reads it in Spanish, which is a way of improving the language, but also because it is a foreign language it forces him to concentrate much more. He reads one chapter an evening, which I find quite impressive, because with all of the other things he has to read it must require an enormous amount of self-discipline and motivation to spend still every evening on reading a chapter from the Bible.

This coming week is going to be quite important, and I stressed to him that he will really have to take the lead in pushing the Israelis toward a clearer definition of their position regarding a peace settlement, especially on territorial issues. Unless such greater precision can be obtained from them, a few months from now we will find ourselves exactly where we are today—talking about the possibility of a settlement but as far away from it as ever before. And if that develops, then it is certain that the situation will begin to deteriorate. Carter indicated that he agreed with this approach, and now we will see how effectively and how persistently he can use the next couple of days to probe the Israelis and to see if we can obtain some greater commitments from them regarding the peace.

The meeting with Rabin did not go well. The Israeli Prime Minister and Carter simply did not relate to each other well as human beings and neither could repress his antipathy. Rabin was stiff, cold, and unresponsive. Carter tried to charm him, to give him some sense of his religious interest in "the land of the Bible," and to engage him as a human being by inviting Rabin, after the State Dinner, to look in on Carter's special pride and joy, his daughter Amy, who was asleep in her White House bedroom. Rabin declined the offer with a curt "No, thank you," thereby ending any chance of establishing a personal rapport with a proud father.

Things went no better on the substantive level. Prior to the dinner with Rabin, I gave Carter a paper outlining the approach he should take on the three key issues: the nature of peace, withdrawal and security, and a solution for the Palestinian problem. Vance also had reported no progress in his talks with the Israelis and told the President that, in his judgment, the Israelis were stonewalling. Carter would simply have to be much more forthright with Rabin. The President handled himself well in the discussions. As I jotted down afterwards: "At the meeting, he laid it down right on the line and was quite direct without being aggressive. He made it very clear that the U.S. was in favor of rapid negotiations, favored minimum border changes, and that the Palestinians (including the PLO) would have to be somehow included in the discussions. It was quite clear that the Israelis were taken aback by this position, and they indicated that they hoped that the U.S. would not make it publicly known since that would weaken their negotiating leverage with the Arabs."

Two days later, responding to a question at a press conference, Carter reiterated his view that the issue of security ought to be separated from the question of territorial sovereignty. Later, at a town meeting at Clinton, Massachusetts, in the middle of March, the President created a sensation by his spontaneous and unexpected public statement that "there has to be a homeland provided for the Palestinian refugees who have suffered for many, many years." Surprised by this formulation, Vance and I huddled on how best to handle this new development, but we received "instructions . . . directly from Air Force One that no elaborations or clarifications were to be issued" on the matter. Nonetheless, to reassure the Israelis, I did tell the Israeli Ambassador, Simcha Dinitz, that in my judgment the word "homeland" had no special political connotation.

The President's public statement, as well as the self-evident absence of progress in the talks with Rabin, brought to the surface the basic disagreement between the U.S. and Israeli positions. At this stage, this did not concern me too much because I felt that it was inevitable that the United States and Israel would go through some period of disagreement before a joint consensus emerged. However, the President's public statements did arouse Jewish public opinion in the United States, and they did so at a time when we did not yet have any Arab concessions to show for our efforts. This helped to create the impression that the new Administration was tilting away from Israel. This suspicion was further stimulated by several other Administration decisions which supporters of Israel viewed as insensitive to Israeli concerns. Very shortly after assuming office, the President decided not to permit the delivery to Israel of cluster bombs, a particularly effective antipersonnel weapon, because of its use by the Israelis against Lebanese civilians. This precipitated a very sharp column by William Safire, the intensely pro-Israeli New York *Times* columnist. Other irritants involved the decision not to permit the export of the Israeli fighter-bomber Kfir to Latin America on the grounds that this would stimulate a further spiral in the Latin American arms competition (and the United States had the right to make such a decision because the Kfir used a U.S. engine), as well as the broader ceiling imposed on U.S. conventional arms transfers abroad. That ceiling was protested vigorously by the Israelis, who feared that it would limit American military aid to Israel. Carter was pressed hard by Mondale, Stu Eizenstat, and Senator Hubert Humphrey to make some accommodation favorable to Israel, and after intense negotiations the decision on conventional arms transfers was revised in a way which we felt met the legitimate concerns of Israeli security and yet did not place Israel, as its supporters desired, in the same category as America's principal allies (NATO and Japan).

The flap over the arms transfers also produced two other minor incidents, each quite revealing of bureaucratic and personal sensitivities. I noted on May 16 that "later in the day I got a rather plaintive telegram from Cy Vance from Iran, who had apparently heard that our press here was reporting that the President reversed his position yesterday on the arms transfers because of Israeli pressure and that in so doing the President allegedly said he had been misled by the State Department. According to Cy, the story originated with a White House aide. I checked all of the stories and was able to inform him that no such attribution in fact took place, that no White House aide was cited, but that an AP correspondent accredited to the State Department did write a story which we had resolutely denied." By then there had been several stories comparing me to Kissinger and Vance to Rogers, and I, in turn, wrote plaintively in my notes that "it really shows the extent to which there are persistent efforts, particularly in the journalistic world, to poison relations between Cy and me, relations which so far have been remarkably smooth."

The other minor incident involved an effort by the Israelis to get the President to phone Shimon Peres, who had replaced Rabin as the Prime Minister of Israel. Mondale was called from Israel by Simcha Dinitz, the Israeli Ambassador, requesting that President Carter phone Peres in order to give Peres personal reassurances on the arms transfer issue. The President and I agreed that this would not be appropriate but that the President would be willing to receive a call from Peres. Mondale then called Dinitz to convey the message, and Dinitz in turn pressed the Vice President to call the Israeli Embassy in Washington to give the Israelis there a restatement of our new assurances regarding arms transfers to Israel. The Vice President was also asked to tell the Embassy that the President would like Peres to call him. As I noted in my journal: "Even Mondale was quite irritated by the whole thing."

Though the initial exchanges with the Israelis were not propitious, we were not discouraged. We expected Israeli opposition, for it was our feeling that the Israelis were essentially playing for time, and were more interested in preserving an exclusive relationship with the United States than in moving toward a broader peace in the Middle East. We were determined to retain close links with Israel, but we knew that we had to widen our relations with the more moderate Arab states, to build on what had been achieved by Nixon and Kissinger in Egypt, and to intensify our collaboration with Saudi Arabia. But the Israelis could not be expected to soften their position unless the Arabs, too, showed some willingness to accommodate, and thus we were prepared to press hard in order to obtain from the Arabs also a more clear-cut commitment to peace.

The next hurdle came in early April, during Sadat's visit. Carter and he hit it off extremely well. Sadat's personality stood in sharp contrast to that of Rabin. Warm, gracious, even ingratiating, he was at the same time poised and confident, and exuded the aura of a man willing to risk much—as in 1973—in order to win much. However, he also had a tendency to let himself be carried away by his own words, and I noted in my journal that "my worry is that Sadat does not seem to differentiate clearly between fact and fiction, and I wonder how much of what he said was just for effect." For example, "at one point he was describing to us with considerable emotion how [in 1973] he had the Israeli armed forces encircled on the West Bank of the Nile, with 400 Israeli tanks ringed by 800 Egyptian tanks which were about to annihilate the Israelis when the cease-fire finally came. . . . I knew that this was simply untrue. Similarly, at the dinner in the evening he gave an account of Qaddafi massacring his colleagues, which seemed to me to be somewhat fictional." At the same time, I sensed from what Sadat and his colleagues were saying that the Egyptians were confronting a rather desperate plight, and that they were extremely eager for a closer relationship with the United States. This gave me some confidence that we could press the Egyptians for the necessary concessions. I was particularly impressed by how well Carter handled the discussions. He showed sensitivity to Sadat's pride, he appealed for his magnanimity, at no point did he make Sadat feel inferior or dependent, and yet he pressed steadily for more and more significant concessions.

While no major breakthroughs took place, Sadat's initial reluctance to consider a formal peace was gradually overcome, and by the end of his talks with Carter he had agreed that normalization of relations with Israel could take place within the next five years. While in retrospect this may seem to have been a modest concession, it was the first substantive breakthrough on the Arab side. Before, Sadat had said that a formal peace was something for the next generation to achieve. In addition, the President obtained from Sadat some personal promises designed to create a more congenial atmosphere. Sadat agreed to return some Israeli bodies to the Israeli side and to tone down his anti-Israeli propaganda. Last but not least, Sadat expressed a willingness to go to Geneva. All in all, we had reason to be satisfied.

The PRC met again on April 19. Vance reaffirmed our view that we should strive to go to Geneva by the end of the year, lest there be serious deterioration in U.S. credibility within the Arab world. Our view was still that we should try to achieve as much prior substantive agreement as possible, and for the first time the question arose as to whether we should deal directly with the PLO. The President had mentioned earlier to Rabin that the PLO would have to be involved at some point, but we had not yet faced squarely the question of how and under what conditions this could be done. We were aware of the extraordinary sensitivity of this issue to the Israelis, who never ceased to remind us that Secretary Kissinger had signed a pledge that the United States "will not recognize or negotiate with the PLO as long as the PLO does not recognize Israel's right to exist and does not accept Security Council Resolutions 242 and 338." It was our feeling that we had to respect that promise, though it was also our view that the promise did not exclude occasional, informal contacts. If Geneva were to involve serious negotiations between Israel and the Arab side, in some fashion the Palestinians, notably the PLO, would have to participate. On April 19, we decided to begin the process of exploring whether the PLO was prepared to make the needed public commitment to UN 242, thereby opening the door to its own involvement in the peace process. Secretary Vance probed for such PLO willingness in the course of his next visit to the Middle East, in mid-August.

As an indication of growing U.S. willingness to be responsive to moderate Arab requests, the President authorized toward the end of April some military items as aid to Egypt. This was designed to be a signal that moderation would be rewarded and that the United States was prepared to parallel its military relationship with Israel by closer collaboration with the anti-Soviet and moderate Arab regimes. Doubtless, this made the Israelis uneasy, but the move was clearly in the U.S. interest.

The President next met with Hafez al-Assad of Syria in Geneva on May 9.

> . . . I must say that Carter was most impressive. After a brief presentation of the issues he would like to discuss he asked Assad for his views. Assad launched into a long discourse on Arab history. After listening patiently for at least one hour, Carter began to ask him pointed questions, but he asked in an extremely pleasant and low-key fashion. This resulted in a really sustained and extraordinarily effective probing exercise in which some areas of flexibility on Assad's part were thereby established. I was really impressed by the skill with which Carter did this. He has the makings of an excellent negotiator. He not only pushed Assad into greater flexibility on such issues as the Palestinians or security arrangements, but at the same time he managed to convey a sense of warmth and concern to the Arabs, which was extremely effective. My only concern was that some of his remarks, if anybody

had taps at the meeting, particularly if the Israelis tapped the meeting, could be misunderstood and played against him. Assad himself is rather pleasant, with a twinkle in his eye when he talks, and a rather warm and engaging person, of really high intelligence; assuming the translations were reasonably accurate, they show a man of very quick mind, effective ability to express himself, and quick adaptability to new circumstances.

The President specifically asked for Assad's assistance in getting the PLO to accept UN Resolution 242. In return, he said that the United States would agree to deal directly with the PLO. Assad was evasive and made no promises, though he seemed to be favoring a Geneva Conference. Although the meeting was congenial, it was not particularly productive. Considering that the Syrians were the most militant party to the Arab–Israeli conflict, one could claim that some progress was made since the discussion was about attaining peace.

The discussions with Assad had one particularly gratifying humane result. Carter asked Assad, at the instigation of Congressman Steve Solarz, to permit a few young Jewish women who wished to marry Jewish Americans to emigrate. Assad at first bristled, but then promised to look into the matter. In midsummer we learned that such permission had been granted and a number of Jewish girls were allowed to leave Syria. It was clearly a gesture of good will, and Carter was genuinely pleased.

The other two Middle East summits held by Carter at this time involved Arab royalty, and that lent them special color. The President met with King Hussein on April 25–26 and with Crown Prince Fahd on May 24. Both men represented the more traditional structure of power: they were more reserved, soft-spoken, and in some ways quite elusive. With both of them the Palestinian issue was much discussed, and Prince Fahd took a particularly strong position in favor of a Palestinian state. However, he did agree to try to get the PLO to endorse UN Resolution 242. On our side, we stressed to both rulers that it was essential that the PLO accept the existence of the state of Israel, for otherwise there was no way of solving the problem of Palestinian representation in the eventual Geneva negotiations.

Begin's Roadblock

While these efforts were in progress, an important event took place in the Middle East which was to profoundly affect the evolution of Carter's policy. In the Israeli elections, the extreme-right-wing coalition headed by Menachem Begin scored a clear-cut victory, and Begin was installed as the new Prime Minister. At an informal meeting with the

President on the afternoon of May 19, Stu Eizenstat and I discussed the implications of Begin's recent victory. I argued that "precisely because Begin is so extreme, the President will be able to mobilize on behalf of a settlement a significant portion of the American Jewish community. . . . This will make it easier for the President to prevail and to have the needed congressional support. I also started pressing the President to insist that Mondale give a major speech on the Middle East because I was becoming increasingly fearful that the President was overly identified as the sole spokesman on the Middle Eastern issue." I noted on May 30 that "it is . . . important that Mondale speak up, thereby showing that the Administration is united on the subject and that any successor to the President would pursue the same policy." I kept pushing for this, in spite of Mondale's understandable reluctance to risk his standing with the Jewish community, and in early June the President approved a speech by Mondale. (It was delivered on June 17 and was a firm statement of our view that a settlement would require Israeli withdrawal to approximately the 1967 lines and the setting up of a Palestinian "entity.")

My concern was heightened by the intensifying attacks by the Jewish community on Carter and, to a lesser extent, on me. In late May, in one of his press conferences, Carter went so far as to talk about reparations for the Palestinians, and that particularly irritated the Jewish community. I spoke to him the next day, suggesting "that in any further discussion of compensation for the Palestinians he stress that he had reconciliation in mind and a comprehensive settlement because otherwise this will become an inflammatory issue, and I particularly recommended that he mobilize Mondale, Humphrey, and Arthur Goldberg to speak up more publicly on behalf of his efforts to obtain peace in the Middle East." I also suggested to the President that he solicit Nelson Rockefeller's assistance, since that would have the added benefit of keeping Kissinger in line. Kissinger in the meantime had phoned me, and had told me that we should be prepared for a massive onslaught from the Jewish community, something that he said he had experienced himself.

Subsequently the President did meet with Goldberg, who was very impressive in his presentation and who basically agreed with the President on the question of the borders. Proclaiming himself to be the father of UN 242, he indicated that he would be willing to do anything the President asked. I subsequently urged the President and Vance to try Goldberg as an unofficial and off-the-record emissary to the Middle East, but Cy did not relish sharing the Middle East with him. Goldberg was later appointed as the head of our delegation to the Conference on Helsinki, which was scheduled for Belgrade. He performed admirably, and I always regretted that we did not involve him more actively in our Middle East venture.

It was during this period that the President first discussed the possibility of a public showdown over our policy toward Israel. One evening in early June, the President met with Mondale, Jordan, Eizenstat,
myself, and others to consider our tactics in response to a large-scale
campaign launched by the American–Israeli Political Action Committee designed to develop pressure against our policy. The President
said that he felt that he had carried too much of the burden himself,
and though Cy and I backed him publicly, others had not done so,
and he now hoped that the Vice President and others would speak up.
We all agreed that Hubert Humphrey was the key in the event that a
public debate had to take place. Later in the evening I spoke with Tip
O'Neill and asked him for his assessment of the situation. He told me
point-blank that if the choice came down between the President and
the pro-Israel lobby, the country would clearly choose the President—
but only if the choice was clearly posed. However, such a choice was
never presented directly. The President felt that it would be too divisive
and that it was not necessary at this stage.

Occasionally Carter would also say that he would be willing to lose
the Presidency for the sake of genuine peace in the Middle East, and
I think he was sincere. Perhaps most importantly, Carter's feelings on
Israel were always ambivalent. On the one hand, he felt that Israel was
being intransigent; on the other, he genuinely did have an attachment
to the country as "the land of the Bible," and he explicitly disassociated
himself from the more critical anti-Israeli view. He once told me with
some distaste that Giscard described the Israelis as "international
bandits" and that in his view Giscard was more anti-Israel than even
the Arabs. Considering his admiration for Giscard, such an observation
was quite revealing of the President's attitude toward Israel.

These mixed feelings contributed to the growing impression that
Carter would not stand fast and that he would accommodate if pressed.
He certainly was warned to be tough and to stand firm. On June 26,
"Fritz Mondale called me and he indicated that [Senator] Abraham
Ribicoff had spoken to him several times urging that we be very, very
tough. The position Ribicoff takes is that the President shouldn't be
intimidated and that he should assert himself." Early in July, Vance
told me that Sol Linowitz, the distinguished Washington attorney, had
said to Cy that "the word is out in the Jewish community that if they
press hard enough the President will yield. This is apparently the effect
of the meeting we had a couple of days ago with the Jewish leaders,"
at which Carter made an impassioned profession of his commitment to
Israel.

As tensions with the Jewish community intensified, and as Israeli
criticisms of our policy mounted, Cy Vance stood firm. He was not to
be intimidated and in some respects was prepared to be much harder
on the Israelis than I. He urged the President to adopt a firm stand on

the expansion of Israeli settlements on the West Bank, condemning them as illegal. Many of the criticisms from the Jewish community were also directed at me personally. Hints of this started appearing in *Time* and *Newsweek* magazines and also in the press. I was presented as anti-Israeli, perhaps even worse than that, and the references to my Polish and Catholic background became increasingly pointed in some of the commentaries on the subject of the Middle East.

Marvin Kalb of CBS was particularly nasty in his frequent hints that I was anti-Israeli. For example, on June 30 he reported that I was urging the State Department to attack Begin and Dayan by name, something which I had never done. I often wondered whether his attacks on me were not due to the fact that I had not taken seriously his offer, made to us in early January, to serve as U.S. Ambassador to Israel, which he reinforced with the argument that his Jewish background would make it easier for us to lean harder on Israel. Feeling beleaguered, I sought the President's sympathy, telling him on June 21 "about the mounting attacks on me and the fact that I am likely to be the fall guy on the Middle East. . . . He kind of laughed and . . . in effect said that 'this is exactly what we want you to be, the fall guy' or something to that effect."

Dealings with the Israelis were further complicated by the vexing habit of the Israeli Ambassador, Simcha Dinitz, of leaking to the Israeli press self-serving or even distorted versions of his conversations with the top officials of the Administration. On more than one occasion, I had to complain to Dinitz about this, and after a while it made serious and confidential talks with him well-nigh impossible. On one occasion, for example, I told Dinitz that "minor border modifications was a desirable formula to use, since the word 'minor' did not spell out precisely the extent of the modifications. Thus it was a source of reassurance to the Arabs that there would be no major Israeli acquisitions, and yet it gave the Israelis the needed opening to press for such rectifications as were necessary from a security point of view. This was then leaked to the press as indicating that I favored major annexations, and I had to issue a clarifying denial." Almost every meeting between Dinitz and the President, Vance, or me was usually followed by an off-the-record tendentious briefing for the Israeli press by Dinitz. This stood in sharp contrast with my dealings, for example, with Dobrynin, who never engaged in such a practice. I was later very much relieved to find that Dinitz's successor, Ambassador "Eppie" Evron, was the epitome of discretion, thereby greatly facilitating a collaborative U.S.–Israeli relationship.

It was in this rather tense atmosphere that the first Carter–Begin meeting was held. The new Israeli Prime Minister came to Washington for a two-day visit on July 19–20. His visit was preceded by a PRC on July 5, held to discuss draft principles that might be adopted before a

Geneva conference. "Cy Vance came across strong, urging a tough position, explicitly stated. If we can hold to it, we may actually get some movement. I have the feeling that the Israelis will be surprised by how explicit and by how clearly spelled out our position is. It is not a blueprint or a plan, but it is a fairly explicit framework, defining our basic approach and indicating our expected and preferred outcomes. We will see whether we can hold to it in the face of domestic pressure," I wrote. The State Department took the lead in drafting these principles and in developing formulations for the participation of the Palestinians in the negotiations.

This meeting of the PRC also marked the departure from the pattern that had been followed up until then. Secretary Vance, who presided and who till then had tended to let me take the lead in defining issues of substance, began to assert his role as chairman more clearly. He prepared the draft principles with his immediate associates at State and argued strongly that they should be discussed with each of the parties. Cy thereby hoped to obtain a commitment to some written formulations, which could serve as the basis for a Geneva Conference.

On the eve of the President's meeting with Begin, I gave the President a memorandum urging that he place heavy emphasis on the American national interest, the danger of radicalism in the Arab world, and the possibility of Soviet reentry into the area if the peace talks were to break down. I also told him that I thought that Begin eventually might be better able than the Israeli Labor Party to deliver the concessions necessary for peace. In the first place, he would not face much domestic opposition if he showed flexibility. Secondly, he might well see the achievement of peace with Egypt as a significant historical attainment for which he could claim credit. Vance and I also met with the President to review what he might say to Begin, and I was struck by the fact that "both Vance and the President seemed to be in some respects more tough-minded than I on such issues as the settlements. For example, I was prepared to make exception for religious settlements. . . . I also felt that in some respects we could concede the historical claim of the Israelis to the West Bank but differentiate that from their claims as a nation-state."

Carter gave Begin an effusive greeting: "Perhaps his best speech of greeting yet—moving, evocative, excellently stated," I noted. But the initial encounter "was somewhat disappointing in that Begin spoke a great deal about history, about suffering, but there was little give so far as procedure and substance." After the meeting, I rapidly dictated a memorandum to the President urging him in the evening discussion with Begin to make it very clear that "the American national interest is involved here and there has to be more give on the Palestinians, more give on the issue of border and security, and more accommodation on procedures pointing toward Geneva."

The next morning the President recounted to me his conversations with Begin the night before. "Begin indicated to him that he plans to meet with some of the top Arab leaders, that he will be somewhat forthcoming on procedures, but on the basic issue of the Palestinians there was still no give." He also exacted from the President a promise that the President would not talk publicly anymore about Israeli withdrawals to the 1967 borders with minor modifications, and that he would refrain from using the formula "a Palestinian homeland." In return, the President asked Begin to exercise greater restraint on the question of settlements, but obtained no commitment from the Prime Minister. When the President put forward the argument that security through territorial annexation would in fact be a formula for insecurity, Begin responded by saying that there would never be foreign sovereignty over the West Bank and Gaza.

Begin's visit involved a particularly moving experience for me personally. I was invited to have breakfast with him at Blair House, and on arrival I found myself confronting a firing line of TV cameramen and photographers. Within seconds Begin emerged and in rather formal fashion presented to me some documents, located in Jerusalem archives, that bore on my father's activity in Germany during the 1930s when, as a Polish diplomat, he was engaged in saving Jewish lives. I was deeply touched by this gesture of human sensitivity, especially since it came in the wake of some of the personal attacks on me and on my role in seeking to promote a peace settlement in the Middle East. Begin and I then sat down to breakfast, and "we talked about Jabotinsky's* influence on him, about his vision of the future and the past. And I stressed to him that I was very impressed by the degree to which he lives the suffering of his people and yet is also the personification of the triumph of Israel. I suggested to Begin that the next phase is to make the triumph permanent through peaceful accommodation. We talked for about an hour and a half, covering essentially the major points previously discussed by him with Vance and the President."

Later in the day (July 20), I reviewed that conversation with the President while we were sitting together on the porch next to the Oval Office. "Carter was very relaxed, I think seemingly pleased at least with the atmospherics of the meeting, and he commented on how much I seemed to be taken by Begin's historical courage and his role. He said that he was quite struck by that and I suppose he is right. In a sense the things which I like about Carter apply to some extent, but only to some extent, to Begin also—courage, principles, belief in God, basic honor, leadership. Begin and I talked a little bit about these

---

* Vladimir Jabotinsky (1880–1940): Militant Zionist leader who advocated armed struggle on behalf of a Jewish homeland in Palestine.

matters, too, and especially about Machiavelli's definition of what is the nature of leadership, the role of *virtù* and *fortuna,* and how in different ways it applies to Begin and to Carter."

When Carter met with the press after the meeting with Begin, he was filled with optimism about convening the Geneva Conference in October. When asked why his meeting with the Israeli Prime Minister had ended slightly ahead of schedule, he replied, "We just had such an unexpectedly harmonious session this morning that we didn't find any reason for arguments." In response to another question about Begin himself, Carter said, "I like him very much. As I said in my welcoming remarks, he's a man of courage and principle, and I have found in my discussions with him that my assessment was quite accurate." Since Carter and Begin were quite suspicious of each other, it prompted Ham Jordan, who was standing next to me during the press conference, to whisper to me, "It's a little bit like tossing dice, isn't it? One wonders what will happen next."

Although the first Begin–Carter meeting was personally cordial, it did little to advance the prospects for peace. Begin had come to Washington determined to avoid discussions of substance, and he was able to turn the negotiations largely to issues of procedure. As a result, in the course of the next four weeks or so our approach toward the Middle East underwent an important transition: away from issues of substance to issues of procedure, and away from a U.S.-backed comprehensive settlement prior to Geneva to an attempt to get Soviet cooperation for a Geneva Conference.

The good will generated by Begin's visit did not last long. Within days the Israeli government approved three controversial new settlements, and the State Department came out with a strong statement in reaction. Since this took place on the eve of Vance's trip to the Middle East from July 31 to August 12, public prominence was thus given to the conflictual aspects of U.S.–Israeli relations and it did not augur well for the success of the Secretary's trip.

Impasse on the PLO and on the Settlements

Vance traveled to the Middle East to work out issues connected with the convening of the Geneva Conference, such as a formula for PLO participation, a decision to hold a pre-Geneva planning meeting, and the setting of a deadline for the start of the Geneva Conference. The Secretary also wanted to secure agreement on five principles that we considered essential to any settlement: (1) that the goal of negotiations be a comprehensive peace settlement which would be embodied in peace treaties; (2) that the basis of negotiations be Security Council Resolutions 242 and 338; (3) that normal peaceful relations between

Israel and its Arab neighbors be established; (4) that there should be a phased withdrawal to secure and recognized borders with a mutually agreed security arrangement; and (5) that a nonmilitarized Palestinian entity with self-determination by the Palestinians be created. Finally, Vance wanted to be able to inform the Russians about the agreements he had reached.

Just before his departure, while I was attending a dinner party in town, I received an urgent call from Cy Vance. "He sounded rather upset. The Israelis have just informed him that they would like him in the course of his visit to the Middle East, which literally begins tomorrow, not to mention our views on the 1967 frontiers, nor the points of our package for Geneva which dealt with Palestinian representation and the question of a Palestinian entity. This is clearly an effort to subvert the mission and in effect to transform the United States into a satellite of their policy rather than an independent force which works for a settlement. Cy felt very strongly about it; in rather intense tones he told me that this to him is an issue of principle, that he has passed this message on to the President, and then he hinted in effect that he did not see how he could go on if the President did not stand firm on this issue."

The President did stand firm, and Cy proceeded as agreed. However, he was going forth with a position which was now somewhat different from what it had been earlier in the year. Geneva was beginning to look more as an end in itself rather than as a device to pressure or induce the parties to move on substantive issues. In effect, substance was giving way to procedure. As the deadline for Geneva approached, we turned our energies to trying to find a formula for Palestinian representation at the conference.

Vance carried four options with him on his Middle East trip: The first called on the countries originally invited to Geneva—Israel, Egypt, Jordan, and Syria—to attend a new session as separate delegations, with the Palestinians permitted to attend as part of the Jordanian delegation. The second proposed that Arab countries would attend as a unified delegation of which the Palestinians would be a part. The third provided that the Palestinian question would be referred to at the beginning of the conference. The fourth deferred it until later in the conference. We ourselves were leaning to the second option.

We were also now more and more inclined to engage in a dialogue with the PLO itself regarding its participation. We hoped that if the PLO accepted Resolution 242, we could end our diplomatic boycott and the PLO could join in the talks in Geneva. In fact, while Vance was in Saudi Arabia he reported a hopeful sign in that direction. He told the press traveling with him that the Saudis had advised him to expect an imminent change in the PLO's attitude toward Resolution

242. On the basis of Vance's report, the President in Plains said that "the Palestinian leaders have indicated indirectly that they might adopt Resolution 242." However, whatever faint optimism had emerged from Vance's signal was quickly shot down by a double volley from Beirut and Tel Aviv. Shortly after Vance spoke, a PLO spokesman in Beirut denied that there had been any shift in the organization's attitude. In fact, the PLO had indicated that it would accept 242 with reservations, if it were interpreted in such a way as to apply to the creation of a Palestinian state by recognizing "that the language of Resolution 242 relates to the right of all states in the Middle East to live in peace." In Tel Aviv, just before Vance's arrival, Begin, either ignoring or unaware of Carter's statement and the PLO's "new" attitude, stated flatly that it would be fruitless to prepare a role for the PLO in the Middle East peace talks by trying to make the PLO recognize Israel. Bernard Gwertzman of the New York *Times*, describing Vance's interpretation of the trip, wrote: "Mr. Vance refused to assign blame for slow progress towards a Middle East settlement, but indirectly he seemed to credit the Arabs with greater flexibility than Israel."

At the end of Vance's trip the idea of trying to reach agreement on common principles before Geneva was basically dropped. This was in part because of stiffened Israeli resistance and in part because the Arabs did not see much merit in a nonmilitarized Palestinian entity and were not willing to make more than minor border adjustments—although they did seem to be considering normal peaceful relations with Israel. We were now more inclined to consider a close dialogue with the Soviets on the Middle East, and Brezhnev was repeatedly urging such a dialogue in his correspondence with Carter.

Another reason for following a different tack was that while Vance was in Alexandria, President Sadat had handed him a draft peace treaty. While leaving much to be desired, the draft did provide a starting point for moving away from general principles toward draft texts of treaties. Without notifying the other parties that we already had an Egyptian draft in hand, we asked each of the negotiating parties to prepare drafts of what they would like to see in a peace treaty. This was an important token of Egyptian willingness to go forward with a peace settlement, though it also did have the effect of bogging us down in detailed textual analysis.

On Sunday afternoon, August 14, the President, Cy Vance, and I met to review the results of Vance's trip to the Middle East. One of the first things the President asked was whether in Vance's view Begin was sincere. "Vance thought that he was, but only in his own sense in that he wishes to promote fully the rather one-sided concept of a settlement he entertains. . . . I was [again] struck in the course of the afternoon's conversation how hard-nosed Cy was in regard to the need to press the

Israelis . . . in advocating self-determination for the Palestinians, including the possibility of a separate and independent Palestinian state.
On the whole I felt that there was much more progress made on this
trip than the press had allowed. . . . It is clear that increasingly we will
have to develop our own proposals and put them forth, including the
need for the parties to settle largely on the basis of the 1967 frontiers,
albeit with minor modifications. All three of us agreed that this will
have to be made clear at some point when the moment is particularly
ripe. I thought that Cy this afternoon gave a particularly good performance. He was to the point, well informed, while effectively making his
case. At the same time, his basic decency and honesty came through,
and this is why he is a very good colleague with whom to work."

My optimism about the progress made on the trip was unfounded,
however. I was wrong in assuming that we would be able to move forward on substantive issues. In fact, even our discussions about the procedure bogged down. We seemed unable to get the parties to agree on
the still unresolved formula for Palestinian representation. While we
leaned increasingly toward a plan for a unified Arab delegation, including Palestinians, Israel preferred that non-PLO Palestinians sit as part
of a Jordanian delegation—an idea unacceptable to the other Arabs,
who wanted some type of PLO representation. The atmosphere became
more tense as Israeli settlements multiplied, the PLO became more
adamant, and fighting erupted once again in Lebanon.

Despite Carter's personal request to Begin to refrain from starting
any new settlements, in July, three days after the Israeli Prime Minister
left Washington, he legalized three controversial settlements. Always
averring that he was only carrying out the policy of the previous Labor
government, Begin a few weeks later extended social services to the
inhabitants of the West Bank and the Gaza Strip, and on August 17
the Israeli government approved the construction of three additional
settlements. Even after the State Department denounced the new settlements as being contrary to international law, on September 2 the Israeli
government was reported to have prepared a security plan for the occupied West Bank that would involve surrounding what were considered
Arab trouble areas with new Jewish urban and rural settlements. At
the time that Moshe Dayan, the Israeli Foreign Minister, arrived in the
United States with a new plan for "functional" arrangements on the
West Bank, there were 77 Jewish settlements in occupied Arab territories and a plan for the next fifteen years calling for the creation of
186 new communities, with 49 yet to be built on the West Bank already
on the drawing board.

On the other side, the PLO seemed to be getting more and more
intransigent, also despite our best efforts. Although he was aware of
increasingly severe criticism from the Jewish community, the President

on a number of occasions sought to show his understanding and compassion for the Palestinian situation. In an interview recorded on August 10 for ABC, he said:

> To the extent that Israeli leaders genuinely want a peace settlement, I think that they have to agree that there will be an acceptance of genuine peace on the part of the Arabs, an adjustment of boundaries in the Middle East which are secure for the Israelis and also satisfy the minimum requirements of the Arab neighbors and the United Nations resolutions, and some solution to the question of the enormous numbers of Palestinian refugees who have been forced out of their homes and who want to have some fair treatment.

Accordingly, we continued our quiet efforts to establish some sort of understanding with the PLO. A prominent American, active in educational matters, was used as the contact with Arafat, and a number of informal messages were thereby exchanged. The President, Rosalynn, and I met with our intermediary, and I was rather interested to see that Rosalynn served here as an informal channel between the President and this particular emissary.

Unfortunately, the PLO maintained its maximum demands, and even wanted additional guarantees from the United States, including recognition. I met with our emissary, and I stressed to him that "the basic point that I wished him to carry to Arafat was that our willingness to talk to him in itself is a very major concession, that Arafat has no reason to insist on additional concessions from us in return for the statement that we desire him to make" on behalf of UN 242.

Our inability to modify PLO demands was matched by our impotence in stopping new settlements. The opening of additional settlements made it increasingly difficult for us to persuade the Arabs to go forward with the peace process, and the settlement policy seemed to us to be one of deliberate provocation. On Sunday, August 28, the President met for an informal afternoon session with Vance, Mondale, Brown, Powell, and me to review progress in various areas of foreign policy. Regarding the Middle East, the President

> indicated his increasing frustration with the Israeli position and his unwillingness to maintain a policy in which in effect we are financing their conquests and they simply defy us in an intransigent fashion and generally make a mockery of our advice and our preferences. He was extremely tough-minded on this subject and he was echoed by Vance, who suggested that if the Israelis open up a single more settlement we proceed to state to them that we no

longer are bound by our self-imposed restraint on not talking with
the PLO and should initiate talks with the PLO. He also advocated
a forthright U.S. statement at the October meeting of the General
Assembly of the UN regarding our views on the Middle East. I
supported that and we also agreed that if further settlements open
we will come out and indicate more strongly than before that we
feel that the '67 frontiers with minor modifications are the just and
realistic outcome of any negotiations that might be contrived.

The next day Cy came over to my office to discuss foreign policy in
general. I noted later that day that "on the Middle East Cy is in favor
of pressing very hard and, indeed, is in favor of having a showdown
with the Israelis. He feels that they have been provocative and intransigent. In one way or another this issue will have to be brought to a head
probably sometime during December."

Our mood at the beginning of September was generally pessimistic,
as reflected in my September 2 weekly report to the President. I saw
four dangers looming increasingly on the horizon: (1) growing evidence
of regional instability and growing internal dissatisfaction in both Egypt
and Syria; (2) the shortsightedness of the PLO and its inability to
respond to our overtures; (3) suspect Soviet behavior, talking peace
while quietly encouraging Arab intransigence; and (4) Israeli tactics
such as de facto annexation of the West Bank designed to make it more
difficult for the Arabs to negotiate. In order to regain momentum and
to establish greater credibility for our willingness to engage in a dialogue,
I advocated some specific steps: (1) a Presidential letter to Assad
reiterating our general approach and asking for his help with the PLO;
(2) a public statement by the State Department addressing the Palestinian issue in general terms and indicating the right of and need for
Palestinian participation in the peace talks; (3) an agreement, despite
the inherent risks, with the Soviets to set a deadline for reconvening
the Geneva Conference; and (4) a counter to Begin's policy of creeping
annexations of the West Bank by drawing on the concept of trusteeship
to prompt interim arrangements.

On September 13, the State Department did issue a new public statement on the Middle East. It said that the status of the Palestinians
must be settled in a comprehensive Arab–Israeli agreement, that this
issue could not be ignored if others were to be solved, and that the
Palestinians had to be involved in the peacemaking process: "Their
representatives will have to be at Geneva for the Palestinian question
to be solved." The Egyptians and the PLO welcomed the statement;
however, it generated a major furor within the Jewish community. We
were again accused of adopting an anti-Israeli position and of betraying
our basic commitments. Much of that attack was directed at me per-

sonally and even the Vice President came around to ask "whether I am depressed by all the criticisms I have been getting, particularly from the Jewish community." Fortunately, a number of distinguished Jewish leaders, notably Hyman Bookbinder, Edgar Bronfman, Sol Linowitz, Arthur Goldberg, Phil Klutznick, and others realized the total injustice of these attacks and rallied to my side.

To explore ways of breaking the impasse, Carter and Dayan met on September 19, 1977. The President stated bluntly that Israel was taking "a very adamant stand and that the Arab side appears to be more flexible." Much of the discussion involved the settlements. Dayan promised that they would be consolidated into military camps and that they would be relatively small in acreage.

Before the meeting adjourned, Dayan said that he would like to suggest that the Arabs not be told that the idea of a unified delegation which had been discussed came from Israel; he would suggest instead that they should be told that the United States might try to persuade Israel to accept such a delegation. "If they know it comes from us they will certainly reject it. You should say that we object, and then you can try to force it on us." The President and Vance agreed to this suggestion.

The unstable situation in Lebanon added another complication to our problems, but ironically in mid-September 1977 it did provide the United States with an opportunity to assert itself over Israel. The latter part of September saw renewed fighting in that tragically devastated country, and on September 20, I told the President in my 7:15 a.m. briefing "about intensifying military activity in Lebanon and about the somewhat disappointing Syrian response regarding our initiatives toward the PLO." During the next several days we watched with growing anxiety the continued fighting. On Saturday, September 25, while attending a formal Washington ball, I was called to the telephone around 11 p.m. The President was on the line inquiring whether I felt that the draft of a proposed message to the Israelis, warning them that unless they immediately terminated their military operations we would halt all military aid to Israel, was too tough. I said I was in agreement but would review it again with Vance and come back to him for his final approval. Vance very firmly stated that he concurred in the message, and the President then approved its dispatch. By the next morning I was able to inform the President that Begin had ordered his troops to withdraw from Lebanon. I was much encouraged by this incident, for I felt that it indicated that a firm and clear position by the United States could be sustained, provided that we persisted.

However, within the next several days it was the United States that had to back down and—unlike Begin on Lebanon just days earlier— it did so publicly. The issue at hand was the joint U.S.–Soviet statement of October 1. In mid-September, Vance and I had discussed the possibility of U.S.–Soviet cooperation on the Middle East, especially in the light of growing obstacles to progress before the Geneva Conference was actually convened. Cy reported, on the basis of his conversation with Dobrynin, that the Soviet position had become somewhat more moderate and that the Soviets no longer insisted on a separate Palestinian state. Reflecting on this talk, David Aaron, my deputy, and I concluded that Begin might be made uneasy by such American–Soviet consultations and this might make the situation more fluid. Shortly thereafter, in keeping with Brezhnev's earlier messages to Carter and perhaps encouraged by the Vance–Dobrynin dialogue, the Soviets took the initiative in presenting the State Department with a relatively moderate draft of a common statement of policy on the Middle East to serve as the basis for reconvening the Geneva Conference. Technical-level discussions with the Soviets on that draft took place at the State Department, though at the time we in the White House did not know about them.

A joint draft was ready at the end of September, and Secretary Vance personally showed it to Dayan a day or so before its issuance on October 1. Dayan refrained from reacting—perhaps deliberately. Cy then forwarded it to me for Presidential approval. Underestimating its potential domestic impact, especially since the contents focused on the formal role of the United States and the U.S.S.R. as co-chairmen, and viewing it largely as a procedural preliminary to the convening of the conference, I forwarded it to the President with Vance's recommendation. It was formally issued on October 1, and instantly produced an angry public reaction, especially among supporters of Israel.

Much of the U.S. press joined in the attack, and the Administration was portrayed as reinjecting Soviet influence into the Middle East. As a result, within days the Administration appeared to be disassociating itself from the statement, thus finding itself tactically on the defensive. The most dramatic evidence of our shift was the document produced after lengthy discussions with Foreign Minister Dayan on the evening of October 4–5 in New York, dealing with procedures for the Geneva Conference. Part of the discussion was conducted by the President himself and at times it was quite tense. "A long negotiating session during the day with Dayan which extended into late at night, interrupted by dinner which the President had to attend, given by U.S. UN Mission. Dayan in effect blackmailed the President by saying that unless he had assurances that we would oppose an independent West Bank and that we would give them economic and military aid, he would have to indicate our unwillingness in his public statements here in the United States. The President clearly indicated that this was impossible but at the same time tried to get Dayan to approve an approach to Geneva which would permit the Israelis to attend." Both men were aware of the psychological value of threatening a confrontation. At one instance, Dayan said, "We need to have some agreed formula, but I can go to Israel and to the American Jews. I have to say that there is an agreement and not a confrontation." To which the President replied, "We might have a confrontation unless you are willing to cooperate. But a confrontation would be very damaging to Israel and to the support of the American public for Israel. If we proceed in good faith, we can avoid a confrontation. If there is a confrontation, and if we are cast in a role against Israel and with the Arabs, Israel would be isolated, and this would be very serious. It would be a blow to your position."

The negotiations dragged on and on in the same vein as Vance and I tried to reach an agreement with Dayan. Vance: "You can say what you want, but let's avoid a public confrontation. You can speak your piece, but I hope you can be positive. I want to go down with you to meet the press." Brzezinski: "Why can't you make three points? You will go to Geneva on the basis of Resolution 242. You will sit down with the unified Arab delegation, including Palestinians. You have reservations on the U.S.–Soviet statement, but you have been reassured by the U.S. President about the commitment to all agreements, and there will be no pressure." Dayan: "That would be misleading if that were all that I said. We have said more than that about the unified Arab delegation." In another exchange with the President, Dayan said: "It would be bad if we did not say anything tonight. It would help if you could say that you adhere to all of your agreements with Israel, and that there will be no pressure." The President responded: "We could do a joint statement. Israel does not have to agree with all of the U.S.–Soviet statement. Let's stay flexible. You could express your disagreement the way that we and the Chinese did in the Shanghai communiqué."

Before midnight the President withdrew. I followed shortly thereafter, and Cy continued the discussions on specific points. The statement which was finally issued did reiterate that Resolutions 242 and 338 remained the agreed basis for the resumption of the Geneva Conference; that proposals for removing remaining obstacles be developed; and that "acceptance of the joint U.S.–U.S.S.R. statement of October 1, 1977, by the parties is not a prerequisite for the reconvening and conduct of the Geneva Conference." As I noted in my journal: "In the end, we got a compromise statement which pledges the Israelis to go, but I do wonder whether Dinitz and Dayan did not emerge from the meeting with an excessively self-assured view of the degree to which the President is susceptible to pressure. In some instances and on some issues he was quite tough; but he didn't go far enough, in my judgment, to indicate that if challenged he would go to the country and there would be an all-out confrontation." Indeed, the impression was now created by these statements that we were prepared to collaborate more closely with the Israelis on matters involving Geneva, and this, in turn, generated increasing skepticism among the Arabs as to the likelihood of Geneva producing any constructive result.

Though I was unfairly labeled by Israel's supporters as the initiator of the U.S.–Soviet statement, I did subsequently feel that I had erred in not consulting our domestic political advisers about its likely internal impact and in not objecting more strenuously to the very notion of a joint U.S.–Soviet public statement. I do not know if my objections would have prevailed, in view of Vance's strong support for such a statement and the President's desire at the time to improve U.S.–Soviet relations, but the net result was to weaken our leverage with the Israelis, to undermine Arab confidence in our determination to obtain a genuine settlement in Geneva, and to increase Soviet unwillingness (if, indeed, any encouragement was needed) to be helpful with the more radical Arab parties, notably Syria and the PLO. Perhaps in reaction to this experience, later in October the President authorized a vote by the United States at the UN critical of the Israeli position on the settlements. He did so despite strong arguments against it by the Vice President, as well as by Stu Eizenstat and Bob Lipshutz, the President's Counsel, "both of whom were very upset and I particularly felt for Stu because I can sense how deeply loyal he is to the President and yet also how very much troubled he was by the position that we were taking." I supported the President in his decision because I felt that otherwise our credibility with both the Arabs and the Israelis would be destroyed. Moreover, "Cy was extremely strong on the proposition that we should not yield but must go through with it. In general, I must say that he is quite tough on this matter. . . ." (October 27).

However, this demonstration of will did little to reassure Sadat or to impress Begin. Begin continued to be unyielding on substance, while, to Sadat's dismay, we kept pressing for areas of compromise on procedural matters. However, contrary to press and Israeli reports, Sadat at first actually welcomed the U.S.–Soviet statement of October 1, telling U.S. Ambassador Hermann Eilts that it was "a master stroke" because it would put pressure on the Syrians to be more accommodating. He was then shaken by the manner in which the United States retreated when the statement came under attack both domestically and from Israel.

In order to try to break the procedural impasse, the President sent Sadat a handwritten note in the third week of October, appealing to him to make a bold, statesmanlike move to help overcome the hurdles on the path to Geneva. Sadat apparently read this as an admission of the President's domestic weakness and thus as a plea for an Egyptian initiative to break the stalemate. It is evident that Sadat attributed a lot of significance to Carter's handwritten note, interpreting it as motivated by despair and calling upon Sadat to prove his friendship.

Sadat's Initiative

Sadat's response came a week later, and it stunned all of us. As I wrote on November 3: "The evening's sensation was the rather unexpected and somewhat droll proposal from Sadat to hold a world summit in East Jerusalem. The President and I wondered how best to deal with this one, and the President rather wistfully said, this was around 8:30 in the evening, that he was now ready to write his energy speech but after such a sensational and exciting proposal he doesn't see how he can go back to writing the speech." Sadat's proposal was nothing if not imaginative: that a meeting be held in East Jerusalem, attended by the heads of state of the United States, the U.S.S.R., China, France, Great Britain, as well as Israel, Syria, Jordan, Egypt, and the PLO. The next morning the President met with Mondale, Vance, and me at the foreign affairs breakfast, and we agreed that Sadat's suggestion was not likely to prove constructive. All of us felt that such a summit would be sterile, quite apart from the specific PLO problem. We worried about Sadat and wondered whether he was not losing his sense of reality.

The next we heard from Sadat was in the second week of November, when he informed us that he was prepared to go to Jerusalem to talk to the Israelis about peace. This, in effect, brought to an end our strategy for going to Geneva, and ushered in a new phase in which the prime mover was Sadat. Although Sadat credited Carter's handwritten letter as the inspiration for his initiative, for the next several weeks the United States was largely a spectator. The President did keep in touch with Begin and Sadat, and both of them made it a point to keep Carter informed. I urged Carter to insist that Sadat visit Yad Vashem while in Jerusalem—I felt that this gesture would be appreciated by the Israelis. On November 20, I recorded:

Sadat in Jerusalem—that was the theme of the day. Living history, full of drama and emotion. One cannot help but admire a leader who is willing to take such risks on behalf of a higher cause. My only regret is that Carter is not doing it. My guess is that until he decides not to follow cautious advice he will not play the pre-eminent role which he could be playing, given his intelligence and the position of America in the world. After watching Sadat and Begin and Peres, Jody Powell and I had a conference call with the President. Much to my surprise he was much harder on Begin than I was. My view was that Begin was forthcoming in his willingness to negotiate everything and in refraining from a rebuttal of Sadat's optimal position. The President rather strongly felt that Begin should have made some conciliatory statement publicly and that he was completely unyielding.

Later Stu Eizenstat phoned me and also expressed concern that Begin had not been sufficiently forthcoming. My hope is that he will be in his private conversations with Sadat, so that Sadat will have something to take back to Cairo. That is the gloss that I put on the meeting today in a number of briefings with newspapermen. These briefings were designed on Sunday afternoon to offset also some of the negative comments that Kissinger was projecting in his observations on the Sadat–Begin encounter. I encouraged Stu to phone Dinitz because comments from him, a person sensitive to the feelings of the Jewish community, might be more effective than if I were to phone him. Incidentally, Cy Vance phoned me yesterday before leaving for Latin America just to say that he had heard that Dinitz in private conversations with newspapermen was lambasting, as Vance put it, us, meaning himself, me, and the President. He was very indignant about it and said he will have [Philip] Habib call Dinitz in and really rebuke him, and he asked me to repeat all of this to the President. I will do so tomorrow.

Sadat's initiative compelled us to reappraise our position, and particularly to define how we should respond to Sadat's proposal for a multilateral conference in Cairo. I took the position that we had no real alternative but to support Egyptian–Israeli negotiations; however, we should use our influence to keep those talks from producing only a separate peace which would be inherently unstable. While starting with Egypt and Israel, we should try to draw Jordan and the Palestinians into the talks as progress was made. The President and Vance were somewhat more reluctant. In a meeting held on the evening of November 28, attended by the President, Mondale, Vance, and me, I urged strongly that Vance go to the Middle East to touch base with the heads of state, and that we use the Cairo Conference as a preliminary to a later meeting in Geneva, in which perhaps the Soviets and the Syrians might also be involved.

"However, I urged the President not to overly engage the Soviets in the first phase. This, in my judgment, precipitates conservative fears, particularly from the Saudis and Egyptians, and is also not popular in this country. I hope he listens to my point of view because Cy was pressing very hard for Soviet participation and for close coordination with the Soviets. We will see whether Cy goes, because I can tell that he is rather reluctant to go. However, he's a good soldier, and when the President said that he favored his going he quickly acquiesced." I then also reported that Dobrynin had stated that the U.S.–Soviet relationship may deteriorate because Sadat is striving to prevent a Geneva Conference. Carter replied to that rather vehemently: "How can he say this? The Soviets have been playing grab-ass for a month instead of helping us all to go to Geneva, including the Syrians."

At the next morning briefing, November 29, "I suggested that the President publicly take a more positive line on the recent Sadat–Begin initiative and that he particularly praise Sadat, who took the greater risks and who offered the more genuine concessions. This would in a quiet way put pressure on Begin but would not single him out for criticism. At the same time, I also told the President that I felt that perhaps we made a tactical mistake in the timing and visibility of the earlier U.S.–Soviet statement on the Middle East and that we should be more cautious than recommended by State regarding Soviet reinvolvement in the Middle Eastern affair. We ought to try to move ahead without the Soviets to the extent that we can and only bring them in in conjunction with the Geneva Conference but only if they at the same time exert their influence to pacify and involve the Syrians and the PLO." I developed this in a more formal memorandum which I submitted on the same day and which argued that we should seek to get the collaboration of the moderates. The Soviet Union should not be deeply involved. As a second phase, the United States and the Soviet Union could begin to work for the reconvening of a Geneva Conference, not as an end in itself but rather as a threat or cover for the actual negotiations.

Shortly thereafter, I wrote another memorandum arguing that we should support the Cairo Conference while developing a strategy to draw in the other Arabs. I recommended that the Vice-President go to Jordan, Israel, and Saudi Arabia, and that he should tell the Saudis in particular that we are worried about the consequences of a separate Egyptian–Israeli peace. Secretary Vance could talk to the Soviets and enlist their cooperation in getting a Geneva Conference underway, and he could urge them to go to the Cairo Conference as a prelude to Geneva. Finally, I suggested that I be sent to talk to Assad, to urge him to go to the Cairo Conference or, at least, to obtain benevolent Syrian abstention. In brief, I wanted the U.S. to regain the initiative, capitalizing on Sadat's move while gradually squeezing the Soviets out of the game.

However, after some additional discussions at Camp David with Cy Vance and me, the President decided not to send emissaries to the region but merely messages to Sadat and Begin backing their efforts and to the Saudis and Syrians encouraging restraint. I would have preferred a policy of greater visibility and action, but the President felt that this was not the time for him to inject himself into the Middle East picture.

In public, I started speaking of a "concentric circles" approach, building on the Egyptian–Israeli accord, then expanding the circle by including the Palestinians on the West Bank and Gaza as well as the Jordanians, and finally moving to a still wider circle by engaging the Syrians and perhaps even the Soviets in a comprehensive settlement.

At this stage, I was mainly preoccupied with finding ways to make certain that the emerging Israeli–Egyptian deal did not produce a situation in which the rest of the Middle East was frozen out of the peace process, thereby creating new openings for the Soviets. I believed that if we were to move forward on the basis of the Sadat–Begin initiative, we should find some ways of making sure that progress on the West Bank was also generated.

That remained my preoccupation throughout much of the next two years. Thus, on December 5, 1977, "at the morning briefing I reviewed with the President the situation in the Middle East. I particularly stressed the importance of moving now favorably to exploit the opportunities that have been opened up by the Begin–Sadat initiative. The Vance mission should be designed to bring in the moderate Arabs and leave the Soviets and the Syrians to the side. In fact, I think we should be very careful not to draw in the Soviets prematurely, even if it means some delay in Geneva. All this, of course, provided that there is movement, particularly by the Israelis, on such matters as the Palestinian issue. We can thereby engage in the process the Jordanians and the Saudis. The critical dimension, therefore, is Israeli flexibility toward the moderates."

Despite his reservations, Vance set out for the Middle East on December 8. On December 10, while attending the Gridiron Club dinner, "I was called out twice by urgent calls from the White House. Vance had reported from the Middle East that Begin would like to meet with the President by flying to Washington quite unexpectedly and then perhaps by proceeding from there to Cairo. The President might even be invited to go along to Cairo. The notion is that this would reinforce peace efforts and give more momentum to the efforts that we have been making. Even though it was late at night, I phoned the President, who was up at Camp David. We consulted on this at length, and I sent an instruction to Vance indicating, in general, agreement with this procedure but also urging him to press Begin for concessions which would meet Sadat's minimum needs and which would go beyond efforts simply to reach a purely bilateral Israeli–Egyptian accommodation. Otherwise it will look as if we are supporting an entirely separate effort, cutting the Israelis and Egyptians off from everyone else, thereby leaving the field open to the Soviets."

A few days later, I talked to the President again about the Sadat–Begin initiative. "I suggested to the President that he consider even the possibility of something as dramatic as flying with Begin to Cairo. If we could get Begin to do something dramatic that would be truly a monumental moment in history. The President was somewhat skeptical and would prefer Sadat to come here, but I think I may have planted a thought in his head. I told him that sometimes in history it is important to seize a unique moment of initiative and exploit it to the fullest."

On December 13, prior to Begin's visit to Washington, I suggested to the President that we should take advantage of any proposal that Begin might make regarding autonomy for the West Bank—and we had some hints that he would make such a proposal—and turn it into an "interim" arrangement. My thought was that at this stage we could not resolve the conflicting Israeli and Palestinian aspirations, and that a transitional arrangement was the best way of breaking the logjam. Moreover, an interim arrangement would create a new political and psychological reality for both sides, making an eventual solution in turn more possible.

Begin's visit prompted more active U.S. reinvolvement in the peace process. In the Washington meetings held on December 16 and 17, Prime Minister Begin laid out before Carter his proposal for an accommodation with the Egyptians on the Sinai and for moving forward on the West Bank issue. I dictated extensive notes of these meetings, and it would be perhaps best if I simply reproduced here my fresh and unedited recollections of the moment:

December 16, 1977. At the morning briefing, I reminded the President of the importance of not committing himself in any fashion to whatever Begin proposes. I warned him that there would be quite a few people in the room and, as I put it in a memo to him, in keeping with the spirit of Cairo, he should be a sphinx.

At the morning meeting with Begin, which lasted two hours, first Begin talked to the President alone, and then the two of them joined us in the conference room. In the meantime, Cy and I worked a little bit in my office, although Cy was quite upset because Phil Habib, his very close friend, was stricken with a heart attack early this morning. In fact, by this evening it is uncertain whether he will survive. During the meeting, which began when the President and Begin joined us, Begin first presented his proposals on Sinai, which were actually quite forthcoming, and then shifted to his presentation on the West Bank. He proposed a home rule arrangement essentially under Israeli control. The President showed me during his presentation a note to the effect that Begin's proposals are inadequate and that he flatly so informed Begin during their private discussions. I listened carefully to Begin and took notes, and as he talked it began to occur to me that there are some openings in what Begin was saying. Accordingly, I slipped a little note to the President saying, "Tactic for us: if they are leaving the issue of sovereignty open, then this is an interim proposal." That referred to the point that I made to the President earlier that whatever Begin proposes, if it is unsatisfactory we ought to tell him that we will consider that not as their final proposal but as an interim proposal. When Begin finished, and he spoke with some emotion and pride, . . . the President made some rather negative inquiries by asking Begin what he meant by the proposal; was it part of a peacemaking process, in which case many of the issues could later be renegotiated (he confirmed that).

At this point I joined the discussion to take advantage of what I had seen as an opening by Begin. I said to the Prime Minister: "Do I understand you to be saying that your security border could be on the Jordan River, but your territorial sovereign claim would extend only to the 1967 line, with this administrative council arrangement ruling over the area where sovereignty is unclear?" The Prime Minister responded: "That is right. There will be autonomous rule for the local population." Brzezinski: "So the sovereignty in that area would be undefined. Israeli sovereignty would only go to the 1967 line." Prime Minister: "Israeli state sovereignty will go to the 1967 line." This was a very important point and one which again in my judgment gave us some opening. I then quizzed him a little on the arrangements he envisioned. Brzezinski: "Who will give the authority to the administrative council?" Prime Minister: "This is a legal problem." Brzezinski: "But it is also a political problem." Prime Minister: "It is more of a legal problem." Brzezinski: "If the authority flows from the military governor, this would be different than if the authority were to stem from the UN or from an international agreement." Prime Minister: "I agree, and this will have to be decided." Brzezinski: "Who would be able to expropriate land?" Prime Minister: "We don't want to expropriate land, but if it will happen this council would do it, subject to the concept of public order." The President: "Who would control immigration." Prime Minister: "This council." In the end,

I said to him that it seems to me that a great deal depends on how this proposal is presented and interpreted. In one sense it could be viewed simply as a proposal for the Arabs to accept the status of a Basutoland under Israeli control, but in another sense it could be viewed as a very forward-looking and serious proposal which could provide the point of departure for constructive negotiation. I could tell from the Israeli reaction that they found my comments helpful. In fact, later both Fritz Mondale and Stu Eizenstat felt that these were very helpful observations. After Begin left, the President told me that he found my earlier memo very helpful when he talked to Begin alone; that he did invoke at my suggestion the name of Jabotinsky, who was Begin's personal teacher, and told Begin that he agreed with Jabotinsky's view that one should always define the end objective first and then focus on details, rather than start first with details. The President told me that Begin was quite responsive to these comments.

After Begin had left, Cy Vance, the President, and I quickly consulted for about fifteen minutes and agreed to meet again tomorrow, having in the meantime reviewed what happened. At my suggestion the President then phoned Sadat, who was extremely pleased by the phone call. He several times reaffirmed his gratitude and at one point said, "I will not fail you, Mr. President, I am really deeply touched." I then went to my office and drafted messages to our Ambassador in Cairo so that he could brief Sadat more fully on what transpired.

I then had several sessions with Fritz, with Stu Eizenstat and others, analyzing the meeting. Both Fritz and Stu felt that it would be very valuable if I talked to Begin separately sometime tomorrow because their feeling was that I had good rapport with him and tended to think the way he does, not in legalistic terms the way his advisers tend to think and the way, to some extent, Cy tends to think, but more in terms of broad historical attitudes, perhaps reinforced by a bit of East European empathy. Accordingly, both Stu and then Fritz indirectly stimulated Dinitz to call me and to invite me tomorrow for a special session, which I accepted. I then informed Cy that I had an invitation from the Israelis to talk to them so that he wouldn't be surprised by it tomorrow. He said fine, and we will meet in any case before I go over to talk to the Israelis in order to develop a common strategy. My own view is that Begin is torn by two conflicting pulls: one, that of a religious and historical zealot, who really wants to hang on to what he calls Judea and Samaria; and the other by a sense of history and opportunity, perhaps even eternity, in the sense that he now has the genuine chance to create peace, which would be monumental in scope. In talking to him yesterday in a preliminary discussion before I had my evening meeting with the President, I played heavily also on the theme that peace right now would exclude the Russians from the Middle East and therefore would have far-reaching positive consequences both for Israel and for the United States from the Cold War political standpoint.

When I wrote my weekly report to the President, I stressed that despite Begin's rhetoric I sensed a real opportunity in his proposals, "which ought to be exploited with as much personal force and drama as possible." I outlined Begin's proposals in the following three columns:

Bad Aspects	Good Aspects	Needed Aspects
1. Authority devolves from Israeli military governor—hence could be revoked by him.	1. Interim solution for five years, hence progress toward peace implied.	1. Authority devolves from two powers with potentially conflicting claims to sovereignty (Israel and Jordan) or from the UN.
2. No formal withdrawal from the West Bank and thus no "return" (UN 242) of territory to Arabs.	2. No incorporation or territorial change, except for Jerusalem (?) since *formal* Israeli sovereignty is same as '67.	2. Some UN military presence on West Bank on the same basis as in the Sinai (subject to veto, etc.).
3. No self-determination. Special status smacks of Basutoland since it is neither Jordanian nor Palestinian.	3. Arabs control their affairs, including land expropriation and immigration.	3. Use formula that Israel will withdraw to a few specific military locations as a continuing security measure.
4. References to Samaria and Judea suggestive of annexationism.		4. Palestinian assembly will meet in East Jerusalem, but final status of East Jerusalem will remain unresolved as part of the five-year interim solution.

I suggested to the President that he should encourage Begin very strongly to correct the "bad" items and to accept the additional points, offering such incentives as his own willingness to attend a special meeting with Sadat, Begin, and Hussein to sign a general declaration of intent to conclude a peace treaty based on the principles sketched out there.

My notes for the next day recall a

full-length meeting with Begin in the evening, preceded by a private meeting with him and myself. . . . After meeting in the afternoon with the Vice President, David Aaron, and Bill Quandt to review the situation and to draft our proposals, I went over to see Begin myself at Blair House. Incidentally, the Vice President decided to warn the President that Begin is going to use public pressure on him in order to force the President's hand. But when I suggested to Fritz that he tell the President, he decided on second thought that I had better do so because it would be held against him by the members of the community, which heretofore has always supported him. At Blair House, Begin and I had a conversation lasting about an hour. We reviewed his proposals, one by one, and I urged him to present them in a more positive light to the Arabs, recommending particularly flexibility on such matters as the devolution of authority to the new administrative council not from the Israeli military governor but through some arrangement involving both Jordan and Israel. I also urged him that he consider the possibility of some UN presence on the West Bank, that he refrain from using the terms Judea and Samaria, or at least adopt a formula whereby these terms are used only in the Hebrew language but more neutral terms are used in English and Arabic, and I also urged him to use the formula that Israeli forces would be withdrawn to military encampments. This would enable the Arabs to claim that there was actually a withdrawal on the West Bank as well. He bristled at the idea of withdrawal, at first apparently thinking that I was urging a general withdrawal from the West Bank; but Ambassador Dinitz, who was present, understood my intent and I think appreciated it. They both acknowledged in the course of their conversation with me their sense that I was generally more positive on the proposals than the other members of the Administration, and this helped a great deal in the discussion that I had.

I then rushed over to the White House, briefed the President quickly on the conversation, and shortly thereafter the meeting with Begin and his associates began. The President opened by a presentation which sounded very much like my own earlier to Begin, and the advantage of that was that Begin had time to reflect and therefore was less negative. All in all, the President took a relatively upbeat attitude and pressed Begin for clarification. The President: "You said something very significant to Dr. Brzezinski yesterday. You said that Israeli sovereignty would be limited by the 1967 borders. That could be a very constructive statement. It could bring you admiration and could help create a proper attitude. . . . Dr. Brzezinski has suggested the idea of UN forces in the area west of the Jordan and has told me of your negative reply. I hope that the question will be kept open. I understand why you are negative, but I hope you will not reject the idea completely. There might be just token forces, but it could be crucial when you talk to Sadat. It might make the difference between an agreement with Sadat."

In my notes I also recorded that the President urged Begin to exercise

flexibility, suggesting to him, as I had done earlier in my conversation with Begin, not to present a blueprint to Sadat but to try to work out this proposal jointly with Sadat so that Sadat would have the feeling that he shared in shaping it. It is very difficult in talking to Begin to tell whether he in fact is willing to be flexible, because he tends to repeat himself and subsequently uses exactly the same words or sentences. Nonetheless, I do have the feeling that perhaps we made a dent on him. In any case, we will communicate what we did to [British Prime Minister James] Callaghan, whom Begin will be seeing on the way home, and hopefully Callaghan can similarly press Begin in the right direction. It was on the whole a very good meeting, with Cy and Fritz Mondale also pitching in and making constructive suggestions. As a consequence, I think that Begin may present a somewhat modified version of this proposal to the Arabs and not approach them with a blueprint precooked in Israel and one which most Arabs, I think, would suspect as essentially entailing permanent Israeli control over the West Bank coated with a thin veneer of autonomy. Incidentally, in this connection, in my conversation with Begin I urged him not to use the word "autonomy," which is usually used for a district or region which is part of your own country but has a special status, but something different, as, for example, "self-rule." This is a term which apparently has been used by the American mass media, and Begin liked it. I seized on it, emphasizing that this is a much better term than either "autonomy" or "home rule." If we can get Begin to go to Sadat with a relatively flexible approach, I think there is a good chance that we can get Hussein on board and then the President could bring Hussein, Sadat, and Begin to the White House for the official announcement of a signing ceremony. It could really mark a major turning point in American relations with the Middle East and also accomplish a very important additional objective; namely, settle the matter without the Russians and relate the moderate Arabs more closely to the United States. Provided Begin is moderate, we can now try to obtain Jordanian and Saudi support, without which the whole venture will not stand.

December 19, 1977 (Monday). In the morning briefing I reviewed with the President the situation in regard to the Middle East and I suggested that perhaps we ought to start leaking to the press our version of Begin's proposals, deliberately emphasizing the positive aspects and perhaps even exaggerating them. This might have the effect of committing Begin to an actually more favorable and flexible version of his proposal than is the case.

Begin's visit to Washington, and the generally positive U.S. attitude toward his proposals, as well as the President's even warmer endorsement of Sadat's initiative, marked a significant turning point in the U.S. strategy. We were henceforth committed to promoting an Egyptian–Israeli reconciliation, though we still hoped to give it a broader regional dimension. Given the fact that the Egyptian–Israeli talks broke down quickly, with Sadat recalling his negotiators in January 1978, the United States increasingly assumed the role of an active intermediary between Egypt and Israel.

The policy on behalf of a comprehensive settlement that we had initially pursued had both a well-thought-out substantive focus and a political strategy surrounding it. We understood the need for an American initiative and for American control over the negotiating process. While realizing that not all issues could be resolved simultaneously, we also understood that they were interrelated, particularly the crucial issues of withdrawal, security, and the nature of peace. The Palestinian issue emerged as the most controversial of our suggestions, and in retrospect it might have been introduced more gradually, and with less emphasis on the role of the PLO. As time went on, we also began to treat Geneva as a more serious exercise, whereas in the first few months it was largely seen as part of the political strategy to get the parties to engage in the negotiating process.

Perhaps the comprehensive approach never had a chance. However, it is also true that the United States did not apply enough pressure during the critical summer stage to sustain momentum, and thus gradually both the Egyptians and the Israelis became more intractable. The Israelis, especially after Begin's ascension to power, became more confident that they could resist American pressure, and their experience with the White House encouraged them in that feeling. In that respect, the first Carter–Begin meeting was probably decisive in conveying the conclusion that the Administration would not force a showdown, and thus Begin could adopt the delaying tactic of focusing on procedure without too much risk. Our own negotiating approach also became increasingly procedural as of the late summer of 1977, and that played into Begin's hand.

The Egyptians, on the other hand, became increasingly discouraged and felt that the United States lacked the will to push through a comprehensive settlement. Moreover, they were more skeptical than we of the possibility of reaching the kind of accommodation with the other Arabs which would enable the Arab side to sustain a common strategy in the course of a Geneva Conference. We probably underestimated in this connection the depth of the Egyptian–Syrian differences. Last but not least, both the Egyptians and the Israelis were suspicious of the Soviets and did not view with favor the U.S. efforts of late summer and early fall to engage the Soviets more actively.

However, it must also be said that Carter's and Vance's efforts did have the effect of unfreezing a previously frozen situation and of stimulating the principal parties into initiatives of their own. Credit is particularly due to Carter for prevailing on Sadat to face up to the need for a formal peace, and for making Begin aware that the only alternative to a dangerous isolation of Israel was for Israel to develop its own peace package on the Sinai and West Bank issues. Thus, without the initial push for a comprehensive approach it is unlikely that Sadat would have gone to Jerusalem or that Begin would have been willing to give up Sinai and to discuss autonomy for the West Bank.

The fact is this: without the United States neither the Egyptians nor the Israelis were able to move the peace process forward on their own. In spite of Sadat's bold and generous initiative, the Egyptian–Israeli bilateral talks quickly bogged down, and it became apparent, even to the Israelis and the Egyptians, that American mediation would be necessary to bring Sadat's initiative to a constructive conclusion. Thus by the end of 1977, both Begin and Sadat again desired an enhanced American role. This created an opening for Cy Vance's truly dedicated negotiating efforts. In the course of 1978, Jimmy Carter, by running major personal risks and by providing effective personal leadership, did succeed in getting Israel and Egypt to take a giant step toward real peace and normal relations.

4

Good Intentions at High Cost

> Because we are free, we can never be indifferent to the fate of freedom elsewhere. Our moral sense dictates a clear preference for those societies which share with us an abiding respect for individual human rights. We do not seek to intimidate, but it is clear that a world which others can dominate with impunity would be inhospitable to decency and a threat to the well-being of all people.
>
> —President Jimmy Carter, inaugural address,
> January 20, 1977

From the very first days of the Carter Presidency, the President had become deeply involved in two centrally important strategic issues: the Middle East and SALT. Both matters consumed an enormous amount of his time. But Jimmy Carter and his foreign policy team had come into office determined to use the immense resources of the United States to serve the wider cause of humanity. We all felt that the United States had a compassionate mission to perform and that American power should be applied not only to serve tangible American interests but, to the extent possible, also to help mankind improve its condition.

Needless to say, there were bound to be contradictions between these goals, and I will not claim that we overcame them fully. Nonetheless, we did succeed in fundamentally reorienting the prevailing conception of national interest and in broadening the focus of American foreign policy to include a greater awareness of global problems and of our capacity to effect change. It was a humanitarian effort which we believed ultimately would also benefit the United States.

With this goal in mind, we approached the various North–South issues with a view to addressing some of the root causes and not just the symptoms of international instability and global injustice. We hoped that in attacking the problems at their most basic level the United States would thus become engaged in shaping a world more congenial to our values and more compatible with our interests. America would no longer be seen as defending the status quo, nor could the Soviet Union continue to pose as the champion of greater equity. This effort was epitomized in our human-rights policy, in the attempt to halt nuclear proliferation, in our determination to resolve the anachronistic "colonial" problem of the Panama Canal through a ratified treaty, and in our firm support for majority rule in southern Africa. This review is not meant to be an exhaustive treatment of each issue, but rather to illuminate my own concerns and approach to these problems. It is true that we did not achieve all our objectives, nor was the effort without serious costs. On balance, however, I am convinced that our commitment was worth the price.

Human Rights and America's World Role

Jimmy Carter took office sensing clearly a pressing need to reinvigorate the moral content of American foreign policy. After an almost unending series of revelations about the abuse of governmental power at home and abroad, the American people were dissatisfied with their government. In international affairs, there seemed to be a moral vacuum. The Carter Administration resolved to make a break with the recent past, to bring the conduct of foreign affairs into line with the nation's political values and ideals, and to revitalize an American image which had been tarnished by the Vietnam experience.

I had long been convinced that the idea of basic human rights had a powerful appeal in the emerging world of emancipated but usually nondemocratic nation-states and that the previous Administration's lack of attention to this issue had undermined international support for the United States. I was concerned that America was becoming "lonely" in the world. I felt strongly that a major emphasis on human rights as a component of U.S. foreign policy would advance America's global interests by demonstrating to the emerging nations of the Third World the reality of our democratic system, in sharp contrast to the political system and practices of our adversaries. The best way to answer the Soviets' ideological challenge would be to commit the United States to a concept which most reflected America's very essence.

By the mid-1970s it became increasingly evident that detente was not the panacea many thought it would be. Mounting public and congressional pressures forced the Executive Branch to make further movement in relations with Moscow contingent on the Soviets' allowing greater freedom to emigrate and easing their treatment of dissidents. The Jackson–Vanik and Stevenson Amendments to the Trade Act of 1974 illustrated widespread dissatisfaction with an American foreign policy that dealt primarily in terms of power. When the Carter Administration came to the White House, the Congress had already enacted the Arms Control Export Act (1976) and the so-called Harkin Amendment, which set some of the parameters of the human-rights issue by placing significant restrictions on security assistance and economic aid to regimes that had exhibited a "consistent pattern of gross violations of internationally recognized human rights." In a speech at Notre Dame in May 1976, candidate Jimmy Carter quoted

John Kennedy, saying that we should not insist on identical governments or all nations of the world accepting our standards exactly. But, Carter added, "we cannot look away when a government tortures its own people, or jails them for their beliefs, or denies minorities fair treatment or the right to emigrate or the right to worship." When the President said in his inaugural speech that "because we are free we can never be indifferent to the fate of freedom elsewhere . . . our commitment to human rights must be absolute," he was expressing the will of Congress and the aspirations of the American people, as well as his own deeply felt moral beliefs. (He was also using words that I contributed to the draft of his speech.)

We were determined to give a greater official voice to human rights, conveying our concerns both publicly and privately. All of Carter's advisers worked to incorporate the concept of human rights into our bilateral and multilateral relations. With the President's full support, I created a Global Issues Cluster on the NSC staff to deal with human rights and the range of problems that cut across traditional foreign policy areas. I specifically chose for that office experts committed to solving these world problems, Dr. Jessica Tuchman and Colonel Leslie Denend. Dr. Tuchman combined technical expertise in nuclear proliferation, political savvy because of her background as a scientist and political adviser to Congressman Morris Udall, and a genuine sense of compassion for the underprivileged. Colonel Denend, a former White House Fellow, was an economist as well as an Air Force officer, and had taught at the Air Force Academy. (Denend subsequently became my special assistant and one of my closest collaborators.) Later in the Administration I brought Professor Lincoln Bloomfield of MIT to the NSC. Linc Bloomfield, an internationally known scholar of world affairs and an experienced Washington hand, gave his particular brand of dynamism to the office. Each member of the cluster made an important contribution to the evolution of American policy, and the creation of this new office on the NSC staff institutionalized the coordination of a sorely neglected issue.

In the first year of the Administration, human-rights questions were pursued with exceptional energy. The President summed up his Administration's fresh approach in comments at a Town Meeting in Clinton, Massachusetts, in March 1977, when he said: "I want to see our country set a standard of morality. I feel very deeply that when people are put in prison without trial and tortured and deprived of basic human rights that the President of the United States ought to have a right to express displeasure and do something about it. . . . I want our country to be the focal point for deep concern about human beings all over the world. . . ."

Translating this broad commitment into effective policy required a sharper focus. The public flap over the Sakharov letter (see Chapter 5) and the Bukovsky affair demonstrated the need to define our terms and objectives more clearly. After a meeting with several people from State on the human-rights issue, I jotted down in my journal for February 18, 1977: "We agreed that there is a need for a systematic review of the issue, more coordination, and the formulation of some principles which can serve as the frame of reference for what we do in the future. Otherwise, we are likely to be dragged into every major civil-rights issue, particularly Soviet ones, and the relationship between us and the Soviets might in fact suffer if this keeps up."

To a large extent our freedom to determine the tactics of policy was constrained by Congress. On June 6, I noted in my journal: "We filed today our reports on human rights and the Helsinki Declaration. It is going to precipitate another round with the Soviets although we had no choice. In fact, we wanted to stop this presentation but Congress forced our hand. As a result we are bound to have another bitter wave of mutual accusations. My own view is that pressure on the Soviets is justified; but it has to be measured in order to be effective. A sheer publicity campaign by itself will not achieve the desired results."

The bureaucratic process in this area reflected the difficulty of expressing in practical terms what a human-rights policy ought to be, and it was not until seven months later that our policy was defined. The President signed the result, Presidential Directive 30, on February 17, 1978. Its essential points were: (1) Priorities were set among U.S. human-rights objectives—reducing worldwide governmental violations of the integrity of the person, and enhancing civil and political liberties. It was also a continuing objective to promote basic economic and social rights. (2) There would be greater reliance on positive incentives that acknowledge improvements; for example, by special consideration in allocating U.S. aid. (3) No U.S. support, "other than in exceptional circumstances," would be allowed for policing functions by governments guilty of serious violations of human rights. (4) U.S. human-rights initiatives in international financial institutions would be geared "so as not to undermine the essential U.S. interest of preserving these institutions as effective economic instruments."

In addition, we organized an interagency group to examine bilateral/multilateral aid decisions from the standpoint of human rights, and to provide guidance on loan support and coordinate policy. This grew into the InterAgency Group on Human Rights and Foreign Assistance, chaired by Warren Christopher. In the first year the Group voted to instruct the U.S. representative to oppose a loan for Guinea and to postpone or abstain on loans to South Korea, Paraguay, and Nicaragua. Other loans to the Central African Empire and Nicaragua were supported on the grounds that they served basic human needs (Harkin Amendment criterion). During the next two years the Group voted to instruct the U.S. delegations to oppose over sixty loans to fifteen countries.

In February 1977, I approved an NSC initiative to curtail arms transfers to egregious human-rights violators. This effort met with a positive response from Capitol Hill, where there was strong support for cutting security assistance to Argentina and the Republic of Korea (although for strategic reasons I favored continued U.S. aid to South Korea). Later, human-rights factors contributed to adjustments in allocations to Indonesia, the Philippines, and Thailand for military training.

The commemoration on December 6, 1978, of the thirtieth anniversary of the Universal Declaration of Human Rights provided a useful opportunity to assess our human-rights policy. I delivered an address in the East Room of the White House which set out my view of what we had achieved. I made three basic propositions regarding human rights. "The first is that human rights is the genuine, historical inevitability of our times. The second is that human rights is a central facet in America's relevance to this changing world. And the third is that there has been progress in the effort to enhance the human condition insofar as human rights are concerned."

I said that human rights was the wave of the present. It was the "central form in which mankind is expressing its new political awakening" and it was essential for the United States to be identified with this. I pointed out that the very essence of the United States was personal freedom and individual liberty. We had succeeded in creating a policy-making structure which "makes certain that human-rights concerns are given new consideration in the shaping of our policy." And we had increased global awareness of the importance of this issue. Nations of the world knew that their record on human rights would affect their relationship with us. I acknowledged the dilemmas and limitations of this policy, but also the fundamental fact that we had made human rights an issue on the global agenda.

The Carter Administration's humanitarian concerns were illustrated by our response to the famine in Cambodia. The situation was already at a crisis stage in later 1979 when we decided that Rosalynn Carter would go to Thailand to dramatize the American commitment to relief —and Mrs. Carter's energetic involvement was a significant factor in galvanizing the U.S. response. Lincoln Bloomfield of the NSC staff worked closely in support of her efforts and achieved a remarkable degree of bureaucratic integration with State and AID on relief activity.

But not all issues were that clear-cut. The dilemmas involved in implementing a measured policy were illustrated in the case of Korea, where an obvious security interest was at stake. When the President visited Seoul on a trip to the Far East in early 1979, he expressed support for South Korea's continued independence and freedom; yet at the same time Cy Vance gave him a list of 100 political prisoners that we were concerned about. In his conversation with President Park Chung Hee, Carter pointed out that Korean disregard for civil liberties was undercutting U.S. public support for a close security link. Later, in October of that year, Harold Brown visited Seoul to consult on defense issues and delivered a letter from the President to President Park that said: "While human rights issues would not affect the security ties between the United States and the Republic of Korea, as a practical matter it would be difficult for us if there was not a return to a more liberal trend." Our leverage was clearly limited, yet we succeeded in preventing some political executions and in encouraging some moderation. Still, in practical terms, our influence was greater with weak and isolated countries than with those with whom we shared vital security interests.

For strategic reasons, I was also concerned that our assertiveness on human rights would combine with our tough nonproliferation posture to produce a backlash in some Latin American countries, particularly Brazil. I noted in my journal on March 14, 1977, that "in talking to the President about Latin American reactions to our human-rights concerns, which have prompted a kind of coalition of Latin American countries against us, I pointed out to him that Brazil is of great importance to us as a potentially new regional stabilizer. Pointing to the globe in his office, I argued that the Carter Administration ought to have as its design the creation of closer relationships with a large number of these emerging regional powers." The problem continued, however, as we searched for an effective way to combine the various strands of policy. Eighteen months later, my journal shows that I raised the issue again. Concerned that our human-rights policy was in danger of becoming one-sidedly anti-rightist, in a talk with the President on August 7, 1978, I said that we are "running the risk of having bad relations simultaneously with Brazil, Chile, and Argentina" because of the way State was implementing our human-rights policy. (Through a personal channel to the very top Brazilian leadership I also tried to develop a strategic dialogue with that important country.)

Though it was difficult for all of us to find the proper balance between human-rights imperatives and the uglier realities of world politics, our human-rights policy did mean freedom for many individuals around the world, particularly in Latin America. It dramatized the issue and gave major impetus to ongoing human-rights efforts by various concerned organizations. It thus had an immediate impact. In April 1977, the Peruvian government released over 300 political prisoners. In Argentina "disappearances" dropped from the thousands to 500 in 1978, 44 in 1979, and even lower in 1980. President Carter raised the case of Jacobo Timerman, the noted publisher, with President Videla of

Argentina and obtained his release. In Chile, "disappearances" ended and President Pinochet ultimately released most political prisoners. The pattern was repeated in Brazil. Our policy contributed to the institutionalization of democracy in Peru and Ecuador. In Southeast Asia the improvement in human-rights conditions was most notable in Indonesia. Over a period of eight months in 1977–78, the government released 15,000 political prisoners and completed the release of the remaining 20,000 over the next two years. In Africa, political prisoners were released in Guinea, Niger, Rwanda, Swaziland, and the Sudan.

Overall, the policy can be counted a success in that it established a climate of global concern that encouraged improvements in human-rights conditions and inhibited as well as exhibited the gross violations. It is interesting to note that our main supporters were the people of the various countries, and especially the victims of political suppression; our main critics, their governments.

Slowing Nuclear Proliferation

The impetus for the Carter Administration's nonproliferation policy originated in the President's personal concern that the destructive potential of nuclear technology posed an immediate threat to international peace and stability. As a former nuclear engineer, he had an impressive grasp of nuclear issues, certainly a better understanding than any previous President and most of his advisers. In a May 1976 campaign speech prepared by Richard Gardner, Carter publicly dedicated himself to a new nonproliferation policy. One of his earliest undertakings after taking office was a review of existing nuclear policy.

Our nonproliferation policy was based on three essential principles: that the highly enriched uranium and plutonium made available in nuclear power programs could be rapidly converted to weapons; that the existing international safeguards were inadequate; and that the technology which would introduce these materials into common use could be deferred for many decades without economic disadvantage. A single fuel charge for a breeder reactor contains enough high-grade nuclear material for hundreds of weapons and, with adequate technology, it takes only one week to make a bomb out of such materials. Yet it seemed clear that the breeder would not be economically significant for many decades.

We confronted two types of problems in this area. First, there were a number of specific cases where potential acquisition of dangerous technology offered an immediate proliferation risk; and, second, we needed a more precisely defined policy on the overall problem of the plutonium fuel cycles being developed domestically and internationally. It was of course easier to define a coherent nonproliferation policy than to implement it. A tough policy required confronting some of our allies and friends in areas where their vital economic interest or national dignity was involved.

Presidential Review Memorandum 15 was issued on January 21 and the response prepared by mid-March. The interagency paper focused on fuel cycle questions and made numerous recommendations, but essentially it advocated an international moratorium on nuclear development programs involving direct access to weapons-grade materials; and the multilateral evaluation of the nuclear fuel cycle. The report called for joint research to develop safer alternatives to the plutonium-fed breeder reactor and recommended that the United States should encourage an international effort to halt these dangerous trends.

I was aware of the President's strong and personal commitment to these issues and supported him fully, but I was becoming increasingly concerned about this issue's potential for straining relations with our allies. In my weekly report of March 18, 1977, I gave the President an opinion piece on "Japan and Reprocessing," alerting him to the extreme sensitivity of the Japanese to any changes in our nuclear policy and the impact these changes would have on U.S.–Japan relations.

Five days later, my concern was heightened by reports from colleagues at the State Department that the President had decided to mention, during his upcoming press conference, that we were adopting a new policy on nonproliferation, particularly in regard to processing plants. My subsequent action succeeded in averting a major international flap and also provided one of the earliest tests of my evolving relationship with Jimmy Carter. I wrote in my journal on March 23:

> I had heard some hints of this at the morning staff meeting, at which the President presided, but I wasn't aware that this was going to come out in such stark degree tomorrow. Dick Holbrooke and Joe Nye pleaded with me to get the President to reconsider. I asked Cy Vance for his view but he was rather bland about the whole thing, stressing that he was not concerned about whether we were in fact notifying our allies literally on six hours' notice. I must confess that I was appalled by Cy's unwillingness to take Carter on when Carter feels strongly about a subject. After a bit of hesitation, I phoned Carter and had a rather prolonged [and quite difficult] discussion in which I insisted on the fact that announcing a policy in a press conference with a few hours' notification to concerned allies and particularly the Japanese would have the worst possible consequences. He rather reluctantly agreed though he did note, "Mark this one up. This is one for you and it won't happen too often." And I imagine that he did resent my being insistent. But then that is what I am being paid for; not just for giving advice that he likes to hear. . . . Later in the day I

noted that many people at State were in touch with me to say how pleased they were by the stand that I took. . . . I think it is probably right that I prevented him from pulling a boo-boo which would have been like the Skybolt affair or even like the Nixon shocks [the unilateral measures imposed by the United States on U.S.–Japanese trade] and would have been quite damaging not only to American foreign policy but to himself individually.

As I saw it, the problem was how to juxtapose the glaring need for a stringent, farsighted policy with the already substantial economic commitment to nuclear reprocessing our allies had made. Essentially, the dilemma was how to put a brake on reprocessing without causing a blow-up in relations with our friends. The British and French already had built large reprocessing plants and signed lucrative contracts for commercial supply users in Japan, Sweden, Switzerland, and other nations. Most of the nuclear fuel was supplied by the United States under agreements which required prior approval by the United States before spent fuel could be reprocessed. Nonetheless, the commercial agreements were arrived at without consulting the United States and took for granted continued routine American approval. When the policy changed abruptly, the allies were, not surprisingly, quite disturbed.

One example, which occurred soon after the inauguration, was the West German government's decision to consider granting export licenses for transfer of nuclear technology to Brazil. The licenses were the initial steps in carrying out a 1975 German–Brazilian agreement for the construction of eight nuclear power plants. The President decided to send the Vice President to Bonn for a discussion with the Germans, and Mondale went in February to express our strong opposition to the deal. The Germans stood firm, and all he received was their assurance that they would observe existing international safeguards. Later in February, Warren Christopher led a mission to Brazil in an effort to patch up relations with the Brazilians, which were strained for other reasons also. He was received very coldly by the Foreign Minister, and his public reception was even worse. Popular anti-American sentiment was running high, and the trip only served to strengthen President Ernesto Geisel's position on this issue.

The Christopher mission did not succeed, and it weakened American credibility, even though the strength of our concern did in large part lead the Germans to announce that they would make no new commitments. In retrospect, the importance of the initial export license was probably overemphasized, and the policy might have been better served if we had waited for a more advantageous moment. Fritz Mondale shared my concerns about the implications of this flap for the larger relationship with the Europeans and Japanese. I noted in my journal on March 3 that "he came in to talk about our relationship with Europe.

He is quite concerned that the issue of nuclear proliferation that divides us from the Germans and the French will be further exacerbated . . . and as a consequence we will go to the summit this coming May with the Western alliance in a state of real disarray."

The new policy was formally announced on April 7, 1977. It reflected the President's decision to discourage the development and spread of dangerous nuclear technologies and to minimize worldwide accumulation of potential nuclear explosives in peaceful power programs. The President announced that the United States would: defer indefinitely commercial reprocessing and terminate support for a pilot reprocessing plant in North Carolina; restructure the U.S. breeder reactor program to give greater priority to alternative breeder designs and defer or cancel commercial projects like the Clinch River plant; and redirect funding of nuclear research and development to explore alternative breeder designs and safer methods.

The particularly negative reaction of the French and Japanese made it harder to reach a compromise with them in order to secure their participation in the International Nuclear Fuel Cycle Evaluation (INFCE), which we launched later in the year. The INFCE, which emerged from the Policy Review Committee's conclusion that a multilateral effort should be undertaken to look at the fuel cycle and alternative methods, provided the backdrop for our nonproliferation policy over the next two years. The U.S. effort was directed by Ambassador Gerard Smith, a knowledgeable and capable international lawyer. On my staff I had initially Jessica Tuchman and then Gerald Oplinger, a career officer with considerable expertise in the field, ably coordinating nuclear issues while educating me on the subject.

Japanese sensitivity stemmed from the fact that they had built a reprocessing pilot plant at Tokai-Mura under the assumption that previous American practices would continue. The Japanese sought assurances that we would allow them to continue to operate the plant. I supported my staff's recommendation that the Japanese be given assurances with two conditions: that operation be geared to actual needs, which were quite small, and that no new initiatives be taken during the course of INFCE. Since we had made a dramatic change in nonproliferation policy, I felt that we had to respect agreements made under the previous Administration.

The President's focus on nuclear proliferation coincided with a growing concern in Congress. Since the Indian explosion of a nuclear device in 1974, there had been numerous draft bills on the Hill. By 1977 there were several that we felt were excessively tough. To head them off and to prevent further legislative initiatives, we introduced our own bill, the Nuclear Nonproliferation Act, which was passed in March 1978 with overwhelming majorities in both houses. The Act set the criteria for licensing the export of nuclear material, and prohibited U.S.

export to any country not accepting international safeguards on all of its plants. Later in the year, American nonproliferation policy was further strengthened by the Glenn and Symington Amendment to the Foreign Assistance Act, which called for a cutoff of economic assistance to any country which did not accept safeguards on dangerous nuclear technology.

The first major test of the new policy was with Pakistan. In early 1979, after it became clear that Pakistan was in the process of developing a nuclear weapons capability, we implemented the requirements of the Glenn amendment and quietly terminated aid. Realizing that the amount of this assistance was too small to give us real leverage, we tried to orchestrate a diplomatic campaign against Pakistan's nuclear policy. None of the allies responded positively, save for Australia. (I should note that the Pakistani record on nonproliferation, and on human rights as well, was a major factor complicating our decisions following the Soviet invasion of Afghanistan as to how much assistance we could get through Congress to help strengthen President Zia's government.)

The Tarapur reactor case with India posed a different dilemma. In 1977 the new Indian government of Morarji Desai promised to be more cooperative with the United States on the nuclear issue. But optimistic initial impressions soon gave way to disappointment, and by the time the President visited New Delhi in January 1978, it was clear that progress would be slow. It was on that trip that the President whispered to Vance—but was overheard by the press—that we should send a "cool, blunt letter" to Prime Minister Morarji Desai, the so-called open-microphone incident.

In the spring of 1979, the Nuclear Regulatory Commission received an application for export of nuclear material to India's Tarapur reactor and voted 2–2, in effect denying the application. The President felt that the Indians were still negotiating on nuclear issues in good faith, so he decided to authorize the shipment. Key congressional leaders sent him a letter saying that they would support him on this as a one-time exception. In March 1980, a license for a second shipment to Tarapur came under review. This time, however, Indira Gandhi, once again Prime Minister, had declared her total refusal to consider international safeguards. The issue provoked contentious internal debate within the Executive Branch, with the NSC alone opposing the application as a clear violation of the Nuclear Nonproliferation Act. Despite our counsel and after much prodding from State, the President approved the shipment, viewing it as a long-standing commitment to India. He sent a letter to Mrs. Gandhi declaring his intention to make a concerted effort to prevent congressional disapproval. Later in the spring the House voted to oppose the license, but the sale was saved by a close vote in the Senate after an intense lobbying effort by the President and Secretary Muskie.

Although the Tarapur decision was inconsistent with our nonproliferation policy, the President's strong leadership on the nonproliferation
issue heightened global awareness of the problem. Coordination among
the suppliers succeeded in preventing the rapid spread of plutonium
processes, and as a result the price of uranium declined to such an
extent that the economic value of breeder systems diminished even
further. Moreover, Carter's personal discussions with Giscard influenced
the French decision not to sell reprocessing plants to Pakistan and
South Korea. But the policy had substantial limitations. We had no
real leverage in cases like Pakistan and limited capacity for dealing
with nations that did not cooperate. We were unable to mobilize
Europe and Japan effectively, and relations with our allies were strained
significantly over the nuclear issue. There can be no doubt that U.S.–
Brazilian reconciliation, which I much favored for strategic reasons,
was set back by the Christopher mission.

Panama, the U.S. Senate, and Latin America

When President-elect Carter met with his advisers at St. Simon in
January 1977, we all agreed that the Panama Canal negotiations should
be an immediate priority. Our view was that if the new Administration
did not move rapidly on the Panama issue, capitalizing on the new
President's mandate, the problem would become unmanageable and
sour our relations with Latin America. I saw a prompt and fair
resolution as signaling to the nations of the region that the Carter
Administration recognized the changed realities in North and South
America and was willing to work constructively to build more mature
relationships based on mutual respect. We were well prepared for the
negotiations and for tackling the broader Latin American agenda due
to the efforts of my NSC staffer Robert Pastor, who had worked on
these issues during the campaign. Bob Pastor was young, bright, and
very industrious, fresh out of Harvard's Ph.D. program in international relations. He served with distinction and extraordinary diligence
throughout the entire four years, coordinating U.S. policy toward Latin
America and the Caribbean, and wearing out several State colleagues
in the process.

Five days after the inauguration, I ordered a wide-ranging review of
U.S. policy toward Latin America, covering both the existing relationships and the available options. The response arrived from State in
mid-March, and a Policy Review Committee meeting was held on
March 24, chaired by Warren Christopher. He and I had discussed the
issue before the meeting and had reached general agreement on what we
wanted the meeting to produce.

I argued, somewhat to the surprise of the Latin American Bureau of the State Department, that we should not have a Latin American hemispheric policy as such, because to Latin Americans that has always smacked of paternalism. There was no need, I suggested, for us to invent a new slogan to describe our policy. Rather, we should deal with the region as a collection of mature states with whom we had diverse relationships. The United States had to recognize the global nature of the region's problems, in some cases working closely with the Latin American nations in the wider context of North–South problems and in others encouraging the development of constructive bilateral relations. I expanded on this approach at the PRC, saying that "the notion of a special policy is ahistorical. In the past, it has done nothing more than lock us into a cycle of creating unrealistic expectations and then having to live with the subsequent disappointments." I added that to most Americans the Monroe Doctrine was a selfless U.S. contribution to hemispheric security; but to most of our neighbors to the south it was an expression of presumptuous U.S. paternalism.

On the key question of U.S. intervention, I proposed that we should not react reflexively, instead responding (to Soviet initiatives in the hemisphere) in terms of the likely consequences if we did not intervene. This was the basic policy line we maintained throughout the four years. The rest of the review consisted of specific proposals, most of which were incorporated into the President's Pan-American Day speech delivered at the Organization of American States on April 14. That speech set down some markers for a major new departure in American policy toward the region.

On April 13, a day before the speech, I recommended to the President that he use the occasion to announce his decision to sign the American Convention on Human Rights and Protocol I of the Treaty of Tlatelolco (prohibiting the placement of nuclear weapons in Latin America). He approved my recommendation, and those two items were most warmly received at the OAS. The speech rejected the traditional statements of "our region" and "our hemisphere" in favor of an affirmation that the United States would treat each nation individually, consulting with all on issues that concerned them. Carter emphasized American support for human rights and democratization, underscoring many of the themes of our policy for the next four years.

We turned immediately to the deadlocked Panama Canal negotiations. President Carter appointed Sol Linowitz to work with Ellsworth Bunker as special negotiator. Linowitz had been Chairman of the Commission on U.S.–Latin American Relations and was well informed on the issues. Ambassador Bunker had been working on the negotiations for some time and provided a measure of continuity. Together, they made a first-rate team. The first few months were spent by them in probing the Panamanians' approach, while we hammered out in the White House our own bargaining positions. We sought to convince

Omar Torrijos, Panama's leader, that we were committed to eliminating the anachronistic "colonial" aspects of our relationship without endangering the operation of the canal. We saw the canal's strategic significance as having diminished while its potential as a source of conflict with the Panamanians had increased. A delay in negotiating a treaty invited violence and also endangered Torrijos's position; and Panama without Torrijos most likely would have been an impossible negotiating partner.

There were three basic issues left to be completed in the negotiations: the duration of the new treaty, guarantees of the canal's neutrality, and post-treaty U.S. defense rights. We were willing to compromise on the duration of the treaty (the Panamanians wanted 1999), but we insisted that the United States had to reserve the right to intervene to keep the canal open even after the treaty expired. Of course, after those issues were settled, there remained the agreement to an economic package for Panama. The talks stalled on the financial settlement. As I noted in my journal of July 27: "My concern is that through the negotiating process we have slid into presenting an economic package which neither the Congress nor the President will be prepared to endorse," and which was still unacceptable to the Panamanians. In a public letter that made front-page news, the President took a firm stand and told Torrijos not to push any harder. We had been looking forward to the problem of Senate ratification and saw it as essential that the American public believe that the President had been a tough bargainer. The tactic worked, and we reached final agreement on August 10.

The campaign for ratification was difficult and personally draining, an uphill fight all the way to the end. I conducted numerous briefings for community leaders from all over the country and met with many senators to lobby for their support. After several ineffective initial briefings, in which I attempted to present a broad conceptual perspective on the agreement and its history, in keeping with my general approach to Latin America, I realized that if the treaty was to pass, the presentation would have to be much tougher and more to the point. This political reality was made clear to me by the reception given my new approach. I gave a briefing in early September to a group of political leaders in the East Room. I noted in my journal that "at the end of the meeting which was attended by Senator [Robert] Byrd, I was asked the question 'But what if after the year 2000 the Panamanian government simply and suddenly announced that it is closing down the canal for repairs?' Without a moment's hesitation I replied, 'In that case, according to the provisions of the Neutrality Treaty, we will move in and close down the Panamanian government for repairs.' This brought the house down and I think assured a great deal of additional support for our efforts on behalf of the Panama Canal Treaty."

Later in the week General Torrijos came to Washington for the signing ceremony. It was a moving occasion. Carter clearly enjoyed his role as the political emancipator of a downtrodden people. For him, this occasion represented the ideal fusion of morality and politics: he was doing something good for peace, responding to the passionate desires of a small nation, and yet helping the long-range U.S. national interest. That he could speak Spanish fluently gave the occasion an added personal touch, and Carter literally glowed. And then there was Torrijos, tough and suspicious, with a popular mandate to achieve his people's burning desire. It was the high point of this shrewd dictator's national life: he knew he was entering Panamanian history forever. Though crude in speech (and I found his Spanish almost impossible to understand because of constant slurring), unpolished in some of his personal habits, with a somewhat checkered history of cooperation with the United States, he was sharing the stage with the leader of the world's most powerful nation and doing so as an equal. It was obvious "that for the Panamanians it was an act of emancipation and not just a settlement of the canal issue." The United States gained much good will from the settlement, but the drive for ratification had a long way to go.

When President Torrijos returned to Washington later in the month, he discussed the reservations deemed necessary to secure ratification. Torrijos made the excellent point that he and the President were engaged in selling the same product to two different audiences and that their approaches should be tailored accordingly. However, this time Torrijos was notably subdued, partly because he expected Carter to react harshly to recent inflammatory statements he had made to the Panamanian people and perhaps partly because some of his family had been publicly accused of drug trafficking. The general accepted our formulation of the reservations and the process moved forward. The two treaties were submitted to the Senate for consideration at the beginning of the 1978 session.

At the end of January, the Senate Foreign Relations Committee voted 14–1 to send the Neutrality Treaty to the floor with amendments that would guarantee U.S. defense rights and priority emergency passage after the year 2000. The full debate began in early February and lasted until mid-March. The outcome was too close to predict, and I made many trips to the Hill to speak with senators. Numerous amendments were offered on the Senate floor. On March 10, an amendment giving the United States and Panama the responsibility for seeing that the canal remained open and secure to world shipping passed 84–5. Three days later, another amendment passed 85–3, giving the United States and Panama priority emergency passage. On March 15, the Senate passed a reservation stating that nothing in the treaty precludes the United States and Panama from agreeing to keep bases in Panama after 2000. With these kinds of conditions being attached and the numbers of senators supporting them, we really could not predict which way the vote would go.

On the night of March 15, the entire effort almost fell apart. The senators' support for these conditions and the rather bellicose rhetoric that the Senate produced had infuriated the mercurial Torrijos. "The President called a meeting in the Oval Office with Cy Vance, Ham Jordan, myself, and the three Panamanian Ambassadors (UN, OAS, and Washington). Torrijos was apparently going to issue a statement blasting one of the amendments and that in all probability would sink the Panama Canal Treaties. Accordingly, the assembled group called up Torrijos and had a lengthy discussion with him. Torrijos finally promised to cooperate and to be silent as a gesture of friendship and cooperation. I must say that Carter and Torrijos were extremely effective in the discussion. It looks like we will get the vote tomorrow if no one at the last minute changes his mind." The next day the Senate adopted another reservation, authorizing the United States and Panama to use armed force to keep the canal open, and then, finally, adopted the Neutrality Treaty 68–32.

The second treaty still remained. Senator Dennis DeConcini introduced an amendment giving the United States the unilateral right to intervene in Panama to keep the canal open, but it was defeated. By April 18 the situation still looked bad and the President was quite dispirited. He felt that several key senators had let him down. I had Bob Pastor prepare two draft statements in consultation with the State Department, one welcoming a positive vote and the other condemning the Senate's action and demanding a reconsideration.

Fritz Mondale explored the possibility of calling the Senate into a special session if the treaty was voted down, but that strategy turned out not to be viable. Mondale's discussions with Majority Leader Robert Byrd offered some hope, however, and we resolved to wait it out. In the meantime, I raised the subject of contingency planning with the President. In the case of a negative vote, we expected massive violence in Panama and I had ordered that military contingency plans be drawn up.

Later in the afternoon of March 18, I talked with the Vice President, who was on the Hill. I noted that "it began to look as if we will get the vote. Around six o'clock I was told by David Aaron that the vote was on because of a sudden shift in the Senate's schedule. I rushed over to the President's office. He was reading, unaware that the vote was going on. I told him that it was on, and we both quickly moved into Susan Clough's office, where we were joined by Jody Powell and Ham Jordan. He sat there, clenching his fists while the vote went on, and finally banged his fists together when we got the required 67th vote. It was a moment of genuine elation and relief. If we had lost, there is no doubt that our policy on SALT and most importantly the

Middle East would have been dead ducks." The treaty passed, 68–32, one vote above the required two-thirds majority. The Senate also approved a leadership resolution disavowing U.S. intentions to intervene in Panamanian affairs. Torrijos accepted the treaty as amended. The battle was won.

On June 16, I accompanied the President on his trip to Panama for the exchange of treaties. My notes for those days described the reception: "An enormous outpouring of emotion. Two hundred thousand people in the streets; a real sense of national liberation and this thanks to the efforts of Carter and his team. I believe that we have set in motion a different pattern of relations with Latin America." Indeed, we had. Ratifying the treaty was seen by us as a necessary precondition for a more mature and historically more just relationship with Central America, a region which we had never understood too well and which we occasionally dominated the way that the Soviets have dominated Eastern Europe. It was a new beginning, and I was proud of our achievement.

Majority Rule

Some of the clearest examples of flagrant disregard for human rights were provided by the white regimes of southern Africa. In June 1976, racial violence in Soweto reverberated throughout the international media, giving immediacy to calls for change in South Africa; and the interminable guerrilla war in Rhodesia seemed stalemated. The President's deep religious commitment to freedom and racial justice as well as his sense of responsibility to the American black community gave these problems a special significance. Jimmy Carter's genuine determination to see majority rule was shared by his advisers. At State, Cy Vance, Andy Young, Assistant Secretary Dick Moose, and Policy Planning Director Tony Lake organized a diplomatic effort under the President's direction. During the four years, my staff members for Africa were: Thomas Thornton, a senior State Department official with broad experience in Third World affairs, who handled South Asian affairs as well; Henry Richardson, an energetic and deeply committed specialist on African affairs, who undertook my education in that vital area; and then Jerry Funk, a talented and extremely effective former labor official, who had extensive experience in African affairs and who brought to the issue a highly practical bargaining approach acquired in labor activities on the African continent.

My own role was of secondary importance. I strongly backed the President's moral concerns, and I supported Cy's and Andy's efforts. My primary focus was on making certain that we did not ignore the Soviet–Cuban military presence in Africa to the point that the conservative whites in South Africa would be fearful of accepting any compromise solution. Moreover, I feared that indifference to the Soviet–Cuban role would eventually maximize U.S. domestic opposition to a policy more sympathetic to majority rule.

I set out my ideas at the first NSC meeting on Africa. "It was a somewhat desultory discussion [focused] too much on detail but toward its conclusion I made strongly the point that our policy toward southern Africa ought to be deliberately designed to promote the social transformation of that society. The point was accepted and, if it sticks, could mark the beginning of a fairly important and consistent policy change insofar as that part of the world is concerned. We will not do anything radical but if we pursue the policy systematically it will entail quite considerable changes from the policies of the last several years." We believed that southern Africa could serve as an illustration of the Administration's new approach to human rights and the problems of the colonial past.

On Rhodesia, the first concrete policy change we made was to secure the repeal of the Byrd Amendment, which had permitted the import of Rhodesian chrome in direct violation of United Nations sanctions. The President signed the bill repealing the amendment on March 18, less than two months after taking office. Moreover, Andy Young's attendance, as the President's personal representative, at the Anti-Apartheid Conference in Lagos, Nigeria, during July was a clear sign of the new American attitude.

As we proceeded to develop an approach to the Rhodesian problem, I became concerned that we were too closely tied to the British position. Thus, in the early months I began to argue for a more independent U.S. involvement. Cy Vance felt that acting through the British was the best method. I maintained my concern and expressed it at the various planning meetings, but resolved to wait until the situation settled a bit more.

By the summer of 1977, I began to think of alternative scenarios for the American role. In July, when British Foreign Minister David Owen came to Washington for consultations, it was apparent to me that the Anglo–American effort was groping. I noted: "At a meeting with David Owen this morning on British and American policy toward Africa it became quite clear that we don't really have any basic concept yet of what it is that we wish to achieve on Africa. I have been staying out of this one on the grounds that it isn't going to be very productive and that any policy at this stage is not likely to be successful. In some ways I am beginning to lean to the notion that we ought to let the so-called internal solution surface and let the moderate Africans take over from [Prime Minister Ian] Smith, because it is only to them that Smith can yield, and then let the internal solution based on the moderate leadership collapse as the more assertive Africans storm in from the outside. If we maintain a policy of benevolent neutrality we can accelerate the process and maintain a positive relationship with the Front Line African states which ought to be the central focus of our efforts." I told the President frequently that I thought the British were "leading us by the nose."

While Vance and Andy Young were focusing on the Rhodesian question, the Vice President turned his attention to South Africa. He developed an initiative that resulted in his meeting with South African Prime Minister Vorster in Geneva later in the year. The President favored the direct approach, and both Vance and Mondale went along although they obviously had strong reservations. I was the only adviser to challenge the desirability of the idea. In my judgment there was no point in plunging the Vice President into the South African problem until and unless we had a coherent plan of action which had a chance of success and on which we could follow through. Without such a plan, a visit by the Vice President would tend to be a one-shot affair, simply raising expectations and ending in disappointments. The original proposal called for Mondale to go to South Africa, but I argued against that because I viewed a direct confrontation between Mondale and Vorster as futile and counterproductive. The meeting which was held in Geneva later in the year established an American position, but the result was much as I had feared.

Despite this lack of progress, our relations with black Africa in general were steadily improving. The President received a friendly reception when we visited Nigeria and Liberia in March–April 1978. It was hard to imagine a more striking contrast to the poor state of relations that had existed only two years earlier when Secretary Kissinger was refused permission to land in Lagos. In both countries we conducted productive discussions of bilateral issues as well as the problems of southern Africa. Much of the credit for the dramatic improvement in relations must go to Cy Vance and Andy Young, whose untiring efforts to find solutions to southern Africa's dilemmas were recognized as a genuine reflection of the President's personal commitment to freedom and racial justice.

Throughout 1977 and 1978, movement toward an internal (Smith-sponsored) settlement in Rhodesia accelerated. The Anglo-American proposals were not working and we really had not made substantial progress. Some senators were increasingly receptive to the idea of an internal settlement, and the President was hard put to justify our policy. I continued to stress my dissatisfaction with the high-visibility strategy of the Anglo–American plan and argued that we should not be out front on Rhodesia. In my weekly report of October 6, 1978, I wrote for the President that an important conclusion of a recent NSC meeting on Africa was that if we could not obtain a moderate solution, we should turn the issue over to the United Nations or the British. Otherwise, the issue would become quite divisive and damaging domestically. In November, I sent the President another piece on Rhodesia, pointing out that conditions there made fruitful negotiation unlikely, that the chances of keeping sanctions were not good, and that we did not have a clear view of where we were headed. I wanted State and my NSC staff to take a fresh look at the options and have a PRC in December. The President wrote on the margin: "Jim Callaghan called me. He wants to move on his own—with some U.S. involvement. I told him O.K." Backed by the President's action, I urged a lowered U.S. profile, a difficult task given the already considerable polarization on the Rhodesian issue in Congress.

The extent of this polarization was evident in the congressional votes in the spring of 1979. When Ian Smith announced that he would be holding elections under the "internal constitution," the Senate voted in March, 66–27, to send election observers. The House defeated the measure by the close vote of 190–180 on April 9. The Rhodesian elections were held in April, and Bishop Abel Muzorewa was sworn in as Prime Minister on May 29. Muzorewa's much-publicized meeting with the President at Camp David on July 9 was intended to placate Senator Jesse Helms, the leader of the right-wing congressional supporters of Ian Smith, and I made the arrangements for it with the senator. Congress passed a variety of resolutions requiring the President to lift sanctions, but each formulation left him enough flexibility to choose his own time to do so.

Initially, the newly elected British Prime Minister Margaret Thatcher gave every indication of supporting the internal settlement in Rhodesia, but she was gradually persuaded by a small group in the British Foreign Office which was convinced that an internal settlement would not work. Thus, Thatcher decided instead to commit herself to a British-organized and -led strategy for an all-parties solution. Prime Minister Thatcher announced compromise proposals at the Commonwealth Conference in Lusaka during the first week of August calling for a new constitution, a cease-fire, and British-supervised elections. In September, the British inaugurated the all-parties conference at Lancaster House in London.

Throughout the fall and into December, we played a supportive role as Lord Carrington, the Foreign Minister, conducted the negotiations. The President was under considerable pressure from Congress to lift sanctions immediately, but he was adamant that the United States should wait until the independence process was firmly in place. On December 3, Vance conveyed the Administration position to Senator Helms in a letter giving the President's commitment to lift sanctions a month after the British Governor arrived in Salisbury. On December 6, the Senate voted 90–5 to end sanctions a month after the British

Governor arrived in Salisbury or January 31, 1980, whichever came first. The United States agreed to help airlift the 1,200-man Commonwealth Monitoring Force to Rhodesia. On December 12, Lord Soames, the U.K. Governor, arrived in Salisbury and the British ended sanctions at midnight. The President ended U.S. sanctions on December 15. Later in the week the United Nations Security Council ended its thirteen-year embargo and the Front Line states followed suit.

The successful settlement of the Rhodesian problem was important not only because it satisfied the legitimate aspirations of the Zimbabwean people, but also because it foreclosed a major avenue for Soviet and Cuban meddling in southern Africa. It seemed to me that we had underestimated the Eastern bloc connection in the region and that Andy and Cy, along with most of those at State, took an excessively benign view of the Soviet and Cuban penetration of Africa, underestimating its strategic implications. It was clear to me that we had to face the fact that Moscow and Havana were exploiting racial tensions to advance their own ideological and strategic objectives. Accordingly, my argument was that our activist policy in southern Africa could work only if on the one hand we convinced the blacks that we were serious about majority rule by pursuing that objective aggressively, even through the use of sanctions; and yet at the same time convinced the whites that there was a future for them, particularly by opposing the Soviets and Cubans and insisting that the Africans join us in that opposition. The whites had to believe that serious social change did not automatically mean a Marxist revolution. I made this point to the President and at various meetings throughout 1979. We were failing to deliver enough to satisfy the black Africans and yet at the same time we were frightening the whites into unshakable intransigence. The South African issue was and is a much more difficult task than Rhodesia, and I felt, as we were leaving office, that we had only just begun to recognize the fundamental outlines of the problem.

Overall, our policy in southern Africa achieved some real successes; the fact that much remains to be done does not diminish the value of what was accomplished. A new, more positive relationship with black Africa in general was established, due in large part to the President's personal commitment to human rights and the efforts of Cy Vance and Andy Young. In addition, through the Namibian and Rhodesian/Zimbabwe negotiations, the United States began to develop mutual respect and a useful working relationship with the Front Line States, a relationship which augurs well for future conflict resolution in the region. Unfortunately, undoing apartheid, breaking the stalemate on Namibia, and improving bilateral relations with Angola and Mozambique all proved more difficult than achieving majority rule in Rhodesia. What is certain, however, is that there was a greater willingness to listen to the African view in Washington and a better understanding in Africa of American dilemmas by the end of the Carter Administration—a major accomplishment in itself.

How Successful the Policies, How High the Costs?

A review of Carter Administration policy on human rights, nonproliferation, Panama, and southern Africa shows that some significant progress was made but also that in some respects our efforts were counterproductive. We succeeded in raising the level of global awareness of human rights and incorporated this awareness into the American foreign policy decision-making structure. As a result, we helped to secure the release of thousands of political prisoners all over the world. Yet at the same time our principles were not always applied with an adequate sense of nuance and specificity. This was due partly to the problems inherent in fitting human-rights criteria into the framework of American interests, but also partly to our own shortcomings. We did not develop a viable method of rewarding governments that improved their records, in policy terms we found it difficult to make necessary distinctions between regimes, and we were pulled in various directions by domestic constituencies. We learned that our policy was most effective in relations with weak or small non-Communist states that were unable to resist our leverage. Notwithstanding its limitations, however, the human-rights policy has had a lasting, positive impact on international relations and American foreign policy. Human rights is a policy that continues to be relevant, an idea that must not be ignored.

On nuclear nonproliferation, we developed some sound theoretical perspectives, but were unable to implement the policy without the support of the Europeans and Japanese. We shifted policies abruptly and unilaterally, thereby straining relations with our allies, who had made major economic commitments to reprocessing. Although we succeeded in diverting the world from a scramble for plutonium, we could not control the serious proliferation risk in Pakistan. Altered strategic realities in southwestern Asia (Afghanistan and Iran) complicated the problem further. We attempted to solve a problem that was unmanageable at best, and the policy has to be judged in that context.

In conjunction with these efforts, the Carter Administration also attempted to generate an international consensus to slow down the sales of conventional armaments to the Third World. This effort was ably orchestrated at the NSC by Robert Kimmitt, my assistant for such matters.

America took the lead in emphasizing restraint, with only a small increase in sales from 6.9 billion to 7.9 billion between 1977 and 1980, or 14 percent over the four-year period. Unfortunately, the U.S. was unable to persuade its major allies, notably France, West Germany, the U.K., and Italy, to do the same. Sales from these four states to the developing countries during the same period jumped from $6.9 billion in 1977 to 12.3 billion in 1980, a 78 percent increase. This was an even larger increase than that of the U.S.S.R., which sold $9.6 billion in 1977 and 14.9 in 1980, for a 55 percent increase during the period of the Carter Administration.

The Reagan Administration has abandoned such voluntary efforts toward cooperative restraint, with the result that arms sales subsequently further skyrocketed.

The Panama Canal initiative capped off almost two decades of negotiations by Democratic and Republican Administrations and was clearly in the American interest. If Carter had not had the courage to bite the bullet, the entire negotiating effort would have gone down the drain. It took a bitter and long campaign in the nation and in the Congress to secure passage; even so, the margin of passage was the absolute minimum. Our policy was a new departure in that the Panama Canal Treaties signaled a change in the American attitude. The Carter Administration eschewed slogans and a paternalistic tendency exhibited by previous Administrations.

In southern Africa, though our intentions were laudable, our efforts were only partially successful. Our support for the British effort on Rhodesia contributed in an important way to the ultimate settlement, but the problem of South Africa still poses some of the toughest questions for American foreign policy. Nonetheless, a constructive dialogue between America and Africa-at-large was opened.

In looking at the global issues together and considering the results, it is apparent to me that we attempted to do too much all at once. This reduced our effectiveness. We did bring about a decline in anti-Americanism abroad, and as a result the United States was not isolated internationally as it had been. The overwhelming support for the United States at the United Nations on Iran and the vehement reaction of the Third World countries to the Soviet aggression in Afghanistan were in some degree influenced by a more positive global view of America's role in the world. At the same time, some of our goals in the global-issues area contradicted our strategic objectives. In the first two years of the Administration, these global concerns tended to overshadow the pressing requirements of strategic reality. In the last two, we had to make up for lost time, giving a higher priority to the more fundamental interests of national security.

5

SALT without Linkage

My preference would be for strict controls or even a freeze on new types and new generations of weaponry and with a deep reduction in the strategic arms of both sides. Such a major step towards not only arms limitation but arms reduction would be welcomed by mankind as a giant step towards peace.

—President Jimmy Carter, speech to the United Nations General Assembly, March 17, 1977

Of the many foreign policy debates within the Carter Administration, that over policy toward the Soviet Union was the most prolonged and intense. Policy toward the Soviet Union raised basic questions regarding not only relations with our allies, or diplomacy toward the Middle East, but also fundamental issues concerning the nature of our defense posture and nuclear strategy. In time, the debate divided the Administration, at first ideologically and eventually personally.

This was not initially the case, since we all rejected the way the U.S.–Soviet relationship had evolved under the preceding Administration. Vance and I both felt that detente had been oversold to the American public. We believed a better agreement than the original SALT I could be obtained. However, each of us reached that conclusion for rather different reasons: Vance hoped that a new SALT agreement would pave the way for a wider U.S.–Soviet accommodation, while I saw in it an opportunity to halt or reduce the momentum of the Soviet military buildup.

The Soviets had gained broad strategic parity (having obtained in SALT I American acceptance of Soviet superiority in certain categories of strategic weaponry) and had become more daring in exploiting openings in the Third World. Soviet reliance on the Cuban military proxy in Africa was a particularly bold gambit, and it was paying off. In general, the sustained Soviet strategic and conventional buildup posed the threat that by 1985 Moscow might attain military superiority over the United States—notwithstanding Mr. Kissinger's casual dismissal in 1972 of the importance of such superiority.

Not surprisingly, in that setting the U.S. public was becoming increasingly uneasy about detente. Support for it remained strong within the Democratic Party, particularly in that "liberal establishment" with which the new Secretary of State was closely connected. Moreover, the memory of Vietnam still influenced public sentiment to the point that there was little opposition to arms control or the SALT negotiations, despite growing skepticism about detente itself.

Carter would be the first to admit that he came to the White House without a detailed plan for managing U.S.–Soviet relations. He was, however, determined to move on SALT, and he firmly supported the concept of detente. At the same time, Carter was critical of the way the previous Administration had allowed the Soviet Union to exploit detente, and in campaign speeches developed by me, he had stressed that detente inevitably had to involve both cooperation and competition and that it had to be both more *comprehensive* and more *reciprocal*. These words were deliberately chosen to convey a more purposeful concept of detente, but I doubt that the new President at first could sense the special significance that these "code" words were later to acquire in some of the debates between the NSC and State. (As the months went on, Vance and his colleagues started objecting to the use of these words, and the drafting of almost every Presidential speech involved Vance crossing them out and me reinserting them.) In any case, in early 1977 Carter was determined to achieve greater stability in the U.S.–Soviet relationship primarily through progress in arms control negotiations.

This was very much the position of Cyrus Vance, who over the years had participated in various joint U.S.–Soviet arms control discussions. These informal joint gatherings of top American and Soviet personalities had made a substantial and positive contribution, and Vance became a powerful and well-informed advocate of the proposition that through progress in SALT we could both stabilize the American–Soviet relationship and generate more wide-ranging American–Soviet cooperation. Paul Warnke, a close personal friend of Vance who subsequently became the head of Carter's Arms Control and Disarmament Agency, was also a forceful advocate of that view.

My View of Detente

My view was that we should redefine detente into a more purposeful and activist policy for the West. The code words "reciprocal" and "comprehensive" meant to me that we should insist on equal treatment (retaliating in kind, if necessary) and that the Soviets could not have a free ride in some parts of the world while pursuing detente where it suited them. In a book which I had prepared for publication in 1977, but which I did not publish because of my appointment, I argued that the policy of detente—as defined by Nixon and Brezhnev—began largely as a defensive response by the two powers to a situation in which their unchecked rivalry had become simply too dangerous. By 1975, however, the policy was acquiring on the Soviet side an increasingly assertive character—stimulated largely by the Soviet perception of the wider political consequences of the "aggravated crisis of capitalism" as well as of the post-Vietnam trauma in America. For the U.S.S.R., the strategic goal of detente was to deter the United States from responding effectively to the changing political balance. Soviet spokesmen began to repeat more and more frequently that "the policy of peaceful coexistence has nothing in common with the 'freezing' of the social status quo, with any artificial mothballing of the revolutionary process."* On the contrary, detente and military parity were now said to facilitate significant political change in Western Europe and elsewhere—a policy of active detente similar in many ways to the policy the United States had pursued toward the Soviet Union and Eastern Europe in the early sixties.

This policy of "decomposition" was flexible in that it left Soviet strategic choices open. At some point, when the "objective" situation became "historically ripe," the Soviets could adopt a more revolutionary policy, exploiting such favorable preconditions for a politically decisive test of will, based on an acknowledged military edge. The policy was equally well suited to promote a prolonged process in which, stealthily, a fundamental change in the political complexion of the world would occur. Thus the Soviets subtly combined elements of cooperation and competition, not to preserve the status quo, but to transform it.

Yet this Soviet thrust toward global preeminence was less likely to lead to a Pax Sovietica than to international chaos. The Soviet Union might hope to displace America from its leading role in the international system, but it was too weak economically and too unappealing politically to itself assume that position. This, I argued, was the ultimately self-defeating element in the Soviet policy; it could exploit global anarchy, but was unlikely to be able to transform it to its own enduring advantage. The Soviet danger was of a different order than that usually stressed by staunch conservatives. And this is why I felt that the proper American response should not be a deliberate return to Cold War tensions, but a carefully calibrated policy of simultaneous competition and cooperation of its own, designed to promote a more comprehensive and more reciprocal detente—one which would engage the Soviet Union in a more constructive response to global problems.

At the same time, I argued that we should move away from what I

---

* See N. N. Inozemtsev in *Kommunist*, No. 18, December 1975.

considered our excessive preoccupation with the U.S.–Soviet relationship, which could only breed either excessively euphoric expectations of an American–Soviet partnership (which would inspire fears abroad of an American–Soviet condominium) or hysterical preoccupations with the U.S.–Soviet confrontation. Instead, I felt that the United States should address itself to a variety of Third World problems, either on its own or through trilateral cooperation with Western Europe and Japan. The Soviet Union should be included in that cooperation whenever it was willing, but should not be made the focal point of American interest to the detriment of the rest of the global agenda.

Finally, I felt strongly that in the U.S.–Soviet competition the appeal of America as a free society could become an important asset, and I saw in human rights an opportunity to put the Soviet Union ideologically on the defensive. Arguing that "human rights is the genuine historical inevitability of our times," I suggested that by actively pursuing this commitment we could mobilize far greater global support and focus global attention on the glaring internal weaknesses of the Soviet system. As early as February 16, 1976, in a memo submitted jointly with Richard Gardner, I tried to summarize for Carter my general approach in the following terms:

1. The East–West detente is desirable, but it is false to argue —as Kissinger has—that the only alternative to it is a war. The detente relationship is by its very nature a mixed one. It combines elements of both competition and cooperation. That is the underlying reality of the Soviet–American relationship, conditioned by strong historical forces, and that relationship is not likely to be dramatically altered in the future.

2. It is in the U.S. interest to strive to make detente both more comprehensive and more reciprocal. Only a more comprehensive and a more reciprocal detente can enhance peace and promote change within the Communist system. The purpose of detente ought to be precisely such a twofold goal: detente should seek to avoid war, but in so doing it ought to be an instrument of peaceful change. Unless the latter takes place, we can never be certain that the former is enduring.

3. It is in the Soviet interest to keep detente limited and rather one-sided. In fact, the Soviets so interpret it quite explicitly. In a number of comments, the Soviet leaders have openly stated that the detente is meant to promote the "world revolutionary process," and they see the American–Soviet detente not only as a means of preserving peace but also as a way of creating favorable conditions for the acquisition of power by Communist parties, especially given the so-called aggravated crisis of capitalism.

4. In seeking to use detente for domestic purposes, both

Nixon and Kissinger have oversold it as having already laid the basis for "the generation of peace." Moreover, they have adopted a stance of moral indifference, as exemplified in the recommendation to the President that he refrain from receiving Solzhenitsyn. The result of this oversell has been rising domestic disappointment with detente, prompting now a tendency to the other extreme, namely to reject detente as a whole.

5.   A comprehensive and reciprocal detente would mean in practice:

i.   Scrupulous fulfillment of the Helsinki agreement. Hence it is important that the fulfillment or nonfulfillment of that agreement be closely monitored, especially in regard to human rights.

ii.   Making it unmistakably clear to the Soviet Union that detente requires responsible behavior from them on fundamental issues of global order and it is incompatible with irresponsible behavior in Angola, the Middle East, and the UN (e.g., stimulation of extremist resolutions such as the one equating Zionism with racism).

iii.   In a more polycentric Communist world, the United States ought to have itself a more polycentric policy, and not deal exclusively with Moscow. Thus more attention should be paid to China, since the Chinese and American relationship bears very directly on the American–Soviet relationship. There should be movement toward the further upgrading of our political relationships. Moreover, the abandonment of the policy of benign neglect toward Eastern Europe is desirable, for the United States ought to be at least as interested in Eastern Europe as the Soviet Union is in Latin America.

iv.   There should be continued efforts to reach agreement with the Soviet Union on arms control, and there should be particularly an effort made to lower the present SALT ceilings. The ceilings are too high and they make possible not only further weapons deployment but they also breed mutual insecurities. At the same time, it would be highly desirable for the Soviet Union to become more explicit about its own longer-term strategic plans, for the very secrecy which surrounds its strategic planning breeds insecurity and suspicion on the American side (which, in contrast, is completely open about its longer-term strategic planning).

This memorandum spelled out the fundamentals of my approach to the Soviet question, providing a consistent guide for the various policy debates in which subsequently I became engaged.

Initial Soviet Testing

The new President favored a broad improvement in U.S.–Soviet relations. He attached high importance not only to SALT but to reactivating the mutual and balanced force reduction talks in Vienna (MBFR). Carter was hopeful that we could achieve a comprehensive test ban (CTB), and he pressed us to develop new initiatives, engaging the Soviets in such matters as limits on conventional arms transfers. The Secretary of State also felt strongly that we should do what we could to lift the trade restrictions that were imposed on U.S.–Soviet trade by the Jackson–Vanik Amendment. Perhaps most important, the Soviet Union was seen as a possible participant in the resolution of such issues as the Middle East conflict and the racial struggle in southern Africa.

Carter set great stock in personal diplomacy. Accordingly, shortly after the inauguration I suggested to the President that he initiate private correspondence with several top leaders of the world, including Chairman Brezhnev. I did not see these letters as a substitute for negotiations, nor was I naïve enough to think that they would, in and of themselves, resolve any outstanding issues. Nonetheless, I felt that they could be a useful mechanism for developing a personal relationship with key foreign leaders. The first letter to Brezhnev was sent on January 26. It was preceded by some drafting negotiations between Vance and me, which foreshadowed later differences. I noted in my journal for January 25 that "the letter prepared in the State Department is just too gushy and naïve. I tried to tighten it up and gave several recommendations to Carter. He accepted most of them, but even so the letter remains, in my judgment, a little too eager and too gushy. I have now written a memorandum to Vance suggesting further changes, and I have given a copy of it to Carter in the hope of making him focus more on substance and less on atmospherics in the U.S.–Soviet relationship. It seems to me that it is important to press this issue even though it injects me a little earlier into central policy matters than I had planned."

On January 27, I jotted down that "on the morning of the 26th Cy Vance called and told me he accepts my letter and we gave this to the President to sign. Moreover, I gave the President my memo to Cy, urging an approach to the Soviets which is more substantive and less atmospheric and also indicating that it is important for him to stress to the Soviets that we take a number of issues very seriously and that accommodation with them will be based to some degree on their willingness to adjust on these issues. The President told me that he had read this memo and had assimilated it."

The letter was generally friendly in tone and the President stressed in it that "it is my goal to improve relations with the Soviet Union on the basis of reciprocity, mutual respect and benefit." Carter noted Brezhnev's speech at Tula in which Brezhnev had stated that the Soviet Union would not seek superiority in arms. He assured Brezhnev that this was the U.S. position as well, noting that "there are three areas where progress can be made toward this goal." The first would involve the rapid conclusion of SALT; the second, an adequately verified comprehensive ban on nuclear tests, accompanied by greater openness about our respective strategic policies (a point that I insisted on inserting into the letter); and the third called for renewed efforts to achieve progress in MBFR. The President also went on to tell Brezhnev that the United States would be actively seeking a peaceful settlement to the Middle Eastern and southern African disputes, and that it was his "belief that the U.S.S.R. can contribute to the realization of progress towards peace in both of these critical areas." Carter concluded the letter by expressing the hope for an early summit meeting.

On February 1, Carter met with Anatoly Dobrynin, the Soviet Ambassador, for the first time. The meeting lasted one hour and was designed to underline some of the points made in the letter to Brezhnev. In my conversations and in a memorandum to the President before the meeting, I urged him to determine very deliberately what overall message and impression he wanted the charming and skillful Dobrynin to report to the Politburo. I suggested that he emphasize his interest in concrete progress: accommodation on SALT, reciprocal restraint in crisis areas, and the mutual reduction of insecurity with regard to each side's intentions and capabilities.

In the course of the meeting the President called for a tangible, drastic reduction in nuclear weapons, reduction of the possibility of a preemptive strike, some reduction of conventional weapons, and a reduction in international arms sales. Carter also told Dobrynin that he preferred to separate the cruise missile and Backfire issues from SALT II (both matters left unresolved in the previous Administration's negotiations with the Soviets). He indicated that he wanted to confine SALT II to numbers, but that the other issues would be open to negotiation later. Following a successful conclusion to SALT II, the President said, he would like to see the total number of nuclear missiles reduced to several hundred.

I was somewhat disappointed in the meeting, because, as I noted then, Carter "went into the general propositions, but he also skipped quite a bit from topic to topic, getting rather involved in specifics. Dobrynin, who at first was quite nervous and was obviously suffering from a certain stage fright, began to assert his diplomatic skills, to pump Carter quite skillfully, probing for his positions on SALT, the Middle East, the Indian Ocean, and so forth. . . . Sensing my unease, Carter later commented when we were alone, 'I tried to stick to the generalities but he kept probing me for specifics.' "

In addition, Vance and I met separately with Dobrynin. My first meeting with the Ambassador was on the evening of January 24, and I was impressed by his persistence in seeking to learn how we would organize ourselves to negotiate SALT and by his hints that it would be useful for him to maintain a back-channel relationship with me. Conscious of Vance's concerns, "I made a point of emphasizing that from now on the Secretary of State will conduct negotiations," though I did not foreclose consultative meetings. I had lunch with Dobrynin shortly thereafter, and meetings over a meal—either at the Soviet Embassy or in my office—subsequently became a frequent occurrence.

Dobrynin and his wife and granddaughter also came to my house, and occasionally we played chess. A skillful and sophisticated debater, Dobrynin always reminded me of an amiable bear, who could all of a sudden turn quite nasty. In his discussions with me he never lost his cool, except—and invariably—whenever I suggested that Gyorgy Arbatov (the director of the Soviet Institute on America) was an influential Soviet figure. Dobrynin would become red in the face and vehemently inform me that Arbatov was a man of no standing and little influence—a creation of the American media.

It is a well-established Soviet practice to quickly take the measure of a new U.S. President by pressing him hard on some issue. Carter was no exception. Brezhnev's initial response of February 4 to the President's letter had been relatively positive. Brezhnev commented—somewhat patronizingly—that he "found it on the whole constructive and encouraging," and he stressed that "to achieve disarmament is, due to objective reasons, the central area of relations between the U.S.S.R. and the U.S. at the present time." He seized upon Carter's earlier references to the Middle East and to Africa, stressing that cooperation in these areas between the Soviet Union and the United States was essential. He also indicated that he would be prepared to discuss the possibility of a meeting with Carter when Secretary Vance visited Moscow. It was evident from Brezhnev's letter that the Soviets hoped to obtain from the new American President a quick SALT agreement, based on the earlier Vladivostok arrangement with former President Ford, including the Soviet version of the understanding on the cruise missile.

Carter personally decided to respond to Brezhnev with a much broader proposal. On February 7, he directed Vance and me to immediately develop a response which would be, according to a handwritten note that he sent us, "personal and specific, including in particular comments on SALT II (less cruise missiles and Backfire?), SALT III (substantial reductions), demilitarized Indian Ocean, prior notice of all missile test firings, throw-weight limits, prohibition of mobile missiles (including SS-20), civil defense limitations, reduced arms sales, Berlin, human rights." I worried that this might be too much at once, and suggested that the draft indicate to Brezhnev that any effort to widen our collaboration and to contain our competition must be based on reciprocity. Accordingly, in the message to Brezhnev, the President noted that the U.S.–Soviet "competition—which is real, very expensive, and which neither of us can deny—can at some point become very dangerous, and therefore it should not go unchecked. To me, this dictates nothing less than an effort, first, to widen where we can our collaborative efforts, especially in regard to nuclear arms limitations; and, second, the exercise of very deliberate self-restraint in regard to those trouble spots in the world which could produce a direct confrontation between us." Finally, I prepared for Carter, and Vance approved, a rather personal paragraph, designed to appeal to Russian pride: "I know and admire your history. As a child, I developed a literary taste by reading your classics. I know also how much, and how very recently, your people have suffered in the course of the last war. I know of your personal role in that war, and of the sacrifices that were imposed on every Soviet family. That is why I believe we are both sincere when we state our dedication to peace, and this gives me hope for the future."

The letter left open the possibility of either a comprehensive SALT II proposal like the one Vance subsequently took to Moscow or, alternatively, a quick agreement which would defer the questions of the cruise missile and the Soviet Backfire bomber. The letter noted that "recently there seems to have been an increasing inclination to create new tensions and constraints in Berlin, which could cause deterioration in the delicate political balance there. I trust that you will help to alleviate these tensions." It also expressed the hope that all of the understandings reached in Helsinki would be respected by the Soviet Union. To reassure the Soviets, Carter added that "it is not our intention to interfere in the internal affairs of other nations. We do not wish to create problems for the Soviet Union. But it will be necessary for our government to express publicly on occasion the sincere and deep feelings of myself and our people. Our commitment to the furtherance of human rights will not be pursued stridently or in a manner inconsistent with the achievement of reasonable results. We would also, of course, welcome private, confidential exchanges on these delicate areas."

Brezhnev responded on February 25 in a chilling manner. Referring to Carter's letter, he began by saying that "I want to talk bluntly about our impression and thoughts it evoked. As I understand, you are for such straightforward talk." He made it plain that any agreement on SALT had to be based on the Vladivostok understanding, including the point that "in January of last year a concrete formula for the accounting of air-to-surface cruise missiles within the aggregate of strategic arms was practically agreed upon." In addition, the letter insisted that the Backfire ought to be excluded from the agreement altogether. This was the Soviet position at its most extreme. Brezhnev went on to ridicule Carter's expression of concern regarding unimpeded access to Berlin by suggesting that "it is sent to a wrong address." To Carter's rather carefully crafted comments on human rights (which were intended to be reassuring) the Soviet leader wrote scathingly that he would not "allow interference in our internal affairs, whatever pseudo-humanitarian slogans are used to present it," and took particular exception to the exchange of letters that had just taken place between the President and the Soviet Nobel Peace Prize winner, Andrei Sakharov. Describing it as "correspondence with a renegade who proclaimed himself an enemy of the Soviet state," Brezhnev rather ominously added, "We would not like to have our patience tested in any matters of international policy, including the questions of Soviet–American relations."

Brezhnev's letter was a jolt to Carter. My private notes for the day, February 28, convey how the key principals in Washington reacted, and —interestingly—they foreshadow Carter's later decision to move on China:

The most important item of the day was the letter from Brezhnev to Carter. It was waiting for me on my desk when I arrived at work this morning in an "eyes only" envelope from Vance. Vance described the letter as "good, hard hitting, to the point." But I read it rather differently. It struck me as being brutal, cynical, sneering, and even patronizing. It certainly was no response to Carter's effort to get a negotiating process going and to establish some measure of even personal correspondence. It was a very sharp rebuff.

Toward the end of the day when General Haig was leaving Carter's office, Carter said for me to stay behind and then we sat and talked for about half an hour to forty minutes. He asked me what I thought of the letter and I told him. He agreed with my diagnosis. He was quite taken aback by the letter. He said he was disappointed by it, but at the same time he indicated that he was not affected by this. He stressed a couple of times that it didn't bother him. I could tell to some extent it was a disappointment. We discussed how we should handle it and in what manner we could best respond. I was also struck by the fact that Carter said that he would like to consider now taking more initiatives toward China, something which clearly must have occurred to him in the light of this rather unpleasant response by Brezhnev. It is quite obvious that the letter was a bucket of cold water and must have been a disappointment if he really expected that there could be very rapid movement toward SALT. In some ways I was made to think of the first encounter between Khrushchev and Kennedy when Khrushchev almost tried to talk

Kennedy down and tried to browbeat him into concessions. The letter from Brezhnev had a little bit of the same tone. In any case, one of its consequences may be that there will be fewer illusions concerning how easy or difficult it will be to resolve some of the outstanding issues in the U.S.–Soviet relationship. In that sense, this may be a very salutary experience.

In spite of Carter's private efforts to reassure both Brezhnev and Dobrynin that he was not planning to use human rights primarily as an anti-Soviet weapon, the incident with the Sakharov letter had clearly touched a raw nerve. One has to concede that this event did not help the relationship between the new Administration and the Soviet Union. But a harsh reaction was not the only course open to the Soviets: they could have simply ignored, or at least played down, the matter. At our end, it is difficult to see, even in retrospect, what other course of action Carter could have pursued. The letter arrived shortly after the inaugural. Sakharov congratulated the new President on his commitment to human rights and drew attention to the human-rights problem in the Soviet Union. We all felt that the President had to reply. The prestige of the author was such that failing to do so would invite adverse comparisons with the widely criticized refusal by President Ford to meet with Solzhenitsyn. Had the Nobel Peace Prize winner been a resident of Chile, the liberal press would have been outraged by Carter's failure to respond. Moreover, American–Soviet relations had not been hurt by Brezhnev's direct contacts with Gus Hall and other pro-Soviet American activists, nor did we take public exception to Soviet proclamations that the world was destined to experience a global revolution. We had every right to insist that human rights was the wave of the future, not to speak of the fact that it would have been cowardly to ignore Sakharov's letter.

Accordingly, Vance and I drafted a carefully worded reply to Sakharov couched in language that made it clear that the President's concern was global in character and not focused specifically on the Soviet Union. Nonetheless, probably to drive home to Carter their sense of outrage, and to demonstrate our impotence, in subsequent months the Soviets stepped up sharply their suppression of human-rights activists.

Seeking Deep SALT Cuts

The initial correspondence between Carter and Brezhnev, in spite of the controversy over Sakharov, set the broad context for our policy efforts. With arms control as our immediate preoccupation, we engaged in the urgent effort to frame a new SALT negotiating approach. This phase culminated in the Moscow talks (March 28–30, 1977) between

Vance and Gromyko and in the Soviet rejection of the two U.S. proposals that Vance brought with him.

On Thursday, February 3, I chaired the first meeting of the Special Coordination Committee on SALT. I was sensitive to the fact that previously the Assistant for National Security Affairs never chaired NSC committee meetings at the top Cabinet level. Since under the new system established by President Carter I was to chair the SCC, I felt it prudent to suggest to the President that he open the meeting himself, and then leave the room, yielding the chair to me. I felt that this would make my role somewhat more palatable to the others, with the chairman's mantle bestowed upon me personally and visibly by the President himself.

This meeting was essentially exploratory. The President underlined his commitment to deep cuts, a position with which all the principals were now familiar.* At this initial meeting there was a consensus that we should pursue a comprehensive SALT II agreement, the framework of which would be along the lines of the U.S. proposal of January 1976, which in turn had evolved from the formulas agreed to in Vladivostok, and then later by Kissinger in Moscow. The key unresolved issues in these negotiations were whether the new Backfire bomber should be subjected to strict SALT limitations, and what range constraints were to be imposed on the cruise missiles that the United States hoped to deploy in the early 1980s. To get an agreement quickly, we explored the possibility of deferring the Backfire and cruise missile issues to later negotiations. Though no substantive decisions were reached, the SCC commissioned an interagency working group to develop alternative packages in two general categories: (1) packages based on the Vladivostok agreement and the January 1976 U.S. proposal; and (2) a package based on significant reductions for both sides (e.g., reducing the overall aggregate tentatively agreed to at Vladivostok from 2,400 down to 2,000 or even less).

In the weeks that followed, several more SCC meetings were held, to review alternative SALT packages that the working group developed and to resolve internal issues. There were wide differences among the various agencies on the preferred opening proposal, although we all agreed that an effort should be made to move beyond the final negotiat-

---

* Prior to the inaugural, the President-elect had met for broad strategic briefings with the Joint Chiefs of Staff on more than one occasion, and he had startled them by asking whether they felt that American security and the strategic balance could be maintained if both the Soviet Union and the United States were to reduce their arsenals to 200 ICBMs each. It was unclear to me at the time whether the JCS were more astonished by this notion or more tempted to exploit it to avoid any progress on arms control altogether. Paul Nitze, a well-known critic of the SALT negotiations, with whom the President consulted on more than one occasion, also pressed for very deep and comprehensive cuts, at least down to the level of 1,000 missiles.

ing positions of the Ford Administration. I limited my role largely to
that of chairing, posing questions, and becoming familiar with the
details of the various options. I felt that I could serve the President best
if I could ensure that the JCS view was fairly taken into consideration
in the shaping of SALT proposals, so that subsequently SALT would
not be opposed by the Pentagon when it came up for ratification.

For example, on March 11, I noted in my journal that "yesterday we
had an excellent SALT meeting, and I was quite pleased with the
way the whole meeting developed. For one thing, I was able to guide
it much more effectively. I got the participants to lay out their positions,
I deliberately asked Paul Warnke to speak first, and then I had him
followed by Harold Brown, and then General [George] Brown [Chair-
man of the JCS], and then I gave the last word to Cy Vance, thereby
balancing the softs and the hards and trying to create a framework
for agreement. I am hopeful that by the end of this week and early
next week we will have several options to lay out before the President,
and then he will have to decide his basic choice and also try to prime
the delegation, particularly Cy, for a firm and unyielding stand in
Moscow. It is to be expected that the Russians will try to be quite
tough, and we should not immediately pull back and start making
concessions, which I suspect some members of the U.S. delegation will
be tempted to do."

By the middle of March, our proposals started to take shape. In
early March, my deputy, David Aaron, Roger Molander, who was
exceptionally knowledgeable on SALT, and Victor Utgoff, a new member of the NSC and a specialist in systems analysis, had come up with
the ingenious notion that we consider an ICBM freeze as an option for
Moscow. This was based on the desirability of limiting the momentum
of Soviet ICBM modernization. At the March 10 SCC meeting I raised
that idea, and Harold Brown responded positively to it. This came to
be a significant element in the later SALT II agreement, providing for
the first time a mutually agreed impediment to the acquisition of a new
generation of offensive weaponry.

The real stumbling blocks remained the Backfire and cruise missile
issues. The State Department and the ACDA (Arms Control and Disarmament Agency) favored an accommodating posture, one which in
effect exempted the Backfire and imposed strict limits on the cruise
missile. Defense and the Joint Chiefs took almost a diametrically
opposing view. In the early meetings, the Defense Department tended
to dominate the discussions, and it was with a touch of relief that I
noted (on March 3) that "in the SALT meeting yesterday the State
Department was more assertive and as a consequence I think we will go
into next week's SALT discussions with options which are a little more
realistic than those that so far have been put forth by Defense."

There was general consensus among all the participants, both civilian and military, in favor of deep cuts, and it is not true, as was subsequently alleged, that the deep-cuts proposal was foisted on Carter by Brown and/or me. Indeed, Vance and Warnke submitted on March 18 to the President a memorandum to that effect. At that time they wrote: "We share your objective of reaching a meaningful SALT agreement as soon as possible. As you have made clear, such an agreement could include substantial reductions in strategic forces on both sides and limitations on the introduction of new weapons. One approach would be to seek to defer the Backfire and cruise missile issues, conclude an agreement based on Vladivostok, and proceed immediately with further negotiations. Another way to achieve the same objective would be to seek an agreement now which includes significant reductions and resolves the Backfire and cruise missile issues. Since follow-on negotiations are likely to require years to complete, a more comprehensive agreement this year would involve less risk than concluding a minimal agreement now and relying on subsequent negotiations to pursue our main objectives."

I favored modest cuts as the most attainable goal. On March 11, I sent the President a memo outlining four basic SALT outcomes: (1) deferral of contentious issues; (2) modest cuts to approximately 2,000 strategic delivery systems; (3) Vladivostok levels; and (4) deep cuts below 2,000. I supported option 2, stating that it was unlikely the Soviets would agree to more than that. I also reported that "Cy and Paul are prepared to accept within that context a separate limit of 300 for Backfire as well as collateral constraints, whereas Harold and JCS feel that without the lower aggregate of 2,000, deployment of Backfire (beyond the limit of 120) should be counted in the aggregate."

The U.S. negotiating position for the meeting in Moscow at the end of March was finally hammered out in two top-level meetings with the President held on March 19 and 22. The March 19 meeting was attended by the President, the Vice President, Vance, myself, and Brown (who had not originally been included but was added at my urging to achieve greater balance), and it was meant to review the draft Presidential Directive which I had prepared. It provided for three options. The first choice called for "deferral" until a follow-on resolution of the Backfire and cruise missile issues, with the rest of SALT II to be based on the Vladivostok levels. The second, and less preferred, option involved reductions to 2,000 (from the Vladivostok total of 2,400) for all ICBMs and to 1,200 (from 1,320) for MIRVed ICBMs; a limit on heavy ICBMs (which applied specifically to the Soviet side) to 150, which they currently possessed; an ICBM freeze; and a 1,500-kilometer across-the-board limit on cruise missiles. Finally, a third alternative essentially split the difference between the other two, and it was to be held back as "the least desirable" outcome.

At the meeting Carter instructed that the deep-cuts proposal be made the preferred alternative. The proposed levels for aggregates were reduced further to 1,800–2,000 and to 1,100–1,200 respectively, while the cruise missile range limit in the reduction proposal was changed to 2,500 kilometers largely on Brown's recommendation. The latter change was done largely to get the JCS to support the proposal, though I did note in my journal that "the position on the cruise missiles was toughened in my judgment somewhat beyond the point of need, thereby reducing the likelihood of Soviet acceptance." Unfortunately, this remark was correct.

The NSC meeting on March 22 was largely pro forma. After I presented various negotiating options, the President led a discussion largely designed to obtain JCS support for the SALT package. As I wrote in my journal: "I was quite impressed by the way Carter massaged the JCS. On the one hand, he made a number of statements which seemed to indicate his concerns for the things that the JCS stress—on-site verification, no free ride for the Soviets with regard to the Backfire, and yet all in all he was able to put through proposals which have rather different consequences insofar as these specific items are concerned. We have also instructed Vance to put forth the two proposals and to stick to them, and I think that is quite important. We also stressed to him that the Soviets are likely to reject and ridicule our proposals, but that he has to stand fast." Specifically, he was told to submit only the first two options, but not the third, even if the Soviet reaction was negative.

I foresaw just such an outcome, and wrote on March 25 that "I expect that the Soviets will not accept our preferred offer and that at best we will come out with our third option. If, however, we can stand fast and not be intimidated and keep pressing, it is conceivable that the Soviets will come around and accept our first proposal, which in that case would mark a really significant turning point in the U.S.–Soviet relationship. If accepted, it would mean a true impediment to a continued arms race, a true stand-down in the level of the arms race, and an arrangement which by and large would ensure political and strategic stability as well as parity." For this reason, I very much favored our not revealing the third proposal until a sufficient time had elapsed to convince the Soviets that we were prepared to stand pat and, if necessary, even to engage in an arms race.

As Vance prepared to go to Moscow, there was a subtle improvement in the tone and substance of Presidential correspondence with Brezhnev. As I have already noted, Brezhnev's letter of February 25 had exercised Carter a great deal, and much of the response was drafted by the President himself. Vance had urged the President "not to let yourself be drawn into a tone of equal harshness in your reply," and suggested focusing on substance alone. The President, however, felt that the State Department draft contained too much of an explanation of his position on human rights, and that "I do not need to explain myself to the Soviets." Accordingly, he rejected the proposed draft (which was actually quite firm) with the somewhat unkind comment that this "wouldn't have been worth the stamp if we were to mail it to Moscow."

My own view was that the President should take some exception to the tone of Brezhnev's letter, and Carter incorporated an introductory paragraph by me which said: "Your letter of February 25 caused me some concern because of its somewhat harsh tone, because it failed to assume good faith on my part, and because there was no positive response to the specific suggestions contained in my previous letter. The differences between our two countries are deep enough, and I hope that you and I never compound them by doubts about our respective personal motives." He went further, adding: "Please do not predicate your future correspondence on the erroneous assumption that we lack sincerity, integrity or a will to make rapid progress toward mutually advantageous agreements. I do not underestimate the difficulty of the substantive issues or the technical details, but we are determined to succeed."

I spent an evening reworking the President's draft because I was concerned that "he is proposing too many things all at the same time, and this is bound to generate unnecessary confusion. It may also make the Russians feel that he is really not serious about his proposals." In a novel departure, the President accepted my suggestion to send the message to Brezhnev through the hot line. The hot line had never been used this way before, and we felt that it might be useful to employ it for direct personal communications, obviating the need to go through our respective Foreign Ministries or Embassies.

Brezhnev's response came on March 15. It was briefer, focused almost entirely on SALT proposals, and was businesslike in tone. However, it reiterated the Soviet position on cruise missiles and insisted again that the SALT agreement should be essentially a reflection of the Vladivostok understanding—as defined by the Soviets. Referring to the earlier exchanges on the tone of correspondence, Brezhnev was conciliatory, noting that "I do not quite understand the meaning of your reference to the tone of my letter of February 25. Its tone is usual— businesslike and considerate." On the eve of Cy's departure to Moscow, I gave the President a memo recommending that he give Vance a personal, handwritten note addressed to Brezhnev. I suggested that the President emphasize his commitment to arms reduction, say that Cy spoke on his behalf and enjoyed his complete confidence and that he hoped to continue the personal correspondence.

In addition, on the President's personal instructions, I phoned Dobrynin to convey a personal message from Carter to Brezhnev. It was to the effect that the President was determined to put through a SALT agreement, but he could only do so in a comprehensive and constructive fashion during the first year, when he had maximum political leverage. The President also told me to tell Dobrynin that negative comments in the Soviet press about him (generated by the human-rights controversy) made it difficult to sustain this positive approach to U.S.–Soviet relations.

The Soviets were unmoved, and turned down the two U.S. SALT proposals immediately. Vance then cabled back proposing that we submit our third option to the Soviets, but (as I noted in my journal on March 30) "both Mondale and I felt very strongly that this should not be so, and the President approved a message to [Vance] indicating that he should stand fast. . . . I was rather surprised that Cy was so willing immediately to retreat to our fallback position." Cy's own assessment, cabled from Moscow, was more consistent with our original expectations: "My view is that they have calculated, perhaps mistakenly, that pressure will build on us to take another position. One of their problems apparently is that they feel we have departed too far from the basic Vladivostok framework. . . . In any case, although the results on SALT were definitely disappointing, we should not be discouraged. A certain testing period was probably to be expected."

Accordingly, I wrote on March 30 that "if the American public stands fast and we do not get clobbered with the SALT issue, I think we can really put a lot of pressure on the Soviets. We have developed an approach which is very forthcoming; on the one hand, we are urging reductions, with the other hand we are urging a freeze, and at the same time we are urging more recognition for human rights. All of that gives us a very appealing position, and I can well imagine that the Soviets feel in many respects hemmed in. However, all of that could begin to collapse if any of our colleagues begins to act weak-kneed and starts urging that we start making concessions to the Soviets."

Unfortunately, within days the press adopted an increasingly critical attitude, arguing that the United States had overplayed its hand. In so doing, it exploited Vance's own admission, made in the course of his return from Moscow, that perhaps we had miscalculated to some degree. The press also played up comments by some members of Vance's delegation, which included Leslie Gelb, to the effect that the United States should have simply gone forth with the original Vladivostok formula. The Washington *Post* led its story with the headline "Some Aides Feel U.S. Miscalculated," with its staff writer, Murrey Marder, writing that American sources had privately conceded that the Administration had made a basic misjudgment. All of that contributed to greater pressure on Carter to revise his position and made it more difficult for us to hold the line.

With the benefit of hindsight, it seems to me that our side perhaps did make the mistake of discussing too publicly its proposals for comprehensive cuts. We hoped it would generate wider understanding of the

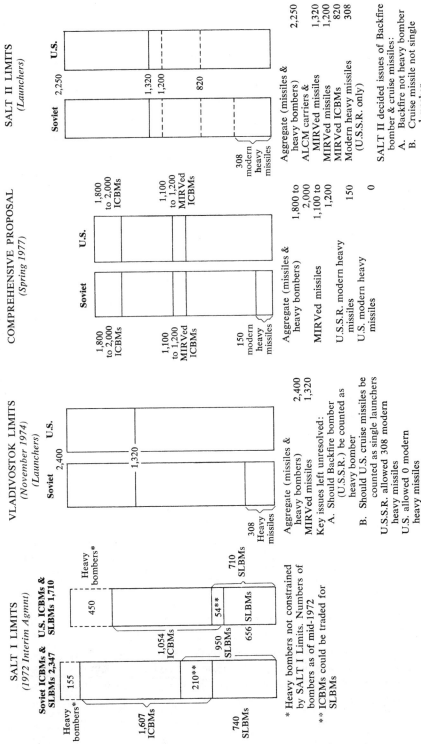

AGGREGATE STRATEGIC FORCE LIMITS

SALT I LIMITS
(1972 Interim Agmnt)

Soviet ICBMs & SLBMs 2,347   U.S. ICBMs & SLBMs 1,710

Heavy bombers*   155   450   Heavy bombers*

1,607 ICBMs   1,054 ICBMs

210**   54**

740 SLBMs   950 SLBMs   656 SLBMs   710 SLBMs

* Heavy bombers not constrained by SALT I Limits. Numbers of bombers as of mid-1972
** ICBMs could be traded for SLBMs

VLADIVOSTOK LIMITS
(November 1974)
(Launchers)

Soviet   2,400   U.S.

1,320

308 Heavy missiles

Aggregate (missiles & heavy bombers)   2,400
MIRVed missiles   1,320
Key issues left unresolved:
A. Should Backfire bomber (U.S.S.R.) be counted as heavy bomber
B. Should U.S. cruise missiles be counted as single launchers
U.S.S.R. allowed 308 modern heavy missiles
U.S. allowed 0 modern heavy missiles

COMPREHENSIVE PROPOSAL
(Spring 1977)

Soviet   U.S.

1,800 to 2,000 ICBMs   1,800 to 2,000 ICBMs

1,100 to 1,200 MIRVed ICBMs   1,100 to 1,200 MIRVed ICBMs

150 modern heavy missiles

Aggregate (missiles & heavy bombers)   1,800 to 2,000
MIRVed missiles   1,100 to 1,200
U.S.S.R. modern heavy missiles   150
U.S. modern heavy missiles   0

SALT II LIMITS
(Launchers)

Soviet   2,250   U.S.

1,320
1,200

820

308 modern heavy missiles

Aggregate (missiles & heavy bombers)   2,250
ALCM carriers & MIRVed missiles   1,320
MIRVed missiles   1,200
MIRVed ICBMs   820
Modern heavy missiles (U.S.S.R. only)   308

SALT II decided issues of Backfire bomber & cruise missiles:
A. Backfire not heavy bomber
B. Cruise missile not single launcher

SOURCE: Author's calculations & U.S. Senate *Hearings—The SALT II Treaty*, July 9–12, 1979, p. 106.

constructive character of our proposals, but it might have been wiser to prepare the ground through confidential discussions with Dobrynin in Washington and with the Soviet leaders through our Ambassador in Moscow. Our public pronouncements regarding the forthcoming U.S. proposals on deep cuts might have created the impression in Moscow that an acceptance of them would be a one-sided concession to Carter. However, it should not be overlooked that the Soviets also rejected our more modest fallback proposal, and it is quite evident that the Soviet side wanted to extract maximum concessions from Carter—concessions that he could not make politically and which could not be justified strategically. The Soviet interpretation of the Vladivostok agreement, particularly as it pertained to the Backfire and cruise missile issues, was clearly one-sided. In fact, two years later, when the SALT II agreement was finally reached, the Soviet side did accept, by and large, the postulates on these two issues that we advanced in March 1977.

Salvaging Detente

The Soviets rejected our two SALT proposals without even making a counterproposal. Responding to Vance's press briefing in Moscow on the U.S. proposals, the Soviet Foreign Minister, Andrei Gromyko, engaged in an angry, podium-thumping speech to journalists calling the U.S. package a "cheap and shady maneuver" to gain unilateral advantage for the United States. This generated widespread international and domestic concern that detente was coming to an end. Given the sharpness of the Soviet rejection, the President decided that I ought to give, for the first time, a public on-the-record briefing on our SALT position, and I did so in the White House on April 1.

In my briefing, I laid particular stress on the proposition that our proposals were designed not only to halt but to reduce the arms competition and that we continued to hope for renewed negotiations. I refused to label the Moscow meeting as a breakdown, thus keeping the doors open to resumed negotiations. In my explanation of the U.S. position, I put special emphasis on the proposition that "the time is ripe for doing something more than creating a framework for further competition" in nuclear weaponry. As Reuters put it, "Mr. Brzezinski's attitude at the White House press conference seemed to reflect the view that detente had not necessarily been derailed."

In private, we confronted a far more difficult task. Were we to stand pat on our SALT proposals or, instead, begin to adjust our position so as to make it more palatable to the Soviets? More generally, how were we to widen detente so as to make it more comprehensive and genuinely reciprocal, thereby also both more stable and more acceptable to the

American people? Finally, in this context, what response were we to generate to the continuing and growing Soviet strategic challenge? The Soviets were making every effort to obtain from President Carter a quick SALT agreement on terms favorable to the Soviet Union. They wanted us to accept detente as the major priority of American foreign policy, with its implied acceptance of Soviet proxy expansionism in Third World areas. On the Middle East, the Soviets were in effect proposing a U.S.–U.S.S.R. condominium. The Soviets must have assumed that Carter's public commitment to SALT gave them bargaining leverage which could be exploited to obtain these ends.

I confess that I was becoming rather skeptical about the prospects for progress. I wrote on April 3: "Today we met in the White House—the President, Cy Vance, Paul Warnke, Fritz Mondale, and myself—to review the Moscow mission. Both Cy and Paul emphasized that the Soviets were quite cordial, in spite of their firm rejection. Nonetheless, I do feel that neither they nor the President really appreciates the degree to which the Soviets are hostile to our proposal and the extent to which they wish to put us under pressure. My guess is the going will be much tougher than any of them realize. Much will depend on the extent to which the press, the mass media more generally, and Congress support us on this issue. And at stake may be the longer-range nature of the U.S.–Soviet strategic relationship, including the capacity of this country to stand up to a challenge somewhere in the early 1980s." Thus, my view was that the ball was in the Soviet court and we should sit tight and wait for a counterproposal.

But Carter was under pressure not only domestically but also from our allies to take a somewhat more forthcoming position. Both Callaghan and Schmidt were in touch with Carter during the late spring and early summer, stressing Brezhnev's allegedly conciliatory attitude and urging Carter to reciprocate in kind. For example, in mid-July, Schmidt told the President that Brezhnev should be viewed as actively promoting detente and needing Western help. The President also told me that he received a letter from Callaghan reporting both Schmidt's and Brezhnev's concerns about Carter's foreign policy and about some of the people around Carter. I laughed and said, "Myself included, of course." The President did not deny it.

One way to resume contact was through an early Carter–Brezhnev summit. Knowing of Carter's interest in an early summit meeting, the Soviets refused to commit themselves to it in advance of "prior agreements." I had proposed in 1976, and I repeated the proposal publicly with the President's approval in mid-April 1977, that both sides adopt the practice of holding regular, informal annual discussion meetings not tied to specific agreements. I felt that such meetings would provide the basis for more serious discussion of contentious issues, without generating public expectation of wide-ranging agreement. My hope was to create a forum for informal, in-depth discussion, so that through a gradually growing understanding it would become easier to resolve negotiating conflicts.

In his private correspondence with the Soviets, the President repeatedly referred to the possibility of a summit. Since the Soviets had again indicated in their oral note of June 3 that they would prefer not to have a summit until the agreement on SALT had been worked out, I urged the President not to repeat the invitation, but he did so again in his letter to Brezhnev of June 9. Carter wrote that he hoped "I can welcome you to our nation at an early date so that you and I can pursue personally our goals of disarmament, peace, trade, and increasing cooperation and friendship. If a formal visit to Washington should prove inconvenient to you, we might consider a less formal meeting, perhaps in Alaska, somewhat similar to your previous meeting in Vladivostok." Although I had reservations about having a summit, the Alaska proposal was my idea, since that would lend itself to a more informal, consultative type of meeting along the lines of my earlier proposal. However, the Soviets were not only unmoved but increasingly graceless in their response. On June 30, Brezhnev wrote to Carter, reiterating the Soviet position on SALT and ending with the following abrupt comment: "Now about our meeting. We have already brought to your attention our considerations on that subject. Therefore, there seems to be no need of repeating them here."

From April on, Carter came to commit an inordinate amount of time to the SALT effort. He would meet frequently with his key advisers on a Saturday morning, in sessions lasting sometimes as much as two or three hours. He carefully monitored the work of the SCC, which met with increasing frequency, and on which I would report to him the same day a given meeting was held. He would review carefully the instructions that I would send to Paul Warnke when he was negotiating in Geneva, or to Cy Vance when he was scheduled to meet either with Dobrynin or with Gromyko. He would meet with the JCS in order to solicit their support, to reduce their concerns, and to give them a sense of genuine participation in the shaping and refining of our proposals. Last but not least, he also engaged himself in direct talks with Ambassador Dobrynin, a development which both Vance and I viewed with some apprehension. We felt it was unwise for the President to become, in effect, the principal negotiator, whereas he probably felt that the issue was too important to be left to Vance or to me.

The first such "negotiating" session was held on April 12. Prior to it, I told the President that Vance and I felt that the meeting should not be too long and that he should try to take the offensive and not let Dobrynin set the pace of the discussion. (What I feared, of course, was a repetition of the first Carter–Dobrynin meeting.) Unfortunately, the meeting did not go well. Dobrynin was surprisingly aggressive, frequently interrupted the President, and tried to score debating points. As I noted afterwards: "I rather feared Dobrynin went away feeling that our first option, which is in favor of a comprehensive reduction and freeze, is no longer viable, and that is what happens when one negotiates on the spot. Subsequently, both Mondale and I agreed that this went much too far and that an effort will have to be made to pull the thing back." To make matters worse, we had not undertaken yet a comprehensive assessment of our position, and I was afraid Dobrynin might transmit a wrong signal to Moscow as to where the United States stood.

In subsequent weeks, Vance and Warnke met further with Dobrynin. I also met with him for an extensive session in which I attempted to put our SALT negotiations in the larger context of American–Soviet relations. I tried to make the Ambassador understand that unless there was progress on SALT soon, we faced the prospect of a slide in the opposite direction. At the same time, we in the Administration continued our substantive work on SALT, with the President providing personal leadership. An important session was held on Saturday, April 25, at which a new position was reached, essentially combining some elements of our initial comprehensive cuts proposal with the so-called deferral option. At this meeting both Harold Brown and I urged somewhat stiffer conditions, and I noted in my journal that "there is a tendency on our side to want an agreement so badly that we begin changing our proposals until the point is reached that the Russians are prepared to consider it."

During this period I also started talking more frequently about this matter with Ham Jordan, in order to get a better feel of the domestic political side. Jordan became an increasingly valued ally in my attempts to maintain a tougher position. He agreed that no further changes should be made, for this would weaken the President politically. I hoped that he would tell the President this directly and thereby make the President more resistant to Vance and Warnke's entreaties for a more conciliatory approach.

The discussions with Dobrynin paid off and, in effect, negotiations resumed in early May. On the eighteenth of that month, Vance and Gromyko met for another SALT session. Instead of dealing with a flat Soviet rejection, we were now engaged in trying to narrow the differences between our respective negotiating positions. These differences at this stage involved: (1) whether the aggregate level of delivery systems would be 2,250 (Soviet position) vs. 2,150 (U.S.); (2) whether the MIRV (multiple independently targetable reentry vehicle) level should be 1,320 (Soviet) vs. 1,200 (U.S.); (3) whether the ALCM (air-launched cruise missiles) limits should be in the treaty (Soviet) or the protocol (U.S.); (4) whether ALCM-carrying heavy bombers should count in the 1,320 (Soviet) vs. a sublimit of 250 (U.S.); (5) whether MIRVed heavy missiles should be further limited to 190 (U.S.); (6) whether there should be a sublimit of 250 on Backfire (U.S.); and (7) whether the ban on new ICBMs should apply only to MIRVed ICBMs (Soviet) or all ICBMs (U.S.). In the meantime, it was jointly agreed that the arrangements regarding cruise missiles would run for three instead of two years, that SLCM (submarine-launched cruise missiles) and GLCM (ground-launched cruise missiles) testing and deployment would be limited to 600 kilometers for that period, and that mobile ICBMs would be banned. This represented some genuine progress.

Throughout the summer I made a sustained effort to obtain JCS support and to mediate the disputes, which largely arose between Harold Brown and Paul Warnke. My notes for August 17 are typical of this concern: "Cy Vance and I tend to represent the middle position and on all of the major issues I think I can say that the middle position came out as the final position of those present. The essential problem is that while our position is a reasonable one it is unlikely that in the short run the Soviets will accept it and it is unlikely that in the long run it is sufficient to meet the threat that the Soviet buildup is posing. We agreed that Paul Warnke and I will talk to Dobrynin in order to try to make the Soviets understand the fundamental nature of our concerns. However, I must say that I am on the whole pessimistic about the short term. I doubt very much that the Soviets are prepared to make the kind of accommodation which will be reasonable. They will probably try once more to split us, either by trying all of a sudden a policy of softness and accommodation, and then of hardening, or by launching major propaganda attacks designed to frighten the Senate and the public and the journalists into thinking that a new U.S.–Soviet crisis is at hand."

On another occasion I jotted: "What was interesting about our SCC discussions on SALT today is the degree to which the military seem to prefer simply to have more and more weapons, irrespective of the strategic consequences. They thus argued at the meeting that our proposed cuts in our mutual forces don't go far enough in reducing the Soviet strategic threat to us and yet at the same time they involve too high cuts of our own forces and therefore higher ceilings ought to be set. On the other hand, Warnke and Vance, who are engaged in negotiating the agreement, and are preoccupied with obtaining an agreement, are more inclined to make accommodations and concessions than the rest of us, who are not directly involved in the negotiations. All the while, the Soviets are sitting patiently on the sidelines, telling us from time to time that their government is not flexible and that therefore it is up to us to make new proposals. This is the standard line that Dobrynin keeps feeding us."

Another major step forward in the negotiating process occurred in September. The President reviewed our various options at a formal NSC meeting, and for the first time the possibility of agreeing to count ALCM-carrying heavy bombers in the 1,320 aggregate in return for a 1,200 MIRV limit was raised. This had been my recommendation as a way of breaking the deadlock on this subject, for by now I was playing a much more active role. Previously I had opposed strongly the inclusion of ALCM-carrying bombers in the 1,320 limit, but I had come to believe that a 1,200 MIRV limit would satisfy our basic interests. The combination of the two limits imposed an identical ceiling on all MIRVed ICBMs for both sides (1,200), while in effect allowing the United States an additional free 120 ALCM-carrying heavy bombers through the imposition of a joint ceiling of 1,320 on all MIRVed ICBMs and ALCM-carrying heavy bombers combined, since the Soviets did not have ALCM-carrying heavy bombers.

The NSC meeting was also preparatory to the forthcoming talks with Gromyko, who was scheduled to visit Washington two weeks later. Vance first met with him in New York, and then Gromyko came to Washington, where he had an extensive session with the President. On the eve of the Washington meeting, Carter received a memorandum from Vance and Warnke recommending additional alterations in our position, but these were strongly opposed by Brown and me. In his meeting with Vance, Gromyko had been surprisingly hard. On some matters he even took a retrogressive position and stuck to it in a totally unyielding fashion. As it turned out, it was a typical Soviet softening-up tactic. On the evening prior to the meeting with the President, I received a call from Cy, who indicated that the Soviets were beginning for the first time to take a reasonable position. Most importantly, they proposed to set a limit on land-based MIRVed ICBMs of 820, which was a concession to us.

The Carter–Gromyko meeting came at a critical time. We had indications that the Soviets were finding Carter hard to understand. From their perspective he was a complicated individual who resented criticism and who was trying to wrest concessions from them which from their point of view would change the strategic balance of forces. Therefore, Gromyko's meeting with Carter was important not only in terms of SALT but also for the Soviet attitude toward U.S.–Soviet relations in general. And the meeting was a personal success for Carter. It is best simply to reproduce my fresh impressions of the day:

> I must say the President could not have been better. He made an excellent presentation, giving an overview of the sort which I strongly felt he needed to do; he did not coddle Gromyko, nor

invite him into a separate session, which initially he was inclined to do but which I urged him not to do. He gave Gromyko a *tour d'horizon* which was extremely effective, both in substance and in tone. He rebutted Gromyko when Gromyko made a counter-response. He did not let him score points. And then when we got to the nitty-gritty of negotiating SALT he was very skillful in presenting our position in such a way that it was projected as a very significant concession which the Soviets must match. I really told him afterwards that I don't usually flatter him, and I certainly don't hesitate to disagree with him, but I was genuinely proud of the way he performed. Gromyko was quite skillful and not as dour as projected, a little too verbose, and I sensed that he was rather impressed by the President's performance. The Russians all watched the President closely and they must have been struck by the fact that he was very much on top of the data, well informed, quite skillful in shooting back immediately any Soviet argument. When the Soviets at one point indicated that they had made a concession by accepting our proposal for lowered aggregates, the President immediately and very eloquently pointed out to them that accepting an aggregate that is lower for both sides is no concession but simply an acceptance of common sense and of genuine and mutual reductions. There was no way that this could be presented as a concession to the United States.

The Carter–Gromyko meeting put new momentum into the SALT process. However, a large number of issues still remained to be re-solved. The next several months saw us concentrate on such matters as what ought to be the overall aggregate limit, how the telemetry issue and concealment question should be resolved, what new types of SLBMs (submarine-launched ballistic missiles) and ICBMs should be per-mitted, how we could resolve the question of cruise missile range defini-tion, what were the implications of SALT for our relationships with our allies (the so-called noncircumvention issue), and what kind of limits could be imposed on heavy mobile ICBMs and heavy SLBMs.

The resolution of these issues involved a tedious process of negoti-ating, and it was well-nigh impossible to accelerate it. In early January 1978, Vance and Warnke wrote a memo to the President summarizing the progress achieved in the course of various SCC meetings during October and November and urging that we move promptly to resolve the outstanding SALT issues by sometime in the spring of 1978. Harold Brown accompanied their memo by a commentary which warned that any agreement that was negotiated must be such that it could be adequately defended to the public. In other words, he warned against undue haste and any one-sided concessions. I supported him on this.

The outcome of these further deliberations was a renewed Vance–Gromyko dialogue, undertaken on April 20 and 21, 1978, in Moscow. This meeting achieved some additional progress; namely, Soviet acceptance of our formula on noncircumvention and a joint agreement on a 2,250/1,200 aggregate and MIRV limit. There was no progress in these talks either on the Backfire or on what new types of ICBMs should be exempted from a jointly agreed freeze. The limited character of this progress meant, in fact, that our hopes for a spring 1978 agreement had evaporated. It was evident that another political push would have to be made sometime in the course of the late summer or early fall, perhaps in conjunction with Gromyko's next visit to the United States. In the meantime, we became increasingly concerned over our ability to achieve ratification in the Congress of the likely SALT agreement. The President met on occasion with Senators Henry Jackson and Sam Nunn and became particularly concerned that they both might reject our SALT agreement because of the cruise missile definition issue.

The central question in this thorny issue was whether the restrictions and bans would apply on all cruise missiles or only on those which were actually carrying nuclear warheads. Almost every key figure had altered his position in the course of the year. The matter was not only extraordinarily convoluted technically, but precisely because we all changed our positions, the President at one point became intensely irritated and chastised me for attempting too persistently to change his mind on the subject.

The internal U.S. debate on our SALT position and the resulting negotiations with the Soviets were accompanied by a major effort to widen the scope of U.S.–Soviet detente. This was in keeping with our earlier belief that it would be a mistake to confine detente purely to arms control. It was the general view of the Administration, and certainly my own, that only in this way could we test the extent to which the Soviet Union was prepared to become genuinely a more cooperative partner in dealing with global problems.

Our efforts were concentrated in five broad areas: (1) through negotiations with the Soviets, we wished to promote the demilitarization of the Indian Ocean; (2) through conventional arms transfer negotiations, we hoped to obtain Soviet agreement to limit the flow of arms, from both the United States and the Soviet Union, to Third World countries; (3) by reconvening the MBFR negotiations in Vienna, we hoped to parallel SALT by mutually agreed reductions on the conventional level in the central theater of any possible East–West military confrontation; (4) by consummating a comprehensive test ban agreement (CTB), we hoped to further strengthen the existing limits on vertical and horizontal nuclear proliferation; and (5) through joint talks regarding the Middle East issue, we hoped to create sufficient

American–Soviet consensus to make possible the resumption of the Geneva Conference between the Arab and Israeli sides.*

I had sent the President a memorandum on the subject "Measures for Stabilizing U.S.–Soviet Relations." It opened by reporting that Secretary Vance "has submitted a memorandum identifying a number of measures which you may want to consider as part of an effort to 'stabilize' U.S.–Soviet relations."

The Vance memorandum proposed the following:

1. An informal meeting with Brezhnev.

2. Use of nongovernmental scientists to encourage their Soviet counterparts to be more forthcoming on SALT.

3. A meeting with the President for Vladimir Kirillin, the Deputy Prime Minister and head of the State Committee on Science and Technology, who will be in Washington in July, and the granting of remote access to the Soviets to the Cyber 76 computer for use in their weather observation system.

4. Increased Soviet involvement in global and North–South issues.

5. Invigoration of U.S.–Soviet working groups.

6. Examination and development of bilateral scientific agreements.

7. A series of minor steps such as permission to the Soviets for opening a banking office in New York; high-level U.S. representation at the sixtieth anniversary ceremony in Moscow in November; expansion of scientific exchanges; our visa policy to be more flexible; greater accommodation with the Soviets on civil aviation arrangements; some U.S. participation and consultation with Japan in the Yakutsk liquefied natural gas project; greater consideration of the effect on the Soviets of our forthcoming announcements regarding weapons procurement or deployment.

In my covering memo, I expressed skepticism over some of the proposed steps (I noted, for example, that the President had seen Dobrynin twice; the Vice-President had seen Foreign Trade Minister Patolitchev;

---

* Actually, I had relatively little confidence that we would make any progress in MBFR and CTB, and throughout the Carter years I was not very interested in these subjects. I saw them as nonstarters, but out of deference to the President's zeal for them, I went through the motions of holding meetings, discussing options, and developing negotiating positions. My view was that the MBFR was too complicated a process, with too many participants, to yield any tangible results; while I saw CTB as a likely embarrassment to any effort on our part to obtain SALT ratification. I feared that our legislative circuits would become overloaded if we tried to obtain both SALT and CTB, but I respected the President's deep moral concern over nuclear weapons and I did what I could to move the bureaucratic machinery toward meaningful proposals—yet ones which would not jeopardize our ability to continue the minimum number of tests necessary for our weapons program.

Brown had had lunch with Dobrynin, who had also met often with Vance and with me; while U.S. Ambassador Toon was still waiting to see Brezhnev and Defense Minister Ustinov). "The recommendations themselves could be interpreted to imply—though that is not their intention—that the cause of current strains is either the result of mis-conceptions or lack of U.S. effort and that we need a series of steps (some of them quite minor ones) to prove our seriousness or sincerity. I must confess that I doubt this premise. If the Soviet leadership views the Administration's more assertive foreign policy as a sign of hostile intentions, then a number of good-will gestures will have little impact. Indeed, there is some risk that the Soviets will conclude that their counterattacks are having an effect." I concluded my memo by saying, "In general, I feel that we should maintain a steady course, pursue those negotiations where progress is to our mutual advantage (SALT, CTB, the Indian Ocean, etc.), and not convey the impression of either haste or concern. U.S.–Soviet relations are the product of long-term historical forces and we should not become too preoccupied with transi-tory aspects, some of them deliberately generated by the Soviets in order to exercise psychological and political pressure on us."

The President indicated that he would not see Kirillin, and he expressed skepticism regarding the very last two items on the miscel-laneous list (7), but did not make any major comments on the others, generally approving them. (The computer, however, was disallowed later.)

In early July 1977, responding to growing press criticism of the stalemate in American–Soviet relations and of our alleged responsibility for such a stalemate, the President asked me to give him a report on the various initiatives that we had taken to improve U.S.–Soviet rela-tions. In response to his request, I reported that we had initiated the SALT proposals, the CTB talks, talks on arms limitations and restraint in the Indian Ocean; a proposed ban on chemical warfare, talks on restraining arms transfers, a program for nonproliferation of nuclear weapons; talks on a ban on radiological weapons; an invitation for the Soviets to sign the Treaty of Tlatelolco; consultations with the Soviets regarding the Middle East, a proposal in the President's press confer-ence of March that the Soviets join in avoiding any interference in Africa; an invitation in the Notre Dame speech for the Soviets to join in aiding the developing world; meeting of the Joint Commercial Com-mission, which had not previously met because of the Soviet involve-ment in Angola; delivery of a supermagnet for joint experiments in energy. I added that "in sum, the foregoing scarcely supports the Soviet claim that we are putting obstacles in the way of improved relations or have embarked on some anti-Soviet course. We have already carried the ball while they have constantly complained in order to build pres-sure for concessions."

During this period, despite some of the press comments which had generated the President's concern, the public tenor of U.S.–Soviet relations somewhat improved. The Brezhnev–Carter correspondence became less abrasive. The President gave a major speech at Charleston, South Carolina, on July 21, in which he incorporated the U.S. initiatives I had listed for him, referred to our policy of competition and cooperation, and optimistically declared: "Beyond all the disagreements between us—and beyond the cool calculations of mutual self-interest that our two countries bring to the negotiating table—is the invisible human reality that must bring us closer together. I mean the yearning for peace, real peace, that is in the very bones of us all." The Soviet side did take a number of public steps in the area of human rights which aroused American concerns, but we deliberately muted our reactions to avoid further friction. Moreover, Secretary Vance formally brought on board a well-known academic expert on Soviet affairs, a former colleague of mine at Columbia University, Professor Marshall Shulman, and his appointment was widely publicized by the New York *Times* and the Washington *Post* as auguring a more constructive and responsible approach toward the Soviet Union.

At that time, I was still "camping" at the Harrimans' and they offered similar refuge to Marshall. On some mornings we would walk to work together, he to the State Department and I to the White House, which gave us a chance to discuss informally the state of U.S.–Soviet relations. In one of our morning walks to work, we lamented the absence of effective coordination within the U.S. government of the various cooperative U.S.–Soviet links. We were both aware that by now many agencies had developed bilateral contacts with their Soviet counterparts and that there were many official and unofficial exchanges in process. This created a situation which was not only somewhat confused but susceptible to deliberate Soviet exploitation. Accordingly, I suggested to Marshall that we create an interagency committee, which he might chair, to monitor all such activities. Having secured his assent, I issued the appropriate White House instructions to create that committee. When its formation was announced, the New York *Times* made it front-page news, adding the amazing interpretation that this was a further public signal to the effect that the Administration was moving toward a more conciliatory attitude toward the Soviet Union, with policy influence allegedly passing from the NSC to Vance and Shulman.

By and large, this period was marked by relative harmony within the Administration, though there was some friction on specific issues. The SCC began working on our proposals for the demilitarization of the Indian Ocean in May 1977, and by September we were ready to move forward with a proposal for a mutual declaration of restraint, our objective being the stabilization of the existing military situation in the Indian Ocean. The proposed declaration was designed at a minimum to ensure that during an agreed period of about five years deployment of Soviet or American naval units into the Indian Ocean would be limited approximately to the current levels on each side. This position was contested by ACDA and State, with both of them favoring reductions from existing levels. On January 24, 1978, the President also approved a recommendation that at the first private meeting between the U.S. representative and the Soviet negotiator, the American side would deliver a protest to the Soviet Union regarding the negative implications for our negotiations of the ongoing Soviet activities in the Horn of Africa and the related buildup of Soviet military presence. Our effort to generate a joint limit on conventional arms transfers also moved forward without any basic disagreements within the Administration. Exploratory U.S.–Soviet talks on limiting the export of arms to other nations were held, but they did not yield concrete results.*

The October 1, 1977, U.S.–Soviet statement on the Middle East was perhaps the high point of this brief period of seeming improvement in U.S.–Soviet relations. The Soviets did not hide their disappointment when, within days, the U.S. side walked away from the statement, and Brezhnev, in subsequent letters to Carter, complained strongly at the growing willingness of the United States to exclude the Soviet Union from the Middle East peace process.

During the summer and early fall, the President also undertook some private initiatives designed to generate greater momentum in the U.S.–Soviet relationship. In July, after reading my memorandum listing our efforts to improve and to widen the scope of the U.S.–Soviet relationship, the President decided to give Governor Averell Harriman the list, which he could convey to Brezhnev in a personal message. Harriman, who undertook that initiative with much encouragement from Vance and Shulman, prepared a letter from the President to Brezhnev in which the President was again to raise the issue of a summit meeting with the Soviet leader, perhaps at Camp David, but I prevailed on Carter to have it redrafted into a proposal from Harriman himself. Brown and I reviewed the proposed letter, and we both agreed that "the letter is too pleading and creates the impression that a U.S.–Soviet summit is a favor that the Soviets are granting us. After returning to my office, I

---

* Later on, I did have an intense disagreement with the head of the U.S. negotiating team, Leslie Gelb, a close protégé of Secretary Vance. Gelb favored talking to the Soviets about U.S. arms transfers to some of our allies, in exchange for their willingness to talk about Latin America and sub-Saharan Africa. I felt that this was no bargain, and Gelb was instructed to confine our discussions to these two neutral regions. At one point, he sent back a cable ridiculing formal instructions to him not to do so. As a consequence, I had to inform him that he would be immediately recalled unless he developed rapidly the necessary enthusiasm for the President's position. He did. Not long afterwards, he left government service and wrote quite critically about me. I was not surprised.

redrafted the letter, making it more of a contribution of Harriman's and more of his own initiative and less a letter on the President's behalf." Brezhnev's response to Harriman was politely unforthcoming.

In early September, the President received a letter from Chancellor Schmidt, "strictly for the eyes of the President only," indicating that, in August, Schmidt had been in touch with Brezhnev to the effect that Carter would be willing to establish a personal and confidential contact with the Soviet leader. According to Schmidt, Brezhnev had responded affirmatively. The President asked me for comments on this, and I gave him a handwritten note on September 14 pointing out that a personally responsible and high-level emissary could be useful in contacts with the Soviets, but I warned against using the Germans. "Arranging it through the Germans raises questions as to their role and interest in this, and also the question of our other allies. Would they be informed? To have such a meeting without their knowledge, but with German cooperation, would be odd; to inform them would guarantee a leak. . . . If the moving force has been Schmidt, then I suspect that he has been put up to it by Egon Bahr, an . . . ex-aide of Brandt's, who already tried something similar on me." As it happened, this initiative, which the President told me was Schmidt's, came to naught, for later in the year Schmidt told me that the Soviets had not followed up on it.

Efforts to maintain a dialogue with Brezhnev continued throughout the year and occasionally generated some disagreements with State. I opposed any further references to a summit meeting. Both the President and Vance desired it, however, and our side kept raising the issue. For example, in November 1977, Vance submitted a draft prepared by Shulman in which the President was to express personal congratulations to the Soviets on the occasion of the Soviet sixtieth anniversary. In the proposed draft the President was to say: "I have a major task facing me in convincing the American public and our Congress that the treaty and other documents we contemplate signing are in the U.S. interest, as I believe they are. Ambassador Dobrynin will have reported to you the efforts I am making here to this end. I will apply my best efforts and political judgment to the task and believe I will, in the final analysis, be successful." The proposed draft also again expressed the hope for a meeting between the two leaders.

In my cover memo to the President on November 1, I objected to both passages. The first seemed to me obsequious; the second was certainly redundant, given Brezhnev's firm brush-off to previous efforts along these lines. The President approved the excision of these passages. However, to convey a positive signal to the Soviets, the President did agree to meet with Soviet Foreign Trade Minister Patolitchev in early November, despite my objections that the Soviets were not providing similar hospitality to our visitors or even our Ambassador. I felt we should insist on strict reciprocity.

The impetus for these growing disagreements with State came from two sources. I was becoming increasingly concerned over the longer-term implications of the Soviet strategic buildup and by the growing Soviet–Cuban military penetration of the Horn of Africa. Both issues came to complicate enormously the management of U.S.–Soviet relations, and eventually brought to the surface, even on the public level, the simmering disagreements between the Secretary of State and me.

We had commissioned a broadly gauged review of the U.S.–Soviet strategic balance as one of our first official acts. I asked Professor Samuel Huntington of Harvard to undertake it, for I wished to obtain not only a narrowly focused accounting of the relative military strength of the two countries but a more sophisticated appraisal of the relative performance—military, political, economic, and ideological—of the two competing systems. The outcome of that undertaking was an ambitious paper, Presidential Review Memorandum 10. Its conclusions were mixed. It identified the military domain as the one in which the Soviets were making the greatest strides, and it registered some urgent apprehension regarding our ability to stand off the Soviets in Europe in the event of a conventional conflict. The report highlighted the need for a more sustained effort to build up both U.S. strategic capabilities and overall allied conventional military power. It also identified the Persian Gulf as a vulnerable and vital region, to which greater military concern ought to be given. At the same time, it was relatively sanguine about our overall ability to compete politically, economically, and ideologically with the Soviet Union. It thus provided the intellectual underpinnings for my own predisposition in favor of an activist, assertive, and historically optimistic policy of detente. Such a policy, however, had to be based on adequate military power, and hence its concomitant had to be a deliberate decision to reverse the military trends of the preceding decade.

PRM-10 led in turn to an important Presidential Directive, PD-18, signed on August 24, 1977. This document directed that we maintain a strategic posture of "essential equivalence"; that we reaffirm our NATO strategy, namely a forward defense in Europe, and the maintaining of a "deployment force of light divisions with strategic mobility" for global contingencies, particularly in the Persian Gulf region and Korea. The interagency debate over the PD-18 draft revealed a sharp dispute within the Administration about the implications of PRM-10. One side preferred to limit our strategic forces to an assured destruction capability and to consider reducing our forces in Europe and Korea. The Indian Ocean–Persian Gulf region was to be addressed through arms control efforts with the Soviets. The other side, on which I found myself, pointed to the momentum and character of Soviet military programs, the vulnerability of the oil-rich region around the Persian Gulf, and the growing Soviet projection of power in Africa, Southeast Asia, and possibly even the Caribbean. The final version of the PD reflected NSC/Defense preferences for NATO and Korea, the NSC initiative for a Rapid Deployment Force, and a stalemate on the strategic forces issue. It left open the final policy decision on nuclear employment doctrine, subject to later analysis and study.

This process gave me additional arguments on behalf of greater caution regarding any U.S.–Soviet collusion on such regional matters as the Middle East, and it reinforced my previous predisposition to push on behalf of an American–Chinese accommodation. I saw in such accommodation, together with our own enhanced defense efforts, the best way for creating greater geopolitical and strategic stability. As the months went on, I became increasingly firm in the view that it would be better not to have a Carter–Brezhnev summit until we had taken some concrete steps to improve relations with China and to enhance our strategic resilience. This is why I subsequently pushed hard not only for diplomatic relations with Beijing but also for the MX decision.

Is There Linkage?

The more immediate source of friction between Vance and me was the Soviet-sponsored deployment of the Cuban military in the African Horn. In the summer of 1977, the long-standing territorial disputes in the Horn of Africa were complicated by the dramatic switch in allegiances of the Ethiopians and Somalis. The increasingly extreme leftist government of Ethiopia broke with the West, while the Somalis, who had been aided by Moscow, turned to the United States. The unsettled situation was of serious concern to Egypt, the Sudan, Saudi Arabia, Iran, and us, because we all had evidence that the Soviets were providing increased aid and using Cuban forces in the already tense border war. Of course, our ability to assist the Somalis was not helped by the fact that they were the nominal aggressors in the Ogaden, having crossed over an established border into territory they claimed belonged to them.

However, in my view the situation between the Ethiopians and the Somalis was more than a border conflict. Coupled with the expansion of Soviet influence and military presence to South Yemen, it posed a potentially grave threat to our position in the Middle East, notably in the Arabian peninsula. It represented a serious setback in our attempts to develop with the Soviets some rules of the game in dealing with turbulence in the Third World. The Soviets had earlier succeeded in sustaining, through the Cubans, their preferred solution in Angola, and they now seemed embarked on a repetition in a region in close proximity to our most sensitive interests.

I was strengthened in my view by the repeated, like-minded expressions of concern by both Giscard and Sadat, leaders with a refined strategic perspective. Both warned Carter on several occasions not to be passive or to underestimate the gravity of an entrenched Soviet military presence so close to weak, vulnerable, yet vitally needed Saudi Arabia. Sadat let it be known that he was afraid the Soviets were seeking to embarrass him specifically by seizing control of territory crucial to Egyptian interests. We had a report from the Shah, who had traveled to Aswan and to Riyadh, that both the Egyptians and the Saudis were increasingly concerned by the increased Soviet activity. In fact, the Shah reported that the Saudis were "petrified" by the prospect of a Soviet presence across the Red Sea. The Sudanese had also expressed to Carter their worries about Soviet activity and U.S. lack of activity. In a personal message the Sudanese President wrote: "We believe that the Soviet Union is pursuing a sinister grand strategy in Africa leading to some definite goals. We are truly alarmed at the extent of Soviet influence in our region; alarmed at the means it uses, and at the ultimate goal it drives at. . . . Against this vigorous Soviet activity in Africa, we notice that the American role is generally quite passive. We expect and hope that the United States in the prevailing circumstances in Africa would respond favorably to requests of help from those countries ready and eager to defend themselves against the Soviet threat."

Yet in spite of such expressions of concern, throughout the late fall of 1977 and much of 1978 I was very much alone in the U.S. government in advocating a stronger response: Vance insisted that this issue was purely a local one, while Brown was skeptical of the feasibility of any U.S. countermoves. But by the late summer of 1977, intelligence sources provided mounting evidence of growing Soviet-sponsored involvement. As a result, I promoted a State-chaired PRC meeting on the subject of growing tension in the Horn of Africa, which resulted in a recommendation to the President, which he approved, to accelerate our efforts to provide support to the Sudan, to take steps to reassure and strengthen Kenya, and to explore means of getting as many African leaders as possible to react adversely to the Soviet-sponsored Cuban military presence.

On November 22, on my urging, the President directed Andy Young to make a speech in the UN against the Soviet–Cuban presence in Africa, and on December 13, there was a mini-SCC on Soviet–Ethiopian airlifts to the region. On December 14, I had dinner with Dobrynin, whom I pressed on the subject, and "he gave me assurances that the Ethiopians will not cross the Somali frontier once they begin to re-capture the Ogaden; that his leaders strongly believe in the conspiracy theory interpretation of what recently has happened in the Middle East, even though he knows it's not true; and he urged that the President write Brezhnev regarding what is of importance to the President with regard to SALT. He also expressed rising concern that SALT will not be ratified. In my conversation with Dobrynin I warned him quite flat out that continued influx of Cubans and of Soviet war matériel to Ethiopia would make us alter our position from that of restraint to that of more active involvement. I told him that we had restrained some of the neighboring countries from sending in their troops, but if the Soviets persist we will stop restraining these neighbors, and after all they are closer and in a better position to pour in much larger numbers of troops. Thus their policy will be self-defeating, while the results would be an intensified crisis in American–Soviet relations. More generally, I told him it seemed to me our relationship on the one hand involves some accommodation (SALT, the Indian Ocean, CTB) but also increasing tensions (in the Middle East, in Somalia, and perhaps on human rights). Accordingly, more of an effort should be made by them to try to improve the relationship."

With Carter's approval, I also started briefing the press on the growing Soviet–Cuban military presence, and by mid-November 1977 articles started appearing, registering the growing escalation of the Communist military efforts. For example, the New York *Times* produced on November 17 a front-page report, including a map, detailing the growing Soviet-sponsored Cuban military activity on the African continent. The President also started referring more frequently to this issue in his public comments, in an effort to make the Soviets more sensitive to the proposition that their conduct was not compatible with the notion of mutual restraint. To drive the point home to the Soviets, just before Christmas I inserted into a letter from Carter to Brezhnev "some reasonably straightforward language regarding Soviet conduct in regional conflicts, notably in the African Horn." The letter stated: "I would also hope that the United States and the Soviet Union could collaborate in making certain that regional African disputes do not escalate into major international conflicts. The fighting that has developed between Ethiopia and Somalia is a regrettable development, one which should be contained and terminated before it spreads further. . . . I mention these concerns because I deeply believe that it is important for us, to the extent that it is possible, to avoid becoming involved in regional conflicts either as direct protagonists or through proxies. . . . I write about this because it is my determination to do my utmost to improve the American–Soviet relationship." I obtained Cy Vance's approval for that language in return for inserting a few paragraphs from Cy's proposed text regarding the Middle East, language which was designed to reassure the Soviets. Specifically, I put in the following at Cy's request: "Without such Soviet help, it might prove difficult to reach the common goals of a comprehensive settlement negotiated in Geneva, as emphasized in your letter of December 16."

As hostilities increased and as more Cuban troops went to Ethiopia, Gromyko suggested the classic Soviet solution to regional disputes—a joint U.S.–Soviet mediation effort pointing to a condominium. I believed that it would only legitimize the Soviet presence in the Horn and suggested instead that we put more effort into urging the regional leaders and other African nations to call for a withdrawal of all foreign troops and for mediation by African states alone. In a memo to the President on January 11, I reiterated my grave concern about the longer-term implications of the Soviet presence, and suggested that the war had to be made increasingly costly to the Soviets in its political and military dimensions. I elaborated on my recommendation on January 18 in a four-page memo to the President: "Soviet leaders may be acting merely in response to an apparent opportunity, or the Soviet action may be part of a wider strategic design. In either case, the Soviets probably calculate, as previously in Angola, they can later adopt a more conciliatory attitude and that the U.S. will simply again adjust to the consolidation of Soviet presence in yet another African country."

By mid-January several thousand Cuban military were deployed in Ethiopia and the number was continuing to grow. Accordingly, I started convening frequent SCC meetings on the grounds that the issue was gradually escalating into a crisis. In the third week of December, I noted after one such meeting: "Everyone is afraid of getting into a crisis, and hence the general tendency is to downplay the seriousness of the issue. . . . You could almost sense the anxiety in the room when I mentioned the possibility of more direct action to make it impossible for the Soviets and Cubans not only to transform Ethiopia into a Soviet associate but also perhaps to wage more effective warfare against Somalia. Yet if Ethiopia and South Yemen become Soviet associates, not only will access to Suez be threatened, and this involves the oil pipeline from Saudi Arabia and Iran, but there will be a serious and direct political threat to Saudi Arabia. This is something we simply cannot ignore, however uncomfortable the thought may be."

It was roughly at this time that Sadat raised with us the possibility of deploying Egyptian forces in Somalia, and we agreed to that initiative. We also informed Giscard of the Egyptian plan, but Sadat did not follow through. I suspect that he hoped for more active American support, both logistical and financial. Neither, however, was forthcoming.

Because I became more and more concerned that we would not respond assertively enough, I urged the President not to make any more public comments on the subject, but privately I continued pressing for stronger reactions. In response to SCC initiatives the President sent letters to Giscard, Tito, General Olusegun Obasanjo of Nigeria, Carlos Andrés Pérez of Venezuela, and Morarji Desai of India, describing his concerns about Soviet–Cuban involvement and urging them in turn to warn Moscow and Havana of negative consequences for East–West relations of continued outside interference. I was very gratified that the President, in meeting Soviet Politburo member Boris Ponomarev, spoke up forcefully on this subject, warning the Soviets that we did not wish a confrontation but that the Soviets were running the risk of creating one in a region which was very sensitive to us.

Encouraged by the President's strong stand, I started pressing again in the SCC for a more direct reaction. I was concerned not only about the foreign implications of perceived U.S. passivity in this strategic area, but also about the effect it would have on domestic politics and what that would mean for SALT. As I had written earlier in January to the President, ". . . failure to pursue such a course could prove to be damaging and will be exploited by your political opponents with considerable effect. Indeed, the Soviet–Cuban offensive could coincide with the signing of SALT." My view was that the deployment of an American aircraft carrier task force near Ethiopia would send a strong message to the Soviets and would provide more tangible backing for our strong words.

I also believed the regional powers had to be motivated by their own self-interest to repel the Cubans. It was the responsibility of the United States to give them confidence in this endeavor. I pursued this line of argument throughout the spring. At an SCC meeting on February 10, I argued that it was important that regional powers not see the United States as passive in the face of Soviet and Cuban intervention in the Horn and in the potential invasion of Somalia—even if our support was, in the final analysis, only for the record. My arguments were corroborated by David Aaron, who, having just returned from a special mission to Ethiopia, believed that some show of U.S. force was important.

Harold Brown and Cy Vance, however, opposed that approach. Vance particularly was against any deployment of a carrier task force in the area of the Horn. For the first time in the course of our various meetings, he started to show impatience, to get red in the face, and to raise his voice. I could sense that personal tension was entering into our relationship. Vance believed that we should emphasize a political settlement that would make it easier for the Somalis to withdraw, but that we should keep our forces out, even if the Ethiopians crossed over the frontier into Somalia. He argued that "we are getting sucked in. The Somalis brought this on themselves. They are no great friends of ours, and they are reaping the fruits of their actions. For us to put our prestige on the line and to take military steps is a risk we should not take." In his opinion, the United States should not put an aircraft carrier in the area unless we were prepared to use it. Vance was supported in his arguments by Assistant Secretary for African Affairs Richard Moose, who expressed the view at the February 21 SCC meeting that "the best protection against invasion of Somalia would be world opinion."

I continued to make my point that more was at stake than a disputed piece of desert. To a great extent our credibility was under scrutiny by new, relatively skeptical allies in a region strategically important to us. I believed that if Soviet-sponsored Cubans determined the outcome of an Ethiopian–Somali conflict, there could be wider regional and international consequences. There would be greater regional uncertainty and less confidence in the United States. But if the United States and France each deployed an aircraft carrier nearby, it would certainly make the Cubans think twice about participating in the invasion of Somalia, while tangibly demonstrating our concern and presence. Just placing the carrier in the area did not mean that we were going to war.

Brown played a particularly cautious role. He agreed with my analysis of the consequences in the short run but with Vance about the long-run outcome. He argued that sending a special task force without a specific purpose would likely have negative consequences outweighing the advantages. He pointed out further that if Somalia were invaded and Siad Barré overthrown, it would be viewed as a failure of the U.S. task force to do its job, and that failure would impair the credibility of such task forces in future crises elsewhere—in short, a U.S. bluff would have been called. As he put it in the NSC meeting of February 23, ". . . if we know the situation will come out all right in Somalia . . . then we might deploy the carrier and take credit for success in preventing an invasion. On the other hand, if we do not know how the situation will come out, or we do not intend to use the aircraft carrier in Somalia, then we should not put it in." Brown did, however, become more receptive when the President himself sounded positive on the idea of deploying an aircraft carrier in the Indian Ocean.

With so much at stake, I felt that I should see whether I had broader support in the Administration. One evening late in February, "I spoke to Bob Strauss about my concerns regarding the longer-range international and domestic implications of the situation in the African Horn. He thoroughly agreed with me; he pointed out that if our foreign policy doesn't succeed, I will be personally blamed because I will be seen as the person closest to the President; and that many people feel that it is weak and indecisive." I then "talked to Fritz Mondale and while he increasingly leans to the idea of putting in a carrier, he is reluctant to recommend this to the President."

In the end, I did not carry the day. The President did not approve at this time the deployment of U.S. aircraft into the area, but indicated willingness to consider moving a carrier closer into the area near Diego Garcia. As I noted in my journal: "Everyone otherwise was against me. The Defense Department speaking through Harold, the JCS speaking through General Jones, and State speaking through Cy— all of them seem to me to be badly bitten by the Vietnam bug and as a consequence are fearful of taking the kind of action which is necessary to convey our determination and to reassure the concerned countries in the region. My argument was that we would not be stepping into a fight but we would be conveying seriousness simply through our presence."

During this period, we were also concerned about how the Horn situation might affect our other relations with the Soviets. Generally the President remained upbeat in his public remarks, believing that relations between the two countries had improved since he came to office. In my memos to him and in our meetings, however, we did consider the Horn within the context of overall U.S.–Soviet relations. On January 18, I wrote to the President: "The Soviet leadership should be unambiguously but quietly advised of potentially destructive impact on the U.S.–Soviet relationship of Soviet military involvement in Ethiopia. Both ongoing and future efforts to improve the relationship could be adversely affected. Note should be taken of the self-imposed U.S. restraint in matters and areas of concern to the Soviet Union (e.g., regarding transfer of militarily significant technology, not to speak of arms, to China), a position which we wish to maintain because of our desire to promote a genuinely comprehensive detente."

In a February SCC we discussed a possible range of responses to the Soviet and Cuban activity. We agreed unanimously that there should be no direct linkage between Soviet and Cuban actions in the Horn and bilateral activities involving either country and the United States. However, positive consideration was given to taking action in the area of space cooperation (future shuttle cooperation) and a greater flexibility with respect to technology transfer to China. (Vance reserved his position on the latter.)

Although the Ethiopian leader, Lieutenant Colonel Mengistu, assured Aaron during his consultative mission that the Ethiopians would not invade Somalia once they regained the Ogaden, we were becoming increasingly concerned about evidence of growing Soviet involvement in the country and the possibilities of expansion of the conflict beyond the borders of Ethiopia. Not only had the number of Cubans increased dramatically to 10,000 or 11,000, but according to our intelligence information about 400 Soviet tanks and some 50 MiG jet fighters had been sent to Ethiopia as part of a major transfer of Soviet arms. Finally, we learned that the first deputy commander in chief of Soviet ground forces, Petrov, was in fact providing direction for the Ethiopian military operations. This at a time when the Soviets were blaming the United States for a cooling in our relations.

On February 24, Brezhnev gave a speech in which he expressed the hope for better U.S.–Soviet relations, which he said were being blocked by certain U.S. actions: slow progress on the SALT talks, decisions on the neutron bomb, and congressional restrictions on trade. The next day the State Department responded with a statement which expressed support for concluding SALT but also said that the character of Soviet–American relations depended "upon restraint and constructive efforts to help resolve local conflicts, such as the Horn of Africa."

On March 1, Mondale asked me to join him in one of his morning press briefings. In response to a question of whether there was "linkage" between Soviet aid to Ethiopia and the likelihood of new limitations on U.S. and Soviet strategic weapons, I said, "We are not imposing any linkage, but linkages may be imposed by unwarranted exploitation of local conflict for larger international purposes." I reiterated my belief that SALT in itself was of benefit more or less equally to the United States and to the Soviet Union. But I also pointed out that "it is only a matter of realistic judgment to conclude that if tensions were to rise . . . then that will inevitably complicate the context not only of the negotiating process itself but also of any ratification that would follow the successful conclusion of negotiation." The press immediately headlined this as advocacy by me of "linkage" as a policy. I did not see in my statement a policy recommendation but merely a recognition of fact: namely, that the American public would not support agreements with the Soviet Union if it saw the Soviet Union as increasingly aggressive.

On March 2, the President spoke at the National Press Club, where he was asked about SALT and the Horn. Expressing his hope for Somali withdrawal from the occupied Ogaden region, a removal of Soviet and Cuban forces from Ethiopia, and a lessening of tension in the area, Carter said: "The Soviets' violating of these principles would be a cause of concern to me, would lessen the confidence of the American people in the word and peaceful intentions of the Soviet Union, would make it more difficult to ratify a SALT agreement or comprehensive test ban agreement if concluded, and therefore the two are linked because of actions by the Soviets. We don't initiate the linkage."

On the same day Vance appeared before the Senate Foreign Relations Committee and said in responding to a question, "There is no linkage between the SALT negotiations and the situation in Ethiopia." All this discussion produced the following headline in the New York *Times*: "Top Carter Aides Seen in Discord on How to React to Soviet Actions; Brzezinski Appears Tougher than Vance—President Leans Toward Security Adviser."

As soon as the linkage issue surfaced, Cy became very angry and agitated. At an SCC meeting on March 2, he firmly insisted that there was no linkage whatsoever between the Horn and SALT. I noted that "the President said in response to a question this noon that there is no linkage but Soviet actions may impose such linkage." Both Brown and Vance responded, "That is wrong," and Vance went on to say, "I think it is wrong to say that this is going to produce linkage, and it is of fundamental importance." I responded, "It is going to poison the atmosphere." The argument continued. Vance: "We will end up losing SALT and that will be the worst thing that could happen. If we do not get a SALT treaty in the President's first four years, that will be a blemish on his record forever." Brzezinski: "It will be a blemish on his record also if the treaty gets rejected by the Senate." Vance: "Zbig, you yesterday and the President today said it may create linkage, and I think it is wrong to say that."

The next day I wrote another memo to the President, in which I once again noted my concern about what our lack of resolve was signaling to the Soviets: "The Soviets must be made to realize that detente, to be enduring, has to be both comprehensive and reciprocal. If the Soviets are allowed to feel that they can use military force in one part of the world—and yet maintain cooperative relations in other areas— then they have no incentive to exercise any restraint. The conclusion to be drawn may be unpleasant and difficult, but I see no other alternative: in brief, our limited actions in regard to the specific conflict must be designed to convey our determination, while our broader response must be designed to make the Soviets weigh to a greater extent the consequences of their assertiveness for detente as a whole."

The debate over Soviet assertiveness in the African Horn in fact raised three key issues: Were we dealing with a local or a strategic question? How should we respond? Was there any linkage to SALT? For Vance, the African matter was largely a local issue, and he was strongly backed by the State Department; I argued that the newly discovered Soviet–Cuban passion for the integrity of frontiers could hardly be analyzed in such narrow terms. Moreover, even if one allowed what seemed to me to be a preposterous notion, namely that the Soviets were acting out of some sort of strange territorial legalism, their presence so close to Saudi Arabia was bound to have strategic consequences, whatever the Soviet intent may have been.

Having disagreed on the diagnosis, it was only natural that we disagreed on the remedy. I strongly believed that a show of force was necessary, that our allies would welcome it, and that it would convince the Soviets that we were serious when we said that detente should be both reciprocal and based on restraint. Finally, I was convinced for political reasons that SALT would be damaged if we did not react strongly, for the American public was prepared to support detente only in the context of genuine reciprocity in the American–Soviet relationship. Had we conveyed our determination sooner, perhaps the Soviets would have desisted, and we might have avoided the later chain of events which ended with the Soviet invasion of Afghanistan and the suspension of SALT.

We will never know, even with the benefit of hindsight, whether my preferred course of action would have been more effective. In any case, the fact is that the Soviets did step up during this time their use of the Cuban proxy in Africa and in a manner which potentially threatened our vital strategic interests. Did they do so because they concluded that the new Administration was so eager for SALT that it would not react? Did they do so because they saw the opportunity for joint collaboration in the Middle East wane and then disappear after Sadat's bold initiative? That complaint was reiterated frequently in Brezhnev's communications to Carter, and it was evident that the Soviets were genuinely disappointed that the Sadat initiative, subsequently backed by the United States, had excluded them from the driver's seat insofar as the peace effort in the Middle East was concerned.

However, it is difficult to argue that the Soviet-sponsored use of the Cuban military proxy in Ethiopia was brought on by Soviet disappointment over the Middle East. Such an explanation fails to take into account the long lead times required in the undertaking of an air and sea lift of the type that was involved in the transfer of Cuban troops to Ethiopia. Thus the most likely conclusion is that the Soviets at this time believed they could probably have their cake and eat it, too. They were thus pursuing a strategy of indirect expansionism while still seeking to fashion a detente relationship with the Carter Administration that would permit the Kremlin to attain its three objectives: a favorable SALT treaty, a flexible and one-sided detente, and a regional condominium in the Middle East.

In two successive weekly reports, I gave the President my views on where our relations stood with the Soviets approximately one year after we took office. In the first report, entitled "Strategic Deterioration," I noted that there were serious dangers on the horizon in U.S.–Soviet relations. I was particularly troubled by the potential Soviet success in the African Horn: first, because it would demonstrate to all concerned that the Soviet Union has the will and capacity to assert itself in the Third World; second, because it would encourage Libya, Algeria, and Cuba to act even more aggressively. "In effect, first through a proxy (as in Angola) and now more directly (as in Ethiopia), the Soviet Union will be demonstrating that containment has now been fully breached." The Ethiopian situation, coupled with what I saw as growing indications of political instability in Western Europe as well as our failure to exploit politically our relatively favorable position in the U.S.–Soviet–Chinese triangle, might contribute to a further deterioration in the U.S. global position. In that setting, I once again warned the President, SALT would not have a chance and our ability to deal with other issues would be severely handicapped.

In a report written a week later, I used the following chart to analyze Soviet behavior since Carter had come into the White House:

Benign	Neutral	Malignant
SALT (tough but serious)	Middle East (not helpful but not overly destructive)	Neutron Bomb (intense propaganda campaign vs. U.S.)
CTB (clearly seeking accommodation)	Arms Transfers (restrained, not actively cooperative and seeking to retain Soviet freedom of action)	Human Rights (suppressed at home and some success in toning down U.S. criticism abroad)
Indian Ocean (seeking rather one-sided proposals)		
Chemical Warfare (positive-exploratory)	MBFR (rigid on key issues)	Conference on Security and Cooperation in Europe (uncooperative and destructionist)
Radiological Warfare (positive-exploratory)		
Nuclear Proliferation (positive-cooperative)		Southern Africa (uncooperative and encouraging extremism)
		Horn (assertive intrusion with demonstrable effects)

I suggested that the chart indicated that the Soviet Union was prepared to be cooperative in those functional areas likely to cement a parity relationship with the United States. At the same time, the Soviet Union is unwilling to accommodate in ideological and political areas; in fact, it is quite prepared to exploit Third World turbulence to maximize our difficulties and to promote its interests.

"In effect, the Soviet Union is seeking, and apparently has had some success in obtaining, a selective detente," I concluded. I wrote that the proper U.S. response should be not to undermine emerging cooperative relations in the "benign" category, but to increase the costs of Soviet behavior in the "malignant" category. In the briefest form, I suggested, this means continued insistence on human rights as part of the ideological competition; countercampaigns on interventionism and more affirmative political initiatives in areas of Soviet sensitivity, such as China. Only thereby could we push the U.S.–Soviet relationship increasingly into the "neutral" or "benign" category.

The President responded to some of the points I had raised in these two weekly reports, and on March 17 he gave another major foreign policy speech at Wake Forest University. The tone was quite different from that of the relatively conciliatory speech given at Charleston in July 1977. It stressed U.S. determination to defend national interests and preserve American values. He declared: "Our strategic forces must be—and must be known to be—a match for the capabilities of the

Soviets. They will never be able to use their nuclear forces to threaten, to coerce, or to blackmail us or our friends. . . . Arms control agreements are a major goal as instruments of our national security, but this will be possible only if we maintain appropriate military force levels. Reaching balanced, verifiable agreements with our adversaries can limit the cost of security and reduce the risk of war. But even then, we must—and we will—proceed efficiently with whatever arms programs our own security requires."

The speech was a good one and set us on the right course. I did not think, however, that it made up for our lack of determination vis-à-vis the Soviet actions in the Horn. (Moreover, our credibility with the Soviets was undercut by an initiative which baffled me: Vance's closest associate on Soviet affairs, Marshall Shulman, reassured the Soviet Embassy—without any White House knowledge—that the President's speech should be viewed primarily as designed for domestic consumption and therefore should not be interpreted as indicating declined U.S. interest in SALT or accommodation.)

Two years later, in March 1980, as we were reacting to the Soviet invasion of Afghanistan, I wrote in my journal: "I have been reflecting on when did things begin genuinely to go wrong in the U.S.–Soviet relationship. My view is that it was on the day sometime in . . . 1978 when at the SCC meeting I advocated that we send in a carrier task force in reaction to the Soviet deployment of the Cubans in Ethiopia. At that meeting not only was I opposed by Vance, but Harold Brown asked why, for what reason, without taking into account that that is a question that should perplex the Soviets rather than us. The President backed the others rather than me, we did not react. Subsequently, as the Soviets became more emboldened, we overreacted, particularly in the Cuban Soviet brigade fiasco of last fall. That derailed SALT, the momentum of SALT was lost, and the final nail in the coffin was the Soviet invasion of Afghanistan. In brief, underreaction then bred overreaction." That is why I have used occasionally the phrase "SALT lies buried in the sands of the Ogaden."

There was, however, in my estimation, one important beneficial outcome from these troublesome months. We started reviewing more systematically the advisability of developing strategic consultations with the Chinese in order to balance the Soviets. As my minutes for the meeting of March 2 show, "everyone agreed that these consultations should focus for the time being on scientific and technological cooperation. Secretary Brown felt they might usefully encompass political issues, specifically the Horn situation as well." I followed this up by initiating an interagency meeting on U.S.–Chinese relations, and I started pressing the President for more sustained initiatives toward China. Thus, on the morning of March 3, "I talked to the President first of all briefly about the situation in Ethiopia. I told him that I will have recommendations for him shortly from our SCC meeting, but in my judgment the basic question was the nature of detente itself. Soviet actions do impose a linkage and the President ought to move now by initiating consultations with the Soviets and with the Chinese. To the Soviets I suggested he consider sending both Vance and Harriman," and I raised the possibility of myself dealing directly with the Chinese.

Handing the President the top-secret Presidential Daily Brief at the morning briefing, April 1977

On Air Force One on the way to the London Economic Summit, May 1977. Left to right: Brzezinski, Secretary of the Treasury Michael Blumenthal, the President, Secretary of State Cyrus Vance. Chapter 8

Consultative luncheon with Soviet Ambassador Anatoly Dobrynin in Brzezinski's office at the White House, June 1977. The President's secretary showed him a copy of this picture, which he returned to me autographed and with the notation: "Now I see why we always get out-traded by the Soviets." Chapter 5

*Breakfast briefing for the President and Vice President Mondale, July 1977.
By arrangement with Carter, the red folder held by Brzezinski was exclusively
reserved for sensitive NSC materials*

*A casually dressed President and Brzezinski meet with the new British Foreign
Secretary, David Owen, in July 1977. Next to Owen is British Ambassador
Peter Jay.* Chapter 8

Greeting Shah Reza Pahlavi of Iran in Washington, November 1977. We had no idea that the Shah was fatally ill. Chapter 10

Vance and Brzezinski conferring, July 1977. "Our personal relations were always good"

Consulting with the President at Camp David on Chinese policy, August 1977

Mrs. Carter meets with Cardinal Stefan Wyszynski, Primate of Poland, December 1977, in Warsaw. Chapter 8

In-flight press conference aboard Air Force One, January 1978

Inspecting the U.S.S. Eisenhower *with Defense Secretary Harold Brown, March 1978*

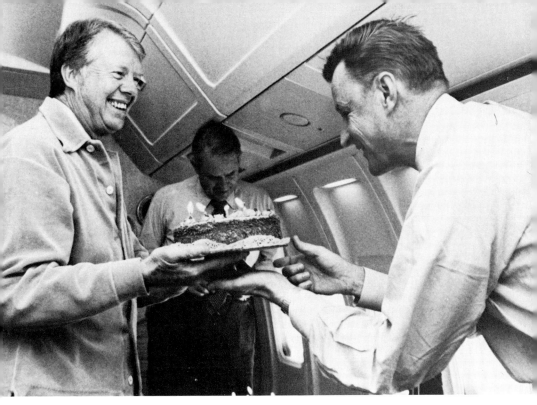

The President surprises his National Security Adviser with a birthday cake on the way to Caracas, Venezuela, May 1978

Press briefing, Caracas, May 28, 1978

Strategic equilibrium: Eyeball to eyeball with the Joint Chiefs, May 1978

The President phoning General Torrijos at a critical stage in the Senate ratification process for the Panama Canal Treaty, May 1978. The Panamanian negotiators are facing the President; Vance and Christopher have their backs to the camera. Chapter 4

Dinner at a lakeside restaurant given by Deputy Chairman Deng Xiaoping for Brzezinski and the U.S. delegation, May 1978. Chapter 6

At the banquet given by Brzezinski for Foreign Minister Huang Hua, Beijing, May 1978. "Much to the surprise of the Chinese, my wife insisted also on making a toast, and the Chinese Foreign Minister was visibly mortified when I asked for his advice. However, his wife rather firmly endorsed my wife's intention, which sealed the matter." Clockwise: Foreign Minister Huang, Brzezinski, Brzezinski's wife Muška, Mme Huang. Chapter 6

Meeting with Prime Minister Fukuda of Japan to urge movement on the Japanese–Chinese treaty following Brzezinski's visit to Beijing, May 1978.
Chapter 6

Briefing of the President prior to a press conference, July 1978. Clockwise: Brzezinski, Jerry Schecter, Gerald Rafshoon, the President, and Jody Powell (back to camera)

The first of a series of chess games at Camp David between Begin and Brzezinski, September 1978. Chapter 7

Business interrupts pleasure at Camp David, September 11, 1978. Chapter 7

The American and Israeli delegations meet for a preliminary discussion. The session lasted late into the night and, smiles notwithstanding, soon became quite heated. Camp David, September 10, 1978. Chapter 7

Brzezinski explains his view on the Israeli settlements to a concerned Prime Minister Begin at Camp David, September 12, 1978. Chapter 7

Part II
MAJOR
TURNING POINTS

During Carter's Presidency, there were five major foreign policy turning points—each requiring either a basic shift in strategy or generating consequences of great significance to the national security of the United States. The effort to achieve SALT without linkage to other issues or events was refuted by "history" or, more specifically, by excessively assertive Soviet behavior. But that, in turn, led to the President's decision to send me to Beijing in mid-1978 to accelerate normalization of relations with China—which then became one of Carter's principal and lasting accomplishments. The goal of a comprehensive peace in the Middle East proved elusive—but Sadat's reactive initiative became the catalyst for Carter's greatest personal accomplishment: the Camp David agreement. Yet almost at the same time, our efforts to invigorate the Western alliance were partially set back—and Carter's personal credibility was unfairly damaged—by the President's decision in May 1978 not to proceed with the deployment of the neutron bomb and not to blame that decision (for the sake of allied unity) on the hesitations and conditions imposed by German Chancellor Helmut Schmidt.

In the meantime, the road to SALT proved longer and more difficult, and by the time the agreement was finally signed in Vienna in July 1979, the deterioration in U.S.–Soviet relations made ratification increasingly uncertain. Soon after, the combined political impact of the "discovery" of the Soviet brigade in Cuba in September and the Soviet invasion of Afghanistan in late December made ratification unthinkable. U.S.–Soviet relations became frozen—a far cry from our early hopes. Finally, the internal upheaval in Iran, culminating by the end of 1978 in the overthrow of the Shah, destroyed the strategic pivot of the U.S.-sponsored shield for the Persian Gulf region and set in motion events that later proved politically most costly to the President himself.

These turning points—a combination of lasting achievements and bitter disappointments—required us to gradually revise our basic priorities and to concentrate our efforts on policies designed to preserve and maximize American power. Inevitably, the resulting shift generated some internal disagreements, in contrast to the more hopeful first phase.

Part II: Major Turning Points

Normalization of U.S.–Chinese Relations

1977	
April–June	PRM-24 formulates China policy goals
August 23–26	Vance trip to Beijing and Chinese rebuff
1978	
May 21–23	Brzezinski trip to Beijing reaches secret understanding
September 19	Carter meeting with Ambassador Chai generates additional momentum
October–November	Secret negotiations by Leonard Woodcock in Beijing and Brzezinski at the White House
December 15	Carter announces normalization of diplomatic relations with China

Middle East and Camp David

1978	
February 4–5	Carter and Sadat fashion joint strategy
March 21–22	Carter–Begin clash in Washington
May 15	Middle East arms package passes Congress
July	Stalemate in trilateral talks
August 8	Carter announces meeting at Camp David
September 5–19	Camp David summit
Late fall	Snags develop in implementation of Camp David Accords

European Relations

1977	
January 23–February 1	Vice President Mondale visits Europe and Japan
May 7–8	London Economic Summit
December 29	Carter embarks on trip to Poland, Iran, India, Saudi Arabia, and Egypt
1978	
April 7	Neutron bomb production deferred
May 30–31	NATO Council meets in Washington; $60–$80 billion long-term defense program approved
July 16–17	Bonn Economic Summit
October 16	Karol Cardinal Wojtyla elected 264th Pontiff
October 18	U.S. announces decision to produce neutron warhead components

U.S.–Soviet Relations

1978	
June	Carter–Gromyko talks in Washington are unproductive
June 7	Carter speech in Annapolis on cooperation or confrontation
Spring	Cuban deployments in Ethiopia
December 21	Vance–Gromyko talks in Geneva resolve some major issues

The Shah and Iran

1977	
November 15	The Shah of Iran visits the White House
1978	
January 1	Carter meets Shah in Tehran
July 20	Shah requests F-14s
July 29–30	Rioting in 13 Iranian cities
October	Khomeini moves to Paris from Iraq
November	Shah forms military government
December 29	Shah names Bakhtiar Prime Minister

1979		1979		1979		1979		1979	
January 1	U.S.–Chinese relations begin	March 1–5	Carter–Begin talks in Washington	January 4–9	Western Summit in Guadeloupe	February	Carter–Dobrynin talks generate further impetus	January 5	General Robert Huyser arrives in Iran
January 29–31	Deng visits Washington to sign scientific and cultural accords	March 8–14	Carter's Peace Mission to the Middle East; Sadat accepts U.S. compromise; Carter announces main ingredients in Cairo	June 26–27	Economic Summit in Tokyo	April	U.S.–Soviet prisoner exchange negotiated	January 13	Regency Council formed
				December 12	NATO agrees to deploy theater nuclear weapons	June	MX decision by Carter	January 16	Shah leaves Iran
		March 26	Begin and Sadat sign peace treaty in Washington			June 18	Vienna Summit: SALT II signed	February 1	Khomeini arrives in Iran
		August 15	Andrew Young resigns			August	Soviet combat troops reported in Cuba	February 2	Huyser leaves Iran
		August 23–24	U.S. Security Council debate on Palestinian rights, vote delayed			September	Soviet brigade in Cuba becomes public issue	February 12	Bakhtiar resigns; Bazargan becomes Khomeini's Prime Minister
						December 26	Soviet invasion of Afghanistan	February 14	U.S. Embassy seized and held for several hours
		1980		**1980**				April 1	Islamic republic declared; U.S. continues relations with regime
		March 1	U.N. Security Council unanimously condemns Israeli settlements on West Bank	March 4	Helmut Schmidt visits U.S. to discuss TNF				
				May 19	Giscard meets Brezhnev in Warsaw				
				June 16	Carter letter to Schmidt on TNF				
				June 22–23	Venice Economic Summit				

6

"The United States has made up its mind"

You should state that the United States has made up its mind on these issues.

—President Jimmy Carter, instructions to
Zbigniew Brzezinski for his mission to China,
May 17, 1978

Normalization of relations with China was a key strategic goal of the new Administration. We were convinced that a genuinely cooperative relationship between Washington and Beijing would greatly enhance the stability of the Far East and that, more generally, it would be to U.S. advantage in the global competition with the Soviet Union. Moreover, normalization was definitely in China's security interest, especially in view of the increasingly threatening Soviet attitude toward the P.R.C.

However, the Soviet dimension was one of those considerations of which it is sometimes said, "Think of it at all times but speak of it never." I, for one, thought of it a great deal, even though I knew that publicly one had to make pious noises to the effect that U.S.–Chinese normalization had nothing to do with U.S.–Soviet rivalry. Soviet disregard for our concerns, especially through the use of the Cuban proxy in Yemen and Ethiopia around Saudi Arabia, made me feel that we should not be excessively deferential to Soviet sensitivities about U.S.–Chinese collaboration. If we should make no linkage between SALT and Soviet misconduct—as Vance strongly argued—then why should we let the Soviets link (negatively) SALT and better U.S.–Chinese relations? Indeed, such U.S.–Chinese collaboration could be valuable in helping Moscow understand the value of restraint and reciprocity. Accordingly, I gave normalization, and later the expansion of the U.S.–Chinese relationship, a great deal of personal attention, and policy toward China represented one of the key issues over which I had the most direct control.

To emphasize the relevance of the Soviet aspects is not to minimize the long-term historical significance of the new relationship between the United States and China. Thanks to it, America came to enjoy at the same time—and for the first time in many decades—a good relationship with the two most important Far East countries, Japan and China. It meant, more broadly, the resumption of the political, economic, and social ties that had been ruptured in 1949 with the most populous, one of the most ancient, and potentially one of the most powerful countries in the world. There were thus good reasons for normalization, quite separate from the Soviet aspect, and those were the ones we stressed publicly. In the words of the special memorandum for the President on U.S. foreign policy goals, normalization was desirable "because we saw that relationship as a central stabilizing element of our global policy and a keystone for peace."

The timing of normalization, however, was definitely influenced by the Soviet dimension. In our goals memorandum, we set 1979 as the deadline, and we achieved the goal as of January 1, 1979.

An Ambivalent Beginning

After the initial Nixon–Kissinger breakthrough of 1972, the U.S.–Chinese relationship had gradually stagnated. The last talks between Ford and Kissinger and the Chinese leaders, held December 1–6, 1975, did not advance American–Chinese relations, and in some respects even caused a retrogression. The Chinese started charging that the United States "had not made up its mind," and they viewed with apprehension the U.S.–Soviet detente.

In this context, our own policy toward China evolved by fits and starts. In the pre-inaugural "informal" NSC meeting, held to define our immediate priorities, the subject of China did not come up. My attention was absorbed by the U.S.–Soviet relationship and by the need to shape a wider Middle East initiative, while State focused on such peripheral issues as relations with Vietnam (and the painful matter of the MIAs) and the question of a claims settlement with China. But shortly after the inauguration, Vance asked a small team of China specialists in State, working with members of the NSC staff, to produce a study on normalization. Their brief was expressly to argue the case for normalization ". . . in a relatively short period of time, including a full discussion of the problems involved." In early April 1977, a formal memorandum (PRM-24) was undertaken to define our policy toward China, and this coincided with a high-powered congressional delegation which was scheduled to visit China in April. (As a gesture of the President's personal interest, his son Chip Carter was added to the congressional delegation.)

I was at first somewhat ambivalent. While I felt strongly that we should open a dialogue with the Chinese that would stress the strategic aspects of the relationship, especially as they bore on the Soviet Union,

I did not have a clear notion of when to seek normalization as such, and I wondered if we could not promote a strategic connection even without normalization. However, both Vance and I agreed that the President should meet with the head of the Chinese Liaison Mission at an early date, thereby underlining the importance we attached to the link with China and balancing his meeting with Dobrynin. This introductory meeting was scheduled for February 8, and I was very pleased with the way it went. The atmosphere was very jovial, and both Carter and the Chinese representative were much more relaxed than Carter had been with Dobrynin. Carter "handled it extremely well. He did exactly what I was urging him to do; namely, to take the high statesmanlike road, to emphasize certain general propositions, including particularly U.S. resilience on the Soviet–American front, and not get bogged down in detail. He handled it much better than his earlier discussion with Dobrynin. In fact, he covered all the major points which I felt were essential." However, nothing specific was said by either side regarding the modalities or conditions of normalization.

Shortly thereafter, I began to get acquainted with our predecessors' voluminous memoranda of conversations with the Chinese. That review was initiated by my NSC staffer for Chinese affairs, Professor Michel Oksenberg. In the months to come, he was to play a central role in moving the American–Chinese relationship forward, in developing the conceptual framework for it, and in helping me overcome some of the key obstacles. Much of the progress achieved in U.S.–Chinese relations is due to him and to his effective collaboration with his very able State Department colleagues, notably, Richard Holbrooke and Roger Sullivan. When it became clear later in the year, and very much so after 1978, that I was inclined to push for more rapid movement in the U.S.–Chinese relationship than was Secretary Vance, this little cluster of senior officials would often meet in my office and coordinate the needed initiatives directly with me.

The initial review of the memoranda of conversations with the Chinese made it clear to me that the point of departure for any progress would have to be a reaffirmation of Nixon's five points as a "pledge" to the Chinese. Accordingly, I sent a memorandum to the President recommending that he endorse these five points, namely that (1) we would acknowledge the Chinese position that there is one China and that Taiwan is a part of it; (2) we will not support a Taiwan independence movement; (3) as we leave Taiwan, we will ensure that Japanese do not come in to replace us; (4) we will support any peaceful solution to the Taiwan situation; we will not support Taiwan in any military action against the People's Republic of China; and (5) we will seek normalization and try to achieve it. The President agreed. Somewhat to my surprise, Vance, on learning of the President's decision, requested a reconsideration, on the grounds that this step was premature. Though

I did not agree with him, I did not contest his request, and the President ordered that there be no transmittal to the Chinese. I went along with this largely because I thought that with our Middle East initiative generating increasing momentum (as well as domestic controversy), with our efforts to move SALT forward requiring an enormous amount of personal attention and probably before too long also stirring public controversy, and particularly with our ongoing efforts to obtain congressional approval for the Panama Canal Treaties, we simply did not need—nor could we sustain—another foreign policy initiative which was bound to be domestically very controversial.

Thus, after a brief flurry in the weeks after the inaugural, the question of China was, in effect, put in abeyance. Nonetheless, the initial conceptualizing, which later served as the point of departure for the push that was mounted in 1978, was done at this time. In mid-April, Vance wrote a memo to the President giving his views on the issue of normalization. He concluded: ". . . in terms of our strategic position, normalization is highly desirable."

At the same time Vance reported that in his April 11 meeting with the head of the Chinese Liaison Mission, Huang Chen, he had said that he would like to visit China in August, when he could focus on a review of world issues and confine any normalization discussions to generalities or hearing out the Chinese. "But," he wrote, "I am convinced, in light of the considerations I have outlined, that we should do more."

Quite early on, I formulated the proposition that we should view the Sino-American relationship as involving three independent aspects: the bilateral contacts, which should be expanded as much as possible, because of the reciprocal stake of both powers in such expansion; our common strategic interest in discouraging Soviet expansionism, which could be furthered by quiet consultations; and the normalization process, which should be moved forward whenever opportune. I also pressed formulations to the effect that China was central to the maintenance of the global equilibrium and that a strong and secure China was in our interest. In his speech at Notre Dame in May 1977, the President, on my recommendation, referred to China explicitly: "We see the American–Chinese relationship as a central element of our global policy, and China as a key force for global peace. We wish to cooperate closely with the creative Chinese people on the problems that confront all mankind, and we hope to find a formula which can bridge some of the difficulties that still separate us."

Within days, the Chinese responded to the President's signal with a signal of their own. The head of the Chinese Mission in Washington invited me to dinner and I obtained the President's approval to accept. At the same time I sent him a rather detailed memo on how I saw the sequence for improving our bilateral relations. By then we had agreed that Vance would go to China in August, and I also told the President that we should take measures to ensure that his visit would produce some movement toward normalization. I wrote: "Our global posture, including our policies toward Cuba, Vietnam, Korea, Turkey, Iran, and southern Africa, will shape the environment in which the Vance talks take place. If we appear indecisive and yielding, then the Chinese probably will be less flexible on the Taiwan issue because it will seem both less worthwhile and less necessary to be accommodating." I then suggested that we immediately test Chinese receptivity to a visit by Harold Brown in the late spring of 1978, which would enable us to sustain our dialogue in the strategic realm should Vance's trip not produce very much in the diplomatic realm. Further, I pushed for the creation of an ad hoc committee chaired by Frank Press (Carter's science and technology adviser) and myself to recommend the advisability of granting four out of thirty pending export licenses. After sending the memo, I noted in my journal that it pointed to a more active policy on China. "I hope this will help also to maintain a balanced approach toward the Soviet Union. On a recent message from the Soviets to the President, a so-called note verbale in which the Soviets in a polite fashion reiterated their firm position, the President indicated that our deteriorating relationship with the Soviets is his principal worry. Perhaps if the Soviets worry a little more about our policy toward China, we will have less cause to worry about our relations with the Soviets."

The President returned my memo full of marginal notes, generally favorable. At the same time, he told me that we should be careful how we went about normalization and that we "should not ass-kiss them the way Nixon and Kissinger did, and also be careful not to antagonize domestic constituencies."

This concern over the likely domestic consequences of normalization caused us to vacillate over the next several weeks. Though it had been decided in late spring that Vance would go to Beijing for talks with the Chinese leaders, it was not yet clear whether that visit would be designed to reestablish contact after the last, and somewhat less than successful, Kissinger visit to Beijing, or whether Vance was to push hard for normalization. Toward the end of June, Vance chaired a PRC meeting to consider PRM-24 on China, and "I came out strongly for a commitment to normalization when Cy goes to China, as well as collateral measures deemphasizing our links with Taiwan and parallel actions designed to convey to the Chinese that we take very seriously our political and strategic relationship." However, at the meeting I was relatively isolated, with most participants feeling that we could not move that rapidly.

Still, I continued to raise the issue with the President himself, using the morning national security briefings as opportunities for stressing the importance of the China connection. In early July, the President was scheduled to meet with the newly designated head of the U.S. Liaison

Mission in Beijing, Leonard Woodcock, and I urged the President to stress to Woodcock "that our policy will move along two tracks: the first is normalization of relations, which will inevitably take a long time; and the second is the parallel deepening of the relationship with China on the political plane through consultations, exchange of information, and so forth, and also through collateral measures, designed to somewhat reduce our relationship with Taiwan and thereby convey to the Chinese our seriousness about normalization." This, I hoped, would lead to some movement in the relationship.

The President was taken by this argument and then moved ahead of me. On July 30, in preparation for Vance's trip, the President convened a meeting which was attended by Vance, Brown, Holbrooke, Oksenberg, and me. The President decided quite abruptly to go for normalization. I was pleased but also worried. The President "told Vance to go directly to the issues and to move as rapidly as is possible. He said his entire political experience has been that it does not pay to prolong or postpone difficult issues. My only concern with the discussion was that it was too heavily focused on how to handle the consequences of normalization in regard to domestic public opinion issues and in regard to Taiwan, and not enough on what happens if Cy Vance's trip does not result in normalization and in fact produces very little progress. In my own judgment, the latter now seems somewhat more probable. Accordingly, we ought to put more emphasis on the preparation of alternative arrangements, including more political and economic connections, but short of normalization." I was concerned since we had not made the basic commitment, especially in regard to the five points previously conceded by Nixon. I anticipated, therefore, that the Chinese might be somewhat less than forthcoming.

Vance left for Beijing the third week of August (and barely two weeks after an exhausting trip by him to the Middle East) with a U.S. position that was somewhat ambivalent. He was authorized to indicate our interest in normalization (and he even had a draft normalization agreement in his pocket), but he was not in a position to cross the Rubicon insofar as U.S. relations with Taiwan were concerned. Moreover, the President, warned by Mondale, started developing second thoughts on how hard we should push for normalization, and on August 22, "when I submitted to him a proposed cable to Vance, who is now in Peking, instructing him to take advantage of any opportunity that develops to normalize relations with China, he pulled back, saying that after talking to Mondale he feels that perhaps it would be asking the Senate too much to handle this and Panama all at once. Accordingly, he again tends to feel that perhaps a somewhat slower, more deliberate pace, still pointing toward normalization, is desirable."

Vance's mission did reestablish the U.S.–Chinese dialogue, but it also generated a faint sense of disappointment on both sides. The Chinese let it be known that they felt the Carter Administration was retreating from previous U.S.–Chinese understandings, while we felt that the Chinese were not sufficiently flexible and that their negative press briefings on the Vance mission were not helpful. In an interview in September with a prestigious Associated Press delegation including Kay Graham of the Washington *Post* and Arthur Sulzberger of the New York *Times*, Deng Xiaoping in fact said that efforts to normalize relations had suffered a setback during Vance's visit.

The U.S.–Chinese relationship was thus once again put on the back burner. Panama was our central domestic foreign policy preoccupation, while the negotiations with the Soviets and the problems with Begin preoccupied us externally. The subject, along with all other issues of concern to the United States and the Soviet Union, did, however, come up in the meeting between Carter and Gromyko on September 23. In his opening remarks, the President said it was our hope that we could normalize relations with China without aligning ourselves with it against the Soviet Union. As part of his response, Gromyko said that it would be a mistake if some sort of "dirty game" were played here in terms of collusion, covert or overt, against the interests of the Soviet Union. Sooner or later this would become known in any event and would have consequences that could only damage Soviet–U.S. relations. He expressed the hope of the Soviet leadership that the United States was not thinking of playing a "China card" to the detriment of the Soviet Union. The Soviet Union had been assured of this by the previous Administration and hoped that this one would do likewise. In fact, we were not seeking merely a tactical relationship with China. The term "playing the China card" was never used by us, but it quickly became the popular phrase of Washington columnists, who insisted on placing any U.S. initiative on China in the larger Soviet context.

I returned to the China issue in mid-October, by holding a review session in my office with Holbrooke of State and Oksenberg of my staff. As I noted on October 12: "I would like to initiate some further movement though it does seem to me that it has to focus more on a politically consultative relationship and less on normalization." With Vance preoccupied with other foreign policy issues, Holbrooke and his State Department colleagues looked increasingly to the White House for leadership.

Who Goes to China?

In early November, the departing head of the Chinese Liaison Mission was entertained at lunch in the Roosevelt Room of the White House by Vice President Mondale. During that lunch our Chinese guests rather pointedly invited me to visit China (an invitation I had quietly encouraged through Mike Oksenberg), repeating this offer in front of the press. I replied that I would be happy to consider such an invitation, a response which provoked a prolonged struggle with State over whether I should make the trip. "Immediately after the lunch there were calls from Holbrooke and Habib, who had been present, to Oksenberg to raise questions about this; and Cy Vance phoned me in considerable agitation, arguing that this will undercut our negotiating efforts with the Chinese. I was quite irritated. . . . I pointed out that the Chinese had invited me in a casual fashion and what was called for was an equally casual but friendly and positive response without any commitment to a date. He finally agreed to some wording about my being delighted and willing to come at some point."

The invitation gave me the needed opening to push more energetically. I pressed within the bureaucracy for the expansion of bilateral relations through enhanced scientific contacts and also through a more favorable attitude toward the transfer of militarily sensitive technology to China. Brown, by and large, helped me on this, and by early February 1978, despite objections from Vance, an interagency system was devised for a more positive handling of Chinese requests. On my own authority, I also arranged for the Chinese to obtain a NATO briefing on the global strategic problem, thereby initiating a tacit security relationship with them. At the same time, I started holding regular consultative meetings with the acting head of the Chinese Liaison Mission, Ambassador Han Hsu, an engaging and good-looking diplomat, whose appearance reminded me of Zhou Enlai. Han Hsu and I developed a warm personal relationship, and our conversations grew increasingly candid and far-ranging. I came both to trust him and to like him. I would brief him on our foreign policy initiatives, and then I would ask him questions regarding Chinese policy. At first, the responses were rather stereotyped and uninformative, but after a while Han Hsu began to reciprocate in some detail and with much benefit regarding Chinese views and initiatives on the international scene.

Meanwhile, I made a sustained effort to obtain Presidential approval for my trip to China. To succeed, I had to overcome strong resistance by State. That resistance, I suspect, was partially institutional: the State Department is probably more "turf-conscious" than any other agency in Washington; and the Secretary of State was, I imagine, concerned about the political symbolism of a mission to China undertaken by the President's Assistant for National Security Affairs. In addition, I felt the difficulty was perhaps also due to the growing disagreement between Vance and me over U.S.–Soviet relations. For Vance, a successful conclusion to the SALT talks was the overriding priority. But although I shared the Secretary's concern, I had by then become quite preoccupied with Moscow's misuse of detente to improve the Soviet geopolitical and strategic position around Saudi Arabia, especially through the Cuban military presence in Ethiopia. I believed that a strategic response was necessary.

To overcome State's resistance, I had to fashion an alliance, and I eventually obtained the support of both Mondale and Brown.. I also made the case that my reputation as the more "hard-nosed" member of the foreign policy team would be helpful in generating greater understanding with the Chinese, and hence it was appropriate that I make the trip. In early February, I started to press the President to approve the Chinese invitation. One snowy day, when "there wasn't much to brief" the President about, "I took advantage of the occasion to tell him that I think it would be useful in order to redress the imbalance against the Far East [in our foreign policy] if I were to visit the Far East at some point, including on the itinerary Japan, South Korea, and China. The purpose of the visit would be consultative, not to negotiate; but I pointed out that the State Department, including Cy, is against it, and he ought to decide on his own whether this would be a useful thing for me to do or not. I also added that strategically maintaining a better relationship with China at this time would make sense. The President answered quite flatly that he felt I should go and he said it twice."

Much to my distress, however, that was not the end of it. A few days later the President casually mentioned the possibility of my going to Japan and China to Vance and Holbrooke, in the course of a meeting with our Ambassador to Japan, former Senator Mike Mansfield. I sensed that both Vance and Holbrooke were taken aback, and shortly thereafter Leonard Woodcock, who was visiting Washington from Beijing, told the President, I suspect with some outside inspiration, that a visit by me to China might not be timely. In the course of the next several weeks, I kept bringing up the issue with the President, and on February 27 I submitted a memo to him entitled "Trip to the Far East." The memo started by saying: "A couple of weeks ago you said that you felt that a consultative visit by me to China would be useful; you mentioned this also to Mansfield in Cy's presence; and this morning the matter was brought up by Harold. Considering the importance of the U.S. maintaining a better relationship with both China and the U.S.S.R. than either of them has with each other, and bearing in mind developments in the Horn and the related need to send a sensitive signal to the Soviets, the time is ripe for a decision on this subject." The memo went on to say once again that "the meeting would be deliberately labeled as consultative." The President was asked to approve or to disapprove. He responded in the margin: "I'll probably decide this week."

Vance made no bones about his opposition to my trip. At the end of February he told me explicitly that "he was strongly against it. His argument is that someone that close to the President as I should not now go to China because it will imply too much about possible normalization." I prevailed on Mondale to talk to the President. Very early in March, Fritz came to my office and yanked me out of a meeting with newspapermen "to tell me, with both of us standing in the hall, the President's reaction. Fritz seemed rather surprised as he recounted the fact that he talked to the President, but the President gave him a rather cold, staring look and simply didn't respond at all. I have the feeling that the President is getting tired of the issue, doesn't want to make a decision on it, and resents being bugged either by me or by Fritz. Fritz was rather abashed and didn't know what to make of it. However, I must say that I rather admired his determination because he told me that on Monday he would try again during lunchtime." I decided then to take the issue directly to the President again. After talking with Brown, who agreed to send a supporting memo to the President, and who backed me very forcefully, I spoke with the President on March 12. "Carter responded by saying that he has been thinking about this, that he hasn't forgotten it, that he is inclined toward sending a mission to China, but he is sensitive to Vance's concerns. As he put it, 'I don't want to be seen as jumping all over Cy, given the fact that he has such strong feelings on the subject. I will talk to him and then try to make a decision on that basis.' "

The issue came to a head because of a move by Vance. In mid-March he told me, with evident satisfaction, that he had discussed with the President the question of a mission to China and that he had obtained the President's approval for Fritz Mondale to visit China as part of his already scheduled trip to the Far East. I was taken aback, and the very next day, after the morning national security briefing, I told the President that if Mondale went, it would generate expectations that we were on the verge of normalizing relations; in contrast, the Chinese had invited me months ago, and a visit by me could be a relatively low-key consultative trip. The President looked at me, smiled rather cheerfully, and said, "Don't talk to the Vice President about this." I said, "Fine, I won't." And as I was leaving he looked up again and said, "Don't talk to him. I'll decide and let you know." Within moments, his private secretary, Susan Clough, walked into my office and handed me an envelope addressed to Secretary Vance. It was sealed with the President's initials written across the flap on the back so that it would have to be opened by Cy himself. A copy was also handed to me, and it said: "To the Vice President, to the Secretary of State: I have decided it would be best for Zbig to go to China."

About an hour later the President phoned me, and I took advantage of his call to ask whether I could now talk about the China trip with the Vice President. He said, "Yes, that's fine," and added, chuckling, "Well, you know Cy phoned me up earlier this morning to tell me that he had arranged everything and that Fritz was going instead of you." I had the feeling that by then he was enjoying both the fact that he had put the issue behind him and the way it had been decided.

I knew that I had badgered the President enormously, but I felt that I was right in doing so. My own talks with the Chinese convinced me that I was the top official in the Carter Administration in whom they had genuine confidence and whose strategic perspectives to some extent they shared. Accordingly, I truly believed that a trip by me would be helpful in giving a new impulse to the stagnating relationship, and that this in turn could pave the way for normalization. In pestering the President, I knew that I had expended some of my own personal capital, but I felt that the rewards of a breakthrough on China would more than compensate for this. His own decision, I have no doubt, was very much influenced by the fact that both Mondale and Brown backed me. Brown did so for solid and well-argued strategic reasons; Mondale largely because he sensed the Administration needed a foreign policy success. Without their support, I doubt that Vance's opposition would have been overridden.

I started planning for the trip immediately after the President's decision, convening a meeting of top State, Defense, and NSC officials dealing with China. Gradually, the trip began to acquire greater strategic significance and more ambitious political goals. Vance and I agreed that we would not announce it publicly until after his return from a scheduled trip to Moscow for a further round of SALT negotiations, though I was subsequently very irritated to learn that when the public announcement was made, the State Department—on its own initiative, and without clearing it with the White House—deliberately gave the Soviet Embassy in Washington advance word.

In the meantime, Vance, Brown, and I reviewed (on April 10) what I might accomplish. "The predisposition is now to move toward normalization but not until after the [congressional] elections. During my trip I will explore the possibility of some progress on normalization even though that is not to be the major thrust of the visit. However, I fear that with the recent indecision on the neutron bomb [see Chapter 8] my visit to Peking will not be quite as felicitous as it might have otherwise been. We will have to develop some initiatives in the arms or security area to fortify the President's image," I noted. Accordingly, I pushed the President for more liberal treatment of China on technology transfer, pointing toward preferential treatment over the Soviet Union, and in my conversations with the Chinese I made it a point to brief them as fully as I could on our SALT negotiations with the Soviets. I also decided to include in my delegation a representative from the Defense Department, Deputy Assistant Secretary Morton Abramowitz, so that he could brief the Chinese on the strategic situation.

The President's own thinking on the subject was evolving in a similar direction. Toward the end of April, he told me "that he would like to make the trip to China meaningful and that he would like to push the process of improving relations forward." Two days later, he again brought up the subject and told me that he wanted the trip to be a serious and substantive occasion and that I should schedule a longish private conversation with him on the subject. In turn, in a memorandum, I raised with him the question whether he preferred to have SALT ratification first and then China normalization, or the other way around. I tended to favor the latter, but the President was noncommittal.

Preparations for my trip were completed in the first two weeks of May. In various meetings Brown pushed aggressively for a mandate for me to engage the Chinese in broad talks and to move forward on normalization. Vance was more reticent, but the President became increasingly persuaded that I should address myself directly to the question of normalization. On the morning of May 12, "I talked to the President about our China policy. He said that he would like to move rapidly, and I should tell the Chinese so. He says he doesn't want to play games behind Cy's back, but he would prefer to tell this to me directly. And if I find the opportunity to move, I should move. At the same time, they have to meet our two basic conditions: no contradiction to our public statement that we trust there will be a peaceful resolution of the Taiwan problem, and our ability to continue military sales to Taiwan."

I was thus empowered to address myself to the question of normalization, in addition to engaging the Chinese in a broad political-strategic review of the global situation. With that in mind, with Mike Oksenberg's help I drafted for myself the President's instructions, which he revised and signed. Dated May 17, and five single-spaced pages long, they dealt with two main issues: the strategic relationship with China and the question of normalization. With respect to the first, I was instructed to tell the Chinese that "we see our relations with China as a central facet of U.S. global policy. The United States and China share certain common interests and we have parallel, long-term strategic concerns. The most important of these is our common opposition to global or regional hegemony by any single power. This is why your visit is not tactical; it is an expression of our strategic interest in a cooperative relationship with China, an interest that is both fundamental and enduring." The President's letter went on to instruct me to stress to the Chinese how determined we were to respond assertively to the Soviet military buildup and to Soviet proxy expansionism around the world. I was to brief the Chinese in detail on our efforts to enhance our defense capability and to strengthen NATO, and I was also to encourage them to be helpful in regard to those regional conflicts where they had a positive contribution to make. We hoped to get them to agree "to provide aid to Somalia, to encourage a peaceful evolution in southern Africa, to initiate contacts with Israel, to improve relations with India, to facilitate the emergence of an independent Cambodian government that enjoys the support of its people, and to promote stability in the Korean peninsula."

The President's instructions to me on the normalization process were historically important: "You should state that the United States has made up its mind" and that it is prepared to move forward with active negotiations to remove the various obstacles to normalization. I was also instructed that I "might indicate informally to the Chinese that the United States is planning to further reduce its military presence in Taiwan this year, to widen the opportunities for the commercial flow of technology to China, to increase direct contacts on a regular and perhaps scheduled basis for our mutual advantage, and to invite Chinese trade and military delegations to visit the United States. These planned steps reflect our seriousness in moving forward with the process of normalization."

Most significantly, I was empowered to tell the Chinese that the United States accepted the three basic Chinese conditions (we deliberately called them "points") regarding normalization; namely, that we would terminate relations with Taiwan, withdraw all U.S. military personnel and installations from Taiwan, and abrogate the U.S.–Taiwan Security Treaty. The President also authorized me to reaffirm the five points previously made by Nixon and Ford, the very five points which in early 1977 I had urged him to reaffirm, which, after some discussion with State, he declined to do, on the grounds that the move was premature. The President and all his advisers agreed that accepting these points need not prevent us from insisting that the resolution of the Taiwan question should be a peaceful one and that the United States would reserve for itself the right to provide arms to Taiwan, as it saw fit. I was to reaffirm to the Chinese our insistence on these conditions and to probe for some formula acceptable to both sides. (With President Carter's permission, these instructions are reproduced in full in Annex I.)

I was thus given a broad and important mandate. The words "The United States has made up its mind" were meant to convey our determination in response to an accusation that the Chinese had previously voiced. From a consultative, low-key mission, the trip thus was transformed into a genuinely major undertaking. As a personal touch, I prevailed on the President to prepare a handwritten note to Chairman Hua, which I would hand him, together with a piece of the moon brought back by U.S. astronauts. The President wrote out in his own hand: "To Chairman Hua—A piece of the moon for you and the people of China—symbolic of our joint quest for a better future—Jimmy Carter."

As I was about to leave for China, I learned that Vance had proposed to the President that Gromyko be invited to visit the White House at the same time as I was to be in Beijing. I strongly objected both to the President and to Cy, pointing out that not only would the Chinese take this badly but it would be interpreted domestically as further evidence of a major split within the Administration. Fortunately, this argument prevailed and Gromyko's visit was postponed until my return. Also, "before leaving, I took the necessary steps to make sure that American planes provide support to the French airdrop to Zaire. This was not only an important step showing our determination, but will convey a useful lesson to the Chinese," I wrote in my journal on May 20. We in fact took this action in response to major unrest in Zaire, apparently fomented with some Angolan and probably Cuban assistance.

The Confidential Commitment in Beijing

I arrived in Beijing on May 20 at midday. I was accompanied by a party of ten, including my wife. In order to engage the Chinese in the kind of broader relationship that I wanted to promote, four members of my party were ready to give the Chinese extensive briefings: Samuel Huntington of the NSC, on strategic issues arising out of our assessment of the U.S.–Soviet balance; Mort Abramowitz of the Defense Department, on overall military intelligence and also on a proposal for an exchange of visits by military delegations; Richard Holbrooke of State, on the expansion of cultural and economic cooperation; and Ben Huberman, who worked on Frank Press's staff as well as the NSC, on the expansion of scientific cooperation, including a possible visit to China by Dr. Press, the President's adviser for science and technology. My closest adviser on Chinese affairs, Michel Oksenberg, worked directly with me on the overall presentation that I was to make on U.S. foreign policy as a preliminary to the more pointed discussions that I was to have with the Chinese leaders.

The experience was a profoundly moving one. I could not help but think of the strange coincidence that the Sino-American relationship was being forged in the course of a single decade by two U.S. officials who were of immigrant birth and who approached this task with relatively little knowledge of or special sentiment for China, but with larger strategic concerns in mind. The opening of China in 1972 had been a bold stroke, of the greatest geopolitical significance, and I was determined to succeed in transforming that still-tenuous relationship into something more enduring and much more extensive.

I was given a formal but very cordial greeting at the airport by Foreign Minister Huang Hua, his wife, and a host of Chinese officials. While on board the plane we had speculated about what kind of greeting I would receive from the very protocol-conscious Chinese, and this greeting by the Foreign Minister himself was a signal that the Chinese had decided to treat the visit on the same level as one by the Secretary of State. After the usual ceremonies, we were driven to an official residence in a luxurious Chinese-made car, very reminiscent of a Rolls-Royce, through the enormously wide and open streets of Beijing, lined with bicyclists and dusty sidewalks.

We were put up in a government guest house, in an isolated compound, surrounded by trees and lawns, though close to a busy street with rather drab and dull apartment houses. We were not given too much time to relax, and after a quick but delightful Chinese meal, we set off for the Great Hall of the People, where we had our first official meeting with the Chinese Foreign Minister and our various counterparts. The building, which dominates the main square in Beijing, is an enormous structure, with cavernous rooms, and its architecture presumably is meant to symbolize the style and the power of the new rulers. It struck me as an architectural hybrid, combining some of the worst features of Stalin's and Mussolini's contributions to monumental architecture.

That evening, the Foreign Minister gave an official dinner in my honor, with an exchange of toasts—ours was carefully crafted to signal the seriousness of our intentions.

Sunday morning began with a visit to the Mao mausoleum. I was not impressed to see that the cultured Chinese had adopted the Russian practice of embalming and displaying their revolutionary leader, an incongruous custom for allegedly scientific materialists. The rest of the morning was spent in further exchanges with the Chinese Foreign Minister, who presented the Chinese position on foreign policy issues. In the afternoon, I was taken on a visit to the Forbidden City. This remarkable complex of palaces and artifacts drives home the degree to which China, more than any other nation in the world, has been a civilization unto itself, quite apart and distinctive. Then I had my first session with Vice-Premier Deng, and the evening was also spent with him, at an informal dinner exquisitely served in Fang Shan restaurant, overlooking a small lake in Peihai Park in the middle of Beijing. Following that, we attended the Beijing Opera, where, apparently in a departure from recent practice for foreign guests, a relatively traditional Chinese opera was staged.

Monday continued with an equally full schedule. I first went on a tourist visit to the Great Wall. While climbing its steep incline with my aides, I said that whoever reached the top second would be sent off to Ethiopia to confront the Cubans. This remark was picked up by someone in the press and reported as a challenge from me to the Chinese. Later on, Jim Klurfeld of *Newsday* even wrote that I issued that challenge to Deng personally, something which my critics then seized upon with glee. Monday afternoon I met with Chairman Hua Guofeng, and in the evening I finally reciprocated the hospitality of my hosts with a banquet. Much to the surprise of the Chinese, my wife insisted also on making a toast, and the Chinese Foreign Minister was visibly mortified when I asked for his advice. However, his wife rather firmly endorsed my wife's intention, which sealed the matter.

Tourism and banqueting soon gave way to substantive talks. On the first day, I had been deliberately lengthy and comprehensive in my opening statement summarizing U.S. foreign policies. My presentation to the Chinese Foreign Minister, which came before the Chinese one, took three and a half hours with the translation. I knew the record would be studied before I met with Vice-Premier Deng or Chairman Hua, and this gave me an opportunity to spell out fully what the United States stood for and what the Carter Administration was trying to do. I was aware that the Chinese felt that our Administration was soft on the Soviet Union, and I therefore stressed our common strategic ends and Carter's efforts to strengthen NATO and to revitalize American defenses. At the same time, I decided not to say anything too specific about normalization because I knew that the Foreign Minister did not have a great deal of flexibility on the subject. It would be better to tackle the matter with the top leaders privately, once we had established some consensus on strategic issues.

I opened by saying: "I have come to the People's Republic of China because President Carter and I believe that the United States and China share certain common fundamental interests and have similar long-term strategic concerns. The most important of these is our position on global and regional hegemony. Thus, our interest in relations with the People's Republic of China is not tactical in nature but it is based on certain long-term and strategic objectives. . . . We have been allies before. We should cooperate again in the face of a common threat. For one of the central features of our era—a feature which causes us to draw together —is the emergence of the Soviet Union as a global power." I went on to summarize Soviet strategy as involving an attempt to achieve strategic superiority, to gain political preponderance in Western Europe, to radicalize the Middle East, to destabilize southern Asia, to penetrate the Indian Ocean region, and to encircle China.

With respect to normalization, I simply acknowledged that "the Shanghai communiqué is the starting point for our relationship. President Carter reconfirms the five basic principles enunciated by the two previous U.S. Administrations. In our view, there is only one China. The President believes that China plays a central role in the maintenance of the global equilibrium. The President believes a strong and independent China is a force for peace in our pluralistic world."

In the course of this presentation, I also made a number of concrete proposals. Aware of frequent Chinese criticisms that the United States was not doing enough to counter "Soviet hegemonism," I deliberately made suggestions for Chinese initiatives, knowing that my opening statement would be distributed within a limited but influential circle of top Chinese leaders. In so doing, I hoped also to counter the image of the Carter Administration as being soft vis-à-vis the Soviet Union. I proposed that we exchange Cabinet-level visits as well as trade delegations and military missions; I told of our plans for troop reduction on Taiwan, though I reserved for the United States the right to sell arms to Taiwan; I urged the Chinese to tone down their anti-U.S. propaganda portraying America as both hegemonistic and weak, arguing that this simply played into Soviet hands; I urged the Chinese to be supportive of our efforts to promote peace in the Middle East, notably to endorse Sadat's initiatives; I also urged them to develop a quiet channel of communication with Israel, pointing out Israel's important security role in stemming Soviet power in that part of the world. I promised Huang Hua that "we shall use our good offices to see whether some relations between Saudi Arabia and your own country may not prove to be in their and your interest." I discussed the possibility of aid to some of our friends in Africa, especially those who would be in a position to increase the costs of the Soviet–Cuban military involvement; I indicated our willingness to modify COCOM procedures in order to facilitate the transfer of advanced technology to China, and I predicted a positive decision on the export of an infrared scanning system to be used in resource exploration by the P.R.C. Finally, I discussed the need to cooperate more closely on such matters as Afghanistan, aid to Pakistan, and assistance to Southeast Asian efforts to check Soviet support of Vietnamese expansionism.

Foreign Minister Huang responded the next day, also with a lengthy presentation. It was a long blast at the Soviets, laced with comments about alleged U.S. softness and naïveté about SALT. But its basic thrust was positive. It indicated that the Chinese no longer held the position that both the United States and the Soviet Union were threats to peace, and acknowledged that collaboration between the United States and China was mutually necessary.

The real negotiations and the truly significant exchanges took place primarily in meetings with Vice-Premier Deng Xiaoping and with Premier Hua Guofeng. I met with Deng in the Great Hall of the People on May 21, from 4:05 to 6:30 p.m. Shortly after the meeting, he took me, as I have mentioned, to a restaurant, where we continued our discussions, in a more informal setting, into the later evening. A man tiny in size, but great in his boldness, Deng immediately appealed to me. Bright, alert, and shrewd, he was quick on the uptake, with a good sense of humor, tough, and very direct. After talking to him, I realized better why he had survived all the vicissitudes of his political career, but even more importantly, I was impressed by his sense of purpose and drive. Here was a political leader who knew what he wanted and with whom one could deal.

At the meeting with the Foreign Minister the two delegations had sat across from each other along a long table, but at this one Deng and I sat next to each other in deep armchairs, with Deng to my left and with Deng's inevitable spittoon to his left (which reassured me, in case he missed), and I was accompanied only by Mike Oksenberg, who spoke Chinese and took detailed notes, and by Ambassador Leonard Woodcock. Other members of the delegation accepted this restriction, except for Holbrooke, who made a great issue of personal privilege out of his exclusion. However, I was bound by the President's clear instructions to keep the meeting small and confidential, and the Ambassador obviously had precedence.

The meeting opened with Deng's solicitous observation, "You must be tired," to which I responded, "I am exhilarated," which accurately expressed my mood. After some additional polite preliminaries, Deng got to the point: "The Chinese side speaks straightforwardly about their views and ideas. Chairman Mao Zedong was a soldier. Zhou Enlai was also a soldier, and I, too." I answered, "Soldiers speak very directly, but Americans have a reputation for speaking directly, too. I hope you do not find Americans difficult to understand or America difficult to understand." I then plunged into the subject which I had previously skirted in my conversations with the Foreign Minister; namely, normalization. I said to Deng that the President had asked me to tell him that "we are prepared to talk seriously not only about the international situation, not only about ways in which parallel actions by us might help to promote the same objectives or to repel the same danger, but also to begin talking more actively about our more immediate relationship."

Deng played the skeptic. He noted, "The question remains now to make up one's mind. If President Carter has made up his mind on this issue, I think it will be easier to solve this problem." Then he added, "What do you think should be done in order to realize the normalization?" In my response, I tried to give Deng a sense of our commitment but also of the difficulties that we confronted at home, particularly on the Taiwan issue. I spoke at some length.

> I can also say, speaking privately and in the confidence of this small group, that the President personally is prepared to resolve this question as rapidly as it proves practical. We have no intention of artificially delaying it. . . . The President therefore is prepared to undertake the political responsibility at home of resolving the outstanding issues between us. He recognizes that this is our responsibility and not a problem of yours. In our relationships we will remain guided by the Shanghai communiqué, by the principle that there is only one China, and that the resolution of the issue of Taiwan is your problem.
>
> However, at the same time we have certain domestic problems and certain historical legacies which we will have to overcome. These are complex, difficult, and in some respects very emotional issues. That is why we will have to find some formula which

allows us to express our hope and our expectation regarding the peaceful resolution of the Taiwan issue, though we recognize that this is your own domestic affair and that we do so in the spirit of the Shanghai communiqué.

In general, we think it is important that the United States be known as trustworthy and that the American presence in the Far East, though we are now continuing and accelerating our military withdrawal from Taiwan, continue in such a manner as not to create destabilizing conditions likely to be exploited by our mutual adversary. This consideration must be borne in mind when resolving the issue of normalization and when defining the full range of relations during the historically transitional period of our relationship with the people on Taiwan.

Throughout, I tried to make our exchange a genuine conversation between friends, and I spoke extemporaneously, interweaving global, strategic, and bilateral issues, edging up to the question of normalization in order to probe for Chinese flexibility, and then returning to the safer global context. In so doing, I made it plain to Deng that our security commitment to Taiwan would continue even after normalization, during the "historically transitional era" (a deliberately vague phrase that I used to describe Taiwan's continued separate status, prior to some eventual reunification).

After some further exchanges I went on to add, "I was instructed to confirm to you the U.S. acceptance of the three basic Chinese points and to reaffirm once again the five points that were made to you by the previous U.S. Administration. I would like to repeat again the phrase that I have used several times since coming to Peking; namely, that the United States has made up its mind on this issue."

I then went on to propose that the two sides begin highly confidential negotiations the following month regarding normalization. Deng immediately accepted the proposal on behalf of China, though he could not resist making a final dig: "I think that is all on this question. We look forward to the day when President Carter makes up his mind. Let's shift the subject." I shot back, "I have told you before, President Carter has made up his mind."

We then returned to a review of the international situation, and Deng reaffirmed with a broad-brush review the points made the day before by his Foreign Minister. He stressed China's interest in obtaining greater access to American technology, though he expressed concern that the United States was not likely to be cooperative. "Perhaps I think you have a fear of offending the Soviet Union. Is that right?" I was somewhat irritated and responded, "I can assure you that my inclination to be fearful of offending the Soviet Union is rather limited. . . . As far as being afraid to offend the Soviet Union, I would be willing to make a little bet with you as to who is less popular in the Soviet Union—you or me." Deng muttered, "It is hard to say. . . ." This gave me the opportunity to raise with him the point that "I honestly do not think it is useful for you to criticize us frequently as appeasing the Soviets; even though your subjective motivations may be good, the objective consequences of that strengthen the Soviets." Deng did not contest me, and, as I reported later to the President, after May 23 no such allegations appeared in the Chinese press.

We went on to review the strategic relationship, with Deng pressing hard the disadvantages of SALT to the United States. I made the point that it was designed to obtain strategic stability, and was being coupled with renewed defense efforts. Deng was not persuaded: "To be candid with you, whenever you are about to conclude an agreement with the Soviet Union, it is the product of concession on the U.S. side to please the Soviet Union." I felt this was the time for a little dig of our own, and I responded by saying, "We are not naïve in dealing with the Soviet Union. For the last thirty years, it has been the United States which has opposed Soviet hegemonic designs, and that is roughly twice as long as you have been doing it, so we have a little bit of experience in this."

It would be wrong to conclude from this summary that the exchanges were acerbic or polemical. They did involve sparring, but the general thrust was positive, and Deng's comments regarding normalization were not as rigid as those of the Foreign Minister. While he conceded nothing in substance, both Woodcock and I felt that there might be some flexibility, especially since Deng chose not to rebut some of my remarks regarding the United States and Taiwan. We continued our discussion into the evening, though our conversation tended to be much more personal. As we talked about our respective families, Deng piled my plate with endless exotic dishes, we exchanged numerous toasts, and Deng made some veiled allusions to his interest in eventually visiting the United States. He also made a mysterious comment to the effect that he had only about three years left as top leader, and as he did that, he seemed to be emphasizing some sense of urgency regarding progress in American–Chinese relations. I told him that I hoped to be able to reciprocate for the dinner with one of my own in my house in Washington. Deng smilingly accepted.

The next day I met with Hua Guofeng, in the same setting, from 5:05 to 7:25 p.m. In contrast to Deng's sense of urgency, Hua seemed less inclined to hint at the need for rapid movement. While Deng appeared blunt and forthright, Hua seemed more gentle and indirect. Hua had the bearing that the Chinese Emperor is supposed to possess. In the West, these qualities are sometimes judged as somewhat effeminate—soft-spokenness, delicate mannerisms, relaxation and gracefulness in personal movement, which suggest an inner serenity of mind.

Yet, at the same time, he was self-assured and presented a masterful overview of the global situation without recourse to a single note, quoting at times verbatim from my earlier remarks to Deng and Huang.

The conversations opened with some small talk about my visit to the Great Wall:

HUA: There is a poem by Chairman Mao entitled "Mount Liupan" in which there are two lines about the Great Wall: "Those who fail to reach the Great Wall are no men of valor."

BRZEZINSKI: "Mount Liupan"—is this the poem "The sky is high, the clouds are pale . . ." ?

HUA: Yes. I have heard that Dr. Brzezinski got to the peak of that section of the Great Wall.

BRZEZINSKI: Yes, it was a challenge which we overcame quickly.

HUA: Are you used to the Chinese food here?

BRZEZINSKI: The cuisine here, quite seriously, is one of the best, perhaps the best in the world. If I stayed in China longer and ate that well, I would have to volunteer for the May 7 school.

HUA: Some Chinese comrades going to the May 7 school have even put on more weight after much exercise.

BRZEZINSKI (ironically): That was muscles.

Hua then delivered a long statement of the Chinese world view, stressing the need to prepare for war so that one is not at a disadvantage if it breaks out and the urgency of upsetting the strategic deployment of Soviet aggression, and proposing that we should call the attention of the world's people to the danger of Soviet aggression. Hua told me that the Soviets "hurriedly sent back [Ambassador] Illichev to Beijing for a few days because they knew that Dr. Brzezinski was coming to China." Referring to the negotiations for the Treaty of Peace and Friendship between China and Japan, Hua noted that the Japanese were hesitant about "the inclusion of the anti-hegemony clause in the treaty."

I responded by saying, "The position of the United States is that close friendship between Japan and China is complementary and reinforcing to the close friendship between the United States and Japan. The Premier mentioned Soviet fears of Japan's signing the anti-hegemony clause. I completely agree with you that if the Soviet Union had no hegemonic aspirations, it should have no reason to object to an anti-hegemony clause." I then went on to promise that I would speak to Prime Minister Fukuda about this matter. I stressed that "we feel that our relationship with China is of historic significance. It is an enduring relationship. It has long-term strategic importance. It is not only a tactical anti-Soviet expedient. . . . We wish to have a relationship of ever-closer friendship and cooperation with China because you are a major, vital force in world affairs, whether the Soviet Union is peaceful or aggressive, friendly or hostile to the United States." Hua agreed with that and said that he had told Kissinger that "you should not, the United States should not go to Moscow on the shoulder of China."

Regarding Taiwan, I said, "There will thus be a historically transitional era in the course of which certain relationships between the United States and the people on Taiwan in some form will continue." I then referred to the fact that Hua had used the phrase "If President Carter has made up his mind," and I said, "The word 'if' is inappropriate in view of the fact that in the course of the past two or three days I have already said three or four times that President Carter has made up his mind."

One of my most important tasks was to establish a public position which would demonstrate that U.S.–Chinese relations had taken a major step forward as a consequence of these consultations. This was done through a formal toast, which was meant to convey the key proposition that the United States and China were now engaged in a new and increasingly significant strategic relationship. It was also meant to reaffirm our commitment to normalize in a manner that would reinforce my private comments to the Chinese, yet not reveal the timetable that we had set for ourselves. Accordingly, and in close collaboration with my State Department colleagues, I prepared and gave the following toast at the evening banquet:

> Our commitment to friendship with China is based on shared concerns and is derived from a long-term strategic view. The United States does not view its relationship with China as a tactical expedient. . . . We approach our relations with three fundamental beliefs: that friendship between the United States and the People's Republic of China is vital and beneficial to world peace; that a secure and strong China is in America's interest; that a powerful, confident, and globally engaged United States is in China's interest. . . . The President of the United States desires friendly relations with a strong China. He is determined to join you in overcoming the remaining obstacles in the way to full normalization of our relations within the framework of the Shanghai communiqué. The United States has made up its mind on this issue. . . .

I also added: "Only those aspiring to dominate others have any reason to fear the further development of American–Chinese relations." The reference to "a secure and strong China" was much highlighted by the world press, and the Chinese media also cited the toast.

I was struck in the course of my conversation with Hua Guofeng, and the issue also arose with Deng and Huang, that the Chinese were frustrated by lack of progress in negotiating the Chinese–Japanese friendship treaty. The obstacle was Japanese unwillingness to offend the Soviets by including in the treaty the so-called anti-hegemony clause, which—though not explicitly mentioning the Soviet Union—was clearly anti-Soviet in its thrust. Accordingly, and on my own initiative, when briefing Prime Minister Fukuda in Tokyo, immediately after my departure from Beijing, on the substance of the American–Chinese talks, I made it a point to urge both him and Foreign Minister Sonoda to go ahead with the treaty, with the clause included in it. I pointed out to the Japanese that the clause mentioned no state, and it could, theoretically, apply to China, to the United States, or to anyone else. More important, I made it clear to them that the United States did not object to the inclusion of that clause and that it favored an expeditious conclusion of the treaty. I believe this statement, including more than subtle encouragement, did impress the Japanese, and shortly thereafter they acceded to the treaty, with the clause included in it. I subsequently reported on my initiative to the President, and he approved. Till then, the State Department had been leery about it.

I reported to the President on the trip both by cable from Beijing and in writing immediately upon my return. The most significant point that I was able to report was that I had told Deng of our need to make a unilateral statement expressing our hope for a peaceful resolution of the Taiwan issue that would not be contradicted by the Chinese side, and that Deng replied that each side could express its own opinion. The Chinese would say that how and when they liberated Taiwan was an internal problem to be solved by the Chinese themselves. We could express our views. I stated that it was important that our two statements not be in direct contradiction. I also reported that we did not talk about arms sales directly. However, indirectly, the subject did come up. I had earlier pointed out the danger that an insecure Taiwan, after normalization, might turn to the Soviet Union. Deng responded that the Chinese had thought about this possibility, but since the United States would maintain economic relations with Taiwan, this would be less of a problem. Thus, on the two subjects of concern to us—arms sales to Taiwan and the Chinese commitment not to contradict our statement— we broke some new and intriguing ground. I reported that Ambassador Woodcock shared this view.

In effect, the Chinese appeared ready to offer us a choice if we wished normalization at this stage—either to continue arms sales to Taiwan after normalization, without receiving a Chinese statement indicating their intent to resolve the Taiwan issue peacefully; or no further U.S. arms sales, coupled with a Chinese declaration of peaceful intent. As Hua put it, for us to sell arms and request China to commit itself to a peaceful resolution of the issue would clearly lead to a "two Chinas" solution.

Finally, I was able to report that our intelligence assessment was that the Chinese viewed the visit as "very successful." Apparently, the initial Chinese plan was to have me engage in a full-scale dialogue with the Foreign Minister only, and to meet with Vice-Premier Deng only for protocol reasons. The schedule was changed when it became evident to the Chinese that I was in a position both to engage in a broad strategic review, pointing toward increased collaboration between our two countries, and to discuss seriously the question of normalization.

The Breakthrough

On my return to Washington, I was greeted at the airport by Warren Christopher in a demonstration of solidarity by the State Department, and in the afternoon the President gave me a genuinely warm, even enthusiastic, greeting. He jumped up from his chair when I walked into his small study, rushed toward me, grabbed my arm, pumped it warmly, and gave me a bear hug. He then called in a photographer to have a picture of the two of us taken. I noted that evening: ". . . I must say I feel certainly very committed to him. He has a manner of conveying warmth and pleasure when I come back from a trip, and I suspect it is genuine. I gave him a highly condensed oral report on the trip and gave him a longer report, which I hope that Rosalynn will also read. The protocols with Deng and Hua are particularly revealing of the Chinese mode of thought."

The President's pleasure was doubtless stimulated by the very positive press reactions to my trip. *Le Monde* called it "a decisive milestone in Sino-American relations"; *Frankfurter Allgemeine* noted that "Brzezinski may consider it his personal success that the Chinese leaders accorded him honors similar to those they used to accord Kissinger"; though Tass warned that I, "as no other American official," had a stake in setting China against the Soviet Union. Within days of my return, the New York *Times* also reported that as a consequence of my visit the United States had quietly agreed to a Chinese request for airborne geological survey equipment using an infrared scanning system, which it would not sell to the Soviet Union because of potential military uses, and that it was also considering approving the sale of an array processor to be used in geological exploration of the ocean bed. Some of the press reported, however, that my visit would bring to the surface the lingering disagreements between me and Secretary Vance, and *La Stampa* reported that "many believe that a confrontation is imminent."

Unfortunately, that prediction proved to be correct. My trip to China did precipitate a renewed clash with Vance, and I regret that I inadvertently contributed to it. Shortly after my return, I was asked to appear on *Meet the Press*, and I should have declined. I was still too much on "Chinese time." I agreed, thinking that I would be quizzed largely about the trip. Instead, the questioning focused almost entirely on the Soviet Union and on the Soviet exploitation of the Cuban military proxy in Africa. In my comments on the air I said: "I am troubled by the fact that the Soviet Union has been engaged in a sustained and massive effort to build up its conventional forces, particularly in Europe, to strengthen the concentration of its forces on the frontiers of China, to maintain a vitriolic worldwide propaganda campaign against the United States, to encircle and penetrate the Middle East, to stir up racial difficulties in Africa and to make more difficult a moderate solution of these difficulties, perhaps now to seek more direct access to the Indian Ocean. This pattern of behavior I do not believe is compatible with what was once called the code of detente, and my hope is, through patient negotiations with us but also through demonstrated resolve on our part, we can induce the Soviet leaders to conclude that the benefits of accommodation are greater than the shortsighted attempt to exploit global difficulties."

The next morning's Washington *Post* had a headline emblazoned across the top of the front page: "Brzezinski Delivers Attack on the Soviets." Underneath it were two articles, both of them overdramatic. The first, entitled "Draws Hard Line Against Breaches of Detente," reported in apocalyptic terms that the United States and the Soviet Union "are now at one of their most critical junctures in the ambiguous relationship known as detente," and "as Brzezinski drew the line in the dust for the United States, the challenge he proclaimed most acutely is in Africa." The paper went on to state explicitly that this also meant that I had now become the principal foreign policy adviser to Carter, overshadowing Vance, unless—the paper rather hopefully noted—the President chose to disown me. The other side of the paper had a subheadline entitled "Voices Sharp Indictment of African, Global Activities." Reporting by the New York *Times* was somewhat more measured, but the approach taken by the Washington *Post* was reflected a week later on the cover of *Newsweek*, where the revival of the Cold War was announced across a portrait of me. Matters were not helped much by a column in the Washington *Post* in early June entitled "Brzezinski Calls the Foreign Policy Shots," which again denigrated Vance and played up my alleged predominance. I noted in my journal that day: "I really felt pained and almost sick when I read it."

The result was predictable. The President was concerned and Vance upset. The morning after the *Meet the Press* appearance, the President said to me during my briefing, while smiling one of his "I like you but I'm really burning inside" smiles, "You're not just a professor; you speak for me. And I think you went too far in your statements. You put all of this responsibility on the Soviets. You said they were conducting a worldwide vitriolic campaign, encircling and penetrating the Middle East, placing troops on the Chinese frontier. All this simply just went a little too far." He went on to say that my comments might even threaten detente and he was wondering whether he shouldn't write a letter to Brezhnev to reiterate his commitment to SALT. I told the President that "it's really important that we discuss this fully, because this raises a question of fundamental judgment. In my view, the West confronts a basic danger, and how we respond may be decisive to the future of this country." I added that I was distressed if my statements went further than he felt they should, and I asked him to review the transcript of what I said and not just rely on the Washington *Post* reporting of it.

Within a day, the President eased up. In the meantime the Washington *Post* had come out with an editorial endorsing the position I had taken and praising the Administration for developing a more coherent and firmer posture in foreign policy, "consistent with the political mood of the country, as we sense it." The President and I rode together to attend the NATO summit meeting, which was being held in the State Department auditorium, and in the course of the drive "he kind of casually allowed that he feels better today about my interview." Later at the NATO meeting, the President called upon me to speak twice, to give a report on the trip to China and then in the course of the NATO debate on Africa. "I was slightly embarrassed because in effect it meant that only the President and I spoke. Cy, who was sitting in the front row, did not contribute. It made me feel rather awkward. I do not wish the relationship to deteriorate."

Though the issue with the President was thus closed, Vance was deeply upset and he called to tell me so. He stated that the Administration should speak with one voice and that my remarks on the air were making it less clear who was articulating the position of the Administration. I pointed out to Cy that I felt that I had spoken in keeping with the President's position, but I knew that he was not mollified. I subsequently learned that he had written to the President and complained to him.

In a cover memo, Vance wrote that he had prepared the letter "before the events and public statements of this weekend." He continued: ". . . sharp and fundamental differences exist within the Administration and are now public knowledge." In the letter itself, while acknowledging the usefulness of my China trip, he questioned how much effect it would have on Moscow's actions, given his assessment of Soviet behavior. He believed rather that "we can help encourage a more cooperative attitude on the part of the Soviet leaders by conspicuous attention to the sense of equality to which they attach so much importance. And if they respond positively, we should refrain from crowing about any gestures they make." Obviously, Vance and I were in serious disagreement.

I regretted the blowup, but in any case, by early June of 1978, Cy and I had found ourselves at odds over two issues: was there linkage between Soviet actions in Africa and elsewhere and the pursuit of SALT, and how should our policy toward China be related to that strategic dilemma? I, for one, felt that the President and the country would benefit by the adoption of a tougher line, and I felt that public perceptions supported my view.

I discussed that issue toward the end of May with Ham Jordan.

He came into my office in the evening all sweaty in his tennis outfit just to chat. The point of the discussion was how to hold the line on the present relatively favorable situation insofar as global and public perception of Carter is concerned. I showed him a memo which I had written to the President in which I pointed out that this week produced a confluence of four positive trends: the first is that for the first time perhaps the major allies take the United States seriously and the meeting was a personal success for Carter; secondly, for the first time the Cubans and the Soviets take our concerns about Africa seriously and are even worried about them; thirdly, for the first time the Chinese now take us seriously, in part because of my trip, in part because of Carter's posture; and finally, for the first time the public takes us seriously insofar as our facing up to global responsibilities is concerned. In view of this, I urged Carter to maintain a steady course . . . to make sure that there are no sudden hints of a desire for detente that's misunderstood by the public as veering from this course. I also emphasized the importance of stressing the long-term congruence of American and Chinese objectives, as well as the fact that detente with the Soviets has to be reciprocal and comprehensive. Jordan agreed with all of that and said that in effect what happened in the last week is that because of Carter's statement last week, then Vance's contradiction of Gromyko last Saturday, and then my own strong *Meet the Press*, the impression has been created that this Administration has pulled its act together. In fact, it's all a big accident, and who the hell knows whether the President will not veer in some direction tomorrow or the day after tomorrow. Jordan thought that the consolation was that the President enjoys this perception of being seen as tough, and this may keep him on course, but he was worried that we might not stay on it. We then talked about how to make sure that he does. One thought was to have a big meeting with everybody in it, but I pointed out that there are real dangers in that. First of all, suppose the consequence of the meeting is that the President decides to go for the soft line. It will be harder to deter him in a larger meeting. Secondly, suppose he decides to go for the hard line and publicly or semipublicly in a group meeting has to reject the advice that Vance is giving. This would really undercut Vance. I rather urged that there be a small meeting with Carter, with Carter being encouraged to define his line himself, preferably the one that Jordan and I favor, and then simply impose it by edict, so to speak, either through a memorandum or by calling all of us in and in effect giving us the order to stick to the line as he has expressed it.

The flap over my television appearance, and the rift over U.S.–Soviet relations with Vance, did not, however, prevent Vance and me from carrying on our work together on the question of China. On June 20, the President met for an important review session of our China policy with Vance, Brown, Jordan, and me. Vance had written a memorandum to the President on June 13, recommending that "the best target date for public announcement of recognition would be mid-December," also adding that the establishment of diplomatic relations "could be marked by a high-level P.R.C. visit to Washington." Vance supported his argument for the mid-December date by writing: "In recommending a mid-December date, I am mindful that if SALT is completed this year, both SALT and normalization would be ready for action by the new Congress at about the same time, requiring careful management from both a foreign policy and a domestic perspective. But I recommend that congressional action on normalization precede SALT ratification debate on next year's legislative calendar. The December date would allow us to proceed with Peking at a reasonable pace and would have some negotiating advantages over a stretched-out process. I have in mind Zbig's remark to Deng that 'the President is prepared to resolve this as rapidly as it proves practical. We have no intention of artificially delaying it.' "

It is important to note Vance's recommendation on ratification, on the deadline, and on the visit, because subsequently I was often charged by critics sympathetic to Vance and hostile to my strategic views with having deliberately contrived the normalization and the invitation to Deng to visit Washington so as to scuttle Vance's efforts to obtain a SALT agreement. The fact of the matter is that at this stage we were working in tandem; the State Department and the NSC shared the same position on normalization of relations with China, especially in view of the momentum generated by my visit to Beijing.

In my cover memo to the President, I agreed with Vance, and I urged the President to insist on utmost confidentiality in the efforts that were now to be undertaken. But I also warned the President that we had to make a careful political assessment as to whether we could really afford to absorb the issue of normalization either before or immediately after the fall elections, "for if you accept Cy's memo, you will have little opportunity to turn back without high cost to our future relations with the Chinese for many years." In addition, I noted that Cy proposed that we discuss the outstanding issues with the Chinese in a sequential fashion, one after another. I was concerned that this strategy might bog us down in detail, the way we got bogged down with the Israelis, and suggested an alternative approach in which we would "lay out our position more comprehensively, perhaps through the device of submitting a draft normalization communiqué." The President wrote on the bottom of the memo: "Cy—Devise special procedures; leaks can kill the whole effort. We should limit the dispatches and the negotiating information strictly—maybe just to the PDB* group. Avoid *any* public hints of degree of progress. I don't trust (1) Congress, (2) White House, (3) State, or (4) Defense to keep a secret. JC."

Thus, the meeting on June 20 included only the President, Vance, Brown, Jordan, and me. We reached the following conclusions, which I jotted down on a sheet of paper and, for reasons of security, did not even have typed:

U.S.–China:

1. Keep very confidential.

2. Chinese anxious to improve relations. Have done everything we wanted prior to ZB visit.

3. Aim for December 15. But keep the info circle very small. Our public position—we do want to improve and normalize relations.

4. China congressional action to precede SALT ratification.

5. Residual relations: would like broader options than private organization. A trade mission? A military sales mission? Cy will get legal assessment.

6. Woodcock to conduct negotiations. Oksenberg and Holbrooke to work on this. Woodcock to initiate discussions by asking for a date. Instructions to follow.

7. Woodcock to go in, propose talks every ten days, propose an agenda: (1) representation; (2) peaceful resolution; (3) U.S. trade with Taiwan; (4) communiqué and modalities.

8. Early next week submit draft on representation instructions.

9. Woodcock to explore the possibility of one year's notice to R.O.C. [Republic of China] as a way out of the dilemma.

---

* President's Daily Brief, accessible only to the President himself, the Vice-President, Vance, Brown, and me.

Our strategy was thus set and we had a target date. Thereafter, I would periodically submit to the President draft instructions for Leonard Woodcock, which would be prepared by Oksenberg and Holbrooke, working closely with me, and which would be reviewed by Vance. The President gave them meticulous attention. He took out sentences and inserted and reworded others. He carefully monitored every single paragraph and every proposal. In his first presentation to the Chinese, Woodcock was instructed to propose a process by which he would meet approximately every two weeks with Foreign Minister Huang Hua to discuss the major issues involved. On July 5 he proposed that these issues be tackled as follows:

1. The nature of the post-normalization American presence on Taiwan.
2. Our statements on the occasion of normalization.
3. American trade with Taiwan after normalization.
4. A joint communiqué and the modalities of normalization.

On July 14 the Chinese responded by suggesting that the United States first make a comprehensive presentation on all the major issues, obviously wanting to smoke out the American position. But we instructed Woodcock to proceed with talking to the Chinese and to simply make a presentation on the first of the four items. Accordingly, Woodcock opened the substantive discussions by presenting the American view of the American presence on Taiwan after normalization. By following this pattern, we tested the Chinese reaction on each sensitive issue before moving to the next. The essence of our negotiating strategy was to table our position when we were fairly certain that the Chinese would not say no. Having already accepted China's "three demands," we were responding with our position on our "three demands":

1. That the Chinese not contradict our unilateral statements at the time of normalization concerning the peaceful future of Taiwan.
2. That we would retain a full range of economic, cultural, and other relations with Taiwan on an unofficial basis.
3. That we could continue to sell arms to Taiwan.

Woodcock conducted these talks with genuine skill, acquired through his many years of negotiating experience as a labor union leader. He was dedicated, effective, and persistent. At our end, we provided him regularly with systematic and extraordinarily detailed instructions, using the White House communications system for direct contact, thus avoiding dispatch of cables through the State Department, which we were afraid would have too wide a distribution. Each cable to Woodcock was sent jointly by Vance and me. Woodcock thus knew that the President personally was engaged.

At the same time, I initiated closer exchanges with the Chinese by setting in motion visits to China by the President's science adviser, Frank Press, and by Secretary of Energy James Schlesinger. I knew that Press was scheduled to visit the Soviet Union in the second half of July, so I told the Chinese they could have him as a guest either in August or in early July. "Oksenberg was sure that the Chinese out of pride would pick August, but I had the feeling that they would choose the earlier date, and they did. Accordingly, shortly after next week, Frank Press will take a fifteen-man delegation to Communist China, including the head of NASA, the head of the National Institutes of Health, and several other heads of major American science/technology organizations. We will really send a powerful signal." In fact, the delegation that he took was the most high-powered science/technology delegation ever sent by the United States to any foreign country. After his return, Press took charge of expanding U.S.–Chinese relations in science and technology, and I thereby gained another important bureaucratic ally.

Shortly thereafter, Schlesinger traveled to China and came back with a glowing account. The Chinese were delighted by his visit, particularly by his views on U.S.–Soviet relations. This, too, generated further impetus, facilitating the difficult discussions that Woodcock was conducting.

While this was going on, I intensified the frequency and scope of my personal consultations with the head of the Chinese Liaison Mission in Washington. I started meeting him at least once a month, and I used each occasion to provide more and more detailed briefings regarding our foreign policy initiatives. Before very long, the Chinese side began posing pointed questions of their own for me to answer. In mid-August, I met for the first time the new head of the Chinese Mission, Ambassador Chai Zemin. Though he reminded me of a teddy bear, Chai proved to be an extremely skillful, persistent, and effective negotiator. He would invariably pull out a little notebook from which he would read his formal presentation. He would then elaborate, and I was able to tell over the longer haul that he not only faithfully reported my views to China but was quite prepared to urge accommodation and adjustment on some issues. Without his sustained efforts, I doubt that we could have made the breakthrough that we did in the early days of December. A great deal of credit ought to go to him and to Ambassador Han Hsu for the establishment of this historically important new relationship.

My first meeting with Ambassador Chai Zemin on August 17 gave me an opportunity to hint at an approach that we subsequently adopted in regard to the termination of our defense treaty with Taiwan. Our exchange went as follows:

CHAI: No doubt, in the final analysis we will come to a successful conclusion. But judging from the current international situation, the earlier that normalization would be realized, the better. But the U.S. bears the major role in reaching a successful conclusion.

BRZEZINSKI: Ah, I consider this part of the negotiations! [Laughter.]

CHAI: Yes, recently China and Japan have concluded a Peace and Friendship Treaty. This is an event of importance and significance and is proof of the historical situation. Public opinion and world opinion acclaim the treaty and feel happy about it. Of course, there is one nation that is upset and has cursed the treaty.

BRZEZINSKI: Of course, that is very sad. [Laughter.] But you have an agreement with the Soviet Union which designates Japan as the common enemy. What will happen to that treaty?

CHAI: In actuality, that treaty is null and void. The treaty will terminate in 1980.

BRZEZINSKI [Expression of puzzlement.]

AMBASSADOR HAN HSU: The Sino-Soviet treaty was signed in February 1950 and will expire in 1980. According to those provisions, we must nullify it one year in advance, which means we must give notice in 1979.

HOLBROOKE: So, you have to give notice.

HAN HSU: Yes, we have to give notice one year in advance.

BRZEZINSKI: I see. Even though it is de facto no longer in effect, you wish to act according to those provisions in order to nullify it. Is that correct? You wish to recognize the juridical dimensions of the treaty.

HAN HSU: Yes. How we shall proceed from this legal point of view precisely, we will see when the time comes.

BRZEZINSKI: Well, your desire to act according to the provisions of the treaty seems a very reasonable approach to me.

In effect, I was deliberately hinting to the Chinese that we might well do the same, instead of abruptly terminating the treaty with Taiwan as they would have preferred.

In the same meeting, I raised with Ambassador Chai the possibility of a summit meeting with the Chinese leader in the United States upon normalization. Chai told me that Hua had visited Europe and that the

Chinese "feel the time has come for them to pay back their debts to others who have visited" them. I seized on that remark to point out to him the enormous political significance of a top-level U.S.–Chinese meeting. Subsequently, I reported on this to the President, and he encouraged me to continue exploring the matter.

But before the new relationship could be consummated, we had to deal with a policy diversion. For reasons which I could never quite understand from a policy standpoint, but which perhaps may be better explained by the psychologically searing impact of the Vietnamese war tragedy, both Vance and, even more, Holbrooke seemed determined at this time to initiate a diplomatic relationship with Vietnam. They did not propose a formal interagency Policy Review Memorandum, but simply preferred to keep the initiative in the State Department, with Vance communicating with the President on this subject primarily through his evening notes.

I found such an initiative untimely, especially given the extremely sensitive state of our negotiations with the Chinese. Moreover, I had already labeled Vietnam publicly as "a Soviet proxy," in keeping with what we had said to the Chinese, though this view was strongly contested by State. Holbrooke kept urging the Vietnamese to demonstrate their flexibility and readiness to move forward in relations with us, so that we would then have to reciprocate. Indeed, normalization of relations was even agreed to in principle at the meeting between Holbrooke and a ranking Vietnamese diplomat, Nguyen Co Thach, on September 29 in New York.

Although for the previous two months I had repeatedly mentioned to the President that such an action would be interpreted by the Chinese as a "pro-Soviet, anti-Chinese move" (briefing of June 23), in early September the President told me that "we should evaluate the pros and cons of diplomatic relations with Vietnam, perhaps aiming at simultaneous recognition of China and Vietnam." Indeed, later that month, on September 28, the day before Holbrooke's meeting in New York, "I pointed out to the President that his comments on the evening notes from Cy last night might imply that he is now giving the green light to the rapid establishment of diplomatic relations with Vietnam. This in my judgment could prejudice our efforts with the Chinese. The President, though somewhat reluctantly, wrote in the margins of the evening note an additional sentence: 'Please first give me the reactions of the Chinese.' I hope this will slow things down somewhat."

That did slow things down, indeed, and in mid-October the President decided to defer the Vietnam normalization. In fact, in the middle of November the President instructed Vance to condemn the Vietnamese for their deliberate promotion of the refugee exodus from Vietnam. "I immediately instructed the State Department to that effect, knowing that Holbrooke would today be making a speech on our Far East policy. The Department came out with a very strong statement, and Holbrooke had no choice but to echo it in his speech. Perhaps this might slow down some of the pell-mell rush toward a rapid recognition of Vietnam while we are at a sensitive stage in our discussions with the Chinese," I noted on November 16.

In the meantime, Woodcock continued his sensitive negotiations in Beijing, closely monitored in Washington by Vance and me, with the President continuously informed and very much in charge. Carter held a brilliant meeting with Ambassador Chai on September 19, which accelerated the process. "The President made a very effective statement of our policy to China and hit the Chinese hard on our right to sell arms to Taiwan and on the importance of a noncontradicted statement by the United States to the effect that we expected a peaceful resolution of the issue of Taiwan." Later on, when the U.S.–Chinese talks appeared temporarily stalemated, especially after a very unsatisfactory meeting in New York between Huang Hua and Vance, in which Huang took a particularly rigid position, the President met on October 11 with just Woodcock and me, and he reached two important decisions: he told Woodcock that we would not move on Vietnam, an issue which I had prompted Woodcock to bring up with the President, and a few days later the President accepted Oksenberg's and my suggestion that we submit a draft communiqué on normalization to the Chinese as a way of establishing the seriousness of our intent. I suggested that we put the date of January 15 on the communiqué, in order to convey to the Chinese that we were prepared to solve the problem quickly; the President on his own advanced it to January 1. (Subsequently, during my visit to China in 1981, senior Chinese officials told me that the tabling of the proposed communiqué dispelled their last doubt as to the seriousness of Carter's intent to normalize.)

Shortly thereafter, I told the Chinese Ambassador that if we missed this opportunity we would have to delay normalization until far into 1979. The congressional schedule would be overloaded, and we would have to move ahead on SALT and a possible meeting with Brezhnev. In the meantime, Dick Holbrooke opened his own, very useful channel with Han Hsu over the unpleasant aspects of our relations. Chinese complaints about our arms sales to Taiwan were delivered through that channel, and were thus excluded from the meetings between Woodcock and Huang or Chai and me, thereby protecting these meetings from unnecessary polemics. Holbrooke also assumed responsibility for developing our congressional consultations strategy, while Vance, consulting former Attorney General Herbert Brownell, developed the tactics for terminating the defense treaty. Things were starting to move rapidly.

On November 2, Woodcock reported that "the Chinese side is paying increasing attention to the details of our presentations. Significantly, too, this is the first session at which Huang avoided a polemical repetition of Chinese positions," instead submitting a series of specific questions. Woodcock gave Huang a draft of the joint normalization communiqué, and he was instructed a few days later to tell the Chinese that we would terminate the defense treaty with Taiwan in accordance with the provisions of that treaty when the joint U.S.–P.R.C. communiqué announcing mutual recognition was issued. Taiwan would thus be given one year's notice. Woodcock completed the presentation of the U.S. position at his sixth meeting, held on December 4, and we now awaited the Chinese response. When it was not forthcoming, in order to elicit a swifter Chinese response I called in the Chinese Ambassador on December 11 and I told him directly that now was the moment when "we should move rapidly on normalization and that they should consider favorably an invitation either to Deng or to Hua to visit Washington in the course of January."

I indicated that such a visit could be scheduled before any meeting between Carter and Brezhnev on SALT. In my journal I also noted the following: "One little footnote symptomatic of the changing times: When Ambassador Chai came to see me today accompanied by his two colleagues in Mao-type suits, he startled me by appearing in a brown suit with fashionably wide lapels, a blue shirt with a long collar, and a very multicolored tie. A total sartorial transformation, symptomatic of the ideological transformation of contemporary China." In that meeting I stressed particularly that the time for formal negotiations had come to an end; the time was now for a momentous political decision. I asked Chai specifically to convey these words to Deng, and he did so.

This conversation with Ambassador Chai—so the Chinese told me later—convinced Vice-Premier Deng that he should also now take direct charge of the negotiations and resolve any last issues. In 1981, during my visit to Beijing, he recalled that, adding: "You and I together overcame the last difficulties."

Things came to a head in the course of the next week. Deng met Woodcock on December 12, having by then received the minutes of my meeting with Chai. The morning of the thirteenth, a cable from Woodcock came in, to the effect that the Chinese had accepted our proposals as well as the invitation for Deng to visit the United States. I immediately went over to the President's office, and as was my right on particularly important occasions, I walked in unannounced. I told him the news and he was visibly pleased. He was sitting behind his desk, and his face broke out into a genuinely joyous grin as he shook my hand warmly. We agreed to move promptly with the public announcement, and I called in the Chinese Ambassador to request that he pass the message to Deng, proposing that announcement be made on Friday, December 15, and that Deng's visit be definitely scheduled for a fixed date in the latter part of January.

In the meantime, the President phoned Cy, who was then in Israel. Cy agreed to fly back for the public announcement on Friday. Later in the day, Christopher, Oksenberg, and I worked in my office well past midnight on the final normalization documents. We were joined later in the evening by the President, who reviewed them line by line. The President was dressed in his blue jeans, a picture of casual intensity, as we sat and drafted word by word the documents which were bound to alter significantly the balance of global power. By early morning we had sent detailed instructions to Woodcock on how to resolve the remaining issues, and the texts of the proposed communiqué and of the unilateral American announcement.

Not everything went smoothly. I noted on December 15: "Unfortunately, at the last minute the arms sales issue has arisen. The Chinese are operating on the assumption that we will discontinue immediately. We made it clear that we will continue after a one-year pause during which the treaty is being abrogated. Late at night, on my instructions, clarifying messages were sent to Deng Xiaoping. This morning, after the breakfast meeting with the President, I called in the Chinese Ambassador to stress to him the historically significant opportunity that we face and therefore the importance that formalistic issues not cloud the immediate international impact of this event. I told him that the sales will go on after 1979, that they can disagree with this, but since we are going ahead with normalization we should try to minimize the difference."

We were faced with the prospect of a last-minute fiasco. Vance was out of the country and the situation called for fast action. Even though Woodcock demurred, believing that a direct statement by the President would force a negative Chinese reaction, I insisted that he tell Deng that "we will try to be as restrained as we can on the subject of arms sales, but that within the United States political process it is simply impossible for the United States not to reaffirm its position on this subject. . . . Recognizing Chinese sensitivities on this matter, we will not make a formal statement but will respond to the inevitable question which will surely be raised immediately both by the press and by opponents of normalization, in the following fashion: 'Within the agreement to normalize, the United States has made it clear that it will continue to trade with Taiwan, including the restrained sale of selective defensive arms, after the expiration of the defense treaty, in a way that will not endanger the prospects for peace in the region. The Chinese side does not endorse the United States position on this matter, but it has not prevented both sides from agreeing to normalize relations.' "

China's willingness to go ahead in the light of my message to Deng constituted, in effect, an agreement to put the issue aside while going ahead with normalization. In retrospect, it turned out that my instructions to Woodcock were significant in that they prevented the Chinese from later claiming that the United States had forsaken the right to continue the military supply relationship with Taiwan. The President, his domestic advisers, and I all felt strongly that normalization would run into major political difficulties in the United States if we were not clear on this subject.

In the afternoon I asked Dobrynin to come to my office, so I could tell him the news personally. "Dobrynin arrived full of cheer at 3 p.m. I tipped Jody off and he in turn tipped some newspapermen off, so they were all outside photographing him. Our hope was to divert newspapermen into thinking that maybe something involving American–Soviet relations would be announced in the evening by the President. By the time Dobrynin arrived, it was known that we had requested television time for 9 p.m. At first I chatted pleasantly with Dobrynin, thanked him for their courtesies to [Secretary of the Treasury Michael] Blumenthal and [Secretary of Commerce Juanita] Kreps during their visits to Moscow, and then out of the blue I informed him that we are announcing tonight initiation of diplomatic, full-scale relations with the People's Republic of China. He looked absolutely stunned. His face turned kind of gray and his jaw dropped. He didn't say anything but then he recouped and thanked me for the information. I added that it wasn't directed against anyone and that American relations with China would now have as normal a character as Soviet relations with China. Formally, a correct observation; but substantively, a touch of irony."

Our consultations with Congress had been limited, primarily on the advice of Majority Leader Robert Byrd. He was afraid of leaks and thought that congressional objections would scuttle any negotiations. In the evening, a congressional group representing the leadership and the Foreign Relations and Armed Services Committees of both Houses was asked to come to the White House to meet with the President, without being told why. Although most of the members were taken by surprise, and were concerned about our commitments to Taiwan, the reaction was positive.

That same evening Senator Sam Nunn and I were at a small dinner party where by complete coincidence we had a Chinese meal. He quipped something to the effect that "I'll have to pay more attention to what kind of food will be served at a dinner party with you so that I can get more hints about foreign policy initiatives."

Late on the fifteenth, at 9 p.m., the President made the momentous announcement, and the next day in Beijing, Hua gave an interview on the normalization, in which he explicitly thanked "President Carter, Dr. Brzezinski, and Secretary Vance" for making all this possible. U.S.–Chinese relations were now formally established.

The pressure was off, but I was still in for a surprise. On Sunday, December 17, "I was taking my children for a walk along the Potomac, when my Pageboy started ringing in my pocket. I made it back to one of the park stations and found out from Signal [White House operator] that the President was trying to reach me from Camp David. When I called him he sounded very cheerful and then he said to me, after asking what I was doing, 'Well, Zbig, the Chinese have just reneged.' I almost shouted into the phone, 'What?' and he laughed and said, 'No, no, no.' Relieved, I gasped, 'Well, you really fooled me,' and he then told me that he would like me to send a member of my staff out to brief Nixon in order to consolidate Nixon's support. I then told him that world reactions are pretty good, and I congratulated him on the decision and asked him how he feels about it. He said he feels very good about it and he wanted to say how much he appreciates what I did, that I was the driving force behind the entire effort. I interrupted him and said no, that it was his decisions that made the difference. He said, 'No, no, you were genuinely the driving force behind the whole effort. Whenever I wavered, you pushed me and pressed me to go through with this.' " Since he rather rarely congratulated anyone, I appreciated the gesture.

7

Uphill to Camp David

Compromises will be mandatory. Without them, no progress can be
expected. Flexibility will be the essence of our hopes. And my own
role will be that of a full partner, not trying to impose the will of
the United States on others, but searching for common ground on
which agreements can be reached.

—President Jimmy Carter, remarks on departing the
White House for Camp David, September 4, 1978

On January 12, 1978, I gave the President my assessment of developments in the Middle East over the course of the past year. I wrote:

The initial phase of our diplomacy involved high-level consultations with all of the principal parties to the conflict, first through
Secretary Vance's trip to the Middle East in February and then
your meetings with the regional leaders between March and May.
These consultations resulted in a much clearer definition of the
issues. You began deliberately to reveal through your public
comments the broad outlines of our strategy—full normalization
of relations, borders and security arrangements, the Palestinian
issue.

The most controversial of the points in your approach proved to
be the idea of the Palestinian homeland. . . . By fall, there was a
very intense domestic reaction . . . it seems fair to conclude that
the Palestinian issue was introduced too early and without adequate care to keep it in perspective. This resulted in a loss of
domestic support for our policy which came at a particularly
unfortunate time in terms of the peacemaking efforts.

The second difficulty which compounded our problems on the
domestic front was the U.S.–Soviet communiqué. Although the
document in fact contained little new and had little substantive
consequence, it set off a storm of protest, bringing together traditional anti-Soviet forces and supporters of Israel.

Sadat's bold initiative brought us into a new phase, and by
December we were embarked on a course which enjoyed much
wider support among the American public and which seemed once

again to hold good promise of moving the parties toward a peace settlement.

In retrospect, it is fair to say that the Administration broke new ground by concentrating on the key elements of an overall peace. Your expression of the requirements of a real peace was an important innovation. The distinction between political borders and security arrangements was also likely to be of enduring value.

The Administration's efforts clearly did help to break the stalemate that had existed throughout 1976, and new momentum was given to the search for peace. The emphasis on negotiations and direct talks was instrumental in ultimately bringing Egypt and Israel together. And, through its largely unpublicized efforts, the Administration helped to limit dangers of the unstable situation in southern Lebanon. Thus, in many respects 1977 was the year of the Middle East.

By early 1978, U.S. policy toward the Middle East had become less ambitious but more focused. We were now resigned to the fact that a comprehensive settlement was years away at best. Instead, we were determined to make certain that Sadat's peace initiative was translated into a tangible accommodation between Egypt and Israel, one that would generate also some progress on the broader, vaguer, and much more sensitive Palestinian issue. We wanted a peace process that would engage the moderate Arabs in such a way that the American position in the region would be strengthened. If we could not do it through Geneva, we were prepared to work with Begin and Sadat, provided we could create opportunities in the process for engaging other moderate Arabs. That goal meant that some clashes between the United States and Israel were inevitable. The Israelis clearly preferred to confine the peace process to a separate Israeli–Egyptian agreement, which would split the Arabs while letting Israel continue its occupation of the West Bank and Gaza. Thus our concern for the Palestinian problem—a concern that Sadat to a degree shared—was bound to be contested by the Israelis, who wished to place the narrowest definition on Begin's proposal for Palestinian autonomy.

When Sadat made his initial grand gesture in Jerusalem, he wanted to reinvigorate the peace process and to help Jimmy Carter out of the corner into which he had been boxed by Begin. Indeed, at first he even saw his Jerusalem initiative as a catalyst for a Geneva-type conference, to be held either in Cairo or elsewhere, and still aimed at a comprehensive settlement. However, by early January it was clear that that was not to be, and that the bilateral Egyptian–Israeli talks were leading nowhere. Sadat now needed American help desperately in order to obtain an accommodation, one that would respect fundamental Egyptian interests while also giving him a fig leaf in the eyes of the other Arabs. Otherwise, Sadat would be politically discredited and regionally ostracized.

Sadat also had a secondary but equally important objective. Sensing in Carter a personal friend, Sadat saw in the peace process an opportunity to fashion a new American–Egyptian relationship, one in which Egypt might even displace Israel as America's closest ally in the region. Failing that, at the very least Sadat would be well on the way to becoming America's favorite statesman in the region—no small accomplishment for a state still technically at war with Israel.

In the emerging three-way U.S.–Israeli–Egyptian negotiations, the Israelis had the advantage of the clearest concept and the most precise goal: to achieve a separate peace with Egypt while leaving Israeli interests on other matters fully protected. This meant, above all, retaining physical possession both of the West Bank and of the Golan Heights while preserving for Israel the privileged status of America's favorite client state in the Middle East. Under Carter, despite the emerging disagreement with the Israelis, American aid to Israel continued to flow, and the Administration made the conscious decision not to intensify Israeli insecurity by using aid as a source of pressure on Israel. As a result, in the words of Ezer Weizman in his *Battle for Peace*, Israel "had received U.S. military assistance of stunning proportions, far exceeding what our forces had possessed in the Six-Day War. By my reckoning, some 20 percent of our defense system is maintained by the American taxpayer, to the yearly tune of a billion dollars in military aid to Israel." This does not include, of course, U.S. economic assistance, which amounted to around $10 billion since 1973, almost $3,000 for each Israeli citizen, an unprecedented level of aid to a single and not a particularly poor country.

Accordingly, the starting point for Israeli policy had to be the preservation of the relationship with the United States. Since 1967, Israeli policy had been to make that relationship an increasingly binding one, and every effort was made by Israeli supporters in the United States to elevate the status of Israel to that of a U.S. "ally." Whenever possible, the words "ally," "special relationship," or "strategic asset" were proposed for inclusion in Presidential statements, in order to reinforce in the American public's mind the special links binding America and Israel.

Another Israeli goal was to extract from Sadat some concessions regarding the Sinai itself, notably with respect to the Israeli settlements and to Sharm-el-Sheikh. The Israelis hoped that Sadat would permit a continued Israeli military presence both in the settlements and in the strategically sensitive peninsula; Begin had made that objective quite clear to us in the course of his earlier Washington visit. However, the overriding objective was that of obtaining a separate peace treaty with

Egypt. Such a treaty would place Israel in a better bargaining position with respect to the remaining issues.

These negotiating stands in turn dictated the negotiating dynamics. Israel, to achieve its goals, had to be intransigent on the broad issues and yet sufficiently enticing not to totally alienate Sadat. Sadat had to protect his flanks with the other Arabs while seeking his main objective, the Sinai. The United States had to help Sadat obtain a justification for a separate accommodation by pressing Israel directly on the West Bank and also, to some extent, on the secondary Sinai issues. As a result, more frequently than not, the United States and Egypt found themselves working more closely together, with Israel appearing as the principal obstacle to peace. Throughout the process, Carter had to play the role of the conciliator, defending Begin to Sadat, and explaining Sadat to Begin. At the same time, the President had to engage in direct, sharp disagreements with Begin, and these were intensified by Begin's legalistic pedantry and by his inclination to take refuge in procedural dodges.

Although Israel enjoyed the advantage of having the clearest and most precise goals, it suffered from having the least cohesive negotiating team. They were, in a word, prima donnas. Begin was the dominant personality, and in the negotiating process the other Israelis clearly deferred to him. At the same time, there was no doubt that Begin, Dayan, and Weizman were engaged in a political contest with one another, and they did little to mask their mutual dislike. To Begin, Dayan was a useful shield, to be put forth in order to obfuscate matters and to give Begin negotiating room. At the same time, the Prime Minister clearly did not trust his Foreign Minister and probably for good reason. Dayan, in personal contacts, tended to be both surprisingly mild and at the same time quite elusive. One could never be certain of the true meaning of his words, and his formulations often seemed to be deliberately obscure. Moreover, without quite saying it, he managed to convey his contempt for Begin, delivering the unspoken message that the Prime Minister was unnecessarily crude and rigid. Begin's attitude toward Weizman was patronizing, conveying the impression that the Defense Minister was not to be taken seriously. Dayan went even further, indicating in private conversations that his brother-in-law was a superficial person, excessively eager to please the Americans and the Egyptians. Weizman completed the circle by letting it be known that Begin was mindlessly missing a genuine opportunity to achieve peace while the deceitful Dayan, for Machiavellian political reasons, was needlessly complicating the peace process.

In the Israeli delegation, Begin generally took the harder positions while the others made it clear that they were prepared to be more accommodating. In contrast, in the Egyptian delegation Sadat generally took the more compromising position while his subordinates sometimes were literally tearing their hair out. On numerous occasions, Sadat had to overrule members of his delegation in front of either the Americans or even the Israelis, a practice which doubtless did not endear him to them. Nonetheless, unlike the Israelis, the Egyptians were relatively united outwardly, with the delegation totally subordinated to Sadat's will and unquestioningly following his instructions. Their dismay at Sadat's willingness to compromise was conveyed more by mood, by gestures, than by words; but there were moments when Boutros Ghali, the sophisticated Foreign Minister, or the highly cultured and soft-spoken Prime Minister Mustafa Khalil, or the legalistic and rather pedantic but brilliant legal adviser Osama el-Baz made it plain that Sadat was excessively deferential to American concerns and needlessly irritating to the rest of the Arab world.

The American delegation was remarkably united. Carter was its outstanding personality, and this was openly acknowledged by both the Israelis and the Egyptians. Carter absorbed all the negotiating issues, and his grasp of the material was extraordinary. Within a few months, he acquired a deep familiarity with all the difficult items that had to be tackled and ever-increasing skill in handling our very sensitive and suspicious Middle Eastern partners. If in the first year he was occasionally insensitive to the special historical and psychological legacies that so conditioned Israeli attitudes, there is no doubt that by the second year he became increasingly adept even at establishing a better personal relationship with Begin.

Carter was ably seconded by Vance, who was at his best in the context of these highly detailed and exhausting negotiations. He was persistent, solid, and well informed. Though often exasperated with the Israelis and even willing to punish Israeli intransigence, he never let his feelings affect his dealings with the Israelis and as a consequence he was able to orchestrate the lengthy negotiations which consumed so much of 1978. Thus, as Weizman put it, "Carter's team functioned with admirable efficiency. It held its internal deliberations and prepared position papers and reports, composing dozens of drafts for every proposal and setting out answers to every conceivable query. The team, orchestrated by Secretary of State Vance, was marked by a high degree of unanimity." That unanimity was especially important on the second echelons, where Roy Atherton, Hal Saunders, and William Quandt collaborated in a joint State–NSC team, making it possible for the President and Vance to be always ahead of the Israelis and the Egyptians in the technical-negotiating efforts. This helped the United States to retain the needed initiative.

During the first two years, Mondale actively encouraged the President to maintain a tough posture and to press hard for a settlement. Though his attitude changed in the course of 1978, in the early period Mondale was in the forefront of those who argued that the time had come for the United States to make its position unambiguously clear and to press Israel to accommodate. More sensitive to domestic political stimuli than Carter, Mondale realized that the period of maximum Presidential leverage was the first or the second year and that thereafter it would become politically too costly to alienate Israel's many supporters—both Jewish and non-Jewish—in the United States. I strongly supported him, and Mondale's view was clearly congenial to Vance as well. Hamilton Jordan was more ambivalent, already thinking ahead to the forthcoming congressional and then to the later Presidential elections. As time went on, and as the attacks from the Jewish community on Carter and his associates mounted, Jody Powell became an increasingly assertive advocate of a tougher line on Israel, but I think that was more out of loyalty to the President than out of any strategic perspective. In contrast, Carter's other domestic political advisers, notably Stuart Eizenstat and Robert Lipshutz, both naturally more sensitive to the sentiments of the Jewish community, urged accommodation with Israel and consistently opposed any actions designed to push Israel into a more compromising posture. While my own relations with Stu Eizenstat remained personally close and our friendship, if anything, became stronger as the years went on, there were times when some frictions between us would arise. I remember one occasion when Stu requested of the Situation Room communications personnel that a member of Stu's staff be given access to the most sensitive cables dealing with Israel, and I had to instruct the Sit Room not to do so on the grounds that the issue was not in Stu's domain.

In brief, the negotiations of 1978 thus involved a clear-minded and purposeful but bickering Israeli team, a charming and tactically bold but rather isolated Egyptian leader, and a well-orchestrated, tactically effective but strategically somewhat ambivalent American side.

Shaping a Secret Strategy

The new post-Geneva U.S. strategy emerged gradually during the first weeks of February 1978. Early in the year the President met with President Sadat at Aswan, on his way to Paris from a state visit to India. While in Aswan, the President and Sadat agreed on a formula (recommended by Hal Saunders) to the effect that the Palestinians have a right "to participate in the determination of their future." The carefully crafted formula was designed to assure the Palestinians that the United States was heeding their desire for political self-definition but that it was also mindful of the Israeli interest in making certain that Palestinian self-determination did not endanger Israel's security.

The stop in Aswan was preceded by consultations in Riyadh with the top Saudi leaders, talks which further enhanced U.S.–Saudi understanding. We felt we were making progress in moderating Arab attitudes on the question of peace with Israel. The visit to Riyadh was memorable also in other ways, notably our trip from the airport to the Royal Palace. My journal summarizes my impressions: "The Presidential caravan from the airport to the Royal Palace involved a headlong race amongst the cars—security cars, cars with dignitaries competing for the road, playing chicken, jamming on the brakes at the very last second, zooming forward, screeching suddenly to a halt. The whole atmosphere was totally surrealistic."

After our return to Washington, and while Vance was on a review mission in the Middle East, Carter and I discussed on January 20— and this was probably the first time the issue was ever mentioned—the possibility of setting up a meeting at Camp David to include Sadat, Begin, and the President. I told the President that I liked the idea. I jotted down in my journal that evening: "I think it might help the negotiating process and it certainly would be a very major accomplishment for the President if he were to generate some genuine progress through such a direct meeting in which he would be playing the central role."

Two days later the President phoned me early Sunday morning from St. Simon, where he had gone for a weekend of fishing. He told me that he would like to have a meeting with Cy as soon as he returned and that I was to include Mondale and Jordan. Speaking cryptically, he indicated that he was leaning more and more to the idea of holding a meeting with Begin and Sadat either in Washington or at Camp David.

Over that weekend a message came in from Cairo from Ambassador Hermann Eilts pointing out that Sadat was becoming increasingly disillusioned with Carter's unwillingness to push the peace process forward. I sent it to the President, along with a memo in which I summarized my assessment of the current situation: "We have reached a point where we may soon lose our ability to shape developments in the Middle East and the chance for peace may slip away. We can slow the process, we can play for time, and we can avoid hard decisions for a while, but the price could be substantial. Alternatively, we can begin to lay the groundwork for a concerted strategy of reaffirming that the basis for negotiations must be Resolution 242 in all its parts, which means that Israel must explicitly accept the principle of withdrawal on all fronts as the counterpart to Arab commitments to peace and security. This will produce a political debate in this country, and we will have to be attentive to timing, but we will be on comparatively strong ground if we stick to 242 and our opposition to settlements."

The memo served as the basis for the high-level discussion of our entire Middle East policy held that same evening. As I noted the very same night in my journal:

The evening was quite fascinating. It involved a meeting on the Middle East which the President asked for yesterday through his phone call. In addition to having the Vice President, Cy, Ham Jordan, and me in it, he also included in the gathering Jody Powell and, much to my surprise, Rosalynn. He came prepared with twenty points, the thrust of which was that we ought to invite both Sadat and Begin to an immediate meeting here. Prior to that meeting, I gave the President a brief memorandum outlining my position and the latest cable from Egypt, suggesting that Sadat is deeply disillusioned with our performance. Cy was against an immediate. meeting involving Begin and Sadat for the good reason that it might not generate enough success to merit such high-level Presidential involvement. The President, however, was obviously sold on this idea and was quite for it. Although I had earlier discussed it with him and initially had favored it, by now I had reservations and I was in favor of inviting only Sadat. In my view this is necessary in order to reinforce Sadat, to give him a greater sense of confidence, and also as a subtle way of putting pressure on Begin. Finally, it buys us some time because we do not wish the crunch to come before the Panama Canal debate is completed. At first there was no support for my point of view at all, but as the discussion went on and as the President reluctantly began to conclude that a Begin–Sadat–Carter meeting may be premature, he started hewing to my position [to invite only Sadat].

. . . the meeting ended with an agreement that we will explore a special meeting with Sadat and that in the meantime we will, at least for the time being, postpone any firm decision on the arms transfers to the Middle East. This will enable us not to have to make a major commitment immediately to Israel, and this may avoid a bruising fight on the Hill with regard to the Saudi request for the latest F-15s. However, I am somewhat less than optimistic regarding our ability to avoid a fight on this issue. My guess is that the Saudis will insist that we go through with our promise and that Israeli supporters will also press for an explicit commitment regarding aid for Israel. However, all in all I was pleased by the position we took, and I was particularly pleased that the point of view which initially didn't have much support in the end was adopted. Let us hope, however, that this approach proves viable. Much will depend on the President's willingness to make a full commitment to Sadat and then to go through with it.

Again, as earlier in the day, I was quite surprised by Fritz Mondale's toughness insofar as Israel is concerned. I do not know what has made him adopt this position but he really sounded quite firm in his view that we have to go through with a very decisive showdown. At one point in the discussion I said that I think that our performance till now appears to Sadat and the other Arabs as being either deceitful or weak or incompetent or a combination of all three. Yet I must state that both Carters laughed at this and the President said, "And they very well may be right in their view."

The decision to invite Sadat to the United States precipitated in turn the emergence of our new and highly secret strategy. In a private conversation with the President on January 14, I suggested that we should urge Sadat to come forth publicly with a reasonable proposal, but that this proposal should deliberately contain one or two maximalist demands which we would subsequently publicly disown. This would enable us to take issue with the Egyptians, and to use the subsequent Egyptian "concession" as the point of departure for joint public pressure on the Israelis. I further developed this thought in a memo, with which the President expressed agreement. Accordingly, we proceeded to flesh out this approach, which was very much favored by our joint State-NSC team. Quandt and Saunders particularly felt that this would enable us to generate the greatest public pressure on Israel, and Vance shared this view.

During the next two weeks we prepared an outline of what might be in such an Egyptian initiative, what elements of it would be deliberately exaggerated, and how the United States might then both "compel" Egypt to compromise and apply maximum leverage on Israel to accommodate. Sadat, in keeping with the President's decision on January 23, was invited to visit Washington in early February so that we could jointly shape the complementary U.S.–Egyptian initiative.

In devising our tactics, both Mondale and Vance felt strongly that the two issues on which we could best confront Begin were the question of the settlements on the West Bank and the applicability of UN Resolution 242 "to all fronts." Their argument was that on these two issues there was adequate domestic support for Carter to take Begin on directly. Even friends of Israel were dismayed by Begin's reinterpretation of UN Resolution 242 and his insistence on setting up new settlements, especially after Sadat's Jerusalem initiative. There had been a particularly strong public outcry in the United States against the recent Israeli announcement that four new settlements were to be established. We also felt that Begin was on weak ground insofar as the UN Resolution was concerned. The purpose of the Resolution was to achieve peace with all of Israel's neighbors, and hence it was strange for Begin, who had resigned from the Cabinet in 1970 to protest the fact that UN Resolution 242 applied to all fronts, now to pretend that it did not apply to the West Bank.

Carter found Begin's attitude increasingly outrageous, and this only enhanced the President's high esteem for Sadat. We all felt that the Egyptian leader had gone out on a limb in order to promote peace in the region and that Begin was busily sawing the limb off. We thus approached our coming meeting with Sadat in a rather determined and grim mood. Carter fretted a great deal and was very impatient.

Toward the end of January, I gave the President a detailed scenario for the proposed two days of meetings with Sadat, including a series of sequential steps designed to indicate our commitment to a just settlement while steadily increasing the pressure on Begin, culminating perhaps even in a showdown with Begin sometime in April or May. I showed it also to the Vice President, and he was quite sympathetic, saying that we had to act firmly on this issue. There was no doubt that the construction of additional settlements irritated not only Carter but Mondale as well, and this made for internal unity on our team.

Carter's mood grew more and more impatient. At the foreign affairs breakfast on February 3, he told all of us that he was disappointed with the slow pace of progress and also with what was being recommended to him. I gave him a ten-point revision of Begin's December autonomy proposals, trying to make them more palatable to both the Egyptians and the Americans, and this the President approved, though again muttering that he wanted more rapid movement from us. At one point he snapped to Ham Jordan, "I don't want to play grab-ass with Sadat all weekend. We need to get moving on this." In any case, the breakfast ended with agreement that we would try to get Sadat to come out first with an Egyptian proposal which in some ways would be evidently unacceptable to the Israelis, and that the United States would then step forth with a more moderate compromise solution. That would enable us to generate the greatest degree of international and domestic pressure on Begin to acquiesce.

On Saturday morning, February 4, our little Middle Eastern cluster, headed by Mondale, Vance, and me, took a helicopter to Camp David. The President was already there with Sadat, and shortly thereafter all of us sat down in a big conference room in one of the lodges.

Sadat spoke up and quickly dropped a bombshell. Speaking in grave terms, and with his face projecting disappointment, Sadat informed us that he had concluded that the Israelis were not prepared to treat him seriously. His meeting with Begin in Ismailia had been particularly distressing, and he was now convinced that the Israeli objective was to acquire as much land as possible. Sadat was especially outraged by the arrogant attitude which Begin had adopted with him. As a result, he planned to announce on Monday the breaking off of the bilateral Egyptian–Israeli military and political talks.

While Sadat's comments were a shock to us, I could not suppress a sneaking suspicion that this was a bluff designed to elicit some sort of U.S. commitment. In any case, the President urged Sadat to exercise restraint and moderation, and he was echoed by both Cy Vance and Fritz Mondale. Mondale was particularly eloquent in saying that Jerusalem had been a historic breakthrough which every American admired and that it was terribly important that this peace process continue. I joined in, saying to Sadat that if he made his announcement on Monday, the American press would view the Camp David meeting between Sadat and Carter as a failure, and this would be damaging to both Sadat and Carter. It would simply make it more difficult for us to support his efforts. I suggested that he announce instead that he was resuming the talks, but couple this with a strong statement on the negative effect of the Israeli settlements policy and on the importance of UN Resolution 242 being applied to all the territories at issue. I added that we could then support him.

After some further exchanges, Sadat accepted our approach, which I suspected he was planning to do in any case, and in return asked Carter whether the United States would be prepared to come out with a firm commitment of its own. That then gave us the opening for suggesting our sequential approach: that the Egyptians come out first and that we then react to the Egyptian proposal with a variant of our own. I elaborated on this more specifically by suggesting a six-point approach: Sadat should come out as a moderate on Monday; on Wednesday we would back him publicly on the question of the settlements and UN 242; later Carter would meet with Begin; following that Sadat would come out with his peace plan; we expected that Begin would reject it; and then the United States would come out with its own compromise formula. Cy Vance also suggested that in the meantime Roy Atherton go back to the Middle East to resume the Israeli–Egyptian talks and to make an effort to draw in the Jordanians. In further discussion it was agreed that our timetable would be for the end of March or early April and that both sides would try to adhere to it.

However, within a day or so, I began to have the uneasy feeling that perhaps neither side fully understood what it had agreed to. Sadat made several public statements while in the United States which seemed to me to be excessively hard and not to contain the moderate components for which we had hoped. The President in the meantime started thinking more systematically about the possibility of a separate Israeli–Egyptian peace treaty, and I suspect that this may have been stimulated by his private discussions with Sadat. Heretofore, the President had felt that such a separate peace treaty would not be in our best interest, but now he asked me to evaluate such a prospect for him, with special attention to the impact on the Soviets. I did so, arguing that an acceptable outcome would have to contain some commitments to progress on the West Bank issue, lest the Arab–Israeli conflict again become stalemated, to the detriment of American interests.

The next stage in our efforts was the March meeting between Carter and Begin. This meeting was preceded by continued irritation over the settlements issue, including some blistering messages from Washington to Tel Aviv. In mid-February, the President met with Dayan, who struck me as extremely nervous, defensive, and unusually ineffective. Perhaps out of compassion, Carter went out of his way to reassure Dayan, and in the process—it seemed to me—walked away quite a bit from our agreed formulas with Sadat. I worried that Dayan might go back with the impression that the U.S. position was not firm and that the President could be swayed.

Carter also met in early March with Defense Minister Weizman, and he made a point of meeting with him privately in order to maximize Begin's uncertainty as to what actually was said. (This meant that Ambassador Simcha Dinitz had to be excluded, and that rather pleased me because in the meantime we had had a series of reports to the effect that Dinitz was using his evening dinner parties in Washington for continuous denunciations of the President, Vance, and me. However, in excluding Dinitz, the President also instructed me to exclude Jordan and Lipshutz, both of whom wished to attend the meeting. That task made me very uncomfortable, for I knew that I would be blamed by them for such exclusion, and I insisted that the President order his Appointments Secretary, Tim Kraft, to do it.) The meetings with Dayan and Weizman were neither productive nor instructive. It was clear from talking with them that the final decisions would be made by Begin and that neither man was in a position to be of much help in coping with the obstacles to peace in the Middle East. One had the impression that both Dayan and Weizman, each in his own way, were also using the visits with the President to bolster their own personal political ambitions, with Dayan quietly insinuating that accommodation with Begin would be difficult to achieve.

The key preparatory meeting for the Begin visit was held on March 12 and included, in addition to the President, Fritz, Cy, Roy Atherton, Jordan, and me. It was at this session that, for the first time, a major disagreement arose between Vance and me on our Middle East policy. All of the participants agreed that the President in talking to Begin should place primary emphasis on the U.S. national interest, and that he make no effort to paper over the differences between the United States and Israel. However, Vance suggested that, if there was no progress, we should go back to the UN and take up Waldheim's proposal for a conference which would also include the Soviets and the PLO. I strenuously objected on the grounds that this not only would reintroduce the Soviets into the region but would be damaging to us in domestic political terms. Instead, we had to face up to the fact that at some point there would be a direct clash with Israel, and therefore we should choose the best grounds for it, namely the question of the settlements and of UN Resolution 242, matters which both Vance and Mondale had previously emphasized. For the time being, Begin was a real asset to us because his low standing in American public opinion made it easier for us to move forward on the other key components of our Middle East policy—the development of a military relationship with both Egypt and Saudi Arabia.

Carter and Begin met on March 21 and 22, and the meetings were generally unpleasant. After a rather chilly greeting, Carter opened with a statement of the U.S. national interest, but in my judgment he did not press Begin very hard. Fortunately, Vance and Mondale joined in, interrogating Begin sharply on the Israeli attitude toward Resolution 242 and on the distinction between genuine Israeli security needs and the question of territorial expansion. Later in the evening, Begin and Carter met alone, and the President told me the next morning that the meeting was completely unproductive. Carter was clearly in a fighting mood, and this showed itself in the next formal U.S.–Israeli meeting, which started at 11:05 a.m. in the Cabinet Room. The President sat down, gave Begin one of his icy smiles, and proceeded in very firm tones to state the following: "I am discouraged about the prospects for the future. I will have to make a report to members of the Congress on our position and yours, and I am going to tell you what I am going to say to them so that you can correct me. My view is that you are not willing to stop expansion or the creation of new settlements; you are not willing to give up the settlements in the Sinai; you will not accept UN protection for the Sinai settlements; you will not politically withdraw from the West Bank; you are not willing to accept UN 242 on all its fronts; and you are not willing to let the Arabs choose between three different alternatives after the end of the five-year transition arrangements for the West Bank."

When he finished, the Israelis looked absolutely shaken. Begin was sitting across from Carter, with a stony expression on his face but looking rather ashen. Dayan leaned back several times in his chair and put his hand to his head, looking obviously pained and very nervous. Dinitz gave me the impression of being in a state of shock. After a brief pause, Begin responded with a rather desultory account of how flexible he had been and how rigid in contrast Sadat had shown himself to be. Dayan then offered some alternative formulas regarding Resolution 242, but Vance intervened forcefully to the effect that the Israeli approach was not acceptable. After roughly an hour of this, the meeting adjourned, with the two statesmen walking out with grim expressions on their faces. I shortly thereafter gave the President two alternative texts of proposed goodbye statements, and he very deliberately chose the one which I had labeled as being the colder.

The next day we called in the top Senate leaders and they were briefed on the talks with Begin first by Vance and then by the President himself. The President was particularly effective and dramatic. He described the new Israeli position on the settlements and on UN 242 as "a shocking change in the Israeli position. The new policy is a shock to me. It undoes everything we have been seeking. Begin was absolutely adamant in his position. Because of the intransigence of the Israeli government, I see no prospects for negotiations." At this point Senator Jacob Javits almost plaintively interceded: "Mr. President, please don't give up." The President went on to say, "We cannot support Israeli policy which is incompatible with the search for peace." The senators were quite shaken. Afterwards, even such pro-Israeli senators as Javits and Clifford Case expressed their support for the President and urged us to stay on course.

The stage was thus set for the execution of our plan. The Israelis were on the defensive, congressional opinion was swinging behind us, and the moment of truth was nearing. Early in April, at a foreign affairs breakfast, following a review of developments in the Middle East, the President and Cy agreed that we would ask Sadat to make his public move toward the end of April, and we would then follow with the U.S. response approximately by the middle of May. This was to be done in conjunction with an address to the nation by the President, in which he would make the case that attainment of a more genuine settlement in the Middle East was in America's national interest. Our timetable was disrupted, however, by the intensifying controversy over the proposed sale of advanced F-15 jets to Saudi Arabia as well as of F-5E fighters to Egypt.

Jets for Saudi Arabia and Egypt

In retrospect, the congressional battle over the proposed sale of the jets to Egypt and Saudi Arabia was a costly diversion, yet winning the battle was absolutely necessary to retain American credibility with the increasingly more moderate Arab states of Egypt and Saudi Arabia. Ever since the Kissinger initiative toward Egypt of the mid-seventies, the United States had a growing stake in furthering a security relationship with that strategically placed Arab country, while the vital economic importance of Saudi Arabia to the West naturally dictated closer security ties. In going forward with the sales, all of us felt that the credibility of the American policy in the Middle East as a whole was deeply involved, even though it was to be expected that both Israel and its supporters in the United States would strongly object. To sweeten the pill, we made it clear that we were also prepared to provide additional planes to Israel. Ezer Weizman, with his characteristic candor, summarized the issue fairly in his book: "The Carter administration contended—with considerable justice—that plane deliveries to all three countries were part of a regional defense plan and of U.S. global strategy. In attempting to block arms supplies to Saudi Arabia, the Jews were widely perceived as supporting petty Israeli interests over global American interests. I was not surprised that the Israeli lobby failed in its campaign."

We had hoped to delay this matter while going forward with our peace strategy, but Saudi demands for the planes, as well as Egyptian insecurity about their defense relationship with the United States, compelled us to make the public announcement in mid-February. In addition, we had some intelligence suggesting that unless we went ahead, the Saudis would buy French planes, with predictable consequences of strengthening the Saudi–French political relationship at the expense of the U.S. one. Nonetheless, we did tell the Saudis in late February that we would like to delay this matter, and their reaction was most adverse.

In any case, we settled in late January on the strategy of combining the proposed plane transfers for all three countries into a single package, making it known that we would not permit the omission of any one country by a congressional veto. The strategy was designed to paralyze the powerful Israeli lobby on the Hill (and, as I recall, the idea for such a combined package originated with Christopher and me). Privately, I urged the President not to give more planes to the Saudis and Egyptians together than to the Israelis, but the President, increasingly irritated by Begin's provocations on the settlements, on his own decided to increase the number of planes to Egypt to a total of fifty. I suspect that his relationship with Sadat influenced his decision.

In subsequent weeks a great deal of time was expended in organizing the necessary bipartisan support on the Hill. The Majority and Minority Leaders were both extremely helpful. Abraham Ribicoff was a tower of strength, in marked contrast to the chairman of the Senate Foreign Relations Committee, Frank Church, who, though he privately promised us support, was extraordinarily susceptible to signals from the Israeli Embassy and in the end failed to come through. His attitude irritated Carter profoundly, and he told me in late April that it was striking the degree to which some senators are afraid to stand up for the American national interest and will simply do the bidding of a powerful lobby.

In order to assuage the Israelis, and thereby also to reassure the American Jewish community, I met for dinner privately with Dayan. My purpose was to gain from him a better understanding of what kind of an agreement on the West Bank might be possible, but also to convey to him our irritation at the lobbying within the United States by Israeli officials against our proposed arms-transfer package. On that point I was quite blunt. I told Dayan that we would win, whatever the Israelis did, but if they lobbied against us they would profoundly irritate the President and he might even have to air publicly the nature of the present security situation in the Middle East, including the sensitive question of who had what kind of weapons. This was meant to be a hint regarding Israeli efforts to obtain a small arsenal of nuclear weapons. On the other hand, if the Israelis were accommodating, I was instructed by the President to tell Dayan, which I did, that we would be prepared to consider a bilateral security arrangement with Israel. Though on these issues Dayan was his usual elusive self, I was pleased by the fact that our discussion regarding the West Bank produced a surprising degree of agreement. We were both of the view that an eventual solution would have to involve some arrangement whereby Israel and an Arab political entity on the West Bank were in a cooperative relationship, involving the free movement of people, opportunity for employment in either place, the right to pray and to coexist together.

During this period all of us were under severe attack from the Jewish lobby, and much time was consumed in meetings and explanations. These were rarely pleasant, even though the top Jewish leaders were more understanding of our need to develop ties with the more moderate Arab states. This was a particularly trying period, especially since all of us felt that in seeking to promote peace in the Middle East, and in weaning the Arab states away from Soviet influence, we were genuinely contributing to Israeli security. Fortunately, passions gradually cooled, and by early May it became clear that the President would have his way. We increased slightly the number of jets offered to Israel, and to reassure the Israelis we imposed some limitations—which came to haunt us later—on the kind of advanced equipment which would be associated with the Saudi F-15s. The Senate vote took place in the middle of May, and by a narrow margin the Administration prevailed.

But it was a costly victory. During this entire period we were virtually unable to move forward on any other front. Thus, it was not until the early summer of 1978 that we could resume our diplomatic efforts. We soon found out that the initial Egyptian proposals required a great deal of additional negotiations. They were simply inadequate and in our judgment would not permit us to proceed forward with the strategy devised in early February. By mid-June we devised an alternative strategy, involving a four-week scenario, to be initiated by an Egyptian proposal, followed by a Foreign Ministers' meeting, and then by a U.S. effort to break the expected deadlock. However, by July, Fritz Mondale, who had just returned from a trip to the Middle East, was beginning to question what he saw as our overly public diplomacy. He started urging the President to appoint a top-level negotiator to serve as a catalyst and shuttle back and forth between the parties. He recommended that Kissinger be chosen. I discussed this proposal with Vance, and Vance told me that he would resign if the President even considered it.

All of this led once again to a fundamental reassessment of our Middle East policy. Prior to our Friday breakfast I gave the President a memorandum (dated July 18, 1978) in which I outlined my basic feeling on what ought now to happen:

> When Cy returns, it would be desirable to hold a broad strategic review of our Middle East policy. Issues are coming to a head, and basic choices have to be made. We have committed ourselves to Sadat to put forward the U.S. proposal. . . . Given Begin's views on the West Bank/Gaza, he will resist a U.S. proposal more strongly than Sadat.
>
> How are we prepared to deal with an Israeli rejection of our proposal? Do we have the political strength to manage a prolonged strain in U.S.–Israeli relations? What kind of forces can we marshal and in what manner in order to prevail?
>
> These are the central questions, and they touch on both international and domestic sensitivities. Above all, you must decide whether at this stage you are prepared to see this matter through to the very end.
>
> I do not raise this issue lightly. It seems to me that if we go "public" and then do not prevail, our Middle East policy will be in shambles, and Sadat and others will be either repudiated or will turn in a radical direction. In other words, if we go "public," *we must prevail.*
>
> It follows that we should not undertake this challenge without considering carefully all the possible consequences and without assessing in advance exactly what it is we are prepared to do in order to make certain that we prevail. This will mean not only major domestic efforts but some advance decisions regarding our international reactions if Israel decides to reject or stall our proposals. You might wish to steer our Friday breakfast discussion along the lines of these questions.

Reacting to the memo at the breakfast on July 20, the President revived his earlier thought of convening a summit meeting with Begin and Sadat. Stressing that instead of working against Begin, we should try to work through him, the President told Cy that he ought to go to the Middle East in order to prepare such a summit. I noted later in my journal that "after the meeting I went into his study and he was standing there looking at the globe. He told me that for political reasons he would like to have a rather dramatic meeting, perhaps somewhere abroad. He suggested I start looking for a historically proper setting. We looked at the globe and talked about Spain, Portugal, and Morocco. I urged Morocco as the most suitable for a variety of reasons. The fact that Hassan needs a boost, that he has had secret dealings with the Israelis, and that there are the precedents in Casablanca of Roosevelt and

Churchill having attended a major and historically significant event or meeting."

Ten days later the issue was again discussed in depth, this time at Camp David. The President asked Mondale, Vance, Brown, Jordan, and me to join him for a complete review of what we should now be doing. Carter started our discussions by returning to his original idea that the summit be held at Camp David rather than abroad because he thought that we could have more effective control over the flow of information. I noted in my journal:

We will invite Begin and Sadat to meet with the President and lay our approach on the table. The question therefore was should Cy go to the Middle East first. I argued that Cy should go because preparation for the summit is needed. We cannot afford a summit in which both Begin and Sadat disagree with us. We ought to have at least one of them on our side so that we can then confront the one who is intransigent. I also stressed the proposition that the President simply cannot afford to fail, and therefore we must be really ready for a showdown. This means we have to be prepared to think through all of the necessary pressures, including even the ultimate sanction; namely, that refusal to accept our proposals will jeopardize the U.S.–Israeli relationship. I also said that in my judgment Begin will not accept our proposals at the meeting; he will say, "I am not President Hacha," that he has to consult with the Knesset and his Cabinet, and hence he will stall at the very least. Thus we have to prepare ourselves for the possibility of massive disappointment, a letdown, and even damage to Presidential prestige.

The President felt that Begin and Sadat both want peace and may be anxious to avoid war. At the present time, they don't take our peace efforts seriously, but if they were to meet with him, there is a better chance that perhaps they would be willing to consider our proposals, especially if they are reasonably moderate and offer the basis for genuine compromise. My proposal that Cy go next week anyway to prepare the groundwork was accepted. I also argued later in the meeting that Cy should go to Begin first and to Sadat second, and not, as we were initially inclined to agree, that he ought to go and see Sadat first and then Begin. My argument was that if he goes to see Sadat first and then invites Begin to the summit, Begin will suspect that he is being set up, that we had coordinated closely with Sadat. Carter read to us a rather effective letter he had prepared to Begin, designed to appeal to Begin's sense of history and destiny. In any case, the die has been cast. The meeting is being scheduled for the third week in August, and after that will come the inevitable showdown which will determine whether our Middle East policy is a failure or success.

The President told us to hold all of this terribly closely. No one should be informed outside of those attending the meeting. The Administration is permeated with those who are only too eager to share information with the Israelis.

The decision to convene the Camp David meeting was made without dissent. We all felt that our efforts had run out of steam and that the proposed secret strategy with Egypt was too complicated to execute. We were not able to contrive the required scenario, and it is also probably fair to say that our State Department negotiators were not comfortable with such a Machiavellian approach. Carter's verbal agreements with Sadat were too vague and tended to be interpreted differently by each side. Moreover, the time lost in the congressional struggle over the plane deal with Saudi Arabia and Egypt had generated Egyptian suspicions that we were not prepared to go through with our side of the bargain. All of these considerations led us to the conclusion that a three-way meeting would be a more effective setting for pursuing a variant of our initial strategy: joint agreement, to be achieved by a subtle combination of U.S.–Egyptian pressure on Israel to make the necessary concessions with regard to the West Bank in order to achieve that which Israel particularly wanted, a separate accommodation with Egypt.

At Camp David

The official announcement of a trilateral summit was made on Tuesday, August 8. The issue was in doubt until the very last moment. Indeed, Vance did not obtain final confirmation of Sadat's willingness to participate until the night of August 7. I called the President out of a dinner party to give him the good news. Despite all these last-minute negotiations we succeeded in keeping the Camp David meeting a secret. The news took the public completely by surprise.

As is often the case in affairs of state, our activities in connection with the announcement ranged from the serious to the ridiculous. In order to gain the support of Congress, the President began a round of intense briefings of congressional leaders. He warned them that failure to generate progress in the negotiations was likely to produce a new war in the Middle East. After one meeting, I urged him to tone down the war threats, fearing that the press would interpret our summit initiative as having been motivated by the fear of war. I worried that, if the summit failed, it would seem as if we had fallen for one of Sadat's ploys. On a lighter note, there was a great deal of jockeying as to who would make the announcement, whether it would be on camera or off camera, what ought to be said, and so forth. Jody Powell was angry that the President decided not to make the announcement on camera and not to take any questions. In the meantime, as I noted in my journal, Presidential media aide Jerry Rafshoon "went around strutting like a peacock trying to decide who should or should not be seen in the pictures." Finally, probably reflecting the tensions under which we were all working, Jody exploded when I told him that the New York *Times* was planning to stress the alleged threat of war in its story on the summit, and he literally shouted, referring to the President, "He is going to destroy his credibility if he keeps filling their heads with this kind of shit."

Over the next several weeks we worked hard to prepare our basic position for the summit. On August 31, I sent the President a memo in which I assessed the situation in this way:

> For the talks at Camp David to succeed you will have to control the proceedings from the outset and thereafter pursue a deliberate political strategy designed to bring about significant changes in both Egypt's and Israel's substantive position.

I suggested that we bear in mind the following:

> Sadat cannot afford a failure and knows it; both Sadat and Begin think you cannot afford a failure; but Begin probably believes that a failure at Camp David will hurt you and Sadat, but not him. He may even want to see Sadat discredited and you weakened, thus leaving him with the tolerable status quo, instead of pressures to change his lifelong beliefs concerning "Judea and Samaria."
>
> Sadat will define success in terms of substance, and in particular on Israel's commitment to the principle of withdrawal on all fronts. Begin will define success largely in terms of procedural arrangements and will be very resistant to pressures for substantive concessions. You will have to persuade Begin to make more sub-stantive concessions, while convincing Sadat to settle for less than an explicit Israeli commitment to full withdrawal and Palestinian autonomy.

I summarized what I believed to be the absolute minimum he should expect from each leader:

> Sadat should agree to an Israeli security presence during the five-year interim period and for an indefinite time beyond; he should agree to defer decisions on the precise location of borders and on

sovereignty until the end of the transitional period. In return he should be able to claim credit for ending the military occupation of the West Bank and Gaza and for establishing that the principle of withdrawal will be applied in the final peace settlement dealing with these areas.

Begin should agree that the principle of withdrawal does apply on all fronts, including the West Bank and Gaza, provided that its application takes into account Israel's long-term security needs in the area; sovereignty will remain in abeyance until a final peace agreement is reached at the end of the five-year period. This will allow Begin to take credit for protecting Israel's fundamental security interests, while not requiring that he explicitly abandon Israel's claim to sovereignty over these areas.

I warned the President not to be diverted by Begin's legalisms or Sadat's imprecision. I considered my agenda to be fairly optimistic, but the President urged us all to set our sights higher. He repeatedly told Vance and me that our planning papers were too modest. At one point he told me privately that he intended to obtain a comprehensive settlement and that he was going "to go for it all the way." However, on the eve of the summit, Carter confided to me for the first time his sense of uneasiness about the prospects for success.

The meetings at Camp David have been amply reported by other participants. Rather than duplicate their efforts, I have chosen to describe those thirteen days through the notes I made at the time with only brief interpolations. It is interesting to note in passing that Ezer Weizman in his memoirs assumes that we "bugged" the cottages of the other participants. In fact, I had proposed such a step to the President, but he, in what I felt was an excess of chivalry, flatly forbade that. As a result, we did not have adequate intelligence on what transpired in the Egyptian or Israeli delegations—though all of them took the precaution of conducting their own business on the porches of their cabins, and not inside.

I should add also that during the thirteen days at Camp David my roommate in one of the several small log cabins (we all doubled up because of space limitations) was Hamilton Jordan, and I could not have had a more pleasant or considerate companion. We got along well, exchanged some laughs, and I adopted his habit of depositing dirty laundry in the middle of our bedroom. I could measure the days spent in confinement by the gradually growing pile! For part of the time, my daughter Mika was also at Camp David, staying with Amy Carter. A diplomatic incident was at the last second averted by the Secret Service as she was about to ram Prime Minister Begin with a golf cart in which she and Amy were driving. (Golf carts and bicycles were our means of transportation within the sprawling camp.)

September 5, 1978

First day of the Camp David summit. I helicoptered to Camp David shortly after noon. A glorious sunny day with a blue sky without a single cloud. Shortly after I arrived, the helicopter bearing Sadat came in. The President and Rosalynn greeted him enthusiastically and took him to his cabin. This was preceded by a brief fifteen-minute meeting with the President alone. Pretty much the same routine was repeated when Begin arrived two hours later. . . . After that the President, Vance, and I sat on the porch of the Presidential lodge and talked about the strategy for tomorrow. Somehow, even though this is truly a grave moment, I do not feel at all nervous or concerned. My feeling is that things will work out well or at least to a satisfactory degree. I am struck again how much, in his conversations with the President, Cy is inclined to agree with him.

Dinner in the main lounge, which was divided by accident into two separate groupings—an American and Egyptian group and a small Israeli group. The Israeli delegation strolled in headed by Dayan and Weizman. The Israelis sat among themselves, except for Weizman, who immediately announced loudly, "I can talk to those fellows anytime." He then joined the Egyptians. There was a lot of bantering, laughing, exchanges of anecdotes. Dayan sat at the other table sulking, obviously irritated by Ezer Weizman's little coup.

Wednesday, September 6

Early-morning breakfast with the President, Cy Vance, and me. The President reviewed his conversations with Begin last night. It was clear that they did not go too well. The President described Begin as rigid, unimaginative, preoccupied with the meaning of words, and unwilling to look at the subject in a broader perspective. He sounded really discouraged. He kept shaking his head and expressing his disappointment.

Later in the morning two meetings: first with the Egyptian delegation, and then with the Israeli. With the Egyptians, Cy Vance tried to make conversation on different subjects, but it really wasn't flowing because everyone knew that at this time the President and Sadat were meeting together. We then had a rather useful discussion with the Israelis. I was struck by how relatively open-minded Dayan and Weizman were. Weizman again stole the limelight, talking most of the time, and Dayan sat there sulking. But when we got to substance both Dayan and Weizman were relatively flexible. Dayan discussed in some detail his conversations with moderate Palestinians, and both he and Weizman indicated a willingness to discuss seriously the question of terminating additional settlements and of finding some formula that would give the Palestinians genuine self-government. Then Cy, Fritz Mondale (who showed up in the middle of this session with the Israelis), and I went to see the President. We sat on the porch and he described to us his morning conversations with Sadat. Again he sounded disappointed. He described to us how Sadat unveiled his peace proposal, which was quite comprehensive but also rather one-sided, with relatively few concessions. In fact, the only concessions he was prepared to make were the concessions which he would have us unveil, but his document was certainly rather rigid, demanding immediate Israeli withdrawals, termination of all settlements, etc., etc. The President said he hadn't realized how far apart these two men still were. At the same time it was quite clear that he was taken by Sadat's attitude, his willingness to consider ideas, his determination to seek peace, his pledge to be cooperative and helpful to the President.

In the afternoon Vance and I played tennis and afterwards we got word that the President had completed his meeting with Sadat and Begin. When we came down to the lodge the President joined us and much to my surprise was very cheerful and pleased. Apparently the meeting with Begin and Sadat went better than expected. Although Sadat's proposals were clearly unacceptable to Begin, Begin, to some extent forewarned by the President not to expect anything forthcoming, responded rather magnanimously, indicated that he is prepared to consider any proposal, and he hopes that the Egyptians would do the same to his proposals. Begin said to the President that at the end of the meeting he hoped they could all say "habemus pacem," a takeoff on the words "habemus Papam," uttered recently at the Consistory which elected the new Pope.

The three leaders agreed to meet again tomorrow, and the fact that they want to continue discussions among themselves is in my judgment a sign of progress. The atmospherics are generally very good. Both the Israelis and Egyptians are making a clear effort to be congenial and to create a positive atmosphere.

The President described Sadat and Begin as initially a little tense but said they quickly relaxed and also tried to be quite affable and cooperative in their attitude toward each other. None of the stiffness and hostility that one might have expected, especially in the light of the comments made this morning by Sadat to Carter extremely critical of Begin, criticizing him personally, describing him as a man without any imagination or flexibility.

I did not keep detailed notes for the two meetings with the Israelis and the Egyptians, respectively, held on the following day. However, I did take notes of some of the exchanges. The first of the meetings involved Carter, Vance, and me, on the one hand, and Begin, Dayan, and Weizman, on the other. It lasted almost two hours and was held first thing in the morning, in one of the small Camp David lodges. It involved essentially a critical review by Begin of Sadat's proposals. Carter repeatedly appealed to Begin to be more accommodating and generous, but to no avail. The issue of the settlements was particularly critical. At one point Carter told Begin, "My reelection is not nearly as important to me as the resolution of the Middle East issue." He then went on to say, "Almost everyone feels that the burgeoning of Israeli settlements indicates that you are planning to stay on the West Bank—creating a societal structure on the West Bank and not a defense system. Each settlement is a nucleus of Israeli control." Dayan then fired, "What does withdrawal mean? Will I be a foreigner on the West Bank? Can they create a Palestinian state?" Carter kept pressing the Israelis to tell him what they meant by peace and under what conditions they would be prepared to settle, but the Israelis refused to become more specific. Begin summed up the Israeli position with the eloquent words: "Sadat wants peace with an Israel that would not only be vulnerable but doomed."

In the evening, our team met with the principal Egyptians: Sadat, Mohamed Ibrahim Kamel, Boutros Ghali, and the Presidential aide El-Tohamy. The meeting started with Sadat denouncing Begin at some length. "The man is obsessed, he's a hopeless case, he keeps citing European precedents, but we have not been defeated. Begin haggles over every word. Begin is making withdrawal conditional on land acquisition. Begin is not ready for peace." Carter doubtless agreed with Sadat, but he admirably maintained his position as a conciliator, responding firmly that "Begin is a tough and honest man. In the past he was quite hawkish. He sees his proposals as a starting point." Carter went on to say that he agreed with Sadat on the question of settlements, but he added that the Egyptians ought to be more forthcoming on security issues. For the first time, the President raised the possibility of an American military presence in the Sinai, if both Egypt and Israel would agree to it.

Sadat was unpersuaded. He returned to his attack on Begin, and he pointedly told us that the Israelis "have spent hours and hours trying to get us to cut you Americans out of these discussions. . . . Begin is full of complexes and bitterness. He has completely ignored my great gesture." But Carter persisted, appealing to Sadat not to ignore the concessions that Begin had already made and urging him to be willing to resolve at least those issues which were more immediate. "We believe that a trial period can work for the West Bank, if we agree on it. If we don't, Moscow and the radicals will rejoice. You must understand our special commitment to Israel—and the Israelis do want peace. They have not adequately responded to Sadat's initiative, but they have offered to leave the Sinai, to give self-government to the Palestinians, and our hope is they will cease the settlements and dismantle the ones in the Sinai. This should be acknowledged. . . . We must find a formula that both Egypt and Israel can accept. I intend not to fail."

The same day I noted in my journal:

Dayan and Weizman separately have sent us word that they think that Begin is too rigid on the settlements. Weizman tried to move him, but to no avail. Dayan proposed last night at dinner that the issue of the settlements be postponed until after all the other issues had been resolved. This might then make it easier to resolve the issue of the settlements. I tend to agree with that.

In any case, yesterday evening and then again this morning we had consultations with the President. He agreed to develop now the American proposal and in the morning we worked on it. These proposals will be reviewed later today, and sometime tomorrow the President will first share them with Begin and then we will give them to Sadat. Thus the issue will be joined because in these proposals we are making our position on borders and on the settlements quite clear.

Incidentally, yesterday at the meeting with the Israelis the only person to speak up firmly on the settlements, as was evidenced later by Begin's comments to the President, was I. Both Atherton and Saunders of State confirmed this fact, and I think it is a pity that the tough statements come mostly from Carter and from me. This could lead the Israelis to the conclusion that the U.S. position on these matters is somewhat idiosyncratic. However, I still remain optimistic. I think in the end we will get some agreed statement because all of the parties have a stake in some minimum agreement. The most difficult will be the Israelis, and help by Fritz Mondale can be quite central here.

Maybe because it's Saturday, maybe because Begin is observing the Sabbath today, but somehow the mood is more relaxed. We played tennis with the President this morning and then sat around the pool talking, having a drink, and generally relaxing. However, to the extent that there is any social mixing, it is almost entirely between the Americans and the Israelis and the Americans and the Egyptians but practically none at all between the Israelis and the Egyptians.

So far also the agreed blackout on news has been observed, but today Jody Powell was strongly suspicious that the Israelis are beginning to leak and to manipulate the news. . . .

In the meantime just had word that Weizman went to see Sadat to discuss the outstanding issues between the Egyptians and Israelis and also he proposed to them that they cut a deal leaving us out of it. Apparently, Sadat refused all of these requests. Thus the issue between the Israelis and Egyptians is being joined ever more sharply. By tomorrow we should have our proposals ready, and the issue will then come to a head.

Saturday afternoon we met in one of the cabins to give the final review to our basic proposal. The President joined us, and I was again impressed how closely he reads these documents and how sensitive he is to nuances and specific points. His textual criticisms are as good as those of any expert. In general his tendency is to make the document tough on the Israelis and more palatable to the Egyptians. In fact, I fear that it is somewhat too tough now. . . .

Later Carter was talking about Begin and Sadat and saying how much he and Sadat have in common, how Sadat is always willing to accommodate him when he calls upon him, and "I feel very comfortable with him. My chemistry with him is good. I feel with him the way I feel with Cy Vance." Cy laughed, and I said, "Yes, because Cy accommodates you the way Sadat does, isn't that right?" Everybody laughed, and the President said, "Yes, and you're just like Begin." . . .

In the evening I went over to Begin's cabin to play chess with him. He announced that this is the first time he has played since September 1940, when a chess game that he was playing was interrupted by the NKVD, which came to arrest him. . . . In any case, he plays a very good systematic, somewhat aggressive, but strategically very deliberate game. In the first game I gained tactical advantage of a pawn and position, but in the end in launching my attack I made a mistake. He took my queen and eventually he won. In the second game, I was more cautious; first consolidated my defenses and then opened an attack against him, especially since in the meantime he had spread his forces thinly. I then won. As a consequence, we ended up one to one. [It was a useful lesson for our Middle East policy, I later mused.]

I suspect that Begin's reference to his last chess game being interrupted by the NKVD was a psychological ploy. Toward the end of the game, Mrs. Begin showed up, and noticing her husband and me deeply engaged, she exclaimed, "Menachem just loves to play chess!"

Monday, September 11
Yesterday afternoon, following a relatively relaxed half day, we met with the Israelis to present them with our proposed document. The situation was somewhat dramatic. We met in a little cottage

around a table, four and four on each side. Begin, Dayan, Weizman, and [Legal Adviser Aharon] Barak; the President, Vice President, Vance, and myself. The President made a rather eloquent opening statement outlining his commitment to peace, his belief in the sincerity of all of the parties and in the reasons for the approach that we were taking. He then asked Begin to read the document through before commenting on it. Begin and his associates then read it, and Begin responded immediately by raising the issue of the inadmissibility of changes in territory through war, wording derived from UN 242 which was in the preamble. . . . The discussions became quite heated. The President was extremely firm in stating that we are here to move toward peace on the basis of established resolutions; that to question these resolutions was to open a Pandora's box which could never again be closed.

The exchanges became quite sharp. Begin at one point averred, "The war of 1967 gives Israel the right to change frontiers," and Carter shot right back, "What you say sounds to me that Sadat was right—that you want land."

Then Begin indicated that he did not wish to discuss the document without further review, and asked that we adjourn till later in the evening. The President somewhat reluctantly agreed. . . .

Cy and I joined the President in his cottage for drinks and we watched the tennis championships on TV. We then had dinner together. I was somewhat struck by the fact that when Stan Turner arrived to debrief the President on his conversation with Sadat, and I was lounging on the floor with a drink while the table was being set for dinner, Turner was not then invited to stay. Given his sensitivity, I am sure this did not make him feel too good.

We met again with the Israelis after dinner at 9:30. This was a heated and prolonged discussion. Begin spoke in somber, grave, and determined tones, registering his objections first of all to UN Resolution 242, particularly in regard to the inadmissibility of the acquisition of territory through war, but also more generally on withdrawals, the nature of the self-government on the West Bank, the issue of the Palestinians, and so forth.

Carter was quite direct. "This is not the time to beat around the bush. If you disavow UN 242, I would not have called this meeting." Begin responded, "We do not consider the resolution to be self-implementing. 'All its parts' includes the preamble. That has been our position for eleven years." Carter responded, "Maybe that's why you don't have peace for eleven years." As the argument went on, Begin began to soften. "We don't want to cause you aggravation. Please be patient with us." And then went on to repeat all of his familiar arguments until Weizman broke in, "Let's go on." The discussion again became heated on the subject of the future of the West Bank. After Begin outlined all of the controls, veto rights, and privileges that he would retain for Israel while giving the Arabs a form of self-rule, Carter exploded, "What you want to do is to make the West Bank part of Israel." Vance added, "The whole idea was to let the people govern themselves. You are retaining a veto." And Carter concluded, "No self-respecting Arab would accept this. This looks like a subterfuge." I joined in, "This is profoundly sad—you really want to retain political control—vetoes, military governor, broad definition of public order. We thought you were willing really to grant genuine self-government. Now it's clear you are not." Dayan responded, "Professor Brzezinski, we are not after political control. If it looks that way to you, we will look at it again." Toward the end of the meeting the President told Begin that he feels that Sadat would be willing to sign a separate treaty with the Israelis, provided the Israelis show some flexibility on the key issues. The President, moreover, pursued my suggestion that the Israeli proposal for home rule be viewed not as a permanent arrangement but as a five-year transitional accommodation, and he pressed Begin to accept that approach. This again led to the question of what the future might be, and the Israelis repeatedly expressed their concern that the Palestinians should not end up acquiring an independent state.

As the evening wore on, it was interesting to note that Weizman first and then Dayan would speak to Begin in Hebrew, and judging from the tone of their remarks, they were inclined either to tone Begin's obduracy down or to actually argue with him. Later on they began to do so also in English. In general the atmosphere became somewhat more relaxed even though the Israelis continued to raise endless objections. The session lasted until after three in the morning. We agreed that the Israelis would submit to us early this morning, by eight o'clock, their proposed changes in writing, that we would reflect on them in the light of the night's discussion, that we would introduce whatever changes we find acceptable into our document and then submit our revised version to Sadat.

We did so early this morning with a meeting of the American cluster again in the same little room. Perhaps because of lack of sleep, Cy Vance was rather abrasive and abrupt. But the President was very much in charge and kept making very useful changes and amendments. In general, I must say his performance was first-rate. Last night he clearly dominated the proceedings . . . firm when needed, and yet willing occasionally to alter the language. Begin probably was not too flattered by the fact that at the end of the meeting at 3 a.m. the President asked Dayan to walk with him to the President's cottage so the two of them could talk separately. I could tell from the rather pained expression on Begin's face that he was troubled and offended by this act.

Rosalynn told me this morning the President described Begin as a psycho, which I think reflects accurately the degree to which Carter was irritated by Begin's performance. An additional element which outraged Carter was that when Carter initially presented our proposals late yesterday afternoon, Begin did not even make a single gracious comment about Carter's efforts in the course of the last eighteen months to bring peace to the Middle East.

It is now noon Monday and the President is meeting with Sadat to present our revised version. I am fearful that we have revised it to a point that may make it difficult for Sadat to accept our document. Carter relies heavily on his special relationship with Sadat to bring him around to a more compromising point of view, and I hope he can pull it off.

Tuesday evening, September 12
Shortly after noon yesterday Cy and I met with the President sitting out on the porch in the glorious mid-September sun to be debriefed on the President's meeting with Sadat. It lasted two hours. Basically it was good. Sadat would be willing to leave the Israeli settlers in the Sinai for three years, and he might be willing to let the Israelis have the two airfields for that period of time. This, however, is not yet to be revealed to anyone, certainly not yet to the Israelis. In spite of this, however, the President feels rather pessimistic and concerned. We all played tennis in the afternoon, and the President was very preoccupied and rather gloomy.

Later in the evening Cy Vance called me and asked me to come to his cabin. He told me how deeply concerned the President and Rosalynn were and how he tried to reassure them yesterday evening, telling them that in such negotiations there are always ups and downs and that things eventually will turn out all right. My own expectation is that we will get a joint statement with the Egyptians, that the Israelis will indicate that it contains some positive elements, but that it also contains elements that are unacceptable to them and that these will have to be considered by the Knesset, in effect neither no nor yes, although they will go to considerable lengths to avoid any direct split between them and us and also by the same token any close linkage in Egyptian–U.S. relations.

This morning I met with the President in the morning; so did

Cy. And he was somewhat more optimistic after his late discussions last night with Dayan and Barak. He found both of them more positive and more willing to compromise. In fact, he even said that he felt now that not all Israeli positions and demands were that unrealistic. . . .

Later in the morning I got a call from Begin asking me to go for a walk with him. We walked around for about forty-five minutes. He started by telling me that he knows that I have been attacked in the Israeli press and by American Jews as being anti-Israeli, that he always defends me, and that he was deeply grieved to hear that in our meetings with the Israelis and again last night I characterized the Israeli settlements as a form of colonialism. He became quite emotional on the subject and spoke at length about the security role that they play and about his commitment to the maintenance of these settlements. He later went on to say that the leading personality on the American side—it was clear from the context of his remarks that it was the President—had also stated that these settlements had to be dismantled or removed. He characterized this idea as "fantasmorphic." I told him that I personally didn't feel strongly about the settlements but I felt that the Israelis should understand that to the Arabs they are a form of colonialism, that the Arabs perceive them as colonialism, and that the Israelis should be more sensitive to the relatively recent Arab exposure to colonial experience. He was quite emotional throughout, speaking about blood and soldiers dying, and referring to Israeli security, and reaffirming that under no circumstances will he ever agree to withdraw these settlements.

At one point during our walk, he exclaimed: "My right eye will fall out, my right hand will fall off before I ever agree to the dismantling of a single Jewish settlement." I thought of this later when Begin agreed to the Sinai deal, which included the dismantling of the Israeli settlements. It reconfirmed my view that Begin can be both pressured and enticed.

He was also very concerned that the United States not adopt a position in favor of removal of these settlements because this would put the United States on the side of the Arabs. We then went and started playing another chess game, which unfortunately was interrupted. I did play a third game with him last night, which I won. . . .

Around midmorning we met again with the President, who reported on his conversations this morning with Sadat. His feeling is that Sadat will be cooperative, provided the Egyptian delegation doesn't influence him too much regarding our draft.

In the afternoon we had a long session with the Egyptians, who on the whole did not raise too many fundamental objections. Thus, as of now, the situation with the Egyptians is on track, relatively speaking.

In the evening, Cy and I met again with the President, who spent the afternoon drafting his own wording for the Sinai agreement. It is a remarkably well-prepared statement, which the Egyptians, with whom the President met shortly thereafter, immediately accepted. Perhaps word of this has gotten to the Israelis somehow, because Begin has requested a private meeting with the President tonight, which he has in advance described as the most important and difficult meeting of his life. The two are meeting right now. Thus the next thirty-six hours are likely to involve the most fundamental confrontation on the central issues.

Wednesday, September 13
The President debriefed me last night on his meeting with Begin. It was apparently quite painful. Begin spoke at length about his inability to accept the words "inadmissibility of acquisition of territory by war." [This was a reference to UN Resolution 242, and Begin was clearly maneuvering to protect his longer-range claims to the West Bank.] Then he again made an impassioned statement about the settlements and generally orated at the President about his position. . . . Carter commented on the fact that he is not quite sure whether the fellow is altogether rational.

We worked yesterday evening in Holly cabin, where we have been meeting most of the time, on a revised U.S. position amalgamating the Egyptian and Israeli points. The President joined us later in the evening, and I walked back with him to his cabin. It was rainy, and very somber. I must say I am immensely impressed by the amount of determination and concentration on detail that the President has been displaying. This morning he has spent more than 3½ hrs., 4 hrs., working with the Israeli and Egyptian legal experts reviewing his own document. Cy has been working with him on this. Sometime later today we will be offering the Egyptians and Israelis this document. It seems to me that the optimum result we can now expect is Egyptian acceptance, though that may not be easy, because it is likely that the other Arabs will object; only partial Israeli acceptance, with strong reservations about major parts of the document. From then on it's going to be a political contest waged before the mass media and Congress. A preview of it was provided by a comment by Dayan. Yesterday at lunch he tried to talk Cy into two concessions by us on the issues of settlements and the inadmissibility of acquisition of territory by war. Cy immediately and rather categorically stated that these were unacceptable. Dayan later on said to someone that this meeting will end up tragically, that there would be no agreement, and that Cy's rejection of his proposals will be the principal cause. ·

Evening of 13th I went to check with the President on his drafting sessions. It turns out that reasonably good progress was made, though the matter still is dependent entirely on Begin's and Sadat's reactions. I am afraid that by now many of the changes we have made may make the document unpalatable to Sadat or at least to the other Arabs, and yet that Begin will still reject it. The President was extremely skillful in unveiling the three-year delay in the termination of the Israeli settlement in the Sinai, and this perhaps might sway Begin.

The President proposed we play tennis [he and Fritz vs. Vance and me]. . . . He was extremely cheerful and friendly. We then had supper together, and the President returned to the drafting session with the Egyptians and the Israelis.

September 14

A rather odd incident occurred at night. At 4:15 a.m. I was awakened by a phone call from the President asking me to come over immediately. I went over (in my pajamas) and found him sitting in the living room with Rosalynn and the head of the security detail. He looked terribly worried. He told me, "Zbig, I am very much concerned for Sadat's life." I was obviously quite startled by that. He went on to elaborate. . . ."

Having noted that some members of Sadat's delegation may be close to El Fatah, the President said that when he went to see Sadat earlier in the evening, at ten o'clock, he was told that Sadat was asleep and could not see him, even though Sadat normally keeps long hours and the light was on in his cabin. Since Sadat is relatively isolated within the Egyptian delegation, with all of its members being more rigid and doctrinaire than he, the possibility of something unpleasant occurring either now or later could not be entirely discounted. After returning to my cabin a few minutes later, I met with the security people to instigate tighter security controls over access to Sadat's cabin, particularly arrangements so that we would know when and who entered and left.

This morning when I met with the President he looked quite grim, but we did not discuss this matter much further. . . . He told us that the Egyptians, that Sadat, would be prepared to sign provided we can get better language on two issues: self-determination and Jerusalem. I then sat with Cy and our other associates and worked on this language. . . .

Around noon I went to see the President again. He showed me

the draft that he has prepared on the Sinai. [It included provisions for demilitarization and for elaborate security zones.] He believes that Sadat will accept it. The Israelis, however, are becoming increasingly difficult. Cy and I feel that we have already made too many concessions to the Israelis and we need to beef up the document to take into account Egyptian concerns. Accordingly, we inserted today a reference to the need for an Arab or Moslem flag in Jerusalem and for direct elections following the peace treaty so that the electorate can express its views regarding the final disposition and governmental form for the West Bank.

After discussing all this with the President at noon, Cy and I went to lunch and we talked to Begin. Begin was extremely agitated and outraged over our proposal for Jerusalem. 'Non possumus,' he flatly stated to Cy and me and in a rather peremptory fashion simply rejected our proposal. He then gave us a long lecture on Judaic rights to Jerusalem and told us, insisting that he was being quite literal, that our new proposal on Jerusalem gave him heart palpitations.

After . . . lunch I went to see the President. He sat in his office and was clearly very disappointed. He showed me the changes that he made in the document. . . . He was, however, very depressed because it became clear that success was now eluding him. . . . He told [Cy and me] rather sadly that he thought the meeting would end in a failure and no matter what, he would be viewed as the scapegoat by the American Jewish community and much of the press. We tried to cheer him up by telling him that this would not be the case. After good tennis, sauna, and a swim he began to be less gloomy, and we began to plot our strategy for the next several days. We are now pointing to a conclusion of the meeting on Sunday and will explain the situation to the country on Monday. The President's mood improved as we discussed how we will coordinate our initiative with Sadat in such a manner as to make it clear that the responsibility for the breakdown rests on the Israelis. If the country supports us, then I believe that after a few months of tension with the Israelis domestic pressures in Israel will make it increasingly difficult for Begin to maintain his unreasonable position on withdrawals, the settlements, and self-determination.

In the evening stopped by the President's for a drink and to hear a report from Cy Vance on his conversations with Begin. Earlier in the day, Cy had been invited to join Begin for a conversation. The President then had told Cy of the need for a tough and direct statement to Begin, especially in view of his peremptory manner during the luncheon discussion of Jerusalem, and in fact the President in his rather disingenuous way suggested to Cy that I accompany him to see Begin. Cy immediately objected and said he would prefer to go alone. And the President said he wanted me there only in case a witness was needed. However, it was clear that he wanted someone to be with Cy so that Cy would be quite tough.

From Cy's report it was quite clear that Cy had gone in there in a fighting mood and had a humdinger of an argument with Begin. According to him, they were both shouting at each other and Cy made it very clear that Begin's position was unacceptable and unreasonable.

On my suggestion the President phoned Mondale and asked him to come in tonight. He will talk to the Israelis tomorrow because it is important that someone who is viewed as sympathetic to the Israelis give them an unambiguous message.

Friday, September 15

Met in the morning with the President, Vice President, and Vance. We reviewed the strategy for the next few days, including the President's appeal to the country on Monday. We agreed that for tactical reasons it would be best to keep the meeting going till Sunday so that the President can be the first on Monday to go to the country and to lay out his view, his version of events.

Subsequently the U.S. group met to define the goals and tasks and assignments for the next several days, the kind of meetings we will have, the kind of speech the President will give, and so forth. . . .

At lunch Harold [Brown] and I were joined by Weizman. Weizman offered us a deal on the airfields in the Sinai which Begin has been refusing to give back to the Egyptians. In effect, if the United States were to build new airfields for the Israelis in Israel, these airfields would then be returned as soon as such construction is completed.

In the afternoon a meeting involving Mondale, Brown, Vance, and me, with Dayan, Weizman, and Barak. Just prior to it I briefed the President on our conversation with Weizman, but he indicated that he would not go along with such a bargain unless the Israelis accepted our total package, including withdrawals from the settlements in the Sinai.

The meeting with the Israelis involved a prolonged discussion of the settlement issue in which they made a determined attempt to obtain either the exclusion of the issue from the agreement or the postponement of its resolution. We made it very clear to them that their approach was not acceptable. However, Barak then came up with an ingenious idea. If Sadat would agree with Begin regarding the overall framework for the West Bank and Gaza and the Sinai, and if the two could then sign also the agreement on the Sinai which the President drafted, it could be stipulated that the peace treaty which the agreement on the Sinai calls for would not be concluded until the issue of the settlements in the Sinai has been resolved. In the meantime, the Israelis would proceed with their withdrawals in the Sinai, in any case, retaining only the thin band of land not far away from the Negev. That they would retain either for three years or pending resolution of the issue of the settlements, while Sadat would refrain from signing a peace treaty with them establishing diplomatic relations or opening the Suez Canal to them. Cy did not think much of this idea, but I feel that it may have some merit if we want to avoid a complete disagreement. In effect, instead of signing a separate treaty with the Israelis over the Sinai, Sadat would be signing an agreement over the West Bank and deferring final agreement on the Sinai. This conceivably could be attractive to him.

I went back and talked to the President about it, and he also saw some possibility in this approach and said he would sleep on it.

Later in the afternoon Vance and I played against the President and Fritz Mondale. We lost in three sets.

This evening I have been reviewing Quandt's initial draft of the Presidential speech.

Saturday evening, September 16

A day of oscillating expectations. It started in the morning on a relatively hopeful note. From 9:00 to about 9:45 the President, Vice President, Vance, and I met to review our framework paper. The President opted for stronger language regarding constraints on the expansion of Israeli settlements on the West Bank. We had a prolonged discussion on the paragraph dealing with the manner in which the Palestinians would participate in determining their future. This has now emerged as a major stumbling block between the Egyptians and the Israelis. The issue is how can one indicate that the Palestinians will have a measure of self-determination. Finally, we reviewed how we can cope with the settlements issue in the Sinai. Could we simply provide that there will be discussions regarding the time of withdrawal? Sadat is insisting on this, whereas the Israelis are arguing that the issue of withdrawal ought to be negotiated perhaps separately after Camp David.

Later in the morning attended a meeting with Dayan and Barak and Dinitz, with Cy doing the negotiating for us. They were engaged essentially in an effort to exclude the West Bank from the provisions of UN Resolution 242. Cy was quite firm in rejecting this approach and we backed him, although I did try to offer some compromise language in order to obtain Israeli accommodation. I must say that throughout these meetings Dayan is skillful at vague and obfuscating formulas. It is sometimes difficult [to tell] what he is trying to convey, although his efforts seem generally to be directed at avoiding any direct or sharp confrontation. Barak has proven to be the sleeper in the Israeli delegation—clearheaded and obviously determined to conciliate. In fact, in private conversations he has told me that many of the Israeli positions have no merit but are essentially psychological in origin. Weizman is bluff, direct, outspoken, an extrovert, occasionally comes through with a real insight, and clearly determined to make the meeting a success. Begin, according to Barak, tends toward total rigidity. His first reaction to any proposal is a curt dismissal with the word "unacceptable." Only later, if pressed, is he willing to concede that perhaps there is some minimum merit in the position that is being offered to him.

After lunch some further consultations and reviews of the situation with the President. I must say that he is driving himself mercilessly, spending most of his time either debating with the Egyptians or the Israelis or drafting and revising texts that are being submitted to him. He has single-handedly written the proposed document for the Sinai formula. . . .

After dinner, a rather moving discussion between Weizman and Boutros Ghali. We sat together chatting, and Ghali made a most eloquent statement to Weizman about the Israeli need to have a sensitivity for Palestinian sensibilities, feelings, and aspirations. Weizman spoke with equal emotion about his desire for peace, what war has meant to his generation, what it has meant for his son who has been invalided by it. The discussion was quite impressive in that it revealed at one time the enormous gulf that separates even people of good will on both sides and yet a genuine determination to seek accommodation. Ghali, however, did make the disturbing point that in his view the Arab world will reject the agreement and that this will put Sadat in an impossible position. In his view Sadat should not sign this agreement, because he will put himself in a most vulnerable position not only in regard to the rest of the Arab world but perhaps even domestically in Egypt.

Regardless of Ghali's assessment, Carter and Vance's meeting with Sadat and El-Baz in the afternoon revealed no significant disagreement except over the settlements, and no disagreement at all between Carter and Sadat. On the comprehensive framework, the delegations came much closer. Carter was able to solve the Palestinian autonomy impasse of earlier in the day by offering wording more acceptable to Sadat, and he induced Sadat to accept the language which had evolved on Jerusalem—provided that there would be an exchange of letters reaffirming the historic U.S. position that East Jerusalem was part of the West Bank.

After a protracted and heated argument, in which Begin shouted "ultimatum," "excessive demands," and "political suicide," he finally agreed to ask the Knesset within two weeks to agree to remove Israeli settlements from the Sinai, provided that agreement was reached on all other Sinai issues.

We also succeeded in drafting language stating that no new Israeli settlements would be established after the signing of the framework, pending the follow-on negotiations. (Begin later repudiated this point and stated that he had agreed only to stop building for three months.)

Sunday morning, September 17

After a long evening session with Begin, it is beginning to look good. We might get a compromise agreement today, though the burden of it will fall on Sadat's shoulders. It will be hard for him to justify it.

Tuesday evening, September 19

The preceding two days seem like months or years away. On Sunday much of the day was spent moving back and forth between cabins and in last-minute negotiations. The burden of the effort was largely on the President and on Cy. The documents were essentially drafted. There was basic agreement, but last-minute hitches developed on the issue of Jerusalem and the scope of rights and opportunities for the Palestinians. The Israelis attempted at the last minute to change wording and raised serious difficulty regarding our proposed statement on the U.S. position on the Jerusalem issue. They even threatened to welch out on the agreement. Nonetheless, we were fairly confident that we would obtain the agreement at some stage but not necessarily on Sunday. . . . Around five o'clock I was in the President's cabin with Cy, El-Baz on behalf of the Egyptians was there, and the President was meeting with Sadat. Around five or so Sadat left and last-minute telephone conversations were held with the Israelis concerning the final statement and exchanges of letters. Begin wanted to go and pay a visit to Sadat, but the President asked him to wait until the final issues were resolved. Around five-thirty, Cy turned to the President and said, "That's it. I think we have it," or "I think you have it." The President sat in his chair, looking rather tired, with a wistful smile on his face, but not particularly elated. No one spoke up, no one cheered, there was a sense of relief and a feeling of genuine admiration for what Carter had achieved. This was indeed his success. He was the one that gave it the impetus, the extra effort and the sense of direction.

Just at that time the weather also turned. Till then it had been generally good; now it became all of a sudden very dark and we were surrounded by the sound of thunder and the occasional flashes of lightning. The lightning seemed almost to be striking us, and there was a slightly eerie atmosphere. One had a sense of something momentous taking place.

It was agreed that I would be the principal briefer that evening. Accordingly, I left early with Fritz Mondale in his helicopter and arrived at the White House shortly before nine. We then went immediately into the press room, where I gave the briefing at which the press for the first time learned of the scope of this agreement. There was an audible gasp when I announced the conditions of the Egyptian–Israeli agreement, particularly the point that the peace treaty would be signed in three months. The newspapermen could hardly believe it. The sense of excitement mounted steadily as the briefing went on. I had difficulty extricating myself. Shortly after ten we went to the East Room. . . .

At ten-thirty the President entered with Sadat and Begin, having landed a few minutes earlier by helicopter. There was thunderous applause as he announced the success. He was followed by Sadat and Begin. Begin made it look much more like an Egyptian–Israeli agreement than is politically desirable, but he too was gracious and warm. As the President was leaving the podium . . . he shook hands with me; we just shook hands very firmly, slightly longer than usual and looked at each other. . . . It was a very special moment in history; and even though the arrangement that we had contrived is fragile, it nonetheless represents an enormous breakthrough.

Later Carter told me in some detail of a critical incident which occurred at Camp David and of which I had not known at the time. He said that he should have told me about it earlier but there simply had not been the time for it. And then he went on to tell me that on the Friday before the end of the Camp David summit Vance had gone to talk to Sadat and "came back looking absolutely ashen, shaken, I've never seen him like that. In fact, when I saw him I thought the Soviets had attacked Egypt. I was so surprised. I forgot that Harold was with me, and Cy did also. Cy simply said, 'Sadat has packed his bags. His bags are packed. He has asked for a helicopter and he's leaving later with his entire delegation.' I was absolutely stunned," said Carter, "and I didn't know what to do. I thought about it for a minute. I thought of calling him and telling him that this would cause us to denounce him publicly, but I decided that this wouldn't do. I therefore decided to go up there. Before going up I actually went and changed my clothes so that I would look more formal, something that I hadn't ever done before at Camp David. I walked up there. His whole delegation was with him on the porch. I asked him to step inside. He looked extremely drawn and nervous. We walked into the cabin, we sat down, and we looked at each other. I didn't say anything for quite a while because I didn't know what to say. I don't think I've ever been so grave or so serious about anything that I have said in my life. I then said to him, 'I understand you're leaving.' He said, 'Yes.' I said to him, 'Have you really thought about what this means?' He said, 'Yes.' 'Then let me tell you. It will mean first of all an end to the relationship between the United States and Egypt. There is no way we can ever explain this to our people. It would mean an end to this peace-keeping effort, into which I have put so much investment. It would probably mean the end of my Presidency because this whole effort will be discredited. And last but not least, it will mean the end of something that is very precious to me: my friendship with you. Why are you doing it?' Sadat looked absolutely shaken and then told me that he was doing it because he is convinced that the Israelis don't want peace and that he would be in a better position to go back and reshape his relationships, reestablish his relationships, with his Arab friends than to try to maintain a relationship of friendship with us. But he will not be in a position of having to listen to Israeli terms which he will now reject but the United States in part might endorse, and which then the Israelis in the future would use as the starting point for any further negotiations with him. I told him that if he does this it will mean the Soviets will reenter the Middle East, that what will happen to him is also uncertain, and that I can pledge to him that if he stays and there is no agreement I will make it very clear that any promises that he has temporarily made to the Israelis and which the Israelis in the future would try to use as the starting point for any negotiations would be null and void, that the United States will support him on it, and that we will support him also on the issue of the settlements. He thought for a while and said, 'Yes, I will stay.' The whole incident took a few minutes. We then shook hands. . . ."

I told him that this was a powerful and, in some ways, a very beautiful story, and I asked him whether he told it to Rosalynn. He said yes. I asked him, has he committed it to paper; he said no, and I said he should. And then I told him, "You know, the implication of this is that you have to be very steadfast on the settlements." He said, "Yes, I hadn't thought of that but that is true."

An Ominous Downturn

The Camp David Accords were not a settlement as such. Rather, they provided the needed framework for negotiating a transitional arrangement for the West Bank as well as an agreement to sign a peace treaty between Egypt and Israel within a specified deadline. Moreover, and it was largely Carter's own handiwork, the Camp David Accords contained a highly specific and complex plan for the gradual return of the Sinai to Egypt, together with arrangements for demilitarizing and internationally policing its more strategically sensitive sectors.

The historic accomplishment of Camp David was to lay the groundwork for an Egyptian–Israeli peace treaty, the first peace agreement ever between an Arab state and Israel. Its worst failure lay in not obtaining Begin's clear-cut acquiescence to a freeze on settlements activity, though on the last day of the negotiations Carter believed he had obtained such an agreement from the Israelis. He rejected an early draft which did not contain the promise explicitly, and he was promised a revised version which would meet U.S. concerns. When the promised Israeli statement was actually delivered a day later, it still contained an altogether different version of what had been agreed: the Israelis limited the settlements freeze only to the time provided for negotiating the Egyptian–Israeli peace treaty—namely, three months—and not for the duration of the negotiations aimed at the establishment of Palestinian self-rule on the West Bank. Moreover, the issue of linkage between an Egyptian–Israeli settlement and the West Bank–Gaza negotiations, which had been flagged at the outset of Camp David as the single most important issue, was not resolved, largely because Carter in the end acquiesced to Begin's vaguer formulas. That came back to haunt us in the subsequent phases of the negotiations.

Nonetheless, the outcome was a triumph of Carter's determined mastery of enormous detail and of his perseverance in sometimes angry and always complex negotiations. He showed himself to be a skillful debater, a master psychologist, and a very effective mediator. Without him, there would have been no agreement. Credit secondly must go to Vance, and I felt strongly at the time that the press did not give him sufficient accolades for his contribution. He was tireless in seeking compromises and persistent in pressing the two sides to accommodate. He was able to match the Israelis in esoteric legal argumentation, and his mastery of the problem at hand was peerless. My own role was quite secondary; it was my idea to turn Begin's initial autonomy plan into a conditional five-year arrangement, and I kept reminding Carter and Vance to insist on tighter linkage between the Sinai settlement and the promised negotiations on the West Bank.

Camp David was clearly a major accomplishment, even though as early as the day after its announcement I had to brief the President about the negative reactions from the interested Arab states, notably Jordan and Saudi Arabia. During the Camp David discussions, Carter seemed more optimistic than either Vance or I that the other Arab states would acquiesce, but in any case we were prepared to live for a while with negative Arab reactions while getting the peace process in motion. At the same time, it has to be acknowledged that the outcome did not conform fully to our initial expectations. The process proved more complex, and it took longer than we had anticipated. President Sadat, who saw Camp David as an opportunity to collude with the United States against Israel, ended with much of the pressure directed at him. His choices were either to walk out or to agree to whatever we could get the Israelis to accept. Sadat chose the latter, particularly after the President pleaded with him personally and pointed out that he had succeeded in getting Begin to agree to full withdrawal from the Sinai and to the removal of the settlements. The United States also obtained for Sadat something of a fig leaf against charges by other Arabs of betrayal of Palestinian interests through the vague "linkage" between the Egyptian–Israeli peace treaty and the West Bank–Gaza negotiations. We did not, however, succeed in getting an explicit commitment from Begin to terminate settlement activity, and that issue boiled up, literally within days of the Camp David success. Perhaps to protect his political flanks at home, Begin proclaimed on U.S. television Israel's right to remain physically on the West Bank for the indefinite future, even beyond the transitional five-year period, and also to go forth with his settlements program. American public opinion was outraged, and the Jewish community was deeply troubled by Begin's intransigence. Some Jewish leaders even said to us flatly that Begin was acting like a madman. Word also came from Tel Aviv that Dayan, Weizman, and Barak felt that it was a mistake for Begin to have stayed behind in the United States, without his more moderate colleagues to keep him under control. Internal Israeli bickering in any case intensified. During one of the lunches I sat next to Ezer Weizman, and he "used the occasion to whisper snide comments about Dayan. It is clear that the Camp David accord between Dayan and Weizman has come unstuck. Weizman blames Dayan for the slowdown of progress in the negotiations. In the meantime, Dayan apparently leaked to the Israeli press a number of nasty comments about the Israeli meeting with the President a few days ago."

During the fall the President continued his efforts to maintain the momentum of the peace process. In mid-October he met with both Dayan and General Kamel to initiate the formal Egyptian–Israeli peace talks. In my journal I mused that for Carter it was "a culmination of a process which could lead to an even more dramatic event—the signing of a peace treaty in the Monastery of St. Catherine in the middle of the

Sinai. The question is, will it endure? I am concerned that if the more moderate Arabs see the Egyptians and Israelis signing a peace treaty under our sponsorship, they may begin to see themselves as deceived, and this may have serious repercussions for the U.S. position in the Middle East." Thus I kept reminding Carter of the importance of obtaining some Israeli commitment to sustain progress on the West Bank issue.

My journal notes during September 1978 reflect our principal concerns. For example, on September 24 I wrote:

Sunday afternoon I chatted with the President by phone. He agreed with my view that we ought to be stressing more the West Bank framework because there is the real danger that Begin, through his statements and public posture, is trying to create the impression that the only accord that really counts is the Israeli–Egyptian agreement. If he can get away with it, he will obtain a separate treaty and then the whole structure of peace in the Middle East will crumble as the Saudis and the Jordanians react negatively.

The thrust of my own remarks on *Issues and Answers* was in that direction, stressing the advantages and the importance of moderate Arab participation in actually now implementing the West Bank–Gaza framework for peace.

Again on Monday, September 25:

The briefing [of the President by me] was followed by the foreign affairs breakfast, held this time on Monday because of Cy's return from the Middle East. Cy essentially gave a brief report on his discussions with Hussein and the Saudis; both cautious and timid. Everyone was very critical of King Hussein; that he is unnecessarily cautious. He wants us to deliver the settlement to him on a silver platter. We agreed that we have to develop cautiously some contacts with the PLO, but it will be done in very, very indirect fashion. Yet Palestinian moderation is absolutely crucial to success. I stressed the importance of moving also now on the West Bank issues. We need to start identifying Arabs who would participate. The President reviewed detailed maps regarding possible lines on the Sinai. It really is amazing how much time and effort he puts into these issues. He spent Sunday night reviewing a detailed disengagement proposal and wrote a number of highly specific comments on these proposals, including suggestions for moving lines between such obscure places as Jabal Libni and Jabal Hilal, apparently two hills in the middle of the Sinai. He also made a number of other detailed comments. . . .

A fair amount of time here was spent reviewing Cy's proposed

speech for the UN. Mondale and Aaron and others are very
agitated over the passages regarding the Palestinians. Cy rather
plaintively said to me on the phone yesterday, "Zbig, please help
on this Palestinian passage; it is important to me." I have tried to
fashion a compromise formula, and the President today approved
it. I think it goes far enough without producing a storm.

We had hoped to obtain a peace treaty by Election Day, but toward
the end of October it was clear that no agreement was in sight. The
President even started mentioning the likelihood of "a showdown" with
Israel, though no tangible steps to pressure the Israelis were taken.
Nonetheless, the President became increasingly concerned that Sadat
might feel that we had betrayed him, and I was struck how pained,
perplexed, and troubled the President looked.

To review where we stood, the President held a meeting on November 8 with Vance, Mondale, Jordan, and me. It was precipitated by a
cable from Samuel Lewis, U.S. Ambassador to Israel, "giving an account of the increasingly firm Israeli demands for money and also of
their stubbornness on the West Bank. I raised the question in the
meeting whether we should in fact be pushing so hard for an Israeli–
Egyptian treaty if it is our intention to resolve also the West Bank
issue. Once such a treaty is signed we will have less leverage. The
President was very tough. He said the Israelis don't want to yield on
the West Bank and that Dayan had seized the PR initiative from us
in terms of interpreting the negotiations to the public. As a result, Cy
should be very tough and yield nothing to them. The United States is
not going to give them any money, and in the meantime he doesn't
want 'Harold Brown wandering around the desert trying to figure out
where to put the airfields for the Israelis, with us having to foot the
bill.' When I said that I thought the Israelis wanted essentially a separate peace, then U.S. payments, and finally a free hand in the West
Bank, the President said that my remarks were brutally frank and perhaps oversimplistically stated. When I sarcastically responded 'Thank
you,' he looked at me very soberly and said, 'Yes . . . but I agree with
you."

The President's pessimism deepened in mid-November. One morning
when entering his office for the national security briefing, I found him
sitting behind his desk with his "nasty smile" on his face. When asked,
"How are things?" he responded, "Lousy." To my natural follow-up
"What's the matter?" he said with some bitterness that the Middle East
peace accord was falling apart and that neither Begin nor Sadat seemed
to want peace as much as we did. Shortly thereafter the President met
with Weizman alone, and he told me that Weizman would urge the
Israelis to accept a postponement in the implementation of the Sinai
withdrawals so that they could be timed to correspond to the initiation

of the West Bank self-governing authority. Actually, that particular formula was not pursued, but we continued to grope for some leverage to accelerate the peace process. At one point the President turned to me and Vance and said, "You, Cy, and I should get out of this. We should find some respected person to continue the negotiations. The most pompous one I can think of is Goldberg. He would wear them down and they would agree just to get rid of him."

On November 30, I wrote a rather lengthy memo to the President in which I laid out my analysis of why the agreements were coming apart. Camp David had worked because Carter had been able to keep both parties under his control; neither dared to assume the responsibilities of failure. The agreements had offered something beneficial to both. The problem by the winter was that Carter had lost control of the negotiations. Camp David had created the impression that a separate peace between Egypt and Israel was acceptable to both the United States and Egypt—in fact, I mentioned to the President that for a while I had even thought that perhaps he and Sadat had secretly agreed to this. I thought that Begin did not want to move on the West Bank because of problems with his domestic opposition and Sadat seemed to be frightened by the Baghdad Conference and the attitude of the Saudis. Furthermore, I believed that both Sadat and the Saudis doubted U.S. resolve to make certain the agreements are implemented. As a remedy, I suggested that the President adopt a strong public posture, be blunt, and push all sides.

Specifically, I recommended that there be a full press effort to get Sadat to accept the treaty. Israel should set a target date to initiate a substantive dialogue with the Palestinians and negotiations with the Egyptians on the scope and authority of the autonomous region. Further, I thought that we should tell Sadat that U.S.–Egyptian cooperation would in effect come to an end unless Egypt acceded to the treaty, but if Sadat did agree, then the United States would engage in long-term military and economic cooperation with Egypt and with Saudi Arabia on behalf of regional security and containment of Soviet influence.

As far as Israel was concerned, I believed it was time to tell Begin that Israeli failure to accept the timetable and to begin positive movement on the West Bank would mean that we would take the entire matter to the UN. I wrote that we should also tell Begin that U.S. economic and military relationships would not be allowed to perpetuate a stalemate which would inevitably radicalize the Middle East and reintroduce the Soviets into the region. I suggested that the President write both the leaders personal letters.

By early December, the stalemated Egyptian–Israeli negotiations revived talk of a showdown between the United States and Israel. Vance, on my urging, was instructed to go again to the Middle East, and the President, looking very sober, told him, "I would be willing to lose my election because I will alienate the Jewish community, but I think it is important to prevent the Arabs falling under Soviet sway. Thus, if necessary, be harder on the Israelis. If there is a breakdown, we will have to go with Sadat." Carter also consulted with Senator Robert Byrd, and asked him point-blank, "Are you willing to face the issue of a showdown with Israel on the question of the settlements in Congress?" Byrd looked at the President with his steel-like eyes and simply said, "Yes."

After a short trip, Cy Vance returned from the Middle East in order to be in Washington for the forthcoming mid-December announcement of our normalization of relations with China. His mood was one of disappointment and bitterness at Begin's tactics, and we were all becoming increasingly grim and dejected. In early 1979, at the January 12 foreign policy breakfast with the President, Vance suggested that we initiate contacts with the PLO as a way of generating momentum. Mondale became quite irritated by this suggestion and strongly objected to it. The President was not prepared to move either, so nothing came of the idea. I did not back Vance on the timing, but I agreed with him on the substance, noting that at some point contacts with the PLO would be necessary and that we must not repeat the mistake of the French, who for years refused to deal with the FLN in Algeria. At that moment, Ham Jordan—always mindful of the influence of the Jewish community in U.S. domestic politics—cheerfully quipped that perhaps one of us might want to be the first U.S. Ambassador to the West Bank, because in two years we would all be unemployed.

The First Peace Ever

This melancholy state of affairs dragged on till the late winter of 1979. As recriminations between Begin and Sadat mounted, it became increasingly clear that the Camp David Accords would not be consummated by a peace treaty unless Carter again injected himself personally and made another major effort. That was not an easy decision for the President to make. The Camp David Accords had been a major personal triumph, and the President was eager to turn his attention to other matters. The Middle East had been an enormous drain on his time and energy, and it had also been an issue of considerable political controversy at home. The signing of the Camp David Accords was thus not only a triumph but also a source of considerable relief.

To make matters worse, the international scene in early 1979 was a highly turbulent one. The recently concluded U.S.–Chinese normalization of relations, followed by Deng Xiaoping's visit to Washington, was suddenly complicated by the Chinese–Vietnamese hostilities, which in turn even threatened a possible Soviet move. The United States had to steer a careful course, and the matter certainly demanded top-level attention. At the same time, and even more dramatically, the strategic pivot of the American position in the Persian Gulf area, Iran, was literally crumbling before our eyes, and a self-proclaimed enemy of the United States was installing himself as the new dictator of that geopolitically crucial country. This development not only represented a major setback for American interests but also posed for the President personally the delicate political issue of the Shah, who was seeking asylum in the United States. Finally, the SALT negotiations were entering their critical stage, and the Administration was still committed publicly to the conclusion of such an agreement and subsequently to its ratification by the Senate.

Given these demands, the President was not eager to engage himself in another difficult round with Begin and Sadat. Yet could he afford not to do so? To let the Camp David Accords slip away would be to turn a triumph into disaster, with unforeseeable consequences for the Middle East as a whole. With Begin scheduled to visit Washington in early March, the issue came to a head.

In the late afternoon of Wednesday, February 28, 1979, the President met in the Oval Office with Mondale, Vance, Jordan, and me. Moreover, as was the case on those special occasions when a decision to be made had considerable personal significance for the President himself, Rosalynn was quietly sitting against the wall, listening carefully. The President asked us to diagnose the situation, and he called upon me to speak first. I was quite blunt. I said that I thought the Israelis were seeking to stall the negotiations so that in the end we would pay them for a separate peace with Egypt, which was what they had wanted in the first place. Moreover, I added that I had now reached the conclusion that the Israelis would prefer Carter not to be reelected and that this objective was influencing their current tactics. I could tell that my comments, particularly the last one, jolted the President and Rosalynn, especially since immediately thereafter Ham echoed them. However, the person who seemed to impress the President most was Mondale, who argued that we should take a passive position, not press Begin at all, and simply let things go on their own. His argument was that anything else would provoke controversy and be politically counterproductive. I was deeply troubled by Mondale's argument, for I felt that his prescription, if adopted, would lead to a general deterioration of the situation in the Middle East, and that would eventually affect the President's political fortunes at home as well. Vance seemed to agree with me, but did not take a forceful position at this meeting. When I left, I was convinced that nothing would be done.

I was wrong. On the following day the President, in a private conversation with me, again registered his concern about the situation in the Middle East, reiterating his unwillingness to become engaged. He made a point of noting that whenever he tried to move the parties toward peace, a significant portion of the American press then portrayed him as anti-Israeli. As a consequence, it was difficult to maintain a steady course consistent with the American national interest. But the President's attitude changed dramatically within a day, following the scheduled meeting with Begin. In retrospect, I suspect that if Begin had not come to Washington, the President would have followed Mondale's advice and not reinvolved himself in the Middle East problem. But the toughness and bluntness of Begin's arguments made Carter's adrenaline flow. He reported to us that Begin, in addition to rebuffing all our pleas for accommodation in keeping with the Camp David Accords, requested massive American help and proposed a defense agreement with the United States, with U.S. planes based in the Sinai airfields. Harold Brown immediately reacted adversely, noting that "the Israelis are pushing themselves as the main U.S. military asset in the region," but without any concomitant progress toward a wider peace. I could tell from Carter's account that he was stirred up and challenged.

The President's debriefing on his personal meeting with Begin was followed by a larger and more formal meeting, at which Begin put on a performance very similar to the one described by Carter. The session was punctuated by statements from Begin to the effect that "I will not sign it under any conditions," or "It is unacceptable," or "We shall never agree," or "It is not written," or even in Latin, "Non possumus." It was really both a remarkable and a dispiriting performance. The President was so discouraged that after the session he suggested to me that he would like to have lunch in my office, where he, Jody Powell, and Bill Quandt, and I discussed how we should react to the overall collapse of the Camp David Accords.

After the luncheon meeting, Quandt and I worked on a scenario for a major Presidential initiative which I submitted to the President on the next day. On Saturday afternoon, the President convened a meeting in his office with Vance, Brown, Powell, Jordan, and me. "I was really struck by the change in Carter's attitude. Whereas over the last couple of days he seemed downcast and almost resigned, he is now again vital, vibrant, and much more confident. He told us that he wants to lead and to act like a President, that he felt bad himself about the attitude that he had to adopt in the last few days, but that he has reached the conclusion that only a bold stroke can actually be the proper response." We agreed that we would propose to the Israelis a security treaty in the context of larger progress toward peace in the Middle East, involving the implementation of the Camp David Accords. I also used the opportunity to tell the President that I thought his foreign policy was too litigational, not dramatic enough, and that as a result he was being drawn into more and more detailed discussions of formulas, paragraphs, and declarations. Genuine breakthroughs, I argued, sometimes require a confrontation. I felt that my remarks had an impact on him.

Our small group met again on Sunday while Begin was still in town. In fact, we met twice on Sunday, with a meeting with Begin sandwiched in between. In the course of these meetings, the President reached a preliminary decision to go to Cairo and then to Jerusalem. The idea was championed most fervently by Jordan and me. Jordan was sensitive to the political consequences at home of a total collapse of the Camp David Accords, while I was worried about the consequences of such a setback for our position in the Middle East. Vance and Jody were lukewarm, while Fritz Mondale maintained his earlier position that the President should not engage in such a risky enterprise.

The purpose of the President's trip would be to overcome personally the remaining obstacles to the conclusion of the Israeli–Egyptian peace treaty. These difficulties involved three major issues: (1) the Israelis wanted preferential access to the Sinai oil and guarantees to that effect from the United States, while the Egyptians were reluctant to give the Israelis a preferential or exclusive status; (2) the Egyptians wanted the Israelis to grant self-government first to the Gaza Strip and to permit an Egyptian political-consular presence in Gaza itself; (3) the Israelis wanted the prompt exchange of ambassadors upon the signing of the peace treaty, whereas the Egyptians wanted to defer that until the full withdrawal of the Israelis back to the internationally recognized frontier. It was these issues that Carter hoped to resolve in the course of his trip, however unpropitious its climate. The meetings with Begin went badly, and Carter recounted that at one point he became so angry at Begin that, as he told us, "if he hadn't been my guest I would have asked him to get the hell out." To overcome Begin's unwillingness to compromise, Carter first had to obtain major concessions from Sadat, and on that basis then try to fashion some agreement with Begin.

The decision for Carter to go to the Middle East was precipitated by a message that we received on Sunday, March 4, from Sadat. Obviously aware that American–Israeli talks were in a stalemate, Sadat simply cabled to inform Carter that he was planning to arrive in Washington in the middle of the coming week, with the intent of appearing before the Congress and on radio and television in order to denounce Begin's intransigence. We all felt that Sadat's initiative was not exactly a constructive one, for its immediate effect would be to underline the degree to which the Camp David Accords had come unstuck. We agreed that a message should be sent to Sadat immediately, asking him to postpone any move for twenty-four hours.

The final decision that the President would go was made early on the morning of March 5, and Carter became increasingly cheerful. At times like that there was occasionally some friendly bantering, and when the phone rang in my office shortly after 9 a.m. (and the only time a phone would actually ring in my office was when the President himself was on the line), I answered by simply saying, "Sorry, Zbig is not here; he has been briefing the President since seven o'clock." Carter laughed and said, "Obviously Zbig is still in bed," and then asked me to come over to his office. It was there that he told me that he felt that the best course of action was for him to go to the Middle East, and he instructed me to bring Begin to his office so that he could inform him accordingly.

Once the decision to go was made, events moved swiftly. Later in the day, as I was having lunch with a group of newspapermen, the President phoned me two or three times to consult on the arrangements for the trip and to tell me that he was sending me ahead to meet with Sadat, so that Sadat would not do anything rash before the President's scheduled arrival by late Thursday. Shortly after 5 p.m., I had a last-minute meeting with the President, Vance, and Mondale, at which I was given my instructions for the trip. In essence, I was told to make certain that Sadat perceived the wider strategic purpose of our initiative, so that we wouldn't get drawn into fruitless legalisms of the kind in which Begin excelled. The President also told me to tell Sadat very privately that the President's domestic political situation was becoming more difficult and that Begin might even wish to see the President defeated.

(My departure for Egypt prompted yet another instance of Carter's personal kindness. I asked the President to let my departure be somewhat delayed, so I could attend my son Mark's confirmation. Unfortunately, because of Sadat's schedule, this could not be so, and Carter, with real feeling, offered to attend the religious ceremony in my stead. Knowing how crowded and exhausting his schedule was, I gratefully declined, whereupon the President wrote Mark a handwritten note, telling him that he was sending his father away on an important mission and expressing the hope that this explanation would partially compensate for my absence.)

I met with Sadat on the afternoon of Tuesday, March 6, until 7:30 p.m. In my opening remarks, I analyzed the security problems of the region, emphasized our determination to enhance Egyptian–American cooperation, reaffirmed the President's commitment to a wider peace in the Middle East, indicated that in our view success in moving toward such a peace was essential to the President's political fortunes, and suggested that Begin's inclination was to stall and perhaps even to contribute to the President's political defeat. This made it all the more important that the United States and Egypt cooperate closely so as to make it more difficult for Begin to prevent the implementation of the Camp David Accords.

Sadat could not have been more cooperative. He showed great concern for Carter's position and with real emotion affirmed his determination to help Carter overcome Begin's obstacles. Several times he repeated, "I have to give the President items with which to hammer at Begin," and as our talk went on, he became more agreeable to the proposals that Carter would make on the key issues at hand. Moreover, and much to my personal satisfaction, I was able to overcome Sadat's resistance to my personal suggestion that he invite Begin to visit Cairo (for I knew how symbolically important such a visit would be to Begin) and give Carter such an invitation to use with Begin. During our talk I was both impressed by the sweep of his strategic interests and amused by the contempt with which he spoke of his fellow Arabs. He kept referring to them as nomads or Bedouins who count for little. Immediately after my session, I cabled on it fully to Carter, who was extremely pleased and instructed me by an instant response not to share my telegram with anyone.

The President arrived on Thursday and immediately went into a session, one on one, with Sadat and then into a wider meeting at which Sadat was flanked by Prime Minister Mustafa Khalil and Vice President Hosni Mubarak, and Carter by Secretary Vance and me. Mubarak during the sessions was silent, though he and I struck up a warm relationship, and I felt that our chemistry was very compatible. I could tell that he would do whatever Sadat wanted, and I was very impressed by his intelligence and determination. Prime Minister Khalil, however, objected vigorously to our compromise formulas, and Sadat had to tell him several times to calm down and not to raise so many difficulties. Our meetings continued in Alexandria, after a memorable train ride from Cairo, during which Carter was cheered along the way by hundreds of thousands of enthusiastic Egyptians. During the train ride I had the chance to talk somewhat more with Sadat's wife and one of his daughters. I was struck both by their beauty, especially by their stunning eyes, and by their intelligence and sophistication. As earlier in China, I could not. help but reflect on the impact on personality and intelligence of the cumulative history of an ancient civilization.

By the time our meetings concluded in Alexandria, an American–Egyptian formula had emerged. In effect, Sadat gave Carter carte blanche for his subsequent negotiations with the Israelis. We agreed among ourselves to arrive in Tel Aviv with a somber demeanor, so that the Israelis would not feel that an Egyptian–American deal had been cooked up, though privately we were quite cheerful and hopeful.

Our mood changed rather quickly after our first meeting with Begin and his colleagues. The atmosphere in Israel was very different from that in Egypt. As noted in my journal, it was "formally correct, with a lot of pomp and military display, but the atmosphere much cooler. We drove from the airport, Weizman, Brown, and I in the car. Few people out in the street; long empty drive from the airport to Jerusalem and then through largely empty streets into Jerusalem; occasionally demonstrators with critical signs. . . . After dinner I went for a walk out on the street with my security people. I ran into some demonstrators who unfurled umbrellas and shouted slogans. I talked to them and said that it isn't raining; they should give peace a chance; that peace can either be that of victors or be based on accommodation. Actually, at the end the atmosphere became much more pleasant and one of the demonstrators asked if he could have his picture taken with me."

The formal discussions started on Sunday, March 11, at 11 a.m. Our little group, composed of the President, Vance, Brown, and me, with our top aides, met with the Security Committee of the Israeli Cabinet, Begin's eight top ministers. Begin started the proceedings by essentially rejecting our positions on the issues at hand. He interrupted Carter several times when the President was making his presentation, and "he was tough, dominating, almost antagonistic." We resumed our debates after lunch, with the President arguing that America had regional security concerns which we could not ignore and which would be helped by a peace settlement. I thought the President was very effective, and I passed him a note saying, "You should adjourn as soon as you finish," because I did not want Begin to rebut at that particular moment. The President followed my advice, and thus we left the meeting with the President's statement on the table. I was hoping that the Israelis would reflect on it and perhaps be somewhat more accommodating the next day.

In my journal I commented on the enormous contrast between a dialogue involving Begin and Carter and one between Carter and Sadat. Carter's discussions with Sadat were punctuated by comments such as "I will represent your interests as if they were my own. You are my brother." Or Sadat saying to the President, "My people admire you. I shall always be proud of our friendship, of our brotherhood." Carter to Sadat: "I hope I will never let you down. You are probably the most admired statesman in the United States." Sadat to Carter: "My people and I are grateful to you." In contrast, exchanges between Carter and Begin were icy, and even mutual praise was formalistic and devoid of any personal feeling.

The next day's discussions were no better. Begin simply took refuge behind the Cabinet, stating that he would be unable to accept any compromise unless the Cabinet accepted it as well, and Begin's Cabinet members made it clear that their attitude toward our proposals was quite negative. To quote from my journal: "Begin and company were completely negative. Begin interrupted me several times, but I rather firmly asked him to let me continue. The second time I said, 'Please, Mr. Prime Minister, let me speak without interruption.' I could tell that Begin was slightly put off, but he yielded and did not bother me again."

In the evening I met with Carter and Rosalynn in their suite, and both were quite dispirited. The sun was setting, it was somewhat dark in the room, the President was lounging on a sofa, and neither he nor Rosalynn made any effort to hide their disappointment. When Jordan joined us, the President made some rather earthy comments about Begin personally, and when Ham asked impishly whether his remarks were for the record, I laughed and said, "The remark is already on the record," pointing at the ceiling. I had no doubt that we were being recorded.

The Middle East roller coaster went upwards dramatically on Tuesday, March 13. Our proposals on oil began to be discussed more seriously, and Begin hinted that he might be willing to take some unilateral steps on the West Bank, symbolic of his commitment to eventual autonomy. In return, the Egyptians were to drop their special interest in a separate arrangement for Gaza and to agree to the earlier exchange of ambassadors. Nonetheless, we had no assurance of Israeli agreement, and we left Jerusalem concluding that Begin did not want to reach an accommodation. Just before our departure, Dayan proposed a last-minute meeting with Begin, who in turn, but in rather reluctant tones, agreed to present our proposals to the Cabinet, provided Sadat agreed. We went on to Cairo not certain whether the Egyptian leader could accept what we had to offer, but determined to make a last effort.

When we landed in Cairo we were greeted by the top Egyptians, who did not hide their apprehension. As we were walking from the plane to a nearby VIP pavilion, Mubarak asked me in a quiet whisper about the state of play. After a few preliminary exchanges, the President, Vance, and I joined Sadat, Mubarak, and Khalil in a separate room. Carter, though playing a weak hand, did one of the best selling jobs of his career. He started off in a very confident tone by saying, "Mr. President, I believe my assignment has been carried out satisfactorily. You will be pleased." Sadat interrupted: "Marvelous." Carter went on to say, "For the first two days Begin behaved the way he does normally. He was unpleasant, interrupted me. But then the moderates began to convince him to be more constructive. Begin now waits to hear your position." And the President went on to outline the proposed compromises, indicating that he substituted a U.S. guarantee of oil supplies to Israel for the demands that the Israelis were making on the Egyptians. On all of these points Carter put the best possible light on the Israeli stand, making it appear as if he had extracted some concessions. He reported that the Israelis were prepared to deal with the Gaza problem first, even though not agreeing to an Egyptian political presence. In return, he obtained Sadat's agreement to exchange ambassadors within nine months of the peace treaty.

Carter concluded his remarkably effective presentation by saying, "I would like to be able to announce today that I have reported to you that on all of those items on which the Israelis have expressed agreement you have also accepted our proposals; that on the other issues the Israelis will now consider them; and that you have, in fact, accepted them. This will enable us to say to the world that there is a U.S.– Egyptian agreement, and the Israelis will have to accept it or reject it." Carter and Sadat then retired to a separate room for a private conversation, and Carter asked me to draft a public statement announcing the agreement. A few minutes later, I rejoined Carter and Sadat and, crouching between them in front of a little table, I read out the proposed text. Sadat took a puff on his pipe, asked that the word "beginning" for a comprehensive peace be changed to "cornerstone" for a comprehensive peace, and then indicated that he was ready to go with it. I stepped out of the room to have the statement retyped and exchanged enthusiastic pats on the back with Ham Jordan.

Immediately prior to the public announcement, Carter phoned Begin to inform him of Sadat's acceptance. It was evident from Begin's reaction that this came as a surprise, and Begin pressed Carter with questions as to how specific the Egyptian commitments were. Carter, who was being photographed while conversing with Begin, at one point asked Sadat sotto voce whether the Egyptian would like to talk personally with Begin. Sadat, in a strong instinctive reaction, waved his hands in a desperately negative gesture and almost fell off his chair. The President and Sadat then walked out of the pavilion and read the announcement of agreement to the assembled newspapermen. It was a moment of tremendous satisfaction, since hours earlier we had been on the brink of total defeat. I was surprised and pleased by the fact that some of the newspapermen even broke into applause.

Almost immediately upon our return to Washington, the President instructed me to fly to Saudi Arabia, Jordan, and Cairo to brief the Saudi and Jordanian leaders on the agreement and to report their reactions to Sadat. While in Saudi Arabia, I obtained a secret Saudi pledge not to adopt any damaging sanctions against Egypt. The Saudis would confine themselves to a formally negative reaction, in keeping with their position against a separate peace treaty. The Jordanian King was much more negative and resentful of having been left out of the process. Incidentally, a revealing little incident took place just before I landed in Amman: I was informed that an assassination attempt against me would be carried out on my way to the Royal Palace. The immediate reaction of a senior State Department official accompanying me was to turn to an aide and say, "We better make sure that we are not in the same limousine as Brzezinski."

Contrary to U.S. press reports, we did not seek either Jordanian or Saudi endorsement of the peace treaty, but we did attempt to convince our hosts that we viewed the treaty as the point of departure for a sustained effort aiming at a comprehensive peace treaty. In both places we underlined the point that attainment of the five-year transitional arrangement for the West Bank and Gaza would create a new political situation, making possible further progress toward Palestinian self-determination in the future. From our point of view, the most important accomplishment was the Saudi pledge that they would do nothing tangible to hurt Sadat, and in subsequent months they kept that promise.

On the way home, we debriefed Sadat on our discussions and pleaded with him to avoid public polemics with his Arab neighbors. I also again urged him to invite Begin to Cairo, for I felt that this would help to create a more positive climate between the two men.

Toward the end of March, Carter, Begin, and Sadat assembled in Washington for the historic signing of the first peace treaty ever between Israel and an Arab state. The signing was preceded, however, by last-minute difficulties. The Israelis pressed us for tighter commitments and guarantees of U.S. support on the remaining issues in future negotiations, and there were also disagreements regarding terminology. The Israelis wanted to use Judea and Samaria and objected to the words West Bank and Gaza. Moreover, in a rather unusual move, Begin requested a private meeting with the President (to which I was invited). He told the President that he had a personal request to make, namely that Carter, as a gesture of friendship for Mrs. Begin, forgive Israel the outstanding debt on the massive $3 billion aid that the United States was extending to Israel. Begin repeated the phrase "as a gesture for Mrs. Begin" several times. Carter, who on financial matters was a bit of a miser, looked at first quite stunned, and then, turning to me, he burst out laughing.

But the dominant mood was one of profound satisfaction, and previous disagreements and bitterness were forgotten. There is no doubt that, each in his own way, both Sadat and Begin made critical decisions and undertook major political risks. Moreover, we all knew that the peace treaty marked a historic turning point and that it might usher in a period of greater hope. As I noted in my journal for Tuesday, March 27:

> Last night in a huge tent in the garden of the White House we celebrated the peace treaty. It was a remarkable evening. Not only was there joy, but a sense of real reconciliation. I sat at a table with the Weizmans and the [Muhammad] Alis and Kissinger. Weizman had his son with him. Badly wounded during one of the conflicts with the Egyptians, to some extent he has been permanently scarred. Yet he was there, partaking of this event, mixing with Sadat's children. Weizman was especially moved when he told me that Sadat had embraced his son, and I could sense that the parents were deeply touched when their son and Sadat's son shook hands and embraced.
>
> All of the participants rose to the occasion. The President was superb: moving, gentle, and yet committed. He opened with a prayer which coming from anybody else would have sounded hypocritical. From him it conveyed sincerity and genuine faith. Sadat made some references to the Palestinians, which he had omitted from the afternoon ceremony. Weizman, sitting next to

me, groaned and said, "Now you will see the Polish character in Begin asserting itself and he will rebut." Much to our joint surprise, Begin's response was peaceful, warm, cordial, especially to the President, but also to Sadat, and made no reference to the Palestinian question or to the firm statement by Sadat that statehood would be the end of the peace process. I was amazed and gratified. Peace can be contagious.

Of the speakers, only Begin praised Vance publicly, and I felt that Carter should have done it himself. After Carter, in the U.S. government Vance deserves most credit for this achievement. I have been saying this right and left to the press and others. The event, though it lasted for hours, was something that no one would have wished to miss. There was electricity in the air, a sense of joy, people mixing, shaking hands, patting [each other] on the back. And for Carter, of course, it was a spectacular and historic triumph.

No other U.S. President has made a comparable personal effort to obtain peace in the Middle East. No other President has ever been as directly involved in the search for compromise. No other President has negotiated as actively to overcome the enormous psychological and historical barriers even to a limited peace in the Middle East. The Israeli–Egyptian treaty, though far short of a comprehensive solution, did reduce the chances of a renewed Arab–Israeli war, a necessary precondition to an eventual settlement, and it created a framework for an interim arrangement for the West Bank and Gaza. Moreover, the Israeli–Egyptian peace treaty established the important precedents of trading territory and the dismantling of settlements for a binding peace treaty and elaborate security arrangements.

8

The Price of Friendship

We have a serious problem in Western Europe and Eastern Europe. The Soviet Union has built up a tremendous quantity of tank force, military force of all kinds, nuclear weapons like the SS-20, which is thirty times more destructive than any neutron weapon we have ever considered and which has a range of more than one thousand miles, where the range of the kind of neutron weapon we're talking about is only fifteen or twenty or twenty-five miles.

—President Jimmy Carter, town meeting, Spokane, Washington, May 5, 1978

The Carter Administration assumed office determined to improve relations with Western Europe and Japan. Enhanced political and economic cooperation with these key partners had been the first objective listed in the foreign policy goals document I had prepared for President Carter. Moreover, all the key foreign policy decision makers of the Carter Administration had previously served in the Trilateral Commission, a private body dedicated to the view that U.S. relations with Western Europe and Japan provide the strategic hard core for both global stability and progress. We assumed office feeling strongly that U.S.–Japanese relations had needlessly deteriorated because of the "Nixon shocks" (the unilateral measures imposed by the United States on U.S.–Japanese trade), and that the Europeans had been pointlessly insulted by Henry Kissinger's patronizing proclamation of a "Year of Europe." In addition, both the Vietnam War and the Watergate affair had jolted confidence in American leadership.

Given the unusually ambitious agenda that President Carter had set for himself during his first year in office, our allies' support for some of our initiatives was important domestically and internationally. In our efforts to promote the SALT and Panama Canal Treaties to reluctant domestic constituencies, we came to rely heavily on the endorsement of our key foreign friends, as well as on the argument that a given initiative was good for allied unity. Similarly, we often used allied backing to reinforce our efforts on such matters as the Middle East initiative and the problems of southern Africa. We also were concerned with strengthening NATO since, during the preceding years, the relative balance of power between the Warsaw Pact and NATO had deteriorated to the

West's disadvantage. In particular, we emphasized enhanced allied capabilities for conventional warfare. Harold Brown applied himself to this task with great energy, and the Carter Administration gradually succeeded in reversing the negative trends of the preceding years.

My own role in all this was essentially supportive. I had no major disagreements with my principal colleagues, and the handling of most inter-allied issues was essentially routine. Thus, I did not play a visible public role, nor was I heavily engaged in any internal foreign policy disputes as far as these matters are concerned. In my academic writing and also in my efforts to help establish the Trilateral Commission, I had focused on alliance issues. The approach that the Carter Administration developed was certainly compatible with my views, reflecting as it did the perception that the alliance had entered a new, more complex stage as Europe and Japan emerged from the era of American tutelage. The Europeans particularly were restless under the U.S. political-military umbrella, yet still fearful of the Soviet threat to their security.

I was especially concerned that this dilemma could strain American–German relations, especially as at the same time Bonn's *Ostpolitik* was gaining a momentum of its own. It was clear that Germany's heightened interest in the Eastern relationship had produced a view of detente that had begun to differ substantially from our own. Before very long, this issue was further complicated by the question of strategic nuclear balance, especially as our SALT negotiations gained momentum. It was on October 28, 1977, in a speech in London, that Chancellor Schmidt first raised the question of "the Euro-strategic balance," pointing out that the deployment of Soviet intermediate-range ballistic missiles, targeted on Europe, was creating a one-sided threat to Europe at a time when the American–Soviet strategic relationship was moving toward greater stability. Schmidt put it bluntly: "SALT codifies the nuclear strategic balance between the Soviet Union and the United States. To put it another way: SALT neutralizes their strategic nuclear capabilities. In Europe this magnifies the significance of the disparities between East and West in nuclear tactical and conventional weapons. . . . Strategic arms limitations confined to the United States and the Soviet Union will inevitably impair the security of the West European members of the Alliance vis à vis Soviet military superiority in Europe if we do not succeed in removing the disparities of military power in Europe parallel to the SALT negotiations."

We were thus faced with a complex set of political, strategic, and economic issues, none of them susceptible of quick resolution. Secretaries Vance and Brown took the lead in the required consultations, and their efforts were facilitated by the excellent personal relations they developed with some of their opposite numbers. I was particularly impressed by the good working relationship that Vance established with David Owen, the young new British Foreign Secretary, and with Hans-

Dietrich Genscher, the genial and wise German Foreign Minister. But my own relationship with Owen, I must confess, had gotten off to a shaky start. Shortly after his appointment, the British Foreign Minister came to the White House one Saturday morning for his first encounter with the U.S. President. As was our custom, on that weekend morning I was dressed in a pair of slacks, a sports jacket, and open shirt. Our guest, slightly stiff and uneasy, was an example of sartorial elegance: a dark pinstripe suit, an immaculate white shirt, an elegant tie. David, whose personal courage and intellect I came to respect greatly, did not disguise his distaste. Wait till you see the President, I thought—and his distaste turned to disdain when the doors opened and in walked the President of the United States, coatless, in blue jeans and jogging shoes.

President Carter soon established a good working relationship with his foreign counterparts. British Prime Minister James Callaghan, for example, displayed remarkable skill in cultivating Carter personally. In fact, I was amazed how quickly Callaghan succeeded in establishing himself as Carter's favorite, writing him friendly little notes, calling, talking like a genial older uncle, and lecturing Carter in a pleasant manner on the intricacies of inter-allied politics. Callaghan literally co-opted Carter in the course of a few relatively brief personal encounters.

It was perhaps fortunate that, during Carter's tenure in office, the Japanese Prime Ministers, Masayoshi Ohira and Takeo Fukuda, were the first genuinely internationalist Japanese leaders. Moreover, the dialogue with them was facilitated by the fact that they both spoke good English. Unlike their predecessors, they were willing to speak frankly and to engage in an active give-and-take, which made for a much easier and more direct relationship. Carter was especially captivated by the fact that Ohira was a practicing Christian.

While relations with French President Valéry Giscard d'Estaing never became warm, there is no doubt that Carter admired Giscard immensely and that this contributed to heightened Franco-American rapport. For my part, I developed a close working relationship and personal friendship with my two brilliant counterparts at the Elysée, Jean François-Poncet and Jacques Wahl, which generated a great deal of quiet but effective Franco-American collaboration on some very sensitive issues.

The only shadow in personal relations was cast by the West German Chancellor Helmut Schmidt, whose inability to keep his tongue under control soured American–German relations to an unprecedented degree and lent respectability to the increasing German propensity to be highly critical of the U.S. President and of U.S. policies more generally. As I have noted elsewhere, we did what we could to contain the problem, and Vance's excellent working relationship with German Foreign Minister Genscher balanced the situation somewhat. For my part, I maintained frequent contact with the solidly pro-American German Ambassador in Washington, Berndt von Staden, and later with his equally dedicated successor, Peter Hermes. Nonetheless, nothing could compensate for the absence of a good personal relationship at the highest level, which vastly complicated the handling of such sensitive matters as the neutron bomb dispute and the later development of a common allied response to Chancellor Schmidt's concern over the "Euro-strategic balance."

Reinforcing Unity

To dramatize his commitment to the improvement of trilateral relations, the President-elect announced early in January 1977 that his Vice President would travel to Europe and the Far East during the first week after the inauguration to discuss the Administration's foreign policy plans and to consult on preparations for the upcoming Economic Summit. During his trip, Mondale emphasized the American commitment to strengthening NATO defenses, reassuring the European governments that the proposed $6–7 billion cut in U.S. defense spending would not affect the alliance. At the same time, Mondale was clear when he stated that increased U.S. spending for NATO would have to be linked to commensurate increases by our allies.

The Mondale visit notwithstanding, relations with the Europeans started off on an uncertain note. Our public criticism of Soviet and Eastern European human-rights abuses and the controversy surrounding the Shcharansky case made many European leaders nervous. Nor were they pleased by our public opposition to German sales of nuclear technology to Brazil, or our new departures on nuclear nonproliferation, which evoked strong protests against American unilateralism. I tried to convey an understanding of the European perspective to the President in a meeting on April 3, 1977. I noted in my journal that when I mentioned Helmut Schmidt's resistance to some of our initiatives, "Carter reacted by saying that 'he's been quite obnoxious to me.' Everyone agreed except me. I shook my head vigorously. He looked at me and looked surprised. He asked, 'Why?' I said to him, 'Well, I suppose in some ways you have been quite obnoxious to him.' I could tell that everyone in the group was quite surprised, including Carter. . . . I wanted him to understand the extent to which Schmidt is under pressure in Germany, in part because of what we have been doing, and we should not underestimate the extent to which we have pushed some Europeans around. It was apparent to me that the upcoming summit in London, scheduled for May, would not be a success if we were not more responsive to European sensitivities."

The London trip actually turned out to be quite successful. The President was thoroughly prepared and held his own in this first exposure to the leaders of the Western world. In fact, Carter clearly emerged as the star. He was scrutinized by the media and hailed by the European press as a dynamic new leader. The President met with large and enthusiastic crowds wherever he appeared. Although differences on the nuclear issue were only papered over, Carter established a personal rapport with the allies. After the Economic Summit, the President addressed a meeting of NATO leaders and issued a firm call for increased defense spending by NATO. His speech set the tone and pace for the entire meeting and demonstrated vital American leadership.

I may add that during the London summit I had an unexpected clash with the German Chancellor. Since I had known him for years, I greeted him warmly. To my surprise, he was rather haughty and distant. Moreover, he visibly recoiled when I responded to his "Zbig" with "Helmut." Perhaps he felt I should have used the more deferential "Mr. Chancellor," but in that case there was no reason for him to call me by my first name as if I were his employee. Then, without any further ado, he lit into me, announcing that he was tired of the U.S.-supported Radio Free Europe operating on German soil, that its presence was contrary to detente, and that he would like to get it out of Germany. I responded merely by saying that the Radio was an important element of the overall U.S. policy toward the East, including our interest in the security of Germany, and that such matters could not be decided unilaterally or outside the larger security context.

Through the winter and spring of 1977–78, the NATO allies developed a long-term plan for increased defense spending. On May 30, 1978, the NATO Council met in Washington and adopted the defense program which stressed the buildup of antitank weapons and the integration of air defenses. The program carried an estimated cost of $60 to $80 billion and required a major commitment to raise appropriations for NATO defense. Harold Brown took the lead in these negotiations and succeeded in securing European compliance. When the 1979 budget was promulgated, it included a 3 percent increase for NATO as pledged. In May 1979, the NATO Defense Planning Committee met in Brussels and agreed to a 3 percent increase through 1985.

Throughout the four years, I made numerous trips to Europe to consult with the allied governments. In September 1977, I spent three days talking with my counterparts in France, Britain, and Germany, and met with President Giscard d'Estaing, Prime Minister Callaghan, and Chancellor Schmidt for about two hours each. As I wrote in my memo to the President reporting on my trip, I sought to convey a deeper and wider sense of Jimmy Carter's thinking on foreign affairs as well as updating them on SALT, the Middle East, and other issues. It was a useful opportunity to assess European views following the London and NATO summits and to give the European leaders a sense of the direction of our thinking. I concluded that the President's policies were "gaining understanding and support, including human rights and East–West, and very much so on the Middle East."

My trip in October 1978 was particularly important because the conversations I had with Helmut Schmidt, James Callaghan, and Giscard d'Estaing foreshadowed some of the difficulties we would have on the question of theater nuclear forces (TNF). In all three countries I discussed the TNF issue, in order to alert them to potential problems. I noted in my journal for October 4 that "what was striking in all three places was the degree to which the gray areas issue [TNF] is likely to become a major problem in alliance relationships in the 1980s. Europeans are worried; yet they are not quite sure what ought to be done about it and are likely to shrink away from any concrete solution. This is why it is so important to prepare them for the problem and yet not confront them with a ready-made solution. The more we can talk to them about it at the highest level, the better."

In my journal, I also commented on the extraordinary security arrangements which my hosts made for me during my trip. "In Germany I was accompanied by several police cars and at one point a massive armored car. In France it was more artistic: three extremely tough-looking detectives followed me wherever I went, on foot or by car, and in addition there were two motorcyclists in elegant dark leather coats and white helmets who would race ahead of my motorcade at enormous speed, weaving in and out of traffic, acrobatically waving cars off the road to the right and left, occasionally even standing up on the motorcycle with both hands pointing in opposite directions in order to make the traffic yield, all this while roaring full speed. They would occasionally pull up to cars which would not yield the way and kick their fenders or pound their windows with their fists—again, all this while going full blast. At one stage, we drove literally on a sidewalk for a brief period of time; at another time we went around a rotary in a direction which met the onrushing traffic head on, forcing it rapidly to pull off to the side. All in all, a spectacular performance."

One of the points that came out of my meeting with Chancellor Schmidt was the need for the leaders of the four nations to meet and discuss strategic issues. Schmidt said it made him feel "uneasy" that President Carter, Giscard, Callaghan, and he never met together in informal, top-level discussion of political-strategic issues. The usual venue was either the larger NATO Summit or the Economic Summit of the seven leading industrial democracies (the United States, Canada, Britain, France, West Germany, Italy, and Japan). What was lacking was a forum where the leaders of the four countries most directly engaged in security problems could meet and discuss frankly, openly, and flexibly matters of common concern. The problem, however, was how to structure such a meeting without giving it the appearance of the *directoire* which de Gaulle had proposed and which had so riled the other alliance members.

I conveyed Schmidt's suggestion to the President in my summary report on the consultations. I noted that I agreed with the Chancellor, pointing out that the respective bureaucracies were moving forward on strategic matters (including TNF modernization), but there had never been a consultation at the top level. We did not want our solutions to these problems to be predicated solely on military concerns. The political element had to be taken into account as well. Carter noted in the margin that at the past Economic Summit in Bonn the leaders had discussed the possibility of meeting informally during the winter and authorized me to explore the matter further. The idea of an informal meeting soon took shape and a date was set for January 5–6, 1979, in Guadeloupe, on an invitation from President Giscard d'Estaing. (The French were anxious to act as hosts and we were only too glad to yield the honor to them, for we realized that there would be resentment from other governments at such an exclusive meeting.)

The discussions were wide-ranging, and although formal notes were not kept, I noted my impressions in my journal: "This afternoon the four leaders sat around a table under a thatched roof in a kind of open veranda with each of us sitting next to our principal. I must say that I was quite impressed by the discussion. It was a thoroughly stimulating and comprehensive review of the security situation, with Carter very effectively taking the lead and pressing the others to define their response to the perceived threat. . . . Giscard was clear, to the point, and quite decisive. Callaghan displayed good political sense, was quite vigorous, and spoke very sensibly." I was very disappointed by Helmut Schmidt, however, after he gave us a rather elementary lecture on nuclear strategy. I noted that "throughout he was the one who was most concerned about the Soviet nuclear threat in Europe and the least inclined to agree to any firm response. He kept saying that he has a political problem and that he is not in a position to make any commitments. I was quite struck by how hard the other three pressed him. However, I could sense that out of the dialogue there was emerging a recognition that a common Western position was needed that has to be more concrete."

Nonetheless, Guadeloupe was not repeated. The discussions were valuable, but, though they contributed a great deal to the shaping of a strategic consensus, the very fact of the meeting was so resented by other governments, notably Italy, that the enterprise would have been counterproductive if repeated. In my view, a better remedy was gradually to transform the annual Economic Summit into something approximating a Strategic Summit, dealing with both political and economic issues. At the Venice meeting in June 1980, half a day was spent on a discussion of the Soviet threat to the Persian Gulf in the light of the Soviet invasion of Afghanistan, and it yielded a useful statement of strategic-geopolitical position (see Chapter 12). The very fact that strategic issues were discussed was a useful precedent, and it led me subsequently to recommend, in a public speech in Paris, that we more deliberately strive to transform the Economic Summit into one in which strategic issues will also be discussed. I urged "a consciously expanded program of sustained strategic consultations between the United States and its principal allies, including Japan," and "the expansion of our yearly Economic Summit meetings into a Strategic Summit which would also address, at the highest political levels, the consequences of Soviet power projection and the mutual security requirements to meet that challenge. A Strategic Summit would provide institutional recognition that the problems of Asia, Europe, and the Middle East cannot be separated from each other, and neither can economic, political, and security issues." It was my view, and it remains, that the West badly needs such an instrument for forging a more consistent, longer-range response to the increasingly threatening trends of global politics.

Courting Eastern Europe

A critical factor in U.S. relations with Western Europe and the Soviet Union was how the Carter Administration would deal with Eastern Europe. The political diversity of Eastern Europe and our emphasis on human rights required that the broad range of policy issues be carefully reviewed and that our choices be made more explicit than they had been in the past.

On April 14, 1977, even as we were pushing hard on SALT and on the Middle East, Cy Vance chaired a Policy Review Committee meeting on PRM-9, the overall study of U.S.–European relations. The interagency memorandum outlined four basic options in our general approach to Eastern Europe. First, the United States could differentiate more sharply within Eastern Europe between those nations which were more independent of Moscow and those that were less so; for example, favoring Rumania over Poland or Hungary. Second, we could be more forthcoming toward those which were relatively more liberal internally; namely, Poland and Hungary. Third, we could limit our ties with the other nations. And, fourth, we could expand contacts with all the Eastern European countries.

The essential choice that emerged in the discussion was whether to favor those states which were somewhat liberal internally or somewhat independent of Moscow or to expand contacts overall without any priority. I argued very strongly for the first approach because it recognized the American interest in encouraging "polycentrism" and pluralism in the region. Some participants, notably from State, favored the fourth option, but I asked what specific U.S. interests were to be advanced by such undiscriminating contacts. After a spirited discussion, Cy noted that there was a general consensus on fusing the first two options and that individual country follow-up studies were needed.

On April 22, I directed that interagency papers be prepared on Eastern Europe issues, clearly setting out the alternatives for U.S. policy. The response was received in midsummer, and on August 23 the Policy Review Committee met to consider the study. This meeting also dealt with the related Conference on Security and Cooperation in Europe (CSCE). I urged that we think through all the options in CSCE and played a bit of a devil's advocate role, as my journal notes indicate. "I pushed hard and I believe effectively for a more assertive U.S. posture in CSCE. In fact, I stunned everyone there by suggesting that we have a paper prepared which deliberately examines the advisability of a confrontationist approach. The State Department types were horrified even by the thought. I suggested to them that we may not accept it, but the idea is we should consider it. My inner hope is that by considering such an approach we will help to stiffen their backs even if we end up adopting a policy which is more designed to achieve compromise. In any case, I pushed hard that the United States take the lead and be perceived as . . . pushing CSCE toward higher standards."

The debate on Eastern Europe was essentially a rehash of previous discussions, but we did agree that a degree of differentiation in our relations with Eastern Europe was needed. As a result, the President signed Presidential Directive 21 on September 13, setting out a policy of giving preference to countries which are relatively more liberal internally and/or more independent of the Soviet Union.

To demonstrate our more forthcoming approach toward Eastern Europe, the President decided that on his first major world trip he would visit Poland. He and I discussed this possibility on several occasions, and I sounded Vance out on the subject as well. I was told that Marshall Shulman, the State Department's principal Soviet Affairs adviser, had cautioned Vance against it, on the grounds that a visit to Poland would be viewed by the Soviets as provocative. While I clearly favored going to Poland, for I felt that it would encourage the processes of liberalization that were gathering momentum there, I also mentioned to the President the possibility of his going instead to Rumania. Carter's reaction was negative. He pointed out that his two predecessors had gone to Rumania and there was no point in a third visit. Poland, he said, was clearly the most important country in Eastern Europe and it made much more sense for him to go there.

We arrived in Warsaw on December 29. My journal notes describe the scene: "The landing was not without a sense of emotion. The American and Polish flags, the two anthems, Carter making an excellent speech, unfortunately marred by a ridiculous translator who somewhat Russified his presentation. Even members of the Politburo objected to the fact that his translation was so Russified. It was bitter cold. I asked the Secret Service to line up behind Mrs. Carter so that she wouldn't freeze to death. A cold Siberian wind was blowing across our backs as we stood on the wet tarmac listening to the welcoming speeches."

The next day, Rosalynn and I visited Cardinal Wyszynski. The Primate of Poland had become over the preceding decades the symbol of Polish commitment to the spiritual and political traditions of the West. His extraordinary courage in facing Stalinist imprisonment and his good common sense had won him a unique standing in Polish society, with even fervent Communists conceding that the Cardinal was a truly world-historical figure. Yet when I suggested to the President that some gesture toward Wyszynski be undertaken, the State Department, notably our Ambassador in Warsaw, felt that this would be provocative to the government. In order not to engage in a quarrel with the State Department, which probably would leak to the press, the President and I contrived to make the decision "on the spot." Shortly after our arrival in Warsaw, we informed the Cardinal's office that Rosalynn and I would like to make a call on him, and the two of us went there without any prior announcement, carrying with us a personal letter from Carter to Wyszynski, which I had proposed and which the President wrote by hand: "To Cardinal Wyszynski, You have my best wishes and my prayers. I share your faith, I admire what you represent, I seek the same goals. Jimmy Carter."

The visit itself started on a slightly amusing note. "The Bishop who greeted us at first thought that [Rosalynn] was my wife, and when they realized that she was the President's wife, there was a great sensation. The Cardinal himself makes a first-rate impression—thoughtful, intelligent, combination of a theologian, a sociologist, and a patriot. He gave a very eloquent and effective analysis of the situation in contemporary Poland, emphasizing the pace of change, modernization, industrialization, and secularization."

At my further suggestion, the President took another important symbolic step. In addition to laying the traditional wreath on the tomb of the unknown soldier, he paid his respects at the monument to the fighters who perished in the Nazi liquidation of the Warsaw ghetto in 1943, and then laid a wreath at the foot of the monument to the fighters of the Warsaw Uprising of 1944. All Poles understood that this act honored the memory of the Home Army, which had borne the brunt of underground resistance to the Nazis, only to be crushed later by the Soviet-sponsored Communist regime. Thus, Carter identified himself with the Polish thirst for independence, a gesture which was much appreciated by the Polish people.

In his formal meetings with the Communist authorities, the President indicated a willingness to increase American commodity credits to Poland. He also took advantage of the opportunity to stress the destabilizing effects on European security of the Soviet deployment of the new SS-20 missile, expressing the hope that the Poles would convey our concerns to the Soviets. Throughout the visit, Carter made a point of stressing U.S. support for Polish independence and for greater ties between Poland and the West. On their side, our hosts were obviously gratified that the first foreign state visit undertaken by the U.S. President was to their country, and they went out of their way to stress their desire for closer U.S.–Polish relations.

Symbolic of the Carter Administration's new approach toward Eastern Europe was the return to Hungary of the Crown of St. Stephen, which had been in the possession of the United States since the end of World War II. Vance and I agreed that it was time to move on this matter, although initially I had been skeptical when the State Department proposed this initiative. After consulting the White House domestic advisers, I feared a negative reaction from voters of Eastern European origin. But Cy convinced me, and in November 1977 the President authorized me to direct the State Department to seek assurances from the Hungarians that the Crown would be placed on permanent display and that full religious participation would be allowed in the return ceremony. After adequate guarantees were obtained, the President approved the transfer. On January 6, Secretary Vance led the U.S. delegation to Budapest and completed the return of the Crown.

This gesture, although ceremonial, had great historical significance for the Hungarians and removed a major obstacle to expanding the U.S.–Hungarian relationship. Negotiations on a bilateral trade agreement were concluded on March 17, extending most-favored-nation status to Hungary. In February 1979, a Double Taxation Treaty was signed in Washington. Our objective in expanding economic relations was to encourage the evolution of Hungarian-style Communism while securing some economic benefits for American business through increased trade and investment.

The President's offer of commodity assistance to Poland was implemented in 1978, and the 1979 budget included the provision of $400 million in direct Commodity Credit Corporation (CCC) credits for Poland, to be administered by the Department of Agriculture. As the enormity of Poland's grain shortfall became apparent, CCC assistance was further increased. In 1979, the President approved a total of $500 million in assistance to Poland, consisting of $200 million in direct credits and $300 million in credit guarantees; in 1980, CCC assistance was increased to $670 million in credit guarantees. We viewed this assistance as essential to prevent the food situation in Poland from deteriorating further. It reflected the Administration's assessment that it was in the interest of the United States to help Poland work its economic problems out on its own.

In courting Eastern Europe, the Carter Administration worked to encourage political and economic trends already very much in evidence. We sought to reward those nations which demonstrated an evolution toward a more liberal internal political system and to call attention to the human-rights abuses in those nations which remained committed to totalitarianism. Through the Conference on Security and Cooperation in Europe, we maintained public pressure on the Soviets and their satellites to comply with the provisions of the Helsinki Accords. To that end, I blocked a relatively unknown State Department nominee for the head of the U.S. delegation and obtained instead the President's approval for the appointment of Arthur Goldberg as our principal delegate. Knowing Goldberg's energy, and also self-assertiveness, I felt certain that he would have a major impact, and I was not disappointed. His leadership gave the United States the visibility and impact we desired.

I also used my office to provide more support for Radio Free Europe. I felt strongly that the Radio offered us the best means for influencing the internal political transformation of Communist systems and that more use should be made of this vital instrument. Accordingly, I pressed for larger financial support and I also used my White House office to free the Radio of excessive political control, notably from State. While the Radio should not be used to foment insurrections in the East, it should, in my judgment, serve as an instrument for the deliberate encouragement of political change. This meant that the broadcasts had to be addressed to the internal problems of the Communist systems and offer a genuine alternative to Communist policies. In my efforts, I was assisted most ably by my NSC associate responsible for the Radio, Paul Henze. Henze was familiar with the Radio network, as well as with Eastern Europe, and had an unfailing zeal for sustained bureaucratic conflict.

Through the years of the Carter Administration, I felt strongly that for the United States to respond effectively to opportunities to promote change in Eastern Europe, we should not treat the Soviet bloc either as a monolithic adversary or simply as a group of uniformly friendly neighbors. Greater diversity in Eastern Europe was clearly desirable. This is why in late 1980 we took such a firm stand in deterring a Soviet invasion of Poland designed to crush the mushrooming Solidarity movement (see Chapter 12). The Carter Administration sought to make careful decisions to advance the larger goal of gradually transforming the Soviet bloc into a more pluralistic and diversified entity. In my view, such a policy was in our long-range interest and offered a better way of dealing with the Soviet challenge than treating the Soviet Union either as the leader of an unmitigatingly hostile coalition or as a partner in an undifferentiated detente.

The Neutron Bomb Explodes

The neutron bomb affair was a major setback in U.S.–European relations, particularly in our relations with West Germany. The President's credibility was damaged in Europe and at home, and personal relations between Carter and Schmidt took a further turn for the worse and never recovered. Clearly, the public blame for the fiasco should have been more evenly shared. Carter's belated reluctance was matched by Schmidt's evasive intransigence. The public perception that the President fumbled is inaccurate and unfair.

The controversy over the enhanced radiation weapon (ERW), or neutron bomb, began when the Washington *Post* published, on June 7, 1977, an article describing the planned deployment of the battlefield nuclear weapon in Europe. Apparently, the reporter had noted the budgetary provision for the Lance missile version of the ERW in President Ford's 1978 budget. The Energy Research and Development Administration had neglected to delete the still-classified term "enhanced radiation" from publicly released congressional testimony. We were quite unprepared for the political storm that hit us only four and a half months after the inauguration. Media portrayals of ERW as the bomb that "destroys people and not property" sensationalized the debate, then spread to Europe, where people had reason to be truly nervous about nuclear conflict on their own soil. Ultimately, Moscow used the material for a propaganda blitz that succeeded in obfuscating the issue of their own deployment of the huge 1,500 kiloton SS-20 missiles.

The program to modernize NATO's aging battlefield nuclear armory had begun during the previous Administration and included plans for developing a Lance missile warhead and a new artillery shell for use against Warsaw Pact tank forces (which outnumber NATO's by three to one). The ERW was desirable because improved accuracy permitted significant reductions in explosive yield, thereby reducing collateral damage because of the lower blast and heat. Civilian casualties would, therefore, be fewer. The deployment of the new weapon in no way signaled a change in tactical nuclear doctrine or altered the strategic nuclear balance. Nonetheless, the *Post* article touched off a political explosion that reverberated throughout the United States and Europe.

After the story broke, the President issued a defense of the ERW, asked Congress to maintain the funds, and ordered a Defense Department study of the issue, to be submitted by August 15. After the review,

Harold Brown recommended to the President that we continue the program. On August 11, I gave the President a memo urging him to support ongoing efforts until a final study had been made. He accepted our recommendation.

At a Vance–Brown–Brzezinski lunch on August 17, we decided to conclude our consultations with the Europeans on the neutron bomb and discussed this with Carter later in the day. It was becoming increasingly clear to me that he was uncomfortable with the idea of ordering production and deployment of the ERW. The President had campaigned on the nuclear issue and his Administration was focusing on arms control and nonproliferation. I noted in my journal for that day that the President told us "he did not wish the world to think of him as an ogre and we agreed that we will press the Europeans to show greater interest in having the bomb and therefore willingness to absorb some of the political flak or we will use European disinterest as a basis for a negative decision." On September 13, a Defense Department team went to Brussels for consultations with the Nuclear Planning Group in NATO. The team was instructed to discuss both sides of the ERW issue and to solicit the views of the allies.

What followed was a diplomatic minuet. We gave the Europeans a balanced presentation of the weapon's benefits and disadvantages and genuinely asked them what they wanted. But without a clear American indication of support for the ERW, they were unwilling to commit themselves and began to waffle. In some instances, the Europeans denied that their governments had supported the neutron bomb in the Nuclear Planning Group (NPG), even though the Ford Administration had been consulting them all along. As the consultation process bogged down, a virulent campaign against the neutron bomb spread on the Continent, which those governments, such as that of Germany, whose very existence depended on left-wing support could not ignore.

The European allies did not want to take the responsibility on their own, and we heard the argument that traditionally the United States had been the leader in NATO nuclear defense. According to Chancellor Schmidt, production of the weapon was solely an American decision. The issue of deployment would be confronted later. Schmidt could not bear the wrath of the Soviets and his own domestic critics and insisted that deployment must be a collective alliance decision and not simply a bilateral agreement between West Germany and the United States. Our own attitude was that both the actual and the political costs did not justify production if the Europeans were not willing to have the weapon. As NATO debated, however, the Soviets' propaganda effort intensified.

In thinking through the problem, it was clear to me that the European governments needed some help in making the issue more palatable politically. I thought that if we linked the ERW to the overall nuclear situation there might be some benefits. We could offer Moscow a commitment not to deploy the ERW in exchange for a withdrawal of some Soviet tank forces, but Chancellor Schmidt's speech on "the Euro-strategic balance" in October underscored the threat from the new SS-20 missiles and criticized SALT II for not addressing this problem. So at an SCC on November 16, I recorded in my notes: "I took a tough line, saying that the President should decide to produce, he should tell the Europeans affirmatively to associate themselves with the decision to deploy, he should generate high-level discussions with the Europeans on security problems and in the light of these discussions offer to the Russians a deferral of deployment of the neutron bomb in return for a Russian decision not to deploy the SS-20. After some discussion, this position was generally adopted. I pushed very hard, even though I was the chairman."

On November 24, I submitted to the President a draft letter to Chancellor Schmidt that called for high-level discussions in which we would take the German suggestion on linking the ERW to arms control. The letter raised the possibility of linking the SS-20 and the ERW, in effect trading Western restraint for a tangible Soviet gesture. The President also suggested that the offer be timed with an announcement that we would produce and deploy the ERW. The letter was sent, and Schmidt responded affirmatively to the idea of consultations. The Chancellor hoped that options on the neutron bomb, however, would remain "open."

Alliance consultations at the staff level continued through the winter, with the Germans pushing their view that the alliance must share the burden of deployment. In practical terms, this meant that another continental NATO country had to be willing to accept the weapon. The potential for this was limited—Belgium and the Netherlands had powerful anti-ERW movements; Italy's Communist Party mounted strong opposition; Greece, Turkey, and Portugal were unlikely, given their shaky internal political situations; and Norway and Denmark prohibited deployment of nuclear weapons on their soil. Moreover, as a battlefield weapon, designed for use against mass tank formations, the ERW made sense only in forward deployment, which made most of these countries irrelevant.

The terms of a compromise gradually emerged from the consultations, however. It amounted to proceeding with the three-part proposal contained in the President's letter to Schmidt. First, there would be a U.S. decision to produce the weapon. Second, an offer to forgo ERW deployment would be made if the Soviets would forgo deployment of the SS-20. Finally, the alliance would announce its intent to deploy the ERW in two years if arms control negotiations with the Soviets were unsuccessful. A meeting of the North Atlantic Council was set for March 28, 1978, to consider the final proposal, and it appeared that the compromise would work.

As a result, Harold Brown and Cy Vance submitted a joint memo to the President reporting this progress. Cy, Harold, and I were in agreement that the time had come to put the issue to rest and, on March 18, I routinely sent their memorandum to the President, who was away vacationing at St. Simon, along with draft statements prepared by State in anticipation of a final agreement, and a companion memorandum by me supporting their assessment. To my surprise, they came back with marginal notations that read: "To Zbig, re: production, etc. Do not act until after consultation with me." On the memo from Cy and Harold, the President wrote: "Do not issue any statement re ERW." The NATO meeting was deferred and we awaited the President's return to Washington.

Cy, Harold, and I met with the President on March 20, and my notes from that meeting describe the situation fully.

In the evening an interesting hour-and-a-half session with the President on the neutron bomb. He was clearly very displeased by the fact that the decision-making process has been moving forward and that we were about to make a key decision. We went back and forth on this issue. I could tell that he would have preferred to back out of this issue. In different ways, all of us were telling him that he could not do so. I told him that, quite frankly, I would like to give him advice which would be more compatible with his moral and political sensitivities, but in my judgment, for him not to go through with what we had proposed earlier to Chancellor Schmidt would contribute to a sickness and then weakening of the alliance. He finally agreed that we will now solicit more explicit statements of support from Schmidt and Callaghan as part of the initiative. If they are willing to make such statements, we will go through with it. If they are not, then we will delay action on this. I don't think that I have ever seen the President quite as troubled and pained by any decision item. At one point he said: "I wish I had never heard of this weapon." He must have been really furious when he got the message from me this weekend that his earlier proposal to Schmidt was about to be implemented. I think that it is quite clear that he had hoped throughout that the whole thing would simply collapse.

At the morning briefing on March 26, it was more of the same: "The President said, in effect, that he did not wish to go through with it; that he had a queasy feeling about the whole thing; that his Administration would be stamped forever as the Administration which introduced bombs that kill people but leave buildings intact; and that he would like to find a graceful way out. I still made my pitch to the effect that his decision, which involves a reversal of everything we have been doing for the last four months, will stamp him as weak and will be so construed elsewhere. I made the point that leadership means making the decisions which the Europeans are not prepared to make. However, he was unconvinced and we will have to search for a way to get ourselves out of the hole." On the morning of March 27, the President announced to us that he had decided against any deployment of the ERW. He planned to send Warren Christopher to Europe to find an acceptable formula for implementing his decision. Carter felt that the European governments were attempting to push all the political costs on him and on the United States and that this was unfair.

Following this meeting, the President left on an official visit to Venezuela, Brazil, Nigeria, and Liberia. On the return flight from Liberia, Cy and I again had a long talk with the President about the neutron bomb. My journal notes indicate that "the President sat in his compartment with his feet on the table, looking terribly preoccupied by this issue. I argued for a compromise position which would commit us to deployment if the Russians did not meet our arms control needs. I could sense that . . . he may resent the fact that he has been pushed so hard on it." (Purely as an aside, it is worth noting that in a private conversation with Vance and his press aide, Hodding Carter, I made the comment that a decision not to go through with the ERW "would be the worst Presidential decision of the first fourteen months." To my chagrin, that comment, which I made only on that occasion, appeared in the very next issue of a weekly news magazine, thereby deepening my suspicions regarding Hodding Carter's conduct.)

Carter was at least partially justified in his view that the Germans were placing the entire onus on him; though Schmidt had not accepted the weapon, and though it had been his insistence that another European country should agree to deployment even though the ERW made sense only if deployed near the East German frontier, the Chancellor had gone out of his way to make it appear as if he had been courageously prepared to have the weapon deployed all along. Soon after Carter's decision he sent Foreign Minister Genscher to Washington for a highly publicized meeting with the President. In preparation for this meeting, I gave Carter a memo urging him to press Genscher for a firm commitment to deploy. Failing that, I urged the President to defer the decision, link it to Soviet arms control, but in effect be willing to produce and deploy it within two years. The memo came back to me with a notation at the top: "Zbig, I must say that you never give up."

The meeting with Genscher did not change anything. No firm commitment was forthcoming. Later in the afternoon, I met with Cy, Harold, Ham, and Jody to hammer out a statement. It was a deferral and not a complete cancellation, at least keeping the issue open. On April 8, the White House issued a Presidential announcement that the United States would defer production of the ERW, pending demonstrations of Soviet restraint in their deployment of the SS-20.

I knew that the impact of this decision would be serious. It was a major setback in alliance relations overall, in particular with Germany. It hurt Carter's public image. Vance and Brown agreed that we should go through with the decision, once the consultations had proceeded as far as they had. As I noted in my journal (April 5, 1978), I told the President that a negative decision "will affect the credibility of his leadership and will sow dissension within the alliance and negative congressional reactions. By the time the day was out, all of that was happening. I also feel that both Vance and Harold should have been stronger in supporting me and that the Vice President particularly should have spoken up. He did not at all, whereas Vance and Brown did support me; they certainly did not do so very strongly. . . . However, I would not be doing my role if I did not make unpopular cases strongly to him."

In fairness, it has to be stated that the President's reluctance, quite apart from its praiseworthy moral concerns, had some political justification as well. Schmidt had obviously maneuvered to make the decision appear a purely American one. To Carter's great credit, he forbade us to engage in any recriminations and willingly assumed the responsibility for the resulting flap, on the grounds that his domestic political problems were smaller than Schmidt's and hence he was better able to ride out the storm. As a result, in all of our press backgrounders we were unable to describe fully the history of the problem or to explain how the issue had come to a head. To protect Schmidt and allied unity, Carter thus paid a high personal price.

I must say that I feel partly responsible myself, for I had obviously misjudged the President's feelings on the subject. When the bureaucratic train was set in motion, I had assumed that we were fulfilling the President's requirements, paving the way toward an eventual decision to produce and deploy the ERW. I had underestimated the degree of Carter's reluctance to deploy this weapon, and as a result the President was clearly caught unprepared when he received the critical memoranda of March 18. In retrospect, it is obvious to me that Vance, Brown, and I misread the President's intentions, and underestimated Schmidt's intransigence. Had we taken these considerations into account earlier, we probably would have reached the same conclusion that was reached in the end: that the United States should proceed quietly with the production of the components of the weapon but that it would be better for the sake of allied unity not to press the issue of deployment. More ominously for the future, the resolution of this issue did not augur well for the more difficult problem posed by theater nuclear force modernization.

Drifting Apart

As the nature and extent of Soviet expansionism became apparent, we sought to galvanize a unified Western response. Iran, Afghanistan, and Central America, in addition to the issues of East–West relations in Europe, became subjects of debate and even dispute among ourselves and our allies. We became frustrated with their unwillingness to make some tough decisions; for their part, they questioned American leadership. The differences that emerged were deep-seated and not merely a reflection of personalities. But the strains were significant and appear to endure.

Differing perceptions of the Soviets and detente were illustrated by the exchange of views during Helmut Schmidt's July 1977 visit to Washington. The main theme of the Chancellor's visit was highlighted at a State Department luncheon on July 13. Schmidt made his argument that we should be more responsive to the "good Brezhnev who is promoting detente and who needs our help." The Chancellor was particularly anxious to set up private, direct contacts between Carter and the Soviet leader, with himself as the intermediary. Perhaps one of the reasons why Schmidt's personal criticisms of Carter continued and even intensified was that the President did not seize on the concept outright. I had the feeling that Schmidt suspected that I talked Carter out of the idea of using Schmidt as the secret intermediary between Carter and Brezhnev, and, as I have noted elsewhere, he was not entirely wrong.

The Soviet Union's deployment of the SS-20 and the Backfire bomber in 1977 also raised new questions about Russian intentions toward Europe, and the need for a NATO response. Both these new weapons systems were capable of hitting targets anywhere in Europe, without any effective Europe-based nuclear counter. The Europeans feared that the Soviets would now be able to exert a greater degree of political pressure than ever before, while at the same time strategic parity and our efforts to achieve strategic arms limitation would limit American willingness to respond to Soviet attack or provocation. These concerns were expressed publicly for the first time in Chancellor Schmidt's London speech of October 28, 1977, in which he pointed out the dangers of the SS-20 and called on the Western alliance to counter this latest Soviet threat.

As a result of this speech and other private consultations on theater nuclear force issues, NATO established a High Level Group in 1978 to consider force modernization and develop an alliance consensus on a proposed program. The President directed the SCC also to review the political and military aspects of theater nuclear capabilities and arms control. Initially, I was doubtful that a military response based on Europe was needed, but I was convinced by my staff, notably Aaron and Jim Thomson, of the political necessity to deploy a European-based nuclear counter. In the SCC, which I chaired, and within which the decisions were reached relatively effectively and quickly, the question of what ought to be the size of our Europe-based theater nuclear force was discussed in July 1979. We were disposed to go for a lower number than the one that we finally recommended to the President, amounting to a total of 572 ground-based cruise missiles and Pershing IIs. Only the JCS and I favored the upper limit of 572, my thought being that we would probably be asked by NATO to scale down or that we would have to engage eventually in some arms control bargaining with the Soviets and that therefore the upper limit was preferable. The President approved my recommendation. In August 1979 our intention was officially announced, and on October 4 the proposal was approved by the NATO High Level Group.

The intense bargaining, maneuvering, and recalculations involved in this issue demonstrate a problem which many outside the policy process frequently forget. In the modern world, at the pinnacle of power, there is no pure, objective analysis of a strategic problem. *All* decisions are made in a generalized decision-making process that is colored by domestic politics, economics, and allied reactions. The question of an objective "need" for a credible response in Europe (TNF) had to be balanced against internal NATO politics, various numbers dictated by a variety of actors (both domestic and foreign), and the need for numbers high enough to give the U.S. bargaining leverage with the Soviets.

Later in October, David Aaron made a trip to Europe for high-level consultations with the allies. The results were encouraging. In my weekly report of October 26, I gave the President a summary of Aaron's trip: "We are much closer to a firm consensus on our proposed TNF program than anticipated. The U.K., F.R.G., and Italy have all taken firm internal government decisions to support the NATO program. The Belgians are prepared to take a vote of confidence on the issue; the Dutch want to change the program. If Schmidt stays firm, others will also."

Whether Schmidt would hold firm was open to serious question. The Soviet response to the NATO decision had been predictably intense. On October 6, Brezhnev warned in a speech that European acceptance of theater nuclear modernization would undermine arms control and threaten the strategic balance. He offered to withdraw twenty thousand troops and a thousand tanks from East Germany during the next year if the West would forgo modernization, and raised the possibility of limiting Soviet modernization as well. This was clearly a propaganda move and did not indicate any specific willingness to withdraw the

SS-20s. It was the beginning of a campaign to mobilize public opinion in Europe against the NATO proposals.

On December 11–12, NATO issued a final plan calling for the deployment of 108 Pershing IIs in place of the Pershing I and 464 new ground-launched cruise missiles. One thousand nuclear warheads would be withdrawn from Europe, to show that NATO was not expanding its reliance on nuclear weapons. This decision was coupled with a renewed emphasis on arms control; hence, the so-called two-track policy decision.

The Soviets withdrew their offer of negotiations on TNF in early January 1980, decrying the NATO decision and calling on us to reverse it. This merely added to the already considerable tension in U.S.–Soviet relations, generated by the invasion of Afghanistan and our preoccupation with the Iranian crisis. As the relationship deteriorated, the Europeans, particularly Schmidt, grew more anxious, and their reluctance to take firm steps on sanctions quickly became clear. We pressed and pulled and prodded, but with limited success. In March, Helmut Schmidt visited Washington, and my journal note for March 4 is indicative of the general attitude: "Schmidt on the whole was positive, but equivocal on concrete support."

The problem of encouraging a stronger European response to Soviet expansionism was exacerbated that spring by a new proposal from Chancellor Schmidt. On June 10, he floated the idea of a moratorium on theater nuclear weapons deployment. Although the proposal actually did not entail a freeze, it was ambiguous enough to create the public impression that it in fact was a freeze. I feared that it would further undercut Western European support for the nuclear initiative. During lunch at the Pentagon the next day, Harold Brown, Ed Muskie (who had become Secretary of State in May 1980), and I agreed that the President should send a toughly worded message to Schmidt on his new idea. The text that I proposed was approved, and I submitted it in the evening to the President.

Schmidt was not pleased, but we all felt that he had to get the message clearly. The President essentially told the Chancellor not to make any commitments on missile deployment during his scheduled meeting with Brezhnev on June 30, 1980. On the eve of the forthcoming Western Economic Summit, I noted in my journal for June 18: "Schmidt is furious over the President's message no doubt, and the President will have a confrontation of sorts with him when the two of them meet in Venice. The problem is that Schmidt has undercut any sympathy for him by his derogatory statements about the President. Even though every meeting produces declarations of friendship, Schmidt then follows it up with back-sniping."

The meeting that did follow on the third day of the European trip was, as expected, a nasty confrontation. Schmidt and Carter met in a tiny room in an extraordinarily elegant old-fashioned hotel, surrounded by the Venice lagoon, with Muskie and me on one side, and Genscher and Ambassador von Staden on the other, with our knees almost touching. Much of the meeting consisted of the American side listening to Schmidt's fulminations. As I described it in my journal for June 21, the meeting "turned out to be quite a humdinger. All last week he has been fuming over Carter's letter on TNF. He started the meeting by loudly proclaiming that he had never let us down, and he repeatedly described the letter as an insult. The President was rather conciliatory, tried to calm him. However, Schmidt persisted, and at some point I weighed in, pointing out that at least we never engage in personal recriminations. . . . Schmidt was somewhat taken aback by this and said, 'Well, I don't mind a fight. If necessary, one has to criticize.' I responded, 'In that case, if a fight is necessary I am quite prepared not to shrink from a fight.' The President then waved toward me to indicate that he didn't want me to pursue this argument with Schmidt. Its effect, however, was to clear the air and the discussion became much more amiable. On my suggestion the two of them appeared before the press and simply stated that they are now in full agreement on Afghanistan and TNF, and again on my recommendation they refused to take any questions." The rest of the Venice summit went somewhat more smoothly.

After the Chancellor's visit to Moscow, following the Venice Summit, Foreign Minister Genscher came to Washington on July 2 to report on the trip. I wrote in my notes that "the main point was that the Soviets seem to be slightly more flexible on negotiations regarding TNF. Genscher right away wanted to characterize that as a serious offer. The President wisely demurred and I supported him strongly, speaking up several times and finally offering a formulation which was accepted by everyone; namely, that the Soviet offer will be examined in a constructive spirit."

An exchange of letters with Brezhnev followed and led to the opening of preliminary talks with the Soviets in Geneva on October 17. The Soviet leader sent President Carter a letter on August 21, raising again his October 1979 proposal as a basis for discussion, and said that NATO must rescind its December 1979 TNF decision. He also wrote that TNF could be discussed in a SALT III framework after the ratification of SALT II, and pressed for a response to his TNF proposal.

The President replied on September 2, stressing that the NATO decision was a response to the deployment of new long-range theater nuclear weapons, particularly the SS-20. Brezhnev countered two weeks later, rejecting our interpretation of events in Europe and in Afghanistan and criticizing our failure to respond to the Soviet proposal. After consultations with Ed, Harold, and me, the President decided that preliminary talks with the Russians on TNF could be a useful undertaking.

Within four weeks of the start of TNF talks, the issue was moot—the election returns foretold a major shift in American attitudes toward the Soviets, or at least it seemed so in November 1980. On November 1, the Germans announced that they would not be meeting the 3 percent annual increase in defense spending as promised. Schmidt's last visit to Washington on November 17 was chilly and thoroughly nonsubstantive.

The Dilemma of Leadership

The Carter Administration recognized that the United States and Europe had been gradually drifting apart since the 1960s. In part, this was a natural evolution as the allies fully recovered from the effects of World War II and developed a set of interests that paralleled our own but were different in important ways. But the OPEC shocks of 1973 and the emergence of detente between Western and Eastern blocs on the Continent foreshadowed major points of divergence between Washington and the allies.

This drift was only partially arrested during the Carter years, despite our efforts to forge a more explicit consensus regarding the common threats faced by the alliance. Differing assessments of the Soviet threat in Europe subsequently led to a disjointed response to repression in Poland. Our allies remained willing to finance Soviet economic expansion, confining their negative reaction to rhetoric only. Conflicting economic priorities also led to a parting of the ways on Middle East policy and on the nature of the Soviet threat to that region. We achieved some successes based on a unified response. The allies for the most part condemned the Soviet invasion of Afghanistan and were helpful during the Iranian crisis, albeit after much coaxing and prodding. NATO took the much-needed decisions on conventional and theater nuclear defenses. The process of economic coordination was improved and the cooperation shown on the issues began to extend to strategic areas as well.

One of the less-known success stories of the Carter years was the U.S. response to the Communist Party threat in Italy. The media generally focused on foreign policy crises, but this was a crisis which did *not* explode—and the reasons why deserve greater analysis.

The Carter Administration took office as the Communist Party (PCI) seemed about to take power in Italy. The PCI had surged to 34.4 percent support in the June 1976 national elections (up from 26.9 percent eight years earlier) versus 38.7 percent for the Christian Democrats (DC), from which increasing numbers of Italians were alienated by its decades-old leadership, its repeated political scandals, and its support for an anti-divorce referendum that was resoundingly rejected by the electorate. Eschewing a continued coalition, the Italian Socialist Party favored a left coalition government with the Communists. The smaller parties also boycotted the DC, and two of them—the Social Democrats and the Republicans—also seemed favorable to Communist participation in the government. Even within the Christian Democratic Party itself, support was growing for the "historic compromise"—Communist leader Enrico Berlinguer's formula for a PCI–DC coalition government.

Many observers viewed Giulio Andreotti's minority DC government as a short-lived expedient to prepare the way for the inevitable entry of the Communists, a clear shift toward neutralism in Italy's foreign policy. Fortunately, America had excellent representation in Italy during this volatile period. President Carter appointed one of his able advisers, Richard N. Gardner, a man who knew Italy well and who spoke fluent Italian, as Ambassador to Italy. After consulting with Gardner, I wrote to President Carter on March 14, 1977, that drift to the left in Italy was "potentially the gravest political problem we now have in Europe."

In response, the President approved a decision memorandum developed by Ambassador Gardner, the State Department, and members of my own staff to the effect that while not interfering in Italy's internal affairs, we would steadfastly oppose the so-called historic compromise, bringing the Communists into the government. The decision to stand fast, coupled with Gardner's effective cultivation of the Italian elite, gradually bore fruit and provided the basis for drawing the line still more sharply a few months later.

In December 1977, Ambassador Gardner warned us that high-ranking leaders of the Christian Democrats (but not President Aldo Moro and Prime Minister Giulio Andreotti) were ready to form a coalition government with the Communists. Gardner advised that our emphasis on noninterference was being deliberately misinterpreted by the PCI and others favorable to their case and that a strong reinterpretation of our policy was urgently needed. After a PRC meeting on Italy, the State Department issued a statement on January 12, 1978, which left no doubt as to our preferences: ". . . Our position is clear: we do not favor such [Communist] participation and would like to see Communist influence in any Western European country reduced . . . we believe the best way . . . rests with the efforts of democratic parties to meet the aspirations of their people for effective, just, and compassionate government."

Events justified this firm stand. The effort to bring the Communists into the government was abandoned by Christian Democratic leaders. The Communists slipped to 30.4 percent in the national elections of 1979. Early in 1980, the Socialist Party broke with the Communists and entered a coalition with the Christian Democrats. Thus, by the end of the Carter Administration, Italy had a five-party government with a majority in Parliament, with the Communists isolated in the opposition. With its courageous decision to accept theater nuclear forces, with its strong support of the United States in the Iranian hostage crisis, with its cooperative attitude on a whole range of U.S. foreign policy priorities, Italy demonstrated both unexpected stability and steadfastness.

Although that transformation was due mainly to decisions which the Italian people took themselves, U.S. diplomacy as well as the carefully tuned policy toward Italy which the President approved in March 1977 were a distinct help. It was such a successful strategy that even the Reagan Administration reaffirmed it upon taking office.

Nonetheless, as the Soviet threat became more extensive, allied strategic perspectives became more diluted. It was easier to agree when the Soviet threat was focused directly on Europe. Allied cohesion began to wane when during the seventies the Soviets acquired increasingly effective global power and the strategic dimension of the confrontation spread to the Middle East and eventually even to the Western Hemisphere. Moreover, it had become clear that both Watergate and the Vietnam War had contributed to a subtle process of cultural de-Americanization of Western Europe, with America no longer being seen either as the wave of the future or as a model to emulate. The waning of America's cultural appeal contributed indirectly to the waning of American political preeminence.

At the same time, French policy also contributed to further weakening of allied unity. France saw itself as a putative leader of Europe, offering in some respects even a genuine foreign policy choice. I favored placing primary emphasis on France in the shaping of our European policy, for I felt that France was the truly organic, integral, and authentic nation on the Continent. French determination to pursue a national policy, based on a separate defense capability, was to me a signal of French vitality, something that should be pursued through closer consultations and a more genuine partnership. I was sensitive to French pride and I admired the French determination to remain independent. I therefore consulted more frequently with my French colleagues than with either the British or the Germans, and I was encouraged by the fact that in some important areas we were able to develop a genuinely collaborative relationship.

But the French desire to assert European leadership could only be effective if backed by Germany, and my fear throughout was that France would prove too weak to exercise such leadership, while in the meantime contributing to the emergence of a separate German road. I once discussed this in some detail with the very cultivated French Ambassador to Washington, François de Laboulaye. I noted in my journal on July 28, 1980, that de Laboulaye "in effect agreed with me when I said that Giscard's policy, quite unlike de Gaulle's, has the effect of stimulating Franco-German competition in a race to Moscow." I felt that France was contributing to the reawakening of the Bismarckian dream, and I made the same point in my farewell call on Giscard in January 1980. Giscard only demurred to the point of saying that he felt confident that France could maintain its position of preeminence, because Germany in the future would be encountering increasing economic difficulties. I did not find that reassuring.

In contrast to Atlantic relations, during our tenure of office Pacific relations improved steadily. Though American–Japanese economic tensions continued, political consultations became closer than ever. This, as I have mentioned, was facilitated in part by the emergence of a genuinely internationalist Japanese leadership, men with a more truly global vision, but also by our farsighted policy toward China, which eliminated a significant divergence in Japanese and American perspectives. Toward the end of our tenure, we started to press Japan for a larger defense effort. However, we were careful not to pose the issue in such an abrasive fashion as to undermine the internal stability of the Japanese government. We took the position that increased Japanese contributions to the development of some strategically important countries would be a good substitute for a more direct defense effort. This had the advantage of encouraging the Japanese to do more in the broader area of security, without the defense budget becoming a major domestic issue in Japanese politics.

I broached the issue with top Japanese officials during the June 1979 Economic Summit. "I did spend some time with the head of the Japanese Defense Agency, sketching out the agenda for the future. I put particular stress on the interdependence of the three key strategic zones: Western Europe, the Middle East, and the Far East, and on the need for Japan to play a greater role in ensuring the stability and security of all three. Such a role need not be necessarily military, but that component will have to grow as well. The State Department official present at these discussions literally had conniptions. His face showed amazement, and afterwards he described the conversations to one of my associates as 'wild.' "

Like our predecessors, we often faced the question of whether we would accomplish more by pressing our allies openly or whether patient and protracted negotiations were the best way of forging allied consensus on behalf of desired actions. By and large, our team was in agreement that the wiser course was to engage in patient negotiations, avoiding head-on collisions. This meant that there would be times when the United States would have to do more than our allies, unpalatable as this may seem to some sectors of our public. If we could demonstrate fortitude and commitment, if we were prepared to undertake the necessary sacrifices (be it through the grain embargo or through the eventual reestablishment of the draft), we would gain greater credibility for our efforts and eventually encourage some of our friends to emulate our commitment. In contrast, a policy of pinpricks or of open sanctions would be likely to exacerbate the inherent contradictions within the alliance, playing into the hands of those who would like to fragment Western unity altogether. My own view has always been that the best way to exercise leadership is to demonstrate it.

9

Neither Dialogue nor Deterrence

The Soviet Union can choose either confrontation or cooperation.
The United States is adequately prepared to meet either choice.

—President Jimmy Carter, commencement address,
U.S. Naval Academy, Annapolis, June 7, 1978

By the spring of 1978, U.S.–Soviet relations were stalemated. The SALT talks were at best creeping forward. The Soviets were steadily increasing their military presence by proxy near the strategically vital Arabian peninsula (notably in Ethiopia and South Yemen), blandly disregarding U.S. expressions of concern. There were first hints of a Soviet military presence in Vietnam, and the beginnings of development of a new Soviet weapons system targeted on Western Europe (the SS-20). More and more domestic and foreign critics were charging the Carter Administration with mishandling U.S.–Soviet relations. Some were citing the neutron bomb case as evidence of Carter's alleged indecisiveness, while others were blaming us for needlessly exacerbating the African Horn issue. We were thus increasingly portrayed as unable either to accommodate or to compete with the Soviets.

Within the U.S. government the solidarity of the activist first year of foreign policy was cracking under the weight of the intensifying debate on how to handle the U.S.–Soviet relationship. A sharp division on SALT was developing between Harold Brown and the JCS on one side and Vance and Paul Warnke on the other. Defense wanted to toughen the existing U.S. position, whereas State, anxious to conclude rapidly the agreement with the Soviets, advocated a relaxation of the U.S. position on the conflictual issues, notably those pertaining to the cruise missile, the Backfire, and new ICBM types.

In early 1978, Vance and Warnke even proposed to the President that the United States initiate immediate negotiations with the Soviets on a production cutoff of fissionable materials for weapons. Since responsibility for nuclear weapons production rested with the Department of Energy, I forwarded the Vance–Warnke proposal to Secretary James

Schlesinger for comment. As I had expected, Schlesinger produced a blistering memorandum, criticizing the proposal for lacking even the most basic supporting analysis and warning that it would prompt questions regarding U.S. stability and resolve. With his aid, I was able to nip this in the bud.

I tended to side with Brown on SALT specifics. We shared the view that any softening of the U.S. position would have the twin disadvantages of making SALT less effective in restraining the momentum of the Soviet strategic buildup and of reducing the chances of Senate ratification. But I had another, deeper concern. I felt strongly that we were making a fundamental mistake in concentrating so heavily on SALT, without engaging the Soviets in a broader strategic dialogue. In effect, I had profound reservations about both the tactics and the substance of Vance's, and to some extent also the President's, approach to the Soviets. They hoped to use SALT as the opening wedge for developing a broader relationship; I felt that Soviet actions around the world required a firmer response and a more direct and sustained dialogue with the Soviets on what was and was not acceptable. Otherwise, I feared that we would end up with neither detente nor SALT.

In early April, I submitted these views to the President in my weekly report. "It is clearly in the Soviet interest, and part of Soviet strategy, to focus attention on SALT and to proclaim the agreement to be evidence of general improvement in U.S.–Soviet relations. This leaves the Soviets free to pursue their political objectives elsewhere and by other means. In addition to *negotiating,* with an agreement being clearly also in the U.S. interest, it is therefore imperative that the United States focus on the larger dimensions of the U.S.–Soviet relationship, emphasizing that it must be *increasingly comprehensive and genuinely reciprocal.* Unless we do that, we enable the Soviets to set the tone and to define the priorities of the U.S.–Soviet relationship, clearly to their own advantage. Moreover, I am quite convinced that unless detente becomes comprehensive and reciprocal we face an increasing rebellion at home, and SALT will not be ratified."

I went on to specify five actions that we should take: intensify international condemnation of Soviet adventurism in Africa; use the forthcoming NATO meeting to repair the damage from the neutron bomb issue; adopt a more positive attitude toward growing Hill pressure for increased defense spending; develop a technology package for China as a warning signal to the Soviets; and use the forthcoming UN Special Session on Disarmament as a forum for exposing the Soviet military buildup.

I discussed this paper with the President on Monday, April 10, and he commented very favorably on it. He "accepted the idea that we should give Cy instructions that in his forthcoming meeting with Gromyko he not only concentrate on SALT but present a toughly stated overall analysis of the U.S.–Soviet relationship." Two hours later the President reiterated these points at the Cabinet meeting.

During the next several days, I returned to this theme in my conversations with the President, for I remained fearful that Vance would focus primarily on SALT intricacies in his negotiations with the Soviets, instead of engaging them in a broader strategic dialogue. Having secured the President's endorsement, I drafted instructions for Vance's talks, emphasizing the need to focus Soviet attention on the deleterious consequences for the U.S.–Soviet relationship of Soviet activities. I also kept up my efforts to influence the President's thinking on this subject. In early May, in another weekly report, I wrote that "my concern for the future is *not* that the Soviet Union will emerge as the dominant world power, imposing a 'pax Sovietica.' I fear something else: that the destructive nature of Soviet efforts will increasingly make it impossible for us to give order and stability to global change and thus prevent the appearance of a more cooperative and just international system. We will become more isolated and fearful and inward-looking. Eventually, the Soviet Union too will suffer, for it is vulnerable in many ways. The East Europeans are restless, non-Russian Soviet nations are becoming more assertive, the Chinese remain hostile. But that is small comfort if Soviet discomfiture is preceded by some decades by our own decline and withdrawal."

I made this argument because I knew that the President felt strongly that Brown and I were inclined to exaggerate the importance of Soviet military power, and I did not want him to feel that my concerns were rooted in a pessimistic expectation of Soviet global domination. Far from it; I felt confident that the United States was by far the more creative and dynamic partner in the competition, and that it should be we who took the lead in shaping the character and direction of that relationship. But the State Department's position of concentrating on SALT alone would not achieve that objective. More importantly, I felt that State was excessively deferential to the Soviets. I resented the debrief of the Soviets on the President's Wake Forest speech (see p. 189), since I felt that it weakened the speech's intent. I was amazed that the State Department had proposed that Brezhnev be informed about the negative neutron bomb decision even before our allies were. I made my feelings known, and that doubtless contributed to the growing resentment in the State Department both over my views and particularly over the role that the President assigned me in developing the relationship with China.

The Policy Conflict Surfaces

Almost immediately after my return from Beijing, the President met with Gromyko. The meeting did not go well. The Russians

were notably and strikingly cold to me. Some of the Russians barely shook hands and looked away. Only Gromyko himself was relatively affable, relatively polite, and Dobrynin quite amiable. Gromyko said, "Oh, you're back already." And I said, "Yes, I was on a little trip." The meeting itself was largely unproductive. It was dominated by Gromyko's mendacity and verbosity. On contentious issues (that is, Africa), he lied like a trooper. On SALT, he was unforthcoming.

The President responded quite well, noting sarcastically that it was early in the morning and perhaps because of that Gromyko's presentation was so unforthcoming on SALT. He said that in the future he would schedule meetings with the Soviets for later in the day. He then discussed SALT quite well, but perhaps even too technically. Toward the end of the discussion, after receiving notes from me and from Hamilton Jordan reminding him of Africa and human rights, he mentioned both. The statements were straightforward; in my judgment perhaps could have been stronger; but he made the mistake of permitting Gromyko to engage in a long rebuttal. In my judgment it would have been more Presidential for Carter to have conveyed a tough message directly and then simply to say that he wants Gromyko to transmit it to Brezhnev and if Gromyko has any comments he can make them to Vance later. Also, at the end the President expressed some hopes that we can sign SALT in the next few weeks and then he can meet with Brezhnev. Hamilton Jordan and I exchanged pained looks at that moment because it seemed to us that he was throwing away some of the credibility for the posture of toughness which he badly needed to convey.

My State Department colleagues were inclined to blame me in part for the tenor of the meeting with Gromyko. On May 29, Vance submitted a memorandum to the President requesting a formal review of U.S.–Soviet relations. He noted that "many are asking whether this Administration has decided to make a sharp shift in its foreign policy priorities" and expressed concern over the possibility of "playing the China card." Without mentioning names he wrote: "Increasingly, we are faced with two differing views of the U.S.–Soviet relationship; although so far we have managed to combine the two in our public statements, it is becoming more difficult to do. We have always recognized that the relationship between the U.S. and the Soviet Union has been a combination of cooperation and competition, with the competition not preventing either side from seeking agreements in our mutual benefit in such areas as SALT. Now, however, we are coming to the point where there is growing pressure on the part of some people to have us portray the competitive aspects of the relationship as taking clear precedence over the search for areas of cooperation. This fundamental issue has begun to spill out into the public domain through recent statements and press interviews. It should be resolved within the government in order to avoid presenting a picture of division which will weaken us." He ended with the recommendation that he (Vance) hold a protracted discussion with Gromyko on the deterioration of relations and that either he or the President give a broadly gauged speech on U.S.–Soviet relations. That memo, as well as the press stories about a rift between Vance and me, led the President to decide to give the famous speech on U.S.–Soviet relations which he delivered approximately a week later at Annapolis.

In that speech, delivered at the graduation ceremonies of the Naval Academy on June 7, the President offered the Soviets the choice of "either confrontation or cooperation." Though on the whole toughly worded, the speech did lay out the basic proposition that it was up to the Soviet Union to choose growing cooperation with the United States or face an eventual confrontation. The President added: "The United States is adequately prepared to meet either choice." The press seized on that formulation to argue that the President had simply compressed into a single draft two alternative versions, one allegedly prepared by Vance and proposing cooperation and one by me emphasizing confrontation. This became a standard cliché, repeated not only at cocktail parties but even by reputable newspapers and columnists.

In fact, the speech was largely Carter's own handiwork. Irritated by the highly exaggerated press accounts of the clash between Vance and me, and particularly outraged by a false story which appeared in early June in the Washington *Post* to the effect that SALT was being abandoned, Carter decided on June 2 to give a formal speech on U.S.–Soviet relations himself. After telling us that he expected all of us to hew to one line, and that Vance should be the principal public spokesman on foreign policy, he then proceeded to develop the draft of the speech entirely on his own. Only three days later did he ask me to convene a group to discuss it, and to summon Vance, Brown, Turner, Andy Young, and Ham Jordan, in addition to myself. We were presented with a 54-paragraph-long manuscript which contained, much to my surprise, a great number of extremely toughly worded statements. Contrary to subsequent press accounts, it was the President himself who labeled the Soviets as having a totalitarian and repressive regime, who inserted unfavorable comparisons between the United States and the Soviet Union, and who posed the stark choice of "cooperation or confrontation." I thought that Vance would object to these insertions, and I therefore did not recommend that they be struck out, though my own inclination would have been to omit them and to insert instead stronger language on Soviet military activities by proxy in the Third World. Expecting hard bargaining over the text, I intended to propose a compromise with such substitute language as soon as Vance had registered his objections to the President's tough statements. Much to my surprise, Vance accepted the draft without any major changes. Accordingly, I limited myself to reworking the portions dealing with detente, adding my usual formulas about reciprocity, comprehensiveness, and the need for restraint.

It should be remembered that at this time the conventional wisdom was to underplay the long-term dangers of Soviet misconduct. Prime Minister Callaghan had used the occasion of the NATO meeting in Washington in May of that year to ridicule those "Columbuses who have lately discovered Africa," while Joe Kraft wrote a number of columns in which my objections to Soviet expansionism were attributed to my ethnic origins. At that time, Kraft praised Vance's restraint and statesmanship, even though two years later he would rage at Carter's failure to respond early enough to assertive Soviet expansionism.

All in all, I was satisfied with the outcome. As I jotted down in my journal for June 7: "Let us just hope that we have now the constancy needed to exploit the signal sent by this speech. I believe the Soviets have overextended themselves and perhaps they realize it now. The speech, as well as my earlier trip to China, will have sent them an unmistakable message. On the way back from Annapolis the President was very chipper and cheerful. I have the impression that he also felt that the exercise of the last few days was useful and necessary."

I was also encouraged by my increasingly close alliance with Harold Brown. My own journal notes reflect that. Though from the very early days of the Administration most of my references to him were highly complimentary, I did have the feeling in the first year that Brown, while assertive and persuasive on specifics and particularly on technical matters, tended to waffle on broader strategic concerns. I had been disappointed that he had not stood with me on the question of the African Horn. But as time went on, Brown and I came to share similar concerns, and his versatile mind, prodigious debating skills, and scientific knowledge of modern weaponry made a great deal of difference in our NSC debates. I felt increasingly less isolated.

I should add that it would be wrong to exaggerate the degree of our internal disagreements. Vance and I continued to work closely together on behalf of SALT, and we both desired a positive outcome, though Vance certainly felt more strongly about it. We were genuinely close allies on the Middle East issue, and I fully backed Cy's efforts to obtain a more flexible Israeli position. We shared a more forthcoming attitude toward the Third World, notably in regard to majority rule in southern Africa. And finally, we both were committed to human rights and felt that it was good for America to be identified with that cause. In brief, the disagreement on the Soviet Union must be viewed in the context of agreement on a larger number of issues. The NSC process of coordination continued to work smoothly, and personal working relations among all of the principals were also good.

However, I was mistaken in feeling that the President's Annapolis speech would set a clear direction for our policy regarding the Soviet Union. Within weeks a new issue arose, generating intense disagreements, though also bringing to the fore in bureaucratic politics the new alliance between the NSC and DOD. The matter concerned the extraordinarily complicated and politically sensitive question of technology transfer to the Soviet Union, and it was brought to a head by the Soviet decision to put on trial their two most prominent dissidents, Anatoly Shcharansky and Aleksandr Ginzburg, both of whom enjoyed enormous popularity in the United States. The Soviet action provoked widespread public outrage. The President's domestic advisers, notably Ham, Jody, Stu Eizenstat, Jerry Rafshoon, and Bob Lipshutz, all became greatly aroused and felt strongly that the President personally should take the lead in responding.

On July 8, I held a meeting in the Situation Room, including in it the President's domestic advisers as well as Marshall Shulman of State. We were in general agreement that the United States should respond by adopting some restraints in the area of technology transfer. However, the next morning Vance informed me rather emphatically that he was against any such action, and it was clear to me that I had been wrong in assuming that Shulman's presence at the meeting, and seeming acquiescence to the emerging consensus, implied that State would go along. Vance clung to his position that the United States should strongly criticize the Soviet Union, but that it would be a mistake to impose any restraints on the transfer of U.S. technology.

The next week or so was a period of intense debate. Brown strongly supported my view that some restraints on the transfer of technology were in any case needed on national security grounds. The debate coincided with the President's trip to Bonn to attend the Economic Summit, and that meant that Secretary of the Treasury Michael Blumenthal and Under Secretary of State for Economic Affairs Richard Cooper also traveled with the President. Both were also strongly against any restraints on technology transfer, and they made their case to the President on Air Force One. Though Brown and I continued to argue the opposite case, I have no doubt that we would have lost the argument if it were not for the very decisive intervention by our domestic advisers. While on the plane, both Rafshoon and Jody told the

President in no uncertain terms that his domestic credibility would suffer greatly unless he was seen as taking a firm position.

I could appreciate the President's dilemmas. Not only were his senior advisers sharply divided, with each side making cogent arguments, but he was also in effect being pressed to make a very explicit, inevitably highly visible choice between his Secretaries of State and the Treasury on the one hand and his Secretary of Defense and his Assistant for National Security Affairs on the other. In addition, while ethnic groups, notably the Jewish community, favored a strong response, the business community generally opposed any linkage between politics and trade. Finally, the President had to take into account the impact of any decision on our difficult SALT negotiations. It was thus with considerable relief that I learned from the President on July 18 that he had finally decided to deny the export license for the sale of a Sperry Univac computer to Tass for use during the 1980 Olympics, to reestablish export controls on oil production technology and issue a directive to the Commerce Department to put oil production technology on the commodity control list, and to defer decision on pending applications for two licenses requested by Dresser Industries for a drill-bit factory and an electron-beam welder. Cumulatively, these steps meant that our highly permissive attitude toward technology transfer to the Soviet Union was now being reversed. On his return from the summit, the President reported on these decisions to the congressional leaders and he was doubtless gratified by their very favorable reaction.

Indeed, at the foreign policy breakfast a few days later, the President reacted quite sharply when I advised him that Blumenthal was objecting to my implementation of the decision and that State and Commerce were considering new trade initiatives toward the Soviets. During the breakfast

> the President turned all of a sudden to Cy and said that he doesn't want new trade initiatives started by Treasury, Commerce, or State with the effect of going around his recent decision on the export controls on technology for the Soviet Union. He doesn't want Marshall Shulman, Juanita Kreps, or others indicating to the Soviets in some fashion that this was just a little slap on the wrist. We want the Soviets to take this seriously, that we can do this to them, that it is meant to hurt. He was quite sharp, and I could tell that Cy was rather surprised. It was obviously precipitated by the memorandum which I sent [the President] pointing out the various initiatives that were being cooked up by Vance and Blumenthal. Later in the day he sent me a memo back with my comments on Blumenthal's objections, writing in the margin, "Tell Mike to support my policies." I phoned Mike and he was quite startled, but I think the effect will be to generate greater

integration and coordination so that Commerce and Treasury don't go behind our backs.

But the bureaucratic battle was still not over. On August 10, I learned from the newspapers that Commerce had approved the Dresser applications. I asked the President directly whether he had approved such a step, and he said he had not, but he told me not to push the issue too hard lest it precipitate the resignation of Juanita Kreps (who might feel thereby repudiated). On further investigation it turned out that State and Commerce had acted on their own. Secretary of Energy Jim Schlesinger had dissented strongly, on national security grounds. Schlesinger then submitted a memorandum alleging improprieties in the procedures followed, and the whole matter, following a very sharp debate between Kreps and Schlesinger, was then referred to the Defense Review Board for analysis. By late August, the report came in, with the conclusion that the proposed transfer would be damaging to our national interests; as a consequence of the report, the Defense Department now requested a suspension of the transfer. To make matters worse, the issue found its way into the press, with the Administration made to look both divided and incompetent.

The President was furious. He bluntly stated that this issue was handled "about as poorly as anything since I became President." He made it plain that in his judgment both State and Commerce should have checked with him before going ahead, though he also indicated that it might have been better if I had let the matter rest. (The Dresser case remained in suspense until 1980, when it was revoked in the context of a dramatically different U.S.–Soviet relationship, but again not without a renewed struggle with State.)

Bureaucratic infighting continued until the end of the year. On November 18, completely out of the blue, a memorandum arrived for the President, signed by Vance, Blumenthal, and Kreps, urging a broad review of our policy on U.S.–Soviet trade, designed to lift restrictions and to enhance the scope of economic cooperation. I noted in my journal immediately after its receipt that "the timing and the substance of this venture completely baffle me; another example of mindless bureaucratic momentum." No prior meeting on the subject had been held, nor had there been any preparatory discussion; but simply a memo to the President from three senior Cabinet members urging a significant change in policy and requesting a formal NSC meeting to that end.

In my cover memo to the President of November 24, I objected to such a meeting on the grounds that it would give the impression "that we have now decided to push for expanded trade, whatever the state of the overall U.S.–Soviet relationship. An expanding economic relationship with the U.S.S.R. is politically sustainable only in the context of genuinely improving overall U.S.–Soviet relations," I argued, and the President wrote in the margin: "I agree." I proposed that the President refuse to hold an NSC meeting but simply sign a directive instructing Kreps and Blumenthal to use the forthcoming meeting with their Soviet counterparts to express "a generally favorable attitude toward U.S.–Soviet trade, indicating a positive but not binding approval of possible projects, and promising expeditious license review, though not revoking the existing controls." On November 28, following a positive Presidential response, I sent a memorandum to the Secretary of State, the Secretary of the Treasury, and the Secretary of Commerce, signed by the President, reiterating those points and, implicitly, rejecting the request for a formal NSC review. Though State and Commerce periodically tried to reopen the issue, the firm principle that there was linkage between politics and trade was finally established.

SALT cum grano salis

Our major preoccupation—and certainly the most time-consuming issue throughout this period—continued to be SALT. The action here was occurring on two levels: between the United States and the Soviet Union in the formal SALT negotiations in Geneva and through the Vance–Dobrynin channel in Washington; and in negotiations between American policy makers in the almost endless meetings of the SCC which I chaired in the Situation Room in the White House basement. Of the two, the latter were often the more lively and outspoken, dominated by head-to-head exchanges between Brown and Warnke. Both occasionally raised their voices as arguments bounced back and forth on such esoteric issues as encryption, ICBM diameters, cruise missile range definitional issues, or specific odometer allowances.

Though generally I tended to support Brown, feeling that we could not weaken our position any further, I concentrated my efforts in the SCC on obtaining consensus, so as to relieve the President of the need to resolve interagency disputes on highly technical and complex issues. I was particularly anxious to make sure that the JCS supported our decisions, for I felt strongly that ratification without their firm support would be impossible. I would often attempt to resolve matters by suggesting a decision when summarizing our discussions, adding that anyone who particularly objected could appeal it to the President. The President himself generally approved unanimous SCC recommendations, on which I would report to him in writing within twenty-four hours of each meeting.

In addition, I kept urging the President himself to temper his public optimism regarding the likelihood of an early SALT agreement. I frequently discussed the politics of SALT with Ham Jordan, and he and I both felt that the prospects of ratification were declining rapidly. In general, our domestic people tended to be more hard-line, and Jordan was particularly outspoken in "bemoaning the fact that Carter appointed Paul Warnke as the head of ACDA. He feels that this in itself is going to cost us dearly in terms of SALT ratification" (note of May 21, 1978). In September, I again noted that "in my weekly report to the President I have also urged him to scale down public expectations of a SALT agreement and also to lower public expectations concerning the consequences of a SALT agreement. Greater realism in regard to both issues is badly needed."

In the meantime, progress in negotiations with the Soviets was quietly being made. Though there were no breakthroughs, each meeting with them tended to resolve some specific issue. For example, in April 1978, Vance in Moscow obtained Soviet acceptance of our position on noncircumvention and also the figures of 2,250/1,200 for the overall aggregate and MIRV levels, respectively. In July, in the meeting in Geneva between Gromyko and Vance the United States offered the "test but do not deploy" compromise on the ICBM new types exemption issue, and Gromyko responded by asking whether the United States would be willing to settle the ALCM numbers, timing for reductions, and Backfire issues on the basis of the Soviet proposals if in return the Soviets accepted our previous position on the new types exemption issue (i.e., to permit testing and deployment of one new type of ICBM, MIRVed or un-MIRVed, through 1985) and drop the idea of limits on new types of SLBMs.

The July meeting was important, for it indicated that the Soviets finally were convinced that the U.S. side was prepared to wait them out and that Moscow too would have to make significant concessions if an agreement was to be reached in the near term. There is no doubt that the Soviet concession on the new types issue at the July meeting was a major break. It had the effect of sanctioning a possible U.S. MX deployment while obtaining for the United States significant limitations on Soviet ICBM modernization. We all sensed that we were entering the home stretch, and our SCC meetings became more frequent, at least three to four a month.

The September 1 SCC meeting was especially important. I was determined to secure a consensus and I chaired it in a very tight fashion, insisting that we reach decisions unanimously so that the following day, at the NSC, the President could approve a series of recommendations. As a result, it was agreed to propose a fourteen reentry vehicle surface-launched ballistic missile (RV SLBM) fractionation limit and a depressed trajectory SLBM testing ban, in addition to agreed positions on ALCM numbers, cruise missile range definitions, and a joint position on the question of dismantling of excess missiles and protocol (on cruise missiles) expiration. We also agreed to emphasize our concern on the telemetry encryption issue, in the light of some intelligence pertaining to Soviet SS-18 tests. The only major disagreement at the NSC meeting on September 2 was actually between the President and me, the President wishing to leave Backfire for the summit and I arguing that we could get more leverage by settling it beforehand, exploiting the Soviet desire for a SALT summit to obtain the desired concessions. This issue was not resolved at the meeting.

The stage was thus set for another round with the Soviets, and at the end of September both Vance and the President met with Gromyko. Unlike the President's preceding meeting with Gromyko, this one was quite amiable. However, I did feel that Gromyko was more explicit in laying out Soviet concerns about China (perhaps the Soviets had some intelligence on our quiet discussions with the Chinese), while our side was not explicit enough in stressing the dangers inherent in Soviet expansionary policies in Africa. I also noted in my journal that "since the Russians watch all of us very carefully during these proceedings, they probably noticed that Harold Brown and I were frequently engaged in conversation, exchange of jokes and notes. They probably feel that we have formed an alliance. On the other side of the President were Cy and Paul, and that probably was also symbolic from the Russians point of view. And, in fact, rightly so."

More importantly, Gromyko offered to drop the 2,500-kilometer cruise missile testing limits in the protocol if the United States accepted the Soviet position on the cruise missile range definition, proposed a six-RV limit on the exempted ICBM, proposed a December 30, 1981, date for completion of dismantling, and indicated flexibility on the new types definition. The United States offered to accept the Soviet settlement on the cruise missile range issue if the Soviets accepted the U.S. position on the cruise missile definition, and we offered an average ALCM limit of 35, and indicated a willingness to accept the December 30, 1980, protocol expiration date if the Soviets dismantle excess systems by June 30, 1981. In addition, the President emphasized to Gromyko the importance we attached to the telemetry encryption issue.

Having made some progress, we could all sense that the end was in sight and we started making plans for a possible SALT-selling ratification campaign. However, the remaining issues proved more difficult than anticipated as each side sought to have the other make the final compromises. Cy and Paul felt that to obtain a quick agreement we should be prepared to be more flexible on some of the remaining issues.

For example, on October 13 in the afternoon I got a telephone call from the tennis court from Ham Jordan, who was playing there with the President, to the effect that Cy and Paul Warnke were coming in to see the President.

On Backfire:

> Cy made again his case to the effect that we should not insist on a written confirmation by the Soviets that they are only producing 30 a year. The President looked rather startled, fixed him with a rather icy stare, and said, "Cy, are you saying that this is good for our country, or is it something that you think the Soviets will simply accept." Both Cy and Paul looked rather startled and then made a case to the effect that if we simply assert that they are producing 30 a year and they do not reject that when they receive our letter, it is in effect a confirmation. The President then indicated that if they do not contradict it that will be good enough. I then spoke up and objected by pointing out that silence is not the same thing as confirmation, that some years from now we will have a hard time proving that they in fact accepted our position, that record of conversations is simply not good enough, and that there ought to be a formal statement. Moreover, if the Soviets are not producing more than 30, then why are they unwilling to confirm it? The President then said that Gromyko is a liar, has lied to him, that he is the only person with whom he has dealt in international affairs who is a liar, and that we do need the Soviet statement in writing. Otherwise, it is a clear vulnerability for him in the ratification process. Paul then said as a compromise, "Why don't we give our proposed letters to the Soviets as illustrative and have them react to it." I immediately indicated that I thought this was a good idea because once we give them the letters we are in fact committed to a negotiating approach which I think is needed, namely one which involves written exchanges of statements regarding the production rate. Moreover, after the meeting adjourned, I agreed with Paul and Cy that in my instructions to them it will be stated that the President has decided that the Soviets need to respond in writing to confirm the U.S. estimate of the Backfire production figure and that we should propose for Soviet consideration . . . drafts of three letters, and one of these letters will be the proposed Soviet response in writing. "Draft" and "proposed" were the words which were designed to accommodate Cy, but it is stronger than illustrative and in any case it commits us to this approach. And once we have submitted it to the Soviets we will have to negotiate on that basis. Thus I am pleased at the way things worked out, but it is another example of continuous hauling and pulling on this issue.

Even more difficult than the Backfire issue was the complex question of telemetry encryption. Stan Turner was clearly not happy with the U.S. position, and we could not find any other solution which would please him save an outright ban on telemetry encryption, which clearly was non-negotiable with the Soviets. He tried everyone's patience during this period. At one point, Turner accepted a compromise at an SCC meeting, and then changed his mind and went past the SCC to the President to change his decision. By the beginning of December, we finally hammered out a formula whereby we would simply provide the Soviets with an example of Soviet behavior which we found incompatible with our interpretation of restraint on telemetry encryption. I was satisfied with this formula, and I felt that "if there is going to be a SALT, the Soviets will have to come across with some concessions. Otherwise, there will be a delay. If the Soviets were smart, they will make the concessions because that might open the door to wider accommodation largely on their own terms."

We came close to wrapping up a SALT agreement in the course of the December 21–23, 1978, Vance–Gromyko meetings in Geneva. At these meetings, we offered to compromise on the cruise missile definition issue provided it was made clear that the (nuclear) "armed" definition would apply only to those cruise missiles limited in the treaty (i.e., not GLCMs and SLCMs). Gromyko raised the unarmed cruise missile issue and proposed that all cruise missile limits apply to these delivery vehicles as well. On ALCM numbers, the Soviets proposed 27 and we countered with 28. On ICBM fractionation, the Soviets accepted our position of a freeze on existing types and a limit of 10 on the one new type that each side would be permitted to deploy. On telemetry encryption, agreement was reached on language for the common understanding, which noted that encryption of that telemetry not relevant to verification would be permitted but encryption of that telemetry relevant to verification would be banned. We also cited an unacceptable example and Gromyko did not respond to this statement.

I spent the night of December 22–23 sitting in my office, spending a good part of the time on the telephone to Cy in Geneva and to the President in Plains. The issue was again encryption. Harold Brown and Stan Turner, who joined me in my office, were absolutely adamant that we could not accept the vague formulations that the Soviets were proposing. Cy felt equally strongly that not to accept the Soviet formula would jeopardize SALT altogether and would deprive us of a major opportunity. He insisted that I review the situation with the President. Though the President was ill, I had him awakened first at 10:30 p.m., following which I wired Cy, reaffirming our firm position. Later that night I got another call from Cy, who insisted that these instructions be revised. I again consulted with Turner and Brown, and woke the President up at 4 a.m. to review the problem for the second time.

I told the President that Cy felt strongly that we might miss SALT if we do not adjust our position, and that Harold and Stan felt equally strongly that SALT would not be in the U.S. interest if our position on encryption was watered down. After some back-and-forth, in which I supported Brown and Turner, the President endorsed our position and instructed me to convey it to Vance. When I tried to reach Vance, he was already in the Soviet Embassy (it was morning in Geneva), and I decided, after some hesitation, to call him there. I knew that the Soviets would be listening, but I confined myself merely to saying to Cy that the previous instruction stands. I could sense Cy's disappointment, and I genuinely felt sorry for him. At the same time, I took the view that a compromise on this position might get us SALT but it would not be in the U.S. interest and it could also compromise the prospects for SALT's ratification.

In fact, later in 1979 the Soviets did accept our position, and anything less than that would have made the agreement worthless insofar as the U.S. Senate was concerned. The question does arise whether the earlier announcement of normalization of our relations with China had anything to do with the Soviet reluctance to make the necessary compromise. The fact of the matter, however, is that a large number of issues remained unresolved at this stage (e.g., Backfire, telemetry encryption, etc.), and they could have been resolved only by U.S. concessions. In subsequent months, by holding firm, we obtained Soviet accommodation on most of them, thereby increasing the value of the agreement to U.S. national security. Revealingly, Dobrynin appears to have shared the view that SALT was not ready by December 1978. In late January 1979, he told me quite flatly that the stalemate in Geneva on SALT was produced not by our normalization of relations with China or our invitation to Deng to visit Washington, but simply by the fact that a number of outstanding issues were still unresolved. I must say that on that point I found Dobrynin's position more credible than the line that some State Department officials were feeding to the press; namely, that somehow or other SALT, which according to them should not be linked to any adverse Soviet behavior, was compromised by our decision to establish normal relations with China.

In any case, as I have noted, the decision to proceed on normalization with China was made on the basis of consensus within the U.S. government, with Vance proposing in a memorandum that ratification of SALT be preceded by normalization of the U.S.–China relationship, since that would enhance the chances of SALT's ratification by the U.S. Senate. I very much concurred in that view, for I felt that an agreement with the Soviets to limit strategic weapons, undertaken in the context of a decade-long Soviet effort to gain nuclear parity and then superiority, must be accompanied by parallel U.S. efforts to improve the U.S. geopolitical and strategic position. I had specifically two goals in mind: I believed that our geopolitical position would be enhanced by a strategic relationship with China, and I felt that our military position would be improved if SALT was preceded by the badly needed decision to modernize our strategic deterrent through the development and deployment of the MX missile. I pressed for both of these objectives while working for an equitable SALT agreement.

By early 1979, it was clear to everyone that SALT would be reached, probably by mid-year. Vance patiently continued his difficult negotiating sessions with Dobrynin, and the President also met with the Soviet Ambassador in late February. Again, as in previous meetings, I used the opportunity to urge the President not only to stress to Dobrynin the importance of resolving satisfactorily the encryption issue insofar as SALT was concerned, but also to register our concern over Soviet activities in South Yemen and the growing Soviet military presence in Vietnam. While the President was making these points, Cy joined in the discussion and, in effect, softened the impact of the President's observations. However, with the President's approval, I reemphasized these points to Dobrynin in personal conversations, which I continued to have with him throughout this period.

By early May, I could note in my journal that "Cy has basically concluded the negotiations with Dobrynin. I expect that we will announce the basic agreement early next week, and we have already started discussions as to the site [of a meeting]. It seems increasingly likely that it will be mid-June in Vienna. That is just as well because it will minimize the chances of a great deal of fraternization," which I feared might occur if the U.S. side was to host the meeting. On May 7, toward the end of a longish meeting that included the President, Jordan, Mondale, Vance, and me, Vance said at 3:15 p.m.: "Mr. President, the basic negotiations for SALT have been completed."

Preconditions for SALT*

But before the SALT agreement could be signed, and the Carter–Brezhnev meeting held, there remained for me two issues to which I had to give personal attention. The first involved making certain that the United States went into the agreement with a relatively favorable

---

* SALT I, signed in 1972, limited ABMs to 100 on each side and froze offensive missile launchers at the 1972 levels—1,710 for the United States and about 2,250 for the Soviet Union.

At Vladivostok in 1974, the United States and the U.S.S.R. had reached a provisional agreement establishing: a common aggregate of 2,400 for strategic nuclear delivery vehicles (heavy bombers, ICBMs, and SLBMs); a limit of 1,320 MIRVed missile launchers on each side; no limits on U.S. forward-based systems (FBS) or

military posture, and that to me meant obtaining a Presidential decision before signing SALT in favor of deployment of the new MX missile. The second matter involved a bilateral U.S.–Soviet accommodation on a sensitive human-rights issue in the hope that the atmosphere of the U.S.–Soviet relationship would be improved. Specifically, I was concerned with Soviet detention of leading dissidents and with the imprisonment, after trial, in the United States of two Soviet UN employees convicted of espionage.

Both Harold Brown and I felt strongly that the United States would be at a strategic disadvantage if SALT II was not accompanied by new strategic deployments by the U.S. side. In the course of the previous decade, the Soviet Union maintained a sustained effort to increase its strategic forces while the United States stood pat. As a consequence, we faced the prospect of genuine strategic inferiority unless SALT II limits were strictly respected by both sides and unless the United States took advantage of SALT II to bring its forces up to approximately the permitted limit. Given the growing accuracy and numbers of Soviet land-based missiles, the existing American land-based deterrent was becoming increasingly vulnerable, and it urgently needed modernization. That modernization required larger, more accurate, and less vulnerable ICBMs than the existing Minuteman III force.

Soviet systems for attack on peripheral targets or on throw weight. The Vladivostok limits were set at levels which required only small Soviet reductions (about 100) in strategic launchers and permitted all U.S. programs. Major unresolved issues included: limits on cruise missiles, treatment of the Backfire bomber, and mobile missiles and MIRV counting rules.

The SALT II Treaty negotiated under Carter imposed equal overall ceilings on the numbers of strategic nuclear delivery systems for both parties through December 1985, with the Vladivostok ceiling of 2,400 delivery systems to be lowered to 2,250 beginning on January 1, 1981. The treaty imposed additional sublimits of 1,320 for each party on the combined number of MIRVed ICBMs, SLBMs, and ALCM-carrying heavy bombers; and 1,200 maximum number of MIRVed ICBMs and SLBMs. Since only the U.S. side was likely to deploy ALCM-carrying heavy bombers, the net result was a bonus of 120 for the United States over the 1,200 MIRV limit on both sides. Each side could deploy a maximum of 820 land-based ICBMs. The protocol to the treaty set out limitations that would be in force through December 1981: mobile launcher deployment was prohibited, as was deployment of ground- and sea-launched cruise missiles capable of a range greater than 600 kilometers. The protocol also prohibited the flight testing and deployment of ALCMs.

The SALT II Treaty was a major step forward. For the first time the two sides were limited to an equal number of strategic weapons systems, and reductions in the number of operational Soviet weapon systems were required. The treaty limits could be adequately verified by existing technology, and it established rules for counting strategic systems that simplified the task of verification. Moreover, the treaty allowed the United States to develop and deploy the systems needed to modernize its strategic triad—the Trident submarine, the cruise missile, and the MX.

From mid-1977 several studies were in progress as to how to deal with the problem. In the fall of that year, the Air Force submitted a proposal to deploy a new large MX missile in hardened tunnels in the Southwest. In a cover memo to the President, I urged him to approve in general the construction of a new missile with solid hard-target kill capability in order to avoid the possibility that at some point in the future the Soviets would have more strategic military options than we did. I feared that if such a situation were to arise, the United States could be forced into significant political concessions in the course of a protracted crisis with the Soviets. However, I also pointed out that the MX tunnel system posed serious problems of verifiability and that for SALT other alternatives would have to be considered.

In 1978, the Defense Department favored the so-called MAP (multiple aim point) basing system involving perhaps twenty or more vertical silo-like shelters for each MX missile. The SALT negotiating group immediately protested that this was an unverifiable system, and the President in early 1978 asked Harold Brown to prepare alternative basing modes more compatible with the evolving SALT agreement. I noted in my journal on July 20 that on the previous day "I briefed the President on the Soviet rejection of our multiple aim point basing proposal in SALT. This is not unexpected as far as I am concerned, and I hope the rejection and the subsequent discussion will force us to focus more deliberately on what are the basic purposes of SALT. The Soviets are clearly trying to constrain our modernization, cruise missiles, and MX, but what is it that we are seeking and how persistent have we been in obtaining our objectives?" After consulting Charles Duncan, Harold Brown's deputy, in late August, I laid out a four-part scenario to force a decision on the MX. We agreed that we would use the Defense budget process to set in motion several studies, to examine the viability of the strategic triad, and to point toward some form of a budget decision by early 1979. This would be reinforced by a parallel effort to refine our existing strategic doctrine to include war-fighting as a necessary element of deterrence. In September, Harold Brown met with the President at Camp David to review our five-year defense program, and he presented him with evidence that modifications in the Soviet SS-18 and SS-19 missiles were making our Minuteman III increasingly vulnerable.

At this time, Brown leaned toward an air mobile system. He and I had a head-on debate on the subject; I noted on December 8 that "earlier in the morning I had a very lively debate with Harold Brown over the basing mode. I favor a ground mobile system; he wants an air mobile system. I don't think this system will work. It will be too costly, too complicated. He was quite exercised. But the debate was fun because he really is very bright." Again, in early April 1979, I noted that in my morning briefing "I urged the President to use an appropriate opportunity to remind Harold that we want a good analysis of the ground-based mobile system for our ICBMs. Both the President and I then talked about it and we agreed that the air mobile system is too complex, cumbersome, and potentially vulnerable. Later in the morning a note came across my desk from the President to Harold asking him who is conducting the study on the ground mobiles and how is it being pursued? Again, a very quick reaction!" By May 1979, Brown had moved away from the air mobile system and instead proposed a land-based trench concept, with a missile launcher moving on tracks. I again raised the possibility of a truck mobile system, and on May 25 in the Situation Room, Harold and I had a lively argument, in which he saturated me with technical data. Shortly thereafter, much to my gratification, Brown came in with a revised concept of the trench basing mode, now generally referred to as the racetrack, in which the proposed MX missile would move on ground mobile launchers.

Throughout this period, the President kept pressing Brown as to whether the United States still needed a triad. In a series of effective memos, Brown reassured the President that a triad was essential to American security and that it would be a great mistake for the United States to move into a defense posture in which our deterrent would be predominantly sea-based. The debates on these matters took place within the PRC, chaired by Brown. On most issues, the State Department took a reserved position, with Warren Christopher representing it. Some of the comments made by Christopher seemed to indicate a slight preference for the dyad over the triad, and considerable concern that any basing mode for the MX might run afoul of SALT verifiability requirements. Nonetheless, State did not oppose the movement which was being generated in favor of an MX decision and thus the issue did not produce intense interagency conflicts.

By May 1979, I felt that the issue was ripe for a Presidential decision, and an NSC meeting was convened on June 4. The topic was U.S. strategic arms policy and U.S.–Soviet relations. When I briefed the President on the proposed agenda prior to the meeting, he "was in an extremely irritated mood. First of all, he complained that the papers came in only the day before the meeting. The fact of the matter is that Defense was not ready to submit such papers and, secondly, he was spending the weekend at Camp David, where he doesn't like to work anyway. Then he told me I was jamming a decision down his throat, namely to build a new big missile and to adopt a complicated trench system for basing it, and that I was not giving him a critical evaluation of this option." However, by the time the meeting convened, the President, who was an extraordinarily fast reader, had digested the basic papers and was more relaxed.

I opened the meeting by presenting seven basic conclusions drawn from our previous work:

1. The United States continued to enjoy considerable advantages in all nonmilitary aspects of the U.S.–Soviet competition.

2. Only in combination with our allies did we have an advantage over the Soviets in the total dimensions of military power. Thus we could not afford to jeopardize the cohesion and confidence of the alliance by any wavering in U.S. power and resolve.

3. With respect to trends in the regional military balance: in the Far East favorable political trends might offset the unfavorable military balance; instabilities in the Persian Gulf–Middle East region had created an adverse balance with an uncertain future; and in NATO the balance was slowly improving.

4. The strategic nuclear balance was deteriorating faster than we had expected two years ago and would continue to do so into the early eighties. The Soviets have been outspending us in defense since the late 1960s, and military investment is important because it is cumulative.

5. In the early 1980s we would face a "strategic dip." We would not meet the criteria established in Presidential Directive 18; namely, to maintain essential equivalence and a balance no worse than that existing in 1977.

6. The strategic gap of the early 1980s could produce damaging political perceptions and encourage assertive Soviet behavior.

7. If these trends were not corrected, the United States would be able at best to wage a spasmic, apocalyptic war rather than one controlled for political purposes. Because of its potential vulnerability to a Soviet first strike, the United States would be less able to bargain stably in a protracted crisis situation, and therefore the United States might be less able in the 1980s to deter the Soviet Union from assertive behavior.

After I finished, "the President rather glumly called on Vance to speak. Vance then much to my surprise agreed with six of my seven conclusions. The only one which he questioned somewhat was the notion that there might be a dip in the eighties, but he did not deny the basic proposition that trends were adverse." I was even more taken aback when Brown stated that the comprehensive net assessment was too pessimistic about the strategic forces balance but too optimistic in its overall assessment. By 1985 the Soviets would have greater strength than the United States in almost every military category, no matter what we do. To my annoyance, at this meeting Brown did not come out strongly for a new missile.

The President reacted to all of this by saying that much of the perception of Soviet superiority had been created by "this group." He stressed that perceptions can affect the gravity of the problem and that the perception was being created that the Soviet Union was stronger than the United States. He pointed out that we had military advantages over them, such as the fact that the Soviets had multiple enemies whereas the United States had solid allies.

In the discussion that followed, both Turner and Jones strongly supported my argument, and the President indicated toward the end that he was leaning toward a decision in favor of the MX, though he was not yet prepared to resolve the basing mode question.

We met again within two days, and at the follow-on NSC meeting the only question to resolve was the kind of MX missile that the United States would undertake to deploy. In the previous months, some consideration was given, largely at Brown's instigation, to the development of a common missile, suited to both ground- and sea-based deployment. I had objected to this concept on the grounds that such a missile would have to be considerably smaller than what the United States could build for land deployment, and I feared that any effort to develop a common missile would run into the same technical difficulties that a previous effort to build a common Air Force/Navy fighter had encountered (the famous FX fiasco). In the final discussions Brown argued that the largest MX missile was already designed, whereas other possibilities, including the common missile, would involve at least a one-year delay. He was backed by General Jones and the new ACDA director, George Seignious. Christopher also went along with the argument. Throughout I had argued on behalf of the largest missile possible, because I thought it would enhance the chances of ratification (since it would give us the argument that our new missile offset to some extent the large Soviet missile) and because it would give us the largest number of RVs allowed under SALT II, thereby enabling the United States to retain its margin in overall deliverable nuclear weapons. Vance also supported this argument, and the meeting ended with my summarizing the President's decision as containing three elements: (1) that we were going to proceed with a verifiable land-based deployment mode, preferably the ground mobile shelter system; (2) that we were going to proceed with the largest missile allowed under the SALT II agreement; and (3) that we would resolve the question of exactly which basing mode we would use within several weeks after the conclusion of the SALT agreement.

I felt good about the decision, believing that we had in one swoop increased American strategic staying power and enhanced the prospects for SALT ratification. I was strengthened in my view by opinions candidly expressed to me by Senators Byrd and Nunn. Both told me flatly that SALT would not be ratified unless the United States increased its defense efforts. The President's MX decision was a token of his firm determination not to let SALT inhibit the further modernization of our strategic deterrent.

The President's willingness to make the MX decision, even in the context of severe budget restraints, was enhanced by the positive attitude adopted on this matter by Vance and Christopher. And that in turn was related to a development which greatly changed the tenor of our internal debates on SALT and defense policy. In late 1978, Paul Warnke, the Director of ACDA, had indicated that the time had come for him to resign. His decision was quietly applauded by the President's political advisers, notably Jordan and Powell. Both felt that he had become a serious liability to our SALT efforts, given the fact that his own confirmation hearings had revealed widespread senatorial opposition to his views. The question immediately arose as to who ought to be his successor. Vance favored one of Warnke's associates or, alternatively, one or two able lawyers from New York, close friends of his. I took the position that whoever was appointed ought to be chosen with ratification in mind and thus ought to be someone seen as sympathetic to our overall efforts to improve our national security. Privately, I wanted also to find someone with whom I could work more closely and who would not view arms control as in conflict with our defense priorities. I therefore suggested to the President that he consider seriously General George Seignious, a member of Paul Warnke's delegation, a man respected in the military as well as in the arms control community.

My suggestion was strongly opposed by Vance. We had several arguments on this subject, but I worked quietly to mobilize support from Ham Jordan, Brown, and Mondale. Ham played an important role in urging the President to act. Brown was solidly in favor of Seignious, and after initial objections the Vice President came around as well. I brought my candidate into the Oval Office, and the President was favorably impressed. He asked me to send a cable to Vance, who was in Moscow conferring with Gromyko, requesting that Cy meet Seignious when he returned. After additional conversations with me, Ham succeeded in persuading the President to send a message to Vance notifying him that Seignious was his choice unless Vance had serious objections. Cy's response was quite negative. I recommended to the President that he "either turn the whole thing off or act on it before it becomes a political football." Two hours later Ham came into my office looking rather pleased and told me that the President had just phoned Seignious to offer him the job.

Seignious joined our deliberations early in 1979, and he played a particularly important role in backing Brown's and my efforts to obtain a quick and firm decision on the MX deployment, especially prior to the signing of the SALT agreement. With his appointment, relations between ACDA and NSC became more cooperative and we no longer had to arbitrate, as we had to earlier, continuous disputes between ACDA and the Defense Department. Moreover, under Seignious ACDA was no longer just an echo for State.

In my judgment, the President's decision to proceed with MX development and deployment, as well as his earlier bold initiative on China, created a proper strategic and geopolitical context for our forthcoming meeting with Brezhnev. There remained, in preparation for it, the need to resolve one more problem; namely the removal of the needless irritant of the imprisonment by the Soviets of some leading human-rights activists. That action conflicted with Carter's commitment to human rights and it poisoned the atmosphere for any U.S.–Soviet dialogue. At least a partial resolution of the issue was the necessary precondition for a successful SALT agreement. Accordingly, I sought and obtained the President's permission in July 1978 to initiate exploratory talks with the Soviets regarding the possible exchange of some Soviet spies for those Soviet dissidents for whom we felt special responsibility. On May 20, 1978, the FBI had apprehended two Soviet UN employees, Valdik Enger and Rudolf Chernyayev, while they were engaging in espionage activities, and on October 13, 1978, they were convicted and sentenced to fifty years in prison. As on most issues pertaining to Soviet affairs, there was some interagency dispute as to whether we should proceed firmly with these two cases. My own view was that the espionage laws should be strictly enforced and that we should not discriminate in favor of the Soviets, even if the Soviets threatened us with reprisals or with the possibility of a worsened relationship. Carter very firmly endorsed that view, overruling some State Department hesitations.

The Soviets kept appealing to Vance and to me to postpone the trial, but once the date had been set and the conviction was imminent, I initiated conversations with Dobrynin about the possibility of an exchange. Dobrynin's first offer was totally unacceptable. He offered me two hijackers convicted in the Soviet Union if the two Soviets were released. I flatly told him that I would not accept that and I pressed for Shcharansky or Ginzburg, though I knew that I probably would not get them at this stage. I also raised the question of clemency for a Soviet citizen sentenced to death for espionage on behalf of the United States.

For the next several months Dobrynin and I had prolonged exchanges on this subject, in my office, in his apartment in the Soviet Embassy, and at my house. At times the arguments were quite heated, especially when I insisted that the execution of the Soviet citizen would jeopardize any possible deal on the Soviet spies. Dobrynin kept insisting that this matter was none of my business, but I pointed out to him that the

Soviets themselves had made it our business by generating a letter from the prisoner addressed directly to Carter, pleading for assistance. That step had been taken presumably to embarrass Carter, but it enabled me to argue that the Soviets had thereby made it also our concern. In addition, I gave Dobrynin a list of dissidents whom I would consider suitable objects of an exchange. I had constructed the list very deliberately to include some leading Jewish dissidents, some outstanding Russian opposition figures, as well as representatives of the Ukrainian minority and victims of religious persecution.

Dobrynin and I continued quibbling over numbers and people for days on end. Soviet offers, in my judgment, were unacceptable, and I at times laughed in the Ambassador's face, telling him that there would be no deal and that the former Soviet UN employees would continue to enjoy American hospitality for the next half century. Finally, with SALT agreement nearing, in the latter part of April, Dobrynin and I were able to strike a deal: the life of the Soviet citizen would be spared, though that would not be part of the official arrangement, and the Soviets would release five leading dissidents in return for the two Soviets. The five to be released were Gyorgi Vins, a leading Baptist; Valentyn Moroz, the most prominent Ukrainian nationalist imprisoned in the Soviet Union; Edward Kuznetsov, sentenced for organizing an aborted hijacking and a leading Jewish dissident; Mark Dymshits, involved in the same case; and Aleksandr Ginzburg, one of the outstanding Russian dissidents.

On Friday, April 27, the prisoners were placed aboard a Soviet airliner in Moscow, without being told where they were going, and at roughly the same time we undertook to deliver to Kennedy Airport in New York the two Soviets (who in the meantime had been confined to the Soviet UN Mission compound in New York, in the custody of Ambassador Dobrynin). Two members of my staff, deeply involved in the exchange, Reginald Bartholomew and Jessica Mathews, went to New York to meet the Soviet airliner. On boarding it, they found the five dissidents cramped in a small cabin, each seated next to several KGB guards. They looked impassive and stunned, and it was only after they had left the plane that Bartholomew, as he later reported to me, "saw the first real signs of animation and excitement."

On Saturday, April 28, while at home resting, I was surprised and pleased to get a phone call from Prime Minister Begin from Jerusalem. "He thanked me from the bottom of his heart and told me that I have earned a mitzvah. Mitzvah apparently is a Hebrew concept of a blessed deed for which one is grateful." I later met with the five, and this entire episode was for me one of the most gratifying experiences of my four years in the White House. Because our side did not appear too eager and had stood firm, a favorable arrangement was in fact negotiated, and the Soviets respected it scrupulously; more importantly, five genuinely heroic individuals and their families gained their freedom, and that injected into the often impersonal conduct of foreign affairs a deeply gratifying human dimension.

The Vienna Summit

The preparations for the Vienna Summit went into full gear in late May. Dobrynin conducted the talks for the Soviet side, while on ours they were mostly handled either by Vance and me or by Christopher and me (when Vance was abroad). The Soviets made it clear to us right away that they wanted the summit confined to SALT, that they desired "no surprises," and that they wished the direct consultations and meetings to be of relatively brief duration. Brezhnev's health was clearly a factor. Moreover, in a sudden burst of candor, Dobrynin one day took me aside and reiterated the Soviet desire to limit all discussion to SALT, adding: "The fact of the matter is that Carter knows so much more on all of these issues than Brezhnev that Brezhnev will be on the defensive and embarrassed if Carter presses him on all of them. Stick to one or two major issues, and don't embarrass the old man. On such matters as encryption, if Carter makes him understand how important it is to ratification, Brezhnev might be helpful three or four months from now."

At my end, I prepared for the President a comprehensive memorandum, outlining the state of the overall relationship and urging the President very strongly to engage Brezhnev in a discussion of the state of the relationship as a whole, placing special emphasis on the negative impact on detente both of the continued Soviet military buildup and especially of Soviet military activities, directly or by proxy, in the Indian Ocean area. I stressed to the President that the summit would be worthless unless we could make the Soviets understand how sensitive these matters were to the American public. It would also be useful if Brezhnev were to agree to continuing consultations on these matters after the summit is over. My hope was that instead of just negotiating SALT we could engage the Soviets in a broader dialogue, and I also hinted to the President that it would be useful for him to use me in that context.

My approach to the summit differed from Vance's. In a memo to the President dated June 8, Vance stressed that "the primary focus of your exchanges with Brezhnev should be to reaffirm the basic framework of U.S.–Soviet relations, which is based on substantial common interest in strategic stability, mutual acceptance of the status quo in the developed world and avoidance of confrontation in dealing with the Third World." This passage shows how important nuances can be. While the

Soviets should share "a substantial common interest" with us, I felt that recent Soviet behavior demonstrated that such a common interest did not yet exist, and that we should make it clear to the Soviet leaders that their actions were not consistent with the notion of a stable and increasingly cooperative relationship.

Quite characteristically, the President kept telling Vance and me that in the various papers we prepared for him we were not sufficiently ambitious. He stressed that he would like concrete accomplishments on a large number of issues. We developed additional initiatives for him, but I was a little anxious. On June 12, I noted that in talking to the President "I emphasized the fact that this is going to be a sober, working summit—one which is not designed to generate excessive expectations. I am giving a memo to the President tomorrow also emphasizing that in talking to Brezhnev he ought to focus on two simple themes— arms cuts and regional restraint. Trying to do more than that is going to be counterproductive." I also succeeded in thwarting a plan, reported to the President by Christopher, for Blumenthal and Kreps to be present at the summit. I pointed out to the President that this would generate expectations of a trade agreement, followed by disappointment if the summit did not generate one. The President decided that neither of them should plan on going.

The first encounter between Carter and Brezhnev took place on the evening of June 15, when they paid their respects to the Austrian President. They then met again at the Opera, and I was introduced to Brezhnev. Brezhnev immediately said, "Oh, I've heard a lot about you," and Dmitry Ustinov, the Soviet Defense Minister and a close associate of Brezhnev, commented that he recognized me from my pictures. During the opera, I sat next to Aleksandrov, Brezhnev's staff assistant. Aleksandrov, a little gnome of a man, kept up a constant chatter: "The opera is too long; the smaller the country, the longer the opera." I said to him, "In that case, have you ever been to Luxembourg?" He laughed and said, "No, but to Liechtenstein and thank God no opera." Then Ustinov leaned back from the row ahead of me and started exchanging humorous remarks with Brezhnev and me, until the fat wife of one of the Austrian ministers sitting next to us, with a typical Germanic sense of order, hissed loudly and asked us all to be quiet.

The substantive discussions opened at the U.S. Embassy on Saturday, June 16. Brezhnev went first, reading his prepared statement, and occasionally turning to his associates to ask how he was doing. "*Khorosho,*" they all assured him. During the discussions, an unexpected problem developed on the Backfire. Brezhnev simply did not act according to script and would not give us the expected assurances on Backfire. The President then pressed him for confirmation that the Soviets would not produce more than thirty a year, and I could hear Gromyko whisper to Brezhnev not to answer.

On Sunday, the President made his presentation on our objectives for SALT III, and he was quite eloquent. His enthusiasm was contagious, and he commanded Brezhnev's interest. In fact, Brezhnev asked the President later for a brief summary of the President's proposals for further cuts and wider limits on strategic weapons, and the President, with obvious satisfaction, wrote these out in longhand on yellow lined paper and gave it personally to Brezhnev. The President's presentation, however, made Brown nervous. He passed me a note expressing concern that the Soviets would misinterpret the President's intent and thus be encouraged to push us even harder. I then received a similar note from Ham Jordan. Fortunately, the Soviets did not misconstrue Carter's initiative.

The best session, in my judgment, took place on the afternoon of the next day, when the President delivered in measured, tough tones a statement of our concerns regarding Cuban activity sponsored and supported by the Soviets, about the Soviet bankrolling of the Vietnamese, and about Soviet hindrances to our peace efforts in the Middle East. The President stated that we had absolutely vital interests in the Arabian peninsula and the Persian Gulf, and that the extensive Soviet sponsorship of Cuban military activities was causing us concern. "We look upon Cuba as a proxy or surrogate of yours, supported and financed by you." He again went on to add, "We now see more Soviet use of Vietnamese facilities and ports, and this causes us grave concern." He elaborated on all of these points, and it was obvious to the Soviets that the President was speaking with deep conviction. The President ended his presentation with a friendly smile, adding teasingly, "I hope you agree with everything I said." The American delegation laughed; the Soviets sat with stony faces.

However, the Soviets listened with rapt attention, unlike at the earlier sessions in which they tended to whisper to each other while waiting for the translation of the President's remarks. The Soviet mood was grim and very sober. Brezhnev responded by reading a prepared statement. At one point, Gromyko gave him an additional page. At first Brezhnev seemed reluctant to read it and pushed it back to Gromyko, but in the end he accepted it and read a brief statement rejecting American concerns regarding Vietnam and launching into a violent attack on the Chinese.

More significantly, in a follow-up session we did obtain Soviet agreement to limit the production of Backfires to thirty per year. Carter pressed Brezhnev hard on this issue, and finally elicited an explicit and affirmative response from Brezhnev. Toward the end of the proceedings I was rather struck by the change in Brezhnev's condition. Though during dinner the preceding night he seemed in reasonably good shape, and he could joke, wave his hands, express mock horror, and from time to time participate in discussion, at the concluding session he seemed to be on the verge of senility. The other Soviets treated him with affection and patience, guiding him gently.

Carter handled himself very well. He balanced his occasionally excessive friendliness with a tough statement on Soviet global activities, which he substantially repeated in a private toast at the small dinner party attended only by eight of us, four from each side (Brezhnev, Ustinov, Gromyko, and Politburo member Konstantin Chernenko; the President, Vance, Brown, and me). All in all, I think the Soviets got a good impression of the President: obvious intelligence, dedication to arms control, but a firm recognition of the Soviet challenge and determination to respond.

On the Soviet side, Brezhnev struck me as a genuinely pitiful figure, struggling valiantly to represent the Soviet Union as best he could in spite of grave physical infirmity. At times, he was quite energetic, and one could sense that in his prime he must have been a man of great ebullience and dynamism. At other times, he appeared almost senile. When Carter met alone with Brezhnev, Brezhnev—as Carter later told me—seemed unable to cope with a direct and informal discussion. His translator had a file next to him, with different topics indexed, and he would reach into the file, pull out an appropriate piece of paper, and Brezhnev would read his response to Carter's comments from the piece of paper.

In the formal discussions in which I participated, Brezhnev deferred a great deal to Gromyko, who would whisper to him instructions in a quiet but firm voice. Sometimes he would also lean over and say, "No, don't agree to this," or occasionally he would point at Brezhnev's script and tell him what to read and where to stop. In general, both Gromyko and Ustinov were very solicitous of Brezhnev, and the relationship between them struck me as being personally quite intimate and warm. Ustinov had a quick and shrewd mind, though he was more deferential to Brezhnev than Gromyko, who was clearly the dominant figure on the Soviet side. Somewhat to my surprise, Dobrynin seemed not to be a member of the inner circle. During the actual proceedings, he sat at the end of the table and did not speak up. During intermissions, he would not join the top Soviet leaders but stood off in a corner by himself. At one point during the proceedings, he rose from the table, walked over to the window, and opened it to let in fresh air; as Dobrynin was sitting down he glanced at Brezhnev, who appeared to be frowning, whereupon Dobrynin walked back to the window and closed it.

I returned to Washington from Vienna feeling fairly satisfied. The meeting had been sober, without the excessive effusiveness which I feared might mislead the American public, which tends to oscillate from euphoria over detente to hysteria over the Cold War. The SALT agreement itself, I always believed and continue to believe, was in the American interest, for it imposed stricter limits on the Soviet side at a time when it had genuine momentum in its military buildup. We obtained the assurances we wanted both on telemetry and, despite initial Soviet reticence, on the production rate of the Backfire bomber. Later, in Washington, Dobrynin told me that Brezhnev in his report to the Politburo spoke in personally warm terms of the President as a person with whom one can have a serious discussion on difficult issues, without acrimony, and as a person who is genuinely interested in arms control. Dobrynin also added that Brezhnev said to the Politburo that "even Brzezinski seems to be a decent fellow."

At the same time, there was at best only a limited dialogue on the issue that I considered most important. We did not succeed in engaging the Soviets more fully in a discussion of our geopolitical concerns, nor was there any agreement to follow up consultations. The exchanges on global-strategic problems, both in the plenary sessions and at the informal dinners, were perfunctory. I doubt that any dent was made in Soviet thinking, nor was there any decrease in the Soviet predisposition to press us as much as possible in areas of vulnerability to us.

The Vienna meeting did put SALT on the rails, and we immediately proceeded to organize ourselves for the ratification struggle. The President invited the highly respected Washington lawyer Lloyd Cutler to join our team as the coordinator of the SALT ratification effort. Cutler established a close working relationship with the pertinent senators, and our initial soundings, and then the actual hearings before the Senate Foreign Relations Committee, proved encouraging. Within the White House, at the insistence of Anne Wexler, the President's assistant, I became the principal briefer on SALT—partly because my reputation as a "hard-liner" made my arguments on behalf of SALT more persuasive to potential opponents and also because I did speak with genuine conviction that the SALT agreement, now accompanied by the decisions which I badly wanted both on China and on the MX, genuinely served our national interest.

SALT Aborted

By late summer of 1979, our campaign on behalf of SALT ratification was making steady progress. Lloyd Cutler was ably orchestrating our congressional efforts, and the hearings before the Senate Foreign Relations Committee were generating wider understanding of the treaty's benefits to U.S. security. Even such prominent opponents as Henry Kissinger and Alexander Haig tended to concentrate their arguments more on the need for a larger U.S. defense effort than on actual criticism of the SALT agreement.

I was encouraged. I wanted SALT ratified, but I wanted also a larger U.S. defense effort. The campaign to ratify SALT, and particularly the position taken by its opponents, was thus creating favorable conditions for a shift in our national priorities toward greater efforts in the national security area. SALT, rather than being the vehicle for acquiescent accommodation with the Soviet Union, was becoming the catalyst for a more assertive posture.

During this period I continued my meetings with Senators Byrd and Nunn to solicit their support for SALT, and also to develop with them a shared approach to our defense policy. Brown also worked hard to influence the President's thinking, and he at times even irritated the President with his insistent arguments that more money needed to be spent for national defense.

The President himself also grew more sympathetic to the case for a larger defense effort. The experience of dealing with the Soviets, and the series of NSC meetings and memoranda stressing the increasing Soviet threat, had a growing impact, even though domestically oriented advisers, notably Mondale and Eizenstat, kept pressing him in the opposite direction. On September 13, the President told me that he was going to discuss SALT and the defense budget with Senator Nunn and he requested some talking points. "I gave him a brutally frank memorandum. I said he's got to sit down with Nunn and talk to him like two Georgians who are willing to talk turkey and who can therefore be totally uninhibited. He should tell Nunn that he is the first Southern President and that Nunn can now make the difference between his reelection and defeat. If Nunn goes for defeat of SALT he (Carter) will also be rejected. At this stage, Nunn doesn't have to endorse SALT but can help stem the tide against SALT. In return Carter later on would be willing to give him more than 3 percent [increase in the defense budget] and it will . . . look like a Nunn victory." The President called me around 6 p.m. to say that the meeting went quite well and that Nunn had agreed to help. This was a major coup.

But while we were intensifying our efforts to obtain ratification of SALT, the Soviets continued to engage in activities which were, to put it mildly, less than helpful. Throughout the year, they continued the buildup of their military presence in Vietnam and increased their support for Vietnamese aggressiveness in Cambodia. We repeatedly registered our concerns with the Soviets, to the point of even warning them that their actions might have some impact on the nature of the American–Chinese relationship. On my initiative, in late January the State Department conveyed an oral message to the Soviets through Dobrynin. This message was repeated in a letter from President Carter to Brezhnev several weeks later. We reminded Moscow of its special responsibility for Hanoi's action and stressed that continued Vietnamese aggression could lead to "serious problems" for the U.S.S.R. These warnings went unheeded.

Our concern over Soviet activity in Vietnam, compounded by the persisting irritation over the Soviet sponsorship of the Cuban military proxy in Africa, was further aggravated by indications of intensifying Soviet involvement in Afghanistan. In late March 1979, I instructed the Director of Central Intelligence to generate more information regarding the nature and extent of the Soviet involvement in Afghanistan, and by early fall more formal meetings were held under NSC auspices to assess the scope and thrust of the Soviet involvement. I also registered our serious concern over this issue in my conversations with Dobrynin.

One cannot deny that Soviet activities worldwide were greatly complicating our efforts to ratify SALT, thereby producing the linkage which was so strongly denied earlier by State. Our ratification difficulties, however, were greatly and almost fatally compounded by a new issue, that of the Soviet troops in Cuba, which surfaced suddenly in late summer.

There had been some fragmentary intelligence earlier to the effect that the Soviet military presence in Cuba was growing. In late 1978 and early 1979, intelligence sources reported increased numbers of Soviet-flown MiGs in Cuba, and we raised the issue in oral messages to the Soviets. In late 1978, I obtained the President's approval for SR-71 flights over Cuba to obtain harder evidence. But we detected no firm evidence of any qualitative change, or of any violation of previous U.S.–Soviet understandings. Moreover, the State Department was not inclined to be very responsive. For example, on November 24, I had lunch with Vance and Brown in the Situation Room. "These are usually very friendly and amiable sessions but this one was a little tense. The reason for it was that first we discussed the MiG issue, the MiGs in Cuba. Cy was for doing as little as possible on the subject. He obviously feels very gingerly about the U.S.–Soviet relationship. We didn't resolve it because Harold was supposed to take the lead on this issue. I promised him privately and separately that I would support him; he was not very forceful. When I brought up the question why the MiGs are considered defensive weapons and we are prepared to accept that definition, but the Harriers which the British might be selling to the Chinese are not defensive even though they have less capability than the MiGs, Cy practically collapsed. He said that if we ever come to the day when we ourselves support arms for China this Administration will have one person less in it."

During 1979, I raised on several occasions the need for more sustained U.S. pressure on Cuba and on the Soviet Union, but relatively little progress was made, especially with all of us heavily preoccupied with both SALT and the Middle East. The situation changed rather dramatically during the summer. In late July, I saw the first report that the Soviets might have a unit in Cuba, and I alerted the President to this on July 24, pointing out that it could have serious repercussions for SALT. A few days later, I sent a crisply worded memorandum to

Stan Turner, the Director of the CIA, requesting the Agency to step up its collection efforts on Cuba. I was frustrated by the absence of adequate intelligence reporting.

Within the next two weeks, we obtained harder and harder evidence. On August 14, "I briefed the President in the morning on the fact that according to intelligence reports there is now an actual Soviet brigade in Cuba, with headquarters and regular organization and that in fact it is scheduled to hold firing exercises within a week. I told him that this is an extremely serious development which could most adversely affect SALT. The President looked quite concerned. . . . I told him also that I would be coming back with a Vance–Brown–Brzezinski recommendation." In the afternoon of the same day, I held a meeting with Vance and Brown, for which earlier I had submitted a memorandum urging concerted action directed at putting more pressure on Cuba. "Brown came back with my Cuba memo rather beefed up, Vance came back with my Cuba memo rather diluted," and we agreed to discuss this issue further, especially if harder evidence becomes available.

I instructed my staff to continue interagency work in order to develop wider bureaucratic consensus for a response to the Cuban problem. In the meantime, since no additional information was coming in, and since the President was leaving on his summer vacation, I decided to take a few days off myself and went to Vermont with my family. In my absence, the sub-SCC committee met on August 29, and the State Department proposed a demarche to the Soviets on the alleged Soviet brigade in Cuba. My staff objected, on the grounds that this course of action could immediately precipitate a Soviet denial, thereby making it more difficult for the Soviets to change their position later on. The group decided that Secretary Vance would be asked to discuss this issue by telephone with me and with Acting Secretary of Defense Graham Claytor (for Brown also was away on his summer holiday).

Vance did not call me, but I was called by my deputy, David Aaron. I asked him to defer any action on this issue until I had returned to Washington around Labor Day, so that Vance, Brown, and I could consult with the President. Much to my amazement, I learned shortly thereafter that Under Secretary of State David Newsom, acting apparently on Vance's instructions, proceeded to brief Senator Frank Church, chairman of the Senate Foreign Relations Committee, on the subject of the Soviet troop presence in Cuba, but Newsom failed to instruct Church how to deal with the matter in public. Secretary Vance apparently felt that the information would leak out and that it would be more prudent to inform Church beforehand.

The result was disastrous: Church, running for reelection in Idaho and attempting to correct his previous image as a dove, immediately convened a rather bellicose press conference on the subject. The issue was thus out in the open, even though at this stage we had neither concluded our intelligence review nor formulated any agreed policy. A stream of front-page headlines, such as the New York *Times*'s "Church Says Soviet Tests U.S. Resolve on Troops in Cuba—Asks Immediate Withdrawal," only served to heighten the sense of crisis. I met with the President immediately on my return to the White House on September 4, and as my notes of that evening indicate, I told him that in my view there was no immediate strategic threat, that we should work quietly but firmly to resolve the issue with the Soviets, and that it would be best if Vance talked it over with Gromyko. Perhaps we could give the Soviets a way out by suggesting to them that this brigade was on a training mission and that would provide the basis for its withdrawal.

My discussion with the President was followed by a PRC meeting, convened on this subject under Vance's chairmanship. Heretofore (and also thereafter) all crises were handled by the SCC, under my chairmanship. However, it was evident that State wished to assert itself on this subject, perhaps bearing in mind the large spate of publicity (generated both by China and by our tougher line on the Soviets) alleging that I was dominant in foreign policy. As a consequence, established procedures were not followed. The PRC typically was a much larger meeting than an SCC, and its staffing was then done by a sub-PRC group, headed in this case by David Newsom. At the meeting, to my astonishment, Vance took the categorical position that "we must have withdrawal" of the Soviet forces. Cutler, whom Vance invited to the meeting as an ally, added that "our position with the Senate must be that if it is a base, we will ask the Soviets to take it out."

I took the position that we should stress Cuban activism worldwide on behalf of Soviet interests as the main problem, that we should hint to the Soviets that we will intensify our relationship with the Chinese if the Soviets are not cooperative, but that "the Soviets will not tolerate a public humiliation in Cuba or a reliving of the 1962 missile crisis." I went on to argue that we should intimate that we were not necessarily calling for a formal withdrawal of the brigade from Cuba, but rather for disaggregation of the allegedly combat-ready brigade and a non-continuation of brigade headquarters. I added that in view of the possibility that the Soviet brigade might have been in Cuba for a number of years and in view of the fact that we had not contested it before, it seemed hard to demand publicly that the Soviets all of a sudden withdraw the brigade. On the morning of Wednesday, September 5, I briefed the President, telling him that "at the PRC meeting surprisingly Cy was arguing that we had to demand a withdrawal of the brigade and I was saying that this is an excessive demand and that its disaggregation would suffice, given the fact that [probably] it has been in Cuba for a number of years." During the next several days, I continued making these points to the President; for example, saying to him (on September 8) that we should be tougher privately than publicly.

Vance took the opposite position. Publicly he assumed an extremely tough stance, whereas privately he moved gradually toward a softer position. He went on public record demanding the withdrawal of the brigade, adding that "the status quo is unacceptable." Presumably he felt that a tough public posture would protect SALT. I immediately went to the President and told him that in my view we should consider the problem to be analogous to the Berlin Wall crisis of 1961 and not to the Cuban missile crisis of 1962. In other words, while the wall was also "unacceptable," we had no choice but to live with it. With the President's permission, I used the same analogy publicly with the press, hoping thereby to take the sting out of Vance's categorical assertion, especially since I had little expectation of a Soviet backdown and I did not wish the United States to be embarrassed publicly.

In the meantime, our internal debate continued to rage. Vance relied heavily on support from Lloyd Cutler, and I balanced that by inviting Presidential adviser Hedley Donovan, who had a distinctly more hawkish outlook, into the Situation Room. These additions made it even more difficult to reach agreement, especially since neither Cutler nor Donovan was very familiar with foreign policy issues. Cutler would opine at length, while Donovan would not say a word. On another occasion, finding the PRC under Vance's chairmanship filled with his more dovish State Department associates, notably Newsom and Shulman, I quickly got in touch with the President and urged him to participate himself in the discussion. The President's unexpected arrival in the Situation Room automatically transformed the meeting into a formal NSC session. This required the departure of the lower-level officials, and the President then asked me, in my capacity as director of the NSC, to report on the discussion that had taken place so far and to spell out the agenda for the rest of the meeting.

Throughout this period, Brown and I collaborated very closely, seeking to obtain a policy decision which would put primary emphasis on the worldwide thrust of Soviet assertiveness and thus deemphasize the Cuban issue itself. In contrast, Vance, Cutler, and Mondale increasingly pressed for confining the issue to Cuba itself, arguing that the wider approach would spell the doom of SALT. I gained also the support of Powell and Jordan, and I felt increasingly encouraged. I also briefed Rosalynn Carter on the subject, and she took, as I expected, a very hard stand. (See also p. 32.)

By the third week of September, the President had decided to give a major speech on the subject, because national concern had greatly increased. It was stimulated particularly by belligerent statements by various senators, all of them demanding U.S. action, some comparing the problem to the Cuban missile crisis of 1962, and most saying that SALT would not go forward unless the issue was resolved in a manner satisfactory to the United States. The President instructed me to start preparing the speech, and I did so with special emphasis on the wider character of Soviet activities in the Third World, stressing that these were not compatible with a stable detente. I also gave the President a memo in which I urged him to stress the need for defense increases, without any reference to SALT; to be very explicit in condemning Soviet–Cuban activities in the Third World; to intensify our worldwide efforts to ostracize Cuba, especially by putting pressure on our Western European allies; to develop a dialogue with China on sensitive technology and military issues; and to increase Voice of America broadcasts to Soviet minorities. I felt that with such a policy we might, first of all, have some credibility with the Soviets, and secondly, we would be in a better position to argue that SALT should be ratified because it was confined to the strategic area and was not a symptom of broader U.S. weakness.

The turning point, but not the one for which I had hoped, occurred on September 23. "Today in the evening after a concert at the White House, on my way home I was called back to the White House to meet with the President in the Oval Office. When I walked in he was sitting there with Vance and Byrd. The basic message: Byrd had been to see Dobrynin and had told Dobrynin that SALT would be jeopardized unless the Soviets are in some fashion accommodating. Dobrynin told Byrd that they cannot be because the issue is a phony one. They have been in Cuba for a long time and there is no reason for them to ac- commodate. Byrd told the President the issue indeed is a phony one and that we have to find some way to get off it in order to save SALT. He said that we have to cool our rhetoric, and he expressed disagreement with what the New York *Times* cited me as saying and also with what earlier the President and Vance had said about the status quo not being acceptable. The President was deeply perplexed. Cy Vance and the President pressed Byrd on how SALT can be saved." It was clear to me that the President was very impressed by what Byrd had told him and deeply concerned that he was about to lose SALT. Within the next few days it became evident that the wider approach would not prevail and that any reaction would be limited to Cuba, perhaps with some cosmetic language on the wider strategic issues.

To make matters worse, Cutler persuaded the President to convene a group of senior statesmen to give him advice on the subject. I objected strongly and told the President that Kennedy, Nixon, and Truman had never consulted with outside panels before they made their decisions and that Johnson had convened panels largely in order to browbeat them into support of his own policies. But the group did meet, and then widely circulated reports of the Administration's alleged disarray. In the meantime, our discussions on the draft of the President's speech became sharper. At one point Cutler said to Brown and me that to consider any options pertaining to the Soviet Union is deliberately to revive the Cold War, and he was backed by Fritz Mondale. In later sessions on the speech, Brown and I succeeded in injecting somewhat tougher lines, dealing with Soviet–Cuban activities in Africa, but by and large the speech that was eventually delivered by the President was an attempt to disengage the United States from the issue. I was particularly irritated by the fact that Cutler told some people in the White House that he succeeded in cutting from the speech the words "Soviet adventurism," because, according to him, the word "adventurism" was a foreign one.

In his television address to the nation on October 1, the President declared that the Soviet brigade in Cuba was a matter of serious concern to the United States, but posed no direct threat. The President pointed out that it was indeed a combat brigade, Soviet denials notwithstanding. The Soviets reconfirmed the 1962 bilateral understandings made after the Cuban missile crisis, but would not change the status of the brigade. He said that the U.S. response would be measured and effective and announced the creation of a special Latin American Military Command to monitor Cuba and coordinate military exercises in the region; increased economic assistance to Central America; and intensified vigilance against Soviet and Cuban activities worldwide. The part of the speech that attracted the most attention in the press, however, was the President's statement that there was "no reason for a return to the Cold War." The President concluded that the real danger was the threat of nuclear destruction and urged ratification of SALT II.

After the President delivered his speech, a small champagne party was held to celebrate the occasion and also his birthday. Neither Donovan nor I attended, for we both felt that his speech was a significant, but unfortunate, turning point in our political fortunes. Indeed, this was the only time that I ever thought seriously of the possibility of resigning. I felt so deeply about this that on October 4 I made what probably were the most disagreeable comments I ever made to the President in the course of our years; namely, that for the first time since World War II the United States told the Russians on several different occasions that we take great exception to what they are doing, that there will be negative consequences if they persist in their acts, be it in Vietnam or in Iran or in the Middle East or in Africa, and more recently in Cuba, and then we did nothing about it. I said that the way we handled this matter could be dangerous for the future because the Russians could miscalculate, and that is exactly what happened with Khrushchev and Kennedy. (Obviously, I overstated my case because of pent-up frustration, but that is how I felt at the time.)

The President looked quite furious, and told me that he had no intention of going to war over the Soviet brigade in Cuba. I responded by saying that I did not advocate that we go to war, but that we lay it on the line more explicitly in regard to Soviet adventurism around the world. I felt that I owed it to the President to be honest, especially since I once told him that I strongly believed that my usefulness to him would come to an end at the moment at which I no longer spoke frankly. And it is to the President's great credit that never during the four years did he discourage me from doing so.

Shortly thereafter I gave the President a more formal postmortem on the Cuban brigade issue. I pointed out that the matter was badly handled, in part because the management of the issue was taken over by State (which itself had inexcusably precipitated the crisis by premature briefings), with large discussion sessions, lack of precision in goals, and deliberate disregard of established procedures for crisis management. Only when the President himself was injected did the NSC machinery function in order to develop for him the needed options. Moreover, the PRC did not function regularly, and instead various other advisers were brought into the process, resulting in changing membership and repetitive discussions. I also strongly objected to the creation of the "senior statesmen" group by Cutler, which contributed little to our discussion but which conveyed publicly the impression of an Administration badly floundering. I urged the President to permit me to manage any such future difficulties through the SCC process, on the basis of established procedures.

I was also not satisfied with my own performance. I was handicapped in being away when Vance and Newsom surfaced the issue, but after my return I simply should not have permitted the crisis to be handled in the unwieldy, excessively large, and State Department-dominated PRC. I should have insisted on my prerogative, convened the SCC, and, if necessary, had a showdown on the procedural issue. Secondly, and more importantly, I should have judged more accurately the extent of the President's concern for SALT and I might have served the President's interests better if I had concentrated my efforts on dampening down the whole issue, even after Vance's "it is unacceptable" statement. Though I did tell Carter not to stress it publicly, and though I did warn him that it was probably a phony issue, I felt instead that the President (especially since the senators had already galvanized public concern) should use the crisis to establish his credentials as a tough-minded, Truman-type leader, focusing the spotlight on the Soviet use of the Cubans to promote Soviet strategic interests in the Third World. Admittedly, this could have had the effect of further reducing the chances of SALT's ratification, but my feeling was that the Soviets were not giving us much choice.

In any case, the Cuban crisis shook public confidence in the Administration and it heightened public hostility toward the Soviet Union. It also deprived us of momentum in the SALT ratification process. Approximately one month of time was lost, and it became increasingly clear that the ratification of SALT would have to slip until the end of the year or perhaps into early 1980. In the meantime, Soviet activities in Afghanistan continued to be stepped up, with the Soviets persistently ignoring our direct and indirect expressions of concern. Moscow also exacerbated the situation in Iran with a program of clandestine broadcasting into that country, carrying strident anti-American propaganda. I resumed my efforts to obtain approval for a wider but informal dialogue with the Soviets, continuing to feel, as I did throughout 1978 and 1979, that we needed to discuss on a more sustained basis the nature of our relationship, not confining ourselves to highly formal negotiations. Dobrynin and I had previously agreed that they would be useful, and my thought was that perhaps a two- or three-day informal meeting, in which both Vance and I could take part, would enable us to discuss more directly with our Soviet counterparts what can and cannot be tolerated by either side. I suspected that the Soviets were being assertive because they felt that they could have their cake and eat it, too, and thus did not believe that at some point the United States would clearly draw the line. In effect, there was neither dialogue nor deterrence in our relationship.

I met for lunch with Dobrynin on November 12, and I stressed to him our concerns about Soviet behavior, while attempting to convince him that their perception of a divided Administration was misleading. More importantly, I stressed to him that the Soviet Union, willy-nilly, might be re-creating the unfortunate experience of Imperial Germany. I reminded him that Imperial Germany was determined to avoid encirclement from East and West, yet its assertive policies eventually generated not only the Entente Cordiale between Britain and France but also the alliance between France and Imperial Russia. Today, Soviet policies were generating growing anxiety, and this could have the effect of creating an alliance, spanning the United States, Western Europe, some friendly countries in the Middle East, and even Japan and China. I had the impression that Dobrynin was concerned but powerless.

Any possibility of a serious U.S.–Soviet discussion came to an abrupt end at Christmas. That very afternoon we started receiving intelligence reports that the Soviets were airlifting troops into Kabul and deploying them throughout the city. My military assistant, General Bill Odom, kept me posted, and at 6 p.m. on Christmas Day I called the President at Camp David to inform him that the Soviets had made their move. Shortly thereafter, a full-scale Soviet invasion of Afghanistan was underway. SALT disappeared from the U.S.–Soviet agenda and the stalemated relationship became openly antagonistic.

The Fall of the Shah

We have made it clear through my own public statements and those of Secretary Vance that we support the Shah and support the present government, recognizing that we don't have any control over the decisions ultimately made by the Iranian people.

—President Jimmy Carter, interview, November 13, 1978

Iran was the Carter Administration's greatest setback. In sharp contrast to the success of the Camp David peace efforts or of the normalization of relations with China and to the eventual adoption of a firmer posture toward the Soviet Union—all representing major and constructive turning points—the fall of the Shah was disastrous strategically for the United States and politically for Carter himself. Perhaps that disaster was historically inevitable, the Islamic fundamentalist wave too overpowering, and perhaps the Shah could never have been saved from either his own megalomania or, in the end, his paralysis of will. But my pained belief is that more could have been done by us on the American side. Historical determinism is only true after the fact.

The crisis in Iran confronted the U.S. decision makers with two fundamental questions: (1) What was the nature of our central interest in Iran, and thus what was truly at stake and must be protected as our first priority? And (2) how to maintain (and encourage from outside) political stability in a traditional but rapidly modernizing state, in which the ruler's absolute personal power was being challenged by an escalating revolutionary situation? These two issues were at the heart of our internal debate, even if the arguments were not always formally cast in such terms; and the disagreements on remedies to be applied were derived largely from differing implicit and explicit answers to these central questions.

My answer to the first question was a largely geopolitical one, which focused on the central importance of Iran to the safeguarding of the American and, more generally, Western interest in the oil region of the Persian Gulf. My concerns were shared most strongly by Jim Schlesinger and Charles Duncan. I often felt during our debates that Secretary Vance or Deputy Secretary Christopher or Under Secretary David

Newsom, while certainly not inclined to reject that view, were much more preoccupied with the goal of promoting the democratization of Iran and feared actions—U.S. or Iranian—that might have the opposite effect. When the crisis became acute, the focus of these State Department officials shifted to a primary preoccupation with the evacuation of Americans *from* Iran rather than to a mounting concern over the American position *in* Iran. To be sure, I shared their humane concerns, but I did not agree with their priorities. The President was thus clearly pulled in opposite directions by his advisers and perhaps even by a conflict between his reason and his emotions.

This disagreement in turn intensified the debate on the second question. Much like the respected historian of revolutions Crane Brinton, I felt strongly that successful revolutions were historical rarities, that they were inevitable only after they had happened, and that an established leadership, by demonstrating both will and reason, could disarm the opposition through a timely combination of repression and concession. Given the central role of the Shah in a system of power that was almost uniquely personal, I argued that the deliberate weakening of the beleaguered monarch by American pressure for further concessions to his opponents would simply enhance instability and eventually produce complete chaos. I simply had no faith in the quaint notion—favored by American lawyers of liberal bent—that the remedy to a revolutionary situation is to paste together a coalition of the contending parties, who—unlike domestic American politicians—are not motivated by a spirit of compromise but (demonstrably in the Iranian case) by homicidal hatred.

My opponents felt that the way to cope with the situation was to reduce the Shah's authority, to move rapidly toward "constitutional rule" (though I never understood how transforming the Shah into a Swedish or British type of constitutional monarch could effectively appease the aroused mobs), and to conciliate the confronting factions by a coalition government. In keeping with this approach, in October 1978 both the State Department and the U.S. Ambassador in Tehran, William Sullivan, even opposed the transfer to the Iranian government of crowd-control devices, since that presumably would have inhibited the needed process of conciliation. As the crisis unfolded, it became evident to me that lower echelons at State, notably the head of the Iran Desk, Henry Precht, were motivated by doctrinal dislike of the Shah and simply wanted him out of power altogether.

In my view, a policy of conciliation and concessions might have worked, had it been adopted two or three years earlier, before the crisis reached a politically acute stage. (It is not clear, however, how the United States could have imposed a prophylactic solution on Iran without the benefit of a visible crisis.) But once the crisis had become a contest of will and power, advocacy of compromise and conciliation simply played into the hands of those determined to effect a complete revolution.*

By and large, during this Iranian crisis, our policy reflected on the rhetorical level more my approach and concerns, although State remained publicly more ambiguous. But the policy was interpreted to the Shah by the U.S. Ambassador in Tehran, and perhaps to the Ambassador by the State Department, in vaguer, more diluted formulas. The Shah was never explicitly urged to be tough; U.S. assurances of support were watered down by simultaneous reminders of the need to do more about progress toward genuine democracy; coalition with the opposition was mentioned always as a desirable objective. This is not to say that Iran was lost by the State Department, for the record does show that the Shah had enough encouragement from Carter and me to have taken—had he wanted to and had he had the will to do so—the tougher line. But he might have been pressed harder to do what he did not do consistently and effectively—to assert his power and afterwards to initiate the needed reforms. The outcome was his personal tragedy, as well as a disaster strategically for America and politically for its President.

The Iranian disaster shattered the strategic pivot of a protected tier shielding the crucial oil-rich region of the Persian Gulf from possible Soviet intrusion. The northeast frontier of Turkey, the northern frontiers of Iran and Pakistan, and the neutral buffer of Afghanistan created a formidable barrier, which was pierced once Iran ceased to be America's outpost. Had the Shah not fallen, it is unlikely that the Soviets would have moved so openly into Afghanistan, transforming that neutral buffer into an offensive wedge, bringing the Russians so much closer to their historic target of the Indian Ocean. The Shah was extremely wary of Soviet designs on Afghanistan, and during his 1977 visit to Washington he spent a good portion of his presentation to President Carter in the Cabinet Room of the White House expounding the shared American–Iranian interest in protecting Afghanistan's genuine neutrality. A strong Iran, backed by the United States, was clearly in a position to make a Soviet invasion of Afghanistan both more costly and internationally dangerous.

During the sixties Iran became our major strategic asset in the wake

---

* In outlining these basic divisions, I do not wish to convey the impression that U.S. policy makers were split during this crisis by bitter and highly divisive animosities. It is to be remembered that our discussions on Iran during the fall of 1978 and early 1979 paralleled ongoing efforts to obtain a SALT agreement, to move the peace process in the Middle East forward, and to advance the cause of normalization with China. Opponents on the Iranian issue were often allies on the other matters, and thus, even though our debates were intense, our "coalitions" were fluid and at this stage personal relations were generally unaffected.

of the British disengagement from "east of Suez." That pull-out created
a power vacuum in the Persian Gulf region, and American policy was
to fill it by building up the military capability first of Iran, then of
Saudi Arabia, and by enhancing their political status as the two
American-backed pillars of regional security. The rivalry between Iran
•and Saudi Arabia over the Persian (or, symptomatically, Arabian) Gulf
notwithstanding, American policy was based on the premise that close
collaboration with both of these states was possible, given their fear
of Soviet Communism and their related desire to contain the more
pro-Soviet tendencies in the pan-Arab circles, notably manifest in Iraq.
The high point of that policy was the decision made by President Nixon
and Henry Kissinger to gratify the Shah's desire for a rapid military
buildup through massive U.S. arms transfers to Iran.

Recognizing Iran's strategic centrality, we chose to continue that
policy, approving major sales of arms to Iran in the course of 1978, but
we also encouraged the Shah to couple his extraordinarily ambitious
efforts to modernize his country with more rapid progress toward
constitutional rule. Our Administration did believe, genuinely so, that
the time had come when all governments should be more responsive
to human rights for simple reasons of morality and decency. But there
were also good pragmatic motives for this feeling: we knew that our
ties with Iran would suffer if our principal regional ally was seen by
the American public as flagrantly violating human rights, and in the
longer run the internal stability of Iran would be undermined if socio-
economic modernization was not paralleled by some evolution from
traditional autocracy toward greater political pluralism. But though we
encouraged the Shah to move toward a more representative system, we
did not have, nor did we feel we should have, a detailed blueprint for
how quick and extensive such political change ought to be. It is hard to
tell in retrospect whether the Shah simply paid lip service to the
goal of democratization when speaking to us or whether he himself
recognized the need for some change. Moreover, the Shah did cause
many positive changes in the role of women, the rights of small peasants,
and through more widespread education. In any event, when the crisis
erupted, this continuing concern of ours certainly contributed to his
inability to define clearly his own priorities or to interpret correctly the
meaning of Washington's exhortations for firm leadership.

The longer-range strategic and political implications of the Iranian
crisis came to be appreciated in Washington only gradually. The domestic political costs became of serious concern to Carter and Mondale
only after the hostage seizure in November 1979; until then, the U.S.
public was not overly aroused by a shift in power from a relatively
unpopular Shah to a group of "reformers," with the Ayatollah Khomeini
exercising his domination initially from the background. The seizure of
the hostages, and with it the rapid radicalization of the Iranian political

scene, changed all that—but these events were still a year away when the Shah's regime was in its death throes.

The strategic dimension worried mostly, as already noted, a cluster of officials more directly preoccupied with national security. In addition to me, James Schlesinger and Charles Duncan voiced the greatest concerns about the strategic implications of what was happening in Iran and urged an engaged and firm U.S. response. They were clearly sympathetic to my view that a military solution in Iran was the only way to avoid complete collapse. As time went on, Harold Brown increasingly came to share that view. Admiral Turner, the CIA Director, initially reflected the Agency's more hopeful perspective regarding the Shah's prospects, and later in the fall, rather like the State Department, he was inclined to rate higher the chances of a moderately pro-American post-Shah coalition government. But it must be noted here that until the crisis became very grave, the attention of the top decision makers, myself included, was riveted on other issues, all extraordinarily time-consuming, personally absorbing, and physically demanding.

Our decision-making circuits were heavily overloaded. The fall of 1978 was the time of the Camp David process and its aftermath. This was also the time of the stepped-up SALT negotiations, and during the critical December days we would literally rush from one meeting, in which the most complex positions on telemetry encryption or cruise missile definition would be hammered out, to another meeting on the fate of Iran. The fall, and especially November–December, was also the period of the critical phase in the secret U.S.–Chinese negotiations, and those took up some of the President's and much of my own time. In addition, the crisis in Nicaragua was beginning to preoccupy and absorb us. Finally, Cy Vance was heavily involved in key negotiations abroad, notably in the Middle East, while for Harold Brown this was the period of most difficult battles with the President over the defense budget, which he conducted with great energy and at the cost of some personal friction with Carter. It was unfortunately not a time in which undivided attention could be focused easily and early on what became a fatal strategic and political turning point.

The Crisis Erupts

On November 2, 1978, at 6 p.m., I called to order in the Situation Room an urgent meeting of the SCC. The committee was summoned to decide on the U.S. response to a cable from the worried American Ambassador in Tehran, reporting that the gradually worsening situation in Iran had caused the Shah to indicate that he might either abdicate or go for a military government. In attendance were Warren Christopher (representing Vance, who could not come), Harold Brown, General

David Jones (who had replaced General George Brown as Chairman of the Joint Chiefs of Staff), Admiral Stansfield Turner, as well as David Aaron and Commander Gary Sick (both of the NSC, the latter responsible for Iran). Without prior warning and contrary to his earlier assessments, the Ambassador requested guidance within forty-eight hours, and our meeting was designed to provide it. Since Ambassador Sullivan had not requested guidance until now, his cable convinced me that we had reached a crisis stage and that the matter required inter-agency attention under NSC control.

The Iranian crisis had been germinating throughout the year, but the recognition of it was slow to mature. Our intelligence as late as the fall of 1978 was predicting political continuity in Iran. So was our Ambassador to Iran, William Sullivan, assigned to the post after an unpleasant stint in Southeast Asia, which had left him scarred by unfair charges that he had "lost Laos." As late as October 27, he was still reporting that "the Shah is the unique element which can, on the one hand, restrain the military and on the other hand lead the controlled transition. . . . I would strongly oppose any overture to Khomeini . . . our destiny is to work with the Shah. He has shown surprising flexibility and is, in my judgment, prepared to accept a truly democratic regime here if it can be achieved responsibly."

A rather different view was held by my NSC officer responsible for Iranian affairs, Commander Gary Sick. A serious and thoughtful analyst, he was my principal assistant for the Iranian crisis and the hostage drama until literally the very last hour of the Carter Administration. He proved himself to be a man of keen insight, and, as I said in early 1981, when awarding him the Defense Superior Service Medal: "Probably neither the American hostages nor their families realize what an enormous personal debt they owe to Gary Sick for the hostages' eventual liberty." On several occasions during 1978 he reported to me that tensions in Iran were growing and that the religious and social forces which had been unleashed were not likely to be easily placated. In late August 1978, he advised me not to approve the draft of a letter from President Carter to the Shah which had been sent in by Ambassador Sullivan, since it was excessively obsequious and flattering and ignored the emerging Islamic fundamentalist challenge.

Gary's expressions of concern, though isolated and in conflict with both Embassy reporting and CIA analysis, reinforced my growing uneasiness about Iran. In late August, I took the initiative to call the Iranian Ambassador, Ardeshir Zahedi, suggesting that the two of us have a private dinner. I knew that he was close to the Shah, especially in view of the role played by his father in saving the Shah's throne in 1953. Ardeshir Zahedi, a dashing, even flamboyant individual, was a popular Washington host. Indeed, he was lionized by the social page of the local newspapers and was a favorite at many social engagements.

When the Shah finally fell, he was immediately ostracized by the same Washington social set and became the object of many unkind jokes. I liked him as an individual, later I admired his willingness to return to Iran in the midst of the crisis in order to oppose Khomeini, and I found him a useful source of information, though I was aware that his perspectives were skewed and one-sided. On that particular hot August evening, sitting in the garden and eating a meal cooked by my host personally, I was struck by the fact that Zahedi did not respond defensively or negatively when I said to him that I thought that something was going wrong in Iran and that I wondered whether the Shah was ready to take the needed remedial actions. I pointed out that to modernize a traditional society is an extraordinarily complex task, and it requires effective political organization. My impression was that the Shah was transforming Iranian society, unleashing new social forces, but without a political framework which could contain them and direct them into constructive channels.

Somewhat to my surprise, Zahedi generally conceded these points, and also acknowledged that there was a great deal of corruption in Tehran, even involving some members of the royal family. He volunteered that he felt the Shah needed to change course dramatically, to clean house, and to engage himself more directly in a dialogue with the people in an effort to project his own personal political leadership. He said that at some point he would like to leave Washington and join the Shah in such an effort, but he was not certain if the Shah was prepared to do so. Without stating this explicitly (though he would later in the year), Zahedi seemed to hint that the Shah was not in fact a very decisive person.

This dinner convinced me, if I needed further proof, that the Shah was in trouble. By then I had met the Shah twice, once when he visited Washington in November 1977 and again in late December of 1977, when President and Mrs. Carter were the guests of the Shah in Tehran. On both occasions, I was struck by the Shah's very obvious intelligence. When discussing issues, he showed a keen analytical bent and he was particularly effective, I thought, in summarizing the geopolitical dilemmas of his region. At the same time, I felt that he displayed megalomaniacal tendencies, that his entourage was excessively deferential to him, and I wondered on what basis he was making his various decisions. I was told by some people who knew the Shah's wife, the Shahbanou, that she was sensitizing the Shah to social concerns and exercising a constructive influence on him, but I had no real opportunity to talk with her at any length. In general, the Pahlavis reminded me of Western-type nouveaux riches, obviously relishing the splendors of wealth and a Western life style, but at the same time the Shah clearly seemed to enjoy being a traditional Oriental despot, accustomed to instant and total obedience from his courtiers. He almost seemed suspended between the two worlds, and there was a strange sense of ambiguity about him. He simultaneously exuded intellectual strength and personal softness. I wondered how the Shah would be able to respond to the social dilemmas which his own program of modernization had produced, but I also felt that we had no alternative but to support him.

A week or so after my dinner with Zahedi, on September 8, violence erupted in Jaleh Square in Tehran, with troops firing on demonstrators, killing scores. Vance and I agreed that it would be desirable for the President to call the Shah and express verbally our support for him. The conversation between the President and the Shah took place between 7:56 and 8:02 a.m., on Sunday, September 10. The President said he was calling to express his friendship for the Shah and his concern about events. He wished the Shah the best in resolving these problems and in being successful in his efforts to implement reforms. The Shah responded that the planning for the disturbances was "diabolical." He noted that he had gone far in liberalizing and that this was now used against him. Nonetheless, he intended to persist and ensure that Iran would have freedom of speech, freedom of assembly, freedom of demonstration according to the law, freedom of the press, as well as free elections. He then added that it would be good if the President could endorse his efforts as strongly as possible because otherwise his enemies would take advantage of it. The interests of America and Iran were so identified that such an action would be much appreciated. The President promised to do just that.

Nonetheless, within two days we had a report from Tehran that, in a meeting with a *Time* magazine writer in which the Shah looked like a shattered man on the brink of a nervous collapse, the Shah had mused out loud to the effect that the United States perhaps had conceded Iran to the Soviets or at least to "a neutral sphere of influence." It was clear that the Shah felt that our human-rights policy had aided his opponents and that he was not certain of American support. Yet shortly thereafter we had another report (September 20), from an Embassy officer, who found the Shah looking the picture of health, confident, almost feisty. He reported that the Shah felt that the current situation would improve and that he would be able to continue with the process of steady liberalization. These conflicting reports created further disagreements within the intelligence community, which had been unable to reach a consensus on the Shah for months. This did not make it easier for us to determine what needed to be done. I should add that, at this stage, neither I nor anyone else in Washington, to my knowledge, was aware of the Shah's illness. Reports from Tehran did not give us any clues. If we had known earlier, it obviously would have made some difference in the kinds of assessments and policy options we formulated.

The rest of the month was taken up almost totally by the Camp

David negotiations, and it was not until the end of September that the Iranian issue again surfaced. In early October, Secretary Vance met with Iranian Foreign Minister Afshar, and assured him that it was not the policy of the United States to support the Shah's opposition. A week later Ambassador Sullivan reported that he had had a long audience with the Shah, in the course of which the Shah said that he was having problems with his military. The generals, according to the Shah, were concerned that if the current disorders continued, they would spread to the troops, and they wanted to clamp down sharply on all disorder. The generals were still loyal but they seemed to think that the Shah had gone soft.

In the meantime, the demonstrations spread, and an oil strike broke out in late October, reducing daily production from 5.8 million to 1.9 million barrels in one week. On October 24, after a visit with the Shah by Deputy Secretary of Defense Charles Duncan, Ambassador Sullivan reported that he and the British Ambassador had told the Shah that in their view a military solution was a nonstarter. To my knowledge, this important judgment was not approved by the White House. On the following day, I received a memorandum from Sick urging that we provide some dramatic example of support for the Shah, perhaps a trip by me to Tehran with a message from the President, or a statement of support or a joint statement of support by America and its key allies. At the same time, however, the State Department prepared an analysis of the situation in Iran, in which, while stressing support for the Shah, the view was expressed that the United States should maintain steadfast opposition to a military regime.

This document, sent over to Tehran for comments, precipitated the message of October 27 from Ambassador Sullivan that there was no current need for more public statements by the President or visits by high emissaries, that the Embassy opposed any proposals for U.S. assistance to the Iranian military for crowd-control purposes, that there should be no contact with Khomeini, and that "our destiny is to work with the Shah," who is prepared to accept a truly democratic regime if it can be achieved responsibly. In the following days, on both October 31 and November 1, Sullivan met with the Shah, accompanied each time by the British Ambassador, and these conversations with the Shah then prompted the message which led to the important meeting in the Situation Room of the White House on November 2.

Earlier in the day, I had briefed the President on Sullivan's cable. It indicated, as I wrote in my journal later that evening, that "the Shah is losing his will while we continue to push him more and more for liberalization. In my judgment, I told the President (he was sitting there with [Charles] Kirbo [Carter's longtime friend and adviser] having a chat), . . . unless the Shah can combine constructive concessions with a firm hand, he will be devastated."

Prior to the SCC meeting, I decided to get a better feeling of the situation and phoned Sullivan in Tehran; the Iranian Ambassador in Washington, Zahedi; and Jean François-Poncet, my opposite number in Paris (later the French Foreign Minister). I also received a worried call from Nelson Rockefeller urging a clear-cut U.S. stand in support of the Shah. Finally, concluding from these conversations that our most urgent need was to bolster the Shah's morale and will, I called Vance just prior to the SCC meeting and obtained his concurrence in the line that I wanted the SCC to adopt.

I opened the meeting by quoting from the message from Sullivan which reported the first signs that the Shah might be thinking of abdication. I then went on to say that I had discussed this matter earlier in the day with the President, with Vance, Zahedi, and Sullivan in Tehran. I reported that Zahedi suggested that Sullivan was being perceived in Iran as being ambiguous in his support of the Shah. I then went on to say that François-Poncet told me that the Shah was suffering from a crisis of will and that the French felt that he needed to regain his determination and authority. I noted that Sullivan consulted closely in Tehran with the British Ambassador, Anthony Parsons, and I wondered what kind of advice the Shah was really getting. Finally, I briefly summarized the call from Rockefeller, who had said that a growing body of opinion in America believed that the United States was doing nothing and wondering where the United States stood.

I then proposed that a message be sent to Sullivan which would reflect the President's view, to the effect that the United States supported the Shah without reservation, that we did not wish to second-guess him with regard to the specific decisions he needed to take on forms of government, but that we felt that the situation called for decisive action to restore order and his own authority. Finally, we hoped he would resume prudent efforts toward liberalization after order had been restored. I added that it was my view that we had pressed the Shah too hard on liberalization and that the Shah himself had gone quite far toward meeting our expectations. If he did not regain the capacity to govern soon, his army would be demoralized. A coalition government was not the answer because its components would be likely to fight among themselves. In conclusion, I read a proposed text of a message, adding that I had discussed it with Vance and that he supported it.

This somewhat surprised Christopher, who pointed out that Zahedi was adept at giving the impression that the United States did not support the Shah and noted that a coalition government might still be the best way to provide movement toward a lasting settlement. (In fact, the State Department paper for the meeting, which I had seen beforehand, recommended a series of concessions by the Shah to mollify his opposition.) Christopher's comment was contested by Aaron, who made the point that the Shah might think that we cared more for liberalization than for his own leadership, and that this ought to be clarified. Brown observed that the move to a military government could be explained in different ways, for example as a step in preparation for elections. This would be more than just support for military repression. Turner observed that coalition would be a better step, but Brown expressed skepticism as to its feasibility.

I was then called out of the Situation Room to speak to the President, and I came back to inform the group that the President had authorized me to call the Shah the next day, to express U.S. support for him, and I said that in the meantime a message along the lines proposed ought to be sent. Christopher suggested that we insert some reference to elections, but I objected that we should not be recommending a specific program to the Shah. Christopher then proposed that a phrase in the telegram referring to "need for action" seemed to tilt in favor of military government, but the SCC agreed with me and let it stand.

The meeting ended with agreement that we should send the Shah a strong message of support, but that the United States should not assume responsibility for decisions that only he could and should make. Accordingly, to underline the importance of the message, it was sent from the White House to Sullivan, under my signature, and contained the following:

> On the highest authority and with Cy Vance's concurrence you are instructed to tell the Shah as soon as possible:
> 1. The United States supports him without reservation in the present crisis.
> 2. We have confidence in the Shah's judgment regarding the specific decisions that may be needed concerning the form and composition of government; we also recognize the need for decisive action and leadership to restore order and his own authority. With respect to the coalition government alternative, our position is that this is up to the Shah if he feels that such an alternative is viable and preferable. We are not pressing for it. The same applies to a military government. Whichever route he goes we will support his decision fully. (FYI: in response to your question: a military government under the Shah is overwhelmingly preferable to a military government without the Shah.)
> 3. That once order and authority have been restored we hope that he will resume prudent efforts to promote liberalization and to eradicate corruption."

On the margins of the cable I scribbled some reflections which summarized my thoughts at the time: "Concerned about progressive disintegration of authority. Morale of Army. Need to combine dramatic gesture of accommodation with firmness."

On the following day, November 3, from 9:05 to 9:11 a.m., with the President's authorization, I spoke directly with the Shah. (I was struck, while I was waiting on the line, by the strange protocol followed at the other end in Tehran: a guard or a functionary of some sort barked out several times in a loud voice and in Iranian the Shah's full title before he actually came on the line.) The conversation, which has been distorted in some accounts of the Iranian crisis, went as follows: I told the Shah that "the United States supports you without any reservation whatsoever, completely and fully, in the present crisis. You have our complete support. . . . Secondly, we will support whatever decisions you take regarding either the form or the composition of the government that you decide upon. And thirdly, we are not, and I repeat, not encouraging any particular solution." I then went on to say, bearing in mind Sullivan's report that he and the Ambassador of the British Labour government had advised the Shah against a military government, "I hope that is very clear and the Ambassador has been instructed to make it very clear that we are not advising or urging you to go in any particular direction." The Shah responded to the effect that he was very appreciative of the message, "but it is a very peculiar situation," and went on to suggest that he had been made to feel that "extreme measures, if at all possible, should be avoided." I then responded by saying, "Well, you in effect, it seems to me, have the problem of combining some gestures which would be appealing in a general sense with a need for some specific actions which would demonstrate effective authority." The Shah simply said, "Yes." I went on to add, "It is a critical situation, in a sense, and concessions alone are likely to produce a more explosive situation." The Shah then asked me to repeat that last sentence, and I did so. Curiously, though of course subsequent events have made clear what the Shah meant, he then asked me, "Is your Ambassador briefed?" I assured him that he had received a message to that effect and that I would call him after this conversation to reaffirm it. The conversation ended with the Shah telling me that he thought the situation was very bad and seemed to be deteriorating further. I asked him to let us know if there was anything else we could do.

My purpose in calling the Shah was to make it clear to him that the President and the United States stood behind him and to encourage him to act forcefully before the situation got out of hand. I made that clear in a subsequent conversation with Sullivan, in which I also indicated that the Shah did not seem to be getting that message clearly from him. Later that day I jotted in my journal: "I am already getting feedback from the State Department reflecting great anxiety and uneasiness that we are offering such a strong backing to the Shah. The draft response by State to Sullivan's urgent request for instructions did after all say that we should press the Shah for a coalition government, that we should press him even to have a referendum on the future of the monarchy, that an opposition leader should be the Prime Minister, and so forth." To me, this appeared to be a prescription for a U.S.-sponsored political upheaval.

The Shah met again with Ambassador Sullivan and Ambassador Parsons on November 4, and Sullivan reported that the Shah opened the meeting by referring to my telephone call. The Shah said it was all very well for Brzezinski to say that the United States would support a military government as a last resort, but he, the Shah, did not feel it was an option even though his generals were pressing him and assuring him that they could easily calm things down by making a number of arrests and by taking really firm measures. The situation was further confused, he went on to say, by an ABC report in Washington that the United States had decided to withdraw support in the event of a military government in Iran. I wondered whether these views reflected genuine anxiety or simply an excuse for not doing what was necessary. In any case, two days later, the Shah announced the military government. The Shah also addressed the nation, promising that the government would continue to move toward democratization as soon as order had been restored.

The news that the Shah had finally opted for a military government greatly relieved me. I saw in this a welcome sign that the Shah had finally faced up to the crisis and was prepared to assert effective leadership. With a large army at his command, I felt that he could prevail if a head-on confrontation developed and that he could use the military not only to establish order but to initiate a comprehensive cleanup of existing corruption. On several occasions during these weeks, I mentioned to Zahedi the need for the Shah to become politically more active and to articulate for the Iranian public a concept of the society that he wished to shape. I felt the Shah's policies had created a fateful conflict between the effects of rapid socioeconomic modernization and the consequences of a highly traditional and excessively personal system of power.

It was in this mood that I attended a PRC meeting on November 6, chaired by Vance. The meeting was convened in order to reassert State control over the Iranian issue (instead of the SCC, which I always chaired), and I was dismayed by the absence at the meeting of any longer-range discussion regarding Iran and by the preoccupation of my State Department colleagues with the evacuation of Americans from Iran. That, to me, constituted sending a signal which could only be interpreted badly for us both by the Shah and by his opponents: the United States was beginning to pull out. To make matters worse, when Charles Duncan proposed that the Iranians be provided with some non-lethal crowd-control devices, Vance put him off by saying that the British were supplying adequate help in that area and that we did not need to do it ourselves. There was also a futile discussion of the nature of the Iranian opposition, with Admiral Turner indicating that, because of prior restrictions on contact with the opposition (restrictions also applied by Sullivan), he did not have much information to share with us.

This exchange brought to a head my own growing dissatisfaction with the quality of both analysis and hard intelligence that we were getting from Iran. The previous day, I noted in my journal: "Reviewing the record of last Thursday's SCC meeting I was really appalled by how inept and vague Stan Turner's comments on the crisis in Iran were. This reinforces my strong view that we need much better political intelligence." Accordingly, I undertook two actions designed to remedy the situation. A few days later, on November 9, I met with an American businessman who had extensive knowledge of Iran and a personal acquaintance with the Shah, and arranged for him to go to Iran to provide us with an up-to-date assessment, relying on his knowledge of the country and his contacts there. Vance and the Embassy were informed of the mission.

Second, I spoke to the President, reviewed with him the woeful state of our political intelligence in Iran, and suggested that he write a note, addressed to Vance, Turner, and me (so as not to single out Turner for criticism and thus not embarrass him), complaining of the President's own dissatisfaction with the state of affairs. On November 11, the President sent the note, which generated some resentment within the Agency but also, belatedly, somewhat more intensified efforts: "To Cy, Zbig, Stan—I am not satisfied with the quality of our political intelligence. Assess our assets and, as soon as possible, give me a report concerning our abilities in the most important areas of the world. Make a joint recommendation on what we should do to improve your ability to give me political information and advice."

My own emissary met with the Shah a few days later, and the Shah urged him to press Washington for the strongest support "in my efforts to restore order and stability and that you look toward me as the key to continued strength, stability, and prosperity for Iran." On his return, my source reported that the Shah found the situation baffling, incomprehensible, and almost overwhelming. He appeared to trust no one and his confidence in his own judgment seemed deeply shaken.

To make matters even more confusing for the Washington decision makers, we received on November 9 a cable from Sullivan entitled "Thinking the Unthinkable." In it the Ambassador speculated on what might happen if the Shah was forced to leave, especially if he decided not to plunge the country into a bloodbath. Sullivan urged us to consider that the Iranian armed forces and Khomeini were anti-Communist and anti-Soviet; that the younger officers were generally pro-Western; that the Iranian economic ties with the West would continue; and that the Iranian military ought to be able to preserve the nation's integrity. He speculated that the religious faction might find it useful to retain the Army because they themselves have no instruments for retaining order; that Khomeini would be likely to return to Iran as a consequence of a religious-military accommodation and that he would play a "Gandhi-like" role; that elections would be likely to produce an Islamic republic with a strong pro-Western influence. Having sketched out this Pollyanna prospect, Sullivan concluded by noting prudently that, of course, something could go wrong and a single misstep could produce unforeseeable consequences. This cable, while carefully neither predicting nor advocating the Shah's resignation, did have the effect of strengthening the views of those in the State Department who were generally inclined to argue that the fall of the Shah would have benign consequences for American interests.

In the meantime, the situation in Iran continued to worsen. The Shah met periodically with Ambassador Sullivan, who in turn was frequently accompanied by British Ambassador Parsons, and Sullivan's messages indicated that the Shah's moods oscillated between extremes of optimism and pessimism. Sometimes the Shah expressed confidence that the military would get hold of the situation; on other occasions he would firmly state that he would not spill blood. Sullivan's cables did not give one the impression that the American Ambassador was exerting himself to reinforce the Shah's willpower. (At one point, this led the Vice President to ask whether Ambassador Sullivan was the right man to be in Tehran. Vance responded, "He is a good man; he's been in some hard spots." Mondale countered: "He has lost all of them, hasn't he?"—referring to Sullivan's previous service in Laos.)

Other reports presented a conflicting picture of the Shah's condition. Secretary of the Treasury Blumenthal met with the Shah and reported on November 21 that the Shah seemed distracted and thoroughly depressed. His conversation was punctuated by long pauses during which he stared despondently into space. Yet a day later the CIA submitted an analysis of the Shah's psychological behavior, which contained the view that "it continues to be our judgment that his mood is not inappropriate to his situation, that he is not paralyzed by indecision, by his emotional reactions, and that for the most part he is in accurate touch with reality . . . reports of discouragement or transient depression should not be read as difficulties with leadership. That he moves first in one way and then in another should also not be considered surprising. It is his way of grappling with pressure from all sides in a situation that has no clear solution." On reading the report, I had the impression that the CIA was grappling with a situation it had difficulty in assessing.

In the third week of November, the Iranian crisis assumed for the first time a more ominous international dimension. Perhaps because of our strong public statements of support for the Shah, on November

18 we received a message for the President from Brezhnev alleging that the United States was planning to interfere militarily or otherwise in Iranian affairs and warning that this posed a security concern for the Soviet Union. I was out of my office when the message came in, but David Aaron phoned me to give me its text and to tell me that the State Department had submitted a proposed response which in his judgment was almost apologetic in tone. It provided assurances that the United States had no intention of interfering, cited some examples of our statements to the effect that we would not interfere, and generally adopted an explanatory posture. I checked immediately with Harold Brown, and his assessment of the proposed State Department response was identical to mine. I concluded that we could not proceed along these lines, for to do so would be to accept the notion that the Soviet Union and the United States had identical interests in Iran, notwithstanding the fact that Iran was our ally.

Accordingly, on Saturday evening I went to my office at the White House and developed an alternative response. I also discussed it with the President and spoke at midnight with Vance, registering my concerns over the earlier text of the proposed response. I also made sure that Brown and Jim Schlesinger phoned the President on Sunday and gave him the same assessment.

On Monday morning, Brown and I met with Vance and Marshall Shulman at the State Department, and we collectively drafted a response which in the main reflected the position which I had wanted to convey. We struck from the text a proposed expression of appreciation for Brezhnev's message, affirmations that the United States had no intention to interfere, and a statement that both the United States and the Soviet Union should respect Iranian sovereignty. Instead we reaffirmed our support for Iran and the Shah and our commitment to the independence and integrity of Iran, noted that we expected the Soviets to conduct themselves similarly, and concluded by insisting that the Soviets should not use their incorrect allegations that we intended to interfere in Iranian affairs as the basis for interfering themselves. The President's message added, "I am sure you appreciate that any such interference would be a matter of the utmost gravity to us." (Since I had raised quite a rumpus with the President over the proposed letter, he left for me in my office a friendly note. It said, with ironic deference, that he was wondering whether I had any difficulties with his proposed changes and whether I had approved the final text. If not, then I should speak to him about it. . . .)

On November 21, I also arranged for the President to meet briefly with Ambassador Zahedi to discuss the situation in Iran. Zahedi, in a display of courage that contrasted sharply with the flight from Iran of other well-placed Iranians, had decided to go back to Tehran to help the Shah in these difficult days. It was not true, however, that either the President or I had urged him to go back there on our behalf and to keep reporting to us. This was entirely Zahedi's initiative, and the President used the opportunity to ask him to convey to the Shah our strong support and the need for the Shah to display firm determination. He also told Zahedi to keep in touch with me, which he did from time to time by telephone. We had, in fact, a total of four or five telephone conversations until Zahedi's return to Washington in mid-January, and not daily contact, as was subsequently alleged.

The firm position taken by President Carter during November regarding both support for the Shah (including strong public statements to that effect) and the rebuff of the Soviets gave me again some short-term relief. I hoped that these actions would provide a reassuring framework for what still needed to be done in Iran, but I was becoming gradually more and more concerned about the Shah's personal capacity for coping with the situation. I noted in my journal on November 24: "The question is what do we do beyond the immediate. We have to concentrate on longer-term and more basic reforms. The Shah needs to develop a pertinent and relevant concept of modernization which will enable the people to identify progress with the system and effective political organization to absorb the shocks of modernization. He has so far been able to do neither. Unless he accomplishes both, his regime and particularly his personal role will be finished."

It was these concerns that led me in late November to propose to the President a bureaucratic initiative which later I came to regret. When Blumenthal came back from Iran, he talked to me about the need for a comprehensive review of what was happening in Iran, so that American policy of supporting the Shah could also be translated into a more effective long-term program. I agreed, and in the course of that conversation Blumenthal mentioned that George Ball might be just the man to do it. I liked the idea, for I had previously worked with Ball and viewed him as having a good grasp of political and economic realities. Accordingly, I proposed to the President and to Vance that he be invited to join us for a few weeks to help develop a long-term program and then perhaps even to go to Tehran to sell such a program to the Shah. When I first proposed this to Vance, he was notably unenthusiastic (perhaps because Ball had been his principal rival for the post of Secretary of State when Carter was forming his new Administration), but I obtained the President's agreement.

Later I wished I had listened to Cy. Ball's participation in our debates sharpened our disagreements while delaying basic choices by wasting some two weeks, and his subsequent willingness to discuss what transpired within the White House and the State Department with members of the press spiced the perception of an Administration profoundly split on the Iranian issue. Moreover, in selecting Ball I violated a basic rule of bureaucratic tactics: one should never obtain the services of an "impartial" outside consultant regarding an issue that one feels strongly about without first making certain in advance that one knows the likely contents of his advice.

Disintegration

In the course of the next few weeks, the issue in Washington gradually ceased being how to help the Shah save himself but became instead how to save Iran even without the Shah. In the earlier phase, I favored pressing the Shah hard to impose a firm military regime as a point of departure for later reforms; during the ensuing phase, I moved gradually and reluctantly to the view that a military government without the Shah was our only viable option. By the same token, those who earlier favored encouraging the Shah to govern somehow through a coalition government now moved increasingly to the view that the Shah should yield power to the more moderate elements from among those who had opposed him in the past. In effect, disagreement within the U.S. government widened as the situation in Iran deteriorated.

Paradoxically, the two sides that periodically met to thrash the issue out in the Situation Room were increasingly agreed on one critical point: that the Shah was becoming an obstacle to any resolution of the issue. The military government that he had installed under General Azhari in early November was not empowered to crack down firmly, and in early December the Shah released some of the top leaders of the opposition, notably National Front leader Karim Sanjabi, and feelers were initiated to determine whether they would be willing to participate in a coalition government. This did not enhance the confidence of the existing military government, and the political situation became worse when, in the third week of December, General Azhari suffered a mild coronary attack. In the meantime, the Iranian monarch kept oscillating between appeals for strong American support for policies he would not define with any precision, and complaints over lack of such support; between predictions of disaster, and dire warnings that the military were about to stage a bloodbath. It became increasingly clear that the Shah wanted the United States to take responsibility for the painful decisions needed to keep Iran intact, and particularly for the decision to use Iranian military force against the opposition.

We thus confronted an acute moral and political dilemma. Vance and Christopher, as well as Mondale, appealed to Carter's humane instincts in warning him against assumption of such responsibility, stressing that a military solution, especially one undertaken without the Shah, would certainly precipitate a massive bloodbath, probably also a civil war. The example of General Pinochet in Chile was at times invoked. At the same time, the argument was made, in keeping with

Sullivan's earlier cables, that the departure of the Shah was likely to produce a transitional period of instability, but with a reasonable chance that the more moderate elements in Iranian politics eventually would be able to consolidate the situation. The case for a military dictatorship, if necessary even without the Shah, had to be stated more cautiously because the very notion of initiating such a coup from Washington went so much against the grain of the dominant values in the White House and State Department. One, therefore, had to argue that a military government represented our best chance of avoiding a destructive and bloody civil war in Iran, with the effect of making the military option our last-resort solution, to be set in motion only if everything else had failed. That, in turn, made it easier for Vance, Christopher, and others to counter that the time to move toward such a drastic solution had not yet come.

In early December, concerned not only by the deteriorating situation in Iran but by the signs of growing Soviet interest, I requested the Defense Department to initiate contingency plans for the deployment of U.S. forces, if necessary, in southern Iran so as to secure the oil fields. I briefed the President on that on December 5, and Brown proceeded to move expeditiously on this matter. I also told the President that I thought his recent public remarks, indicating pessimism regarding the Shah's chances of survival, were counterproductive, and he had me issue a corrective statement. Moreover, the President approved my calling Zahedi in Tehran to reassure him that we were steadfast in our support of the Shah, and several days later the President himself made strong public comments to that effect. Finally, on December 11, I suggested to the President that it might be useful for either Schlesinger or me to go to Tehran, to give the Shah the needed political-moral support, because it was becoming increasingly doubtful that the Shah could act on his own. Schlesinger had made a very similar suggestion. I brought that idea up again on the following day, but the President was noncommittal on both occasions.

In the meantime, the alternative strategy, favored by Vance, Sullivan, and Ball, took shape. Reversing himself, the Ambassador proposed that we consult with the Shah regarding contact with the oppositionists, including a U.S. approach to the Ayatollah Khomeini. The purpose of approaching Khomeini would be to establish whether he would be willing to agree to some form of civilian government which preserved a titular role for the Shah. Almost at the same time, Ball concluded his report by suggesting that the Shah yield effective power to "a Council of Notables," a political pastiche that would represent the various feuding elements of Iranian politics. In effect, both recommendations amounted to a transfer of power in the midst of a revolutionary situation. Moving rapidly to implement the preferred State options, Sullivan reported that he met with the Shah on December 13 and discussed with him the difficult choices confronting Iran. According to the cable, the Shah set out three choices: a national coalition; a surrender to the opposition and the creation of a regency council; or a military junta, with an iron-fist policy. Sullivan reported that he expressed the view that the first was the only logical choice, encouraging the Shah to continue with his efforts to find a compromise solution to the crisis.

Back in Washington, the Ball report was discussed in the Situation Room on December 12, with no formal recommendation, and Ball himself presented it to the President on December 15. The discussion of the Ball paper became largely a debate between its author and me. I expressed the view that setting in motion a process of political change was desirable, but I also argued that there are circumstances in which a military government, which in time can become increasingly civilianized, as in Turkey or Brazil, might be the best solution. The Ball approach would have the effect simply of transferring power to the other side, and I did not think that Iran as a country was ready yet for a democracy, certainly not in the midst of a revolution. At the meeting with Ball, the President reserved his position, but seemed to agree when Ball argued that it would be inappropriate for me or for anyone else to go to Tehran on the President's behalf since that would excessively involve the U.S. government in the internal Iranian crisis.

One major effect of the Ball exercise was to precipitate a more pointed effort to force the Shah to think through his options. A message was sent "eyes only for the Ambassador" entitled "Questions for the Shah." It asked Sullivan to see the Shah at the earliest opportunity and tell him that the President had continued to follow events in Iran with deep concern in the context of our support for the Shah and his courageous effort to restore peace and stability. The last phrase was repeated for emphasis. It asked for the Shah's own considered judgment on a number of important questions to assist the President in offering helpful comments or suggestions. It asked what actions the Shah believed necessary to restore oil production and return the economy to normal operation. It asked how long the military government could function effectively and maintain order, and if the addition of some civilian Cabinet members was feasible and would politically strengthen the government in dealing with civilian disorders and government operation. To what extent and at what pace was the Shah prepared to move toward a government of national unity and devolve power to a predominantly civilian Cabinet? To what extent might military officials participate in a civilian government or provide leadership of some of the ministries? What role would the Shah see for himself; would he be prepared to retain the role of Commander in Chief but devolve budgetary authority to the Parliament and Cabinet? By what mechanism would a Cabinet in a government of national unity be chosen—by appointment, by a representative body, elections, or otherwise? Did the Shah believe the United States could be helpful in consulting with serious and responsible leaders of the opposition and, if so, how best could we conduct such consultations? Would he be prepared to let his endorsement of such consultations be known to opposition leaders? If his answers to these questions indicated that it would be appropriate, Sullivan was to say that we had compiled a list of names of individuals who might be helpful in providing leadership or advice to a newly formed government.

Our purpose in sending this message was to establish whether the Shah seriously considered any solution short of a military government to be feasible, and, if so, how it could be organized. Personally, I had great reservations about the message. I feared that it might push the Shah into concluding that the United States was pressing for a coalition government, but I had no choice but to go along with the preponderant view in the White House. Moreover, I felt that the best way to establish the case for my preferred solution was to exhaust all alternative avenues, thereby demonstrating that the time had come to opt for the last resort.

With the Shah continuing to waver, our own debates became sharper in the course of the next several days. After General Azhari's coronary, it was clear that the passive, semi-military government was beginning to fall, and the Shah was engaged in a last-minute, but floundering, effort to paste together some civilian alternative. The National Front leaders were unwilling to participate unless the Shah left the country. The Shah, while still telling Sullivan that he did not favor the drastic military solution, began to speculate aloud about the possibility of taking "a vacation" away from Tehran, during which the military would solve the problem in their own inimitable way. Since Sullivan had reported that he had warned the Shah against such an approach, I made it a point to insist in our Situation Room discussions that Sullivan be explicitly instructed not to indicate either approval or disapproval of such a course of action.

This was done in a message sent out on December 22, after a lively debate in the Situation Room. Originally, Christopher came in with the draft of a telegram which seemed to me to say that we ought to encourage the Shah more strongly on behalf of a coalition civilian government. Concerned that prolonged ambiguity regarding the situation in Iran would simply destroy the loyalty of the Army and produce overall fragmentation, I strongly objected, and I was supported in this both by Brown and by Turner. At the same time, our group agreed that it would be wiser to encourage the Shah to stay in Tehran, since a sudden departure might contribute to even greater instability. Accordingly, in a follow-up telegram from Christopher to Sullivan (since Vance was in Geneva), Sullivan was instructed to urge the Shah to stay in Tehran to provide "greater legitimacy and perhaps moderation to the alternative that then might become unavoidable."

The continued weakness and indecision of the Shah was painfully demonstrated in his meeting on December 26 with Sullivan. In the course of it, the Shah asked point-blank what the United States wanted him to do. Sullivan reported that the United States supported his efforts to reestablish law and order. The Shah asked then whether he was being advised to use the iron fist even if it meant widespread bloodshed and even if it might fail to restore law and order. Sullivan reported that he responded by saying that if the Shah was trying to get the United States to take the responsibility for his actions, he doubted that he would ever get such instructions from Washington. He was the Shah and he had to take the decision as well as the responsibility.

This exchange left me dissatisfied, for I felt that we were failing to provide the Shah with the needed guidance. On December 28, I spoke about it with the President, who concurred. I then held a meeting in my office with Vance, Turner, Brown, and Duncan, and we prevailed on Vance to agree to a strongly worded telegram which would have the effect of giving the Shah the needed reinforcement. Brown was particularly effective in backing me and in overcoming Vance's hesitations. The following telegram was then approved and sent out from Vance to Sullivan:

I have just finished talking with the President and we wish you to convey the following message to the Shah:

1. Continued uncertainty is destructive of Army morale and of political confidence.

2. If a civilian government is possible soon that is moderate and can work with the United States and with the Shah and maintain order, then obviously it is the preferred alternative.

3. But if there is uncertainty either about the underlying orientation of such a government or its capacity to govern or if the Army is in danger of becoming more fragmented, then the Shah should choose without delay a firm military government which would end disorder, violence, and bloodshed. If in his judgment the Shah believes this alternative to be infeasible, then a regency council might be considered by him.

4. You should tell the Shah the above, clearly stating that the U.S. support is steady and that it is essential repeat essential to terminate the continued uncertainty.

This message represented the clearest and most direct effort to get the Shah to do what needed to be done, without the United States assuming, in effect, the responsibility of governing Iran on his behalf. Yet just as the Shah was receiving our message, he was moving in the opposite direction. Sullivan reported that he had asked a leader of the National Front, Shahpur Bakhtiar, to form a new government. While

seeking parliamentary approval, Bakhtiar made it clear that one of the
conditions for his government was that the Shah must leave Iran.
Sullivan reported he had a long and doleful audience with the Shah
on January 2 in which the Shah said that he wanted the President to
know that he was pushing fast on a civilian government and that he
hoped to swear Bakhtiar in by January 4 or 6. He then again agonized
about the iron-fist option as an alternative in the event that Bakhtiar
failed. Sullivan conveyed to the Shah personal assurances that he and
his family could visit the United States or accept an invitation issued
by Sadat. In effect, the possibility of leaving the country was now
being formally discussed, though it was obvious that the Shah was still
flirting with the iron-fist solution as a last resort.

These conflicting actions by the Shah resulted in two significant conclusions in Washington: that it was now in our interest for the Shah
to leave and that the United States should send a senior military
official, General Robert Huyser, to Iran to assist the Iranian military
in retaining their cohesion once the Shah left. The climactic meeting
resulting in these decisions was held on January 3, first in a session of
the SCC, and then over lunch with the President. Perhaps the most
authentic way to report on that meeting is simply to reproduce the
notes from my journal for that day:

> The situation in Iran has become critical. Our Ambassador has sent
> a cable announcing the moment of truth has come, asking in
> effect whether we should tell the Shah to step aside and to leave
> the country so that a civilian government can take over. The
> discussion in the group was rather desultory, with Vance pre-
> dictably leaning in favor of doing this. This discussion was then
> followed by a meeting with the President himself over lunch. In
> addition to our group, the Vice President and Jordan also took
> part. The President asked those present whether in their view
> we should ask the Shah to step aside. I immediately said that in my
> view if the question is whether we should ask him to step aside,
> and not whether it is desirable that he should step aside, the
> answer is clearly no. In other words, I was differentiating between
> the desirability of his stepping down, which might in fact be
> desirable since he is unable to make up his mind, and the de-
> sirability of the U.S. asking him. In my view this could be
> damaging to us in the future. Turner and Vance indicated that he
> had to leave, and Vance said that we should simply support a
> decision that he is leaning toward taking, since it would give
> Bakhtiar more of a chance to succeed. The President said we could
> posture it in such a way that it would be simply an approval for
> the Shah's decision. I argued that we should not delude ourselves;
> that the above would be interpreted by the Iranians as a recom-

mendation that the Shah should step aside. The Iranians are psychologically dependent on us and we have to take into account the likely consequences of this for our friends in Iran. Seeming U.S. disengagement, which they would interpret as disengagement, could plunge the country into anarchy and even civil war. Vance argued that the military could not govern. The President said the Parliament could be a source of stability, and he said . . . that a genuinely nonaligned Iran need not be viewed as a U.S. setback.

The discussion was punctuated by Vance leaving the table and phoning the State Department to arrange for exile for the Shah in the United States at the [Walter] Annenberg estate [in California]. The Vice President then said that we should encourage the Shah to leave without appearing to have said so. The President stated that the central issue is whether the Shah's early departure was favorable to the United States. Turner said he wasn't sure the Shah wants to leave. Duncan suggested that General Huyser, deputy to Haig, be sent to reassure the Iranian military of continuing U.S.–Iranian military arrangements. I then argued that if the Shah has to leave we should compensate for this by a clear-cut commitment to Iran, to the Iranian military, so that the Iranian military feel that the United States will support them if there is a military showdown. I said quite frankly that we ought not to be hesitant in supporting the Iranian military. Finally, we decided to send a cable to the Shah that we support his decision to leave the country when the civilian government is confirmed and that he will have hospitality here. At the same time it was also agreed that General Huyser would leave for Iran from Brussels with a message for the Iranian military that the United States supports them completely no matter what trends in the political circumstances may arise and that we urge the Iranian military leaders not to leave the country. We were beginning to get rumors that they are planning to leave the country while others are planning to stage a last-minute coup. At the end of the meeting I said to the President that we should not lose sight of the fact that every overt U.S. action with respect to Iran seems to be indicating disengagement. Civilian evacuation, the removal of personnel and equipment, indirect encouragement of the Shah to leave. This is bound to have political ramifications in the region and eventually domestically. . . .

After that I received finally the proposed text of the message to the Shah from Vance and to General Huyser from Duncan. I succeeded in stiffening the message to the Shah by insisting that the new government maintain a close U.S.–Iranian relationship and also particularly in stiffening the part in the telegram which

urges the Iranian military leadership to remain cohesive and that
the United States attaches importance to the Iranian military
leadership remaining united and in close touch with the United
States. The instruction to General Huyser goes even further because it urges the Iranian military in effect to be the guarantor of
a stable and strong government which keeps close ties with the
United States. Duncan, who talked to me about the cable to
General Huyser, told me that General Haig phoned in a state of
great emotional outrage and concern. He feels that we are being
much too soft, that we should have put an aircraft carrier task
force in the Indian Ocean, deployed some aircraft in Saudi
Arabia, and indicated firmer support. When I went in to talk to
the President at 6 p.m. with the cables, I also told him that I
felt we were not doing enough and that this could backfire very
gravely. He was rather irritated and asked me what I wished to
have done. I told him we should have encouraged the military to
stage a coup. He told me that we couldn't do this, not only
because of the [historical] record but also because there is no
military leader we could identify who would lead such a coup.
He has a point in a specific sense, but my view is that we do not
need to identify a leader. What we need to do is to give a clearer
signal and a leader will emerge. My hope, however, is that the
telegram to General Huyser, who is supposed to fly to Tehran
with a message of assurance to the Iranian military and with the
request that they stay behind and guarantee a close relationship
with the United States, will be interpreted by the Iranian military
as encouragement to take firm action when the moment of truth
arrives. In any case, the changes that were made in the telegram,
in part by the President and in part by me, I hope will have that
effect and will be so interpreted by the Iranians. In the cable to
the military, for example, we have such wording as "It is of vital
United States interest that the Iranian people have a strong and
stable government which is friendly to the United States. The
Iranian military today have a role of overriding importance to the
future of Iran and can only carry out this responsibility if they
remain cohesive and work closely together. No Iranian military
leader should leave the country now. The Iranian military should
do all it can to remain strong and intact in order to help a
responsible civilian government function effectively." I also prevailed on the President to omit any specific references to Bakhtiar
which could imply that we are supporting him specifically. I hope
all of that will give the Iranian military the needed signal.

The formation of the Bakhtiar government meant that the Shah's
regime was finished. The question now was whether the new regime,

still relatively moderate even if anti-Shah, could endure, given the collapse of the old political order and in the face of religiously aroused masses and radicalized urban youth. The strategy on which the group in Washington did agree was to make every effort to keep the Iranian military intact as the Shah prepared to leave. Our fear was that the military high command, composed of individuals hand-picked by the Shah for their personal loyalty to him, might disintegrate on his departure, plunging the country either into a devastating civil war, which the Soviet Union would then exploit, or into chaos, resulting in the seizure of power by Khomeini. Since the late November exchanges with Brezhnev, the foreign policy dimension was of increasing concern to us, and we were especially mindful of the certainty that a civil war in Iran would be a windfall for the Soviet Union.

But while agreeing on the importance of keeping the Iranian military in readiness—and that was the point of departure for the Huyser mission—our group differed as to the ultimate purpose of the exercise. Huyser, a ruddy-faced, direct, and confident officer, was recommended because of his previous service in Iran and his many personal contacts with the top Iranian officers. To Vance, Christopher (who in Vance's frequent absence played a leading role during this stage), and Mondale, the purpose of the Huyser mission was to help preserve a post-Shah civilian government in power. I agreed, and I publicly stressed firm U.S. support for the Bakhtiar government, but I also stressed that Huyser should prepare the Iranian military for a coup in the likely event that Bakhtiar should fail. Brown, Duncan, and Schlesinger concurred, and Huyser's instructions specifically contained such a provision.

The question was when the right moment might come. I wanted it understood that the coup would come if Bakhtiar faltered, and that we would not go on supporting a series of increasingly more radical civilian regimes while the Army disintegrated. Our divergence on this matter quickly surfaced over two issues: Should we back a coup even before the Shah left the country? Should we initiate dealings with Khomeini?

These questions arose immediately after the President arrived for the allied four-power summit meeting in Guadeloupe. Shortly after my arrival, on Thursday afternoon, January 4, 1979, I was summoned to the President's cottage. Carter was wearing only a bathing suit, as was I, and he was sitting on a small icebox in an alcove next to the informal sitting room, talking on the phone and looking rather concerned; Hamilton, also in a bathing suit, was sprawled on the sofa. The President was talking on the secure phone to Cy Vance.

It clearly transpired that Cy was phoning in a state of considerable agitation. Apparently the Iranian military have told Sullivan that they are now determined to move, that they will not let the Shah leave the country, and that they are prepared for a massive crack-

down which will involve a lot of blood being spilled. He and
Mondale had a meeting on it, and they were both obviously arguing with the President to the effect that we should make it clear
to the Iranian military that we will not support this. I indicated
right away to the President that in my view what had to be done
ought to be done and that we would shoulder massive historical
responsibility if we prevented the military and the Shah from
doing what they had finally decided to do. The conversation lasted
a long time, with me passing notes to the President, but much to
my satisfaction . . . the President took a very firm line. He told
Cy that he did not wish to change General Huyser's instructions
in order to water them down, that Ambassador Sullivan should
ascertain the Shah's attitude regarding the coup, that he should
not deliver the last message to the Shah, which was urging him
to leave the country. In effect, unless the Shah completely dis-
owns this effort, this would mean that we would be prepared to
back it.

The conversation lasted from 6 to 6:30 p.m., Guadeloupe time, and
I took quick notes as the President spoke. I was gratified by his firmness and dismayed that anyone at this late stage would actually wish
to prevent what was clearly in the collective interest of the West. I
could tell that the President was quite concerned about possible bloodshed, and I mentioned to him after the conversation was over that,
unfortunately, world politics was not a kindergarten and that we had
to consider also what will be the longer-range costs if the military failed
to act.

Alas, nothing happened. Vance conveyed the instructions orally to
Sullivan, and I have no doubt that he did so faithfully. At the other
end, the military and the Shah simply procrastinated, with the Shah
explaining that the coup scenario was meant to put pressure on Bakhtiar.
A few days later the Shah decided that he would leave in the middle of
the month.

The other issue which faced us in Guadeloupe was whether the
United States should initiate contact with Khomeini. Vance called
several times to make such a recommendation, in keeping with Sullivan's
pleadings. The President and I discussed it, and I instructed Vance to
make sure that the Shah approved such an initiative. Vance called back
and informed us that the Shah concurred; to gain time, I then requested that the final decision on the matter be postponed until the
President had returned to Washington. This would give us, I said, a
full opportunity to discuss the matter. My concern was that such an
approach would demoralize the top military leaders and accelerate
their exodus.

The President, Mondale, Vance, Brown, David Aaron, and I met on the morning of January 10. Vance renewed his recommendation, arguing that such a dialogue was necessary, supporting it with the case made by Sullivan, and referring to the Shah's concurrence. I objected on the grounds that such an approach would leak, that the seventy-eight-year-old fanatic was not going to be swayed by a single conversation with an American emissary, that the American public would not understand such an initiative, and that it would undermine confidence in Tehran in the Bakhtiar regime. Our discussion raged back and forth, and the President in the end decided that we would ask the French to initiate discreet contacts with Khomeini on our behalf.

I then proposed that we give Bakhtiar ten days to obtain evident support from other political leaders, and particularly support from them in standing down the strikes, and that otherwise we would move with a military coup. I argued that such a threat would give greater credibility to our position and might even induce the Iranian civilians to pull their act together. This recommendation was not accepted. Finally, the meeting concluded with a decision to proceed with arrangements to receive the Shah, who would leave Iran within just a few days. As I noted in my journal later that day: "I acquiesced to the Shah's departure largely because I feel that he has become an impediment to any decisive action. At least this way the situation will be brought to a head and we will know where we stand before the armed forces become altogether demoralized."

The President's decision not to initiate direct contact with Khomeini, but to do so through a French intermediary, precipitated a hysterical telegram from Sullivan. He described the President's decision as "insane" and requested that Vance and Brown attempt to get it rescinded. I showed the telegram to the President, and he in strong terms reaffirmed the original decision and had Vance send a cable to that effect to Sullivan, indicating that the decision was made on the basis of a unanimous recommendation to the President by all of his advisers. Sullivan's erratic behavior during these weeks, and particularly the telegram, did not do much to heighten his standing in the President's eyes.

This was a tense period for all of us, and tempers occasionally became frayed. My relations with Cy became more strained, especially since in the meantime our normalization with China was moving ahead well while our SALT negotiations with the Soviets were stalled. The President, under pressure from all sides, was also becoming somewhat short-tempered, and he reacted quite critically to my weekly report of January 12, in which I wrote that I disagreed with the views of Iran experts that the Shah was entirely the problem and that when he departed the National Front would run the country while Khomeini returned as a venerable sage. I portrayed Khomeini as uncompromising, the military as hating the National Front, and the left as growing in influence. In the scramble for power, we might soon have to throw our weight behind one of the sides to protect our interests. The President, obviously irritated, wrote in the margins: "Zbig—After we make joint decisions, deploring them for the record doesn't help me."

My purpose, however, was not to deplore our policy but to persuade the President of the need for a coup. I felt very much alone, especially since I suspected that my urging of a coup—for broader strategic concerns—was undermining my credibility with the President, who found my advocacy of a coup morally troublesome (as well as irritating). Two days later I reported that we had received a longish cable from Huyser in which he described his initial activities and in which he provided also an interpretation, as he understood it, of his instructions. Noting that "I consider a military coup as an absolutely last resort," Huyser indicated that the sequence of events might involve a successful Bakhtiar government, a Bakhtiar government that is successful for a while but eventually fails, another civilian government more acceptable to Khomeini, and even "this alternative could repeat itself under certain circumstances," followed only then by a coup. In my cover memo to the President, I noted that I believed that Huyser was following his instructions correctly but that "I feel uneasy about his list of desirable governments. I do not believe we can afford to go down a slippery slope of one civilian government followed by another more to the left. The armed forces will be demoralized and we will have no more leverage. . . . If Bakhtiar fails, we must make a decisive change and Huyser's 'C' will have to be implemented with U.S. backing" ("C" being a reference to the military option in his instructions).

The Shah left Iran on January 16. The question now was whether the Iranian military had the capacity, and Washington the determination, to implement option "C."

Collapse

But the execution of option "C" required both logistical planning and political determination on the part of the Iranian military—and a signal from an accepted authority. It was Huyser's mission to ensure readiness for action and, with the Shah gone, only Washington could give the signal. There were divided opinions on the ability of the Iranian military to act. Sullivan, who had always been against a military coup, argued that the military could not pull it off, and his views were echoed by the Department of State. By late December, Gary Sick wrote me that the military were in a fragile condition and that it was doubtful that they could assert themselves in order to govern effectively. The intelligence community did not give us any firm views on the subject. From time to time, I arranged through Sick to meet with various

Iranians, and on the whole they tended to the view that the Iranian military could still act, if purposefully led. Zahedi was also of that view, though I had to discount his views as biased in favor of the Shah.

The uncertainty regarding the state of the Iranian military made Huyser's professional and disinterested appraisal all the more important. He arrived in Tehran on January 4, and within days we started receiving reports from him. The usual procedure was for Harold Brown and General Jones to talk to him on a secure phone, raising questions which were prepared in advance by them as well as on the basis of instructions from me. On a few occasions, I joined Brown in the telephone conversations. In addition, Huyser would occasionally report by telegram, and at times both he and Sullivan would talk together. Most often, however, Huyser reported through Brown, while Sullivan kept in touch with Newsom or Christopher. Brown would submit to the President, through me, written reports on these conversations.

Huyser's first major assessment came in on January 9, one week prior to the Shah's departure. He warned us that the major concern in the military was that the senior officers might depart with the Shah and that the military would then fall apart. The military were particularly concerned about destructive anti-Shah BBC broadcasts, which were galvanizing the Iranian public, and they urged us to encourage the British government to do something about the BBC. Moreover, the top Iranian commanders admitted that their planning to support Bakhtiar's government was inadequate, and Huyser reported that he would be working with them on the logistical requirements of any eventual military action. On January 10, Brown reported to the President that the military were not prepared to conduct a coup at that time and that in Huyser's view it would be useful for the religious and the military to get together (though Brown added that he viewed that recommendation as unrealistic). Surprisingly, Huyser reported that for the first time in his long relationship with the Iranian military the top Iranian command seemed united. The President wrote at this point in the margin: "I hope he is right."

As the date for the Shah's departure, January 16, approached, Huyser started reporting that the military were becoming restless and leaning toward a coup to coincide with the Shah's departure. Huyser said that he held firmly to the line that the military must give Bakhtiar a chance to form an effective government. Brown conveyed the above to the President on January 12 and 13, and Brown added in his January 13 report that "I then said to General Huyser that it remained very important that we not imply to the military that there would never be a basis for strong military action, or that any civilian government would be better than a military coup. I repeated that he needed to walk a narrow line to prevent a military coup against the Bakhtiar government, but not encourage the military to stand idly by if the situation deteriorated continuously." This was in keeping with what I told Brown earlier in the day, having read Huyser's initial report and having become concerned that Huyser might interpret his instructions as meaning that we were committed indefinitely to any kind of civilian government.

A day later, on January 14, Brown reported to the President that Huyser had asked the Iranian military to tell him when they thought they might be approaching the point where they would lose the option for military action. His judgment and theirs was that the point was not at hand. Each day perhaps 500–1,000 of the Iranian military were moving over in sympathy or in person to the religious and political opposition, but that was out of a force of 500,000. On the following day, I joined Brown and Jones in a conversation with Huyser, and I asked Huyser whether the military had developed a plan for use if the Bakhtiar government faltered. Huyser stated that the military had been working on it for four to five days, but they already had a marginal capability. I also inquired about the attitude of middle-level officers, from the level of division commanders down to brigade and regimental commanders, and Huyser stated that they appreciated the fact that the senior Iranian military were working in greater unity than ever before and that this was a positive factor.

After the departure of the Shah on January 16, Brown reported to the President that the military in Tehran were still holding together. At the same time Huyser's reports reflected a growing anxiety over what would happen if and when Khomeini returned. Brown said that in Huyser's view Khomeini's return was likely to generate widespread disorder, Khomeini himself might get killed, and there would certainly be a coup attempt. Brown also reported to the President that I had discussed with Huyser the planning necessary to assure that the military option remained open: "Zbig pointed out the values of explicitly planning for this option: making the political opposition aware that the support of the Bakhtiar government was the best way of avoiding a military coup; discouraging Khomeini from returning; putting the military in a psychological situation that would allow the option to be exercised if necessary. Huyser indicated that if he were to describe the planning to the military as a takeover of government functions it would be hard to keep them from executing a coup. He added that the nature of the detailed planning is similar and urged that we proceed on the previous basis. This was agreed."

On the following day, Brown reported to the President that the military continued to be very worried about Khomeini's return, but that they were gaining in planning and physical capability for action and should be much readier in a week than they were today. Two days later, Brown informed the President that he had received the most encouraging report to date, in that the military and Bakhtiar seemed to be getting together well. But the tone of the reports changed for the worse in the third week. On January 22, Huyser reported by cable that the prospective return of Khomeini represented the greatest potential for complete disaster and that Khomeini's return would prompt Bakhtiar to go "down the drain." Huyser went on to add that he now had real doubts as to whether the military were sophisticated enough to administer the country if they seized power. On January 24, he told again of growing worries within the military about Khomeini's prospective return. The increasing likelihood of that return was the subject of Duncan's report (Brown was away) to the President on January 29, in which Huyser stated that Khomeini's return was likely to lead to Bakhtiar's fall. That would be the moment for a military move, though Huyser added that his conclusion was not shared by Ambassador Sullivan.

On February 5, Huyser reported personally to the President in the Cabinet Room of the White House (the circumstances of his return are described below). In his report, Huyser stated that he differed with Ambassador Sullivan regarding Iranian military capabilities and regarding the desirability of military action. He said that Sullivan felt it was probably better to get the military forces aside and to let the political elements fight it out among themselves and for the United States to accept whoever won. Huyser stated that Sullivan believed that if Khomeini established an Islamic republic, the drift would be eventually toward democracy. Huyser added that in his view the drift would be toward Communism. At the end of the meeting I asked Huyser for a direct answer to the question of whether the military would and could execute a coup if given a signal from Washington, and Huyser responded in the affirmative.

Thus, by and large, until the very last moment, we had some reason to believe that military action was possible. We had no way of telling the extent to which the military were demoralized by the fragmentation of the political order, and on this score we tended to be somewhat more pessimistic than Huyser, though not as defeatist as Sullivan. I noted in my journal on January 17: "We are getting increasingly conflicting reports on military morale," but the signal, which would have tested the accuracy of Huyser's judgment and preparations, was never given.

My growing fear that we would never give such a signal prompted me to write, on January 18, a long and personal memo to the President (it comprised seven single-spaced pages—an unusual length for a personal memo), and I accompanied it with a handwritten note telling the President that he had the only copy. In the memo I argued that we were not likely to be presented in Iran with the luxury of a simple black-white dichotomy, but rather with a gradual deterioration which in the end would produce disastrous international consequences for the United States. I warned that the military would become more politicized, demoralized, and fragmented. I argued that Iran was likely to shift piecemeal to an orientation similar to that of Libya or into anarchy, with the result that our position in the Gulf would be undermined, that our standing throughout the Arab world would decline, that the Israelis would become more security-oriented and hence less willing to compromise, that the Soviet influence in southwestern Asia would grow, that our allies would see us as impotent, that the price of oil would increase, that we were likely to lose some sensitive equipment and intelligence capabilities germane to SALT, and that there would be severe domestic political repercussions.

I outlined alternative courses of action, which I defined essentially as: to continue as at present, to push more actively for a coalition, or to stage a military coup. I argued that the second alternative simply would produce all of the negative consequences I had outlined, and that was also likely to be the effect of pursuing our present course of action. I told the President that I was not arguing for an immediate decision to stage a coup, but that I felt that within the next two weeks we would have to make a deliberate choice to that effect. The concluding part of the memorandum argued that we should be prepared to ride out some initially negative domestic reactions, and that it was wrong to contend that the military cannot make the economy in Iran work. I cited examples of other military coups in which the military proved capable of providing an effective government. Finally, I urged the President to consult with former President Ford and Kissinger, as well as Senators Byrd and Baker, on the needed action so that we could galvanize maximum political support.

I considered this memo to be quite important, and on a very private basis I showed an initial draft of it to Brown. He endorsed it, and gave me a number of helpful suggestions which I incorporated into the final draft. The President read it very carefully, but his overall reaction was limited to the observation that the memorandum was sensitive. He did not comment directly on my specific policy recommendations.

In the meantime, to make certain that Huyser and Sullivan worked closely together, I drafted an instruction providing guidance and obtained Vance's and Brown's concurrence. It was sent out on January 19 to both Huyser and Sullivan and stated:

1. U.S. position unchanged. We support the Bakhtiar government in its effort to reestablish stability within a constitutional framework.

2. To that end the military support is necessary. Military should continue to support Bakhtiar.

3. Military unity is essential to support existing government, to maintain domestic order and stability, to protect the security of Iran, and to deal with other problems which may develop in the future.

4. Success of Bakhtiar regime requires dealing with the Army and non-Communist forces. We recognize the need of Bakhtiar to gain support of additional forces, including the religious. To this end talks with various groups may be necessary, including people like Bazargan. As we see it, the purpose of this dialogue is not to transform the nature of the Bakhtiar regime into a coalition with Khomeini, but to give it a wider popular base and support, especially through some of the clergy and other key groups who support the constitution.

5. Any efforts to broaden the Bakhtiar government must be measured by their effect not only on stability and government's ability to govern but also on the government's attitude toward the West and on military unity. We wish to avoid a slide into a government which would act against the interests of the West or cause the fragmentation of the military. To this end Bakhtiar and the military should be very cautious about bringing in opposition members.

During this period, prompted by the increasingly frequent and alarmist reports from both Huyser and Sullivan, Vance, Brown, and I, as well as occasionally Mondale and from time to time the President, started meeting with increasing frequency on the Iranian issue. At the Friday-morning breakfast on January 19, the President said, "We should tell Bakhtiar that we will not accommodate any more to the left; we support the military in their position and in their effort to maintain stability, but we are not in favor of bringing Khomeini and his people into the government." Cy then asked, "Does it mean we don't broaden the political base?" and Carter responded by saying that we had only the military and the remnants of the Shah's supporters on our side left in Iran and we could no longer undermine them. Vance then argued that this might imply that we were encouraging the military to move, but the President snapped, with unusual sharpness, that if the word got back to Iran that we did not support the military, the effect would be to undermine the military's morale. Mondale joined the discussion by saying that Bakhtiar had to broaden his base and we had to recognize the fact that Khomeini represented the most powerful force, and I could sense from his remarks that he and Vance were very much on the same wavelength. I was accordingly very gratified when Carter concluded forcefully: "We never agreed among ourselves to a coalition government. Yet all people hear abroad is the implication that we favor a coalition government. We will back the military in their support of Bakhtiar but we don't want it to slide any further to the left. The threat of a military coup is the best way to prevent Khomeini from sliding into power."

Actually, prior to our breakfast, I had told the President that there was increasing consensus here and abroad that the United States was sliding into support of a post-Bakhtiar coalition government, including perhaps Khomeini, and that this was devastating to our credibility. Accordingly, immediately after the President's comments, I suggested that the President approve a directive codifying what he had just said. Later in the afternoon I obtained Brown's and Vance's agreement to a draft, and it was sent out to Tehran. Brown told me in an aside after our afternoon session, "You got ninety percent of what you wanted. Your memo obviously had an impact on the President."

But while our position stiffened, it did not prompt the needed action. The issue of how to deal with the threat of Khomeini's return came to a head, in a rather dramatic fashion, in the course of the next two days. On January 22, Brown reported that he had been advised by Huyser that Bakhtiar was prepared to confront Khomeini as Khomeini attempted to return to Iran. His plane would be diverted and he would be arrested. The question for us was whether we were prepared to encourage Bakhtiar to undertake this action and to stiffen his determination to carry it out. The issue was actively debated over the next two days among Vance, Brown, and me. To make matters more complicated, we received on January 23 a request from Huyser and Sullivan that we change their instructions to permit the possibility of a coalition between the military and the religious elements, something which Cy strongly favored and which I very much opposed. We had an even sharper disagreement on how to respond to Bakhtiar's initiative. Cy was strongly against it and felt that we should simply advise both Bakhtiar and Khomeini that Khomeini should not return and that a confrontation would be a disaster for both sides. Both Brown and I had a different reaction, feeling that if Bakhtiar now had the will to stand up, he should be supported.

On January 23 and 24, we had several meetings on the subject among ourselves and also with the President. The President's initial reaction was extremely positive; he exclaimed, "Great," when I advised him of Bakhtiar's plans. Cy, however, argued strenuously that the result would be massive disorders and that Khomeini might even get killed in the process, setting in motion altogether unforeseeable consequences. We continued our meetings throughout the twenty-fourth, with Brown and I arguing that if Bakhtiar wished to arrest Khomeini he should be encouraged to do so and that it would be a great mistake for us to give any contrary signals. Because of our disagreement we could not draft a proposed instruction, and I had to take to the President several alternative versions. The President decided not to approve Cy's draft urging Bakhtiar not to go through with his plan, but chose, after calling me several times into the Oval Office, a modified version of the text favored by Brown and me, in effect giving Bakhtiar the green light to do what he had proposed. Unfortunately,

Khomeini chose to delay his return, and though in that initial skirmish Bakhtiar perhaps won a limited psychological victory, the issue remained unresolved.

Bakhtiar's display of determination was short-lived. By the end of the month Khomeini was on his way to Tehran, and on the morning of January 31, I was startled to discover in my office a cable informing me that Huyser was planning to leave Iran. Apparently while I was at breakfast with the President and congressional leaders, Brown and Vance approved Sullivan's rather panicky recommendation that Huyser should leave immediately, especially since he had been threatened with assassination. As I wrote later that day in my journal: "I blew my stack, phoned Brown, who wasn't there, so I really ripped into Duncan. Then I spoke to Vance. I told him that this was not coordinated and in my judgment it was a bad decision—the U.S. general fleeing Tehran ignominiously two hours before Khomeini arrives, and what signal does it send to the Iranian generals? That the United States is backing out?" Fortunately, Cy agreed, and I phoned Duncan with the order to rescind the instruction.

Khomeini's return to Tehran created in effect a situation in which two governments were competing for power, with growing turmoil in the streets and with increasing signs of demoralization within the Army. Two days later, on Saturday, February 3, our group met under my chairmanship in the Situation Room at 7 a.m. and received a request directly from General Huyser, reinforced by Sullivan's anxious plea to State, that he be authorized to leave. Everyone in the room except me favored this decision, and I phoned the President at Camp David to inform him that all but me favored Huyser's withdrawal. I also reported to the President that Sullivan did not wish option "C" implemented but was urging Huyser's immediate departure, since Sullivan felt Huyser's presence was endangering the lives of other Americans. The President made the decision at 8:15 a.m. to call Huyser back and to have his deputy, General Philip C. Gast, continue with the preparations in which Huyser had been engaged.

Two days later, on February 5 (as I have noted), Huyser reported to the President, and his account of the situation in Tehran resulted in a strong public endorsement of Bakhtiar by the President, designed to maintain military morale and Bakhtiar's confidence. Two or three hours later, the evening television news reported that State Department officials expected Bakhtiar to last only two or three more days, and this incident greatly enraged the President and Jody Powell. It led to the highly publicized meeting between the President and middle-echelon State Department officials, in which the State Department was castigated for disloyalty and excessive leakage. Officials at the State Department blamed me for engineering the meeting, but in fact it had been recommended to the President the very evening of the incident by Ham Jordan, who wrote (on his own initiative) the President a memorandum urging such a meeting and also the summary dismissal of a number of State Department officials.

The next few days were painful. The reports from Iran indicated increasing disintegration, while my State Department colleagues were urging an accommodation between Bakhtiar and Khomeini's chosen political leader, a relatively moderate Iranian opponent of the Shah, Mehdi Bazargan. I was convinced that under these circumstances the military would disintegrate. The culminating meeting of the SCC took place on Sunday, February 11, from 8:30 to 11:30 a.m. It might be best simply to give a synopsis of what transpired at the meeting based on my journal notes dictated that evening as well as the minutes of the meeting itself. They convey the extent to which the situation in Iran was out of control and the degree to which events outpaced our deliberations.

The situation in Iran was critical; we faced the final collapse of the Bakhtiar regime. It was clear that we had to make some tough decisions on the basis of incomplete and often confusing reports from the field. Warren Christopher, assisted by David Newsom, represented State; Charles Duncan and General David Jones headed a group from Defense and the Joint Chiefs of Staff; Stan Turner and Frank Carlucci were there from the CIA; and my assistants Gary Sick and Colonel (later General) Bill Odom and other agency officials rounded out the group of a dozen or so men.

We discussed three options: first, to urge the Iranian military to pursue accommodation with Bazargan, who was emerging as Khomeini's choice for Bakhtiar's successor; second, to recommend that the Iranian military acquiesce in the transfer of power and concentrate on remaining united, staying in the barracks; third, to encourage the Iranian military to undertake a direct action to restore order and take control of the political situation, assuming that they had the capability and will to do so. Before moving to a consideration of these options, I raised the issue of preparing for evacuation. The initial questions dealt with the logistics of moving a platoon of Marines and six helicopters to the Azores for possible forward deployment to bases in Turkey. The Marines could be used to strengthen the security detachment at our Embassy in Tehran and the helicopters would be used to evacuate Americans in an emergency. In addition, I raised the advisability of moving the 82nd Airborne to alert status. Early in the meeting, however, we were interrupted by a secure phone call from the President at Camp David, where he and Vance were spending the weekend. Duncan and I briefed him on the morning's developments. We had just received reports that our consulate in Tabriz had been sacked and that several Iranian generals had been executed. Duncan told the President about the contingency planning for evacuation, and I outlined the issues we were discussing. The conversation ended at 8:46, and I returned to the meeting.

With the President's approval, we decided against putting the 82nd Airborne on alert status because it would exacerbate the situation. We discussed the number and location of Americans in Iran. I asked what Sullivan was proposing. Christopher said that the Ambassador had not recommended evacuation and had suggested that the best course was to get agreement from the successor government to protect Americans. The SCC decided to continue the current disposition of American citizens as directed by the Embassy. Americans would be urged to stand fast in their homes and not to concentrate in large groups. The Embassy would continue its contacts with all parties in Iran to assure the safety of U.S. citizens.

I turned the discussion toward a consideration of the Iranian military's status. It was my understanding, from reports, that the military had decided that they could do nothing under the present circumstances and they were not willing to support Bakhtiar. But did that mean they were willing to support a Khomeini government? Christopher suggested that we urge the Army to stay together and defend whatever government was in place. He wondered if there was any different view. I responded by saying that if the new government was clever, they would not purge the military all at once but take them one at a time. First Badrai, then Rabii, and so forth. I wondered what the long-range result would be. I feared that it would be the piecemeal dismantling of the military. I then went on to say that if the military had the will and the capacity to take control of the situation, we should be prepared to act like a major power and support them. Frank Carlucci, Turner's deputy, suggested that the military go to Khomeini and say that they would accept him with the following guarantees: for example, maintaining the status of the intelligence sites for the national security, specifying who would be the Minister of War, and so forth. They had some bargaining power.

The discussion was interrupted at 9:40 by a Situation Room staffer relaying a report that the Tehran military governor had been seized and was being held prisoner at Khomeini's headquarters. At the same time the Joint Chiefs called via secure phone from the Pentagon to ask approval for moving the Marines to the Azores.

Christopher pointed out that Bazargan was not the first choice of the military. However, he was better than what existed to the left of him. He noted that the military were not willing or able to stand behind Bakhtiar. How could they stand by themselves now that Bakhtiar was apparently gone?

I wondered what the long-term outcome of the situation would be. I said the military could not act in a political context. They were not particularly sophisticated. They would be better off acting directly to restore law and order. I wondered if we should not ask General Gast and General Huyser whether option "C" was still viable at this point. Our previous guidance was that we would support the Iranian command in using force to protect Bakhtiar or to protect the existence of a pro-Western Iran. Christopher said that the military did not have enough cohesion to stand on their own. I asked if we could influence that situation. I went on to say that if the military joined with Khomeini, it would eventually lead to a general deterioration as well. I argued that we should still consider option "C," though admittedly at this late hour it would be a major and a very risky action. If it was successful, it would reinforce the U.S. position in the region. General Jones said he was not optimistic about option "C." Duncan said that he did not think option "C" was viable, but if those in the field did, then it should be considered. I then said that we ought to consider the implications of handing over Iran piecemeal to an unstable situation. There would be major repercussions strategically and domestically as a result of such a decision. I went on to say that if the Army asserted military discipline and acted, it should be able to do it. It is possible that the very lack of action would breed a breakdown. I then suggested that calls be placed to General Gast, Ambassador Sullivan, and General Huyser to get their assessment of the situation.

At 10:10 we received a press report that Iranian radio and television had been seized because the tanks had pulled back. A minute or so later the communications officers informed us that there was no link to the Military Advisory Assistance Group (MAAG) compound, Gast was no longer reachable. I called the President at Camp David to update him and Vance. I learned that they were at church and could not be reached.

Back in the meeting, I said that in any conversation with Sullivan and Huyser they should be asked if a military option, among others, is still viable. They should be asked what would be the effect of moving sensitive equipment to the port of Bandar Abbas and what would be the advisability of Huyser's returning to Iran. I emphasized that if option "C" was clearly not viable, it would be stupid to attempt it. But if it was, we should pursue it.

At 10:37 the President called, and I briefed him on the situation. In this conversation I noted that if the military made an accommodation with the Bazargan government, the armed forces would disintegrate, with major domestic and foreign implications. I said that the military were still relatively united and that they were passive now. The President said that we should consider sending more Marines to the Azores and that we should approach Bazargan for the purpose of protecting the lives of the Americans in Iran. As I finished briefing the President, Charles Duncan was called to a phone to speak with General

Huyser. Huyser's view was that option "C" was not feasible without a massive U.S. commitment. The Iranian military would need a great deal of encouragement.

The meeting resumed at about 11:00. I noted that Huyser's analysis indicated very limited options for the United States. His conclusion carried more weight with me than Sullivan's, given the general's calmer demeanor. I was very pessimistic about the outcome since the Iranian military evidently did not have the will to act. Newsom then suggested that we go directly to Bazargan and tell him that we wanted a stable, peaceful Iran. I said in response that if we talked to Bazargan we should remind him that we had leverage with the military. The way we would use that leverage would be influenced by the kind of assurances we got of Iranian cooperation.

After this discussion, the meeting adjourned until later that evening. It was clear to me that we were faced with a fait accompli. My journal notes for the next few days speak for themselves. On February 12, I reported, after another SCC meeting on Iran: "I was rather struck by how eager Christopher and Newsom were to emphasize that the new regime in Iran is treating Americans well. I suspect that the outcome in Iran is one that not only fulfills some of their prophecies but also expresses some of their preferences." On February 16, I noted: "The first executions have already started, with four top generals being shot earlier today." And on February 20, I wrote: "A depressing story of chaos and confusion. The more I hear of what is going on, the more depressed I am over the fact that I did not succeed in getting the U.S. government to approve and, if necessary, to initiate an Iranian military coup."

Denouement

The Shah did not act; the military did not move; Washington never ordered a coup. Could Iran have been saved? Who "lost Iran"? Pointing a finger at a culprit is easier and certainly psychologically more rewarding than acknowledging that a historical drama like that of Iran is a complex process, with few precise causalities and with many contradictory turning points. Nonetheless, my summation of our internal policy struggles in Washington must explicitly address—even if not conclusively answer—three key questions:

1. Could Iran have been saved by a timely coalition, and did Washington have sufficiently early warning that such a coalition was the only way out?

2. Could Iran have been saved by a military coup, and did the Iranian military have the capacity and the will to undertake it with, and later without, the Shah?

3. Should Washington have been more explicit in pressing the Shah to adopt a particular solution, and particularly should we have triggered a military coup even in spite of, or without, the Shah?

My own answer is that coalition was not a practicable solution by the time we in Washington or even the Shah himself became aware of the depth and scope of the crisis. As late as August, Ambassador Sullivan was away from his post on a vacation, clearly a sign that in his view nothing dramatic was in the offing. Our political intelligence indicated continuity in Iran, and later still, by the end of October, Sullivan was reporting that "our destiny is to work with the Shah" on behalf of a controlled transition. Yet within ten days we in Washington were confronted with the sudden report of a serious crisis, with the Shah said to be considering abdication. Strikes continued to spread, violence escalated, the very existence of the system was suddenly in jeopardy. Islamic fundamentalism—a phenomenon largely ignored in our intelligence reports—was now openly challenging the existing order.

From that moment on, the gut question for the Shah was not that of reform but that of survival. Iranian history after the fall of the Shah tells us eloquently how viable any contrived coalition would have been: the successors to the Shah spent the subsequent months in literally killing one another, in widespread executions, in repeated and increasingly murderous assassinations, in an intensifying civil war.

I felt then, and I still feel, that our task was to help the Shah regain effective authority—and then to launch the needed reforms. I believed that the ruler with a strong and still disciplined army could assert himself—and the sooner, the less costly the effort. In any case, that effort would certainly have involved less spilling of blood than was subsequently inflicted on Iran by that "Gandhi-like" figure, to quote Sullivan's quaint description of the Ayatollah Khomeini.

Moreover, from the international standpoint, American interests dictated supporting the Shah strongly. Other rulers in the region, friendly to the United States, were watching us closely. How we responded to the crisis was a guide to them how we might react if they were threatened. They were certainly discouraged by the seeming inconsistency between our public statements of support and our apparent hesitation in pressing the Shah to assert effective authority. They could not tell whether Sullivan's less than hearty transmittal to the Shah of our encouragement reflected in fact the genuine inclination of the Carter Administration. After the fall, the Shah assiduously disseminated, especially with Sadat and Hassan of Morocco, this latter version in order to justify his own indecision.

But could the military have saved Iran? I find it inconceivable that in the early stages of the crisis a strong display of leadership by the Shah would not have resulted in effective and relatively bloodless imposition of control over the country. The military were disciplined, well organized, and powerful. Their counterparts in Pakistan, Turkey, Brazil, Egypt, and elsewhere have proved in equally difficult circumstances capable both of seizing power and then of governing. There was no reason to believe they could not do so in Iran, especially if ordered to do so by the Shah.

The question becomes more difficult in regard to the later phases of the crisis—when the military became increasingly contaminated and demoralized, especially after the Shah's departure, and when faced with massive mobs and paralyzing strikes. There is no doubt that each passing week increased the difficulty and the human costs of any military action. I have no basis for arguing categorically that the military could have still prevailed, though in a head-on confrontation involving brute force the balance of power would certainly have favored the military. It is a fact that even on the very eve of Khomeini's return some of his supporters, notably Bazargan, remained fearful of a military coup. That indicates that they thought it was feasible. General Huyser reported more than once that adequate preparations for the seizure of power had been made and that a coup could be undertaken. In retrospect, he was clearly too optimistic in presenting a picture which made us feel that the military were more cohesive than in fact was the case and that, therefore, we could afford the luxury of delaying the final decision regarding "last resort" action. Others, notably the State Department and our Ambassador, disputed the proposition that the military could effectively assert themselves, but these colleagues of mine were always against a military coup. The truth is that we will never know who was right.

But we do know—and this was of decisive importance to the tragic outcome—that the Shah proved weak, vacillating, and suffered from a paralysis of will. Perhaps his fatal illness, known only at the time to him, affected him in ways which deserve human compassion. Our Ambassador, abetted by State, instead of strengthening the Shah's morale, contributed to his indecision by diluting our urgings that the Shah act. Should we have, therefore, taken the needed decisions for the Shah? I believed at the time that we should, because of the enormous stakes involved, and I still feel that way. Accordingly, I fault myself for not having been more convincing and persuasive in regard to the President. I should have perhaps exploited more effectively Schlesinger's and Duncan's support of my views in order to pose the issue more sharply. Brown, in critical instances, proved a strong ally, but on the larger issue of the military coup he tended to agree in principle but then to argue that the right moment for action had not yet come.

Our political intelligence did not help matters, for it did not emphasize to the President the strategic dimensions of the challenge. This was left largely for me to do, but I suspect my strong advocacy of a forceful course of action made the President skeptical when I painted a grim picture of the strategic consequences for us of Iran's—and of the Shah's —tragedy. The intelligence system gave the President little preparation for the shock that the sudden disintegration of Iran was for him, as well as for the rest of us. Preoccupied on a daily basis with other major issues, deeply involved particularly in the Camp David process, we simply did not have the time to reflect more deeply and from a longer-range perspective on the broader strategic and geopolitical ramifications of the Iranian crisis. In a sense, it was these broader considerations that were in the back of my mind when I pressed over and over again for a solution in which the primary emphasis was placed on the preservation for the United States of our strategic position in Iran. I do not know what historical assumptions guided Carter's or Vance's approach to the subject, but I assume that their assumptions were different from mine and involved a somewhat different scheme of the world. To me, principled commitment to a more decent world order did not preclude the use of power to protect our more immediate interests; to the others, it was not for America to decide what transpired within Iran.

Vance and Christopher, supported by Mondale, simply played for time, always arguing that the next concession to the Shah's opponents was less dangerous than the difficult and dangerous decision for Washington to stage a coup. As the Shah's fortunes declined, they also made their general dislike of the system more evident, while the lower echelons of State, on the Iran Desk, were clearly cheering the Shah's opponents. Even when Bakhtiar was falling, the argument was made that his successors would not be too bad, that some accommodation could be struck with Iran (and within Iran), while a military coup would at best plunge the country into a civil war and by failing it could even deliver the country to our sworn enemies. The decision to support Bakhtiar, so as to maintain stability as the Shah was leaving, while giving Huyser time to prepare the military for an effective coup, simply led to our procrastinating until it was too late.

But their most persuasive argument, I think, was the moral one. They felt that the United States—and notably the President himself— should not assume the responsibility for plunging another country into a bloody and cruel confrontation. I was not unsympathetic to this argument, for it was a compelling one, and hence my clear preference was for the Shah to make the decision that I favored. But while we encouraged the Shah to do so, and some of us even prodded him to act, the Shah chose not to or, perhaps more correctly, was simply too weak a person to make the decision himself (and found it useful to blame America by pointing to Ambassador Sullivan's ambiguous conduct). Thus I gradually came to believe that we had no choice but, for overriding strategic and geopolitical factors, to make the decision for him.

The President, for reasons that I respect but do not entirely share, felt otherwise and would not cross the elusive line between strong support (which he provided to the Shah quite consistently) and the actual decision to embark on a bloody and admittedly uncertain course of action. Carter felt that we gave the Shah all the backing and encouragement that he needed. but that it was historically and morally wrong for the United States to go any further. Moreover, the President also felt that a civil war in Iran would benefit the Soviet Union, and for this reason as well we had to draw the line.

It is painfully clear that all the choices facing the President were grim. It was not only that the options available to us were limited, but the one that I preferred involved in some respects the most risky course of action. Suppose the coup had failed and Iran then exploded into a violent civil war, from which the Soviet Union had benefited? Part of my own inner agony stemmed from the fact that I knew that I could not give a categorical answer to that troubling question— though in fact that is exactly what later happened, without an attempted military coup. Nonetheless, on balance, I did feel that our interests were so vital that we should make the effort, and the sooner we did it, of course, the greater the chances of success. This was both a moral and a political decision—and clearly a fateful one for all concerned.

In the deepest sense, the collapse of the Shah thus involved on the American side a failure of political intelligence in the widest meaning of the term "intelligence." That failure is not so much a matter of particular intelligence reports or even of specific policies. To be sure, it would have been better to know sooner that the Shah was mortally ill, that his willpower was gone, and that his highly personalized political system was not capable of generating effective alternatives to him. But a deeper intellectual misjudgment of a central historical reality was involved here: that rapid modernization of a very traditional society breeds its own instabilities and revolutionary dynamics, that it requires a political system that can gradually enlarge political participation while providing safety valves for social dissatisfaction, that old religious beliefs should not be uprooted without gradual public acceptance of more modern values, including some genuine connection with the national past. The Shah's regime violated these basic rules, and U.S. policies throughout the seventies, including our own four years, could not and did not provide effective remedies. Carter's effort to make the Shah more responsive to human rights was a step in the right direction, but it came at a time when the basic problems of Iran were beginning to get out of hand and the structure of authority was beginning to crack.

At that stage, the decision to go for a military coup, in my view, was necessary because the alternative was turmoil, with destructive consequences for our regional interests. But, admittedly, one could not be sure if the coup would have worked, and by itself it was not a solution to the deeper problem. Nonetheless, in my view, we had no alternative, and we could couple the reassertion of authority with some of the needed reform, but in that sequential order. Nonetheless, it was a decision that preferably the Shah had to make, and not the President of the United States acting on his behalf and relieving him of that responsibility. Under the circumstances, one has to understand, even if one does not share, Carter's unwillingness to embark on a bloody and uncertain course of action.

The fall of the Shah was clearly a political calamity for President Carter. It undid the political benefits of his effective leadership in obtaining the Camp David agreements, it obscured public appreciation of his boldness in achieving normalization of relations with China, and it weakened the credibility of his efforts to oppose the Soviet occupation of Afghanistan. It hurt his image as a world leader in the very mid-point of the first Presidential term. Finally, by setting in motion circumstances that led eventually to the seizure of the American hostages in Tehran, the fall of the Shah contributed centrally to Carter's political defeat.

Before the dinner for Chinese Chairman Deng Xiaoping at the Brzezinski home, January 1979

Presidential working luncheon for King Khalid of Saudi Arabia, October 1978. The Americans are (clockwise) Atherton, a translator, the President, Blumenthal, Saunders, Ambassador West, Brown, Vance, Brzezinski

One of the rare amiable encounters with Chancellor Schmidt, Bonn, October 3, 1978. Chapter 8

General Robert Huyser reporting on the disintegration in Tehran, February 1979. Chapter 13

President Carter, deeply worried that the Camp David process has ground to a halt, at a brainstorming session in Brzezinski's office with Jody Powell and NSC staffer William Quandt, March 1979. Chapter 7

Jogging in Jerusalem, March 1979. The President later sent Brzezinski an inscribed copy of this picture, noting on it: "At least once we were in step."
Chapter 7

President Carter on the phone to Begin in Cairo, March 12, 1979, informing the Prime Minister of the breakthrough. A moment later the President covered the receiver and asked President Sadat if he would like to exchange greetings with Begin. Sadat recoiled in horror, waving both hands in emphatic negatives

Greeting the leading Soviet poet Andrei Voznesensky in April 1979. Chapter 9

A mood piece—the signing of the SALT agreement, Vienna, June 1979. Chapter 9

Departing for the Tokyo Summit, June 1979

Greeting Valentyn Moroz, one of the five dissidents whose release Brzezinski negotiated on the eve of the SALT agreement

Inspecting a Chinese-made AK-47 automatic rifle at the Khyber Pass, February 1980. This is the picture which was widely misrepresented by some as a bellicose gesture against the Soviets. Chapter 12

Meeting with Pope John Paul II in Rome, June 1980

Late afternoon briefing on likely outcome of the Presidential election, Election Day, 1980. Chapter 13

A quiet walk in the White House garden after the 1980 elections. Chapter 14

Part III
PROGRESS AND FRUSTRATION

The last phase of Carter's foreign policy involved the shaping of a new balance between the priorities of power and of principle. The higher recognition of the centrality of power in world affairs emerged gradually, through intense internal debates sparked largely by the impact of Soviet expansionism and the crisis with Iran. The result was a tougher policy vis-à-vis the Soviet Union, a major effort to shape a new regional security framework for the Middle East, and a sustained commitment, which paralleled during 1979 the deterioration in U.S.–Soviet relations, to forge a broader relationship with China. The third phase thus overlapped chronologically with the second, and some of the issues treated in the chapters which follow date back to early 1979.

The new balance in U.S. foreign policy was expressed first in the President's 1980 State of the Union Address, especially in regard to the security of the Persian Gulf, and elaborated most fully in the Presidential address delivered in Philadelphia in May 1980. There, the President reaffirmed our continuing commitment to moral objectives but placed special emphasis on the need to respond strongly to tangible threats to vital U.S. interests. However, the inevitable price of this accommodation to the unpleasant realities of world politics meant the quiet postponement, until, hopefully, a second Presidential term, of such ambitious goals as a comprehensive peace in the Middle East and SALT II ratification, the latter to be followed by an even more ambitious arms control treaty. Nonetheless, significant progress was achieved in U.S.–China relations, key decisions were made regarding U.S. defense strategy, and—most important—the momentum generated by the Camp David Accords was translated by March 1979 into the first peace treaty ever between Israel and an Arab state. All of that, however, was obscured by the daily frustrations produced by the detention of the fifty-two American hostages in Tehran, a detention which posed agonizing choices between moral and strategic priorities.

Part III: Progress and Frustration

Developing the Chinese Relationship	The Carter Doctrine	The Hostage Crisis
1979	**1979**	**1979**
January 29–31 Deng visits Washington	February 14 U.S. Ambassador to Afghanistan Adolph Dubs killed in Kabul	October 23 Shah enters U.S. for medical treatment
February 18 Chinese invasion of Vietnam	Spring–Summer mid-1979 Soviets step up involvement in Afghanistan	November 4 U.S. Embassy in Tehran seized, hostages taken
Spring–Summer Internal debates between top U.S. officials on scope of U.S.–Chinese ties	Brzezinski begins receiving explicit signals from Polish leaders that the situation was deteriorating greatly	November 6 Prime Minister Bazargan resigns
August 25–September 1 Mondale trip to Beijing	August 2 Brzezinski warns U.S.S.R. on deeper involvement in Afghanistan	November 14 U.S. freezes Iranian accounts
Fall Expansion of economic ties; intimation of limited secret links	December 26–28 Soviets invade Afghanistan	November 28 Carter on TV: U.S. will seek peaceful solution
		December 4 UN Security Council unanimously passes resolution demanding hostages' release
		December U.S. seeks economic sanctions against Iran
		December 31 UN Security Council calls for release in seven days or sanctions
1980	**1980**	**1980**
January 19 Brown visit to Beijing	January 4 Carter's address to the nation on the Soviet invasion announcing anti-Soviet steps	January 1 UN Secretary-General Waldheim in Iran
May 27–29 Chinese Vice-Premier and Defense Minister Geng Biao visits Washington	January 7 Soviets veto UN Security Council resolution calling for withdrawal of all foreign troops from Afghanistan	January 13 Soviets veto UN sanctions
	January 23 State of the Union Message: the Carter Doctrine	January 25 Bani-Sadr elected President
	February 1–4 Brzezinski and Warren Christopher visit Pakistan and Saudi Arabia	February 23 UN Commission arrives in Iran
	February 20 Carter urges U.S. withdrawal from 1980 summer Olympic games in Moscow	April 7 U.S. breaks relations with Iran
	May PD-59 becomes public knowledge	April 17 U.S. declares sanctions against Iran
	Spring–Summer U.S. develops and implements plans for Persian Gulf security framework, including facilities access agreements with nations of the region	April 24 Rescue attempt
	June 22 Venice summit calls for complete Soviet pull-out from Afghanistan	April 28 Vance resigns
	October Polish crisis and U.S. contingency planning	Summer–Winter Negotiations ongoing
	December 7 Carter warns Soviets against military intervention in Poland	September 22 Iraq invades Iran
		1981
		January 20 Hostages released
		January 21 Carter meets hostages in Wiesbaden, Germany

11

Toward a Strategic Relationship

> . . . we have found that we share many common perspectives. While we pursue independent foreign policies, our separate actions in many places can contribute to similar goals. These goals are a world of security and peace, a world of both diversity and stability, a world of independent nations free of outside domination.
>
> —President Jimmy Carter, remarks after signing of agreement between the United States and the People's Republic of China, January 31, 1979

The visit of Deng Xiaoping to Washington at the end of January 1979 was a clear signal that the U.S.–Chinese relationship was rapidly moving beyond just diplomatic normalization. Although American–Soviet negotiations on SALT were moving forward, the cumulative effect of the relentless Soviet strategic buildup, of Soviet indifference to our expressions of concern over Soviet–Cuban activity in Ethiopia and South Yemen and ever growing Soviet involvement in Vietnam and Afghanistan, had transformed Deng's trip from what initially was conceived of as a formal diplomatic act into a summit meeting of global geopolitical significance.

Deng's visit to Washington, and the drama associated with it, was a political triumph for Jimmy Carter. Coming, as it did, in midst of the growing Iranian crisis, of continued delays (as well as uncertainties) over SALT, and of frustrating obstacles to the implementation of our Camp David Accords, it provided the President with a timely and major foreign policy success.

The very fact of Deng's visit, the extraordinary interest it evoked among the mass media and the public, and the international attention focused on it, all brought to a head the question of how far the United States should go in developing the new relationship with China. Should it be confined to the diplomatic realm alone, thereby undoing the bitter legacies of the preceding thirty years, or should it be transformed into something with greater strategic significance?

Secretary of State Vance favored a narrow definition of the relationship. His clear preference was for confining it primarily to the diplomatic sphere, to be accompanied by a gradual but careful expansion of the economic relationship. Cy was strongly opposed to any links in the military-strategic area, not only by the United States but also by our allies. He felt that any arms sales to China would be "provocative" to the Soviets and was concerned when, on the eve of the official initiation of diplomatic relations (which took place on January 1, 1979), the President received a blistering message from Brezhnev, expressing worry over any possible U.S. arms sales to China. (When the Soviet chargé delivered the message to me at my office in the White House, I asked him when we might expect the Soviets to be more responsive to our previously expressed concerns regarding their activities in Africa, the Persian Gulf, and Cuba. Alas, he did not have much of a response.) Vance and his associates also favored balancing the evolving U.S.–Chinese relationship with some accommodation with Vietnam, an initiative which doubtless would have troubled the Chinese, who at this stage were reacting to the growing Soviet–Vietnamese military ties with a pathological intensity very reminiscent of early American reactions to Soviet–Cuban military links.

Vance's view was opposed largely by Brown and me. My view was that it would be a mistake to confine the new relationship to a narrow accommodation, for two reasons: (1) a narrow relationship would give greater salience to continuing disagreements over such matters as Taiwan (especially the arms sales issue), and this could eventually poison the new relationship; (2) there was a genuine strategic opportunity in the relationship to offset the Soviet military buildup and to prompt the Soviet Union eventually into a greater recognition of its stake in a reasonable accommodation with the United States.

I therefore favored a deliberate policy of steadily but significantly expanding the relationship. That expansion should take place first in the economic realm, so that both countries would have a major stake in tangible benefits, with China being treated quite explicitly on a more favored basis than the Soviet Union. At the same time, but more cautiously, we should gradually expand the security relationship, so that China would become less vulnerable to Soviet military threats, and so that the Soviets would become concerned that the U.S.–Chinese military relationship not become a counterpart to our NATO ties. Most important, I felt that the normalization of U.S.–Chinese relations gave us an opportunity to build a long-term, lasting relationship with one of the potentially most important global powers, and that this ought to be pursued for its own sake, even if at some point the U.S.–Soviet relationship were to improve.

On December 28, I forwarded the Brezhnev message to the President with an accompanying memo to the effect that the Soviets clearly wished us to help them ostracize China. I knew that Vance was going up to Camp David to spend some time with the President, and I was fearful that we might give the Soviets excessive assurances. As it turned out, the response that was sent to Brezhnev some two weeks later was properly noncommittal about U.S. intentions, while making the point that every country had the right to sell defensive weapons to China and that China had the right to buy them.

On the eve of Deng's arrival, I also evened the score with the President regarding the trick he had played on me immediately after normalization (see p. 233). In briefing the President on Deng's requirements, I noted that we were specifically requested to maintain a temperature of 71 degrees Fahrenheit in Deng's bedroom in Blair House, and I told the President that, in keeping with his earlier injunction that all federal buildings were not to have their thermostats set above 66 degrees, I had informed the Chinese that the President said this was impossible and that Deng's bedroom would be kept at the cool temperature of 66 degrees. Evidently alarmed, Carter responded with genuine concern, "You must be kidding." I then reminded him of his telephone message to me of a few weeks earlier and reassured him that Deng's reception would be suitably "warm."

The Visit to Washington

Deng's visit began on a highly personal note. Shortly after his arrival on Sunday, January 28, on his first visit ever to America, Deng, his wife, and key members of his party motored out from Blair House to my home in McLean, Virginia, for a private supper. We had made that date provisionally when Deng entertained me at a banquet in Beijing and told me of his hope someday to visit America. I was delighted to be able to welcome him with a personal dinner, to which I also invited Mike Oksenberg of my staff, as well as Cy Vance, Leonard Woodcock, and Richard Holbrooke. The evening was a thoroughly informal affair (my children waited on table), with an American menu, though reinforced with some very good Soviet vodka, given me earlier by Dobrynin. Deng was greatly amused when I told him that he was being toasted with Brezhnev's favorite drink.

The evening started, however, with a near disaster. Literally as Deng's party was pulling into our driveway and I was going out to greet him, the main fireplace in our living room backed up, and the house slowly filled with black smoke. While I was trying nonchalantly to welcome Deng, exchanging two-handed handshakes with him and his colleagues, my wife, Muska, and Mike Oksenberg were frantically rushing around, placing electric fans near the windows to eject the smoke and sealing off the living room from the rest of the house. Despite inevitable fatigue, Deng and his wife displayed excellent humor throughout the evening, and Deng proved himself a master at quick repartee. At one point, making small talk, I told him that President Carter had encountered political difficulties at home with the China lobby over normalization, and I asked him facetiously whether he had similar difficulties in China. In a flash, Deng responded: "Yes, I did; there was some opposition in the province of Taiwan!"

The next morning I briefed the President on the more substantive conversations which also took place during the dinner. I informed the President that Deng told Vance and me that China approved of our decision to support the Shah in Iran, that in the Chinese view the United States should be more active in strengthening Pakistan, and—somewhat ominously—that Deng wished a private meeting with the President on Vietnam. I sensed from the tone in which Deng asked for this that we would be hearing something significant, especially given mounting indications that the Chinese would not sit by idly as the Vietnamese continued their military occupation of Cambodia. I took advantage of the briefing to suggest to the President that he remove from the proposed drafts of his toast and planned press comments the various assurances that the new American–Chinese relationship was not directed against anyone else. I felt that this gave his remarks an excessively apologetic tone and the President agreed.

On Monday morning, January 29, Deng made his first appearance at the White House. The atmosphere was charged with electricity, and I could not recall a comparable sense of excitement in the White House. After an effusive exchange of greetings, the two sides spent much of the day in direct talks. The discussions were very frank and focused largely on world issues, in a manner more characteristic of friends or even allies than of countries which four weeks earlier had no formal diplomatic relations with each other. Deng minced no words, and after a vigorous denunciation of Soviet activities in the Middle East and southern Asia, he urged joint American–Chinese cooperation against the Soviets, though carefully adding that he was not proposing at this stage a formal alliance. Nonetheless, the import of his remarks in the private meetings, and even more so in his public statements, was clear and pointed: the United States and China had a common enemy and therefore should collaborate closely.

The President, quite understandably, was somewhat more cautious, though his analysis of world affairs did not diverge sharply from that of Deng. He, too, stressed Soviet assertiveness, agreed that close consultations between our two countries were necessary to stem Soviet expansionism, but carefully avoided any reference to Deng's overture. I was worried that Deng might feel somewhat rebuffed, especially since I knew that there would be opposition toward the end of his visit to any joint communiqué, and so I passed to the President in the course of one of our meetings a note saying, "At the end, it might be useful to pick up Deng's words 'not a formal alliance' to recapitulate where we can cooperate and consult: (1) Africa—Zambia, Somalia; (2) Pakistan—

also dialogue with India; (3) Middle East—Camp David (China–Israeli relations?); (4) Non-Aligned Movement; (5) Korea. It would be a useful summary and a positive cap on the session." The President did just that in a very effective manner, and thus at the end of our formal discussions with Deng I felt greatly encouraged that the basis for enhancing our relationship had been laid.

In addition to these formal and rather sober exchanges, there were a few light moments. At one stage, when Carter registered his concern for human rights, requesting Deng to be flexible on emigration from China, Deng leaned forward toward Carter and said, "Fine. We'll let them go. Are you prepared to accept ten million?"

The formal talks were complemented by a gala reception at the Kennedy Center and probably the most elegant dinner given at any time during Carter's four years in the White House. The high point of the televised festivity at the Kennedy Center was the joint appearance on the stage of the American and Chinese leaders. Both events were brilliantly orchestrated by Anne Wexler, who used all her talents in the development of a suitable program and audience. Deng and his associates still recalled the evening with warm gratitude almost three years later when I visited them in Beijing.

One of the issues which arose prior to the State Dinner was whether former President Nixon should be invited. The President agreed that the proper thing to do would be to invite him and instructed me to do so. But as I was concluding my conversation with Nixon, Mondale came into my office saying that he objected and wished to talk to the President about it. It was too late. Nixon was quite gracious and asked me whether his appearance would cause embarrassment, but I assured him that President Carter appreciated his role in initiating a new U.S.–Chinese relationship and felt the invitation was appropriate. During dinner, Nixon sat with me, and I was quite struck by how warmly he was greeted by the White House service staff. At the conclusion of the dinner, the former President passed around the menu, which was in both English and Chinese, asking all those sitting at the table to autograph it for his wife, Pat.

Before Deng left Washington, I had to negotiate both with the Chinese and with Cy Vance the proposed joint press statement. The Chinese, as I had expected, wanted to insert in the communiqué a reference to the threat of "hegemony"—their code word for the Soviet Union. Cy was adamantly against using that term, viewing it as a concession to the Chinese and a provocation to the Soviets. He was unmoved by my argument that we had previously used that word in American–Chinese statements. Accordingly, I proposed to Cy a compromise formula; namely, that we incorporate in the communiqué a reference to "hegemony or domination over others," the latter words being our preferred wording. I was confident that the Chinese would accept that, since the formula incorporated their preference and that was all that counted to them. Much to my surprise, Cy accepted it as well, and as a result the communiqué came out rather strongly on the central strategic issue.

The next day, however, the State Department came up with a new wrinkle. At the Presidential foreign affairs breakfast held on Friday, February 2, Cy started the breakfast

> by reading the text of a proposed statement which would be issued on the termination of Deng's visit. It will stress that an improvement in our relationship with China can contribute importantly to a stable structure of peace, but then it goes on immediately to say that equal emphasis is to be given to the need for improved relations with the Soviet Union. It stresses the need for such Soviet–U.S. cooperation and then reiterates the importance of SALT and expresses confidence that when the President meets with Brezhnev it will help to build a foundation for more constructive bilateral relations. When Cy handed it to the President, the President even before reading it muttered, "Is it another apology?" Cy was quite taken aback and put off. The President started editing it to cut out the more apologetic parts, but I spoke up, and I must say rather strongly, to the effect that we are already seen as weak and zigzagging and this statement will simply contribute to that impression. We issued only yesterday a joint communiqué with the Chinese and we deliberately accepted use of the words "hegemony or domination," and now we are backing off. Cy was rather angry, but the President, after thinking about it, and with Brown and Mondale silent and clearly not supporting Cy, finally and very firmly stated he did not wish such a statement issued. . . . I was amazed that Cy would even go to the President with such a statement. I don't think it helped to further the President's confidence in his tough-mindedness. . . . I was absolutely incredulous when it was brought up, and I was really relieved by the President's tough-minded decision.

The Vietnamese Lesson

Deng's visit was clearly a major success both for the Chinese leader and for his host. However, before departing the Chinese leader dropped a small bombshell at our feet. As I have noted earlier, Deng had requested a private meeting with the President, and it was held on Tuesday at 5 p.m. and lasted about an hour. On our side, the Vice President, Vance, and I also attended, and Deng was accompanied by a Vice-Premier, the

Foreign Minister, and the Deputy Foreign Minister. The subject, as I expected, was Vietnam.

We knew from previous conversations with the Chinese that they were gravely concerned over the Vietnamese occupation of Cambodia, seeing it as a Soviet-sponsored aggression designed to strengthen Vietnam as a base for Soviet operations in Southeast Asia. In various conversations with top U.S. officials, the Chinese leaders stressed that this represented a strategic threat to China's security, as well as a longer-range threat to the stability of Southeast Asia. The Cambodian regime that the Vietnamese displaced, that of the murderous Pol Pot, had been closely allied to China, and the Chinese were determined to retaliate against the Vietnamese.

When we sat down together in the Oval Office, I had a general sense of what was coming, and so did the other members of the American side. Nonetheless, there is a difference between anticipating a situation and actually experiencing it. There was something grave and very special in the calm, determined, and firm way in which Deng Xiaoping presented the Chinese case. China, he said, had concluded that it must disrupt Soviet strategic calculations and that "we consider it necessary to put a restraint on the wild ambitions of the Vietnamese and to give them an appropriate limited lesson."

Without detailing at this stage what the lesson specifically would entail, he added that the lesson would be limited in scope and duration. He then calmly diagnosed for us various possible Soviet responses, indicating how China would counter them. He included among the options "the worst possibility," adding that even in such a case China would hold out. All he asked for was "moral support" in the international field from the United States.

Though we had had some preliminary discussions earlier, I wondered how the President would react. Prior to Deng's arrival, I had mentioned to the President the growing Chinese concern over Cambodia and how important it was for us not to convey to the Chinese any excessive U.S. alarm over possible Chinese actions. I was worried that the President might be persuaded by Vance to put maximum pressure on the Chinese not to use force, since this would simply convince the Chinese that the United States was a "paper tiger." Accordingly, I was quite relieved when the President responded in a matter-of-fact fashion, simply pointing out that this was a serious issue which he would like to discuss with his advisers before giving his reaction. He did register the view that the Chinese action could be highly destabilizing and that restraint was desirable in such a difficult situation.

Deng responded by saying that if the Vietnamese were not restrained, they would expand their activities. China would undertake a limited action and then withdraw its troops quickly. Citing the Chinese–Indian clash of 1962 as an example, Deng insisted that the Vietnamese must

be similarly punished. He concluded by saying that he did not expect
United States endorsement, and indeed appreciated that sometimes one
had to do things one would prefer not to do. It was obvious that the
Chinese had weighed all the alternatives and decided to undertake the
action, even if it involved a confrontation with the Soviet Union. I must
admit that I was impressed with the deliberate and resolute tone of
Deng's presentation.

The next day the President met with us to discuss how best to respond.
We agreed that he should meet with Deng alone and urge him in
restrained terms to reconsider. In addition to international repercussions,
we were concerned that military action by China could undermine U.S.
domestic support for normalization. The President himself drafted by
hand a letter to Deng, moderate in tone and sober in content, stressing
the importance of restraint and summarizing the likely adverse international consequences. I felt that this was the right approach, for we could
not collude formally with the Chinese in sponsoring what was tantamount
to overt military aggression. At the same time, the letter did not lock
the United States into a position which could generate later pressures
to condemn China in the UN.

When the President met alone with Deng, the Chinese leader expressed
his appreciation for the President's comments, but reiterated his view
that "China must still teach Vietnam a lesson." Otherwise, he argued, the
Soviets might use Vietnam the way they had used Cuba, adding
prophetically that later on Afghanistan would suffer the same fate. Deng
reasserted his confidence that China had the necessary strength to carry
the operation through and again assured us that it would be short,
lasting only ten to twenty days. He expected divided international reactions but felt that in the longer run world opinion would gravitate in
China's favor. Deng concluded by saying, not disingenuously, that it
was good to have a friend with whom these things could be discussed so
frankly. The President said that he wanted Deng to understand that our
position was not based on fear of the Soviet Union; rather, we felt that
it was better to isolate the Soviet Union and Vietnam internationally
than to engage in actions which could gain them greater worldwide
support.

I held separate meetings with Chinese Foreign Minister Huang, an
engaging though extremely assertive and somewhat polemical diplomat,
and I shared with him my concern that the Chinese might be forced to
withdraw by a Soviet nuclear threat or that their operation might become more protracted than they had planned. Although Huang was
silent and apparently not very much alarmed, I hoped that my warning
would encourage the Chinese to concentrate on a swift and decisive
move and not undertake a prolonged engagement. As a particular
gesture of friendship, I went out to the helipad near the Washington
Monument to bid goodbye to Deng personally. I wanted to underline

Presidential support,* and Deng gave me the impression of being quite pleased. We had the traditional two-handed handshake, and Deng urged me to visit China again.

The Chinese did not give us a precise date for the forthcoming "educational experience" that they were planning for Vietnam. Within days of Deng's departure, I outlined my views on how the United States should react. I wanted to avoid a situation in which we would be pressured, both by world opinion and by the State Department, to condemn the Chinese as aggressors. Accordingly, I developed a proposal that the United States should criticize the Chinese for their military action but should couple that criticism with a parallel condemnation of the Vietnamese for their occupation of Cambodia, and demand that both China and Vietnam pull out their forces. I knew that such a proposal would be totally unacceptable to the Vietnamese and to the Soviets, and hence would provide a partial diplomatic umbrella for the Chinese action without associating the United States with it, thereby permitting the United States to adopt publicly a somewhat critical position.

As is usually the case with contingency planning, this proposal did not provoke much controversy as long as it was still in the hypothetical stage. Thus, at least in a formal sense, an agreed position emerged, in anticipation of the Chinese action. An indication that it was imminent came to us in the unlikely setting of the banquet for President López Portillo given by President Carter during his visit to Mexico City. In the course of the banquet, held on Thursday, February 15, I was called out of the room to receive an urgent message from Washington. The Chinese Ambassador wished an appointment with either Secretary Vance or me to convey an important message. I instructed my NSC China aide, Michel Oksenberg, to accept it, but the Chinese responded by saying that their instructions were to deliver it precisely at 9 a.m. Friday morning. The combination of urgency and a fixed time was very suggestive, and I went back to the banquet and whispered into the President's ear my conclusion that the Chinese military action was about to be undertaken.

Since both Vance and I were away, the Chinese had no choice but to deliver their message to Oksenberg, who received it in my name on the President's behalf. Friday morning, while driving from the U.S. Ambassador's residence to a breakfast with President López Portillo, I phoned Washington from the President's car and was briefed on the Chinese message. The Chinese were informing us that they had considered carefully our objections, but in view of the deterioration of the

---

* Subsequently Carter told me that he found Deng extremely likable and impressive; that his feelings toward him were like those he had toward Sadat—in Carter's lexicon the highest praise indeed.

situation on the frontier with Vietnam, they were now undertaking the necessary "self-defense measures" which they had previously discussed with us. After briefing the President and Vance, I called Washington back and spoke to the Vice President. On the President's instructions, I told him to hold an immediate meeting of the SCC, with principals only, to review the situation and to report back later in the morning.

Later in the day, I received the proposed text of the message to the Chinese, which we had earlier developed and which I now reviewed again with the President and Vance. There was no disagreement among us: we should register our disapproval but not do so in panicky terms and certainly not in a manner which would in effect put us on the side of the Soviets, who most certainly would be condemning the Chinese once the action had started.

Immediately upon returning to Washington, the President convened a meeting of the NSC. He was more formal than usual and began the meeting by saying: "This is a meeting of the National Security Council. Will the National Security Adviser please proceed." We reviewed at length what attitude we should adopt in the event the Soviet Union should forcefully react to the hostilities. Everyone concurred with the view that our demand for the withdrawal of Chinese forces from Vietnam should remain coupled with the demand for a Vietnamese withdrawal from Cambodia. It was further agreed to send a message to the Soviets urging them not to take actions which could exacerbate the situation, particularly through military deployments or other forms of military action. I urged that we include in the message a phrase to the effect that the United States was prepared to exercise similar restraint. Some in the room felt that this sounded excessively concessionary, but I argued that it was important to give the Soviets some sense of reciprocity. (Privately, I felt that the phrase implied also a willingness to respond militarily if the Soviets acted.) The addition was finally approved, and the message was sent to the Soviets immediately thereafter. Somewhat to my surprise, Cy and others did not object to a passage in the message to Brezhnev which seemed to hint at some connection between SALT and the need for restraint on the part of the Soviets.

I spent Sunday, February 18, in my office, for the hostilities had now broken out and additional meetings needed to be held. Late that afternoon I phoned former Presidents Ford and Nixon to brief them. Nixon emphasized the need not to take any action which would give the Soviets a green light against the Chinese. To solicit his advice, I read to him our message to the Soviets, and he immediately spotted the subtle allusion to SALT and commented very favorably on this, calling it "linkage." I doubt that this was the intention of everyone in the NSC meeting when the message was approved. I should note that, to add to the prevailing atmosphere of crisis, the U.S. Embassy in Iran was seized that day by violent demonstrators, while a day later the U.S. Ambassador in Afghanistan was killed by terrorists, a tragic event which involved either Soviet ineptitude or collusion.

As the Chinese action against Vietnam gathered momentum, and as it became the subject of greater international concern, the State Department began to shift its position. At a meeting of the SCC, the proposal was made that the forthcoming trip to China by Michael Blumenthal, the Secretary of the Treasury, be canceled as an expression of our disapproval. I was told that Marshall Shulman and Peter Tarnoff, Vance's assistant, had told the Secretary that such an action was appropriate because earlier we had canceled Cabinet-level trips to the Soviet Union because of Soviet misconduct. On the same day we also received a strongly worded message from Brezhnev, which, like our earlier one, came over the hot line. It arrived as the President and Vance were honoring Ambassador Adolph Dubs on the return of the body to Washington from Afghanistan; the moment the funeral cortege had taken off, the President, Vance, and I went into the Presidential helicopter to consult on the message. I translated it verbatim from the original Russian while the three of us sat there shivering in the unbelievably cold temperature which had struck Washington. We were absolutely frozen stiff.

I was very impressed by the President's reaction, which seemed to match the temperature. He was not at all perturbed by the message, and told us to stay on the course we had previously determined. In effect, a slight tilt in favor of the Chinese. However, among his advisers, cleavages soon became sharper. On Monday, February 19, at the SCC meeting the issue of Blumenthal's trip again came up. However, anticipating this, I suggested that we first agree on the general principle that the crisis between China and Vietnam should not be permitted to affect our respective bilateral relations with either the Soviet Union or China. This formula was unanimously approved, and thus when the issue of Blumenthal's trip to China came up, I was in a position to argue that its cancellation would be inconsistent with the broad approach just approved, which was not to let our bilateral relations with either major power be affected. Though Vance favored cancellation, I was pleasantly surprised by Holbrooke's guts in standing up and supporting my view that Blumenthal should proceed as planned. I drew the group's attention also to a cable from Prime Minister Callaghan, which, among other things, indicated that the British Minister of Industries was leaving the same day for China and that Callaghan had decided not to cancel that trip because it would not have been in Britain's best interest. On the written report of the SCC meeting, which I submitted later in the day to the President, the President scribbled in the margin: "Blumenthal should go."

Curiously, during his Chinese visit, Blumenthal made a number of public statements rather more strongly condemnatory of the Chinese than our formal position, as announced in Washington and as stated in the UN debates. I had no idea whether Blumenthal was doing this on his own or whether he had been encouraged to do so by some instructions (from State?) from Washington. In any case, after checking with the President, I sent him a strongly worded cable to the effect that he should concentrate his public comments entirely on trade matters. As a precaution, I told Cy that I was sending this cable to Blumenthal, and the Secretary did not object.

In Washington, we continued our deliberations while closely monitoring Soviet reactions. The President's advisers agreed that we should warn the Soviets that any organized Soviet military presence, particularly naval presence, in Vietnam (notably in Cam Ranh Bay), would force us to reevaluate our security position in the Far East. The implication of this message was, of course, that a U.S.–Chinese relationship of some sort would develop as a consequence of such Soviet involvement. Again, this message represented an implicit step toward a wider American–Chinese relationship.

Throughout this crisis, I felt that the Chinese action in some respects might prove beneficial to us. For one thing, it revealed some limits to Soviet power by demonstrating that an ally of the Soviet Union could be molested with relative impunity. This was a lesson bound not to be lost on a number of observers, notably those potentially threatened by the Soviet Union. I also felt that a steadfast U.S. position would convince the Chinese that we were not a "paper tiger" and that the relationship with us had certain longer-range and reciprocal security benefits.

As they had told us from the beginning, the Chinese after some twenty days terminated their operation and withdrew their forces. The Soviet reaction throughout was confined to threats and bluster. From a military point of view, the Chinese operation was not as efficient or as effective as apparently the Chinese had anticipated. The Vietnamese proved more resilient, while Chinese command and control, as well as logistics, were more cumbersome than expected in conditions of modern warfare—but the political point was effectively made. The Vietnamese were forced to redeploy some of their forces from Cambodia, the conflict imposed very major costs on them, produced a great deal of devastation, and, above all, showed the limits of their reliance on the Soviets. Most importantly, thanks to Carter's steadfastness, the new American–Chinese relationship had successfully weathered its baptism of fire.

Not "Evenhanded" but "Balanced"

Had Carter wavered, it is doubtful that the U.S.–Chinese relationship would have blossomed. The Chinese learned in the course of the three critical weeks that they now had a reliable friend: they could confide in us, we could keep a secret, and our public reaction—formally critical but substantively helpful—was firm and consistent. We learned that the Chinese trusted us, that they were not easily intimidated, and that their determination could be strategically helpful.

But the question of how far to go in the relationship, and how to define it, was still to be resolved on the level of practical policy. As is often the case, labels are not only meant to serve as definitions but can also be screens for other objectives. This was certainly so in our internal deliberations. Vance and his associates argued that we should pursue an "evenhanded" policy toward both the U.S.S.R. and the P.R.C., carefully moving in tandem, granting trade privileges to both, especially the most-favored-nation privilege, but not engage in a military relationship with either. Clearly, the priority of good relations with the Soviets was uppermost here. Brown and I ostensibly agreed that we should be "evenhanded," and we did not try to argue explicitly for a policy of favoring China. Instead, we simply made the case that since China was so much weaker than the Soviet Union—posing no immediate military threat to us—and since it was helpful to us in various parts of the globe, greater consideration for China was necessary. Otherwise a "mechanically evenhanded" treatment would in effect mean favoritism for the stronger Soviet Union. The relationship with China should be a "balanced" one, taking not only Soviet concerns into account but also the significant disparities between the Soviet Union and China. Clearly, the need for a strategic response to the Soviets was a major concern here.

This somewhat esoteric debate provided the intellectual framework for concrete policy decisions that had to be made in the aftermath of normalization. The early weeks of 1979 were especially frenzied. Normalization had come with such suddenness, and the circle of people involved had been kept so tight, that adequate preparations for the various issues cascading upon the bureaucracy could not have been undertaken earlier. The State Department handled the severance of diplomatic relations with Taiwan, as well as the preparation of the Taiwan omnibus legislation. Perhaps some of our subsequent problems, such as the ambiguities and disagreements with China over the Taiwan Relations Act, can be attributed to the lack of planning, but it must be remembered that under very trying circumstances the State Department did extremely well. Roger Sullivan, Deputy Assistant Secretary of State, who later joined the NSC, was especially effective in dealing with the problems which appeared so suddenly and in such abundance.

The White House limited itself to making certain that the normalization agreement was carried out precisely. On the basis of the Taiwan Relations Act, the American Institute on Taiwan was established for dealing with "the people of Taiwan." At the same time, to make certain that the ball kept moving on the relationship with the P.R.C., I established a number of structures within the U.S. government through the NSC: the Committee on Science and Technology, the Committee on Economics, the Subcommittee on Culture, etc. There was good interagency coordination and a general sense of satisfaction with the progress made.

The debate between an "evenhanded" and a "balanced" approach was joined more directly on the larger issue of whether China should be granted most-favored-nation status (MFN) by itself or whether that should be done only in conjunction with the Soviet Union. That issue, in turn, was precipitated by the skillful trade negotiations which Blumenthal initiated in early March with the Chinese and which culminated in the signing of a very constructive U.S.–China trade agreement on July 7, 1979. Taking advantage of the protracted negotiations on this subject, with their inevitable ups and downs, Vance and Blumenthal toward the end of March came forth with the proposal that the time had come for the granting of MFN to both China and the Soviet Union. It is to be remembered that negotiations for SALT were now at a delicate stage, while the Soviets at the same time were rather actively agitating against America within turbulent Iran and also backing the Vietnamese military activities in Southeast Asia. Accordingly, I feared that the Senate would simply refuse to grant MFN to the Soviet Union but in so doing would also derail any effort for China. At a meeting held on March 31, Mondale—uneasy about a bruising fight with Senator Henry Jackson over the Soviet MFN—rather skillfully raised a number of questions regarding the kind of assurances we might be able to obtain from the Soviets regarding emigration and human rights, and that for the time being deferred any movement on the subject.

By April, some slack in the momentum of relations with China had developed: negotiations on trade were still unresolved, and there was growing Chinese anxiety over the arrangements that were being worked out with Congress regarding Taiwan. To complicate matters further, the State Department proposed in early April that former Senator Joseph Clark be sent to Vietnam to initiate talks with the Vietnamese, and I precipitated a Presidential query (which he scribbled on Cy Vance's evening notes) which had the effect of halting this initiative. Nonetheless, both Vance and Holbrooke remained committed to the idea of generating some movement on Vietnam, and the issue prompted a rather sharp discussion at the Presidential breakfast held on May 18. Cy forcefully made the case that our neglect of Vietnam was driving Vietnam into the hands of the Soviets, and became visibly angry when I responded by saying that the Soviets and the Vietnamese were promoting their own interests, which at the moment happened to be complementary. I argued that we should not rush to embrace the Vietnamese at a time when they were suppressing the Cambodians and our relationship with the Chinese was still quite unsettled. In late July, the State Department came back with a proposal for American–Vietnamese talks on the subject of Cambodia, but the President approved my recommendation that we first consult on this subject with the Chinese (with predictable results).

To counter what I feared might become a backward slide in American–Chinese relations at a very early and still highly delicate stage of that relationship, I repeatedly briefed the President in the course of April on the need for wider-ranging initiatives toward China, notably for flexibility regarding MFN. I also urged calls by our naval ships at Chinese ports, as a response to the growing Soviet military presence in Vietnam. Moreover, in some ways an even more important bureaucratic ploy was for Oksenberg and me to schedule a number of trips to China by various members of the Cabinet, thereby involving every key policy maker and every major bureaucracy in a constructive relationship with China. This created a wider constituency, and the list of those who sooner or later visited China in an official capacity eventually came to include Mondale, Blumenthal, Kreps, Strauss, Brown, and Schlesinger.

The high point of this stratagem of "trip diplomacy" was Vice President Mondale's trip. The Vice President was clearly eager to go, for such a visit would afford him good exposure. It was difficult for Vance to object, though Carter himself showed some hesitancy. Nonetheless, after some back-and-forth, in mid-May the visit was approved, though "I could tell that the President wasn't too pleased that he was planning to go in late September–early October to participate in the thirtieth anniversary of the Chinese Revolution. In general, I sense that the President is not too happy about Mondale going, and later today (on Wednesday) he finally approved a different schedule for late August–early September. It's much hotter and less pleasant to be in Peking then," I wrote in my journal on May 30.

The Vice President was very pleased by this decision, and I was glad that I could be helpful to him, in return for his earlier efforts on behalf of my trip to China in 1978. We had consulted on several occasions on how best to convince the President that such a trip would be timely and that it would not conflict with any eventual trip by the President himself.

I assumed throughout that the Chinese were sensitive to some of these bureaucratic conflicts, and indeed they not so subtly tried to exploit personal vanities. The Chinese Ambassador made a point of inviting Mondale to dinner and then of expressing great delight at his visit, and the Chinese made every effort also to cultivate me. A somewhat embarrassing example occurred in the course of Vice-Premier Kang Shien's visit to the White House in late May. I was given the task, together with Secretary Schlesinger, of greeting him in the Cabinet Room, and he went out of his way to praise President Carter and me for having achieved normalization. Then, making no effort to whisper, he turned to the translator and said in Chinese, "I suppose I should also mention the Secretary of State; what's his name?"

By midsummer, the cumulative effect of Soviet rigidity on a number of international issues, as well as of our own discussions, made the President more inclined to consider MFN status for China alone. Though he made no firm decision, on a couple of occasions in June and July he indicated that it was nearly time to act on this issue. At a Presidential breakfast on July 27, the President decided that we would move on MFN for China once SALT had advanced in the Senate. In effect, for the first time, the explicit decision to decouple China MFN from Soviet MFN was made, though still without a precise target date.

Moreover, as I had calculated, Mondale's trip became a catalyst for further movement. With the date for his journey approaching, Mondale became more and more concerned with making his visit a genuine "success." In bureaucratic terms, this meant shaping a cluster of initiatives which would be seen as significant and which could generate some headlines. The Vice President prepared himself meticulously, and David Aaron, my deputy, became deeply involved in putting together a package of proposals that would be both impressive and substantive. Aaron's closeness to Mondale was quite important in overcoming bureaucratic resistance. Mondale extracted a promise from Vance that we would propose MFN for China before the end of 1979, that China would be declared a friendly nation and thus freed from some restrictions applicable to Communist countries, and that special credit would be made available for Chinese economic development. These decisions were confirmed at the Presidential breakfast on August 3. Immediately after the breakfast, I called in the Chinese Ambassador to inform him of the promised movement of MFN, thereby sealing the matter. After a personal appeal to Vance from Mondale, Cy promised that China would be declared a friendly nation, adding, "I will hold my nose and do it for you."

As expected, Mondale's visit was a great success. He appeared on Chinese television, and a great deal of positive publicity was generated by the concrete announcement of expanded economic cooperation, notably the decision to grant most-favored-nation status (the agreement was completed in October). On his return, he made an enthusiastic report to the President, describing the visit as the high point of his

Vice Presidency, concluding with the words: "We unlinked China and the Soviet Union!"

In the course of the following year, momentum was maintained through the successful conclusion of consular, aviation, maritime, and textile negotiations, for which both State and Commerce deserve a great deal of credit. In keeping with these developments, by the latter part of 1979 the White House stopped using the word "evenhanded" to describe our relations with China and the Soviet Union and adopted the formula of a "balanced" approach.

Not a Balance but a Tilt

Mondale's trip to China had one more specific purpose. In late July 1979, when discussing with the Vice President his proposed agenda, I suggested to him that the Chinese would be most pleased by a visit by Harold Brown. The Vice President, eager to make his trip substantively significant, seized on this idea even though earlier he had been inclined to side with Vance against any expansion of U.S.–Chinese ties into the military realm. Brown, needless to say, was extremely eager to go. I felt that a visit by him was timely, and I was also eager to repay him for the help he gave me during the controversy preceding my own trip to China.

Here, too, the Soviets proved helpful. The new U.S.–Chinese relationship might well have been confined to good diplomatic relations and growing trade ties—in brief, a balanced relationship—if the Soviet Union had not been so determined to extract concessions from the United States on SALT, less inclined to use the Cuban military proxy, and quicker in exploiting the eagerness within some sectors of the Carter Administration to reach a broad accommodation. More restrained Soviet behavior would have left little room for those who favored a closer relationship with China on the grounds that that was in keeping with U.S. national interest.

The security relationship between China and the United States emerged very slowly and tentatively. Deng's solicitation of an informal alliance was very cautiously received, though since 1978 both Brown and I felt that some defense cooperation was desirable and that we should move step by step in that direction. We certainly felt that it would be unwise for us to wholly exclude security cooperation, since this would be tantamount to providing gratuitous insurance for the Soviet Union. During Deng's visit the President authorized me to initiate some special negotiations with the Chinese, and I conducted these myself until an informal agreement was reached by the end of the year. In addition, at the weekly Vance–Brown–Brzezinski luncheons the question of technology transfer to China was frequently raised and debated. Here, as in the case of economics, the question was where to draw the line: should we very carefully make certain that any technology transferred to China was not susceptible of military use, or should we take a somewhat less restrictive attitude, on the grounds that China was both weaker and more friendly to us than the Soviet Union? The issue was further complicated by Chinese efforts to obtain arms from some of our Western European allies. The allies, anxious not to provoke Soviet wrath, came to us for advice. Vance and the State Department were inclined to discourage such sales. Brown and I argued that our position should be that of "benign neutrality"—i.e., make it clear to the Western Europeans that the decision was up to them but that we did not object to such sales and we would certainly not permit them to be intimidated by the Soviets.

Our internal discussions on a possible security relationship started as early as 1978, but they gained in intensity in the course of 1979, after normalization and especially after Deng's visit. Growing Soviet involvement in Afghanistan, with the potential threat to the Persian Gulf, the consolidation of the Soviet presence in South Yemen, the mounting crisis in Iran and the very active Soviet public exploitation of it against the United States, all contributed to my feeling that it would be wise gradually to increase the pressure on the Soviet Union's eastern flank. Moreover, by the spring of 1979, we had more intelligence concerning increased Soviet use of Vietnamese naval and air facilities (constructed by the United States), thereby introducing a new dimension to the strategic equation. By late April, Brown and I had prevailed on Vance at one of our weekly lunches to tell the British that we had no objection to their selling weapons to China and that we would prefer them not to submit such a sale for approval to the inter-allied Coordinating Committee (COCOM), where it might become a matter of dispute. Earlier, in January, the President met with the leaders of Britain, Germany, and France for an informal discussion in Guadeloupe, and in the course of it the view was conveyed that we would not be unhappy with a more relaxed Western attitude regarding Chinese arms purchases.

By early May, approximately a month and a half prior to the conclusion of SALT but in the context of growing tensions in U.S.–Soviet relations, the President met with the Chinese Ambassador in a lengthy session. This was an important meeting. Earlier, I had submitted a memo to the President suggesting that a high-level signal of a positive American attitude regarding the gradual expansion of U.S.–Chinese security links was timely, and the President, taking into account the overall global situation, agreed. In the meeting he made some proposals to the Chinese side, and thus an important threshold was crossed. The next day, on May 4, the President debriefed Harold Brown on his discussions with the Chinese, adding significantly, "It is not bad for the Soviets to think that there is an embryonic U.S.–Chinese military relationship."

That relationship proceeded to develop more rapidly thereafter, but there were obstacles. We proposed to the Chinese, as a counter to the Soviet naval presence in Danang, that U.S. warships visit Chinese ports, and in early June, Ambassador Chai came to tell me that this was untimely because his government was disturbed by some aspects of our legislation on Taiwan. I was somewhat irritated, and I asked Chai who in his view benefited from the Chinese response on the proposed naval visits? I reminded him of various earlier Chinese digs to the effect that we were afraid to provoke the Soviets, and I hinted that perhaps now the shoe was on the other foot. My good friend, with whom I had worked so closely on behalf of normalization, was clearly embarrassed and came as close to agreeing with me as diplomatic constraints would permit.

But far more important to our efforts was the Presidential blessing for greater flexibility. On July 11, I sent a memorandum to both Vance and Brown stating: "The President sent a note from Camp David indicating agreement with the view that we owe it to ourselves as well as to the Soviets to indicate to the Soviets that we may have no choice but to counter their moves (Third World Cuban activities, the buildup of an arsenal in South Yemen, reinforcement of Cuban military potential in Central America). . . . The protocols of the Vienna meeting are not particularly encouraging, and it would be a mistake to let matters rest there." This memorandum, precipitated in part by the stonewalling response of the Soviets in Vienna to our emphasis on the need for greater moderation, was designed to force the issue. I also hoped to press the State Department to engage in a more serious discussion with the Soviets on what ought to be the appropriate code of detente. Shortly thereafter, Vance, Brown, and I agreed to give the Chinese some civil advanced imaging systems as well as some small jets with sophisticated navigational equipment of the type that we would under no circumstances sell to the Soviets. But even then, this decision was not made without a hard debate. Brown proposed the transfer of five items, Vance objected to all of them, and the outcome was a compromise.

In this context Brown's trip to China became an important catalyst as well as the new focal point of our internal debates. I had originally proposed it to the Vice President, who was enthusiastic and who in turn obtained the President's blessing. In early August, I hinted to the Chinese that we would suggest a trip by Brown during the Mondale visit, and I urged them to be prepared to give a quick positive response. However, by early September, Vance decided to oppose the visit by Brown on the grounds that it was "inopportune" and also that he had not been sufficiently forewarned that it was coming. I responded by saying, according to my notes, that "we have so informed the Chinese, and we would look rather silly reneging on this matter. After the meeting I checked and I discovered that the original memorandum from Mondale to the President on this subject, which I helped to draft and in fact somewhat inspire, was coordinated with Holbrooke, who was acting on Cy's behalf." Holbrooke was with Mondale in Beijing when Mondale made the proposal to the Chinese, and thus it was strange for the Secretary now to argue that he had not been informed, when his own Assistant Secretary of State had participated in the drafting of the proposal. Nonetheless, the issue was sharply debated in mid-September. I warned the President that unless the matter was quickly resolved, it could leak in the press and be presented as another indication of internal discord. Accordingly, on September 14, at the foreign affairs breakfast, the President simply stated, "In the next week or so we should announce Brown's trip to China." He then asked Brown when he would like to go, and Brown indicated that mid-October would be his preferred date. Vance again immediately objected, saying that it was important to keep a sense of balance in our relations with the Soviets and the Chinese and that such a visit would be a needless irritant.

It is to be remembered that these discussions were taking place in the midst of a tense and very difficult situation for all of us: the crisis involving the so-called Soviet brigade in Cuba. The debate over Brown's trip to China was thus inevitably linked to the question of how best to respond to the Cuban crisis, and that crisis was itself straining relations among key participants (see Chapter 9). Vance felt so strongly about this issue that on September 18 he submitted a long memorandum to the President "to give you my overall perception of where we stand and where we should be going in our relations with China." He acknowledged in that memorandum that normalization was an important achievement and that it had strategic value, but he expressed concern that we were now showing a "tilt" toward China, instead of a balance in our relations with China and the Soviet Union. Coming to the point directly, he argued that we should not "move into a military security relationship with China, for there is an element of finality in moving toward an agreement. Such a policy would suggest that we have given up hope of improving relations with the U.S.S.R. To create such an impression would not only increase U.S.–Soviet tension but could precipitate policy changes by our allies in Europe and Japan." After laying out his case with his usual clarity, Vance concluded by "in effect" conceding that Brown's trip would take place but pleading instead that it should be delayed until the following year, after Chairman Hua's still unscheduled visit to the United States.

In an accompanying memo, which I also forwarded to the President, Brown made the opposite case, stressing that consultations with the

Chinese would be timely, especially in view of current difficulties with the Soviet Union. Brown reminded the President that we had earlier invited Soviet Defense Minister Ustinov to visit the United States in exchange for a Brown visit to the Soviet Union, and that the Soviets had turned us down. In my covering note on the two memoranda, I recommended that the President approve Brown's trip, suggesting also that Cy be authorized to give a preview of this fact to the Soviets and to tell them that the substance of the trip would be influenced by Soviet behavior. On September 19, evidently determined not to let the issue get out of hand, the President pulled from his pocket a handwritten note addressed to Brown, Vance, and me, which he read aloud to me: "Acting on my instructions, the Vice President suggested to the Chinese that Harold might visit the P.R.C. this fall. Deng accepted immediately and Fritz accepted the resulting invitation. My suggestion is that Cy remind the Soviets of our long-standing offer of an exchange of Defense Minister visits with the U.S.S.R. and inform them that Harold will be accepting such an invitation from the Chinese. Fritz announced publicly in Peking that we would have no substantive military relationship with China. Proceed accordingly. J.C."

Once Brown's visit was approved, the next policy debate was over the substance of the trip. The date for it slipped in any case, because of the combined impact of the crisis with the Soviets, the growing difficulties in Iran, and the need to coordinate schedules with the Chinese. Accordingly, it took place in January 1980, immediately after the Soviet invasion of Afghanistan. That in itself gave it additional significance, though our internal discussions regarding its substance took place mostly in December, just prior to the Soviet invasion.

In mid-December, the President received major memoranda containing conflicting recommendations, from Vance and Brown. The opening salvo was fired by Vance on December 9, with the central point being that in Vance's view "the implied security aspect of our relationship with China (with its unspoken threat of greater development) has been an important factor in deterring Soviet adventurism. But developing it is less likely to produce moderation in Soviet behavior than strategic claustrophobia and irrationality. . . ." Conceding that he was no longer advocating "a policy of mechanistic evenhandedness," Vance argued that we should move very slowly and that we should not authorize further exports of technology for military end use or when such technology transfer might have destabilizing consequences.

In keeping with established procedures, this memo was shown to Brown, who responded on December 13 with a series of concrete suggestions designed to loosen up export controls and technology transfer in favor of China. While not advocating "at this time" military arms sales, he argued that we should not foreclose it, and that above all we should give tangible expression to our aim of achieving "a strong, secure and friendly China." In forwarding these two memoranda to the President, I particularly emphasized that in many specific instances Vance and Brown were in agreement, notably in the conviction that balance rather than evenhandedness should be our posture. I felt that stressing consensus rather than disagreement would make it easier to pursue a stable course.

On December 19, the President signed a memorandum to both Cy and Harold, which I had prepared, outlining certain common principles of our China policy. Most importantly, the President approved my proposal that before Harold's trip Cy should present an initiative liberalizing regulations regarding China. In addition, Brown was empowered to engage the Chinese in broadly gauged strategic consultations pointing toward some complementary approaches. Since a week later the Soviets invaded Afghanistan, the remaining disagreements between Vance and Brown were in effect resolved in Brown's favor. On January 18, 1980, reporting from Beijing, Brown was able to say that in the course of his trip "we have taken a significant step in our strategic relationship with the Chinese."

In the weeks that followed, in part as an element in our reaction to the Soviet invasion of Afghanistan, the State Department liberalized regulations for some thirty types of support equipment that could be licensed for export to China by the Office of Munitions Control, including air defense radar, radio, tropospheric communications equipment, transport helicopters, truck tractors, and electronic countermeasure devices. In April 1980, China was transferred by the Commerce Department from the Warsaw Pact country group "Y" category to a new country group "P" category, making China eligible for wider exports, particularly in such sensitive areas as transport aircraft, long-distance communications equipment, and military-type helicopters. This was followed in July 1980 by further liberalization of licensing criteria announced by the Commerce Department, which by then was working in close collaboration with me under the extremely effective and loyal leadership of Secretary Philip Klutznick. Finally, in September 1980, a high-level Pentagon delegation visited China, and approval was given for export licenses for some 400 items in the area of advanced technology in military support equipment.

In late May 1980, Vice-Premier Geng Biao, the head of the Chinese Military Commission, visited Washington, symbolizing the expanding security relationship. He was a guest of Harold Brown, and he called on me in the White House. I used the occasion to discuss in some depth and detail our respective reactions to the Soviet invasion of Afghanistan, and I stressed to him that in my view the Soviets were pursuing a two-pronged offensive strategy, one pointing through Afghanistan at the Persian Gulf and one through Cambodia at the Strait of Malacca. Geng Biao very much liked that analysis, and I was amused to hear him, as well as Deng Xiaoping, repeat it to me as the Chinese view of Soviet strategy when I visited Beijing in 1981. Mondale's and Brown's visits to China thus provided the key catalysts to a process of consolidation and expansion of the U.S.–Chinese relationship. What had started as an exercise in evenhandedness by 1980 became demonstrably a tilt, driven by stark strategic realities.

12

The Carter Doctrine

Let our position be absolutely clear: Any attempt by any outside force to gain control of the Persian Gulf region will be regarded as an assault on the vital interests of the United States of America and such an assault will be repelled by any means necessary, including military force.

—President Jimmy Carter,
State of the Union Address,
January 23, 1980

Christmas of 1979 was grim and full of foreboding. The lights of the national Christmas Tree remained unlit as a symbol of America's solidarity with the hostages in Tehran, captive already for more than seven weeks. Special Soviet radio transmitters targeted on Iran were broadcasting inflammatory anti-American material, while Soviet military involvement in Afghanistan was steadily expanding. Prior to the President's foreign affairs breakfast on December 21, I used the early-morning national security briefing to share with the President my view that the growing Soviet involvement in Afghanistan was pushing us toward a wider regional crisis. The President agreed, accepting my recommendation that Secretary Vance be immediately instructed to chair a formal Policy Review Committee meeting.

This move was designed to generate a broader and more energetic response to the deterioration in our position brought on by the collapse of the Shah's regime and the growing Soviet intrusion into the area. During the preceding months I monitored with mounting apprehension the intensifying Soviet military involvement in Afghanistan and I pressed for stronger U.S. reactions. It should be remembered this was the time during which SALT was negotiated and these successful efforts (followed by our intense campaign to obtain senatorial ratification for it) produced a natural reluctance, especially on the part of those most directly involved in these delicate activities, to concentrate on the more unpleasant aspects of the U.S.–Soviet relationship.

Nonetheless, toward the end of March 1979, Brown and I prevailed on Vance and Christopher, both of whom were less than enthusiastic, to register formally our concern over the Soviets' creeping intervention in Afghanistan. I also raised this matter repeatedly with the

President, most frequently at my morning national security briefing. My notes show, for example, that I brought this issue up several times in late March and early April, and that in early May 1979 I warned the President that the Soviets would be in a position, if they came to dominate Afghanistan, to promote a separate Baluchistan, which would give them access to the Indian Ocean while dismembering Pakistan and Iran. I also reminded the President of Russia's traditional push to the south, and briefed him specifically on Molotov's proposal to Hitler in late 1940 that the Nazis recognize the Soviet claim to preeminence in the region south of Batum and Baku. The President then instructed Vance to have the State Department brief all of Afghanistan's neighbors on the situation.

In the months that followed, the NSC continued to press for a more vigorous U.S. reaction and State continued to comply reluctantly. In April 1979, I pushed a decision through the SCC to be more sympathetic to those Afghans who were determined to preserve their country's independence. Mondale was especially helpful in this, giving a forceful pep talk, mercilessly squelching the rather timid opposition of David Newsom, who was representing the State Department. By midsummer we had received numerous intelligence reports of widespread resistance throughout Afghanistan to the Soviet-supported regime, but the Soviets rebuffed all our warnings that their growing intrusion would jeopardize the American–Soviet relationship. On the President's orders we began to publicize our concerns, in order to give greater credibility to our private admonitions.

On July 23, I warned the President that the Soviets would probably unseat Prime Minister Amin (who later in September seized complete control from his fellow Communist President Taraki), since Amin's Communist terror tactics were proving counterproductive. The President approved my recommendation that the State Department be instructed to publicize this analysis. (When I phoned Vance to give him the President's message, he rather abruptly told me that he knew what to say and did not need to be told. I simply repeated that I was conveying a Presidential instruction.) In addition, with the President's approval, I gave a public speech, which the New York *Times* reported (August 3) prominently on page 1 under the headline "U.S. Is Indirectly Pressing Russians to Halt Afghanistan Intervention." The *Times* paid particular attention to the passage which urged the Soviets to abstain "from efforts to impose alien doctrines on deeply religious and nationally conscious peoples."

By early September, the situation had become sufficiently grave for the President to ask me to prepare contingency options in the event of an overt Soviet military intervention in Afghanistan. I had my staff immediately develop such papers, and I also consulted with the Saudis and the Egyptians regarding the fighting in Afghanistan. On September

19, in the midst of the "Soviet brigade in Cuba" flap, I informed the President that a direct Soviet invasion of Afghanistan was becoming more probable and again recommended further public statements by the Administration. In my weekly report of September 13, I included a personal five-page essay, entitled "Acquiescence vs. Assertiveness," in which I outlined the reasons for the increasingly pervasive feeling in the United States and abroad that, in the U.S.–Soviet relationship, the Soviets were becoming more assertive and the United States more acquiescent. I was critical of the way the State Department had, through inaction or opposition, diluted some of the President's decisions designed to demonstrate American firmness, and recommended that in our public posture we stress that the defense buildup was being undertaken on its own merits, not just to buy the SALT treaty. I suggested that we be less hesitant in explicitly condemning Soviet–Cuban exploitation of instability in the Third World and that we ostracize Cuba and share intelligence more widely on Cuban activities. I further argued that we should consider the transfer of sensitive technology to China and the opening of a military dialogue with the Chinese, since we needed to convey to the Soviets that their use of the Cuban proxy would entail severe costs for them. I urged expanded broadcasts to the Moslems and Ukrainians in the U.S.S.R. and the initiation of broader talks with the Soviets on the general theme of the need for "reciprocal restraint."

The President agreed with my analysis, and a few days later responded to my memo of September 19 with a note addressed to both Vance and me, instructing that greater publicity be given to the growing Soviet involvement in southwestern Asia. The issue kept percolating throughout the fall, with the State Department still reluctant to press the matter. As late as mid-December, a senior State Department official, Under Secretary David Newsom, objected to a proposed press backgrounder on the Soviet intervention in Afghanistan, prepared by the NSC, on the grounds that this might be seen by the Soviets as U.S. meddling in Afghanistani affairs.

A week before the Soviet invasion, I again raised the matter with the President, outlining how in my view the United States should react. I argued that we should again register our concern with the Soviets so that there would be a clear-cut record of our position, publicize Soviet activities so that the Islamic world would be mobilized, and also continue to demonstrate our sympathy for the Afghan freedom fighters. On the morning of December 17, at an SCC meeting, I obtained approval for my approach, though again with considerable opposition from the State Department but with support from both Brown and Turner. I then went back to the President with a formal recommendation to that effect.

But events moved more rapidly. During the night of December 25,

Soviet forces invaded Afghanistan and occupied Kabul, and a new President was installed to replace the one murdered during the Soviet coup. Creeping intervention had become overt invasion and occupation. On the morning of December 26, instead of the proposed PRC meeting, I chaired a session of the SCC, convened in its crisis management mode. The issue of Afghanistan was added to the regular SCC Iran crisis agenda. I proposed at the meeting that we should immediately tell the Russians, through a Presidential message to Brezhnev, that SALT was now in jeopardy and that the scope of our relationship with the Chinese would be affected. Vance and Christopher objected strongly. Accordingly, after the meeting I phoned the President, who was at Camp David, and told him that in my judgment the Soviet action had initiated a regional crisis of strategic significance. I recommended that he return from Camp David to hold a formal NSC meeting on this matter.

The meeting was held in the Cabinet Room on Friday, December 28. The mood was grave, for we all knew that a major watershed had been reached in the American–Soviet relationship. To some, it meant the burial of hope for a wide-ranging American–Soviet accommodation, with SALT as its centerpiece; to the President, it was no doubt a political blow, though it also represented an opportunity for him to demonstrate his genuine toughness; to me, it was a vindication of my concern that the Soviets would be emboldened by our lack of response over Ethiopia. Still, I remained apprehensive regarding our ability to demonstrate credibly our resolve at this late juncture. Past disagreements were quickly buried, however, under the impact of the Soviet aggression, and there was general consensus that we needed to respond with a broad strategy. Our objective had to be to ostracize and condemn the Soviets and to reinforce regional confidence.

The President made it very clear at the meeting that he wanted a tough message sent to Brezhnev directly, and he even sharpened the proposed NSC draft (since the State Department did not submit one for the meeting). The message labeled the Soviet action as "a clear threat to the peace," and it added that "these actions could mark a fundamental and long-lasting turning point in our relations." We also decided at the meeting that Pakistan must be reassured, our earlier disagreements over nuclear nonproliferation notwithstanding. A preliminary decision was made to send Christopher to consult with President Zia of Pakistan, and plans were also made to further enhance our cooperation with Saudi Arabia and Egypt regarding Afghanistan.

Two days later we received a mendacious and arrogant rebuttal from Brezhnev, which so exercised the President that he wrote a number of polemical comments in the margins. When Brezhnev asserted that the Soviet presence was invited by Afghan leaders, Carter wrote in the margin, "The leaders who requested Soviet presence were assassinated."

He returned the message to me dotted with such ironic comments, and later in the day, in a meeting with a group of newspapermen, the President strongly emphasized that we were now facing in the Persian Gulf a wider strategic challenge which would require a similarly wide response. This was a crucial point, for I was concerned that the President might be prevailed upon—as he had been earlier in the Cuban case—to view the Afghan problem as an isolated issue.

I discussed that issue at some length with the President and showed him the text of a briefing that I had given the day before to a group of editors, in which the strategic dimensions of the new crisis were emphasized. In it, I had stressed that the issue was not what might have been Brezhnev's subjective motives in going into Afghanistan but the objective consequences of a Soviet military presence so much closer to the Persian Gulf. The President's approach served as the point of departure for a wider response which, in the course of the next several weeks, took three forms: (1) the adoption of sanctions directed at the Soviet Union; (2) the formulation of a doctrine linking the security of the region with that of the United States and a U.S. effort to shape a regional security framework; and (3) the acceleration of our strategic renewal, in terms of both doctrine and defense budget.

Post-Afghanistan Sanctions

The first sanctions designed to penalize the Soviets for their invasion, and thus to serve as a deterrent against further action, were adopted in a series of meetings held in a five-day period, starting with the NSC meeting of December 30. We had no illusions that sanctions in themselves would force the Soviets out, but we all felt that the Soviet Union had to pay some tangible price for its misconduct. Rhetoric alone would not suffice. Both the NSC and the State Department drew up a "menu" of possible responses, numbering in toto some forty punitive steps. In my cover memo, I suggested to the President that he adopt a combination of unilateral U.S. actions, some multilateral responses involving our allies, as well as regional initiatives designed to minimize the intimidating impact of the Soviet action. I also attached a brief memo outlining how President Johnson had reacted to the Soviet occupation of Czechoslovakia, since I felt that that established a minimum possible response on our part.

As it turned out, my concern that we might underreact was unwarranted. For reasons more explicable on the level of psychology than politics, those who previously were reluctant to react strongly to growing indications of a likely Soviet move against Afghanistan now urged actions stronger than those I proposed. As a result, in the sessions that were held between December 30 and January 3, my own role was mainly that of guiding the discussion, suggesting possible combinations of responses. I felt at the time, as I noted in my journal, that an adequate message to the Soviets would be conveyed by some limit on U.S. grain sales to the Soviet Union, some further transfer of advanced technology or even defensive arms to China, and a large aid package for Pakistan. This combination, I felt, would be both sufficiently punitive and strategically significant.

At the NSC meeting on December 30, to my surprise, Vance came out in favor of registration for the draft and for a deep cut in U.S. grain deliveries to the Soviet Union. He was immediately opposed by Mondale on the grain issue. The Vice President pointed out that this could be damaging in the forthcoming Iowa primary and, as a result, the President decided to defer his decision. In the meantime, at a subsequent NSC meeting on January 2, the assembled group, chaired by the President, agreed on some twenty-six specific reactions, severely limiting the scale of U.S.–Soviet contacts, Soviet fishing rights, exchanges, cooperative projects, and so forth.

However, sanctions on grain and the possibility of a closer cooperative relationship with China remained unresolved. The discussion continued for the next several days, and it was not until January 4 that the President made his key decision to couple a ban on the transfer of advanced technology to the Soviet Union with a grain embargo. There is no doubt that Vance's strong support for the grain embargo influenced the President and prompted him to dismiss Mondale's political concerns. The President was also influenced by the Agriculture Department's firm opinion that no other country could replace the United States as a major seller to the Soviet Union—a conclusion which within days was shaken by Argentina's announcement that it would partially replace the American grain shipments.

Another bone of contention involved my proposal that we use the Soviet invasion of a country in a region of strategic sensitivity to Asia as a justification for opening the doors to a U.S.–Chinese defense relationship. I was supported in this by Brown, who was about to embark on his China trip, as well as by Hedley Donovan. Vance, Christopher, and Cutler opposed us, with Vance arguing that such a step would set back American–Soviet relations for many years. The President concluded that under the present circumstances it would suffice for Brown to indicate to the Chinese that the United States would be willing to provide China with over-the-horizon radar and would give China more favored treatment in trade than the Soviet Union, but that "it would be a quantum leap to go to arms sales" at this time. It was better, he concluded, to leave that option open.

On Friday evening, January 4, the President announced the U.S. decisions. SALT was the principal casualty, and the President stated that our efforts to ratify the agreement would have to be postponed because there simply was no longer sufficient Senate support. I knew that this was personally and politically painful to him. At the morning briefing the day before, he had stood by the fireplace in the Oval Office and ruminated sadly about the Soviet move. Usually our briefings were quite businesslike, but this time we simply reflected on the significance of the events of the past two weeks. The President told me that he saw the Soviet move as a far-reaching challenge to which he had to respond in a firm and credible way. It was here that he mentioned for the first time his conclusion that SALT would have to be indefinitely postponed. I responded by saying that in my judgment the Soviet move was the most direct case of Soviet military aggression since 1945, and that we needed to mount a broader strategic response.

Knowing how deeply Carter felt about SALT, and sharing with him a genuine sense of regret about the way things had developed, I commented that I understood his desire to go down in history as a President Wilson but added that "before you are a President Wilson you have to be for a few years a President Truman." By that I meant that the President first had to convince the American public and the world of his toughness, and only then, during his second term, could he adopt a more Wilsonian approach. Shortly thereafter I repeated that formula, "first be like President Truman and then be like President Wilson," to Rosalynn, who I felt both understood me well and was politically sympathetic to that view.

In my own journal, I jotted down my private view: "Had we been tougher sooner, had we drawn the line more clearly, had we engaged in the kind of consultations that I had so many times advocated, maybe the Soviets would not have engaged in this act of miscalculation. As it is, American–Soviet relations will have been set back for a long time to come. What was done had to be done, but it would have been better if the Soviets had been deterred first through a better understanding of our determination."

In his January 4 speech, the President announced the following additional steps: The United States would impose a grain embargo on any further sales to the Soviet Union above the eight-million-ton five-year agreed minimum level; there would be a tighter ban on the export of high-technology items to the Soviet Union in areas of possible military application; Soviet fishing privileges in U.S. waters were to be severely curtailed; the United States intended to provide military equipment and economic assistance to Pakistan; and the U.S. Ambassador was recalled from Moscow, while all U.S.–Soviet official exchanges were suspended.

Though the President's speech exuded determination and firmness, our internal debates on the Soviet issue soon resumed. I noted that "Harold Brown, who is in China . . . is making very tough anti-Soviet statements. Had I been making them the press would certainly be on my back. He is describing them as killers, who express their friendship for the Afghanis by killing their government; he is talking about common or complementary U.S. and Chinese responses to the Soviet aggression." Yet at the same time, Vance, in a joint appearance with the President before some 120 distinguished Americans, who assembled at the White House for a special briefing on Afghanistan, went out of his way to say that the United States would not transfer or sell arms *either* to the Soviets or to the Chinese. Donald Rumsfeld, the former Secretary of Defense, who was in attendance, at that point rose and asked Vance with pointed sarcasm, "Is anybody in any seriousness suggesting or even contemplating selling arms to the Russians?!"

Moreover, within the White House there arose increasing concerns about the grain embargo. Some officials were inclined to blame me for it, even though the decision had been advocated by Vance and Cutler as well as Ham and Jody. Actually, I did not object to the proposed grain embargo, for I feared that without such an embargo the business community would be more effective in lobbying against the more stringent controls on technology transfer that I strongly favored. My judgment was that with the grain embargo in effect, the President would be in a better position to resist efforts to relax controls on technology transfer.

Our internal debates became even more acrimonious when it was learned within days of the President's speech that Argentina might be in a position to replace the United States as a seller of grain to the Soviets. It is a distressing fact that the senior officials of the Agriculture Department underestimated the extent to which Argentina could do that. Nonetheless, the suspension of additional U.S. grain deliveries to the Soviet Union had a negative impact on Soviet stock feed, disrupted Soviet shipping arrangements, and caused some reductions in Soviet meat consumption and in livestock inventories. Full relief from this painful sanction was not obtained until the Reagan Administration lifted it early in 1982.

The other issue that generated controversy involved the question of U.S. participation in the forthcoming Summer Olympics in Moscow. We were aware that the Soviets saw the event as an opportunity to stage a major propaganda festival. The Kremlin leaders were determined to make the Moscow Olympics the most successful ever and had committed themselves to large economic and political efforts. When the possibility of U.S. abstention was first raised by Mondale, Vance objected strongly and at the January 11 breakfast became even quite heated in arguing against Mondale's proposal that we recommend a shift to some other, more acceptable, site such as Munich or Montreal. Moreover, Christopher, on a mission to Europe to urge our allies to join in collective sanctions, was under instructions to tell them that for the moment we were not considering abstention from the Olympics.

But domestic pressure steadily mounted for an Olympic boycott, with Vance himself publicly saying that such a move was under consideration and noting that he personally would not have favored U.S. participation in the Berlin Olympics of 1936. The matter came to a head at the Presidential foreign affairs breakfast on January 18, with everyone agreeing that the President, in a public television interview scheduled for Sunday, should indicate that the United States would withdraw from the Olympics and would urge other states to do so as well.

Our initial inclination was to organize a competitive international athletic event, and Lloyd Cutler was put in charge of the enterprise. However, by late February it became clear to me that his efforts were getting nowhere and that at best we would obtain only a partial boycott by other states of the Moscow Olympics. I briefed the President on February 22, and soon thereafter we dropped our efforts to organize an alternative event, concentrating on making certain that in addition to the United States some other key countries refrained from participating. We had only partial success in so doing, but the absence of the United States, and also of such key countries as Germany, Japan, China, and a number of others, did make the Moscow Olympics an empty event from an athletic as well as a propaganda point of view.

In the weeks that followed, my own activities focused on three matters: to make sure that the Soviets paid some price for their invasion of Afghanistan; to initiate a quiet negotiating channel with the Soviets to determine if at some point they were prepared to reconsider their involvement in Afghanistan; and to prevent the sending of misleading signals to Moscow that the United States might reconsider its tough line on Afghanistan.

On the President's instructions, I pursued some of these matters with friendly governments, including a confidential meeting with President Giscard of France, in order to generate a common political stand. I met also privately on several occasions with Dobrynin to probe for Soviet flexibility. At the same time, with the President's approval, I used various channels to suggest to some Islamic countries, and then later directly to our Western European allies, that the proposal be made to the Soviets that neutral Islamic countries create an international contingent which could replace the Soviet forces in Afghanistan, perhaps under UN auspices, and permit the restoration of a genuinely neutral but not violently anti-Communist government. My thought in making this proposal was that such an interim arrangement would make it easier for the Soviets to leave, if at some point they should conclude that their venture in Afghanistan had become counterproductive. In the meantime, such an initiative would be likely to win endorsement even from the relatively anti-Western Islamic governments and thus help to shape a united Moslem front. As I noted in my journal on February 25: "I do not exclude the possibility that the Soviets may eventually want to get out of Afghanistan, but only if for a longish period of time the West remains united, the Islamic world remains outraged, and Afghani resistance persists. I will give a memo to that effect to the President."

The discussions with Dobrynin were not productive, though at one point it appeared that the Soviets might be prepared to dump their newly installed puppet President, Babrak Kamal. At one meeting with me, after Dobrynin had adamantly insisted that we should deal with the new regime, he pointedly hinted that this need not be obstructed by the question of a single personality. It is not clear whether Dobrynin was acting under instructions, but the Soviets refused to return to this matter throughout the rest of the Carter term.

This, however, did not prevent the State Department from generating pressure to revive detente through a new American–Soviet dialogue at a higher level and in a more open forum. On February 28, I got a phone call from the President instructing me to attend a meeting with him and Vance on Afghanistan in the Oval Office at 10:30 a.m. When I arrived, I found the President accompanied by the Vice President, Secretary Vance, and Vance's principal Soviet affairs adviser, Marshall Shulman. The conversation was already in progress and the President was recapitulating what he had apparently been told; namely, that there had been some indirect communication from Moscow, through Brezhnev's son, to the effect that the Soviets might be willing to consider withdrawal from Afghanistan if the United States reconsidered its position on the Olympics. Vance strongly reaffirmed that point, saying that Soviet Party Secretary Ponomarev also had said "to someone," otherwise unidentified, that the Soviet invasion had been a mistake. Soviet Foreign Trade Minister Patolitchev allegedly had made similar comments. Accordingly, Vance felt that this should be explored through a high-level meeting.

I remained silent, though I was appalled at the thought that two months after the Soviet invasion of Afghanistan we might be taking the initiative to open up a dialogue with the Soviets even while pressing our allies to maintain a united front. To my relief, Mondale's reaction was negative: "I don't think Patolitchev or Ponomarev are significant actors. We can lose everything by appearing to want a meeting. They might conclude it's a sign of weakness on our part. I don't see any hopeful signals. In brief, I am skeptical." Vance responded by saying that he also had a message from Dobrynin favoring a formal Gromyko–Vance meeting. Shulman added that the time to relax our pressure would be "when the Soviets are stuck," and that eventually, when an Afghan army and government were in place, the Soviets would leave. The President somewhat sarcastically noted that this meant "they will withdraw when they can leave a puppet government in place," and asked for my comments.

I said that while I did not object to talking to the Soviets, we should proceed very carefully lest we project the image of uncertainty and be accused of new zigzags. If we persisted in our course and carefully explored the possibility of Soviet withdrawal, we might get somewhere. But right now a Vance–Gromyko meeting would confuse our allies and would be politically devastating at home. As a fallback position, Vance then proposed that Carter communicate directly with Brezhnev and that Shulman go to Moscow with such a message. After the meeting, Mondale and I agreed that such an initiative would be a disaster. At my urging, Mondale went back to the President to register his concerns, but the President simply did not respond.

I confined my own reaction to a formal memo, which I attached to Vance's draft of the proposed letter to Gromyko, sent in for Presidential approval on March 2. I pointed out that the proposed draft addressed itself to such matters as neutrality for Pakistan and Iran, with whom we had not consulted, and that Pakistan would hardly be reassured by such a U.S. move. I said I failed to see what U.S. interest would be served by making the Soviet Union in effect the co-guarantor of neutrality in the Persian Gulf region, especially after the Soviet military intervention in Afghanistan. I also expressed the view that our message could be exploited by the Soviets to split allied support and that it involved a misunderstanding of Russian psychology. The Russians, I argued, tended to respect the strong and had contempt for the weak, whereas the President was considering sending an emissary who is clearly identified with the dovish side of the American decision-making process. In brief, the whole initiative struck me as harmful. Finally, I reiterated my own position: that to get the Russians out of Afghanistan we had to maintain allied unity, we had to have an aroused Islamic world focus its hostility on the Soviet Union, and the Afghani resistance had to be sustained for a sufficiently long period of time.

To my amazement, when I met Dobrynin at a party at the Japanese Embassy a few days after submitting the memo to the President, I learned from the sardonically smiling Soviet Ambassador that he had already been asked to approve a visa for Shulman and that the Soviet side had rejected the initiative. He added cuttingly that somebody at Shulman's level might be able to see the Soviet Deputy Foreign Minister but certainly not Brezhnev. To rub it in, Dobrynin added: "We want to talk to someone who shapes policy, not to a messenger. This is not serious. Did the President actually approve it? I really thought the whole idea was an effort by you, Zbig, to indicate to us that you are not serious about negotiating." I was deeply embarrassed, for I thought that the President had not given his final agreement to this initiative and that he had not been informed that an approach had already been made to the Soviets. As it happened, whatever the impact of Mondale's objections and of my memo might have been, and perhaps independently of the negative Soviet reaction to the Shulman initiative—on which I reported to the President—the President within days turned the entire project off. He had me reiterate to Vance his firm view that our position on Afghanistan had to stick, that there would be no changes in it, and that this view should be communicated unambiguously both to the Soviets and to our allies.

On the human side, it is appropriate to recall that all these decisions were being made in a highly charged atmosphere. The President's political stock was low, and he was irritated by the Kennedy challenge and frustrated by our inability to break through on the Iranian hostage issue. The time of decision on the rescue mission was nearing, and that must have weighed very heavily on his mind. Moreover, privately he gave increasing signs of dissatisfaction with Vance, especially in the wake of the political fiasco of the UN vote on Jerusalem, which was proving very damaging to Carter in the New York primary contest. Vance, too, was clearly unhappy, feeling unfairly blamed on the Middle East issue, resentful of White House political criticism, and also deeply disappointed by the turn of the U.S.–Soviet relationship. Most of our key strategic decisions, be it on relations with China, on our defense policy, or on the response to the Soviet action in Afghanistan, were not pointed in directions that he would have naturally favored, and his discomfort was doubtless compounded by increasingly frequent press stories greatly exaggerating my preponderance in the policy-making process. Brown's relations with Vance had also deteriorated because of Brown's China trip and Brown's statements while in China. Mondale's judgment on foreign policy issues was more and more colored by domestic political interests, and I could sense that he was frequently dismayed by Carter's unwillingness to give a higher priority to electoral concerns than to foreign policy considerations. This was not a happy time.

Middle East Stalemate and Vance's Distress

The signing of the peace treaty between Israel and Egypt in late March 1979 marked the high-water mark of Carter's involvement in Middle East affairs. Thereafter, we largely restricted our efforts to preventing excessively negative reactions to the treaty by such moderate Arab states as Saudi Arabia and Jordan, and consolidating the peace agreement through the gradual implementation of the Sinai accords and through quiet negotiations on the future of the West Bank. Increasingly, we were preoccupied with the region's security as a whole, particularly in view of the turmoil in Iran and the subsequent Soviet invasion of Afghanistan.

After the signing of the peace treaty, the President made it clear to us that he no longer wished to play a highly visible role in Middle East affairs. He indicated that his political interests would be well served if we could agree on a negotiator who would provide him with a political shield at home. It was then that the name of Robert Strauss was raised, and a week later the President informed us that Strauss had agreed to serve as our Middle East negotiator. On May 4, 1979, Strauss took part for the first time in our review of the current status of our Middle East policy. I wrote that "the whole session was really a charade. For one thing, Vance and Strauss were elaborately polite to each other, laughing endlessly at each other's jokes. Secondly, there was no substantive discussion whatsoever. The President conveyed as clearly as he could that he is totally disinterested in any further discussion of Middle Eastern strategy. Cy brought up the question of Israeli settlements on the West Bank and what we ought to do about it, and the President raised his hand and said, 'Strauss, take care of it,' which was, I think, meant half to be a joke and half an indication that he really doesn't want to be bothered with this problem if he can help it."

In the weeks that followed, Strauss proved rather hard to handle. He had apparently taken on the assignment expecting that it would make him into a Democratic Henry Kissinger, a mass-media star, the new peacemaker in the Middle East. He plunged into the job with great enthusiasm, going out of his way to make certain that everyone knew that he was not taking directions from Vance and that he would shape our policy on his own. But later, when the going got tough, Strauss became quite discouraged and was only too eager to get out of the assignment. He was from the outset particularly concerned with the domestic implications of our Middle East policy, and he (along with Mondale) made it clear to Carter that any pressure on Israel would be damaging politically at home.

Strauss's desire to assert his independence from Vance produced tensions from the very beginning. In mid-May, Cy chaired a meeting on our next moves. One of the proposals was for Strauss to accompany Vance to the Middle East. As soon as the meeting was over, Strauss phoned me and said, "I don't want to be a prop for Vance. I will not sit down at meetings with nothing to say." He simply refused to go. Some weeks later, at the foreign affairs breakfast held on August 3, the President said that the Middle East issue ought to be left to Strauss, because otherwise we would be faced with increasing difficulties within the Democratic Party. Vance, who had been sitting quietly, became extremely aroused and for the first time actually raised his voice in speaking to the President. "There is Lebanon, there is the Palestinian question, there is the question of the UN. Do you want me literally to do nothing?" He then paused, lowered his voice, leaned back in his chair, and added, "Mr. President, I am not going to be a figurehead for you. If you don't want me to do this, I am going to resign as

Secretary of State." Carter was quiet for a second, then gave Vance one of his icy smiles and in a very quiet voice said, "Cy, I don't want you to resign. I would rather drop the whole issue. But I do want Strauss to be up front because I need him as a political shield."

Two weeks later, Strauss embarked on his first major visit to the Middle East. The Strauss trip coincided with the Palestinian issue again heating up. The UN Security Council had been scheduled to consider the rights of the Palestinian people at the end of August. It was clear to us that the United States would have to acknowledge the fact that the Israeli record toward the Palestinians was poor. The political situation became even more delicate when Andy Young's meeting with a PLO representative became public and Young had to resign. (I was genuinely sorry that Andy had to go, but his violation of standing policy was so clear that the President had no choice.) The Security Council adjourned without reaching agreement on a resolution, and the President, deploring this lack of progress, instructed Strauss to take up the matter with both Sadat and Begin. He was to tell them that the United States was itself prepared to move on the Palestinian issue in the UN. Since Strauss earlier had indicated to the President some reservations about our approach, the President told me to prepare a written instruction, which he would sign prior to Strauss's departure. I spoke to Christopher about the subject on August 16, and the State Department prepared an initial draft. To toughen it, I inserted a last sentence which read: "I count on you either to obtain Israeli support for a moderate U.S. resolution or to explain fully to them the reasons why we will have to proceed in any case." I gave the finished draft to the President to sign, and he added in his own handwriting: "Be firm." Fearing that Strauss would phone the President to try to obtain alternate instructions, I arranged for the instructions to be delivered to the envoy after his plane had taken off.

Within a day I got an outraged phone call from Strauss in the Middle East. He told me that he would have turned right around if he had received this instruction before boarding the plane. I told him flatly that these were the Presidential instructions and that he was expected to carry them out. He not only informed me that he had already obtained a negative Egyptian and Israeli reaction to what we were proposing but on his way back briefed the press on the instructions, complaining bitterly that Vance and I had engineered it and that I was responsible for the failure of his mission. When I reported his message to the President, the President quite shrewdly asked, "Do you think that perhaps Sadat was against this initiative because Bob Strauss in fact talked him out of it?"

After Strauss's return, a session of reconciliation was held in the Situation Room, chaired, at my suggestion, by the Vice President. The press had by then become increasingly critical of Strauss's performance;

one newspaper called him the Jewish Andy Young. As a result, Strauss was in a very conciliatory mood, and we managed to bury the hatchet. A few weeks later, when Strauss embarked on his next mission to the Middle East, I gave one of my aides who was accompanying him a sealed envelope, addressed to him, again with my name on it. As instructed, my aide handed it to Strauss immediately after takeoff; Strauss visibly blanched, rose from his seat in the front compartment, and locked himself in his stateroom before opening it. The envelope contained a message from me saying, "Have a wonderful trip, Bob." I have to add that one of Strauss's permanently endearing qualities is his genuinely decent and charitable attitude toward other human beings. I enjoyed crossing swords with him, but more importantly, I both respected and liked him.

In late October, the President told me that Strauss would shift to domestic politics and asked for my advice on whether our Middle East policy should be handed back to Vance. I told the President quite frankly that I thought not; that Vance did not have the time to negotiate the Palestinian issue and that it might be better, to maintain momentum, to appoint someone like Clark Clifford or Sol Linowitz. After a round of consultations, the President settled on Linowitz, who applied himself with considerable energy to the tedious task of negotiating the autonomy issue with both the Egyptians and the Israelis. By the end of 1980, the envoy had made quiet but substantial progress. Indeed, by the time our Administration left office, Linowitz had developed a plan for the equitable sharing of water rights, for an arrangement whereby new settlements would not be established without the permission of both the Israeli and Palestinian sides, for Israel to retain responsibility for protecting the Palestinian area against external attack but also for a Palestinian force responsible for internal security. Moreover, he managed to skirt Begin's efforts to limit Palestinian autonomy only to administrative responsibilities. Though the West Bank issue was far from resolved by the time we left office, Linowitz's efforts at the very least provided the necessary political shield for the continued implementation of the Egyptian–Israeli accord.

However, one unintended effect of the appointment first of Strauss and later of Linowitz was the undermining of Vance. By midsummer of 1979, Vance was determined to press hard on the settlements issue. On June 12, he told me that he intended to urge the President to approve reductions in U.S. economic aid to Israel every time the Israelis moved forward with an additional settlement. Later, Vance appeared to have acquiesced in Austrian Chancellor Bruno Kreisky's decision not to let Jews from the Soviet Union leave Austria to go to Israel unless the Israelis gave assurances that these immigrants would not be settled on the West Bank. This matter became a source of considerable political embarrassment to us, and in the end the President instructed

Vance to make it clear to Kreisky that this was purely an Austrian matter, with which we did not wish to be associated. I could tell that the President's decision bothered Vance a great deal, and his unhappiness was compounded by Strauss's increasing assertiveness. In July, Vance resumed the effort to obtain approval for U.S. condemnation of Israeli settlements, but the President was reluctant to grant it. Differences also surfaced between Vance and Strauss on how the United States should react to Israel's having used American military equipment in Lebanon without formal U.S. permission. Vance again favored a tougher line, and Strauss, though in a carefully modulated fashion, opposed it.

The appointment of a special aide to Hamilton Jordan to deal specifically with Jewish affairs also upset Vance. In mid-August, he called me in great irritation to complain that the appointee, Ed Sanders, a very intelligent, pleasant California lawyer, had sent the President a memorandum recommending that Strauss be given authority for our Middle East policy, and to complain that Sanders would accompany the envoy on his upcoming trip. I reported Vance's unhappiness to the President, and he reacted very strongly, issuing orders to Hamilton Jordan that henceforth Sanders would have to clear all foreign travel with me and that he was not to submit memoranda dealing with foreign policy. Vance was mollified, but I could sense his deepening unease.

Vance's unhappiness must have been magnified by the general trend in U.S. policy. The fall of 1979 and early 1980 saw the collapse of SALT, a worsening crisis in Iran (refuting the State Department's view that the Shah's fall would produce a stable coalition government), and a widening U.S.–Chinese cooperation against the Soviets. All of that went counter to Vance's assumptions, while the assignment of responsibility for the Middle East to a highly visible and self-assertive figure like Strauss must have been humiliating both personally and professionally. This unhappy situation came to a head in early 1980 with the highly publicized snafu over how the United States voted at the UN on the Jerusalem issue.

On the last day of February, the upcoming UN vote was discussed at the foreign affairs breakfast. It was decided that the United States would support a proposed resolution, to which the Israelis objected strongly, but only if some objectionable wording, especially on Jerusalem, was removed. Ambassador Donald McHenry urged an affirmative U.S. vote, and Vance was clearly leaning in the same direction. Later that day, Cy phoned me to say that the wording of the resolution had been modified satisfactorily and that he therefore felt free to instruct McHenry to support it. He said he assumed that I concurred. Having been burned earlier on the U.S.–Soviet declaration (see p. 108) and sensing Vance's desire to vote for the resolution, I told Vance that he should transmit the revised text to the President or at least speak to him personally just to be sure. I then left for a scheduled speaking engagement in the South, and on my return discovered that we were faced with a massive political problem. The UN resolution, for which the United States had voted, turned out to be replete with references to Jerusalem and included a call for the dismantling of existing settlements.

In my absence, both Strauss and Mondale went to the President and insisted that our vote be retracted and that Vance be required to state that the U.S. vote had been the product of an internal misunderstanding. On Monday evening, Vance met with Mondale, Strauss, and Jordan in a session which lasted late into the night, and he was pressured into a public retraction, including the admission of bureaucratic error. I was appalled by this outcome. Whatever the merits of the vote, and it was obvious that the vote did not reflect accurately the decision made at the Presidential breakfast, I felt strongly that it would have been wiser to make no retraction, but merely to state that we had voted in keeping with our traditional position on Jerusalem and the settlements, and that the specific language—though objectionable—was of secondary importance. The admission of error, in my judgment, made the Administration look silly and the President look weak.

The outcome was shattering for Vance. I could tell from his demeanor, even from his physical appearance, that he was crushed. I sensed his deep resentment and disappointment, and from then on I was convinced that his days as Secretary of State were numbered and that he was simply waiting for an appropriate moment to resign. Moreover, his unhappiness was aggravated a few weeks later when he was requested by the White House to state in forthcoming Senate testimony that our recent vote on the Jerusalem issue had been incorrect. My suspicions were confirmed by a conversation I had with the President on the morning of Thursday, March 20, 1980. When my briefing ended, the President all of a sudden said that he was "very troubled by Cy. I don't know what's the matter with him. He is absolutely dogged on the settlements issue." He told me that he would invite Cy up to Camp David to see if things could be worked out, but he made no secret of the fact that he was generally "very distressed with him."

Carter's unhappiness was intensified by a memorandum which Mondale submitted, urging in strong terms that our previous policy on the settlements be repudiated in time for the New York primary, and I was struck later in the day by how very emotional Vance became when I quizzed him on the subject. Vance flatly refused to disavow the resolution as a whole, pointing out that parts of it were in keeping with traditional U.S. policy. His Senate testimony was followed shortly by the New York primary vote, in which Jewish voters swung heavily over to Senator Kennedy, ensuring Carter's defeat. This setback prolonged the Carter–Kennedy contest, and the politically minded White

House officials blamed Vance. I was convinced that Cy would seize the next opportunity to tender his resignation.

It would be wrong to conclude, however, that the gradual loss of momentum in our efforts to obtain a more comprehensive peace was due entirely to a lack of will in Washington. For one thing, Sadat's attitude was critical. He obviously did not want a final showdown on the Palestinian problem prior to the return of the Sinai to Egypt. The experience of the last two or three years had made him more appreciative of the need for a gradualist approach. Accordingly, he did not press us hard to assert our position either on the question of the settlements or on progress in the West Bank negotiations. And without pressure from Sadat, our own incentive to push Israel hard was much decreased.

Moreover, the President could push hard and risk a massive public clash with Israel only if he had a reasonable expectation of a genuinely impressive success to justify the effort. In the circumstances prevailing in late 1979 and early 1980, such expectations were hardly justified. Begin proved himself to be a skilled manipulator and a determined negotiator, adroit in delaying tactics and in diversionary public appeals. Moreover, by mid-June 1980 it was clear even to Mondale that Begin wanted Carter to be defeated. Mondale stated this directly on July 26 at the foreign affairs breakfast. Thus a decision to confront Begin involved major risks not only for the stability of the region but also for the President's domestic position. Last but not least, by late 1979 the Soviet threat to the Middle East, magnified by the Iranian disaster, demanded our urgent attention.

A Regional Security Framework

"Any attempt by any outside force to gain control of the Persian Gulf region will be regarded as an assault on the vital interests of the United States of America and such an assault will be repelled by any means necessary, including military force." With these words, addressing a joint session of Congress on the State of the Union, Jimmy Carter on January 23, 1980, committed the United States to the security of the Persian Gulf region. The President's words represented a formal recognition of a centrally important reality: that America's security had become interdependent with the security of three central and interrelated strategic zones consisting of Western Europe, the Far East, and the Middle East–Persian Gulf area. For me it was a particularly gratifying moment because for more than a year I had been seeking within the U.S. government the adoption of such a policy, based on a formal recognition of the interdependence of these three central strategic zones.

The Carter Doctrine was modeled on the Truman Doctrine, enunciated in response to the Soviet threat to Greece and Turkey. On a number of occasions I had drawn the President's attention to the significance of that Doctrine, and after the Soviet invasion of Afghanistan, I urged him explicitly to emulate President Truman's historic act. The collapse of Iran, and the growing vulnerability of Saudi Arabia, dictated the need for such a wider strategic response. Moreover, I wanted the President's statement to contain a reference to "a regional security framework," since in my judgment we needed a concept which could then be bureaucratically implemented. I felt that something much looser than a formal alliance was needed to convey our recognition of the political sensitivities of the countries in the region and yet at the same time provide a sufficiently explicit assurance of American involvement.

When the concept of a security framework was first broached in the spring of 1979, it had few adherents; but gradually, after numerous SCC sessions held on the subject, support grew, particularly from Graham Claytor, Brown's very energetic deputy. Thus by the time of the Soviet invasion of Afghanistan, some of the basic work had been done, notably by my military assistant, General William Odom, who most energetically enlisted the support of key officials in the Defense Department, notably Under Secretary Robert Komer. Vance and Christopher remained skeptical, while Brown maintained a position of ambiguity until late 1979, when, with Claytor and Komer's help, he was won over to the concept.

In early January 1980, after the Soviet action in Afghanistan, I gave a comprehensive interview to *The Wall Street Journal*, in which I spelled out the views which had been previously discussed in the SCC on the three interrelated central strategic zones and on the consequent need for a new "regional security framework" for the Middle East. Almost simultaneously I submitted a memo to the President on January 9, outlining in detail a long-term strategy for coping with the consequences of the Soviet action in Afghanistan, with specific emphasis on how we could flesh out a regional security arrangement with the Egyptians, the Saudis, the Pakistanis, and the Turks. I warned the President that our response would have to be a sustained one and that it would be costly from a budgetary point of view, but I argued that there was no choice. I also encouraged Stan Turner to write a similar memorandum, which I gave to the President concurrently with my own.

A week later, on January 16, the President informed me that he had decided to make the Soviet regional challenge the main theme of his forthcoming State of the Union message. He assigned me the responsibility for developing the initial draft, in coordination with Vance, Brown, and others. That gave me the opportunity to include wording modeled on the Truman Doctrine and also to insert into the speech my notion of a "regional security framework." At the very last moment, quite literally a few hours before the speech was to be delivered, both Vance and Cutler made last-minute efforts to cut out that reference, but I caught Jody on his way to the Presidential residence with the very final version of the speech, and he and I, standing in the semidarkness of the portico linking the West Wing with the main part of the White House, simply penciled in again those three words. In his speech Carter declared that ". . . we are prepared to work with other countries in the region to shape a cooperative security framework that respects different values and political beliefs, yet which enhances the independence, security and prosperity of all."

The President's speech was well received, and its significance was immediately appreciated, both at home and abroad. Press editorials were generally favorable, and—even more importantly—some of the key governments in the region, notably those of Egypt, Saudi Arabia, and the smaller Gulf states, privately conveyed to us their sense of relief. The United States was seen as finally drawing the line and as making its engagement in the security of the Persian Gulf region unambiguously clear.

However, two criticisms surfaced: that the Carter Doctrine was not backed by sufficient force and that it had not been preceded by adequate interagency consultations. The first criticism was made by a number of columnists and was then picked up in the Presidential campaign by Governor Reagan's supporters. After Carter's electoral defeat, the second criticism was voiced by David Newsom, who during the latter phases of the Carter Administration served as Under Secretary of State.

I did not find either criticism very persuasive. It is true that when the commitment to the security of the Persian Gulf was made the United States was not in a position to meet the Soviet Union on the ground, so to speak, matching man for man or tank for tank. Geography and logistical complexities made that impossible. But President Truman also did not have the capacity to match the Soviets man for man or tank for tank either in Greece or, a year or so later, in Berlin, when he responded firmly to the Soviet threat. The point of both the Truman Doctrine and of what later came to be called the Carter Doctrine was to make the Soviet Union aware of the fact that the intrusion of Soviet armed forces into an area of vital importance to the United States would precipitate an engagement *with* the United States, and that the United States would then be free to choose the manner in which it would respond. In fact, in our private contingency preparations, I made the point of instructing the Defense Department to develop options involving both "horizontal and vertical escalation" in the event of a Soviet military move toward the Persian Gulf, by which I meant that we would be free to choose either the terrain or the tactic or the level of our response.

In addition, the criticism involved a basic misconception of how a democracy responds to a crisis. As a practical matter, there is no way for the United States to reach the conclusion secretly that the Persian Gulf is in our vital interest, then to build up our military forces in order to have the capability of responding locally, and only then to announce that the United States is committed to such a defense. In a democracy such as ours, only a public commitment is capable of generating the necessary budgetary support and the other decisions that are needed to implement a commitment. In the meantime, the very awareness in Moscow and elsewhere of America's engagement serves as the immediate deterrent.

The charge that the decision was not sufficiently vetted through the interagency process is simply factually wrong. The fact of the matter is that on a number of occasions the President discussed the need for a more sustained American engagement in the region with his principal advisers, of whom Under Secretary Newsom was not one. A key instance was a formal meeting of the NSC held on December 4, 1979, in which the deteriorating situation in Iran and the growing evidence of Soviet involvement in Afghanistan were carefully assessed. Prior to that meeting, I gave the President a one-page memorandum urging him to approve preliminary work which had been undertaken throughout the summer and fall of 1979 within the SCC and which led me to conclude that the time had come for the United States to seek access to military facilities in the Indian Ocean area.

I brought up the matter formally at the NSC meeting by recommending specifically that the United States now approach Oman, Somalia, and Kenya with a proposed contingency arrangement for granting us naval and air basing facilities. This, I argued, was necessary to inject effectively American power into a region that had become "an arc of crisis," and in which the Soviets were both militarily and politically on the offensive. With Vance and Brown not taking a strong position either way, but with General Jones and Admiral Turner backing me strongly, the President instructed the Defense and State Departments to develop joint initiatives to the countries concerned. Later, a cooperative arrangement was also concluded with Egypt, and thus the retrenchment of Western military power from the region was reversed. The United States during 1980 acquired access to Masirah Island, located very close to the Persian Gulf, with supporting bases further back in Berbera, Mombasa, and Ras Banas in southeastern Egypt.

The President's speech of January 23, 1980, as well as the NSC meeting of December 4, 1979, were in fact the culmination of a longer process of interagency discussions and debate which had started about a year earlier. By late 1978, I began to press the "arc of crisis" thesis, and on February 28, 1979, I submitted a memo to the President urging a new "security framework" to reassert U.S. power and influence in the region, thus abandoning our earlier plans to demilitarize the Indian

Ocean, an objective to which the State Department was still dedicated. With the earlier British disengagement from "east of Suez," and with the collapse of our strategic pivot north of the Persian Gulf, I felt that a wider response by the United States was needed, and I used my memorandum as the basis for a number of SCC meetings. Moreover, Brown went to the Middle East in early February 1979, and I used the occasion to draft for him Presidential instructions which put particular emphasis on the strategic concern and on the need not only to involve core countries of the Persian Gulf but also to engage friendly peripheral states, such as Morocco, Sudan, and Turkey, in a wider response.

These efforts coincided with a growing threat to Saudi Arabia from South Yemen. In early March 1979, the President, by prearrangement with me, showed up unexpectedly at an SCC session that I was chairing in the basement Situation Room and approved the recommendation to dispatch immediately the aircraft carrier *Constellation* to the Arabian Sea and two AWACS to Saudi Arabia, as well as an emergency airlift to North Yemen. Until the President's appearance, the State Department representatives at the SCC had been reluctant to act, and the President's decisions marked a significant step toward America's involvement in the security of the region.

Throughout 1979 I persisted in holding SCCs in which, though it was like pulling teeth, a number of incremental decisions were made regarding preparations for prepositioning of military stockpiles, holding of joint exercises with some of the friendly countries in the region, and enhancing U.S. naval/air deployments in the area. All of that gradually generated bureaucratic momentum, with the NSC staff in firm control. Thus the idea of the regional security framework was already quietly being fleshed out by the time the Afghan crisis had erupted.

A series of particularly important meetings was held in the middle of June 1979, in which the overall strategic issues were sharply debated. Vance and Christopher generally argued that the United States should not become more involved, while Brown, Schlesinger (who attended as Secretary of Energy), and I argued for a more active American policy which would combine efforts to move the Arab–Israeli peace process forward with wider security arrangements. At one point in that debate, Schlesinger argued forcefully that American military presence in the Indian Ocean–Persian Gulf area should "balance" the Soviets, and when Vance and Christopher reacted negatively, I not only backed Schlesinger but stated that in fact our objective ought to be military preponderance, since the area was vital to the United States while not of equal significance to the Soviets.

Thus by early 1980 the ground had been laid for a more formal American commitment to the protection of the region from Soviet intimidation. In fact, if this had not been the case, I might have been more sympathetic to a suggestion made to me by Jim Schlesinger over lunch on January 10. Schlesinger shared my very grave view of the unfolding situation in the Persian Gulf, and at the lunch he urged me to resign from the Administration in order to jolt the President into making the needed response. But by early January 1980 I felt that the President's response was producing a genuinely balanced and effective foreign policy. We remained committed to such morally desirable ends as human rights and nonproliferation, and, at the same time, we were demonstrating our willingness to use American power and to assert vital American interests. That was the kind of foreign policy I wanted the United States very much to pursue.

This is not to say that all things moved as well as I had hoped. Shortly after the Soviet invasion of Afghanistan, I showed the President the exact wording of the security assurances that the United States gave to Pakistan back in 1959, again drawing a parallel between the present crisis and the one faced by President Truman in regard to Greece and Turkey. Since I was scheduled to appear on *Issues and Answers* on Sunday, December 30, I suggested that the President authorize me to read out these assurances and to reiterate on the President's behalf that the United States stands behind them. The President approved this suggestion, and after my appearance the President phoned me at home to tell me that this had worked out well. Since the Pakistanis were rather concerned that they might be the next target of Soviet military aggression, such a public reiteration of the U.S. commitment was an important reassurance, which in turn should have been expressed more tangibly. I had hoped, and I was supported by Defense on this, that we might be able to put together a large package involving both military and economic aid. Much to my frustration, growing budgetary stringencies, as well as Pakistan's dubious record both on human rights and on nonproliferation, made that impossible, but we did come up with an initial package of $400 million. To make matters worse, the President of Pakistan chose a public occasion to express his dismay, dismissing the American proposal as "peanuts." The President was understandably annoyed, but more important was the damaging effect of what appeared to be a U.S. unwillingness to treat its commitments seriously.

To reassure the Pakistanis that we were still in earnest, I proposed to the President and to Vance that I join Christopher on his planned visit to Pakistan. Vance did not object, and the President approved the proposal, agreeing that this would signal to the Pakistanis that our approach was not merely a diplomatic one but that we were prepared to deal seriously with the security dimensions of the challenge. Christopher and I met with President Zia in Islamabad on February 2 and 3. I was delighted by how well Christopher and I worked together and by the genuine harmony that prevailed in the course of the delicate mission. Each of us reinforced the other, and I felt that both in Pakistan and then on the way back in talks with top Saudi leaders we succeeded in making our hosts understand that the United States was serious about its security commitment to the region. Moreover, in both places I held separate negotiations regarding cooperative responses to the Soviet action in Afghanistan, and these yielded tangible results.

However, on the question of U.S. assistance to Pakistan little progress was made. The Pakistanis repeated their request for much more substantial assistance, and they coupled it with the request that the U.S. assurances to Pakistan be interpreted to include a possible Indian attack as well. We made it plain that this could not be the case, and that our commitment involved the Soviet Union only. The Pakistani leaders then took the position that in such a case their security interest would be better served by a broad understanding with the United States, reinforced by the public U.S. reaffirmation of the 1959 assurances, but with Pakistan publicly distancing itself from the United States and instead collaborating more closely with other Moslem countries in opposing the Soviet occupation of Afghanistan. In a private conversation, the Pakistani President emphasized to me that this approach would serve best both American and Pakistani interests, and he indicated that on more sensitive matters he did not wish to deal with the State Department, which he viewed as motivated by an anti-Pakistani bias. He also stressed the importance of enhancing Saudi–Pakistani cooperation and asked for our good offices. Both Christopher and I used our stop in Riyadh on the way back to emphasize that point to the Saudis, who did undertake to facilitate Pakistani arms purchases, in return for a Pakistani military input to Saudi security.

While in Pakistan, Christopher and I paid a visit to Afghan refugee camps, where we were saturated with very emotional and moving appeals for American arms. Separately, I paid a visit to a Pakistani military outpost in the Khyber Pass, where the commanding officer showed me a Chinese version of the Soviet automatic AK-47 rifle. As requested, I inspected the weapon (muzzle downward) and returned it to the Pakistanis, declining the suggestion that I fire it. On my return to Washington, I was amazed to find that a great furor had developed over the picture of me with the rifle in my hands. According to some press reports, I had aimed the weapon at Afghanistan; others had me firing it. Those who particularly resented my role in shaping our response to the Soviet actions in the region and who would like to see the United States conduct its foreign policy purely through a display of good intentions seized on this picture as symbolic of my "hawkishness"—while I saw in that emotional reaction a symptom of the malaise besetting some American liberals.

The stopover in Saudi Arabia was my second visit within less than a year, and I was struck by the degree of apprehension among the Saudi rulers. Prince Fahd, the sensible and very pro-American head of government, and even Prince Saud, the articulate but somewhat more distant Foreign Minister, both stressed the grave security threat that the region now faced, and they were much more prepared than before to consider, on a quiet basis, enhanced American–Saudi military cooperation. They made no bones about stating their desire for closer military ties, they asked for better intelligence regarding Soviet activity in the region, and they particularly stressed the growing threat to Saudi Arabia from the growing Communist military presence in South Yemen. We agreed in principle that the United States would look more favorably on additional Saudi arms purchase proposals and that in return we would expect greater Saudi assistance both for the Afghans, especially the refugees, and for the Pakistanis.

The President's State of the Union message of January 23 defined our position; during the rest of the year I concentrated my efforts on fleshing out the approach. Step by step, progress was made, with each, usually biweekly, SCC meeting generating some additional decisions. The initiative continued to rest primarily with the NSC staff, particularly the relentless General Odom, ably assisted by Major Christopher Shoemaker, though by late summer and early fall the Defense Department, spearheaded by the energetic Bob Komer, started to develop its own initiatives. Throughout, the State Department, now usually represented by either Christopher or Newsom, continued to show considerable disinterest, and later in 1980 it again adopted a more actively critical posture. Tedious negotiations on the facility in Somalia continued throughout the spring, and it was not until late in the year, through a more direct Presidential intervention, that the State Department abandoned its efforts to have this part of the initiative scuttled.

All in all, however, concrete progress was made during this period. American force capabilities were enhanced by the acquisition of access to regional facilities and by increased Navy and Marine presence; contingency planning with some key countries was initiated and combined exercises were scheduled; defense capabilities of the regional states were to be improved and more streamlined Foreign Military Sales (FMS) procedures were adopted; and our NATO allies were pressed to codify shared responsibilities through an enhanced effort to make up for the consequences of the U.S. "swing" strategy pointed at the Middle East–Persian Gulf area. The President also approved my idea for developing a very small rapid intervention force, capable of very quick reaction, for the purpose of helping a friendly government under a subversive attack. My view was that such a force, even if only of battalion size, could prove politically more valuable than a full-scale division deployed ten days or two weeks later. I summarized our progress to the President in a memorandum of June 3, entitled "Persian Gulf Security Framework." The President liked it and instructed me to circulate it among the other departments. That, in turn, gave additional legitimacy to our efforts.

A more substantial debate over our efforts to give substance to the concept of a regional security framework developed in the fall of 1980. It was precipitated by indications that the commitment solemnly undertaken earlier in the year might in fact soon be tested in the field. By late August we had mounting intelligence that the Soviets were deploying forces on the Iranian frontier, in a mode suited for intervention in Iran. Shortly thereafter, the Iraqi–Iranian war commenced, posing what appeared to the Saudis to be an immediate threat to the security of their oil fields.

The State Department was now headed by former Senator Edmund Muskie, and he—relying very heavily on Christopher's expertise—used the occasion to raise some fundamental questions regarding the nature of U.S. vital interests in the region and the credibility of U.S. commitments. Indeed, Muskie's presence injected new vitality, and in some respects more heat, into our internal discussions. As a trained politician, skilled in debate, he relished the open give-and-take of an argument much more than Vance, and he was particularly inclined to the Socratic method of probing questions. At the same time, he was much less informed about international affairs and for substance had to rely heavily on Christopher. Though clearly enjoying the role of a critical questioner and sharp interrogator, he was at the same time highly sensitive to any rhetorical counterattacks. As a consequence, discussions with him tended to be punctuated by occasional flare-ups, loud voices, even some shouting and table pounding. But the redeeming, even personally attractive, feature of his temperament was that after the heated debate was over, there were no lingering resentments.

A particularly sharp discussion took place at the SCC meeting on September 5, held to assess the policy implications of the intelligence regarding a possible Soviet military intervention in Iran. I argued that we should explicitly tell the Soviets that any Soviet military action would lead to a direct military confrontation with the United States. I objected to the "softer" proposals made by State that the United States promise not to intervene in Iran but be ambiguous about any U.S. resort to military action if the Soviet Union did so. I was strongly supported by Brown, and the argument developed into a very pointed exchange between Brown on the one side and Muskie and Christopher on the other. Muskie offered the judgment that Congress would not feel that a nuclear war was worth 11 percent of our oil, and Brown rather sharply responded by asking what would happen if the Soviets invaded Iran and we did nothing. Did Muskie really believe that our losses would be only a percentage of our oil supply? Muskie retorted that the American people might even accept the loss of Europe rather than risk nuclear war. I then joined in by asking Muskie if he accepted the proposition that the loss of the Persian Gulf might lead to the loss of Europe, and Muskie reluctantly agreed that that might be the case. In that case, I asked, isn't it vital that we deter the Soviets from moving into Iran?

The discussion on September 5 became even more dramatic at one point: as we were heatedly arguing in the windowless Situation Room in the basement of the White House, the electricity suddenly went off and the room was plunged into total darkness. We decided to go on, though one could not see a thing. As I presided, all I could hear were disembodied jabs between Muskie and Brown.

Fortunately, at the NSC meeting the following day, both Muskie and Christopher took a more balanced position, and the President approved a firm message to the Soviets, in keeping with the Carter Doctrine. I was encouraged by the President's attitude at the NSC, for I saw in it a reaffirmation of America's strategic credibility. Muskie was scheduled to meet with Gromyko in the second half of September, and the President, at a subsequent meeting of the NSC on September 12, had approved talking points for Muskie, reiterating our strong interest in the stability of the region; he also decided that we should develop military options both for the defense of Iran itself and for retaliatory military responses elsewhere, in the event of a Soviet move. In addition, after a separate consultation with me, the President approved an instruction to Muskie that he should read his talking points to Gromyko and actually hand over a so-called nonpaper to him. I felt that this would be a desirable precaution, given that Muskie had previously not engaged in international negotiations and that it was important that he convey accurately to Gromyko, both in substance and in tone, the message we wanted.

In the meantime, Iraqi–Iranian border skirmishes had escalated into war, and American resolve to act firmly in order to reassure our friends was tested anew. The mounting violence just to the north of Saudi oil fields precipitated by late September urgent Saudi requests for American military protection. I was alerted on Friday, September 26, at 10:55 p.m., by a call from the Duty Officer in the Situation Room to the effect that the Saudis had just urgently asked for the deployment of American AWACS, enhanced air defense, and greater intelligence support. Apparently the Iraqis were planning to stage an attack on Iranian facilities along the Gulf from the territory of some of the Arabian Gulf states, and the Saudis feared a retaliatory Iranian response, directed at their oil fields.

I convened an SCC meeting the next day, and we decided to press the Gulf states to stay neutral. At the same time, at this and at subsequent SCC and NSC meetings, held between September 27 and October 7, Brown and I favored an immediate and positive reaction to the

Saudi request, while both Muskie and Christopher argued that we should hold back and not act in a manner that might be seen as provocative to either the Soviets or the Iranians. Brown and I made the point that a positive response to the Saudis, with whom we shared a common interest in protecting the oil fields, could not be viewed as provocative to the Soviets since it was merely an expression of U.S. determination to protect our vital interests. Christopher countered that the United States should be neutral in the Iraqi–Iranian war and that, therefore, it should not respond favorably to the Saudi request. Mondale seemed to be leaning toward Muskie and Christopher. Moreover, both Muskie and Christopher were advocating a joint U.S.–Soviet effort to promote a settlement, which I felt would legitimate the Soviet position in the Gulf and thus objectively undercut our vital interests.

On the morning of Sunday, September 28, the President, having reviewed my report on what was taking place, phoned me from Camp David and authorized me to proceed with the movement of AWACS toward Saudi Arabia, with the final decision on their deployment to be made later, on the basis of fuller SCC discussions. The SCC met the same day, and I took secret delight in informing it that I had already instructed the Defense Department to proceed with the initial movement of AWACS on the basis of the Presidential decision. Muskie exploded and said that we are plunging headlong into World War III. He and Brown then got into an intense debate, though Brown clearly more than held his own. At one point, Muskie even declared that he was not aware of any governmental decision to inject American military presence into the region or to tie the security of the Persian Gulf area to the United States. I could not resist the temptation of pointing out to him that American foreign policy did not start on the day that he became Secretary of State, and I suggested that he reread the President's State of the Union message. However, when it was all over, Muskie and I exchanged friendly punches on the shoulder, and on the personal level all was well again.

We also agreed that the matter should be resolved on the NSC level by the President himself. That meeting was held on the following day, with the President approving formally the deployment of the AWACS, which in any case was already underway. In addition, the President sent a message to Giscard, proposing a joint American–French naval presence in the Arabian Gulf, to keep the Strait of Hormuz open. Giscard was quite responsive, and we proceeded to reinforce our naval deployments, even while continuing to debate among ourselves on how to answer the rest of the Saudi request.

Additional discussions took place in early October, with both Muskie and Christopher insisting that no further U.S. military actions designed to reassure the Saudis be undertaken. Muskie again became quite heated and on several occasions literally shouted at Brown. The session of October 7 was especially testy, with both Brown and Muskie contesting each other's versions of the last NSC meeting and the President's decision. However, as before, once the meeting was over, everyone concerned became quite relaxed, and personal relations between Muskie, Brown, and me were not adversely affected.

These SCC discussions reflected conflicting strategic assessments. Brown and I were now firmly united in the view that the United States had to sustain its commitment to the security of the Persian Gulf, while Muskie and Christopher appeared inclined to use the Iraqi–Iranian war—arguing that the United States was neutral—as an opportunity to dilute the commitment made earlier in the year. Fortunately, the President agreed with Harold and me, and approved decisions to enhance Saudi–U.S. military cooperation, to dispatch an American military-diplomatic team to engage the Saudis in longer-range security planning, and to consider the further upgrading of Saudi military capabilities.

The cumulative effect of the events and decisions of 1979–80 was a strategic revolution in America's global position. Until the 1970s, U.S. foreign policy was anchored on the principle of interdependence with Western Europe, and then later with the Far East. The Middle East was viewed as a semi-neutral zone sealed off from Soviet power by a protective belt composed of Turkey, Iran, and Pakistan, with a neutral Afghanistan providing a buffer. America's interest, as well as the security of the Persian Gulf, was seen as resting on two secure pillars, Iran and Saudi Arabia. Soviet political penetration of the Middle East was greatly reduced by Sadat's switch in 1973–74 to a pro-American orientation, and America's political centrality in the region was underlined by Carter's Camp David negotiations. The peace process, it was hoped, would undercut political opportunities for Soviet-backed radicalism.

However, the collapse of Iran and the Soviet move into Afghanistan, preceded by the unimpeded Soviet military intrusion into Ethiopia and South Yemen, created an urgent security problem for the region as a whole, prompting by 1980 formal U.S. recognition of the security interdependence of three, instead of two, zones of central strategic importance to the United States: Western Europe, the Far East, and the Middle East.

Strategic Renewal

The recognition of America's widened geopolitical responsibilities, generated both by the collapse of Iran and by the more menacing implications of growing Soviet power, also required a redefinition of America's defense strategy. The most notable step in that direction was the issuance by the President in July 1980 of Presidential Directive (PD) 59, designed to update in the light of the new circumstances our strategy of deterrence.

Clausewitz defined war as "an act of violence intended to compel our opponent to fulfill our will." To me, deterrence was the threat of counterviolence designed to negate the capacity of our opponent to compel us to fulfill his will. In my judgment, an effective deterrence theory had to take fully into account not only the capabilities of the opponent whom we wished to deter but also his psychological-political predispositions as well as war doctrine. Over the years I had become increasingly concerned that our existing deterrence doctrine, based on the principle of mutually assured destruction, had been formulated largely in a setting of actual U.S. superiority in the early sixties, and thus, in fact, "mutual" destruction was really one-sided; namely, the United States could inflict much worse damage on the Soviet Union than vice versa. That asymmetry in turn allowed the United States the luxury of disregarding the other side's doctrines as not very relevant to the other side's capabilities. In a setting of Soviet strategic inferiority, our doctrine of deterrence, derived largely from psychological assumptions based on our own experience and perspectives, seemed adequate to prevent a situation in which the United States could be compelled to do something against its will.

But that asymmetry had gradually changed in the course of the preceding decade and a half. The Soviet Union, first of all, significantly enhanced its conventional-war fighting capability; secondly, it energetically sought a long-range deployment capability and started more actively exploiting the Cuban proxy in the context of Third World turbulence; finally, the Soviet side appeared to be reaching out for a genuine nuclear-war fighting capability, through its command, communications, control, and intelligence structures (C31), hardening of key command sites, etc., and was on the professional military level articulating a doctrine to the effect.

Accordingly, I felt that the United States could no longer afford to disregard the Soviet doctrines guiding the possible use of the growing Soviet capability. I was not alone in that view, for in the mid-seventies Secretary of Defense James Schlesinger, motivated by rather similar concerns, initiated a review of our strategic posture. I was convinced that our old doctrine was politically and psychologically credible only as long as America was in fact superior, and that it might not deter an opponent capable of conducting both a major or a more limited nuclear conflict and a significant conventional conflict, or some combination thereof. Defense planning, I felt very strongly, had to accommodate itself to this new reality, and our defense doctrine and programs should be adjusted accordingly.

I started expressing these concerns as early as 1977. They were intensified by the findings of Policy Review Memorandum (PRM) 10, submitted for Presidential review in midsummer of 1977, and by the requirements set by the President in his PD-18, postulating strategic equivalence as our major objective. In PD-18, the NSC initiative for what later came to be called the Rapid Deployment Force was also approved, and during the next two years I kept pressing the Defense Department for progress on that score. By 1979, I had become discouraged by DOD's slow reaction, and I proceeded to send Harold Brown a number of requests in the President's name for progress reports. This helped to spur the Defense Department into greater activity, especially since I would frequently return Brown's reports to him with Carter's marginal notations expressing dissatisfaction with the rate of progress. At one point, conversing with me in the White House corridor, Brown asked what we might call this new force which was capable of rapidly projecting American power into areas where American forces were not permanently stationed, and I quite spontaneously suggested, "How about a Rapid Deployment Force?" The name stuck, and with Harold now energetically pressing the matter, by late 1980 the United States was beginning to acquire the ability to project its power much more rapidly into such vital regions as the Persian Gulf.

The Rapid Deployment Joint Task Force (RDJTF) was officially established in March 1980 at MacDill Air Force Base in Florida. By spring 1981, the RDF had assigned to it four Army divisions (about 100,000 troops), the equivalent of two Marine divisions, and associated airlift, sealift, and logistical capabilities. In preparation for any potential deployment to the Middle East, we secured access to facilities for en route, rear, and forward basing. Equipment was pre-positioned on land and on special ships. Elements of the RDF undertook battalion-sized amphibious, air, and land exercises with the armed forces of various Middle Eastern states in the course of 1980.

PRM-10 and PD-18 led also to the initiation in the Defense Department of two major studies, one dealing with our nuclear targeting policy and the other focusing on the Secure Reserve Force. In addition, on March 31, 1977, I asked Brown to provide the President with three items: a succinct statement of our nuclear war doctrine; a brief statement of the procedures for conducting war beyond the initial stage, particularly the location for the President and the C31 capabilities in light of some previously identified deficiencies; and a statement of the basic objectives to be achieved through limited nuclear options, including their military and political assumptions. My hope was that these memoranda would spur within the Defense Department a broader review of our strategic doctrine and also interest the President himself in this difficult and complicated issue.

The takeoff phase for many of these efforts was mid-year 1978. At that time I strengthened the NSC cluster dealing with military issues, and in Colonel William Odom, Fritz Ermarth, Victor Utgoff, and later General Jasper Welch, I acquired a team of collaborators with considerable expertise and capacity for doctrinal innovation. Their impact on their colleagues in DOD was significant, and Harold Brown's associates worked closely with them. There thus developed a fruitful and constructive interchange, with Harold Brown gradually becoming himself more involved in the effort to generate genuine strategic renewal.

A major watershed for me was my trip (with Colonel Odom and the JCS chairman, General Jones) in August 1978 to the Strategic Air Command and to NORAD (North American Air Defense Command), which convinced me of the acute weakness of our C31 and of the urgent need to correct that deficiency, in the context of a broader review of our basic doctrinal assumptions. I reported to the President on my trip at the end of August, and I used his reaction to my report to request a further speed-up in the ongoing work. In my journal I noted on August 22 that I decided "to engage myself more heavily in strategic doctrinal issues. This issue has not been given adequate attention . . . yet our strategic doctrine is based largely on the experience of the sixties, which is less and less relevant to the late seventies and is likely to be altogether irrelevant in the eighties. Moreover, the Soviets . . . are developing a war-fighting capability and we have to think through the implications of this doctrinal asymmetry."

A series of PDs were issued. In September 1978, the President signed a directive to the effect that defensive capabilities are part of the strategic balance. Previously, we had considered only offensive forces as relevant to that balance. This was followed in November 1979 by another directive, setting forth for the first time certain goals for national C31 objectives and providing for more endurance, flexibility, and ability to manage a prolonged conflict. Here we had a document in which for the first time the United States deliberately sought for itself the capability to manage a protracted nuclear conflict, and it recognized that supporting activities in such areas as mobilization, continuity of government, and intelligence would be critical. In March 1980, the President issued a further directive, developing a more comprehensive mobilization guidance, with this document being the first national-level guidance on mobilization planning in more than two decades. Subsequent to its issuance, actual mobilization exercises were held for the first time and they revealed very major deficiencies in our capabilities. Finally, in the summer of 1980, the President authorized a wholly new conceptual approach to ensuring the survival of the national command authority. It provided for special emergency arrangements for the continuity of government under conditions of war, updating old plans and seeking a new and survivable basing mode for the senior officials.

In seeking to define our revised strategic doctrine, I posed in the course of 1979 and early 1980 three central questions which I felt needed analysis, and the answers to which I hoped would result in a significant revision of our strategic thinking. I asked DOD and JCS: What would it take to maintain stable deterrence in the 1980s? What would it take for the United States to be able to engage in stable crisis bargaining in the likely conditions of the 1980s? And what would be the requirements of politically effective management of a nuclear war under the likely conditions of the 1980s? In addition, I suggested that to answer these questions appropriately one would have to answer first the last question, for only by answering what requirements would have to be met to manage a war effectively could we provide a meaningful answer to the question regarding the requirements of stable crisis bargaining. Otherwise, we could not bargain stably, but would have to either preempt or concede. And only if we had answered the questions regarding the requirements both of war and of stable crisis bargaining would we be in a position to meet the requirements of sufficient deterrence. I used the occasion of a closed lecture at the National Defense University to disseminate some of these ideas more widely, and my staff continued its collaboration with its counterparts in Defense in developing the needed responses.

By late spring of 1979, I could note in my journal that "Harold Brown has now become much more interested in greater flexibility and is clearly moving away from a rigid deterrence posture. Cy Vance remains concerned and skeptical." By this time, the Defense Department had submitted its papers on strategic targeting policy, and our discussions on the subject, over which Harold Brown presided, moved our thinking a great deal forward. At a meeting held on May 15, 1979, I argued that we now needed a new document, codifying our review, and Harold Brown strongly agreed with me, though he was contested by Christopher, representing State.

With all of this work under our belt, in very early 1980 I instructed Colonel, soon to be General Odom of my staff, together with his associates on the NSC, to develop an initial draft of a new doctrinal statement. Once this was ready, Harold Brown and his associates worked it over, inserting additional references to the notion of a countervailing posture, an idea which Brown on his own had started to articulate, and thus our efforts came to be joined together. By mid-May 1980, I was in a position to submit the document for Presidential approval.

In so doing, I noted that it might be useful for the President to convene a formal NSC meeting on the proposed doctrinal revisions, so that other principals could become acquainted with the proposed changes, or alternatively that a briefing be held just for the President and the Vice President, with Brown later following it up with a separate briefing for Muskie. The President chose the second alternative, and the subsequent, though I strongly believe unintentional, delay in Brown's briefing of Muskie later prompted a public flap to the effect that Muskie had been deliberately excluded from the process. Fortunately, Vance went on public record as indicating that while serving as Secretary of State he had been fully involved, and the issue gradually faded from the scene, though not without some bitter press attacks on me, alleging that I had deliberately excluded the Secretary of State from the exercise.

PD-59 marked an important new step in the evolution of American strategic thought. As publicly reported, flexibility was expanded beyond preplanned options. Greater targeting emphasis was placed on military targets, on C_3I, and on war-supporting Soviet industries. C_3I was treated as a broader requirement, for control of both strategic and general-purpose forces in a protracted conflict, and it called for a "look—shoot—look" capability for identifying new and moving targets. The Secure Reserve Force was to be increased for influencing military campaigns and not only for psychological coercion. Finally, and very importantly, acquisition policy was tied to employment policy for the first time.

Till PD-59 was issued, American war planning postulated a brief, spasmic, and apocalyptic conflict. It was based on the presumption of a short war, lasting a few days at most. The new PDs that the President issued marked a departure from this earlier pattern, so reminiscent of allied planning prior to the outbreak of the war in 1914. The new directives were concerned with mobilization, defense, command, and control for a long conflict, and with flexible use of our forces, strategic and general-purpose, on behalf of war aims that we would select as we engaged in conflict. All of that, in my view, gave the United States a more coherent and more effective *doctrine of deterrence*, designed in keeping with both the capabilities and the doctrines of our potential opponent and thus more likely to deter him effectively. Finally, assuming sustained progress in the development of the Rapid Deployment Force, the new strategic doctrine would provide the necessary deterrence umbrella for the needed application of American conventional force if some regional interests vital to the United States were threatened. The Carter Doctrine thus had important geopolitical as well as strategic dimensions.

Checking Soviet Assertiveness

By 1980, Carter had a foreign policy that, in my judgment, combined the good virtues of Wilson's and of Truman's. Like Wilson's, it was focused on a longer-term objective of shaping a world order that would be increasingly just and more responsive to the aspirations of politically awakened peoples no longer willing passively to accept the domination of a few imperial states. Whatever might have been the imperfections of application on the level of practical policy, Carter had succeeded in identifying America worldwide with human rights, with sympathy for majority rule, with the objective of nonproliferation. But, like Truman, he was also prepared to rebuff Soviet expansionism, to demarcate clearly what were our vital interests, and to commit American power to the goal of political as well as strategic deterrence. It was thus a balanced policy, recognizing the importance of principle as a long-term beacon but also of power as the necessary tool of effective policy.

The best statement of this balanced approach was the speech that Carter delivered on May 9, 1980, in Philadelphia. It was meant to be a conceptual statement, building on the much earlier statements made in May 1977 at Notre Dame, but taking into account the developments that had taken place since then. The Notre Dame speech was a philosophical statement, expressing our objectives and projecting our optimism. The famous sentence that we should eschew "inordinate fear of Communism" was not a dismissal of the reality of Soviet power but an optimistic recognition of the greater appeal of liberty and of the superiority of the democratic system. In the Philadelphia speech, the President put major emphasis on the new strategic challenge confronting the United States as a result of the Soviet threat to the Persian Gulf and on the need, therefore, for the West to apply its power in a firm fashion in order to deter the new surge of Soviet assertiveness. The President's message was that foreign policy "must be based simultaneously on the primacy of certain basic moral principles—principles founded on the enhancement of human rights—and on the preservation of an American military strength that is second to none. This fusion of power and principle is the only way to ensure global stability and peace while we accommodate to the inevitable and necessary reality of global change and progress. . . . Americans must be mature enough to recognize that we need to be strong and we need to be accommodating at the same time."

Unfortunately, with the notable exception of such more thoughtful writers as James Reston, most American commentators on foreign affairs did not focus on the speech but reported on some casual remarks that Carter made shortly after its delivery, comparing the personalities of the new Secretary of State, Muskie, and of the recently resigned Vance. This was regrettable, for the speech represented a summary of the lessons learned during the preceding three years and an augury of what policy Carter might have pursued if he had been reelected.

The firm U.S. reaction to the Soviet invasion of Afghanistan, followed by the more consistent foreign policy line that now emanated from the White House and the State Department, helped to overcome the widespread impression of an indecisive America. This manifested itself most dramatically at the Economic Summit held in June in Venice. On the way to the summit, the President turned down a recommendation from Fritz Mondale that the grain embargo be lifted. "I made the point that if it is lifted after Reagan had recommended its lifting, the farmers will conclude that they owe the lifting to Reagan and thus we will get no political benefit from it while the rest of the country will consider it as additional evidence of the President's zigzagging. The President told Muskie and me flatly that if he were to alter his position on the grain embargo both his wife and Jody would 'resign.' "

On the way to the Economic Summit, Carter first flew to Rome for a state visit, and used the occasion of the visit to Rome to deliver a major speech, repeating some of the themes of his Philadelphia address. This was designed to provide the point of departure for the discussions in Venice with the other top leaders of the Western industrialized democracies.

The stop in Rome gave me a unique personal opportunity to spend close to seven hours with Pope John Paul II. I was again struck in our conversations (we had some earlier one-on-one discussions during the Papal visit to Washington in October 1979) by how political the Pope's thinking was. Indeed, at one point he mentioned that when he first met Carter he had the impression that it was two religious leaders who were consulting together, and I could not resist the temptation to respond that for the last several hours I had had the impression that it was two political leaders who were consulting together. In his comments, the Pope reviewed carefully the political situation in the Middle East, which we feared might become stalemated; relations with China; and the internal situation in the Soviet bloc, with special attention to Poland. I wrote in my journal: "The most impressive personality of the trip was clearly the Pope. Having spent seven hours with him was the high point of the trip for me. He came across clearly as a man of extraordinary vision and political intelligence. In a sense, I think it is fair to say that today he is *the* outstanding Western leader. I particularly appreciate his sense of authority and his understanding that Western man does crave a sense of direction which is firmly and clearly defined."

The Venice meeting was more productive on Afghanistan than we had anticipated. Carter asked me to sit in on the sessions dealing with political-strategic matters, and I was delighted to see that none of the Western leaders objected to our efforts to have the meeting issue a strongly worded statement dealing with the Soviet aggression in Afghanistan. The statement was tough and to the point. The seven nations agreed that "the Soviet military occupation of Afghanistan is unacceptable now and that we are determined not to accept it in the future." The occupation of Afghanistan "undermines the foundations of peace both in the region and in the world."

However, Venice was not without its unpleasant moments. Carter and Schmidt had a particularly nasty meeting, in which the testy German Chancellor came close to being abusive. By then Schmidt had let it be known to all and sundry what a low opinion he had of the U.S. President. In turn, Carter, who had tried to avoid public polemics, had concluded that Schmidt was unstable, egotistical, and unreliable. After the United States adopted sanctions against the Soviet Union over the Afghanistan invasion, Vance had seen Schmidt on February 20, and in his report to the President (contained in a long memo of February 25) he indicated without quite saying so that Schmidt's earlier determination to stand fast with us was melting as quickly as snow in a late Rhineland winter. This was particularly ironic because Schmidt had previously used numerous occasions to tell newspapermen and foreign visitors that he felt that Carter was not steadfast enough. The President was deeply annoyed by what he learned from Vance and noted on the memo: "Cy, Zbig—Overall, I see nothing encouraging here. F.R.G. opposes any sanctions against Iran or Soviets, are continuing business as usual with S.U., refuse to commit publicly to Olympic boycott, and privately and in press are very critical of us. However, we need each other. Schmidt's visit should help. J." The visit did not help, and by Venice a new issue had arisen to poison the relationship even further (if that was still possible).

It involved the allied decision, reached in December 1979, to move forward with the deployment of theater nuclear weapons (TNF) in Europe, as a response to the progressively more menacing deployment by the Soviets of their highly advanced triple-warheaded SS-20 missiles. As previously stated, it was Schmidt himself who earlier, in a public speech, had pointed to that danger, arguing that the "Euro-strategic balance" was being threatened, with the result that American–European security interdependence may be "decoupled." It was to meet that threat that the TNF initiative was developed after a number of discussions with Schmidt, in which he insisted that such a response was needed. However, in the late spring of 1980, Schmidt, reacting to domestic pressures and perhaps anxious to preserve his self-appointed role as the West's interlocutor to Moscow, made ambiguous public statements to the effect that it might be better to impose a freeze both on Western and on Soviet theater nuclear weapons deployments.

Since such a freeze would have legitimated and made permanent the situation of "a Euro-strategic imbalance," shortly before the Venice summit I phoned Schmidt's principal national security adviser, asking him for a clarification of this statement and pointing out that it was inconsistent with the NATO decisions. These decisions clearly had stated that the West would proceed with the deployment of counter-vailing TNF forces while at the same time being prepared to negotiate with the Soviets equitable arms control arrangements. Schmidt's assistant assured me that the Chancellor had been misinterpreted by the press. At the same time, David Aaron, my deputy, who had been primarily responsible for negotiating with the Europeans on TNF, initiated, in collaboration with Walter Slocombe of Secretary Brown's office and Reginald Bartholomew of Muskie's office, a formal message from Carter to Schmidt, pointing out that Schmidt's statements, presumably incorrectly reported by the press, could be harmful to our collective efforts and that it was important for all of us to stand unambiguously on the NATO decisions. Both Muskie and I thought the proposed message was needed to set the record straight and recommended to the President that it be dispatched. Carter approved it, and shortly thereafter someone in the State Department leaked it to both an American and a European journalist.

Schmidt was infuriated and requested, on the eve of the Venice meeting, a private session with the President. It was an angry and at times an altogether unpleasant session, with Schmidt striking me as occasionally not being quite balanced. (The meeting is described more fully in Chapter 8.) Fortunately, Carter kept his cool, and at the end of the meeting the two leaders appeared before the assembled press to underline their continued friendship and unity.

However, not long thereafter Schmidt fulfilled an invitation from Brezhnev to visit Moscow, to discuss Afghanistan and other issues. He knew that we were opposed to the visit, but all we could do was to prevail on him not to undertake it before the Venice meeting. Accordingly, the trip took place on June 30. Shortly after his return from the Kremlin, Schmidt requested, through an intermediary, an opportunity to speak privately with two of Carter's Cabinet members, both also political confidants of the President. As Carter later told me, on each occasion he used the opportunity to urge that the President dismiss me, arguing that I had had a negative influence on the President, particularly on the East–West relationship. I could not tell whether Schmidt's extraordinary initiative, unprecedented in German–American relations, had anything to do with his earlier visit to Moscow, but I was gratified by the President's contemptuous dismissal of it as well as by the fact that the President personally told me about it.

The firm posture taken by the United States in response to the Soviet invasion of Afghanistan proved its worth later in the year, in the case of the historically important developments in Poland. For the preceding year and a half, the economic and political situation in Poland had been deteriorating, in large measure because of the unsoundness of the economic policies pursued by the Polish leadership but also, more broadly, because of the growing national resentment against both Soviet domination and the overly bureaucratized and sterile Communist system.

Carter's Administration displayed considerable interest in Polish affairs, and from early 1977 on we took advantage of every opportunity to demonstrate our sympathy. The President chose Poland to be the first country to which he paid a state visit. American economic aid was maintained and gradually increased, and contacts with Polish leaders, both governmental and nongovernmental, were cultivated. By mid-1979, I was receiving quite explicit signals from some Polish leaders that the situation was deteriorating greatly and that the pro-Soviet elements in Poland were deliberately interfering with Polish economic programs so as to keep Poland dependent on the Soviet Union. Considering the fact that these messages were from highly placed and official sources, I felt that the situation in Poland was moving toward a critical stage. I briefed the President in early September 1979 on my conclusion that developments in Poland represented "a significant change in the Soviet world and a sign of decreasing Soviet control," and I said that we should intensify both our contacts with Poland and our economic assistance. In late 1979 and early 1980, meetings to that effect were held in both the PRC and the SCC, and we continued our policy of quiet assistance.

By August 1980, the situation in Poland had become quite volatile, with the Solidarity free trade union movement asserting itself more and more effectively against Party control. There was no doubt that a national resurgence was occurring, and that the authorities in Warsaw, and even more so in Moscow, were perplexed as to how to respond. On August 25, I urged the President to underline American interest in these developments through Presidential letters to Prime Minister Thatcher, President Giscard, and Chancellor Schmidt, as well as to the Pope, and to initiate an exchange of views on this subject so that a common Western policy would emerge. The letters also noted our concern over possible Soviet intervention, and that in turn led to initial State Department consultations with our European counterparts on possible contingency measures in the event the Soviets moved in.

In early September, the AFL-CIO decided to provide financial assistance to the fledgling Polish trade union movement, and I was distressed to hear that the President approved Muskie's initiative to call in the Soviet Ambassador to tell him that the U.S. government had nothing to do with this action. I phoned Muskie and prevailed on him at least to call in the Polish Ambassador as well so that the appearance would not be created that we accepted Poland as a vassal of the Soviet Union and that we owed such explanations to the Soviets alone. Internally, our interagency discussions on aid to Poland moved forward, and by mid-September we were ready to announce additional credits for Poland. Throughout, on this issue there was good collaboration between the NSC and State, Defense, and Commerce; everyone concerned recognized that the consolidation of a freer system in Poland would significantly affect the East–West balance, and some felt that it might create preconditions for the fading of the post-World War II division of Europe.

However, toward the end of September and certainly by early October, the situation began to look more ominous, with portents of possible Soviet intervention. Accordingly, I started convening the SCC in order to review contingencies for a possible crisis, and that gave me additional opportunity to influence the shaping of our policy toward Poland. I made certain that, in a forthcoming meeting with Gromyko, Secretary Muskie conveyed in clear and unambiguous tones that the United States would view any Soviet intervention as a grave threat to peace, and Muskie did that with considerable élan. By the third week of October, the SCC was in a position to approve a series of specific steps designed to penalize the Soviet Union severely in the event of military intervention, and we used these decisions as the basis for allied consultations.

Throughout this period I was guided by the thought that the United States must avoid the mistake that it made in 1968, when it failed to communicate to the Soviets prior to their intervention in Czechoslovakia the costs of such an aggression to East–West relations and to the Soviet Union specifically. Accordingly, my strategy was to generate advance understanding on the various sanctions that would be adopted, and to make as much of that publicly known as possible, so that the Soviets would know what would follow and that we were politically bound to react. I realized that this would not be a decisive factor in Soviet calculations, but I felt that under certain circumstances it could make more than a marginal difference in the event of any internal Kremlin disagreement. In keeping with that, in late November I sent both Muskie and Brown a memorandum, which I assumed would be circulated among their associates and might eventually leak, stating that in my judgment Soviet intervention would produce a rupture in the political detente in Europe, disrupt East–West economic cooperation, generate increased NATO budgets, produce severe strains between Western European Communist parties and the Soviet Union, further alienate the Non-Aligned Movement from the Soviet Union, possibly precipitate turmoil elsewhere in the Soviet bloc, and probably lead to overt American–Chinese military cooperation. I was also hoping that in their public comments Muskie and Brown might make use of this list, and I myself gave background briefings to some members of the press.

The situation came nearly to a head in the first two weeks of December. We learned that Soviet forces had been deployed in an offensive mode, sections of the East German–Polish and of the Soviet–Polish frontiers had been sealed off, and we had mounting indications of accelerated preparations in airfields, depots, and even hospitals. On December 3, I convened a meeting with Brown, Muskie, and Turner in my office. We agreed that the President should issue a public statement reiterating for the record that any Soviet action would have far-reaching consequences for East–West relations and that American policy toward the Soviet Union would be directly and very adversely affected.

In addition, we decided to send a message to Brezhnev repeating these points, while also underlining our established position that the United States had no intention of exploiting the developments within Poland itself to threaten legitimate Soviet security interests. I was happy that the United States was now on record, quite unlike our passive stance prior to the Soviet action in Czechoslovakia, and I was further reassured by growing indications that our allies would stand equally fast. Especially important was the assurance I received from the German Ambassador in early December that West Germany would adopt economic sanctions against the Soviet Union in the event of Soviet military intervention. Given the scale of German credits and trade with the Soviet Union, this was an extremely important reinforcement for our efforts to deter the Soviets.

On Friday, December 5, at 9:10 a.m., I received a secure call from Turner informing me that according to reliable information a number of Soviet divisions were scheduled to enter Poland on Monday morning. I immediately informed the President and advised him that I would hold an SCC meeting the next day if further information confirmed the report that an invasion was imminent. The President told me to schedule also an NSC meeting in the White House for Sunday, to which he would return from the planned weekend in Camp David. At the SCC meeting, held at 4 p.m. on Saturday, Turner informed us that it was anticipated that Soviet divisions would enter Poland in the next forty-eight hours and that this would be accompanied by a crackdown by the Polish Communist regime on the Solidarity movement. The Agency judgment was that there would be national resistance and considerable bloodshed. I was somewhat skeptical that the Polish leadership as a whole would be prepared to collude in any such action, and therefore I suspected that news of a possible crackdown would spread before any actual intervention took place. Accordingly, we sent instructions to our Embassy in Warsaw to step up political reporting from Poland.

The NSC convened at 9 a.m. on Sunday in the Cabinet Room. We again reviewed intelligence information indicating that the Soviets would move into Poland under the guise of a "peaceful exercise" and that this would be combined with a simultaneous massive crackdown against the Solidarity movement. The President decided to issue a stronger public statement and also to send messages to key foreign governments urging them to respond both publicly and privately for the purpose of deterring the Soviets. In the early afternoon, I chaired an SCC meeting at which these messages were drafted, a press briefing was held, and congressional leaders were informed on what might soon occur. In addition, through my own channels, I arranged for telephone calls to alert the Solidarity leaders in Warsaw, so that they could take personal precautions so as to avoid being swooped up during the night.

Finally, with the President's approval, I phoned the Pope and briefed him on the situation. (I do not know if the Pope had ever been phoned from the United States before, but I reached him late in the evening, Vatican time, and his secretary's first response, when I identified myself and asked to speak to the Pope, was to say, "I will see if I can find him." The Pope came on thirty seconds later, and in a way the conversation was historically unique. Here was the Assistant for National Security Affairs to the President of the United States conferring with the Roman Pontiff in the Vatican in Polish about peace and Poland.)

The situation remained tense for the next several days, with intelligence agencies indicating that the scope of the Soviet intervention might be even greater than anticipated. Additional divisions were identified as ready to move, and—according to press reports—preparations included advance storage of fuel supplies, the unfolding of tents next to field hospitals to provide more space for likely casualties, and the forward deployment of assault forces, including paratroopers. In our efforts to deter the Soviets from moving, we undertook three further steps. With Brezhnev about to visit New Delhi, Mrs. Gandhi was prevailed upon to register strongly with the Soviets Indian concerns over such a move; I conferred with Lane Kirkland of the AFL-CIO, and we agreed that a worldwide boycott on the shipment to the Soviet Union of any goods, by air, rail, or sea, should be organized—Kirkland seemed reasonably optimistic that there would be widespread international support—and I sent a memorandum to the Department of Defense instructing it to prepare lists of weapons that might be transferred by the United States to China in the event of a Soviet invasion of Poland. Knowing the Defense Department, I felt fairly confident that the substance of this memorandum would rapidly become more publicly known.

On December 8, I wrote in my journal: "I see four objectives to what we are doing: One is to deprive the Soviets of surprise. This we have already done. Two, perhaps to encourage the Poles to resist if they are not taken by surprise, for this might somewhat deter the Soviets. The publicity is already doing that. Thirdly and paradoxically, to calm the situation in Poland by making the Poles more aware that the Soviets may in fact enter. The Poles have till now discounted this possibility and this may have emboldened them excessively. Here in effect we have a common interest with the Soviets, for they too may prefer to intimidate the Poles to a degree. And fourth, to deter the Soviets from coming in by intensifying international pressure and condemnation of the Soviet Union."

A key element in political deterrence of the Soviets was the President's tough-minded decision to accept my recommendation that all of the information cited earlier be disseminated as widely as possible. Allied and even some neutral governments were fully informed, and I briefed the press on the details of the Soviet military preparations. Turner's timely intelligence was thus put to good use in depriving the Soviets of secrecy and surprise.

During the next several days, our efforts were reinforced by a very strong message from Giscard to the Soviets, though we had some indications of a wavering German attitude. Our public alarm generated considerable international anxiety, and precipitated further expressions of concern to the Soviets, even from Western European Communist parties. Last but not least, we also deprived the Soviets of the critical element of surprise insofar as the Poles were concerned, and some Poles undertook preparations for national resistance, including the flooding of mines, the closing down of blast furnaces, the disruption of communications, as well as the occupation and lock-ins by workers of industrial plants, from which resistance would have been offered. Thus the costs of an intervention to the Soviets were increased, though there is no way of knowing whether in fact the actual decision to intervene had been reached by the Kremlin and then rescinded because of this massive reaction. What we do know is that military moves were afoot, that preparations to move had been completed, and that initial implementing actions were on the way and were terminated after the U.S.-led global reaction. Moreover, one cannot discount the overall impact on the Soviets of our earlier response to the Afghanistan aggression, which must have contributed to the greater credibility of our response to the Polish challenge.

The Polish crisis was the final major test of American–Soviet relations during the Carter Presidency. The President handled it well, firmly and calmly, and there is no doubt that he had digested fully the lessons of the U.S. underreaction to the Czechoslovak crisis of 1968. During the critical days of December, Carter did not need to be convinced of the historical importance of deterring a Soviet move, and in this effort he was quite prepared to exercise the full weight of American influence and to take a public position designed to convince the Soviet Union that the reaction of the United States, and of the world more generally, would be even more severe than it was in the period after the invasion of Afghanistan. Moreover, all of his principal advisers were supportive, and on this issue there was a notable absence of internal dissent.

In the waning days of the Administration, the last national security issue requiring a Presidential decision involved our continuing preoccupation with the threat to the Arabian peninsula. Harold Brown and Robert Komer took the initiative in fashioning a comprehensive document outlining a long-range military plan for the Persian Gulf, in keeping with our earlier efforts to generate a regional security framework. The document was a bold and forward-looking statement, and both Brown and Komer deserve a great deal of credit for leaving it on our successors' agenda. It also represented the high point of Brown's gradual and initially reticent involvement in strategic matters. In line with our new Persian Gulf strategy, Brown also prevailed on Carter, Muskie, and Mondale to adopt a positive attitude on the Saudi request for the sale of AWACS in order to ensure the safety of the vital Arabian oil fields.

These final debates indicated, however, that Carter's reelection probably would have precipitated a major argument within the Administration on our overall defense and strategic posture. Muskie, Christopher, and probably Mondale would have been pitted against Brown and me, with Carter having to make the final decision. My journal notes for December 21, reporting on an SCC meeting held on Harold's strategy paper, are revealing. Brown had outlined the strategic challenge we were likely to confront in the years ahead, and he concluded that the United States had to acquire the capability to fight either one full-scale war or two "half wars." This in turn would require not only an augmentation of American military capabilities in the Persian Gulf region but quicker rearmament of Japan and a closer security relationship with China. "Muskie was very upset at first. His hands were literally quivering when he questioned the appropriateness of discussing this paper as a preliminary to the NSC. However, with Brown asserting himself strongly, with Komer backing him, and with me encouraging at least a discussion of the key issues raised by Brown, the discussion did move forward. Nonetheless, the reaction is typical of what we might have expected had we been reelected."

The concluding act in fashioning a comprehensive strategy designed to meet Soviet assertiveness in the dangerous and turbulent decade of the 1980s involved codifying all that was done into two last Presidential Directives—PD-62 and PD-63. Brown and I felt strongly that it was appropriate, and in keeping with precedents, for the President to issue such directives, which summarized our new strategic doctrine and our efforts to promote the regional security framework. These documents were meant to provide our successors with a useful point of reference, even though they would obviously not be binding on them. Secretary Muskie objected to their issuance, and even refused to comment on the preliminary drafts, arguing that the action was inappropriate and likely to be politically misunderstood. There may have been more substantive reasons for his reluctance, in view of the positions that he and Christopher took on these matters in the various SCC discussions. But with the President's signing of these two directives in the last days of his Administration, I felt we completed an important year during which we had fashioned a new geopolitical doctrine, a revised nuclear strategy, and a foreign policy in which our continued commitment to principle was reinforced by a more credible emphasis on the role of American power.

13

Lives and National Interest

What's right for our nation and its interest and principles, on the
one hand, is closely interrelated to what's best for the lives and
safety of the hostages. I have never had to face any difference between those two, and I try in my own mind to keep them compatible and I think every action that I've taken so far and every
action that I would contemplate in the future would not be to
abandon either one of those commitments of mine: our nation's
prestige and interest on the one hand, the hostages' lives and safety
and freedom on the other.

—President Jimmy Carter,
interview, April 21, 1980

The final year of the Carter Presidency started for me in the dark hours
of the morning on Sunday, November 4, 1979, at 5:10. The red phone
on my night table rang sharply. Early-morning calls were by no means
unheard of, and I had no premonition that this one would be so fateful.
The calm, professional voice of the Duty Officer in the Situation Room
informed me that the U.S. Embassy in Tehran was being taken over by
a mob.

This was not the first time that this had happened. On February 14,
the Embassy had been stormed by Iranian radicals, but the Iranian
government succeeded in restoring order and in removing the demonstrators. Moreover, in the months that followed the Shah's departure,
we had undertaken cautious efforts to stabilize the American–Iranian
relationship. My colleagues at State, after all, had felt all along that the
departure of the Shah might lead to a somewhat more distant but still
not hostile Iran, with Khomeini—that "Gandhi-like figure," according
to Ambassador Sullivan—exercising his benign influence from the background. Though my own prognosis for Iran was far less rosy, I did feel
that we ought to try to tap the anti-Communist sentiment of the now
dominant fundamentalist clergy, and on several public occasions both
the President and I made thinly veiled appeals to the Iranians which
underscored our common interest in containing Communism.

During this period our central strategic objective was to help Iran
preserve its national integrity and independence. Even though Iran was
openly hostile to us, we continued to feel that during the difficult phase

of consolidation it would be wiser for us not to engage in policies designed to destabilize the new Iranian government but, on the contrary, to remind the Iranians that their security required a stable relationship with the United States. In addition, in the wake of the Shah's fall, I initiated within the Administration increasingly intensive efforts to fashion a security framework for the region to supplant our prior reliance on Iran.

As I feared, however, the revolutionary dynamic within Iran worked against stability and compromise. The enemies of the Shah, united only by their desire to get rid of him, were torn by conflicting objectives: the moderate reformers and secular radicals hoped, by and large, for some form of social-democratic regime, though this group also contained many who believed much more in social engineering by compulsion than in democracy; the Islamic fundamentalists ranged from old-fashioned religious fanatics to those who tried to blend somehow Islamic values and modernity; finally, the extreme left contained a strong and disciplined Communist element. All of these groups were busily arming themselves, since, in addition to slaughtering the Shah's supporters, they were engaged in growing violence against one another. To this day no one knows the scale of the executions in Iran, but at times literally scores of people were being executed daily after mock trials (a toll far in excess of anything that ever took place under the Shah). In addition, there were mass incarcerations, public floggings, and even executions by stoning, as well as assassinations.

During the first year after the overthrow of the Shah, most of the victims of the bloody butcheries were adherents of the previous regime. The radical elements exploited the common anxiety of the Shah's successors that the former monarch might somehow stage a comeback. Exaggerated claims concerning the Shah's wealth deposited abroad, notably in the United States, were also useful in stirring up the masses and creating an atmosphere of hatred both for the former ruler and for his principal sponsor, the United States. The issue of the Shah as a person and his wealth was thus a convenient tool not only for keeping America and Iran apart but also for radicalizing Iranian politics. The hostage crisis was an extension of this internal Iranian turmoil, and for us in Washington it posed a painful dilemma: could we save the lives of the hostages without sacrificing our principles and regional interests?

The Unwelcome Guest

Initially, it was taken for granted by the President's top advisers that the deposed monarch, who had been our ally and whose retention of the throne the United States had actively sponsored in the early fifties, would be welcome on our shores. In early January 1979, when President

Giscard d'Estaing of France suggested to us that it might be wiser for the Shah not to come to the United States but to stay in the Middle East, all of us reacted adversely. On the afternoon of January 14, Vance, Christopher, Brown, and I met in my office to discuss the situation in Iran, and after I had reported on Giscard's suggestion to Carter, Brown flatly stated, "If we seem to be backing off on our invitation, our name would be mud." I wholeheartedly agreed, adding that if the Shah "hangs around [the Middle East], everyone will think he's coming back. That's not good for us if we want action. The difficult choices would be postponed." Cy agreed, and actively solicited for the Shah the hospitality of a wealthy American, Walter Annenberg.

But suddenly, without consulting us, the Shah decided to postpone his arrival in America and to linger first as a guest of Sadat and then of King Hassan of Morocco. Perhaps he was so advised by others, perhaps he considered the situation in Iran to be still fluid and hoped for a sudden reversal. In any case, the Shah put some distance between himself and us, and that pause in his journey of exile to America proved to be disastrous. While earlier it was seen as axiomatic that the Shah could enter America, before too long his arrival began to be regarded, particularly by the State Department, as a needless complication in our efforts toward improved relations with Iran and a pointless provocation to the radicals. The Shah's own procrastination thus generated an issue where none should have existed.

My position never wavered. I felt throughout that we should simply not permit the issue to arise. This was a matter of both principle and tactics. I felt strongly that at stake were our traditional commitment to asylum and our loyalty to a friend. To compromise those principles would be to pay an extraordinarily high price not only in terms of self-esteem but in our standing among our allies, and for very uncertain benefits. I was aware that Sadat, Hassan, the Saudi rulers, and others were watching our actions carefully. Moreover, I felt that, tactically, we could not be blackmailed if we made it clear that what we were doing was central to our system of values, that the matter was not one of weighing pros and cons or costs and benefits, but was integral to our political tradition.

The issue was joined as a policy dispute in the late spring. In March 1979, it became clear that first Sadat and then Hassan had begun to feel that the Shah was overstaying his welcome and they began to urge him to move on. The Shah himself had apparently reached a more pessimistic conclusion regarding his future prospects and started hinting strongly that he would like to resume his journey to the United States. By then, the view had jelled among Vance, Christopher, and Newsom that his arrival would complicate the process of improving relations with the post-Shah regime and that it could pose a threat to the safety of

Americans in Iran. Their views were strongly contested by influential friends of the Shah in America. On Monday, April 9, I told the President of a phone call I had received on April 7 from Henry Kissinger, who in rather sharp terms had complained about the Administration's seeming unwillingness to permit the Shah to enter the United States. The President was visibly irritated by my comments and asked me quite flatly, "What would you do if you were President?" I told him that in my judgment this was not only a pragmatic question, which called for a careful assessment of the impact of our decision on Hassan or Sadat, but above all a question of principle. We simply had to stand by those who had been our friends.

It was evident to me that the President was not happy with my reaction and was torn by the political and human dilemma with which he was now confronted. Shortly thereafter the President told me that he had had a call from David Rockefeller, and again I sensed that the President was deeply troubled. A few days later, the matter became public knowledge when a front-page story in the New York *Times* revealed that Rockefeller, Kissinger, and John McCloy were pressuring the Administration to admit the Shah, and that the Administration was concerned that this decision might trigger mob action against Americans in Iran.

The question of the Shah kept percolating, though at this time I was more preoccupied with other regional issues as well as with U.S.–Soviet relations. I was also not involved in the various discussions between State and the Shah regarding alternative refuges. But our stance on this matter troubled my conscience, and in early May I suggested to the President that we should at least be flexible on the question of the Shah's wife and children. They ought to be guaranteed a safe haven, even if for the moment political conditions did not permit us to have the Shah come with them. Cy Vance agreed, and not long afterwards some arrangements were made for study here by the Shah's son.

On July 23, I informed Vance and Brown that Mondale had sent a memo in which "the Vice President has recommended that the time has come to review our policy on residence in the U.S. by the Shah. The Vice President moreover notes that 'to deny an individual entry to the U.S. runs against the instinct and traditions of most Americans. . . .' While he does not prejudge the outcome of the review, he feels it should be undertaken and I concur. Perhaps we could discuss this during our forthcoming lunch, but I thought it might be helpful to raise this issue with you both beforehand. We will need to reflect on it carefully."

This resulted in renewed discussions with Brown and Vance, as well as with Mondale. I sensed that Mondale was coming around to the view that it would be better to let the Shah come, and that he would speak to the President about it. Vance remained strongly opposed, while Brown reserved his position. In late July 1979, I was called by both Kissinger and Schlesinger, who urged me to promote a reconsideration of our position on the Shah. Kissinger in his subtle fashion linked his willingness to support us on SALT to a more forthcoming attitude on our part regarding the Shah. I realized, immediately after reporting this conversation to the President, that it was counterproductive to have done so, since the President strongly resented such outside pressures.

Perhaps for this reason, our next collective discussion on the future of the Shah became rather testy. It occurred at the foreign affairs breakfast of July 27. Mondale expressed the view that our policy should now be changed. He even went so far as to compare our refusal to admit the Shah to President Ford's refusal to meet with Solzhenitsyn, commenting that it would play very badly politically. Both Carter and Vance became rather heated. The President noted that Kissinger, Rockefeller, and McCloy had been waging a constant campaign on the subject and that "Zbig bugged me on it every day." I interrupted the President and said, "No, sir," and Carter relented somewhat, muttering, "Well, not every day but very often." He then went on to make the prophetic comment that he did not wish the Shah to be here playing tennis while Americans in Tehran were being kidnapped or even killed.

When I raised the point that we should not be influenced by threats from a third-rate regime, and that at stake were our traditions and national honor, both Vance and Carter again became quite angry. We did agree, though, to reassess the situation after a new report (which Vance said he had requested) came in from our Embassy in Tehran.

As far as I was concerned, the issue remained dormant for the next several weeks, though in mid-August Princess Ashraf, the Shah's sister, wrote a highly personal letter to the President, quite literally begging him to grant asylum to the Shah. The President asked Christopher to draft a response, and Warren sent over a draft which was rather curt and cold, to the point of being addressed to "Ms. Pahlavi." I felt this was uncalled for, and redrafted it in a somewhat warmer fashion, with a more appropriate salutation. By then, I had a strong feeling that the issue of the Shah had become in some ways symbolic of our earlier disagreements over policy toward Iran, and I stopped raising it with the President.

The matter took a dramatic turn in mid-October. Early in the month, we received the first vague intimations that the Shah was seriously ill. On October 18, the President was quite suddenly advised by Vance that it had been established that the Shah was suffering from a potentially fatal illness and that he needed further diagnosis and treatment in the United States. By then the Shah was in residence in Mexico, though still knocking at our door. Cy reported also that we had asked the

Iranian government for protection for our Embassy and that the official Iranian response had been positive. In a preliminary discussion which followed on Friday, October 19, between the President and his senior foreign policy advisers, the President concluded, "We ought to make it clear that the Shah is welcome as long as the medical treatment is needed."

The President's formal decision was then made in response to a memorandum sent on October 20 to Camp David by Christopher (Vance was away on a trip), referring to the Shah's "malignant" illness and recommending examination in the United States. Warren reported that this was Vance's view, adding that we should inform the Iranian government accordingly and obtain their approval. Needless to say, I concurred with the recommendation, but in my cover memo to the President I noted that it was inappropriate for the United States to ask the Iranians for approval. I felt that we should simply inform them of our decision, especially in view of the earlier preliminary exchanges. The President decided that same day to go ahead, though he instructed me simply to inform the Iranians of our decision. It was clear to me that the President felt morally ill at ease over the exclusion of the Shah and that Mondale's earlier change of heart had had an impact. Vance's flat recommendation that temporary admission be granted on compassionate medical grounds clinched the matter.

The Shah arrived in the United States on October 23. The day before, Cy reported that the initial reaction of the Iranian government was moderate. This was also the case with the Iranian public reaction immediately after the Shah's arrival. Despite our concern, and contrary to some subsequent reports, in the days immediately following the Shah's admission to the United States there was no increased hostility in the daily protests outside the walls of the Embassy compound. (This was pointed out later by our heroic chargé d'affaires in Tehran, Bruce Laingen, after his release, in a letter to the New York *Times.*)

A week later, on November 1, I was in Algiers, heading the American delegation to the twenty-fifth anniversary celebration of the Algerian revolution. During this visit, the Iranian Prime Minister, Mehdi Bazargan, requested a meeting with me. I agreed, and we met in his hotel room that afternoon. Bazargan was accompanied by his Foreign Minister, Dr. Ibrahim Yazdi, and his Defense Minister, Mustafa Ali Chamran. Our discussion did not focus on the question of the Shah as such but dealt rather with our overall relationship. I made the point that the United States was not engaged in, nor would it encourage, conspiracies against the new Iranian regime and that "we are prepared for any relationship you want. . . . We have a basic community of interests but we do not know what you want us to do. . . . The American government is prepared to expand security, economic, political, and intelligence relationships at your pace." This produced some exchanges on the possibility of cooperation in the security area, with Chamran raising the question of American assistance to the Iranian military. Without making promises, I did not rule that out.

It was then that the question of the Shah arose. Yazdi, an American-trained doctor cultivating a radical sartorial style but with a rather ingratiating manner and quick wit, first referred to our previous support of the Shah, then added that his presence in the United States "disturbs us." He went on to say that even if the Shah might not personally be active, his people were, and "his presence in the United States leaves our people with the conclusion that the United States is involved." He also mocked the idea that the Shah sought asylum for medical reasons.

I responded to that quite strongly: "This discussion is humiliating and demeaning. I am not certain whether it is more humiliating for me to listen or for you to raise this. It is your country's tradition to give refuge. Many Polish refugees were welcomed in Iran in 1941. Iran acted honorably. The man is sick, and we will not act contrary to our principles." It was only then that Bazargan, an elderly Iranian liberal with an elegant goatee and a courtly manner, joined in, suggesting that perhaps Iranian doctors could examine the Shah so that the Iranians could be reassured that he really was ill. I responded by reiterating that "the Shah is not a political factor; he's a sick man and he will be treated according to our laws and our principles," though I did not flatly rule out Bazargan's suggestion. When the question of the Shah's assets was raised, I told my Iranian interlocutors that the doors to our courts were open and that they could sue for them anytime they wished. The discussion ended very amiably, and actually throughout the Iranians were surprisingly cordial. I reported on it immediately both to the President and to Vance.

Within days, however, an altogether new situation developed in Iran itself. On November 4, the Iranian militants stormed the Embassy, and two days later Bazargan was forced out of office. I do not know the motives for Bazargan's overture to me. Had I refused to talk, the Iranian radicals would have been provided with additional proof of American hostility, and the U.S. government would have been charged with rebuffing an important overture. Moreover, it is likely that by the fall of 1979 the more moderate of the Iranian successors to the Shah were beginning to feel increasingly isolated and were attempting to reach out. Alas, the internal dynamics within Iran doomed their efforts to failure. They simply lacked support. The logic of the revolutionary situation was at work, driving Iran more and more into the hands of extremists.

Patience and Pressure

Having received the news of the seizure of the Tehran Embassy on the morning of November 4, I consulted by secure phone with both Warren Christopher and Harold Brown. The Situation Room staff had told me that the President had been informed directly, and therefore I did not call the President myself until shortly after 9 a.m., having obtained some additional information from my NSC staffers. I told the President that Brown and I agreed that no immediate military response was possible and that we felt that we should avoid at this stage any publicized military deployments since the situation was very fluid. I noted that experience indicated that kidnappers were most volatile and trigger-happy in the early stages of hostage-taking. Moreover, on February 14 the Iranian government had acted properly, and Harold and I thus concurred with Warren's view that we should use friendly intermediaries to demand that the Iranian government take appropriate action. A regular SCC was promptly scheduled for the next morning, by which time we expected to have a clearer picture of what was happening in Tehran.

When the SCC convened at 10:30 on November 5, none of us had the slightest expectation that this act of kidnapping was the start of a fourteen-month-long crisis. During the many months that followed, we continued meeting several times a week, and the SCC served throughout as the central coordinating mechanism, directing our response. I chaired scores of such meetings, and they were attended frequently by the Vice President, the Secretary of State, the Secretary of Defense, the Director of the CIA, the Chairman of the Joint Chiefs, the Secretary of the Treasury, the Attorney General, the Counsel to the President, the President's Press Secretary, and the President's Chief of Staff. The SCC thus became a broadly gauged body, coordinating all the facets of our response, from the diplomatic, the military, and the financial to the spheres of public relations and domestic politics.

In time, more specialized subgroups were formed. Lloyd Cutler, the President's Counsel, did a superb job in coordinating the legal matters involved in our response, which ranged from domestic constitutional issues to laying our case before the International Court of Justice. Moreover, he collaborated very closely with Bill Miller, Blumenthal's replacement as Secretary of the Treasury, and Bob Carswell, Miller's deputy, in fashioning our embargoes as well as in the seizure of Iranian assets. Ben Civiletti, the Attorney General, was also deeply involved in both these matters. Vance and Christopher focused on diplomatic responses, and also collaborated closely with Ham Jordan in initiating confidential and informal negotiating channels to the Iranians. David Aaron provided continuity and supervision over implementation by frequently chairing the so-called mini-SCC, composed of senior inter-agency officials. Finally, I presided also over a small and highly secret group, involving only Harold Brown, General Jones, and Stan Turner, which was concerned with the development of military options. None of the other members of the SCC were permitted to take part in the meetings of this group, and we often met in my office rather than in the Situation Room.

Though the hostage issue was inevitably charged with much human emotion, and though the Iranian issue earlier had generated deep policy splits among us, our work throughout the crisis itself was conducted in a spirit of remarkable harmony. The division of labor worked effectively, coordination was maintained throughout, and SCC direction was loyally respected. The President was kept informed on a daily basis by reports on the SCC meetings (which were normally held at 9 a.m.), delivered to him in writing by the afternoon of the same day. Moreover, Vance, Brown, Mondale, and I would meet additionally with the President whenever a more important issue had surfaced, and we were joined quite frequently by Cutler, Miller, or others. Of course, the morning national security briefing also gave me a daily opportunity to update the President and to obtain guidance from him, which I would then transmit to the morning SCC meeting.

At the first SCC meeting, I focused our discussion on the diplomatic initiatives the United States needed to take and on the importance of mobilizing Islamic support for our efforts. I requested that contingency plans for military action be undertaken, for implementation in the event the hostages were killed or if Iran started falling apart. In addition, prior to the meeting I spoke with the President and suggested to him that we consider sending a private emissary to Khomeini to see if our people could be gotten out quickly. The President crinkled up his nose and was visibly reluctant to approach the aged tyrant, but did not veto the idea. I brought the matter up at the SCC; later in the day Christopher came back with a memorandum nominating two emissaries, and he and I decided to go ahead with this initiative.

At this very early stage, we were inclined to feel that the issue would not confront us for very long. We were all concerned that the Iranian government was practically nonexistent, especially after the fall of Bazargan, and we worried about what might happen to the remaining Americans in Iran. We agreed that their evacuation ought to be ac-celerated, since the political situation was visibly unstable. We were also all irritated by the violent demonstrations in the United States carried out by pro-Khomeini Iranian students, and a few days later, on November 11, I received a firmly worded note from the President stating: "When we get Americans out of Iran, I want all Iranian 'students' who are not enrolled full-time in college to be expelled. Tell Ben to prepare optimum implementation of this enforcement of U.S.

law." The note was generated by my report to the President that the Department of Justice was finding it difficult to expel Iranian students because of various legal loopholes, and I immediately phoned Ben Civiletti, the Attorney General, to read him the President's note.

Our hope that the hostage issue would be a transient one started evaporating by November 6. The Ayatollah Khomeini publicly endorsed the seizure of the hostages and refused to treat with any American emissaries. Moreover, there was mounting public hysteria in Iran, with increasingly violent threats being made publicly against the American "spies." We began to fear for the lives of the hostages. This anxiety prompted very intense diplomatic efforts, both conventional and unconventional, the latter including the PLO and later even the Libyans. One of those efforts involved the much-publicized conversation between me and Billy Carter, who had been cultivated by the Libyans. Both the Libyans and the PLO actually did urge the release of the hostages, but their influence was not significant.

The growing danger to the lives of the hostages, as well as the increasingly evident support of the Iranian authorities for the outrage perpetrated against the Embassy, not to speak of rising domestic fury in America, caused the SCC to recommend to the President a series of escalating sanctions. They were designed to punish Iran as well as to generate wider international pressure on the authorities in Tehran. The President himself was anxious for more action, and he used me to press the other principals in the SCC to come up with more effective and biting measures. While my colleagues were cooperative and eager to do their best, I could not help but be struck by how on specific matters every major department had excuses for inaction. The Department of State was appalled when I suggested that Iranian diplomats be punished in some reciprocal fashion; the Justice Department was always ready to explain why no action could be taken against Iranians resident in this country; Treasury came up with complicated reasons why economic sanctions would be counterproductive; and so forth.

Nonetheless, with helpful cajoling by Jody Powell, Ham Jordan, and Lloyd Cutler, a series of measures were adopted. On November 10, a day before the President penned me the note about deporting all Iranian "students," we announced the beginning of deportation proceedings against all Iranians who were in the United States illegally. Two days later, the President ordered the discontinuation of oil purchases from Iran; the Iranian government countered with an oil embargo against the United States. In reaction to reports that the Iranians were about to pull deposits out of American banks, the President ordered the blocking of all official Iranian assets. This move was promulgated in an Executive Order on November 14 and applied to assets in United States banks, foreign branches, and subsidiaries. The Iranian government announced on November 23 that it would not repay its foreign debts and proceeded to file suit in New York State Supreme Court against the Shah, seeking $56.5 billion in damages.

Clearly the pressure for more comprehensive action was intensifying. Apart from the military option, the logical next step was to tighten the economic noose around Iran. At the December 4 meeting of the NSC, the President decided on a further development of economic sanctions. Teams of State and Treasury Department officials were sent out to consult and coordinate action with our allies. This planning ultimately would lead to the break in diplomatic relations and the ban on most exports and financial dealings with Iran announced on April 7. The threat of sanctions was intended to add leverage to our position with the Iranians, though our allies urged us to be restrained, since in their view the negotiations for release could be set back by the application of sanctions.

We also took action against the Iranian diplomats accredited to the United States. The Iranian Embassy in Washington was ordered to reduce its staff from sixty to fifteen, and the staffs of their four consulates around the country were cut by half. Our efforts were given added impetus by the International Court of Justice decision on December 15 which declared unanimously that the hostage-taking violated international law and ordered their release. On December 27, a United States Court of Appeals upheld the President's decision to deport Iranians who were in the United States illegally. (The decision had been challenged and was held unconstitutional by a lower court.) Therefore, on January 3, the Immigration and Naturalization Service began to search for the 9,000 Iranians who had not reported their whereabouts. Two days later, the State Department gave the Iranian diplomatic staff seventy-two hours' notice to report to INS.

Although we acted in concert on behalf of our colleagues incarcerated in Tehran, disagreements within the SCC did surface fairly quickly on two issues. The first involved the question whether we should encourage the Shah to leave the United States, thereby perhaps depriving the Iranian militants of their rallying point. Cy first raised that question at the SCC meeting on November 8, and did so again two days later. A rather sharp exchange developed, in which, in addition to Cy and me, Mondale and Brown also participated. Cy and Mondale felt that we would be better off if the Shah left; Brown thought that the Shah perhaps could be prevailed upon to make a statement of his intention to leave as soon as he was well, and he volunteered a military Medivac C-9 aircraft to help to speed the Shah's move.

I was deeply dismayed by these reactions. Though I shared Cy's concern for the hostages and I admired his personal commitment to them, I felt that in the end our national honor was at stake. It bothered me—and after the SCC meeting I confided these feelings to some of my NSC staffers—that the one to speak up for American honor was a naturalized American. I wondered what this indicated about the current American elite and whether we were not seeing here symptoms of a deeper national problem. To mask my feelings, I spoke up in a deliberately low voice, saying that were we to ask the Shah to leave we would be giving in to the demands of a student mob in Tehran. "A month ago we backed down to the Soviets and the Cubans after declaring that we found the status quo unacceptable. Now we shall back down again. What will this mean for our international role as a global power? Who will find us credible hereafter?" I was supported only by Civiletti.

Fortunately, when the issue was taken to the President, he flatly declared in a smaller meeting (just Vance, Jordan, Brown, myself, and one or two more) that he would not force the Shah out of the United States as long as Americans were being held prisoner. (This session was punctuated by an amusing interlude. In the midst of our discussions, one of the President's aides stepped into the Cabinet Room to tell him that Rosalynn was calling him from Thailand, where she was on a mercy mission among the refugees. Carter stepped out of the room to take the call, and Ham Jordan, referring to Rosalynn's reputation as a super-hawk, laughingly said to the rest of us, "When he comes back he will probably declare war on Iran.")

The issue did not rest there, however, for Cy continued to raise it with the President. Cy clearly was motivated by a personal sense of responsibility for his imprisoned colleagues, and his compassionate feelings were stirred by meetings with their families. The President was similarly moved. (I deliberately decided to avoid such meetings in order not to be swayed by emotions.) On November 14, I found Cy talking to the President at 7 a.m. when I came into the Oval Office for my regular briefing. Such a one-on-one meeting was quite unusual. It turned out that Cy had convinced the President that the Shah's departure for Mexico would be helpful in resolving the hostage issue, and the President had agreed that an exploratory approach should be made to the Shah. Not much came of this, however, because the Mexicans first announced that the Shah would need a new visa to reenter Mexico on the completion of his medical treatment and then, toward the end of November, they bluntly announced that the Shah was no longer welcome. (The behavior of the Mexican President, López Portillo, was particularly hypocritical, for he had earlier made a great deal out of his magnanimity and courage in granting asylum to the Shah, contrasting his conduct not too subtly with American equivocation.)

With the Mexican door shut tight, the Shah stayed, for the simple reason that he had nowhere else to go. However, the Mexican final refusal, announced on November 29, precipitated a most disagreeable conversation between the President and me. The Shah, increasingly desperate, was inclined to accept Sadat's invitation to go to Egypt. Cy

Vance and I agreed that, with emotions in the Islamic world running high from Karachi to Tripoli, it would be dangerous for Egyptian stability for the Shah to settle in Cairo and that we should accordingly discourage the Shah from accepting the invitation. On Sunday, December 2, Cy called me and told me that he had spoken to the President on the subject and urged me to talk to him as well. I also received a phone call from Averell Harriman, much to the same effect and presumably generated by a conversation between him and Vance. Cy warned me that the President was thoroughly irritated, but I felt I had no choice but to call him at Camp David. When I reported that I concurred with Vance and that Harriman had called me with the same advice, the President was absolutely outraged. He accused me of conspiring with Kissinger and Rockefeller to get the Shah permanently into the country, he said that Cy "was sitting on his ass and doing nothing," and he terminated the conversation simply by hanging up on me. It was probably just as well because I was becoming somewhat angry myself, and I should have been more conscious of the enormous pressure under which Carter was operating.

In any case, the fate of the Shah continued to be negotiated quietly, though this time more by Ham Jordan and Lloyd Cutler than by anyone else, and the two of them succeeded in reaching an arrangement with Omar Torrijos for asylum in Panama for the Shah. When informed of this at the Friday foreign affairs breakfast on December 14, "I asked what Torrijos would be charging the Shah, but got the answer that Torrijos said when asked, 'I don't talk about costs of drinks when I have someone to dinner.' I am afraid he is going to skin the Shah alive once he has him in his hands," I noted in my journal. The Shah left the United States on December 15, never to return. The hostages remained incarcerated for thirteen more months.

The other issue on which some internal disagreement surfaced in the days immediately after the seizure of the hostages involved the extent and character of preparations for military action. At the second SCC on the hostage crisis, held on November 6, I recommended that we look at three military contingencies: a rescue operation; a retaliatory action if any or all Americans were killed; and in the event that Iran disintegrated as a political entity, a military reaction focused on the vital oil fields in southwestern Iran. Both Brown and General Jones quite correctly stressed the difficulties involved in undertaking any of these tasks, while Vance and Christopher were notably cool to any serious consideration of military options.

The President himself became directly involved on November 9, following a wider strategy session on the Iranian issue. By prearrangement with me, at its conclusion Brown was asked to join the President and me in the Oval Office and the President flatly stated: "I want to punish them as soon as our people have been released; really hit them.

They must know they can't fool around with us." Later in the morning, General Jones and Mondale joined us, and we all sat down on the armchairs and sofa near the fireplace, with a little coffee table in front of us on which General Jones spread various maps and outlined alternative military actions. They were essentially retaliatory in character, designed to inflict economic damage with minimum loss of life as punishment for the abuse meted out to our people.

Our thinking on the military option changed in character shortly thereafter, for it soon became clear that a post-release retaliation was not in the cards, for the simple reason that the release was not forthcoming. Instead we started worrying increasingly about the hostages being killed and how we might prevent this from happening or, alternatively, punish Iran for it.

Our planning, which continued to be conducted under the supervision of the special small committee that I chaired in confidential meetings in my office, moved forward fairly rapidly. By the middle of the month I noted in my journal that we had identified initial targets and would be ready to act within two days if ordered by the President. With Khomeini publicly threatening to place our people on trial, the military option became more urgent, and a special meeting of the NSC on November 20 focused on the matter. The President flew down from Camp David and at the meeting approved several steps recommended to him: to move another aircraft carrier to the area, to begin to deploy tankers which would sustain our aircraft in the event of long-range attacks into Iran, and to place some helicopters in Diego Garcia. The following day, I sent my military assistant, Colonel William Odom, to Camp David with a sealed envelope containing a chart outlining all of the military options developed by Defense and summarizing for the President their scale and likely impact.

On Friday, November 23, an important meeting of the NSC was held at Camp David. The Vice President, Brown, Vance, Jody Powell, Ham Jordan, General Jones, Stan Turner, and I flew up by helicopter, and we undertook a two-hour assessment of the situation. In the course of the session, the President outlined the options open to us: he listed them as involving a series of escalating steps, which he summarized with the words "condemn, threaten, break relations, mine three harbors, bomb Abadan, total blockade." Military dispositions taken were designed to give us the ability to act accordingly. The President also decided to continue to pursue the political path, but at the same time, after a lively debate, he concluded that we should warn the Iranians that any trials of Americans would result in retaliatory action. The President made that decision with only Ham, Jody, and me backing it explicitly, and Ham whispered to me that Carter simply would not be reelected President if he did not act firmly. Mondale and Vance, backed by Brown, argued that it would be unwise to issue a public warning, for it might polarize the situation. After returning from Camp David, Cy and I consulted by telephone on the public statement that we would issue and also on the wording of the grave warning that we would convey to the Iranians confidentially. We made it brief and direct, so that there would be no misunderstanding of the import of the message.

The NSC met again on December 4, and in preparation for it, I shared with the President my judgment that time was not working to our advantage. I expressed the fear that the issue was becoming increasingly a matter of America versus Islam (because of increasingly frequent anti-American demonstrations in the region, generating in turn anti-Moslem feelings in America) and that we faced a general deterioration of the situation in the Persian Gulf. As a result, we had to focus not only on how to save the hostages' lives but also on the larger strategic issues. I recommended a number of steps designed to enhance our security presence in the region and to place greater pressure on Iran, including the possibility of assisting efforts to unseat Khomeini. In effect, I felt that the question of the lives of the hostages should not be our only focus but that we should examine as well what needed to be done to protect our vital interests. I was painfully aware that at some point perhaps a choice between the two might even have to be made.

In addition, I forwarded to the President a strongly worded memorandum from Brown, dated December 1, 1979, in which the Secretary made it clear that he, too, felt that the time had come to consider seriously some military option: "My own judgment is that we can go for a period of 10–15 days along the diplomatic route if it appears to be moving in a promising way and if there is not evidence or grave suspicion that any hostages have been harmed. If strong economic measures against Iran are taken by our key allies acting with us, that might give us another week or so. But even then I do not think we can delay facing up to at least the mildest military action for more than about a month from now."

At the meeting, the President took a firm stand, formally approving the deployment of AWACS to Egypt (to serve in the event of a larger regional contingency and as backup for potential action against Iran) as well as some of the additional measures that I had proposed. On some of them, he instructed Vance to consult with our allies to see if a collective effort would not be more effective.

By the middle of the month, I began to be concerned that our approach to the Iranian crisis was becoming increasingly routinized. I mentioned that to the President, noting that the departments were again becoming sluggish in the application of pressure on Iran and that international support was not having a sufficient effect. To be sure, we were encouraged by the unanimous vote of the International Court of Justice in favor of the American position, but how effective that would be in Iran was very problematical. Accordingly, at the SCC meeting on

December 19, I raised the question whether we should not reassess our overall strategy. I asked whether the application of pressure should not be accelerated, for otherwise we might be "inoculating the Iranians" against graduated escalation of sanctions. With that thought in mind, at our separate, smaller meeting on military options, I raised the question to what extent covert activity ought to be related to the development of our military options since no amelioration was to be expected as long as Khomeini was in power. In my weekly report to the President on December 21, I emphasized the same themes, pointing out to him that we were approaching the stage of having to make truly difficult choices.

However, the strategic context changed dramatically in the fourth week of December. The Soviet invasion of Afghanistan meant that henceforth any action taken by us toward Iran had to be guided, to a much larger extent than heretofore, by its likely consequences for regional containment of Soviet ambitions. More specifically, the Soviet invasion of Afghanistan made it more important to mobilize Islamic resistance against the Soviets—and that dictated avoiding anything which might split Islamic opposition to Soviet expansionism. In turn, it was more important than before to avoid an Iranian–American military confrontation.

In other words, until the Soviet invasion of Afghanistan, the trend was toward more and more serious consideration of military action. The Soviet aggression against Afghanistan arrested this trend, and our strategy increasingly became that of saving the hostages' lives *and* of promoting our national interest by exercising military restraint. As a result, during the next three months, the primary emphasis of our efforts was on gradually intensifying the sanctions while engaging in more active direct and indirect negotiations.

Unfortunately, we did not get much help from the international community. As I noted in my journal on January 7, 1980: "Yesterday afternoon from 5:00 to after 7:30 the President met with Waldheim. It was meant to be a 15-minute meeting, but the first hour plus 20 minutes involved an almost compulsive account by Waldheim of the travails that he encountered in Tehran. He repeatedly referred to the 'plot against my life' and gave graphic descriptions of the risks he had run during his three-day visit. On substance, he said in effect that he didn't think sanctions would move things forward and urged the President to hold back. Fortunately, the President was quite tough and said to Waldheim without any ifs or buts that there will be no extradition of the Shah and if the Panamanians try to extradite him he will invite the Shah back here to the United States. . . . In the meantime we want the Security Council to vote the sanctions because if it doesn't do so then the UN will prove that it is irrelevant."

My role during this period was largely that of a coordinator of the

SCC process, and I was not involved directly in the negotiating efforts, except for a brief attempt to establish contact with the Ayatollah Beheshti through my new Algerian contacts. The negotiations were supervised largely by Vance, with Ham Jordan becoming increasingly involved in the confidential channel. Toward the end of February, however, the Iranians started escalating their demands as the negotiations became more concrete. This led me to reactivate the somewhat dormant planning for the military contingency, including the rescue option, though I did not press the matter with the President. On March 11, at an SCC meeting, I did raise the question whether at some point we should not consider blockading Iranian ports if our economic sanctions did not work. Alternatively, I proposed that the United States seize Kharg Island in the Persian Gulf (an important Iranian oil outlet) and hold it until such time as the Iranians were prepared to trade the hostages back. In both cases, I felt, the burden of a more direct military response would then be on the Iranians, and such self-contained action would not create major openings for the Soviets.

My growing sense of impatience was shared by the President. Although Vance and Cutler felt that the negotiating track was making progress and that we should expect some positive developments by April, at the March 18 NSC meeting the President said that we needed to increase our pressure on Iran. He noted that the American people were getting sick of the situation and added that he was sick of it as well. In his judgment, the United States had been too quiet and had not taken sufficiently direct action to create the most favorable circumstances for a settlement. As a result, we seemed to be accepting the status quo. We simply could not sit until May without placing greater pressure on Iran to release the hostages. At the foreign affairs breakfast three days later, the President stated that we should give the Iranians a deadline so that the negotiations do not keep dragging out indefinitely.

In fact, during the next ten days the negotiating channel came to a dead end, and shortly after April 1 the effort collapsed altogether. It became clear that the Iranians either had been negotiating in bad faith or were unable to deliver on the promises they had made. The deal contrived through various intermediaries, with Ham and Cy contributing in a selfless fashion an enormous amount of time and energy to the effort, simply collapsed. This did not surprise me. While I supported Ham's confidential negotiations (and met once with his secret interlocutors), I personally was very skeptical about the chances of success. I felt that the left-wing Parisian lawyers might be able to strike a bargain with their left-wing Tehran friends (like Ghotbzadeh) but that the fundamentalist mullahs would block it. To get a real agreement we had to negotiate with the key power figures like the Ayatollah Beheshti, and our efforts to get to him got nowhere.

The President convened a meeting of the NSC on Monday, April 7, and announced that the time had come to take firmer steps. Full-scale economic sanctions and a break in diplomatic relations were to be adopted. Moreover, American public opinion was now quite restive, and voices everywhere were being raised in favor of more direct action. I noted in my journal on the evening of April 7 that the President "realizes that we have passed a watershed and that the next phase will have to be the use of coercion unless our allies concert more effectively with us so that the Iranians are forced to accommodate. . . . I think at some point force will have to be used." Pressure did not work, and we were running out of patience.

The Rescue Mission

The decision to try to rescue the hostages by force crystallized in a three-week time span, approximately from March 21 to the final decision day of April 11. On Saturday, March 22, the President met with his key advisers (Vance, Mondale, Brown, Turner, Jones, Aaron, Jody Powell, and myself) at Camp David. As was customary at Camp David, we were all dressed most casually—jeans, sports jackets or sweaters.

The meeting with the President lasted a long time, from 10:40 a.m. until after 4 p.m. At the conclusion of our deliberations on the diplomatic strategy, General Jones gave the President the first comprehensive and full briefing on the rescue mission which had been developed over the preceding months. The President authorized a reconnoitering mission into Iran, designed to advance our plans for executing a refueling mission in the Persian desert as well as the transfer of the rescue team from the refueling aircraft into helicopters.

However, no decision regarding the mission was made. We were hopeful that the negotiations would succeed, and Vance in any case went on record at the meeting as opposing any military actions against the Iranians. The President asked with some impatience whether that meant that he was willing to sit and wait until the end of the year, while the hostages continued to be imprisoned. Carter also agreed with a point that I made; namely, that we were more likely to increase the chances of our allies joining us in sanctions against Iran if they became convinced that we were planning some sort of a military action.

The briefing on the rescue mission was the outcome of a prolonged planning process. It was initiated on November 6, the day after the hostages were seized, when I telephoned Brown and instructed him to have the JCS proceed with the development of a plan for a rescue mission. My thought at the time was that we needed such a contingency scheme in the event, which at the time appeared quite possible, that some of the hostages either were put on trial and then sentenced to death or were murdered by their kidnappers. Accordingly, in such circumstances, we would have to undertake a rescue mission out of a moral as well as a political obligation, both to keep faith with our people imprisoned in Iran and to safeguard American national honor.

By November 8, with Brown and Jones providing energetic leadership, the military came back to me with a briefing, held in the Situation Room, in which we carefully reviewed aerial photographs and examined the schedule for a possible airborne helicopter assault directly on the Embassy compound by a specially trained team, to be followed by extrication from an airfield not too distant from Tehran. Our problem at this time was inadequate intelligence regarding the disposition of the hostages as well as the enormously complex problem of logistics. Our target was distant from the United States, remote from any American-controlled facilities, and helicopters were not usually used for long-distance assault missions. Nonetheless, the military worked to overcome these difficulties, and on November 11 I went to the Pentagon for a much more comprehensive review of how the mission might be executed.

It was here that for the first time I started to think of the need to combine the rescue mission with a retaliatory strike. My view was that casualties in the rescue mission would be unavoidable and we had to face the fact that the attempt might even fail. Accordingly, it would be better if the United States were to engage in a generalized retaliatory strike, which could be publicly described as a punitive action and which would be accompanied by the rescue attempt. If the rescue succeeded, that would be all to the good; if it failed, the U.S. government could announce that it had executed a punitive mission against Iran, because of its unwillingness to release our people, and that unfortunately in the course of that mission an attempt to rescue the hostages had not succeeded. I mention this point now because it became the subject of more intense debates later, when the rescue mission was finally approved.

It should be made clear in this context that my concern over the possible failure of the mission did not pertain to something like what finally happened—its early abortion—but rather to some totally unexpected setback during its execution in Tehran involving heavy casualties for the team, for the hostages, or for both. The probability of such a setback seemed to us relatively low, but we could certainly not exclude it entirely.

At this stage I also felt that the rescue mission should be a last-resort action, to be undertaken if the hostages were being killed or were about to be killed. I leaned at this stage more toward a generalized military response, designed to put Iran under pressure to release our hostages. I was particularly drawn to the notion of seizing Kharg Island and imposing a military blockade on Iran, combined perhaps with some air strikes. However, after the Soviet invasion of Afghanistan, as already noted, I came to the view that such a military action would be strategically damaging, and would simply give additional opportunities to the Soviets in their drive toward the Persian Gulf and the Indian Ocean. It now seemed to me more important to forge an anti-Soviet Islamic coalition. It was in this context that the rescue mission started to look more attractive to me, especially as the negotiating tack gradually came to prove fruitless.

Throughout this period, our small group, composed of Brown, General Jones, Admiral Turner, one or two of their and my immediate associates, met regularly in my office. I chaired the meetings and took only handwritten notes on the proceedings. My gravest concern was that any eventual rescue mission would have to be assured maximum secrecy and surprise. I feared that the pattern of massive leakage in the U.S. government, the endless multiplication of papers, the rather loose enforcement of limited access to restricted information, as well as the unavoidable penetration by hostile agents, would compromise our mission. The specter that haunted me was that at the critical juncture the Iranians would be forewarned, probably by the Soviets, and the mission would be destroyed because it lacked the essential elements of surprise and secrecy.

By the latter part of February, I was noting in my journal that I sensed increasing pressure from the public and from Congress for more direct action against Iran. On February 28, I met with a group of some forty congressmen, and I reported on my return to the White House their growing frustration over the absence of progress in the negotiations. Accordingly, I raised with the President the rescue option and I asked him to approve a flight into Iran to do the necessary reconnoitering of possible landing sites. The President declined to do so, out of concern that such a mission might fail and thereby jeopardize the ongoing negotiating process.

Early in March, I succeeded in obtaining Vance's concurrence for such an intelligence operation, and I went back to the President on March 7. I knew that the President would be more impressed by a joint recommendation. The President again reserved his decision, on the grounds that negotiations still might succeed and the reconnoitering would provide a needless provocation in the event that something went wrong. The rescue issue, however, was becoming more urgent, not only because two or three weeks later we were to discover that the negotiating process was not proving fruitful but also because the success of the mission depended on nighttime darkness being of sufficient duration to provide cover for the complicated process of deep penetration into Iran's airspace. A very comprehensive review of the rescue plan undertaken by Brown, Jones, and me in mid-March led me to the conclusion that the rescue mission had a reasonably good chance of success, though there probably would be some casualties. There was no certain way of estimating how large they might be; a great deal depended on the degree to which the mission would enjoy the advantages of surprise and secrecy. At this stage, I also informed both Powell and Jordan of some of the details of the rescue mission and discussed it more fully with Mondale. All three were feeling increasingly frustrated and concerned about rising public pressures for more direct action against Iran as a whole.

We were faced essentially with three choices: to continue negotiating ad infinitum, even if the Iranians gave no indication of a willingness or ability to accommodate, or perhaps with the prospect of eventually accepting humiliating conditions; to undertake a large military operation against Iran, essentially punitive in character, with the likely prospect that the Iranian response to it would be to do something brutal or murderous to the hostages and perhaps even to invite the Soviets to provide military assistance; or, finally, to undertake the admittedly risky but increasingly promising scenario of a rescue mission. With the political climate heating up, and with our political opponents deliberately exploiting the Iranian issue to embarrass the President, public pressures on behalf of the second option were clearly on the rise. Yet, at the same time, it was evident to us that this represented perhaps the worst option of all. It would not free the hostages, and it would tip the strategic situation in this vital region in favor of the Soviet Union. Thus the choice increasingly was one between endless negotiations, with the public clamoring for more direct action, and a more surgical solution, which the rescue mission provided.

Perhaps surprisingly, there was never any explicit discussion of the relationship between what we might have to do in Iran and domestic politics; neither the President nor his political advisers ever discussed with me the question of whether one or another of our Iranian options would have a better or a worse domestic political effect.

With the passage of time, we were all becoming more confident that possible kinks were being worked out of the rescue plan and that its probability of success was increasing. It was in this context that the President, on March 22, listened to a full briefing on the rescue mission and then authorized the reconnaissance into Iran. While the final decision clearly had not been made, consideration of the rescue option became more serious.

The plan, as developed after weeks of careful analysis, involved a two-day operation. Eight helicopters would rendezvous with three C-130s in the middle of the Persian desert during the first night, to be refueled and to transfer the assault team; the helicopters would then continue to a site near Tehran, where the team would conceal itself for a full day. The actual assault would take place during the second night, with the team transported by vehicles that were previously prepared, with a separate mission directed at the Foreign Ministry, to release Chargé Laingen and his two associates. Following the well-rehearsed penetration of the Embassy compound, all of the hostages, and perhaps some prisoners, would be moved to a nearby stadium, from which the helicopters would then move the entire group to an airport near Tehran, which in the meantime would have been occupied in the course of a sudden landing by American military transport aircraft. The extrication of the entire mission would be completed in darkness. After frequent rehearsals and personal assessments of the leadership quality, morale, and training of the team, and with increasingly effective intelligence support provided by Turner, we all felt that the operation was feasible, provided the Iranians had no advance warning.

To execute the mission, we obtained the generous cooperation of one friendly country in the Middle East, and we engaged the unwitting cooperation of some other countries in the region. President Sadat, as we expected, was courageous and fully supportive, but we had to take into account the internal vulnerabilities of other friendly countries. We thus did what was necessary, feeling that their resentment at not being consulted would be less than their embarrassment at being asked in advance. Finally, I have to note that some other countries were helpful to us in some aspects of the internal preparations in Iran for the execution of the mission, and we owe them a debt of gratitude which someday doubtless will be acknowledged.

The negotiating track collapsed in the very first days of April. On Monday, April 7, at 9 a.m., the President, presiding at a formal NSC meeting, stated that in his view it had been a mistake for him not to have acted more assertively sooner. The discussion, which moved rather briskly, resulted in the decision to adopt more economic sanctions and also to break diplomatic relations. Vance objected to such a break, suggesting instead that we simply expel the Iranian diplomats. However, Mondale, Brown, and others felt strongly that we should leave no ambiguity on the subject, and the President approved the decision formally to break relations. In addition, the possibility of military action was discussed. Special attention focused on a naval blockade. However, no decision was made, though Carter indicated clearly that in his view the time had come to bring things to a head, and we should either get other countries to join us in collective sanctions or consider more direct action ourselves. He concluded by saying that we were no longer dealing with kidnappers who were holding the hostages in the face of a weak Iranian government but were, in effect, dealing with a hostile government whose belligerent actions were coming close to the point of forcing us to respond forcefully.

The meeting of April 7 was the curtain raiser for the decisive meeting of the NSC held on Friday, April 11. The day before that meeting

I gave the President a memorandum entitled "Getting the Hostages Free," in which I argued that the negotiating track had come to an end and that we were left essentially with the choice of either the rescue operation or direct application of force. Since the latter would be likely to drive Iran into the hands of the Soviets, I therefore recommended that the President consider seriously reaching a decision on the rescue mission. I wrote: "In short, unless something is done to change the nature of the game, we must resign ourselves to the continued imprisonment of the hostages through the summer or even later. . . . The above recommendation is not easy to make. It is even more difficult for you to consider and accept. However, we have to think beyond the fate of the fifty Americans and consider the deleterious effects of a protracted stalemate, growing public frustration, and international humiliation of the U.S." I also noted that any rescue operation should be accompanied by a contingency plan for an almost simultaneous retaliatory strike, to provide a broader context in the event that the rescue mission should fail. Finally, since I was greatly concerned over secrecy, I recommended to the President that he convene a full-scale NSC meeting, including some of his key domestic advisers, at the end of which he should announce for the purpose of deception that he had decided *against* a rescue mission. We would then hold a separate, smaller meeting, confined only to the people who "needed to know," at which the actual decision to undertake the rescue would be reached.

When Carter told me on that fateful Friday morning that he wished to convene urgently a meeting of the NSC, I asked him what its purpose was. He said that he had concluded that the time had come to act. The meeting lasted from 11:30 a.m. to 1:20 p.m. Despite the solemnity and importance of the occasion, for some reason the President chose to give it a somewhat informal format: instead of sitting in the middle of the Cabinet table, he sat more casually at the end of the long table, with his back to the door leading to his office, with me on his left, Christopher (standing in for Vance, who was on vacation) on his right, and then the Vice President, Brown, Turner, Jones, and Jody Powell completing the semicircle on both sides. The President opened the meeting by stating that in his judgment the likelihood of release of the hostages soon was remote, that we needed to assess our options, and that the time had come to decide on specific actions to be taken and on the timetable for them.

The first to speak was Christopher, who outlined a number of non-belligerent options which he felt we could consider. We could go back to the UN, we could blacklist Iranian ships and aircraft, we could strive for the adoption of an international telecommunications embargo, all of which would give the Europeans more time to support us. Brown immediately spoke up, dismissing Christopher's suggestions as not impressive. He then reviewed the punitive options and concluded that the blockade would push Iran toward the Soviets, and thus he came out in favor of a rescue attempt, though he hedged this point by saying that a decision should be made in the course of the next two or three weeks. An important contribution was made by Mondale, who said simply and forcefully that rescue offered us the best way out of a situation which was becoming intolerably humiliating. The President asked me to comment, and I said that the President knew my views, and therefore I would limit myself to saying that we ought to attempt the rescue as early as possible because the nights were getting shorter; that we should consider taking prisoners back with us, so that we would have bargaining leverage in the event that the Iranians seized other Americans as hostages; and that we should consider a simultaneous retaliatory strike in the event the rescue failed.

After further contributions by Jones and Turner, which focused more specifically on how the rescue would be implemented, the President spoke at some length, saying that he had reviewed the matter fully with Rosalynn, with Ham, with Fritz, with Jody, adding also that he had discussed it extensively with me, and that his conclusion was that we had to take strong action. In passing, the President remarked that Vance, prior to leaving for his vacation in Florida, had told the President that he opposed any military action but if a choice had to be made between a rescue and a wider blockade, he preferred the rescue. Our national honor was at stake, Carter said, noting that Sadat had told him that our international standing was damaged by our excessive passivity. Accordingly, we had to go forward and we would proceed to attempt to rescue our hostages. The mission should be undertaken at the earliest possible date, which General Jones indicated was April 24, and at 12:48 the President decided: "We ought to go ahead without delay."

The die was cast, though there was to be one more debate on the subject. In a way, the decision had been foreshadowed by the discussion initiated at the March 22 briefing at Camp David. From that date on, the rescue mission became the obvious option if negotiations failed —and on that point there was almost unanimous consensus within the top echelons of the Administration. However, shortly after Vance came back from his holiday, he and I discussed the decision briefly while standing outside the President's Oval Office, on the White House portico facing the Rose Garden. Some sort of public function involving the President was in process in the garden, and Vance and I could be observed by photographers and newspapermen from a distance. I remember covering my mouth with my hand so that no lip-reader from afar could tell what was being said. Vance told me that he had learned from Christopher of the decision, that he was dismayed and mortified by it. I responded that in that case he ought to register his objections with the President immediately, and I would back him in requesting a formal NSC meeting to review the matter once more, though I added that I favored the decision because the only other alternative left to us would be wider military action.

The NSC met again from 12:45 p.m. to 2:50 p.m. on Tuesday, April 15. It was a secret meeting, since we did not wish to publicize the fact that the NSC was meeting with increased frequency. The President first met with Vance alone so that Vance could register his objections personally. A grim-faced Carter opened our meeting by asking Vance to summarize his objections. Vance stressed that in his judgment progress was still being made in negotiations, that our allies were beginning to join us in sanctions, and that the rescue mission would probably result in the loss of some lives. Brown again was the first to speak up by pointedly asking, "When do you expect the hostages to be released in that case?" Vance responded that he did not know and that he feared that the rescue mission would result in some of them being killed. I limited my comments to the observation that we should attempt the rescue now or it would be too late, because we would not have the nighttime necessary for the mission, and that we needed to lance the boil through a rescue mission, since otherwise we would be pressed into actions, either blockade or an embargo, which would deliver Iran to the Soviets. After some further exchanges the President simply said, "I will stick with the decisions I made."

The rest of the meeting focused on the two questions that I had previously raised: should there be a concurrent retaliatory strike and should we take prisoners? On the prisoners, I was supported only by Brown, Claytor, and Jones. My view was that having prisoners might give us some leverage, especially if some Americans were detained. Prisoner exchanges were a frequent occurrence in the Middle East and it might be prudent to gain some bargaining power. All the others felt that this would be a needless encumbrance, and finally the President authorized Jones to take some prisoners along until the final takeoff from Iran, at which point the mission commander would presumably release them, unless there was some compelling reason to take them along.

A sharper discussion developed on the wider retaliatory response. The President felt that we should try to limit casualties, since that reduced the chances of any hostile actions against other Americans, and he was very strongly supported by Vance. Both Brown and Turner joined me in favoring some concurrent action in the event of a failure, though at this stage our presumption was that "failure" meant the collapse of the mission in the course of the actual assault in Tehran or in the course of subsequent extrication. None of us had in mind an early abortion of the mission as implying failure. In any case, the upshot of the discussion was that we were authorized to develop some contingency planning along these lines, with the final decision to be made closer to the actual D-day.

On the following day, the President presided at a secret meeting in the Situation Room from 7:37 to 9:55 p.m. with the mission commanders. Carter's performance was very impressive. He not only carefully examined every aspect of the mission but emphasized particularly that he would not interfere with operational decisions, that he would give the military maximum leeway for doing what was necessary within the framework of the approved plans. He and I had earlier discussed John Kennedy's interference with military planning for the Bay of Pigs operation, and Carter was clearly determined to make certain that his personal concerns did not interfere with the mission's chances of success. It was approximately at this stage, though I am not certain if it was at this meeting, that we decided to increase the number of helicopters planned for the mission from seven to eight. We had been told by the military that the absolute minimum for success was six, and that repeated exercises and careful examination showed that seven would give us sufficient redundancy. However, in the course of one of our meetings General John Pustay, at the time an assistant to General Jones, whispered to my deputy, David Aaron, that we needed to take a closer look at the helicopter part of the mission. Aaron passed the comment on to me, and as a consequence we decided to increase the number of helicopters to eight. This had the advantage of not necessitating any increase in the number of refueling aircraft destined to rendezvous with the helicopters inside hostile Iranian terrain.

(Some have argued subsequently that the mission should have been composed of, say, twice as many helicopters; but if the Iranians had discovered the mission as a result of the size of the air armada penetrating their airspace, we all would doubtless have been charged with typically excessive American redundancy, with unwillingness to go in hard and lean—the way, for example, the Israelis did at Entebbe. Moreover, the implication is that if the United States had sent, say, twelve helicopters for a mission that required six, we could have afforded to lose on the way to Tehran as many as six. But that simply fails to take into account the fact that surprise and secrecy would have been compromised if as many as six U.S. helicopters, and crews, were sprayed over the Iranian countryside.)

During the next few days, the small group which I chaired continued meeting daily, consulting frequently with the President. Carter was very emphatic in insisting that every effort be made to avoid wanton killings, and he requested General Jones to give this his personal attention. We also stepped up our efforts to deceive the Iranians by initiating a new round of negotiations while pressing publicly for all Americans to leave Iran. Deployments of men and matériel were moving forward, and so far everything was proceeding smoothly.

The only cloud on the horizon was Cy Vance's very evident disaffection. It is to be remembered that the rescue mission decision was taken in the context of growing bitterness between Vance and the White House over the UN vote flap (see p. 442). Vance clearly felt set upon, and I sensed in my bones that he was ready to quit. He looked worn out, his temper would flare up, his eyes were puffy, and he projected genuine unhappiness. I confided that thought to the President on April 21, and he quite flatly told me that Cy seemed to be burned out and determined to quit. He asked me not to tell anyone about it, since he intended to discuss the matter with Cy again, but he doubted very much that Cy's decision could be altered.

On April 23, the day before the rescue mission, Carter decided that no concurrent attacks on other targets would be undertaken. His decision was based on the view that this could needlessly complicate the execution of the rescue mission as well as heighten international tensions to a counterproductive degree. At 11:30, the President, Mondale, Turner, and I sat together around a little table in the Rose Garden, in beautiful sunshine, reviewing the status of the operation. Everything was go, and as of that time there had been no security leakage or any unexpected technical or international problems. The President decided that during the following day, D-day, he would conduct business as usual in the Oval Office, I would operate out of my office, and Brown would be in touch with me from DOD, while General Jones would conduct the operation from the National Military Command Center. I noted in my journal: "The first critical phase of the operation will begin fourteen hours from now. I feel good about it. I realize that if it fails I will probably be blamed more than anybody else, but I am quite prepared to accept that. If it is a success, it will give the United States a shot in the arm, which it has badly needed for twenty years."

The longest day of my four White House years started on a hopeful note. At 10:20 a.m., General Jones reported to me that the weather was good and that all eight helicopters were on the way. Earlier Turner reported that we had additional information on the location of the hostages and that our team inside Tehran, which would play a critical role in assisting the assault on the Embassy, was extremely optimistic about our prospects. Not much came in during the rest of the morning, and I met with the President, Mondale, Vance, Brown, Jordan, and Powell for lunch. We reviewed the progress to date and discussed at some length how to undertake congressional consultations. The atmosphere was low-key; we were all preoccupied but taking refuge in routine. It was probably the best way to avoid contagious tension. In the middle of the lunch Brown was called out of the room and came back to report that two helicopters were short of the landing site but they might simply be delayed.

There was no further information until 3:15 in the afternoon. I was in my office when Brown called to report that the two helicopters were down (one landed and was abandoned after warning signals indicated a potential malfunction; the other returned, unauthorized, to the carrier *Nimitz* because of navigational problems in a dust storm), but initial indications were that the needed minimum six were on schedule. In any case, all of the C-130s had already landed in darkness at Desert One, the rendezvous site. But there was an unexpected wrinkle. The site was near a road because that provided us with the best opportunity for selecting an adequate desert landing field. Shortly after the landing of the three C-130s, however, three vehicles were observed: one of them got away, while one of those stopped was a bus with some forty people on board. Brown and I reviewed the situation. Since it was pitch dark, we had no reason to believe that the Iranians who got away knew that something major was afoot, especially since the region was known for various incidents of smuggling. And as to the bus passengers, we felt confident that we could simply evacuate them. Brown and I agreed there was no basis for aborting the operation.

I went to see the President at 3:30, reported these latest developments, and told him that in my judgment there was no reason to terminate the mission. Carter was more disturbed than I and very carefully reviewed all the possible consequences. We were so preoccupied that I did something which otherwise I would never have done: while talking with the President I sat on the edge of his big desk in the Oval Office. We were soon joined by Mondale, and I told both of them that we would simply evacuate the unexpected Iranian "visitors" on one of the C-130s and release them after the mission had been completed. To make certain that this would work, the President called General Jones at 3:38, and after consultations with him agreed that there was no problem with going ahead.

To maintain our regular office routine I then attended a PRC meeting in the Situation Room on the Middle East, barely listening to a discussion between Vance and Linowitz. At 4:20, I was called out of the room and received a report from Brown to the effect that everything was under control at the rendezvous site. Four helicopters had already completed their refueling, while two were still being refueled. The commanding officer's expectation was that in about forty minutes everything at Desert One would be completed and the next phase of the operation would begin. I felt good and confident.

However, everything changed dramatically at 4:45 p.m. Brown called again: "I think we have an abort situation. One helicopter at Desert One has a hydraulic problem. We thus have less than the minimum six to go. We can use the C-130s to extract our people from

Desert One." I was stunned and quizzed Brown sharply on whether the abort was necessary. Why couldn't we go ahead, given the emergency, with five? Brown insisted that planning indicated that six was the minimum. I told him to consult with General Jones, and particularly to obtain the opinion of the commander in the field. I had met Colonel Charles Beckwith earlier, at the dress rehearsal in the Situation Room, and I had the utmost confidence in his courage. I figured that if he was prepared to go with five helicopters I would back him all the way. I told Brown that I would inform the President but I expected him to give me the answer by the time the President called him.

I immediately proceeded to the President's office. Carter was in the Oval Office conferring with Christopher and Cutler. I entered at 4:50 and told the President that I needed to talk with him immediately and alone. He looked quite startled, waved the other two out of the office, and together with me headed for his small study, linked to the Oval Office by a short corridor. In the corridor I told him the news and the reasons why according to Brown the mission had to be aborted. Carter merely muttered, "Damn, damn."

After we entered his small office, Carter sat behind his desk and called Brown. I stood in front of his desk with my mind racing: Should I press the President to go ahead with only five helicopters? Here I was, alone with the President. Perhaps I could convince him to abandon military prudence, to go in a daring single stroke for the big prize, to take the historic chance. And at the same time, a contrary thought flashed through my mind: Would I not be abusing my office by pressing this man into such a quick decision after months of meticulous planning? Would I not be giving in to a romantic idea?

The President reached Brown at 4:55 p.m., and I knelt in front of his desk so that I could take notes while he spoke. He asked for the latest report, and Brown presumably repeated what he had said to me. I whispered to the President, having resolved in my own mind how to act: "You should get the opinion of the commander in the field. His attitude should be taken into account." I had decided to urge going ahead with only five if Colonel Beckwith was prepared to do it, but not to press for it without the field commander's concurrence. The President asked Brown for the field commander's assessment, and then I heard the President say, "Let's go with his recommendation." He hung up, looked at me, confirmed that the mission was aborted, and then put his head down on top of his desk, cradling it in his arms for approximately five seconds. I felt extraordinarily sad for him as well as for the country. Neither of us said anything.

The President then asked me to convene a meeting of all his principal advisers, and the rest of the day was spent in informing the various foreign governments of what had transpired and in coordinating the extrication of our men.

At 5:58 p.m., the President was called by General Jones and told that one helicopter had run into a C-130 and burst into flames, and that there were casualties. The President looked as if someone had stabbed him; pain was evident all over his face, but he remained very cool and in complete control of the meeting. He instructed Vance, Christopher, and Jody to leave and to prepare a public statement on the failure of the mission. They were joined in the Cabinet Room shortly thereafter by Turner, who very strongly urged that no public statement be issued until he had made certain that his people in Iran had been secured. I admired the way Turner fought for his agents, and we agreed to delay any public announcement until 1 a.m. I was struck by how lined everyone's face was (and I assume mine was as well) but also by how calm and low-key the atmosphere was. There were no recriminations, no raised voices; there was not even much tension. Carter particularly was very controlled and businesslike, though he must have sensed what a personal as well as political calamity he had just suffered. Although we knew shortly after 6 p.m. that there were fatalities at Desert One, it was not until approximately eleven o'clock that we learned that eight men had sacrificed their lives so that other Americans would go free and so that America's honor would be redeemed. They were the real heroes of this tragic day.

The next morning Harold Brown gave a superb briefing to the press, explaining in cool and precise terms how the operation was planned, how it was executed, and what went wrong. Since the mission was aborted at an early stage, I did not raise the question of any concurrent retaliatory action. Such action would have simply given the aroused and emotionally unstable Iranians an opportunity to take revenge on our hostages.

On the morning of April 26, I convened a meeting in my office, on the instructions of the President, to plan another rescue mission. While not knowing at this stage what precisely had gone wrong—beyond the fact that three helicopters had allegedly failed—we decided initially to undertake the next time a simpler mission, based on the injection of a larger force right into Tehran, combined with the seizure of a nearby airfield. Any effort to attempt such a rescue would have to await the outcome of renewed diplomatic initiatives as well as the reassembly of the hostages, who in the meantime had been dispersed throughout Iran. I also met with the commanders of the operation and verified that they had all concurred in the view that the mission should be aborted once they were down to five helicopters. This greatly relieved me, for I had continued to worry that perhaps we should have gone ahead, adjusting our plans "under fire," so to speak. However, I could not suppress the suspicion that in the case of two of the helicopters—the one that went down and the one that turned back—an excess of prudence contributed to the outcome.

Needless to say, the failure was the most bitter disappointment of my four years in the White House. Could we have done it differently? Should we have tried sooner? Should we not have tried at all? These questions are not easy to answer, even with the benefit of hindsight. Carter perhaps would have improved his political fortunes by having been more willing to toy with, or even to sacrifice, the lives of the hostages—but this he refused to do, rejecting any resort to peremptory and demagogically appealing actions. The political costs of failure might have been smaller if we had tried the rescue mission sooner, but we felt that we had to give the negotiations a chance to succeed.

For my part, I thought we had to exhaust the negotiating track and that the Administration had to be almost united in the view that the rescue mission was timely before we actually undertook it—for otherwise any failure would have been demoralizing and profoundly divisive.

The rescue attempt, paradoxically, did have one immediate benefit: it relieved public pressure for a large-scale American military action against Iran, and thus permitted the resumption of our diplomatic efforts, reinforced by sanctions, to obtain the release of our people. Personally, I never had any political or moral regrets about the rescue mission. I felt that we owed it to all concerned to try to rescue the hostages once we had a reasonably good chance of being successful. My greatest worry was that we would not succeed in preserving secrecy and in achieving surprise. I knew throughout that there were risks involved, but that was unavoidable. I felt then, as I feel now, that not to have tried, while having the capacity to try, would have been shameful and unworthy of America.

Restraint under a New Secretary of State

The failure of the rescue mission left us with only one alternative: negotiations. The larger military option, either blockade or mining, was unpromising. Not only did the public clamor for action quickly subside, but the potential for Soviet political exploitation of any major U.S. military action continued to provide an irrefutable argument against such an initiative.

Carter was painfully aware that this meant that the hostage crisis would drag on into the fall elections. His political image would inevitably suffer, and there was no doubt that the issue would be exploited by his political opponents. And, indeed, it was. As the Presidential election neared, the Republican candidate and his associates did everything they could to deprecate the possibility of a constructive settlement. Public expectation of "an October surprise" was deliberately fanned, thereby making negotiations with the Iranians more difficult. Nonetheless, there was no other way of resolving the issue and of obtaining our twin objectives: preserving lives and protecting our national interest. We had to be patient, even though the political costs would be enormous. To Carter's credit, he had the fortitude to exercise that patience, and on this issue he had the unanimous support of his Administration.

That Administration now contained a new Secretary of State. At a morning briefing in late April, Carter told me that Cy would definitely resign and he added quite straightforwardly that he would like me to stay where I was. Our conversation was very matter-of-fact, and I told the President in return that I was prepared to help him by resigning. He simply laughed, waved his hands, and said, "No, I want you to stay." He then asked me in great secrecy whom I preferred as Secretary of State, Muskie or Christopher. I told him that I thought I could work well with either, that Christopher knew more about foreign policy and that Muskie could help him more politically. The President told me that Christopher indicated willingness to serve as Muskie's deputy, and I sensed that Muskie was his first choice.

That Muskie's style as Secretary of State would be different from Vance's, seeking and asserting much higher public visibility, was demonstrated on April 29, the day of his appointment. I had earlier urged the President to involve Vance somehow in a ceremony, in order to show continuity and to reduce likely attacks on the Administration from Vance's disappointed supporters. Shortly before Muskie's swearing-in ceremony, Carter phoned and asked whether I thought it would be possible and appropriate to invite Vance to stand on the podium, together with the President, Muskie, Brown, and me, as a sign of unity. I strongly endorsed that, and Vance, though doubtless with some ambivalent feelings, readily consented. When the President finished swearing Muskie in, Muskie launched into a protracted speech, which then turned into a press conference. We all stood around for a while, wondering when it would end, and finally drifted out of the East Room of the White House, leaving the new Secretary of State to his one-man show.

Vance and I went to my office, while the President disappeared into the Oval Office. As we sat down to chat, I turned on the closed-circuit television, and lo and behold, there was Muskie still holding forth. Both Vance and I were stupefied as the show went on and on. After a while, neither of us could suppress laughter, and there we were, alleged bitter enemies, sitting together in my office, giggling uncontrollably as the new Secretary of State reveled in his moment of glory.

Contrary to prevailing Washington gossip, Vance's resignation left me neither pleased nor triumphant. For one thing, for quite some time now Carter's foreign policy was more in keeping with my strategic priorities and concerns than with Vance's approach. Thus I had no policy reasons to be pleased by his departure. Moreover, I believed that

Vance was unfairly victimized because of his strong stand on the Middle East question, and I feared that his departure would create even more of a paralysis in that vital region. Finally, I took seriously the warning Henry Kissinger conveyed to me shortly after Vance's resignation. At a lunch that the two of us were having, Kissinger all of a sudden remarked, "You are now in the same position that I was when Jim Schlesinger was forced out as Secretary of Defense. The press and everyone else saw me as completely in charge and turned against me in full fury. You, Zbig, never had the press behind you the way I had, and thus you are even more vulnerable to the attacks that now will concentrate on you."

How right he was. Within days of Vance's resignation, a torrent of nasty personal attacks on me, some openly penned by Vance's close associates, started to appear in the Washington press, claiming that I had forced Vance out and that I had engaged in a sustained personal campaign against him over the preceding three years. To make matters more difficult, Muskie's elevation to the Secretaryship inevitably re-opened some of the procedural questions which had been settled by practice and by fiat. Egged on by his subordinates, Muskie began to voice publicly his discomfort over my alleged "preeminence" and to request changes in existing arrangements. This campaign unfortunately contributed to the public's image of the President as not being effectively in charge, though it had the paradoxical internal effect of making Carter somewhat more sympathetic to me than to Muskie. When Muskie actually forced a formal discussion of existing NSC arrangements, at a special meeting convened for that purpose at Camp David, the President, in spite of the case laid out by Muskie, Christopher, and other State Department officials, strongly backed me by expressing satisfaction with most of the existing procedures.

As public attacks on me mounted, Carter's sense of personal loyalty was demonstrated in many ways. When Ambassador Donald McHenry delivered a speech which by implication seemed to be a shot at me, the President sent him a sharply worded handwritten note of disapproval (with a copy to Muskie). On another occasion, he came to one of my NSC staff meetings to praise the NSC for its performance and quite explicitly to support me, describing me as a personal friend. And finally, when Muskie made a point of circumventing established procedure by handing to the President directly his memorandum of a conversation with Gromyko, rather than forwarding it through me, the President simply waved his hand and told the Secretary of State, "Give it to Zbig."

None of that gainsays the fact that Muskie's appointment was a political coup. He brought to the office strength of character, an ability to articulate, and strong congressional support. At the same time, his grasp of foreign affairs was relatively general, and he was joining an

Administration which had worked together on a number of issues for some three years. As a consequence, on the Iranian hostage issue, the burden of coordinating and conducting the complicated negotiations was shouldered almost entirely by Warren Christopher, who continued to serve as Deputy Secretary of State, and by Lloyd Cutler, the President's Counsel.

My own role during this last phase of the hostage drama became quite secondary. I continued to chair the SCC meetings that dealt with Iran and to coordinate our continuing efforts to maintain effective and painful sanctions against Iran as our negotiators were seeking to find a way out of the impasse. I did not involve myself in these negotiations in any detail. For one thing, I concentrated very heavily on trying to shape and flesh out the regional security framework, to push for a more active development of the Rapid Deployment Force, to refine our strategic doctrine, and also to develop an approach to the Central American problem that would combine genuine commitment to social reform with more effective impediments to Cuban penetration. On the Iranian issue, my basic feeling was that not much could be done directly by us until after the elections, and that in the meantime my main responsibility was to make sure that we did not agree to a negotiated settlement that would tarnish our national honor.

In mid-May, Giscard, despite the Soviet invasion of Afghanistan, undertook a bilateral, and rather frivolous, meeting with Brezhnev. It yielded absolutely nothing and later on it hurt Giscard's standing in France. In any case, after his encounter he informed us that Brezhnev might be willing to make a demarche to the Iranians provided he was asked, not by the U.S. government, but by the families of the hostages. At first the President toyed with the idea of passing this message to the leaders of the informal organization of the families of the hostages, but I told the President that in my judgment we should not dignify the Giscard proposal by any reaction. Later in the day he sent me a note instructing me not even to reply.

In June, we received some signals that the Iranians might again be planning to put our hostages on trial, and we agreed in the SCC to convey a strong warning to the Iranians, reiterating our earlier commitment (made on November 23 of the previous year) to react strongly if that should happen. My notes show that in the course of July I told the President several times that I thought that the negotiations by the State Department were moving slowly and that he needed to prod them. On one or two occasions the President sent a note or phoned Muskie in my presence, asking for a summary of the efforts being undertaken and of their progress.

The Shah, a tragic figure abandoned by his friends, died in exile in Cairo on July 27. I made certain that the U.S. Ambassador attended his funeral, though the initial intention of the Administration was not to be represented at all. His death did have the effect of removing a major obstacle to our negotiating efforts, and in early September we received the first serious probe from people close to Khomeini regarding a possible settlement. The President designated Christopher to conduct the negotiations, which, at this stage, were being pursued through German intermediaries. I was hopeful but also suspicious. When we met in the President's office at 2 p.m. on September 11, with Muskie, Christopher, and the Vice President also in attendance, I warned Carter that "it could be a trap. The Iranians may be fearful that he is planning to move in October and hence they are holding up the possibility of the hostage release as a way of preventing us from moving. Then in late October or early November the whole thing may simply fall apart and the President could end up by being humiliated. I told him there is no way of knowing whether this was the case, but we should at least prepare ourselves for that possibility."

For the next several weeks it looked as if my fears were exaggerated. The Iranians seemed to be negotiating in good faith, and Christopher seemed to be making progress. Moreover, the outbreak of the Iran–Iraq war created in Iran a need for American spare parts, and we began to hold out that option as a way of enticing the Iranians into a prompt settlement. By the middle of October, we were even discussing among ourselves the possibility of pre-positioning some of these spare parts in Germany, Algeria, or Pakistan, so that the Iranians could then promptly pick them up with their own aircraft.

It was at this juncture that we learned, much to our dismay, that the Israelis had been secretly supplying American spare parts to the Iranians, without much concern for the negative impact this was having on our leverage with the Iranians on the hostage issue. Muskie and I discussed this at some length and decided that the Secretary would make a strong demarche to the Israelis, since this was obviously undercutting our sensitive efforts. He did so, and, as far as I know, at least for a while the Israelis held back. In any case, in retrospect it seems clear that the Iraq–Iran war created less of an opportunity for negotiations than we may have thought and more of a complication for the Iranians, who became even less capable of focusing on the resolution of the hostage issue.

A continuing source of frustration as well as anxiety during this time was our uncertainty regarding the fate and disposition of the hostages. I was oppressed by the thought that some of the hostages might even be dead, and that we would discover this only after negotiating a settlement. In addition, we did not have good information regarding the whereabouts of the hostages. On several occasions, I raised this matter with Turner, complaining of inadequate intelligence penetration of the chaotic Iranian government. The President, too, felt strongly about it and even wrote Turner a rather sharp note early in August, stating that he found it difficult to understand why so little information was being provided to him regarding the whereabouts and condition of the hostages. Turner was understandably annoyed by the note, but it did have the effect of intensifying CIA efforts.

I have to add that throughout the Iranian crisis, and particularly during the preparation of the rescue mission, Turner and his colleagues worked with great intensity and much imagination, and succeeded in developing an organization that would have played a critical role in the rescue mission. However, when it came to longer-term political intelligence, especially conventional espionage, the admiral seemed to show less interest, and as a result the performance of the Agency was more sluggish.

Our hopes for a positive resolution of the hostage issue were dashed in late October. On the twenty-seventh, at 10:30 a.m., just prior to Carter's departure for Cleveland, where he was to make a campaign speech, Muskie, Christopher, and I met with him to tell him that the Iranians had postponed any decision and that all we had were some hints that the Iranians might release a portion of the hostages and then wait to see whether we were implementing our part of the bargain. This would be clearly unsatisfactory. The President listened, instructed us to keep him informed, gave us a wave, and abruptly terminated the meeting.

We met again on Sunday, November 2. I was awakened at 4:15 a.m. with word from Tehran that the Majlis, the Iranian parliament, had finally voted the conditions for the release of the hostages. I made a few phone calls and then left for the office to meet with the President, who was making a special return flight from Chicago. I stood in front of the south portico together with Fritz Mondale when the helicopter landed. Mondale and I walked up to the President and I handed him a piece of paper with the Majlis resolution on it, which I wanted him to read before our discussion. He looked grim and did not even say hello. As we walked to the Oval Office, he read the dispatch. (Later, some claimed the event—which was televised—was orchestrated for electoral purposes; this is simply not so.)

In the Cabinet meeting, Christopher gave us a comprehensive briefing on the state of the negotiations. It was evident that the hostages would not be released by election day, and it was still unclear whether the Iranians were acting in good faith or simply setting us up. We met again the next morning, November 3, the day before the elections. Turner told us that we had intelligence that buses had been assembled outside the Embassy, which might imply that the transfer of the hostages was about to occur. At the same time, Christopher informed us that conversations held by German intermediaries with the top Iranian leaders had not yielded any resolution of the issue. The President terminated the meeting by telling us to make clear to all that we would not compromise our national honor and that we remained hopeful that events were moving in the right direction. When the formal meeting broke up, the President's more immediate associates remained in the Oval Office with him: Hamilton Jordan, Patrick Caddell, Jerry Rafshoon, Stu Eizenstat, Jody Powell, and I. The President sat behind his desk while we all lounged around on chairs and sofas. The atmosphere was very informal, and I was struck by how much genuine affection there was between those closest to him and Jimmy Carter the man. When we broke up, knowing that tomorrow was *the* Tuesday, the handshakes were just so much stronger and warmer than in the Cabinet Room a few minutes earlier.

As I had feared, nothing happened. Election day passed with the hostages still incarcerated. And Carter was defeated. The Iranian debacle was clearly one of the three major factors contributing to that defeat: it generated a sense of national frustration and contributed to the unfair conclusion that Carter was indecisive; the related challenge by Senator Edward Kennedy destroyed Democratic unity and undermined the party's finances; while inflation undermined public confidence in the President's economic policies. In my view, these three factors together resulted in Carter's decisive defeat; the subtraction of any one of the three would have made for a close election; and in all probability he would have won quite strongly if handicapped by only one of the three.*

After the election, the only question facing us was whether we would resolve the hostage issue before leaving office. Not only was this a matter of personal pride for Carter; it also stemmed from the President's desire not to leave the new Administration encumbered by a painful dilemma. During this period Christopher and Cutler continued their effort at negotiations, and I recommended that we send signals that we might be inclined to provide some military aid to the Iraqis if the Iranians were not more forthcoming. Brown backed me on this last point in the course of some meetings in December.

We continued to be worried that at some point the hostages might be put on trial, and this issue was debated at an NSC meeting on December 19, 1980. The President took a hard line: "We mustn't rush into a response, and the fact they are bargaining with us rather than breaking with us publicly indicates that they still may be interested in

---

* In early 1982, I shared that judgment in the course of a conversation with former President Richard Nixon. Nixon's eyes lit up, he nodded vigorously and said, "You are absolutely right. Those three beat him. You should quote me in your book as agreeing with you."

negotiating. It is hard to tell when they will put any of our hostages on trial. I agree with Zbig that we cannot go out of office with a whimpering situation. We should therefore inform our allies as to what we would do if the trials start. We should recapitulate our plans to them and state the consequences of such trials or of any injury to the hostages."

The logjam in the negotiating process was broken between Christmas and January 20. Our intermediary now was Algeria, and in day-and-night negotiations Christopher and his associates were able to put together a package in which the release of the hostages was a quid pro quo for undoing our punitive sanctions against Iran. There would be no formal apologies, no restitution to Iran of the Shah's alleged fortune, no humiliating one-sided concessions. But even then the Iranians were not to deny themselves one last gesture of human pettiness: they made certain that the hostages were not released while Jimmy Carter was still President of the United States. As I noted in the last entry of my White House journal, dated January 20:

The last day of the Carter Presidency. . . . That tragedy which so poisoned everything about the Presidency continues to dominate. Yesterday shortly after one o'clock I went into the Oval Office and found in it the President, Vice President, Rosalynn, Civiletti, Jody, Cutler, Sick, [Gordon] Stewart (speech writer), Turner, [G. William] Miller, [legal adviser Michael] Cardozo standing around in a semicircle discussing the timing of the possible announcement of release. The Algerians apparently wanted to delay the announcement for several hours because of last-minute technical difficulties. The scene was one of anticipation and hope. I asked Rosalynn whether the President was still planning to go and she said he hoped to be able to go later in the day. I told her that he could still take the Concorde if necessary because that would cut flying time considerably. She went over and whispered to him but he said that he would not have the special communications required. However, as the day lingered on, it became clear that there would be no release on Monday, and the Presidential trip to Wiesbaden to greet the hostages as President of the United States is out. I talked to [Richard] Allen in the afternoon and he told me that an arrangement has been worked out whereby Reagan will designate Carter as a special emissary, provide him with Air Force One, and Carter would go to Germany immediately after the inaugural.

Tuesday morning, as I went in to brief the President at 9 a.m., my last scheduled briefing, I found in the Oval Office a large group of people. The President, sitting behind the desk with the red phone in his hand, listening to direct intelligence reports pertaining to the two Algerian aircraft parked on the runways at Tehran airport, said to me, "They have been ready to take off since 8:35." Everybody is standing around or sitting. The Vice President on the sofa, Rosalynn coming in and out and looking concerned, [Presidential assistant Jack] Watson, Gary Sick, Muskie, Jordan, Phil Wise, Pat Caddell, Jody in and out, Cutler, Kirbo. The President called me over and whispered that he wanted to go to Europe with me later today. . . .

We stood around for an hour or so. At 9:25 we started speculating as to why the planes are sitting on the runways and not being permitted to take off. The President called Christopher in Algiers and Christopher told us that there is concern in Algiers that perhaps there has been too much talk in the U.S. about the planes taking off and the hostages being released and the Iranians are deliberately holding back. At 9:55 the President talked with the operator monitoring Tehran. No flight plan has been filed yet. Moreover, the Iranians apparently have asked the Algerians not to announce any departure until the plane is outside of Iranian airspace. It is just possible that they are deliberately delaying taking any action on this so that the takeoff coincides with the end of the Carter Presidency. If so, it would be an additional mean blow by people who have proven themselves to be unusually capable of duplicity.

Shortly after 11 a.m.: Word just received from the Swiss that the Swiss Ambassador has been summoned by the Iranians to the airport to witness the takeoff of the hostages. I increasingly suspect that the timing is deliberately contrived so that it will coincide with the swear-in.

1:18 p.m.: Airborne in Air Force One to Atlanta. Until the very last minute the transfer of power and departure of the President dominated by the Iranian affair. I went down to the Sit. Room before leaving my office to monitor the latest developments from Iran. The plane as of 11:30 was still on the ground. It became clear that the Iranians were deliberately holding it up so that the transfer of the hostages would not occur while Jimmy Carter is President of the United States.

Yet it was in these trying months that the moral strength of Jimmy Carter stood out, and that deserves history's acknowledgment. A lesser man, faced with the enormously compelling task of reelection, vilified by the press and by his opponents as weak because of the humiliation inflicted upon us by Iran, might have been tempted to do something dramatic, irrespective of the effect on the lives of the hostages or of geopolitical consequences. Had Carter decided to embark on a series of punitive actions, actions which might have resulted in the death of some or all of the hostages but given the American people relief from their mounting frustration, his electoral chances would have been greatly increased. Instead, he remained steadfast and strong in his view that until we had another practical option, we should persist on the negotiating path. And Jimmy Carter succeeded in preserving both lives *and* our national interest, but at the cost of his Presidency.

CONCLUSIONS

14

The Past: A Critical Appraisal

> There have been Presidents in the past, maybe not too distant past,
> that let their Secretaries of State make foreign policy. I don't.
>
> —President Jimmy Carter, October 9, 1980

After the 1980 elections, I was standing with President Carter on the portico outside the Oval Office, looking at the White House garden while waiting for Prime Minister Begin to arrive. It was a gloriously sunny day, one of those rare late-November days which exude joy. The President pointed to his favorite tree right next to the Oval Office and then wistfully said, "I planted four trees in the White House garden. I hope Reagan doesn't cut them down."

The outcome of the election obviously left us unhappy and worried about the future. On December 4, after the morning briefing, the President and I chatted about the incoming Reagan Administration: "The President said that he was disturbed that Reagan for almost a month hasn't met with any of his advisers, either on domestic or foreign policy. He wondered how Reagan was going to govern. In effect, is he going to have a government of old millionaires who are assembled together in an informal kitchen cabinet? The President leaned back in his chair behind the desk in the Oval Office, his hands folded behind his head, and mused out loud: 'Is Reagan going to try to govern this country the way that GM is run?' I said, 'No, Mr. President. They are going to govern it the way Chrysler was run.' "

On January 20, 1981, a few minutes after noon, I walked out of my White House office, no longer the President's Assistant for National Security Affairs. During the preceding four years I had often reminded myself—deliberately—that being in the White House was an exceptional and very transitory period of my life. Frankly, I enjoyed it enormously but I also sensed how easy it would be to become attached to the trappings of power and to become totally enveloped by its aura. I was determined not to become the captive of my temporarily exalted status, or to take it for granted, or to yearn for it when it was over. I conditioned myself to view my White House experience as a unique chapter in my life, self-contained and not repeatable. This helped me to retain some sense of perspective about it all and to be more detached about its end. "Decompression" was not a problem.

To be sure, had Carter been reelected, I would have liked to continue on, but only for two more years. Family considerations aside—and a high government post simply leaves little time for normal family life—I was very conscious of the degree to which my intellectual arsenal was becoming depleted in the course of a continuous race against time. There was hardly ever any time to think systematically, to reexamine views, or simply to reflect. A broader historical perspective and a sense of direction are the prerequisites for sound policy making, and both tend gradually to become victims of in-house official doctrine and outlook and of the pressure toward compromise. Furthermore, as time goes on, the President himself tends to become increasingly a remote institution and less and less a person, and in dealing with him one becomes thus less inclined to be frank, direct, and critical. In brief, one's usefulness declines. The recognition of this made me determined to quit after at most two more years.

I have to confess that Carter's electoral defeat came as a surprise to me. I knew that he was in deep political trouble, largely because of the economy, and also because the Iranian issue and the mini-crisis over "the Soviet brigade in Cuba" had undermined public confidence in his leadership. Nonetheless, I expected Carter to win by a narrow margin, and I was reinforced in that belief by watching the Presidential TV debate a week or so before the election. Reverting, I suppose, to my academic past, I sat and listened to the debate, grading the participants on their mastery of the subject and on their skill in refuting each other's arguments—and I felt that Carter had won hands down. I failed to take into consideration that what really counts in these debates is the vague public perception as to which candidate sounded more self-assured and projected greater "Presidentiality" as well as personal warmth. I should have known better and earlier that my White House years were coming to an end.

In the course of those years I at no point wanted to become Secretary of State. As I said repeatedly (though in Washington no one would believe me), I preferred my position, and I hope my memoirs make the reasons for this clear. The fact was, for better or for worse, that Carter was *his own* Secretary of State. Working closely with him was therefore the bigger challenge. I had not expected, however, that my own role would evolve quite the way it did. I genuinely expected that the "team" approach would endure, and I did not anticipate that our internal policy disputes would propel me to public attention to the extent that they did. On the other hand, I was always conscious of the degree to which coordination of policy meant shaping policy, and I was intent from the start on influencing our priorities and policies.

Since history is not like a tape recorder—it cannot be rewound and replayed—I doubt that there is much value in speculating on "what might have been." In any case, it is probable that I would have been better off personally had I avoided policy disputes and thus been less controversial. But the issues were too important for me to be passive, and I felt increasingly vindicated by events and encouraged by the growing national consensus in favor of a firmer handling of the Soviet challenge.

In any case, it is a point of fact that in the area of foreign affairs President Carter achieved a historically impressive record. In four years his Administration—and the credit for this has to go largely to him personally—contributed significantly to world peace, to greater global justice, and to enhanced national security. It was Carter's major accomplishment that, by the time he left office, there was more widespread appreciation worldwide that America stood again for principle and identified itself with the movement for more social and political justice. It is no exaggeration to say that, thanks to Carter, America was again seen, after the years of Watergate and the Vietnam War, as standing for its traditional value of freedom. That is an asset in world affairs that cynics are wrong to dismiss.

At the same time, our principal rival, the Soviet Union, came to understand that Carter's foreign policy rested not only on more appealing principle—and the human-rights emphasis was seen by the Kremlin as especially dangerous—but also on the revival of American power. The decisions to shape the Rapid Deployment Force and to deploy the MX were taken seriously by the Soviet leaders. Especially in the last two years, the Carter Administration was mounting an increasingly effective response to Soviet assertiveness, and it was doing so by mobilizing the human spirit as well as by bolstering U.S. power.

Even more significant, perhaps, were the philosophical and historical underpinnings of Carter's foreign policy. The various specific moves toward China, or on the peace process in the Middle East, or toward the Third World more generally, were derived from the view that the world had entered a new post-Eurocentric era; that concentration either on the Atlantic alliance or on the U.S.–Soviet competition would not suffice to assure both international peace and increasing global justice in a world that has become politically awakened and active. We felt that we should strive in that context to temper as much as possible old ideological and power conflicts, especially through arms control with the Soviet Union, but we should at the same time even more actively address ourselves, without waiting for the resolution of U.S.–Soviet differences, to the many new problems that emerged in the wake of the collapse during two world wars of the Eurocentric world order.

Our determination to move on a broad front, thereby downplaying somewhat the U.S.–Soviet relationship, was at the root of our efforts to develop a more equitable relationship with Latin America, to promote majority rule in southern Africa, to obtain a peace that would ensure Israeli security while obtaining for the Palestinians the political dignity to which they are entitled, to deepen a new relationship with China, and to advance the various and highly complicated negotiations on economic relations with the Third World. Some observers later claimed that American–Soviet relations returned to center stage with the collapse of SALT and the Soviet southward push toward the Indian Ocean. However, such criticism misses the key point. U.S.–Soviet relations were and will remain central insofar as the largely negative agenda of world peace is concerned, for their essence is the mutual interest of the two competing superpowers in avoiding a nuclear war. But the truly positive agenda of world order and progress cannot wait until the United States and the Soviet Union are prepared to cooperate on a broad front, and so we felt that it behooved the United States to be more constructively engaged in moving to define the new global agenda.

It was Jimmy Carter's significant contribution to have made the United States a more positive force in the painful and difficult process of seeking a new cooperative framework for an increasingly turbulent world. That world has simultaneously experienced during this century the collapse of the existing, largely Europe-centered world order and the birth of so many new participants in the new and highly unstructured global political process. This engagement was difficult for many Americans to appreciate, for contemporary global change involves also painful adjustments for the hitherto dominant nations. But without such a change of emphasis and direction, there was growing danger in the mid-seventies, as there is again in the mid-eighties, of America becoming increasingly isolated and lonely in the world.

The fall of the Shah and the hostage crisis obscured much of that accomplishment, reinforcing the view that Carter's Administration was hesitant and reluctant to assert American power. After Carter's electoral defeat, even the more liberal Democrats, who normally have been unwilling to face up to the more brutal realities of power politics, joined in the conventional consensus that Carter's foreign policy was excessively moralistic and insufficiently militaristic. Harry McPherson, a leading liberal Washington Democrat, epitomized the prevailing wisdom in an interview with the New York *Times* (August 2, 1981), when he stated (though he did not single out Secretary Vance): "One of the problems President Carter had with the voters was that he and his administration conveyed the view that there were almost no circumstances under [which] we would defend any interests with our own troops. And while the country is not war-mongering, it does not want to have quite that message delivered."

The fact is that, outside of the Iran crisis, there were no circumstances during the Carter four years when the dispatch of American forces into combat was clearly required. There were times, as I have tried to suggest, when a firmer line, backed by U.S. military force, might have been more effective in containing Soviet expansionism. But to say that is not the same as to charge that Carter underestimated the importance of power. Indeed, such an argument overlooks the fact that for the first time in peace the U.S. defense budget actually grew, reversing the trends of the preceding years. It was President Carter who decided to create the Rapid Deployment Force, to deploy the MX missile, and to commit the United States to a military reaction in the event of a Soviet threat to our interests in the Persian Gulf region.

Nonetheless, myths about our supposed lack of toughness persisted even among staunch friends. I was startled one day in late 1978 when the very able and acute British Ambassador, Peter Jay, representing a Labour government not noted for its martial fervor, pressed me at some length on whether our Administration had the will to apply American power. Knowing of Vance's and Christopher's aversion to the use of force under most circumstances, Jay specifically asked whether Carter had "the guts" to invoke America's might. I found his inquiry disturbing, for it came at a time when we were fiercely debating our response to the Iranian crisis, and I knew that Jay's British counterpart in Tehran was advocating acquiescence to the anti-Shah movement. Jay's questioning reinforced my view that at stake in the Iranian crisis was our overall credibility.

The Administration's other major setback was unquestionably the failure to confront early enough the Soviet policy of combining detente on the Central European front with military expansion (first by proxy and then directly) in areas peripheral to our sensitive geopolitical interests. Had we responded more assertively through credible political-military reactions, while engaging the Soviets in wide-ranging discussions on the nature of the U.S.–Soviet relationship, perhaps we might have succeeded in stabilizing the American–Soviet relationship and in giving it an increasingly constructive content. American–Soviet detente would thus have become gradually both more comprehensive and reciprocal.

However, any criticism of our performance here has to be coupled with a recognition of the major Soviet responsibility for the downturn in the American–Soviet relationship. The Soviet Union not only pressed forward with its expansionist moves, but it flatly turned down U.S. overtures which could have had the effect of tempering the confrontationist aspects of the relationship. It was the United States which proposed significant cuts in strategic forces, and a more positive Soviet response would have immediately created a much more favorable political climate. The Soviet turndown was total, brutal, and fateful. Moreover, the Soviet Union repeatedly rejected our proposals for annual summit meetings between Carter and Brezhnev, which could have resulted in the development of a genuinely consultative relationship between the two governments. Here again, the Soviets, for shortsighted reasons, opted in favor of a rigid posture, which prevented an amelioration of the U.S.–Soviet relationship.

I am convinced that the adoption of a firmer line sooner, coupled with the willingness to pursue arms control and to widen U.S.–Soviet cooperative relations, would have presented the Soviet leaders with a clearer choice. I do not know if they would have chosen to opt for more cooperation, but at least the issue would have been posed. Instead, during the first half of the Carter Administration our almost fetishistic pre-occupation with obtaining a SALT agreement made the Soviets feel that they could press us for concessions while one-sidedly exploiting detente elsewhere. Vance fueled the President's desire to speedily conclude an arms control agreement by reinforcing Carter's view that Brezhnev and he, in Vance's words, "have similar dreams and aspirations about the most fundamental issues." I recall irritating Carter by disputing that view and arguing that it ignored the cumulative influence of history and ideology in shaping a leader's outlook.

But events tended to confirm my view of the U.S.–Soviet relationship, and by mid-1978 public opinion was also drifting toward a more realistic appreciation of the Soviet problem. An editorial in the Washington *Post* (May 30, 1978) put it succinctly: "In a sense the Administration is arriving collectively at a point not far from where Zbigniew Brzezinski has been all along. It is a point consistent with the heightened apprehensions raised in the last year or so by Soviet power plays in Africa, and by Soviet strategic programs. It also happens to be a point consistent with the political mood of the country as we sense it. . . . We see no special unmanageable policy tension between Mr. Brzezinski and Mr. Vance, who, with his aides, is more problem solver than theoretician. . . . Mr. Brzezinski's trip to China seems to have produced a measure of consultation and understanding well suited to reminding the Russians that the United States is not without friends in its efforts to induce Soviet restraint."

Within the Administration, Harold Brown came to share my concerns, but the debate continued. According to an entry in my journal for September 13, 1979:

I spent much of the morning working on my rather tough memorandum to the President urging that he adopt a much more assertive tone in foreign policy and take some assertive decisions. I toned down the memorandum so that it doesn't sound so much like a critique of the State Department, but there is no doubt that the President will resent it. I showed it to Brown, who very much agreed with me. He also told me that in his judgment the President has a simplistic and naïve view that the Soviet leaders are like ourselves and that I should include that point in my memorandum.

I told him that there is no point in my continuing to preach to the President, especially since he knows how I feel about the Soviets. However, [Harold] has negotiated with the Soviets in SALT I and perhaps it might be useful for him to write such a tough memo to the President. By this evening a memo came in from Harold to the President making these points rather forcefully. I sent it in. I am sure that by tomorrow morning the President is going to be furious at me. But I think he needs to be told this. I showed my memo to Jody and to Owen and both agreed that it was needed.

I believe it is fair to say that on the Soviet issue we simply did not resolve during the first two years the difficult question of what should be the proper mix between cooperation and competition in the relationship. In speaking to the press, I would often use the formula that the American–Soviet relationship is "a mixed one, involving both competition and cooperation," and I would explain that the two superpowers were doomed by history to an inherently contradictory relationship. Competition between America and Russia was ordained by history, geography, and philosophy, while the imperative of cooperation is the consequence of nuclear weaponry. But such a formula, designed to make the press more sensitive to complexity, did not by itself provide a clear guideline for resolving our internal policy choices. These had to be made on a case-by-case basis, and it is here that subtle differences of nuance, emphasis, and priority among Carter's advisers presented the President with a continuing dilemma.

I reflected on this issue at mid-point in our Administration, when I wrote:

In general, as I look at our foreign policy, it seems to me that eighteen months after we took office we can define it in terms of two alternative models: model #1 would involve placing primary emphasis on relations with the Soviet Union, making SALT the centerpiece of our foreign policy accomplishments and generally attempting to broaden the American–Soviet relationship. This would obscure our second emphasis on close relations with our allies. We would also make a major effort to solve the Middle East problem, but by doing it together with the Soviets. Perhaps to some extent the same would be true of southern Africa, while China would take very much a back seat. An alternative model, perhaps called #2, involves putting primary emphasis on our allies, downgrading the relationship with the Soviets and restricting it essentially to SALT, upgrading our relationship with China to a more or less equal level, solving the Middle East problem but without Soviet participation, and seeking to resolve the southern African problem. The first model comes closer to what Vance would favor. The second one comes closer to what I would favor and have been favoring. The second one also comes closer to what we are now doing.

But I continued to worry about the inclination of my colleagues over at State to equate foreign policy with endless litigation and to confuse detente with acquiescence. I wrote on November 27, 1978:

First snow of the year; a gloomy dark day. On a day like today everything looks less promising. I was struck that David Aaron had very much the same reactions as I: that our foreign policy with regard to Africa is stalemated; that the Israelis are thumbing their noses at us; that the Soviets no longer take us seriously and are asserting themselves in Iran and South Yemen and southern Africa and Cuba. All of this was reinforced by the proposed response to the Soviets on the MiG-23s [in Cuba] which was submitted by the State Department. It sounded practically apologetic and as if it was designed to explain the Soviet behavior to the American public rather than to insure that the Soviets remain restrained and fulfill their previous obligations.

From time to time, I also meditated on my own position, especially on my relationship to Carter. In late 1978, on December 28, when the issue of how to deal with the Soviet Union was still not resolved, I observed:

The interesting point about my situation here is that unlike Kissinger, who had in Nixon a clear ally in shaping a grand strategy for the country, I have to do it through indirection, although increasingly Brown supports me. Cy basically is in disagreement, particularly on our relations with the Soviet Union, and he doesn't like to think in broader conceptual terms. The President on specific issues tends to be tough, and sides with me when there is a show-down, but at the same time he is very much tempted by the vision of a grand accommodation with Brezhnev.

That temptation was derived from Carter's intense and instinctive desire to go down in history as the peacemaker. On more than one occasion, as I have noted, I used with him the formula "You first have to be a Truman before you are a Wilson" in arguing that our first priority must be to revive global respect for American power, after the debacles of Watergate and Vietnam, lest our pursuit of principle be confused with weakness. Carter agreed cerebrally, but emotionally he thirsted for the Wilsonian mantle—and this was sensed on the outside and generated the unfair but damaging charge of vacillation.

Contrary to what his critics asserted, Carter was tough, cool, and determined. Cerebrally, he knew that the President had to use power and to project confidence in doing so—but reliance on force was not instinctive with him. And that showed. This sense of reluctance which Carter conveyed was translated in the public mind into a perception of weakness. The President's public credibility suffered accordingly. Though he moved steadily toward a firmer reliance on power, he was increasingly perceived as indecisive. This was devastating politically, especially after Iran.

Actually, in foreign affairs, contrary to public perception, Carter was a dominant President. His personal involvement in the foreign policy process was assertive and extensive. He engaged himself deeply and he mastered impressively the technical arcana of the key issues. He dominated our discussions, and in some cases, especially the Sinai pull-out agreement, he himself devised the complicated formulas for a constructive resolution. He made it clear to all that he was in charge, and for it to be so he worked extremely hard, mastering previously unfamiliar material. The U.S. taxpayer had in Jimmy Carter a truly dedicated Chief Executive.

Moreover, he was prepared to make tough decisions. Never has a President engaged himself as deeply in the Middle East problem. On the Panama Canal Treaties and on normalization of relations with China, he bit the bullet because he felt strongly that it was in America's historical interest to do so, even if it was domestically costly in political terms. He adopted stringent sanctions against the Soviet Union following the Soviet invasion of Afghanistan, and it was his reputedly tougher successor who lifted the most significant sanction because it was domestically unpopular. When Carter became convinced that the strategic balance needed reinforcement through the deployment of the MX, he did not hesitate to take the required decision on the basing mode, even though he knew it would hurt him politically in the states in which the MX would be based. When national security was involved, political considerations always took second place in Carter's decision making.

Indeed, Carter made hardly any effort to disguise his disdain for domestic politics—and that certainly contributed to his one-term Presidency. On many occasions he spoke disparagingly about political expediency; he resented having to deal with interest groups; his heart was not in the give-and-take of bargaining politics. Often I would discuss his speeches with him because I felt strongly that he needed to make more formal addresses and that he had to improve his delivery of them. After his State of the Union Address of January 1979, I complimented him on the parts dealing with foreign policy, but I noted critically that I thought he delivered the other sections of the speech in a listless fashion. To drive the point home, I added that he read these sections as if he was not even interested in what he was saying, and the audience could sense it. Carter was not offended; on the contrary, he disarmingly agreed, saying that the foreign affairs part engaged him, while in the rest of the speech all he was doing was "handing out goodies to interest groups" and he had no stomach for it.

As a highly active President, with an intense personal interest in foreign affairs, Carter was not only the central U.S. decision maker but ultimately also the key political mobilizer of national support for our foreign policy, the principal manager of the bureaucratic process, and, occasionally, even the ultimate foreign negotiator. His involvement in these four roles was intense, probably more so than was the case with any of his post-World War II predecessors.

As decision maker, President Carter displayed good balance and a genuine sense of historical-moral responsibility. He fashioned an active foreign policy, infused with principle, and designed to move on a broad front: SALT, the Middle East, southern Africa, China, Panama, to mention just the first year's agenda. He was compassionate and felt that America should also project that feeling to a world grappling with the blight of poverty, hunger, and disease. At the same time, he came to recognize more and more the central role of American power in the preservation of peace and became increasingly committed to the re-invigoration of America's military might. In my judgment, his only fatal error was in regard to Iran, though that is, admittedly, debatable. I cannot prove that the approach I favored would have avoided the debacle, while Carter's own efforts to buttress the vacillating Shah were diluted by State.

Before making any decision, Carter would immerse himself deeply in the subject matter. He would first read a great deal about it, then often discuss it informally with me and also with his other advisers, review the preliminary reports sent up from our Cabinet-level SCC or PRC meetings, and then either decide and respond to me in writing or make his final decision at an NSC session. Throughout, he would keep up with the critical issues and make a serious effort to master their nuances. He did not make uninformed decisions, nor is it fair to say that he zigzagged once a basic decision had been made. However, determined to stay on top of issues, he had a tendency to become excessively involved in their continuing discussion, with the effect that he would at times overrefine his approach and occasionally alter it by simply sticking with it for too long. At times, I thought he was like a sculptor who did not know when to throw away his chisel.

But because he was so intelligent, he did tend to see more sides to an issue than perhaps occasionally was necessary, and on two of them— Iran and the U.S.–Soviet relationship—he was pulled in opposite directions by conflicting advice from his immediate associates. In that respect, it would have been better if a sharper choice had been made by the President earlier on. Certainly, neither Vance nor I, as the protagonists of rather differing perspectives on those two issues (though in agreement on many others), had any reason to quit, thus leaving the field to the other. Each of us must have felt—I certainly did so—that the predominant consensus on issues justified working on together, with each of us hoping that the President would side with him on the specifically contentious matters.

Moreover, the fact is that we on the inside underestimated the political damage created by the public perception of Presidential indecision which the so-called Vance–ZB split was generating. Because on so many issues the working relationship was good, and particularly because the President felt strongly that he was benefiting from the occasionally contradictory advice he was getting before he himself made the final decisions, we all tended to discount the press reports from the outside as simply exaggerations, which in fact in most cases they were, not taking into account their increasingly damaging effect on public perceptions.

I recall being genuinely surprised one day in late 1979 when the President's adviser Hedley Donovan came down to my office and told me that he had come to see what could be done about the controversy surrounding Vance and me. As I noted in my journal: "He then described it as the most serious problem that he thinks the President confronts." I suspect that Carter, who saw on a daily basis that Vance and I were collaborating in a fair-minded fashion and who knew that neither of us was complaining to him regularly about the other, also felt that the situation was better than perceived outside. In one of his press conferences, he explained how he viewed the situation: "We discuss the important issues around the world, 150 nations, trouble spots in different parts of the world, and what our nation should do to address it. We sometimes have differences of opinion among us. I'd say 95 percent of the time the National Security Adviser and the Secretary of State agree in making a recommendation to me. On those times when they do disagree, I make the judgment. . . . And I can tell you that I will always have strong advisers around me, sometimes they are inevitably going to give me conflicting advice, but I'll be the one to make the judgment on what should be the foreign policy of our country and let it be known to the American people."

Precisely because Carter did dominate the process, he did not feel troubled by the disagreement. He considered that normal and in some respects even useful. I remember once discussing with him how President Roosevelt took advantage of conflicting advice and how he played one adviser off against another. I think Carter saw himself as doing the same, but without the Machiavellian touch. Moreover, because Vance was not assertive or excessively innovative, Carter needed me; at the same time, as he once noted, he needed Vance to restrain his own activism as well as mine. Beyond that, I suspect that Carter worried that if he got rid of Vance the press would proclaim me a victor in the

Kissinger mode, and he had come to office determined that there no longer be any domination by a "Lone Ranger." At the same time, as he testifies in his memoirs, I was useful to him as an energizer as well as a coordinator, provided I was not perceived outside as dominant.

Carter also felt that I was helpful as a public spokesman, largely because Vance was reluctant to play that role. Under normal circumstances, the Secretary of State should have been the principal spokesman, and later Muskie tried to be one (with greater relish but with less expertise). Vance's heart was not in it. Moreover, there were times when Carter felt (and so did I) that the Secretary of State was articulating not so much the President's foreign policy as the State Department's. Though the public craved a President who was perceived as firm, only too often the voice emanating from State made his foreign policy sound maudlin and indecisive. When I spoke up, the press had a field day, playing up real or imagined differences of emphasis between NSC and State.

Moreover, a system of decision making that was highly centralized in the White House under a dominant President created a situation in which the Assistant was increasingly the bureaucratic beneficiary of active Presidential predominance. By the final year of the Carter term, the outside world tended to see me in fact as more predominant than I actually was. *U.S. News & World Report* even listed me in its 1980 poll as "the third-most-influential" official after the President and the Federal Reserve chief, "a degree of power never before enjoyed by a White House aide." But this perception was in conflict with the simultaneous emphasis put on the formal preeminence of the Secretary of State as the President's principal associate in the area of foreign policy. To make matters worse, the deliberate use of me by the President as his occasional spokesman on foreign policy prompted various press attacks on me as a usurper of the Secretary's prerogatives. Thus, while on the inside the reality was far from one of continuous conflict, on the outside the misleading impression was one of almost never-ending Vance (Muskie)–Brzezinski strife.

Had the President been more effective in shaping public opinion, or had I spoken up less and Vance more, this problem could have been perhaps overcome. Given the centrality of the Presidential office in foreign affairs, the President needs to be an effective mobilizer of political support, a persuasive educator who simultaneously enlightens the public about global complexities and generates support for his policies. It is certainly easier to obtain public support if one is willing to oversimplify issues and to reduce foreign affairs to a confrontation between good and evil. But Carter was too responsible and intelligent to seek refuge in demagogy; he had contempt for simplistic solutions and had faith in his ability to explain complex matters to the public. This he did especially well in informal, spontaneous situations, in which his quickness of mind and his personal appeal could excel. His press conferences were generally impressive, and he was usually in command both of the audience and of the subject under discussion. He was equally good in on-the-record TV interviews.

Surprisingly for a political leader who scored such an unexpected and meteoric electoral success, Carter was a much less effective speaker. His delivery was uneven, his emphases often wrongly placed, his pauses and articulation not evoking enthusiasm. Perhaps because he sensed that weakness, Carter tended to downgrade the importance of formal speeches, arguing that few people listened to them and even fewer read them. Moreover, and on this point I was more than once deeply frustrated, he fancied himself to be a good draftsman, with the result that finely crafted statements, combining the eloquence of his speech writers with (so I felt) serious reflections on the state of the world as well as carefully nuanced policy statements prepared by me, would be rewritten or chopped up by him beyond the point of recognition. The language would come out stilted, with elegance of expression yielding to simple, flat, declaratory assertions, often with completely unrelated paragraphs colliding gracelessly.

I suspect the absence of historical perspective played a role in Carter's attitude toward speech making. I felt strongly that a President should speak not only to his people but on some occasions also to history. Moreover, I also wanted the elite of other nations, and even their peoples, to note what he had to say—and therefore both style and substance were important. Also, there were times when I felt it was appropriate and even noteworthy for the President to give a lengthy address on foreign policy, one lasting at least three-quarters of an hour, so that complex issues could be fully analyzed and so that the President's own depth would be effectively conveyed. But Carter would have none of that. Most speech drafts that went into the Oval Office came out amputated, with fifteen minutes usually set as the maximum, no matter how important or complicated the subject. By prolonged negotiations, we managed occasionally to stretch this to twenty or twenty-five minutes.

On balance, Carter was not good at public relations. He did not fire enthusiasm in the public or inspire fear in his adversaries. He was trusted, but—very unfairly—that trust was in him as a person but not in him as a leader. He had ambitious goals for this nation, both at home and abroad, and yet he did not succeed in being seen as a visionary or in captivating the nation's imagination. His personal qualities—honesty, integrity, religious conviction, compassion—were not translated in the public mind into statesmanship with a historical sweep. This was not only very costly; it unduly elevated the importance of some disagreements among his key lieutenants.

In fulfilling the role of the supreme manager of the bureaucratic process, Carter developed and sustained a more centralized system than that of other Presidents, with his principal foreign policy advisers continuously engaged in collective discussions and frequent consultations with him. Under his overall direction, genuine coordination by the NSC was achieved, especially between State and Defense, to a greater extent than had previously been the case. At the same time, the President spent too much time on foreign policy in general. In part this was my fault, especially in the first year. I not only welcomed his involvement but I stimulated it with a comprehensive agenda that the NSC developed for our foreign policy. Moreover, he involved himself excessively in too many secondary matters, and to make matters worse, he resisted, and quite sharply at times, any effort by me to promote genuine delegation of authority.

At the same time, and curiously so for a leader who insisted on being very much in control, Carter did not insist sufficiently, in my judgment, on the maintenance of political discipline within the secondary echelons of his team. Especially among some political appointees at State, there was relatively little personal loyalty to Carter, in time a great deal of anti-Carter gossip, and in some cases in 1980 only barely masked sympathy for the Teddy Kennedy challenge. A manager has to be also a disciplinarian. And Carter should have done what President John F. Kennedy did. Kennedy, after two years, decided that he had to have more self-evident loyalty in the State Department, and he cleaned house. For reasons I could not understand, Carter never asserted himself in that respect.

But Carter has to be given credit for personally assembling a team of able top associates. Whatever my disagreements with Vance or Christopher, or less frequently with Brown, there is not the slightest doubt that Carter in selecting them—and he was deeply involved in the selection process—chose individuals of great integrity, high intelligence, and genuine ability. They, in return, respected him and worked in a highly dedicated fashion. Moreover, both in supporting the President and in trying to make decisions on his behalf, we were able to collaborate closely, to maintain very close contact both personally and through more official meetings, and on the overwhelming number of issues to generate genuine consensus.

During the four years, on many occasions Carter acted as the principal U.S. foreign negotiator. He did so spectacularly during Camp David, displaying extraordinary patience, occasional flashes of anger, and genuine empathy for Sadat's and Begin's dilemmas. He dealt skillfully with Gromyko on SALT, revealing a mastery of the subject which must have surprised that old veteran of some two decades of arms control debates. He developed a curious relationship of personal closeness with Torrijos of Panama and used it at sensitive junctures to obtain Panamanian cooperation in our own ratification process. At a key point in our negotiations with China, he intervened personally to convince the Chinese that the United States meant what it was saying, and later Deng told me that the intervention had been critical in accelerating the normalization process. Not only did Carter make policy; at critical junctures he also negotiated it.

As our principal negotiator, Carter was truly superb. He had a unique gift for projecting empathy for the other man's point of view even while attempting to get him to change it. I recall my amazement when in May 1977 he charmed the shrewd and experienced President Assad of Syria while skillfully probing for flexibility in Assad's position. Here was the brand-new U.S. President, fresh out of Georgia, never before engaged in serious foreign negotiations, first listening patiently to Assad's lengthy catalogue of complaints and then to his even longer discourse on Arab history—both lasting about an hour—and then quietly steering him into a more productive discussion of possible security arrangements, of the need for more flexibility on the Palestinian question, and of the wider significance of Arab–Israeli peace. I was genuinely impressed by his ability to marshal facts and by his subtlety in dealing with a highly skilled and intransigent protagonist.

When need be, he could be very blunt—and yet manage not to offend needlessly. In early October 1977, the Marxist President of Mozambique, Samora Moises Machel, opened his meeting with Carter with a five-minute tirade on the subject of alleged American support for European colonialism. Carter listened without blinking an eyelash. When Machel finally came to a stop, Carter leaned forward, looked his guest straight in the eye, and said very quietly, "Mr. President, you have a very distorted view of my country." Machel, taken aback, lapsed into silence, and Carter then, in the same relaxed tone, went on to say that he did not need a lecture from someone running a totalitarian society (and he used the word "totalitarian") on how to govern America and what America's world role ought to be. Unbelievable as it may sound, the discussion thereafter became quite amicable, and later our relations with Mozambique even improved somewhat.

The truly substantial foreign policy accomplishments of the Carter Presidency are thus largely the product of Carter's own intelligence, drive, and dedication. Despite the very major setbacks suffered in Iran and the continuing stalemate in U.S.–Soviet relations, in an overall sense Carter left the U.S. position in the world considerably better than what he inherited. The Middle East moved toward peace. American–Chinese relations were normalized. NATO was being reinvigorated. A crisis in U.S.–Latin American relations was averted because of Carter's willingness to pay the political price involved in the ratification of the Panama Canal Treaties. And America was no longer viewed by the Africans as hostile. In a deeper, more philosophical sense, because of his Administration's commitment to human rights, America was again being seen not only as a major power but as a moral force for human progress.

To conclude, President Carter was innovative and activist in the area of foreign policy, enhancing America's power and recommitting America to principle. Foremost among his accomplishments were:

The reidentification of America with certain basic ideals: justice, equity, majority rule, self-determination, dignity of the individual —and here our human-rights policy was essential

The Camp David Accords, prompting the first peace treaty ever between an Arab state and Israel, and the creation of a process for dealing with the Palestinian problem

The normalization of relations with China and the growth of a more comprehensive political and even an incipient strategic relationship   —

The Panama Canal Treaties, ushering in a more equitable relationship with our Latin American neighbors and avoiding a nasty confrontation in a strategically sensitive area

Commitment to majority rule in Africa and the revival of constructive relationships with key African countries

A policy of differentiation in Eastern Europe, developing U.S. relations not only with those Eastern European countries that defied Soviet foreign policy but also with those that engaged in quiet domestic liberalization, as well as the deterrence in 1980 of a Soviet military move against Poland

The revitalization and modernization of American strategic doctrine and military posture, including PD–59, the RDF, and the MX

The reinjection of American military presence into the Persian Gulf and the Indian Ocean and the initiation of a regional security framework for the area, including the Carter Doctrine

The negotiation of a comprehensive international trade agreement, averting a relapse into destructive protectionism

International energy agreements designed to give the West increased capacity for dealing with future energy crises through conservation and increased production

Partially effective restraints on nuclear proliferation and worldwide sales of arms

Lifting of the Turkish arms embargo and the reintegration of both Greece and Turkey into a more positive relationship with NATO

Firm, even if politically costly, sanctions against the Soviet Union after the Soviet invasion of Afghanistan

A SALT II agreement (not ratified but mutually honored), involving a considerable improvement on the asymmetrical arrangements negotiated by Nixon and Kissinger in SALT I

This list speaks for itself. And it guarantees that President Carter will be appraised more generously by posterity than he was by the electorate in 1980.

15

The Future: Power and Principle in American Foreign Policy

A major problem we confront in the shaping of our foreign policy is the difficulty of combining a commitment to principle with a realistic appreciation of the importance and deep centrality of American power in the world. Our thinking about world affairs since America became deeply engaged, roughly around the time of Wilson, has oscillated between an idealistic commitment to a world order yet to be shaped and a periodic swing toward fascination with Realpolitik.

—Zbigniew Brzezinski, speech at
Georgetown University, April 23, 1981

Our world is becoming increasingly turbulent. The factors that make for international instability are gaining the historical upper hand over the forces that work for more organized cooperation. The unavoidable conclusion of any detached analysis of global trends is that social turmoil, political unrest, economic crises, and international friction are likely to become more widespread during the remainder of this century.

In this context, a stable American–Soviet relationship is all the more important to maintain and all the more difficult to attain. Soviet military power is likely to increase, while, at the same time, internal tensions within both the Soviet system and the Soviet bloc will become more acute. There is every reason to believe that without major structural adjustments the Soviet system will be unable to cope with the problems of modernity, that its overly bureaucratized structure will continue to stifle creativity, and that the imposed maintenance of such a system over Eastern Europe will generate rising resentment. The contradiction between the poor internal performance of the Soviet system and the growth of Soviet external military capabilities is likely to create a much more unpredictable pattern of Soviet behavior. Erratic opportunism by a world power in the setting of global turmoil will pose an increasing threat to international peace.

Moreover, in the years ahead regional conflicts not involving the major powers are likely to become more threatening. Already in the late seventies and early eighties regional conflicts have acquired immunity from effective international containment. As American power receded, it became more difficult to terminate local conflicts quickly. Their persistence and increasing frequency is likely to be especially debilitating to American interests, for American society, more so than the Soviet system, requires international stability for the promotion of its interests and its values. In contrast, low-level, regionally disruptive violence is seen by the Soviet leaders as generally more conducive to the spread of Soviet influence. This is especially the case now because the end of U.S. nuclear superiority means that the Soviets have less cause to fear that in a local conflict the United States might act assertively (as it did earlier in the Cuban missile crisis). Of course, this entails the enormous risks of miscalculation, and that is one important element of heightened danger in the evolving international situation.

More generally, the combination of demographic pressures and political unrest will generate, particularly in the Third World, increasing unrest and violence. Much or maybe even most of this will be internal, but it will inevitably impose major strains on international order. The population of the world by the end of this century will have grown to some 6 billion from about 4 billion people. Moreover, most of the increase will be concentrated in the poorer parts of the world, with 85 percent of the world's population by the end of this century living in Africa, Latin America, and the poorer parts of Asia. The dramatic change in the demographic character of the world, pregnant with political consequences, is best illustrated by the following table listing the most populous countries of the world in 1900 and by the year 2000:

	1900 (in millions)		*2000* (in millions)
1	China 440		China 1,165
2	India (not independent) 285		India 1,080
3	Russia 132		U.S.S.R. 306
4	United States 76		United States 265
5	Germany 56		Indonesia 255
6	Austria-Hungary 45		Brazil 215
7	Japan 44		Pakistan 155
8	United Kingdom 41		Bangladesh 145
9	France 40		Nigeria 135
10	Indonesia (not independent) 35		Japan 135
11	Italy 33		Mexico 135
12	Ottoman Empire 30		Philippines 95

Most of the Third World countries listed are likely to continue to suffer from weak economies and inefficient government, while their increasingly literate, politically awakened, but restless masses will be more and more susceptible to demogogic mobilization on behalf of political movements.

Moreover, it is almost a certainty that an increasing number of Third World states will come to possess nuclear weapons, and some are likely to use them in the course of a conflict. Terrorist groups may also before very long try to advance their causes through a nuclear threat, either by theft of such weapons or by surreptitious production. In any case, the probability that nuclear weapons will be used in anger is becoming ominously high.

To make matters worse, it is problematical whether in the short run some advanced industrial democracies will overcome their internal socio-economic difficulties initiated by the revolution in the cost of energy. The dislocations caused by that upheaval—itself a symptom of the political redistribution of power that has been taking place in our age— are still to be assimilated by the advanced economies. The resulting slowdown in the economic performance of the industrial West not only has contributed to a global recession but has sharpened tensions among the advanced industrial economies themselves. One symptom of this trend is the upswing in domestic support for protectionist measures, diluting further the political consensus of the most advanced and democratic sector of the global community.

Though the Soviet Union is likely to exploit all of these difficulties, the danger confronting the world is not, at least in the short run, that of global domination by the Soviet Union. The U.S.S.R. simply lacks the capacity to impose its will on the world in a manner even remotely reminiscent of the predominance enjoyed by the United States during the Pax Americana of the 1950s. That predominance not only rested on American military superiority but was derived from the economic, political, cultural, and even ideological appeal of America. The Soviet Union is simply not competitive in any of those latter domains, and military power alone will not suffice to impose a Pax Sovietica on a turbulent world. Soviet power, used in a shortsighted and dogmatic fashion, can, however, intensify global unrest and stimulate increasing fragmentation of the global order. The menace confronting humanity, in brief, is not Soviet hegemony but global anarchy.

As the world becomes increasingly turbulent and inhospitable to American interests, the problems confronting Washington in assuring U.S. national security will become increasingly complex and overlapping. At the same time, the available reaction period to external crises will shrink because of the revolutions in communications and in weapons technology. Finally, our difficulties will be compounded by the increasingly direct connection between our nation's foreign and domestic affairs.

During the 1970s, the United States experienced severe and perplexing problems that demonstrated the close interrelationship between historical-cultural, political-military, and socioeconomic factors: In the Middle East, the OPEC oil embargo had an acute effect on the daily life of virtually every American; never before had we felt such an impact in peacetime. The resurgence of fundamentalist Islam throughout the region, culminating in the fall of the Shah and the convulsions of Khomeini's Iran, created a continuing danger to our interests in a region on which the well-being of the West as a whole very much depends. In Central America, the populist call for land reform and the progressive social transformation again caught us without a national consensus on how to react. These foreign policy problems are new and different from those of the previous decades.

A historically adequate response will require a sustained national effort, a highly focused national policy, and an effectively centralized decision-making process. Given the nature of our political system, any effort to generate a meaningful sense of direction will have to originate with the President. He alone can mobilize the national will and also educate the country to the dilemmas—and imperatives—of the new world situation. The logical implication of this is that the initiation and coordination of policy—as well as the shaping of a broader strategy—has to be coordinated by an individual closely and directly associated with the President himself. Even an active President, deeply interested in foreign affairs, needs someone—given the enormous demands on the President's time also for domestic issues—to act as his adviser, as his eyes and ears, and as his bureaucratic coordinator. The President himself does not have the time to integrate the key departments, notably State and Defense. The perspectives and priorities of these departments diverge so often and so widely that coordinating them is a full-time job, and it can be done only if the individual assigned the task is known to enjoy the President's personal confidence and can speak authoritatively on the President's behalf.

There are basically two ways of making certain that this is done. One is by enhancing the established "Secretarial" mode of making policy; the other is by legitimatizing the bureaucratic implications of direct "Presidential" leadership in foreign policy. There may be times and circumstances when the President wishes to concentrate on domestic policy or when a powerful Secretary of State, strongly backed by the President, can provide much of the needed initiative and coordination. In the case of such a "Secretarial system," the office of the Assistant for National Security Affairs should be deliberately downgraded. The Secretary of State should be seen as fully in charge, and the President must then make certain that potential rivals to the Secretary of State accommodate themselves to his primacy. This is clearly a more difficult system to make work, especially given the emergence over the last two decades of a highly complex interrelationship between diplomacy, security, and intelligence and the increasing relevance of international economics and commerce. Indeed, to make such a system work, a combination of a relatively domestically oriented and personally highly secure President and a very gifted and assertive Secretary of State will be needed—as in the case of Truman and Acheson or Eisenhower and Dulles.

On the basis of my own experience, and reflecting on the historical relationship between Presidents and Secretaries of State, I think the "Secretarial system" is likely to be more and more difficult to operate efficiently. As the United States moves into the twenty-first century, with its global involvement so intense and so central to our national survival, the nerve center for national security is bound to be increasingly the White House. It is there—close to the President—that relevant national objectives are most likely to be defined and bureaucratic discipline is most likely to be imposed on a highly complex governmental structure. Few people outside the government realize the extent to which policy is hammered out through bureaucratic and personal rivalries, and how rarely it springs from the mind of a single dominant individual. This makes it all the more important that a single individual be the final arbiter, the source of national direction, lest security policy become simply the amalgam of bureaucratic compromises. Under the U.S. system, it has to be the President who is that final decision maker. That constitutional fact inherently drives decision making back into the White House.

Nonetheless, given the weight of tradition and also the controversy created in recent years by the roles played as National Security Assistants by both Kissinger and myself, it is likely that efforts will be made to maintain and even enhance the role of the Secretary of State. It is certainly the popular convention to assert that that is how things ought to be done—and a system of Secretarial, rather than Presidential, predominance in foreign affairs can work. The difficulty that any such arrangement is likely to encounter is apt to be less on the level of public articulation and even policy initiation—for a dominant Secretary of State can hold his own in these areas, especially if visibly backed by a supportive and secure President. The problem is likely to arise on the level of coordination, with the Defense Department and the CIA traditionally opposing coordination by State, since coordination also means subordination. Accordingly, to make such a system work, the President will have to sanction formal arrangements making the Secretary of State his principal coordinator in the NSC committee system, including the sensitive responsibility for crisis management.

Nonetheless, political and international realities are likely to work increasingly against the effective assertion of the "Secretarial" model. The inevitable fact is that in modern democracies making foreign policy is becoming less and less the exclusive prerogative of professionals. With mass media and communications producing a greater sense of global intimacy and with increasing economic interdependence, the borderline between the foreign and the domestic has become blurred.

It is no accident that in the U.K., in France, and in Germany chief executives have felt compelled to create their own foreign policy staffs at 10 Downing Street, in the Elysée, and in the Chancellor's Office, respectively. Integration of policy and responsiveness to public opinion simply could not be generated by their more professional, admittedly better informed, yet domestically more isolated foreign ministries.

In addition, Secretaries of State only too often (especially with the passage of time), and their State Department professionals almost always, tend to confuse diplomacy with foreign policy. What they forget is that diplomacy is a technique for promoting national objectives abroad and not an end in itself. This is why most recent Presidents have tended to become disillusioned and frustrated by "Foggy Bottom," gradually concentrating foreign policy decision making more and more in the White House, where it is likely to recoil less from the occasional need to employ compulsion and where it is likely to be more responsive to sensitive domestic, economic, and other concerns.

Even on foreign policy matters the President needs someone close to him who shares his larger "Presidential" perspective and can rise above narrower bureaucratic concerns. This is why coordination is easier to achieve if attempted from the White House than if it is undertaken from one of the key departments, even if a given Secretary possesses a strong personality. Moreover, such coordination is manifestly easier to impose if it is openly associated with the shaping of policy as such, for the making of policy inevitably tends to become the coordination of policy. Bureaucracies do not respond to visions; they respond to clear-cut and enforceable directions—and these have to come from one source and from the top.

The centralization of national security policy in the White House can also facilitate a closer integration of foreign and domestic policy. The President's key domestic political advisers tend to be located in the White House. Secretaries of State frequently have difficulties with them. During my service in the White House, I initially tried to restrict their involvement in truly sensitive matters, but as the months went on, I discovered that it was actually helpful to forge an alliance with the President's domestic advisers. More attuned to domestic sentiment, they tended to be more "hard-nosed" than the foreign affairs experts pro-duced by academia or diplomacy, and certainly better able to judge what was both feasible and desirable from the standpoint of domestic political support. On more than one occasion I would note in my journal that on the key issues both Jody Powell and Ham Jordan were willing to urge the President to adopt a firmer line. Typical was the entry of November 8, 1979: "I huddled several times today with Ham and Jody. We all agreed that for political reasons as well as for substantive reasons the President should be tough on the Iranian issue. Ham is pressing to bring Kirbo up here because he thinks that Kirbo will stiffen the President's back and cancel the weak advice likely to be given by Vance or Cutler. In general, on all of these issues, I find the domestic people to be more tough-minded than some of my colleagues in the foreign affairs area."

In the event that foreign policy decision making is deliberately concentrated in the White House, the central role of the Assistant for National Security Affairs should be openly acknowledged and even institutionalized. Conflict is generated when lines of command or even of influence are not clear. It is minimized when authority is seen as "legitimate." Part of the problem that I faced, especially vis-à-vis the Washington establishment and the press, was that I was perceived as having usurped Vance's legitimate prerogatives. This could have been avoided if it had been openly acknowledged that the President actually approved and encouraged my occasional appearance as the spokesman for the Administration's foreign policy.

The same consideration should apply to the Assistant acting as a negotiator. I performed this role only on three occasions: I negotiated the swap of Soviet spies for leading Soviet dissidents; I prompted the secret negotiations on normalization of relations with China and managed the critical final stages; and I negotiated some sensitive relationships. In all three cases there were special circumstances warranting some departure from the norm that negotiations are the exclusive prerogative of the Secretary of State. In these three instances, the Assistant's proximity to the President, as well as my own inclination to force issues to a head when the moment seems timely, helped to resolve matters. In fact, I did not feel at the time that my role was resented. I kept the Secretary of State informed of what I was doing, and the Secretary in turn knew that I was acting with the President's blessing. In the future, there may be special occasions when it would be appropriate for a White House official to become involved in negotiations, though on the whole that area of activity should remain the primary responsibility of the Secretary of State as the chief diplomat, even if the White House is openly dominant in the shaping of policy.

To legitimate the Assistant's central role in coordination and thus also in shaping national security policy, consideration should again be given to making the nomination of the Assistant for National Security Affairs subject to senatorial confirmation. This would also warrant his occasional formal appearances before congressional committees. When I was in the White House, a bill to that effect was proposed, though its intention was actually to curb my influence. At the time, both the State Department and the President's legal advisers opposed this initiative. In both cases, the argument was made that it would involve an excessive limitation on the President's prerogative to appoint his key advisers and that it would interfere with the role of the Secretary of State as the President's primary spokesman on foreign affairs.

There is, however, a precedent for such an institutional development:

the Director of the Office of Management and Budget (OMB) is subject to congressional confirmation, and the incumbent does testify before the Congress. This enables him to play the needed coordinating role, and provides a useful precedent for the institutionalization and political legitimation of the office of the Assistant for National Security Affairs. If the President wishes to make the White House the center of decision making, the source of policy initiation, and an effective instrument for coordination of the extremely complex governmental machinery in the area of national security, then a step along these lines would greatly enhance clarity and the legitimacy of White House preponderance. The National Security Adviser might also be redesignated as the Director of National Security Affairs, to underline his central role.

The need for more formalized central direction is the consequence of America's increased global involvement. It is to be recalled that in the late 1940s the experience of World War II and the pressures of the Cold War led to the creation of the office of the Secretary of Defense. It was superimposed over existing service departments, despite considerable resistance from their Secretaries. No one would now think of reverting to the old system of Army and Navy departments. Today, foreign affairs, diplomacy, and global security need above all to be coordinated. They cannot be made subject to decisions by a single department. Rather, someone close to the President has to make certain that the President does not become a prisoner of departmental briefs.

Moreover, the close interconnection between domestic policy and foreign affairs makes it imperative that the President be actively involved in those foreign policy decisions which are domestically sensitive. This again dictates arrangements which enhance the central role of the White House in the shaping of national security policy. Thus under ideal circumstances the best system would be one in which an engaged President provides both strategic and tactical direction, with the definition of strategic priorities and the practical coordination on the President's behalf of the work of the key national security agencies originating from his Director of National Security Affairs.

However, in any system, tensions between competing individuals and bureaucracies are unavoidable. It is also almost inevitable that the press in a democratic society will thrive on reporting and exaggerating such competition. Thus it is simply impossible to design—and truly naïve to think that it can be done—a system in which there is no rivalry in the process of decision making and no public gossip about such rivalry. When the President has predominated in foreign affairs, the axis of conflict has tended to be between the National Security Assistant and the Secretary of State; when the Secretary of State was dominant, the conflict tended to be between himself and the Secretary of Defense. People preoccupied in recent years with the rivalries between Kissinger and Secretary Rogers or between me and Secretary Vance have tended to forget that in the years past there have been intense conflicts between Secretary of State Kissinger and Secretary of Defense Schlesinger as well as between their respective predecessors.

No matter which arrangement is chosen, whether the "Secretarial" or the "Presidential," in the years to come the President will need a more deliberate mechanism for national security planning. Currently there is no such organ in the U.S. government. Each department plans on its own, in the light of its own inevitably narrow departmental perspective. To a degree, especially in the first year, I tried to use the NSC as the President's "think tank," and I often referred to it as such. We produced the basic guidelines for Carter's foreign policy, and by and large the Administration stuck to them. In my view, whatever system of decision making a future President adopts, it will need an institution in which on an integrated basis longer-term national strategic and diplomatic plans can be formulated. It is important that such a body be an interagency organ, including international economics. It is also important that early in the life of a new Administration the President should be personally involved in a comprehensive review of our strategic-geopolitical priorities.

In the past, planning agencies have tended to be headed by "planners," divorced from policy making. My own experience leads me to the view that anyone responsible for longer-term planning relevant to Presidential decisions has to be a policy maker, closely involved in day-to-day affairs. Otherwise, "planning" becomes a remote and irrelevant exercise. Accordingly, depending on which system a President prefers, either the Assistant (Director) for National Security Affairs or the Secretary of State ought to develop a small interagency staff, drawn from senior officials of other departments, for the purpose of formulating and reevaluating longer-term national priorities in the area of national security. Obviously, one cannot be mechanical about such an exercise, and our global and highly turbulent reality does not permit the luxury of conducting a foreign policy based entirely on plans dreamed up by a small body of advisers. Nonetheless, without such a deliberate effort to set priorities, to define timing, to reexamine historical trends, it is likely that our foreign policy will be increasingly reactive, responding to challenges and crises rather than shaping the world around us.

To cope with the problem of survival in a turbulent world, American policy will have to be derived from an efficient organizational structure; it will also have to involve a sustained and even draining effort to shape a wider framework of global cooperation. Such a framework is needed to replace the Eurocentric world order that collapsed during two world wars and the Great Depression. Its place was taken briefly by a Pax Americana that endured only for about a decade and a half; it was followed by an uneasy period of almost a de facto condominium, which informally restrained global violence. That condition is in the process of collapsing—and in any case it could never endure because of conflicting philosophical and national aspirations. The vital question for the era ahead is whether the world will move haltingly toward some wider cooperative arrangements or whether it will plunge into destructive chaos.

To promote wider global progress, the United States must be actively engaged. Without the United States there is no force in the world capable of stimulating and sustaining a serious effort to enhance genuine international cooperation. And that means in turn shaping and applying a policy guided by a historically sound moral sense of direction and backed by credible and applicable American power. An internationally passive America will simply contribute to greater global anarchy. A morally indifferent America also runs the risk of becoming increasingly isolated. There is no escape from the need for an active, broadly gauged American foreign policy to cope with the problems inherent in the emergence of a decolonized and politically more awakened world. At the same time, precisely because American power has relatively declined, it is all the more necessary that America cooperate more closely with its key friends, despite politically appealing domestic pressures in favor of protectionism and unilateralism. It will take strong Presidential leadership to offset such pressures and to keep America committed to the concepts of collective security and international cooperation.

The first two years of the Reagan Administration have been troubling in this respect. The United States is perceived as turning inward. It is seen as increasingly indifferent to misery in the Third World and unconcerned about human rights. The President himself appeared to concentrate on domestic affairs, while his decision-making process seemed to fit neither the "Presidential system" (White House control) nor the "Secretarial system" (Secretary of State in charge). His domestic advisers were seen as checkmating the Secretary of State, while the other two major participants in the process, the Secretary of Defense and the National Security Adviser, had no major expertise in the area of national security. U.S. foreign policy became more and more reactive, with the result that the peace process in the Middle East significantly slowed down and American influence in the region visibly declined. The Third World increasingly saw America as indifferent or even hostile. On the strategic level, the MX deployment—so necessary to narrow the "window of vulnerability"—was greatly delayed, entirely for political reasons (so as not to offend the voters of Utah or Nevada), while movement toward a closer strategic relationship with China came to a near halt.

In the years ahead, without wider trilateral cooperation it will also become more difficult to temper and contain regional conflicts. Of these, the conflict in the Middle East is likely to pose the greatest threat to vital U.S. interests. Iranian–Arab conflicts over the Persian Gulf, the growing Soviet threat to the region as a whole, and the radicalizing as well as destabilizing consequences of the Israeli–Arab dispute will confront U.S. policy makers with highly complex and difficult dilemmas. The United States will have to be engaged actively in seeking Arab–Israeli reconciliation, for without assertive American involvement there will be no progress. Our policy on the Arab–Israeli dispute as well as on Persian Gulf security must also be fitted into a larger consensus, in which the common stake of the Western world prompts also a common policy more actively supported by our European and Japanese friends. In such a wider context, we are also likely to prompt a more positive response from the more moderate Arab countries, without diluting America's traditional commitments to Israel's security.

The President will have to be engaged personally in seeking peace in the Middle East. One of my strongest impressions from my four years in the White House is that on this issue there is no such thing as delegation of authority. Not only are there so many psychological and historical complexes to be overcome, but the problem is so domestically sensitive in the United States itself that the President has to be involved in reassuring the parties and in charting the needed initiatives. Without Carter's involvement in the Camp David process, there would have been no Israeli–Egyptian peace treaty. Without direct and genuinely sustained Presidential participation, there will be no resolution of the bitter dispute over the Arab West Bank and Gaza.

In seeking progress and eventually in achieving peace in the Middle East, Presidential leverage is likely to be the greatest during the first phase of the Presidency. By the third and fourth years any President becomes enmeshed in his own electoral efforts, and his foreign policy becomes increasingly hostage to domestic political concerns. This means that on the extraordinarily difficult and sensitive Middle East question, a President should move rapidly, so that he has time to demonstrate to his domestic constituencies that his efforts are bearing fruit. In seeking such peace, American goals may occasionally have to be in excess of what is actually feasible. One of the paradoxes of Carter's early efforts to achieve a comprehensive settlement in the Middle East was that these efforts gave both the Israelis and the Egyptians an incentive to reach the more limited accommodation which Carter's efforts later made possible.

The American role will also remain central in the shaping of the North–South relationship. In recent years, America has lagged behind the other advanced democracies in recognizing the moral and political imperative of promoting a more equitable world order. Yet what is happening today on the world scale is replicating recent American domestic experience in coping with our racial dilemmas. A previously excluded portion of mankind is entering into more active participation in the global political process, and it behooves America to promote a gradual redistribution of existing political and economic power to take that new reality into account. In doing so, one should be careful not to embrace such slogans as the new international economic order (NIEO), which implies that a fundamental change can be effected by fiat. The shaping of a wider cooperative framework will involve a protracted and incremental process, but it is important in that context that the United States not be viewed by the Third World as inherently indifferent or even hostile to its aspirations.

In the years ahead, the most ambitious and taxing goal of American foreign policy will be to prevent Soviet exploitation of global turbulence while at the same time encouraging evolutionary change within the Soviet orbit. The U.S.–Soviet relationship will thus continue to be a mix of competitive and cooperative elements, with the former predominating. The rivalry between the world's two greatest powers is not likely to fade during the remainder of this century; it is motivated by too many historical, philosophical, and even psychological impulses. But it can—and should—be maintained, controlled, and cooled. With careful management, it can also be guided toward increasing accommodation on such matters as arms control and regional restraint, while the expansion of cooperative links can very slowly encourage internal changes within the Soviet orbit itself. Such evolutionary changes, however, are more likely to occur first in Eastern Europe, and the West should persist in its efforts to create ever closer links between Eastern and Western Europe.

Educated opinion in Russian society traditionally has been conscious of the gap separating Russian civilization from the West. Pyotr Chaadaev, writing in 1829, observed: "We are one of those nations which do not appear to be an integral part of the human race, but exist only in order to teach some great lesson to the world. Surely the lesson we are destined to teach will not be wasted; but who knows when we shall rejoin the rest of mankind, and how much misery we must suffer before accomplishing our destiny?" Today that gap is, if anything, wider than it was in 1829, and it is in the world's interest that it should gradually be closed. Our long-term goal must be to encourage the Soviet Union to become eventually a constructive world power.

How to deal with the Soviets will thus continue to be the litmus test of U.S. statesmanship. The experience of the last thirty-five years, and certainly of the Carter years, teaches some pertinent lessons. The first is that the negotiating process with the Soviets should not be confined to the litigation of specific contractual relationships but should involve also a protracted dialogue, even a debate, on the proper rules of restraint and reciprocity that must guide the relationship. Only through such a sustained dialogue can, in time, shared perspectives emerge and moderate the conflictual aspects of the relationship. Secondly, there are moments when it is appropriate simply to hang tough, and not to yield too quickly when the Soviets reject U.S. positions or proposals. The fact is that there is no premium in the public's esteem for adopting initially a soft position and then gradually toughening it up. On the contrary, as the experience of the Reagan Administration shows, there is some real advantage to sustaining first a reputation as a hard-line ogre and then softening one's position. The opponents, as well as interested opinion here and abroad, tend to respond gratefully to such belated concessions.

Third, and above all, it will be essential for the American public to appreciate the long-term and historical character of the Soviet challenge to America. Ultimately it involves different conceptions of the human being's relationship to society and to government, and a different notion of history. The Soviets in their concept of the rivalry have a long-term view and they are pursuing their policies with genuine persistence and patience. The American public must learn to support a sustained defense effort and a long-term policy of assertive competition, without its periodic swings from hysteria about the Cold War to euphoria about detente.

In seeking to structure a stable relationship with the Soviet Union, the U.S.–Chinese relationship will remain very important. It would be wrong to make it merely conditional on the state of the U.S.–Soviet relationship, for good relations with China have a long-term historical and strategic value in and of themselves. Nonetheless, as long as the American–Soviet relationship remains essentially antagonistic, closer American–Chinese strategic cooperation can offset some of the existing disparities in conventional power, compelling the Soviet Union to divert a significant portion of its military effort to the Sino-Soviet frontier. There is little doubt that U.S.–Chinese normalization has contributed to greater stability in the Far East, making in turn more possible Japan's increased but more relaxed involvement in security problems. Given the likelihood of major internal changes in China, in the years ahead the United States will have to be especially sensitive to Chinese concerns and not needlessly aggravate Chinese suspicions by appearing to favor a de facto two-China policy.

The foregoing is not meant to outline a U.S. foreign policy for the eighties but to refine the proposition that America will have to be engaged in global affairs in a sustained fashion, responsive to the complexity of the global condition, and pursuing long-term objectives with patience and a sense of historical direction. But that raises the fundamental question: Is American democracy capable of conducting a protracted and subtle policy in a turbulent and complex world?

Several perplexing conditions justify concern about America's capacity to sustain such a long-haul effort to compete with the Soviet Union while simultaneously seeking to shape a wider cooperative system. They can be summarized under five broad headings: historical *tabula rasa;* escape from complexity; political discontinuity; collapse of bipartisanship; and congressional usurpation.

The American approach to the world is profoundly unhistorical. The almost automatic inclination of the media, the analysts, and even the decision makers is to focus on every foreign event as a disparate happening—"newsworthy" to some (and the word is symptomatically derived from "new"), troubling to others, but most often perceived as a novel development. The absence of historical perspective afflicts analysis as well as daily reporting. There is relatively little effort to identify trends, to catch the essence of historical phases. As a result, while the U.S. public probably has more information potentially available to it, it in fact inadequately understands much of what is happening in the world, and our political leaders generally reflect that condition as well.

The mass media are rarely interested in deeper analysis. Typical was the press reaction in May 1980 to a major foreign policy speech by President Carter. It was meant to be a conceptual speech, summarizing the underlying principles of U.S. foreign policy in the wake of the Persian Gulf crisis and the Soviet invasion of Afghanistan. The European press understood its significance and gave it considerable publicity in both news and editorial reporting. But the American press concentrated almost entirely on some casual remarks that Carter made two hours later, comparing Vance with Muskie. Our newsmen were simply not interested in a broader analysis. They found it much more rewarding to focus on ad hominem gossip.

The preoccupation with personalities and personal infighting is the logical extension of a lack of interest in history. Personalities are more interesting and their coverage intellectually less demanding than the clash of ideas. Hence so much focus on personal and bureaucratic struggles but so little serious attention to historical and philosophical assumptions on the part of the Washington press corps.

This condition is intimately related to the difficulty that a mass democracy confronts in trying to cope with the reality of global complexity. Early in the Carter term I gave a speech in which I said the following: "If there is a single common theme to our efforts, it is this: after World War II our foreign policy, by necessity, was focused primarily on issues connected with the Cold War. This gave it a sharp focus, in some cases making it easier to mobilize public opinion. A concentrated foreign policy could be supported by public emotion. Today we confront a more difficult task, one that calls for support based on reason. We must respond to a wider range of issues—some of which still involve the Cold War—issues stemming from a complex process of global change. A concentrated foreign policy must give way to a complex foreign policy, no longer focused on a single, dramatic task—such as the defense of the West. Instead, we must engage ourselves on the distant and difficult goal of giving shape to a world that has suddenly become politically awakened and socially restless."

For the mass public, it is easier to understand problems if they are reduced to black/white dichotomies. It is easier to understand policies if they are attached to individuals who are simplistically labeled as hawks or doves. Yet in today's world any attempt to reduce its complexities to a single set of ideological propositions, to a single personality, or to a single issue is in itself a distortion. Such a distortion also raises the danger that public emotions could become so strong as to make the management of a genuinely complex foreign policy well-nigh impossible.

These cultural impediments to an informed involvement in global affairs are compounded by political handicaps. Foremost among them is the discontinuity of recent American politics, with six different Presidents shaping American policy over the last twenty years. Each President has striven to fashion his own foreign policy, identified with himself. It has even become unfashionable to speak of American foreign policy; one speaks instead of Nixon's foreign policy or Carter's foreign policy or Reagan's foreign policy. Moreover, the frequency in the change of Presidents has been accompanied by equally frequent changes of top foreign-policy-making personnel, with hardly benign consequences for the acquisition of experience and for the establishment of enduring foreign contacts. In addition, American foreign policy has tended to become hostage to domestic politics usually after the second Presidential year in the excessively short four-year Presidential cycles, and this has further distorted the shaping of a sustained American foreign policy which could be understood by our friends and respected by our enemies.

Every Administration goes through a period of an ecstatic emancipation from the past, then a discovery of continuity, and finally a growing preoccupation with Presidential reelection. As a result, the learning curve in the area of foreign policy tends to be highly compressed. Each Administration tends to expend an enormous amount of energy coping with the unintended, untoward consequences of its initial, sometimes excessive, impulses to innovate, to redeem promises, and to harbor illusions. In time, preconceptions give way to reality, disjointedness to intellectual coherence, and vision to pragmatism. But by the time this happens, the Presidential cycle is usually coming to an end. That the four-year election process has a pernicious influence on foreign policy is evident, but it is also clear that this structural handicap is not likely to be undone.

The four-year Presidential cycle makes the need for bipartisanship even greater. Bipartisanship could compensate for Presidential discontinuity, but in fact bipartisanship faded coincidentally with the beginning of the period of frequent changes of Presidents. The United

States has not had a genuinely bipartisan foreign policy in almost twenty years. I tried to encourage such bipartisanship under Carter by seeking on several occasions to bring Carter together with Senator Howard Baker, for whom I gained enormous respect. Yet unfortunately the chemistry between the two men was so incompatible that even discussions of subjects on which they were of like mind tended to become unproductive and occasionally even acrimonious. President Reagan had a real opportunity, given his initially widespread appeal, to fashion a bipartisan foreign policy with centrist Democrats, but his inclination toward doctrinaire rhetoric prevented him from taking advantage of it.

Inherent in the disintegration of bipartisanship is the disappearance of the nonpartisan foreign policy elite that reinforced and helped to shape the policies of America in its first phase of post-World War II global engagement. That elite faded roughly at the same time as the collapse of bipartisanship, and it has been replaced either by partisan dogmatists within the extreme wings of the two parties or by a new generation of foreign policy technicians who are adept at shifting from one orientation to another, without any deeper philosophical commitment.

In the past, the springboard for involvement in foreign affairs tended to be the Foreign Service itself, the legal profession, or more recently academia. In all cases, the individuals involved engaged themselves from a position of relative independence of judgment and professional security. They tended to stand for something. The more recent pattern has been for a floating attachment usually to some semi-academic research organization during the out-of-power years, while prudently waiting until a new candidate surfaces. Carter suffered from that particularly, since a whole layer of his second-echelon appointees was hardly committed to him personally and did not share his basic philosophical predispositions. Moreover, some of them felt free to disclose to the press the internal workings of the decision-making process whenever it served their own interests, grinding personal or ideological axes. Such leakage further fragmented policy cohesion.

The prospects for bipartisanship have also been reduced by the breakdown of the seniority system in Congress. Whatever the benefits of this change for Congress itself, the leadership on both sides of the aisle can no longer deliver their respective parties. Congressional power has become more dispersed, making Executive-Legislative cooperation more difficult to sustain. At the same time, with the proliferation of staff support, individual senators and congressmen have acquired their own in-house foreign and defense policy experts and the yen for making foreign policy (or, at least, headlines).

The main impulse for the enhanced intrusion of Congress into the actual making of foreign policy was, of course, the Vietnam War and the crisis of confidence in Executive leadership that it generated. The more frequent changes of Presidents and the increasing injection of partisanship into foreign policy also stimulated this trend, with eventually a Democratic Congress legislating a series of limits on the conduct of foreign policy by a President who happened to have been a controversial Republican. Though limitations on Presidential power to wage war are not unjustified in the nuclear age, Congress has mandated a series of obligations in the form of certifications, reports on the behavior of other states, restrictions on the sales of military equipment, checks on intelligence activities that gradually evolved into attempts to co-determine sensitive or covert operations, cumulatively producing a situation in which discretion, flexibility, and rapidity of response have come to be thoroughly lacking in the conduct of U.S. policy. The result has been an unprecedented degree of congressional involvement in the conduct of foreign policy, intensifying some of the difficulties that a mass democracy faces in seeking to conduct a subtle and complex policy.

It will take time to remedy the factors that so complicate the shaping of a historically relevant American policy toward the world. Of the ones mentioned, the cultural ones are clearly the most deep-rooted. Only through sustained public education, in which the mass media will have to play a central role, will America acquire the capacity to shape and sustain a policy that does justice to the complexities of our age. In my years in the White House, I cooperated closely with several younger journalists who showed, in my judgment, the relatively rare inclination to combine an interest in facts with intellectual curiosity to discern their historical meaning. I would hope that newspapers and television in the years ahead will more deliberately encourage such analytical reporting, with more emphasis on the centrality of historical experience to our day-to-day affairs.

But the main opportunity for remedy lies in the area of bipartisanship. I believe that the first President who succeeds in elevating foreign policy again above partisanship will greatly enhance his chances for overcoming the recent trend toward a one-term Presidency. A President with vision and political skill could accomplish a great deal, and relatively quickly, to revive a broad coalition on behalf of nationally shared goals. To be sure, this is easier said than done. But in recent years no President has really exerted himself and been ready to make the necessary compromises to persuade leading figures of the other party (especially from Congress) to participate in the process of actually shaping policy. As a practical matter, such a policy would have to be an essentially centrist one, along the lines of Carter's during the last two years of his Administration, committed to the maintenance of American power, to the projection of American idealism, and to the shaping of wider cooperative relationships with the many new participants in the global political process. Such a policy would embrace moderate Democrats and liberal Republicans; it would not fully satisfy either the liberal Democrats or the conservative Republicans. Such a bipartisan foreign policy would create the preconditions for greater continuity in American international conduct and thus regain for America the needed reputation for constancy.

A genuinely bipartisan foreign policy would mitigate some of the negative consequences of excessive congressional intrusion without necessarily requiring either the formal retrenchment of congressional control or the explicit restoration of Executive prerogatives. The very fact of bipartisanship would create an easier Executive-Legislative relationship, making foreign policy more immune to opportunistic extremism and elevating national security policy almost to a national consensus.

To make relevant American principle to a world in which the craving for political freedom (the central challenge in East–West relations) is reinforced by the yearning for social dignity (the key problem in North–South issues), it will also be necessary for Americans to accommodate themselves both to a more crowded and eventually to a somewhat more egalitarian world. This will be especially difficult for a people whose own accomplishments were derived from an age in which relatively splendid isolation was combined with almost unlimited space and resources. But in a world soon to be populated by more than six billion politically activated people, respect for some general rules of conduct and some minimum standards of livelihood will be the essential preconditions of global order, indeed, the only alternative to global disaster.

The effort to shape a foreign policy based on a fusion of American principle with American power will be intellectually and politically taxing. The prevailing tendency has been for American democracy to swing from excessive moralism to morally insensitive realism. In one phase, Realpolitik is extolled as the highest virtue; in another, the enhancement and application of American power is denigrated as immoral and unwarranted. The effort to blend the two in a pragmatic fashion is condemned either as inadequately responsive to the imperatives of power or as inconsistent with its moralistic underpinnings. Yet rigid moral consistency is not possible in a complicated world, nor is a single-minded focus on power justified in a world in which morally legitimate aspirations are the source of much political and social unrest.

Just as it is impossible intellectually to encapsulate the reality of a complex world, so it is impossible to reduce foreign policy to a neat formula in which power and principle will be precisely blended. Yet a combination of the two is clearly necessary to translate into historically meaningful terms America's mission in our contemporary age.

ANNEX I

President Carter's Instructions to
Zbigniew Brzezinski for His Mission
to China, May 17, 1978

May 17, 1978

To Zbigniew Brzezinski

My purpose in sending you to China is two-fold:

1. To continue the consultations called for by the Shanghai Communique;

2. To reassure the Chinese that my Administration is serious in seeking normalization.

With reference to the first, and central, purpose of your trip, you should stress that we see our relations with China as a central facet of the U.S. global policy. The United States and China share certain common interests and we have parallel, long-term strategic concerns. The most important of these is our common opposition to global or regional hegemony by any single power. This is why your visit is not tactical; it is an expression of our strategic interest in a cooperative relationship with China, an interest that is both fundamental and enduring. You should emphasize this point at the very outset of your visit.

Your basic goal should be to convey to the Chinese our determination to seek peace with the Soviets, to compete effectively with the Soviets, to deter the Soviet military challenge, and to protect our interests and those of our friends and allies. Equally important, you should probe the Chinese for their views, seeking to establish a shared perspective and, where desirable, develop political collaboration. You should emphasize reciprocity and stress that the pursuit of our shared objectives requires mutual efforts.

To accomplish this goal, you can begin by giving the Chinese my assessment of the Soviet challenge. You should stress that I see the Soviet Union as essentially in a competitive relationship with the United States, though there are also some cooperative aspects. That competitive relationship is enduring, deep-seated, and rooted in different traditions, history, outlooks, interests, and geopolitical priorities. Hence the competition will not be terminated quickly -- and the United States is prepared to compete for as long as necessary. At the same time, the reality of nuclear weapons dictates not only the need for restraint but also for greater cooperation, especially in arms control. SALT is not a product of weakness but the consequence of prudence.

With the above as your point of departure, you should then share with the Chinese my view of the nature of the Soviet threat. To state it most succinctly, my concern is that the combination of increasing Soviet military power and political shortsightedness, fed by big-power ambitions, might tempt the Soviet Union both to exploit local turbulence (especially in the Third World) and to intimidate our friends in order to seek political advantage and eventually even political preponderance.

This is why I do take seriously Soviet action in Africa and this is why I am concerned about the Soviet military buildup in Central Europe. I also see some Soviet designs pointing towards the Indian Ocean through South Asia, and perhaps to the encirclement of China through Vietnam (and even perhaps someday through Taiwan).

The United States, however, is determined to respond. My overall foreign policy seeks the following goals:

Wider cooperation with our key allies, and also with the new regional influentials;

Comprehensive and genuinely reciprocal detente with the Soviet Union, and also a closer relationship with Eastern Europe;

Sufficient military capability to support our
global security interests, particularly through
an adequate strategic deterrent, through the
preservation of the conventional balance in
Europe, and through the development of a
quick reaction global force for rapid deployment in areas of central importance to the
United States;

The involvement of the United States in all
major regions, through closer cooperation with
Japan and China in East Asia, through collaboration with the moderate states in Africa,
through more mature and bilateral ties with
Latin American countries, and through our efforts to obtain a settlement in the Middle East;

Development of constructive and cooperative
solutions to emerging global issues, the promotion of more open international trade, and
the prevention of the drift toward nuclear
proliferation;

Mobilization of stronger domestic support
for our foreign policy, relating that policy
to values and beliefs deeply held by the
American people.

Taken together, these goals are designed to shape
an international system not subject to hegemony
by a single power.

You should then speak more specifically of our
efforts to strengthen NATO, to find a peaceful
solution to the problems of South Africa, to resolve the Middle Eastern conflict, to strengthen
U.S. ties with the moderate African countries,
to reinforce our friendship with the countries
of the Western Hemisphere, and to create a stable
Southeast Asia and Far East -- all of which shall
reduce openings for Soviet intrusion. In so
doing, you should not gloss over our difficulties
but speak of them candidly, so that the Chinese
will have the sense that we approach these matters
realistically, responsibly, and with confidence.

Moreover, you should share with the Chinese our analysis of internal Soviet weaknesses (both economic and political) and of their external difficulties (notably their waning ideological appeal, and the continued hostility of East Europe). In so doing, do not betray confidences nor take an anti-Soviet posture.

You might indicate in this overall context that the United States does not object to the more forthcoming attitude which our allies are adopting in regard to trade with China in technology-sensitive areas. We have an interest in a strong and secure China -- and we recognize and respect this interest.

Finally, in the consultative part of your discussions, you should brief the Chinese on the strategic balance, the conventional balance (both East-West and in the Far East), and also on the status of SALT negotiations. You should indicate to the Chinese in some detail how SALT II will not reduce but in fact enhance our ability to maintain our security and the security of our friends and allies.

Just as the Chinese are not reticent about reminding us of our responsibilities, you should indicate where we think they have positive contributions to make: to provide aid to Somalia, to encourage a peaceful evolution in Southern Africa, to initiate contacts with Israel, to improve relations with India, to facilitate the emergence of an independent Cambodian government that enjoys the support of its people, and to promote stability in the Korean peninsula.

With reference to the second purpose of your trip -- the reassurance on normalization -- you should convey to the Chinese our determination to move forward with the process of normalization. In this connection, you should reiterate U.S. acceptance of the three Chinese key points and reiterate the U.S. five points. You should state that the United States has made up its mind on these issues. You should also add that Ambassador Woodcock is instructed to pursue normalization more actively and that he will be prepared to participate in appropriate negotiations as of this June.

At the same time, in your discussions you should make clear to the Chinese that at the time of normalization the United States will make a unilateral statement calling for a peaceful settlement of the Taiwan question by the Chinese themselves and that there will have to be an understanding with the Chinese that such a statement would not be contradicted; and that the United States will continue to provide Taiwan with access to military equipment for defensive purposes.

Moreover, if an informal opportunity allows it, you may explore with the Chinese the possibility of developing "an American formula" for a continuing non-diplomatic relationship with Taiwan. In this connection, you should remind the Chinese of the importance to both the United States and China of the United States being known to be trustworthy. The peace of the Far East, indeed of the world, depends on continued U.S. military presence in the Pacific area, and a crisis of confidence in U.S. credibility could be destabilizing. It would certainly be exploited by our common adversaries. This consideration must be borne in mind when resolving the issue of normalization and our future relationship with the people of Taiwan.

In addition, you might indicate informally to the Chinese that the United States is planning to further reduce its military presence in Taiwan this year, to widen the opportunities for the commercial flow of technology to China, to increase direct contacts on a regular and perhaps scheduled basis for our mutual advantage, and to invite Chinese trade and military delegations to visit the United States. These planned steps reflect our seriousness in moving forward with the process of normalization.

Jimmy Carter

The Honorable Zbigniew Brzezinski
Assistant to the President for
    National Security Affairs
The White House
Washington, D.C.

ANNEX II

Reflections for the
President

A month after the inaugural, I initiated the practice of submitting to the President a weekly report on NSC activities and on related developments. Unlike the weekly reports that the President requested from other Cabinet members, this one contained not only information which I thought ought to be brought to the President's attention but often also a personal "opinion" piece of approximately a page or so. In it I shared with the President my thoughts on matters of major importance either to him as President or to U.S. national security. In these memoranda I drew the President's attention to world trends and developments which might not have reached him through the daily paper flow and also expressed my own views on broader issues. The President occasionally commented on my opinion pieces or issued instructions by writing directly on the report and sending it back to my office. A few of his notations are indicated below, when appropriate. I should note that the President was the only recipient of these weekly reports. What follows are abstracts of selected opinion pieces.

Weekly Reports

#1. *February 19, 1977: U.S.–U.S.S.R. Relations and the Human Rights Debate.* The media is not picking up your efforts to start serious discussions with Leonid Brezhnev and is focusing instead on whether we should be commenting on human rights in the U.S.S.R. I am concerned that the press may characterize your posture on human rights as an anti-Soviet tactic. It is important to correct this impression in the media.

#3. *March 5, 1977: Foreign Policy Design.* You should seek to present a vision of what we are trying to accomplish in the foreign policy area and articulate a coherent approach to the problems the U.S. confronts. The public must be made aware of the complexity of these problems, in particular relations with our allies. There is a strong possibility of short-term setbacks in relations with France and Germany on the nuclear nonproliferation issue and with the U.K. and France on the Concorde. We are also likely to encounter a rocky road on the SALT negotiations. You need to make a comprehensive statement of your policies. [The President wrote: "Plan for 3/17 at UN."]

#4. *March 11, 1977: SALT and the Summit.* (1) SALT: We have essentially four options for the SALT proposal: (i) deferral; (ii) modest cut in aggregate levels; (iii) Vladivostok levels; (iv) deep cuts. I favor option (ii).

(2) Summit: The Western allies are in a difficult position because of the protracted period of political stagnation and economic decline. The London Summit must have a positive outcome, but we should build only modest expectations. We should not try to do too much. [The President wrote: "I agree."]

#5. *March 18, 1977: Japan and Reprocessing.* I want to alert you to the extreme sensitivity of the Japanese over the impact of our nonproliferation initiatives. Our new policy has seriously complicated Japan's nuclear power planning and objectives.

#6. *March 25, 1977: India's Political Future.* A cautioning note on the prospects for the new Janata government of Morarji Desai. India may be more receptive to Western views, but will not quickly align itself with U.S. interests.

#7. *April 1, 1977: Assessment after Two Months in Office.* After two months in office your Administration has made an affirmative commitment to certain basic human values. Human rights, broadly defined, has great appeal. We are coordinating policy more closely with our Western allies, seeking to develop North–South relations, working to reach accommodation on East–West relations to avoid war and attain wider "trans-ideological" cooperation, and attempting to halt the spread of arms, conventional and nuclear. The results are mixed so far, but trends are positive. In specific areas: (1) U.S.S.R.–Eastern Europe is ideologically on the defensive. Moscow is concerned that the human-rights idea has been taken over by the U.S.; (2) SALT—we have proceeded with a package of reduction proposals; (3) Middle East—your basic statement provides a flexible framework for dealing with hitherto intractable issues; (4) China—we have time to develop our policy this spring; (5) Latin America—bilateral relations are generally looking up; (6) Africa—we should press the Soviets to desist, but do so outside of Africa through diplomatic leverage, trade denial, etc., but not through direct involvement on the continent; (7) Defense issues—we are undertaking a comprehensive reassessment of current force structure and strategic concepts.

#8. *April 9, 1977: The "Architectural" Notion of Carter Foreign Policy.* The United States should provide leadership to the European alliance with a first step being an improvement in personal relations between the President and Schmidt and Giscard. In addition the Administration should concentrate on improving relations with the new emerging powers.

#9. *April 16, 1977: Human Rights—For a Broader Interpretation.* Some in the Congress are using human rights as an excuse to block aid or attach restrictions. This is being viewed abroad as excessively rigid and moralistic. I believe the human-rights idea is morally justified and historically relevant. It must be a broad concept, however, encompassing social and economic existence as well as political liberty. This is why the words have such universal appeal. There is no single definition and we must be more flexible.

#11. *April 29, 1977: Peace in the Middle East.* You should adopt a more assertive and positive public position concerning a return to the Geneva Conference. [The President wrote: "I agree—let's get together with Pat and Jody to plan how to do this."]

#15. *June 3, 1977: Stocktaking.* The Administration has defined its broad purposes. Your objectives are clear, but tactics and strategy are running out of steam. With the Soviets we are moving on a broad front —Comprehensive Test Ban (CTB), Indian Ocean, chemical warfare and trade—but what about Soviet and Cuban behavior in Africa? While our focus is on SALT, Moscow is becoming increasingly assertive. On SALT we need to come up with an intermediate proposal and approach Brezhnev for a visit to the United States. On the Middle East the Vice President's statement was very good, but we need to garner support for our position and perhaps invite Begin to Washington. In Africa, the British seem to be running our foreign policy for us. The Cubans and Soviets may be consolidating their position in Ethiopia. On North–South issues we seem to be slow in moving.

#16. *June 10, 1977: Domestic Aspects of the Middle East Issue.* We should give those Jewish Americans who believe that Israel must take risks for peace more encouragement. We should carry our case to the American people, but be careful not to overreact or to be overly optimistic and thereby contribute to a crisis atmosphere.

#20. *July 8, 1977: A Time of Testing.* You face a time of testing in three critical areas—relations with the Soviets, with the Europeans, and with the Israelis. On relations with the Soviets, we try to conduct business as usual—CTB, Indian Ocean demilitarization, etc.—and all Moscow does is complain. The Soviets tie everything to our accepting *their* SALT position. The Europeans are always nervous. When U.S.–

U.S.S.R. relations are good they fear a condominium, when they are bad then the Europeans feel threatened. The Soviets are seeking to drive a wedge between the U.S. and Europe. In the Middle East, there is strong Israeli and domestic American opposition to our objectives. Here the issue is steadfastness.

#24. *August 19, 1977: U.S.–Soviet Relations.* Brezhnev's recent statement indicates that the U.S. policy of quiet firmness is beginning to pay dividends. The Soviets want to avoid heightened tensions and want to talk about extending the Interim SALT Agreement. It is time for serious discussion with them of bottom-line concerns about strategic postures. Cy Vance will need some flexibility in Vienna. U.S.–Soviet relations once dominated everything in foreign policy. If there was no progress in that area then everything else was in bad condition. This centrality is no longer the case.

#26. *September 2, 1977: Middle East Policy.* I am concerned about our policy becoming unstuck. We need to regain momentum by (1) your sending a letter to Assad for help in dealing with the PLO; (2) State Department making a statement on the Palestinian right to participate in peace talks; (3) reaching an agreement with the Soviets to reconvene the Geneva talks to set a deadline; (4) developing a trusteeship concept for the West Bank. [The President wrote "OK" after each item.]

#30. *September 30, 1977: Prospects for Geneva.* To get to Geneva, both sides will have to make concessions about the type of PLO participation and the framework for discussions of the Palestinian issue. The Soviets will have to go along with our proposals, thus putting some pressure on Syria and the PLO. The Arabs will have to accept the fact of no separate PLO delegation and the Israelis will have to stop insisting that the PLO be a part of the Jordanian delegation.

#33. *October 21, 1977: U.S.–Soviet Relations.* It is of utmost importance that you develop and convey to congressional leaders a coherent strategy for managing U.S.–Soviet relations on arms control negotiations, CSCE (Conference on Security and Cooperation in Europe), human rights, and the Middle East. Your foreign policy will be judged on how the Soviet connection is managed. You should not back down on human rights. [The President wrote: "Brezhnev attacks on Goldberg are helping us."] Soviet behavior on the Middle East could affect SALT and its public perceptions. [The President wrote: "Agree."]

#36. *November 11, 1977: SALT Issues.* I am concerned about the inadequate response to continued public attacks on our SALT position. [The President suggested that ZB go over suggestions with Ham Jordan and start with a Senate and then a public outreach program.] I propose that Cy, Harold, and I meet with Scoop Jackson and his staff and that Jackson provide a paper on our SALT approach. [The President noted that this "may be a good idea."]

#37. *November 18, 1977: Foreign Policy Strategy.* Public perception of your foreign policy is that it is "soft" because of Cuba, Vietnam, Korea, SALT, B-1. You should consider taking some "tough" decisions, i.e., European security and the neutron bomb, reasserting human rights. Combinations of realism and idealism will generate support for complex matters such as Panama, SALT, Middle East, etc. [The President commented on my point that Republicans and others will focus on Panama and SALT as "soft" with "Don't chicken out." On the point that public pressure on Cuba in regard to its activities in Africa came none too soon, he noted: "It took me 6 months to get it done."]

#39. *December 9, 1977: U.S. Position in Asia.* I am concerned that our position in Asia may be unraveling on the eve of Ambassador Ushiba's visit. We should press for (1) a turnaround in Japan's current accounts position; (2) the preservation of the integrity of the Korea troop withdrawal; (3) forward movement on China policy; (4) adoption of defense decisions which do not undercut the rhetoric of the U.S. remaining an Asian power. I have received an invitation through the Chinese here to visit Peking early next year.

#40. *December 16, 1977: Begin's Proposals on the West Bank.* I sense a real opportunity in Begin's proposals and recommend that you might exploit Begin's sense of historical drama and get him to accept additional points by suggesting special meetings with Sadat and Hussein and you to sign a general declaration of intent to conclude a peace treaty.

#46. *February 9, 1978: Strategic Deterioration.* There are three serious dangers which cumulatively might affect the United States' overall position. I urge you to become involved in their discussion. (1) The political instability in Western Europe. (2) The consequences of major Soviet–Cuban success in Ethiopia. [The President commented that Iran, Saudi Arabia, and Egypt should stand firm on the issue of Ethiopia crossing the Somali border.] (3) Failure to exploit the U.S. position in the U.S.–Soviet–P.R.C. triangle. [President commented: "Later, post-Panama," agreed that part of the slowdown was due to Chinese rigidity, and disagreed with my assessment that it is also due to our excessive sensitivity to the Soviets.] I suggest that you instruct me to go to Peking to consult with the Chinese.

#47. *February 17, 1978: Soviet Behavior.* With major decisions ahead on SALT, the Horn, the P.R.C., I conclude that the Soviets are seeking a selective detente. U.S. actions should seek to maintain the emerging cooperative relationship in certain "benign" areas, while increasing the costs of Soviet behavior in the "malignant" group.

#48. *February 24, 1978: The Psychology of Presidential Power.* A President must not only be loved and respected, but also feared. I suggest that you try to dispel the impression that you and the Administration are too cerebral by picking some controversial subject and acting with anger and roughness to demonstrate that no one can pick a fight with the U.S. If we do not do this soon, Begin, Brezhnev, Vorster, Schmidt, Castro, and Qaddafi will thumb their noses at us.

#53. *April 7, 1978: Foreign Policy Objectives: U.S.–Soviet Relations.* We need to orchestrate our efforts more effectively to achieve increasingly comprehensive and reciprocal detente. The United States must make clear to the Soviets that their activities in Africa are unacceptable. Cy should be instructed not to allow his upcoming session in Moscow to be merely a bargaining exercise. Increases in defense spending should be pushed on the Hill. [President indicated general agreement.]

#54. *April 14, 1978: SALT Uncertainties; Begin.* (1) I am concerned that attacks on SALT will intensify between the treaty signature and delayed ratification. The process could be helped along if you take some decisions conveying toughness: MX, trade cutoffs to Soviets on petroleum technology, trade-off proposal on the neutron weapon, or open access to the P.R.C. on technology. (2) Begin: Since his return from Washington, it seems that he intends to ignore us as much as possible. He has determined that he cannot gain our endorsement for his approach, but does not want a public break. He seems to listen politely and then do precisely what he wants. His strategy appears to be designed to secure his domestic base by running against "U.S. pressure."

#56. *April 28, 1978: SALT and Congressional Negotiations.* If we are to make substantive changes on SALT to accommodate the congressional concerns, it must be done before the signing. If we pursue a stronger defense program, that would help alleviate many of the senators' concerns. I suggest that you consult closely with Senator Nunn. [The President agreed and commented that negotiations with Scoop Jackson are seen as a sign of weakness.]

#57. *May 5, 1978: Geopolitical Overview.* I am not concerned that Moscow will be able to impose a Pax Sovietica, but that the Soviet efforts will make it increasingly difficult for the U.S. to give order and stability to global change. Western confidence must be restored, and the NATO summit offers a good opportunity. A possible meeting with Brezhnev should be exploited to express much more firmly our will to respond to challenge.

#64. *June 23, 1978: Overview of Central Issues of the Next Six Months.* We will confront two kinds of issues during the next six months, those over which we have some control and those over which our control is only marginal. Some control: (a) The Economic Summit will provide an opportunity to reaffirm U.S. leadership in regard to the global economy, Western security, and East–West relations. We should present an image of confidence and determination. (b) U.S.–Soviet relations—a successful conclusion on the prisoner exchange issue will remove a significant irritant to relations and help us move more rapidly on SALT by late summer–early fall. The major decisions on the FY 1980 budget will reassure Congress that we are determined to maintain strategic equivalence. (c) China normalization—we must have a consistent line on Soviet adventurism, so the Chinese do not think that we are letting the Soviets dictate the terms of detente. Marginal control: (a) In the Middle East, we should seek to draw Jordan into the peace process, but if that fails we should consider a temporary disengagement. (b) On southern Africa, we should prepare contingency plans in the event that a peaceful solution is not possible and get ready for greater Soviet and Cuban involvement. (c) With the Non-Aligned Movement, we should encourage growing criticism of Cuba and focus attention on the Cuban presence in Africa.

#66. *July 7, 1978: Foreign Policy Choices.* You are now confronting four key areas where major decisions are impending. In China, the development of a relationship between our two countries will bring a major change in the international balance. I think that moving ahead on relations with Vietnam would only be an irritant to expanding our understanding with China. In the Middle East, a special negotiator may be necessary to provide continuity. With the Soviets, we should expand the scope of negotiations and work toward coming up with "rules of detente," particularly with regard to Africa. In Africa, we should consider quietly disengaging from the Rhodesian negotiations if the British do not succeed with Nkomo.

#70. *August 11, 1978: U.S.–Soviet Relations.* In connection with the letter to Brezhnev, it is important to remember that periods of friction in U.S.–Soviet relations have usually led—whenever the West was steadfast—to new "rules of the game" codifying and restraining overall behavior. We are now in such a process for the Third World.

#72. *September 22, 1978: SALT cum grano salis.* Although SALT is useful, it is not likely to alter profoundly the nature of U.S.–Soviet relations. [The President noted: "I'm not sure about this—provided a summit meeting is held to conclude SALT II."]

#73. *September 29, 1978: Gromyko Meeting.* It is important to use this meeting to give the Soviets a broader message—detente should be genuinely comprehensive and reciprocal. The United States is determined to seek SALT, but the overall relationship is not immune to events in key parts of the world, i.e. Africa, attacks on Camp David. I am also concerned about Soviet development of what might be a nuclear-war fighting capability.

#75. *October 13, 1978: Our Asian Policy—Or the Making of a Carter Doctrine.* We are faced with an opportunity to create a genuinely stable relationship with Asia similar to that with Europe. To do so we must be deliberate about: (1) Timing of the P.R.C. normalization. I recommend that you authorize me to mention the December–January window to the P.R.C. Ambassador. [The President commented: "Don't be too specific, but ok."] (2) Timing Vietnamese normalization. Vietnam should come after China normalization. [The President commented: "OK if PRC doesn't delay" and "Zbig—you have a tendency to exalt PRC issue."] (3) P.R.C. trade issue. (4) P.R.C. factor taken into account in SALT and military posture planning. If we can achieve a new stability, it will be easier to generate a more stable U.S.–Soviet relationship and SALT III.

#77. *October 27, 1978: Human Rights.* The Pope's election can be viewed as part of a new era of human rights. The worldwide demand for human rights is a growing political force, and you should reaffirm the U.S. commitment. [The President agreed.]

#78. *November 3, 1978: The Dollar and the Administration.* Recent problems in international economic policy indicate clearly that the government is not well organized to integrate international economic and political issues. We need more centralization within the White House. I have asked Henry Owen to set up an informal mechanism.

#79. *November 9, 1978: SALT and Middle East.* I am increasingly concerned about drift in these two areas and suggest: (1) Message to the Soviets that we cannot back down more and we must sign a treaty in the December–January window; we should also begin talks with Byrd about an agreement vs. treaty or abiding by the provisions if the Soviets do until it is a good time to bring it to the Hill. (2) We should either quietly phase out our central role after the signing of the Israeli–Egypt treaty or bring the West Bank issue to a head in 1979.

#84. *January 12, 1979: Iran—the Conventional Wisdom.* I disagree with the views of some Iran experts that the Shah is the entire problem and when he departs the National Front will run the country, while Khomeini returns to become a venerable sage. I see Khomeini as uncompromising, the military as hating the National Front, and the left as growing in influence. In the scramble for power we may soon have to throw our weight behind one of the sides to protect our interest.

[The President commented: "Zbig—After we make joint decisions, deploring them for the record doesn't help me."] (See also pp. 381–2.)

#86. *January 26, 1979: Midterm Assessment.* As we move toward the 1980 electoral year, some of the major issues and questions which will dominate foreign policy are: (1) What will be your principal foreign policy success in 1980? SALT will most likely end up in an inconclusive debate without a clear-cut victory. Perhaps a MBFR agreement focusing on U.S.–Soviet reductions in Central Europe with a summit of all the participating nations? (2) The Middle East will drag on unless we make a maximum effort now through the late spring, with a gradual easing off during the second half of the year. (3) How to maintain the relationship between the U.S., U.S.S.R., and P.R.C. The normalization of relations with Peking will obviously carry the danger of an overreaction in Moscow and/or miscalculation in Moscow and Peking. The Germans are already nervous about potential Soviet pressure on Berlin. You should insist on close personal control of relations with the U.S.S.R. to maintain the delicate and crucial balance of relations. (4) How to overcome the deep-seated perception of disarray in the national security process, an image which gravely undermines the very real and substantial successes of this Administration. Many in the bureaucracy feel free to talk to the press, discuss and distort the most intimate decision-making process, and generally promote themselves or their personal policy preferences. A significant shake-up of the bureaucracies may be in order.

#87. *February 2, 1979: Islamic Fundamentalism.* The conclusion from several studies done in the intelligence community is that we should be careful not to overgeneralize from the Iranian case. Islamic revivalist movements are not sweeping the Middle East and are not likely to be the wave of the future. The foreign policy consequences of this strengthening of Islamic sentiment are mixed. It is more difficult to resolve the Arab–Israeli disputes; moreover, conservative Muslims are often xenophobic. If we emphasize moral as well as material values, our support for diversity, and a commitment to social justice, our dialogue with the Muslim world will be helped.

#91. *March 23, 1979: Middle East after the First Peace Settlement.* I think it is advisable for you to reduce your involvement in continuing negotiations and appoint a top-level negotiator to pursue a comprehensive follow-up on Camp David. I am concerned about negative Arab reactions to current stalemate and suggest that you stress our goal of comprehensive peace, the resolution of the Palestinian problem in all its aspects, and the unchanged U.S. stand on settlements. We should also be focusing on Saudi Arabia, the Gulf, the Sudan, and North Africa.

#93. *April 6, 1979: Forthcoming U.S.–Soviet Summit.* I would suggest that you use the formal sessions to convey your overall foreign policy design and how the U.S.–Soviet relationship fits into the design. In personal talks, you should seek Brezhnev's commitment to lower aggregates in SALT II, which would be a personal coup [the President agreed], or his commitment to genuinely ambitious cuts in SALT III.

#94. *April 12, 1979: Foreign Policy and Domestic Politics.* In 1980 you must be recognized as the President of *Peace* and *Resolve.* You should stress your role as Commander in Chief and can do so on the Korea trip. A speech at a service academy would be a useful vehicle as well. And you should make decisions on additional strategic systems. This all will help SALT.

#104. *July 27, 1979: Cuban Problem.* Cuba's foreign military and subversive activities have steadily intensified since the mid-seventies and might become a domestic political issue. Our response must be on several planes: (1) reinforce democratic trends in Latin America, (2) increase the cost to Cuba of its revolutionary activity, (3) make clear by action that we hold the Soviets accountable for Cuba's activities, i.e., transfers to the P.R.C. Cy Vance is reluctant.

#107. *August 17, 1979: Middle East.* I agree with your assessment that the current "crisis" in relation with Israel results from Israel's decision to push us hard. Political loyalties are rarely motivated by gratitude, more often they are influenced by respect, confidence, even fear. We must demonstrate that we don't fear confrontation.

#109. *September 13, 1979: Acquiescence vs. Assertiveness.* You may not want to hear this, but I think that the increasingly pervasive perception here and abroad is that in U.S.–Soviet relations, the Soviets are increasingly assertive and the U.S. more acquiescent. State's handling of the Soviet brigade negotiations is a case in point. I recommend that in the future we will have to work for greater White House control. [The President commented: "Good."]

#110. *September 21, 1979: The Parallel—1961, but not 1962.* In the Soviet brigade issue a comparison is being made with the Cuban missile crisis, but actually the situation is more like that of the Berlin Wall. JFK called it "unacceptable" and responded by taking a number of steps designed to indicate to the public that he would assert U.S. interests and be prepared to use force. He did not pretend through some cosmetic formula that he had solved the problem. If you do so now, it will be self-defeating, undermine public confidence in our firmness, and endanger SALT. We need more defense, more intelligence, limited steps on the P.R.C., and a tough line on Soviet adventurism.

[The President agreed with the Berlin Wall analogy and noted that we should begin using it.]

#111. *October 5, 1979: Our Recent Conversation on China.* I do not favor "playing the China card." The long-range strategic significance of the U.S.–Chinese relationship stands on its own, and is not a tactic. Soviet behavior can be compared to Germany in the pre-World War I period when, driven by a fear of encirclement, it actually created such an encirclement. I think that you should use this historical analogy. The Chinese relationship is useful in showing the Soviets that their assertiveness is counterproductive and not cost-free.

#112. *October 12, 1979: The Process.* In reviewing the Soviet brigade issue postmortem I see the following conclusions. There were too many participants in the decision-making process, some made unsustainable statements, and there was a lack of precision in goals. The formal machinery (SCC) was used sporadically, and the issue was left to State with the Policy Review Committee. The SCC was not convened, because Cy wanted to retain control over process as well as U.S.–Soviet negotiations. You should insist if similar crises arise that the SCC manage them.

#122. *December 21, 1979: Difficult Choices in Iran.* As a follow-on to our morning discussion, I will seek to define some military options which reinforce our political strategies rather than being either retaliatory or merely an extension of economic pressure. [The President noted that we needed to list everything that Khomeini would not want to see occur and which would not incite condemnation of the United States by other nations.]

#123. *December 28, 1979: Soviet Invasion.* Our response in southwestern Asia ought to send not only a clear diplomatic signal to the Soviets but also the broader strategic message that the U.S. remains strategically committed to the independence of the region. The Soviet action will affect the passage of SALT and thereby TNF. If we blame the Soviet invasion of Afghanistan for the delay of SALT, it will be less a political setback for us and will enable us to insist to the Europeans that we all proceed with TNF. We haven't come to that point yet, and hopefully won't at all, but you might want to think about this and consult with Byrd.

#125. *January 11, 1980: Pakistan.* Whatever we do let us not create in Zia's mind the same ambiguity that clearly existed in the Shah's mind. This is not an argument for a massive aid program, but it is an argument for a very clear statement of our position.

#128. *February 8, 1980: Public Pronouncements on Iran and Afghanistan.* I suggest that you issue a written reminder that the bureaucracy stick to State of the Union themes. The Soviet invasion has broad strategic significance for U.S. vital interests, and there will be no quick return to business as usual. [The President wrote: "OK. Do so for me with a copy of S of U speech. Mark key passages as a reminder."] We should seek to avoid the recurrent swings in public opinion from euphoria to hysteria that have plagued U.S.–Soviet relations.

#131. *February 29, 1980: U.S.–Soviet Relations.* As you consider the possibility of exploring further with the Soviets the probe made in the Tito letter [which urged renewed U.S.–Soviet talks], I think that you should be extremely cautious and deliberate. It would be useful to have indirect probes first, i.e. the VP at Tito's funeral with senior Soviets, me with Dobrynin. An explicit U.S. initiative might be exploited by the Soviets to undermine allied support. It is also important to keep in mind that the Soviets have only contempt for the weak. I do not agree with the view that the Soviets have concluded that it is time to pull out of Afghanistan. Before they are ready to consider a neutral Afghanistan, three fundamental preconditions must be met: (1) a united West; (2) an aroused Islamic world; (3) continued Afghani resistance.

#134. *March 28, 1980: Afghanistan—an Aberration or Symptom.* Although there is Administration-wide agreement on measures adopted after Afghanistan, there is continuing argument among those who disagree on explaining Soviet behavior. I lean toward those who see the invasion as part of the current phase of Soviet assertiveness. Soviet behavior is symptomatic of the long-term historical drive, with military power supplanting Marxist ideology as its basic dynamic source. The drive toward the Persian Gulf is a historic element of Soviet foreign policy. (In the Molotov–Ribbentrop negotiation in November 1940 the Soviets stated that their territorial aspirations would be in the direction of the Indian Ocean and Persian Gulf.) The ongoing argument could have policy implications: how long should the present U.S. policy be maintained, should the Allies be pressed to respond more to the Soviet challenge, how energetically should we try to reinforce the Western presence in the Persian Gulf–Indian Ocean, how important is it to beef up Pakistan, is there more urgency in dealing with the Palestinian problem, how fruitful are efforts to improve relations with the Soviets?

#137. *April 18, 1980: Consulting with "Europe."* We find ourselves behind the power curve in trying to develop common perceptions with Europe. The reason is that the Europeans meet regularly and frequently on a multilateral basis at relatively high levels and have many bilateral meetings at various levels. We have only two NATO ministerials a year and one summit. We need to do more to correct this imbalance.

#144. *June 6, 1980: ZB–Muskie Relationship.* The relationship seems to be evolving well. On substance we have no real disagreements; the issues of a Middle East speech and letter to Gromyko were resolved amicably. Muskie has good political sense and is more secure. The press and his staff may stimulate conflict.

#149. *August 7, 1980: Foreign Policy and the Elections.* Foreign policy should provide the greatest opportunity for the exercise of Presidential leadership in a manner that could influence the election. We must do more to make the country understand the constructive nature of Carter foreign policy and the dangers inherent in Reagan's approach. (1) The distinctive nature of Carter foreign policy is reflected in your concern for moral principles and recognition of the importance of American power. Your foreign policy combines a recognition of global complexity with an understanding of the need to restore American military and economic strength. We must reach an accommodation with the Soviet Union as well as with the Third World. We can neither run the world nor run away from it. You have reversed the decline in defense spending under the Republican Administrations (3–4% per year in real terms) and obtained agreement from NATO for 3% increase in spending over the long term. (2) The dangers in Reagan's approach—it is escapist as well as dangerous. Reagan's talk of strategic superiority is a repudiation of past Republican foreign policies. The focus on U.S.–Soviet struggle is one-dimensional. Overall, Reagan is unrealistic, and his policies would reflect his indifference to the central issues in American foreign policy.

#151. *August 29, 1980: Protecting the Flanks.* My basic feeling is that I should play a low-key role, essentially to help protect you from likely Reagan attacks that we have been soft. The Assistant for National Security Affairs has traditionally not taken an active political role in campaigns. In selective and infrequent appearances, I could be useful to help rebut charges that we have been insufficiently sensitive to the Soviet political and military threat.

#155. *September 26, 1980: Iran–Iraq.* It is important to differentiate between short-run danger to the oil supplies, which we are right in minimizing, and the longer-range threat to the region—which we should not underplay. The country must understand that the long-term effort in the area requires fortitude and sacrifice to accomplish there what Truman did in Europe.

#156. *October 3, 1980: Long-Term Implications of Iran–Iraq War.* The war is likely to be one of attrition which could generate more tensions and at some point could involve other Gulf states. The threat to the Gulf gives us a unique opportunity to consolidate our security position. We need to begin more subtle initiatives to help Iran enough to put pressure on Iraq in order to push it back from most if not all occupied territory and safeguard Iran from Soviet penetration or internal disintegration. We should enlist the help of Turkey, Algeria, Pakistan, and the P.R.C. Private and secret initiatives are needed. [The President wrote: "You, Ed, and Harold advise me on how to pursue this."]

#158. *October 17, 1980: Foreign Policy Consequences of Reagan's Victory.* The implications of a possible Reagan victory are disturbing in seven key areas: (1) Latin America—greater polarization between right and left in El Salvador and Honduras and probably the immediate loss of Nicaragua to the extreme left (because the moderates will be unable to secure U.S. assistance). In the Caribbean a general left-wing drift will be exploited by Castro. Increasing coolness from the Andean Group will be matched by better relations with Argentina and Chile. (2) Africa —we will lose most of the gains in Nigeria, Tanzania, and Zimbabwe. Africa will become generally more unfriendly. The potential for a U.S.– Algerian relationship will fade. Relations with South Africa might improve. (3) Middle East—the Camp David process will stall, with Sadat's loss of personal confidence in us. The Saudis will become uneasy and the regional security framework efforts will be handicapped. (4) Far East—relations with China will suffer gravely. Most of the historical gains and progress of the last two years will be jeopardized. (5) Western Europe—the democratic center and left will become very uneasy. Relations with the European heads of state will not be very positive. The European left will become more vociferously anti-American. The Europeans will set out on their own in relations with the U.S.S.R. and in the Middle East. (6) Eastern Europe—there will be a great fear that the U.S. is once again writing off Eastern Europe. This will be felt particularly in Poland. The Soviets will have no alternative but to conclude that U.S.–U.S.S.R. relations have become one-dimensional. SALT will be abandoned and an arms race will begin. (7) Third World— hostility toward the U.S. will be widespread. The U.S. will be viewed as a status quo power, indifferent to global changes. The United States will find itself alone in a more hostile world.

ANNEX III

The NSC Staff and Organization, 1977-81

The White House Staff

Zbigniew Brzezinski, Assistant to the President for National Security Affairs

David L. Aaron, Deputy Assistant for National Security Affairs

Henry D. Owen, Special Representative for Economic Summits (*see also* Economic Cluster)

The National Security Council Staff

OFFICE OF THE STAFF SECRETARY

†Michael Hornblow, Acting Staff Secretary, 1/77–5/77

Christine Dodson, Staff Secretary, 5/77–1/81
  Deputy Staff Secretary, 1/77–5/77

OFFICE OF THE APNSA

Special Assistant to the APNSA
  Karl F. Inderfurth, 1/77–4/79
  Robert M. Gates, 4/79–12/79
  Leslie G. Denend, 1/80–1/81
Military Assistant to the APNSA and Crisis Coordinator
  William E. Odom

National Security Planning

  Samuel P. Huntington, 2/77–8/78

---

† Indicates staff members who were held over from the previous Administration or stayed after we left.

Press and Congressional Liaison Office

Press Officer and Associate Press Secretary
    Jerrold Schecter, 1/77–2/80
    Alfred Friendly, Jr., 3/80–1/81
Congressional Liaison Assistant
    †Jane Pisano, 1/77–8/77
*Congressional Liaison Office (created as separate entity in 3/78)
Congressional Relations Officer
    Madeleine Albright, 3/78–1/81

The Situation Room

Director
    †Denny Chapman†
Deputy Director
    †Manny Rubio†

Security Office

    †Jerry Jennings†

Legal Counsel

    Robert Kimmitt,† 8/78–1/81

The Geographical Clusters

WEST EUROPE
    Robert Hunter, 1/77–8/79
    Robert Blackwill, 9/79–1/81
    Gregory Treverton, 1/77–8/78
    James Rentschler,† 10/78–1/81

U.S.S.R./EAST EUROPE

    †William Hyland, 1/77–10/77
    Reginald Bartholomew, 11/77–4/79
    Marshall Brement, 5/79–1/81
    Robert King, 7/77–8/78
    Stephen Larrabee, 9/78–1/81

MIDDLE EAST/NORTH AFRICA

    William Quandt, 1/77–8/79
    Robert Hunter, 9/79–1/81
    †Gary Sick†

EAST ASIA/CHINA

> Michel Oksenberg, 1/77–2/80
> Michael Armacost, 1/77–7/78
> Nicholas Platt, 7/78–11/79
> Donald Gregg,† 1/80–1/81 (*see also* Intelligence Cluster)
> Roger Sullivan, 2/80–1/81

North/South Cluster

SOUTH ASIA/UN MATTERS

> Thomas Thornton

SUB-SAHARAN AFRICA

> Henry Richardson, 2/77–11/78
> Gerald Funk, 12/78–1/81
> Nicholas Spiliotes, 8/79–1/81

LATIN AMERICA/CARIBBEAN

> Robert Pastor
> Richard Brown, 12/78–6/79

The Functional Clusters

DEFENSE COORDINATION

> Victor Utgoff
> Fritz Ermarth, 9/78–11/80
> Jasper Welch, 11/79–1/81
> †John Marcum, 1/77–7/77
> †Randy Jayne, 1/77–5/77
> Roger Molander
> James Thomson, 4/77–1/81
> Charles Stebbins, 5/77–6/80
> Horace Russell,† 7/80–1/81
> Jake Stewart, 4/78–10/80
> Sydell Gold,† 9/80–1/81
> Chris Shoemaker,† 8/80–1/81

Intelligence Coordination

> Paul Henze, 1/77–12/80 (also covered Cyprus/Turkey/Greece
>   and Horn of Africa nations; international broadcasting)
> †Robert Rosenberg, 1/77–3/80
> †Samuel Hoskinson, 1/77–5/79
> Donald Gregg,† 6/79–1/81
> Michael Berta,† 1/80–1/81

International Economics

> †Robert Hormats, 1/77–10/77
> Henry Owen, 10/77–1/81 (also Special Representative for Economic Summits)
> Guy Erb, 9/77–1/80
> Tim Deal, 1/77–4/79; 1/80–1/81
> James Cochrane, 12/78–12/79
> Rutherford Poats,† 9/78–1/81

Global Issues*

> Jessica Tuchman Mathews, 1/77–6/79
> Lincoln Bloomfield, 6/79–8/80
> †Robert Kimmitt,† 1/77–6/77 (*see also* Legal Counsel)
> Leslie Denend, 7/77–6/79 (*see also* Office of the APNSA)
> Gerald Oplinger, 7/79–1/81

Science

> Benjamin Huberman† (joint appointment with Office of Science and Technology Policy)

Freedom of Information

> †Ted Carrou, 1/77–6/77
> †Gary Barron, 5/77–6/78
> Beverly Zweiben, 2/78–2/80
> Brenda Reger,† 2/80–1/81

---

* Cluster covered arms transfers, security assistance, chemical warfare, nonproliferation and nuclear cooperation; human rights; refugees.

Index

Note: ZB in the following items refers to Brzezinski

9:00	Dr. Zbigniew Brzezinski - The Oval Office.
10:30	Greet President-elect and Mrs. Ronald Reagan. North Portico.
10:35	Coffee Reception - The Blue Room.
11:05	Depart North Portico via Motorcade en route Capitol Building.
11:30	Inaugural Ceremonies - West Front of Capitol.
12:30	Inaugural Ceremonies Conclude.
12:40	Depart via Motorcade en route Andrews AFB.
1:00	Military Honors Departure Ceremony.
1:20	Air Force One Departs en route Robins AFB.
2:55	Air Force One Arrives Robins AFB.
3:30	Helicopter arrives Plains High School Field.

To Zbig -
4 years ! from
the first one -
Jimmy